♡ Valentines
Day 2015
Love you Blakey
xo Paigey

Strong Inside

STRONG ● INSIDE

———

Perry Wallace
and the Collision of
Race and Sports
in the South

———

ANDREW MARANISS

VANDERBILT UNIVERSITY PRESS • NASHVILLE

Published by Vanderbilt University Press
Nashville, Tennessee 37235
First printing 2014

This book is printed on acid-free paper.
Manufactured in the United States of America

Library of Congress
Cataloging-in-Publication Data on file

ISBN 978-0-8265-2023-4 (cloth)
ISBN 978-0-8265-2025-8 (ebook)

For Alison, Eliza, and Charlie,

my home-court advantage,

and for my parents,

David and Linda

Contents

List of Illustrations

One day the South will recognize its real heroes. They will be the James Merediths, with the noble sense of purpose that enables them to face jeering and hostile mobs, and with the agonizing loneliness that characterizes the life of the pioneer.
—MARTIN LUTHER KING JR.
"Letter from a Birmingham Jail"

Forgiveness

Bob Warren sat alone in the back of a taxi, bound for Massachusetts Avenue and the law school at American University, where he planned to deliver a message nearly forty years in the making.

As his cab sped through the streets of Washington, DC, far from his home in western Kentucky, Warren's mind raced back to the 1970s, before he became a preacher—when he was a professional basketball player—a crew-cut farm boy passing red, white, and blue basketballs to "Ice Man" Gervin in the freewheeling American Basketball Association, sharing locker rooms for nine seasons with Afro-coiffed men from places like Tennessee State, North Carolina A&T, and Jackson State University.

It was in those ABA days—in hotels, buses, cabs, restaurants, flights, and conversations with his many black teammates, in becoming familiar with their perspective on the world—that it dawned on Warren what hell one of his "brilliant and hardworking" teammates at Vanderbilt University, Perry Wallace, must have been going through in 1968, when Warren was a senior and Wallace, a sophomore, was the first and only African American ballplayer in the entire Southeastern Conference.

Warren's cab reached its destination, and the basketballer-turned-country-preacher made his way up to the fourth floor of the law school. Standing there to greet him was Professor Wallace; it was the first time these old teammates had seen each other in thirty-eight years.

"Forgive me, Perry," Warren said. "There is so much more I could have done."

Short 26th

Long before the day Bob Warren came to visit, there was the day Perry Wallace was elected captain of the Vanderbilt basketball team, the day when he was voted as the university's most popular student. There was the day he graduated from Columbia Law School, the day he delivered a lecture on global warming entirely in French, the day when he represented the Federated States of Micronesia before the United Nations. There was the day he watched his jersey hoisted to the rafters at Memorial Gym.

But before any of that, there were days when dorm room doors were slammed in his face, accompanied by cries of "Nigger on the floor!" There were days when grown men dressed in maroon, or orange, or red, white, and blue, threatened to castrate or hang him. There were days when he cried with frustration, days when blood flowed but no referees' whistles blew, days when so-called friends laughed at his pain.

But before any of this, before Perry Eugene Wallace Jr. even came into this world, there was Short 26th. His story begins in a little shotgun house on a dead-end street on the other side of the tracks.

His parents, Perry Wallace Sr. and Hattie Haynes Wallace, had come to Nashville from rural Rutherford County, Tennessee, not long after their marriage in 1928. Perry Sr. moved to Nashville first, to furnish and decorate the three-room house on Short 26th before his wife arrived. The Wallaces, both twenty-two years old, were eager to enjoy the benefits of city life. The South remained overwhelmingly rural, with only three out of ten people living in cities, but the migration had begun, and while many blacks headed hundreds of miles north to places like Chicago and Detroit, others, like the Wallaces, made the shorter journey to nearby southern cities.

Perry Sr. was just eleven years old when his mother died in childbirth, and his father, Alford Wallace, raised twelve children with a tough-love attitude, and the help of his sisters, on a farm near Murfreesboro, about thirty-five miles southeast of Nashville. It was a typical farm in many ways, full of fruit orchards, corn, cotton, hogs, and chickens; and there was a rock formation that seemed like a vast canyon to the kids, who would run through it barefoot. But the farm was unusual in one important way—Alford, a black man whose father had fought with the US Colored Troops in the Civil War, *owned* it. Perry Wallace Jr. wouldn't be the first pioneer in his family.

Hattie Haynes grew up close to Perry Sr. in the Blackman community near Murfreesboro. As children they played together, went to church together, and walked together across an old wood-and-rope bridge on the way to the one-room schoolhouse they attended through eighth grade. Hattie's teachers considered her the smartest student in the school, and they often let her do lessons on the chalkboard as an example to the others. Most of all she loved music: a traveling salesman had come through her parents' neighborhood selling affordable organs, and Hattie's father bought one for her mother. Hattie learned how to play, and from then on the Haynes house was full of music, her young fingers flying through a fast melody she called "Racing Horses."

Hattie was twenty years old when her mother died, and just two years later Perry Sr. came calling on her father to ask for Hattie's hand in marriage. They were married on April 1, 1928—their children would later joke about the April Fool's Day wedding—and soon they were on their way to Nashville, a bit apprehensive about the people and the pace of the city but excited about the opportunities. Two of Perry Sr.'s older brothers were already there; Joe and James Wallace helped the young couple get settled. Perry took jobs at a granary, then a chemical company, then with the railroad, then as a bricklayer, while Hattie rode the bus to clean homes and offices. Perry and Hattie were doing the best they could; these were the standard jobs available to blacks in Nashville at the time—and for decades to come. As late as 1940, nearly 80 percent of working black women in the city were employed as domestic servants or waitresses.

The city where Perry and Hattie began their lives together had been settled after the Revolution, emerging as an important frontier town in the mid-nineteenth century. As the young nation entered an era of Manifest Destiny, Nashville served as a key launching point in the western expansion. Up until the time of the Civil War, most Nashvillians considered their town more western than southern. Located roughly halfway between Chicago and New Orleans, about as close to parts of Missouri, Illinois, and Indiana as to Georgia, Alabama, and Mississippi, Nashville's crossroads location made the city more open to new people and new ideas than its Deep South peers.

It also made the city a major railroad hub for the occupying Union army during the Civil War, an especially important depot for General William T. Sherman's march on Atlanta. More than fifty thousand Federal troops occupied the city from 1862 to 1865 (more than three times the size of the city's 1860 population), what one historian called "perhaps the first, continued occupation of a city by any American army." While those troops cleared the city of thousands of trees—needed for firewood—they did leave some things behind: namely themselves. Dozens of Union soldiers married southern belles and remained in Nashville after the war, and one Federal fort was converted into a "college for Negroes" in 1866: Fisk University, named for Brigadier General Clinton B. Fisk.

Ten years later, the first medical school for blacks in the South, the Medical Department of Central Tennessee College of Nashville, was established. The school later became known as Meharry Medical College, and for generations afterward it produced most of the black doctors in the country. In 1912 another black college was founded in the city, Tennessee Agricultural and Industrial State Normal School, which later became known as Tennessee A&I State and then simply Tennessee State.

Clustered in what locals call North Nashville but what is more accurately the near-west side of the city, these three institutions gave Nashville a larger concentration of highly educated, upwardly mobile blacks than most cities in the South. Still, most blacks in Nashville lived in deep poverty, many in a near shantytown just yards from the state capitol building downtown.

The center of black life was near those universities, and one road—Jefferson Street—was the place where everything happened. In a segregated society, the Jefferson Street area was where Black Power flourished long before the slogan was invented. Living in the "black cocoon," as Perry Wallace would describe it decades later, meant patronizing black-owned businesses, entering the front doors of black movie theaters, eating in black restaurants. Inside the cocoon, poor as it was, there were no whites-only lunch counters or back-alley entrances. Rather, there were institutions like Isom's Beauty Shop, Frank White's Cleaners, Green's Grocery, and the Ritz Theater. The leading black entertainers of the mid-twentieth century, from Duke Ellington, Count Basie, and Nat King Cole to Little Richard and Ella Fitzgerald, included Nashville on their itineraries, playing at the Silver Streak and the Del Morocco and staying at the Brown Hotel.

Perry Sr. and Hattie, the laborer and the cleaning lady, made a life in this cocoon. It was humble—this was *Short* 26th after all, just a stub of a road around the corner from Jefferson Street, not even the *real* 26th Avenue. Their house was small—living room, bedroom, kitchen, bedroom, porch—but soon enough it filled up with kids. First there was Annie, who became known simply as Sister, and then along came James, known as Brother, and Bessie, Jessie, and Ruby Jean.

While some neighbors succumbed to the temptations born of the marriage between a new urban existence and poverty—moonshine, gambling, and violence among them—Perry Sr. and Hattie lived a straight life, and they were determined, in the face of significant peer pressure, that their children would do the same. Of all the traditions and values in the Wallace home, the two most important were religion and education, and church life was especially important to Hattie. She was a regular at the Jefferson Street Church of Christ, a conservative congregation that forbade drinking, dancing, and instrumental music in the sanctuary.

The children went to Sunday School, read the Bible, and attended services with their mother. Mrs. Wallace brought the lessons of the church back to Short 26th, and the kids experienced what they would later call a "home-based" religion, a "vehicle for motivation and inspiration and healing when that was necessary," said Jessie. Much of that motivation and inspiration was directed at schooling. The Wallaces believed that a strong education was a necessary ingredient if their children were to succeed in a society that was not only becoming more urban and fast paced but also was engineered to restrict the opportunities for black people. The Wallace kids were smart, so smart that they encountered more than a little jealousy, more than a few strange looks from friends, neighbors, and other parents. Were those really French-, Spanish-, and German-language records you could hear Annie practicing with when you walked past the little shotgun house on Short 26th? What was *that* all about? That family is *different*.

On February 19, 1948, this straitlaced family of seven got quite a surprise: Perry Eugene Wallace Jr. was born at Meharry Hospital.

Can a birth really be that much of a surprise?

For some it was quite unexpected, given that the oldest Wallace child, Annie, was a sophomore in college and the youngest, Ruby Jean, had been born ten years earlier.

For Jessie, then thirteen, it was a real shock. She had had no idea that her mother, who wore billowing smocks around the house, was pregnant; when she heard her mother was in the hospital, she thought she must be dying. So traumatized by the thought, Jessie didn't ask anyone for days what was going on. Just then learning about menstruation in school, she thought about how this baby was made, and she was traumatized all over again. For Perry Sr. the birth of a healthy baby boy was no small pleasant surprise. Jessie's fear that her mother was dying was closer to the truth than she could have known. For Hattie, then forty-two years old, childbirth was life threatening. She was in the hospital for more than two weeks before Perry was born, and doctors discovered a tumor on her colon, which at the time they believed to be benign. Still, they took special precautions when Hattie gave birth to Perry. "Daddy was tickled to death," Jessie recalled, "because his wife had survived and he had gotten a little boy."

When mother and son were healthy enough to return home, Perry Sr. drove them back to Short 26th. As they rolled down Jefferson Street and neared the house, a train passed overhead on a railroad trestle. "Oh, son," Perry Sr. whispered to his infant boy, "before you could even get home you've gotten run over by a train." Jessie would later say that she believed her father's joke foretold "the trials and tribulations of life" that her baby brother would endure.

The girls gave little Perry baths, brushed his hair, and hauled him around everywhere, using the infant to draw the attention of boys at Hadley Park. The only time they let go of him was when Daddy came home from work. "Have to have my boy, have to have my boy," he would say, and then he wouldn't let his son out of sight all night, putting the "miracle baby" to sleep in a white bassinet at the foot of his and Hattie's bed.

Nearly as soon as one boy arrived in the house, the other left. Brother James, realizing that his parents would be struggling to put the girls through college while raising another child, enlisted in the air force as soon as he turned eighteen the November following Perry's birth. "He sacrificed for the family," Jessie recalled. "He was gone, and that was devastating."

As his sisters grew older and eventually all moved out of the house, Perry became even closer to his mother. He developed an uncommon sensitivity and was called a mama's boy; the love and values Hattie passed along to her son began to shape his behavior. In a world of chaos, much of it soon to be directed squarely at him, he would remain above the fray. Some observers would later remark on Perry's unflappable character when they saw him remain cool under pressure in places like Oxford, Mississippi, and Auburn, Alabama. They should have seen him in kindergarten.

Perry Wallace's education began in 1954, the same year as the *Brown v. Board of Education* school-desegregation decision, at a school for black children named Jewel's Academy. Every day Perry the kindergartner walked from Short 26th down Howard Street over to the complex of chapels and schoolrooms at the academy, a private school run by the Church of God and Christ. Along the way, he passed by a factory and railroad tracks and, most exotic to him, a retirement home and its constant parade of elderly people with canes, walking by "real slow."

Run by a female bishop known as Chief Jewel, whom Perry considered a "big, strong, charismatic woman," the school included a mandatory, mid-day chapel session. Whether it was the imposing figure of Chief Jewel or the lessons on respect he had learned from his parents, Perry was the most even-tempered kid in kindergarten. This didn't necessarily sit well with his sister Jessie, who occasionally picked up her little brother from school.

Jessie arrived at Perry's classroom one day, and the teacher, Miss Davis, was nowhere in sight. With free reign, the kids were going berserk, running around screaming, bouncing off walls and windows—total pandemonium.

All but one kid, that is. As his classmates went bonkers, there at his tiny desk sat Perry Wallace, not saying a word, waiting patiently for his sister.

"I was just enraged, not at the children, but at the teacher," Jessie recalled. "But my strongest feeling of all was, 'Is my brother going to be a wimp? Is he going to stand up for himself with these rougher guys? Is he going to be able to defend himself?'"

Her mind flashed to a poem the Wallace children had been given, "If" by Rudyard Kipling, which begins with the line "If you can keep your head when all about you are losing theirs," but she thought that at just five years old, her brother was too young to be heeding the poet's advice on self-discipline.

"I think I would have preferred at that moment for him to be running around, too," Jessie recalled. "But looking back, this is when I saw the first instance of that self-control, this discipline, and not only that, this desire to do the right thing and not follow the crowd. He learned all that so early."

If those traits would later serve him well as a pioneer, he didn't need to look far to see another example of a trailblazer—however unheralded—in action. It was Perry Sr., who despite long odds was making a living as an entrepreneur in the "good ol' boy" field of commercial and residential building construction.

Nashville in the 1950s was in the midst of what was known as its "Central City Renaissance," a postwar building boom that saw the construction of the city's first skyscraper, the thirty-story L&C Tower, as well as several new department stores, government buildings, and the continuation of the Capitol Hill redevelopment project to remove the shacks that circled the statehouse. And, as the county's population ballooned from 257,000 in 1940 to 400,000 in 1960, residential construction—much of it brick—created increasing demand for Perry Wallace Sr.'s services as a bricklayer.

This middle-aged man from the country, father of six children, saw his chance at the American Dream. Just as that dream was fueling the development of these suburban brick homes, Perry Sr. seized on a fundamental truth: the dream required that these houses look beautiful. In the world these new homeowners wanted to live in, the lawns needed to be manicured and the bricks needed to sparkle. Through his bricklaying experience, Wallace knew that the crews often did a quick, sloppy job of removing unsightly mortar from the face of the bricks and the joints in between.

And so with an optimism far exceeding what was expected of a man of his standing, Perry Sr. started his own brick-*cleaning* business. For years, the Wallace kids called it "Daddy's business in a bucket," and that was no metaphor. Perry Sr. had no car when he first got started, so each morning he would wake up early and load his steel brushes and acid into his bucket and ride the city bus to jobs all over town. Eventually, as business improved, he was able to buy a car—a 1952 Chevrolet—which allowed him to work jobs as far away as southern Kentucky and northern Alabama. This at a time when merely pulling over for gas was a risky proposition for a black man in the South. It wasn't until decades later that Perry Jr. could fully appreciate the risks his father took to provide for his family.

"Here he was in a very tough situation, making his money doing work for white general contractors in the South," Wallace recalled. "The construction industry is tough enough if you're a privileged white male. But to be a black man with his own business in the 1950s in the South, not everybody would cotton to that. So my father was a pioneer. We understood he was working hard, but didn't understand at the time just what kind of world he had to go out into."

As Perry Sr. began to make a little money, he saw an opportunity to improve his family's lot. Boxes were packed and Short 26th was home no more; the family moved to a bigger, nicer house at 1110 Cass Street. The new neighborhood was integrated—the all-white North High School was across the street—but was becoming increasingly black as whites moved to the suburbs.

It was around this time that young Perry's own view of the world and its possibilities began to expand. He was now living at the fringes of the cocoon, old enough to take note of the disparity between certain things that he heard or read about and the environment in which he lived. One of the few benefits of his mother's job as a cleaning lady downtown was the fact that she brought home magazines she found in the trash at the Bennie Dillon office building and the Maxwell House hotel: *Life, Look, Ladies' Home Journal, Redbook.* Flipping through the pages with the children, Hattie would say, "'Oh, look at this, look what you can have if you want it,'" Jessie recalled. "She didn't say, 'We wish you could have it,' or 'We wish we could give it to you,' but 'Oh, look what you can have if you go to school and if you want it. There are things you don't have now, but that's what they are used for.' So we learned about things that we didn't actually have. And we always had a *National Geographic.* Thank God some doctor subscribed to that."

Perry was mesmerized by Madison Avenue's portrayal of the ideal American lifestyle, fascinated by the photos, the advertisements, and the articles, all pointing to a world he did not know. "A person would wonder why you would spend your time looking through *Ladies' Home Journal* or *Redbook* or whatever," he recalled. "But the idea was that you were locked out of the American mainstream. So if you wanted to live a life of meaning, you looked at whatever sources you could, within the black community and outside it, into the great American mainstream. How many other ways could you peek into it?" The seeds were planted that this was a life he wanted to have.

And then he found another way to peek into this other world—literally. He could see the white students walking to and from North High School across the street, and on Friday nights in the fall, there were the football games.

Perry and his buddies would walk over to Robertson's corner store and buy some Cokes and cheese and bologna and crackers, and then make their way over to the chain link fence that sat atop a hill overlooking the floodlit football field. Invisible to the crowd below, they popped open their Cokes, stood at the edge of the fence, built their sandwiches, and watched the spectacle—one they were prohibited from seeing any other way. As they peeked through the chains, Wallace later concluded, he and his friends were in effect looking through what W. E. B. DuBois called the "veil that separates the races." It had a profound impact.

"We stood there for two or three hours on Friday nights and we watched the games, but we also watched the people," Wallace recalled. "We watched whites live and enjoy being an American. They had popcorn and candy and a band and cheerleaders and hot dogs, and it just looked like they had a better place than we did. And I think the subtle signal that was sent was that even though they were poor, they were better than we were and they were more a part of the real America than we were."

Perry became interested in finding other ways to escape the rigid boundaries society had placed around him, some superficial, some more meaningful. The family's black-and-white television brought a new world into their home, with Perry watching Steve Allen, Perry Como, *Leave It to Beaver*, *The Dick Van Dyke Show*, all programs that depicted a certain image of the American middle class that intrigued him. When a black performer like Sammy Davis Jr. or Harry Belafonte appeared on *The Ed Sullivan Show*, it was a stop-what-you're-doing event, with Perry calling out to the rest of the family, "There's somebody colored on television!" For a black kid in the Jim Crow South of the 1950s, mistaking Hollywood sets for a real America and daydreaming about the idyllic scenes depicted in magazines were no faulty pastimes. Reality, after all, was insane, even in a "moderate" city like Nashville.

In his voluminous study of Nashville-based civil rights activists, *The Children*, David Halberstam wrote that "the racial texture of [Nashville's] daily life seemed less edgy than that of comparable cities in the Deep South." Here was a capital city in which blacks had a history of voting and had representation on the City Council. The city's morning newspaper, the *Tennessean*, had a long liberal tradition. "Nashville's segregation was largely of a soft kind, administered, it sometimes seemed, not with the passion of angry racist officials but more as a cultural leftover from the past," Halberstam wrote. True as all this may have been—Nashville was different from Memphis or Birmingham or Selma, so much so that one disgruntled segregationist declared Nashville "the worst city in the world"—the fact remained that there could be no soft segregation, no genteel Jim Crow.

"By the 1950s," historian Don Doyle noted, "the races in Nashville had never been more segregated," as tens of thousands of whites moved out of the city into the surrounding suburbs. And yet even as they came to make up a greater percentage of the city's population, Nashville's black residents were excluded from most white-owned restaurants, forced to enter the downtown movie theater through the alley entrance and sit in the balcony, barred from public parks, pools, and golf courses. They were made to sit in the back of the bus and in special sections at the Ryman Auditorium and Sulphur Dell baseball field, steered to segregated bathrooms in the basement of city hall and the county courthouse, relegated to segregated schools and confined mostly to service occupations.

In this context the big question for Nashville's power brokers was how they would handle the issue of school desegregation in the wake of the *Brown* decision. Following a successful 1955 lawsuit brought by the prominent black Nashville attorneys Z. Alexander Looby and Avon Williams, Nashville's Board of Education was ordered to implement a desegregation strategy by 1957. In what became a national model dubbed "The Nashville Plan," the system called for one grade to be desegregated each year—starting with first grade in year one, adding second grade the following year, and so on. As gradual and conservative as the plan was, it still included convenient "outs" for white parents, including the ability to transfer their children to other schools with a written request and a gerrymandering of school districts that would cluster black students even closer together.

And yet there was still significant organized opposition to this cautious plan from elements of white Nashville. Vanderbilt English professor Donald Davidson (an aging former member of the fugitive and agrarian literary movements) and some downtown business leaders formed a coalition opposed to "federal intervention in southern race relations," and a group of parents created a committee calling for the creation of a three-tiered system: one set of schools for whites, a second for blacks, and a third that would be integrated. The plan was endorsed by the state legislature before it was declared unconstitutional.

With local segregationists splintered into various ineffective factions, an outsider stepped into the mix. His name was Frederick John Kasper, a racist and anti-Semite from New Jersey who found support in pockets of the south. After sparking a bout of violence in Clinton, Tennessee, that required National Guard intervention, Kasper arrived in Nashville in 1957, passing out literature urging parents to "keep the niggers out of white schools" and placing threatening phone calls to black families. The KKK arrived from out of town, too, with bands of young toughs riding around Nashville in cars emblazoned with Klan stickers. Had these groups not been so hateful, the situation might have been comical, a kind of supremacist family feud. The Klansmen couldn't quite embrace a Yankee like Kasper, and the more intellectual segregationists of Davidson's ilk were put off by the tactics of both Kasper and the Klan. No true leadership emerged, but still there was violence.

As an elementary school student in Nashville, Perry Wallace was often accosted by young white kids on his way to school. "I had to figure out the basic law of the jungle," Wallace recalled. "It was fight or flight." Courtesy of Perry Wallace.

When the first black students and their parents arrived at previously all-white schools on September 9, 1957, they were greeted by a "crowd of whites who hurled insults, sticks and stones." Later that night an entire wing of Hattie Cotton Elementary was destroyed by a dynamite blast.

In hindsight, Doyle concluded, the violence instigated by Kasper and the Klan had the ironic effect of galvanizing support for peaceful integration among most white Nashvillians. Their city was "on the brink of chaos," and support for desegregation became a necessary element in a "defense of Nashville's integrity as a community."

In the midst of this charged atmosphere, one that he was only vaguely able to comprehend, Perry Wallace, an asthmatic kid who had been taught by his parents to stay out of trouble, had to walk to elementary school. And to get there, on his way from Cass Street to Elliott Elementary, he had to walk through white neighborhoods, past white schools.

Sometimes the white boys threw rocks at him. Sometimes they called him names. Sometimes a carload of teens sped by, throwing things *and* calling him names. And at least one group of punks surrounded him and threatened him with a knife. In those moments, Wallace later recalled, he "had to figure out the basic law of the jungle. It was fight or flight. It was classic and it was raw." Sometimes he fought, sometimes he ran. Sometimes he took the bus, just to avoid the hoodlums.

But even that plan didn't always work. Nearly fifty years later, Wallace vividly remembered one incident. Late on a spring afternoon, he stood alone at the corner of 5th Avenue and Madison Street near Elliott Elementary waiting to take a bus downtown, where he would transfer to another bus back home.

A car packed with young white males rolled down the street toward him, the teens shouting insults as they approached. Perry had endured this before, and he stood his ground, just waiting for the car to pass by. But this time, as the car got closer, one of the guys leaned out and pointed a gun right at him. Time seemed to slow down, the shouts now just so much white noise, and Perry's eyes grew large as he stared down the barrel of the gun. The car slowed to a crawl as it turned the corner in front of him, and the guy just kept pointing the gun at Perry—pointing it, pointing it, pointing it—everything in slow motion. And then he didn't shoot.

"Maybe they were just kidding, because people just didn't shoot people in Nashville in those days," Wallace recalled. "But who knew? Who knew?"

Faced with no easy solution—ride the bus or walk, it made no difference; trouble could lurk anywhere—Perry lost himself in other pursuits. There were chores at home: feeding and grooming his father's hunting dogs out in the back yard, waking up early in the winter to fill up a freezing-cold bucket with coal for the stove. He found comfort in attending church with his mother, ignoring the taunts of the neighbor kids as he clutched his Bible on the walk over to the 15th Avenue Church of Christ.

Where you going, Preacher?!

I'm going to church!

And he came to love music. Perry's father, no musician himself, had surprised him one day in fifth grade by bringing home a trumpet. Though Perry was never told exactly why he received the gift, he later got the sense that his father wanted him to enjoy the benefits of the study of music, believing that he would enjoy music as a source of expression, that it would serve as a safe way to help him forget the troubles he encountered and escape to new worlds.

As Perry's trumpeting skills blossomed, he was invited to participate in the All-City Band, made up of kids from various elementary schools around town. To today's ears, that sounds like some sort of All-Star ensemble, but back then it was the only band available to black schoolchildren in Nashville. Since the schools didn't have their own bands, this was a way for music teachers to give their students the opportunity to play concerts. It was while playing in the All-City Band that Perry met a small, cheerful, neatly dressed clarinet player named Walter Murray. Though at the time they were just a trumpet player and a clarinetist who happened to play in the same band on weekends, Wallace and Murray would become best friends a few years later in high school ("the black Mutt and Jeff," some friends kidded them, with Wallace so tall and Murray so short). It was a friendship that would grow deeper when they entered Vanderbilt together and continue all the way to Murray's deathbed, when Perry was one of the last people to sit with Walter and to console his wife, Donna, Walter's high school sweetheart.

Perry's love for the trumpet continued as he graduated from the Elliott School and enrolled at Wharton Junior High School, one of two schools that fed into the legendary Pearl High, a major source of pride in North Nash-

Reverend James Lawson is arrested after organizing student sit-ins at downtown Nashville lunch counters in February 1960. A Vanderbilt Divinity School student, Lawson was expelled from the university after his role in the nonviolent protests became known. Lawson's arrest and expulsion set in motion the events that led to the hiring of the progressive Alexander Heard as chancellor, the integration of Vanderbilt's undergraduate schools, and the recruitment of Perry Wallace. *Nashville Banner* Archives, Nashville Public Library, Special Collections.

ville. Almost immediately, Perry noticed one comforting advantage to attending Wharton: the walk to school was peaceful. While the journey to Elliott had taken him through some white areas, the walk to Wharton took him in the opposite direction, closer to Fisk and Tennessee A&I and deeper into the heart of black Nashville. "My life shifted into the black world," Wallace recalled, "and I encountered no problems once I started heading in that direction."

As the scenery changed, so too did Wallace's curiosities. The year was 1960, and Nashville was the stage for some of the first, dramatic scenes of the civil rights movement. James Lawson, a black divinity school student at Vanderbilt, had been teaching the principles of nonviolence to students from Fisk, Tennessee A&I, American Baptist Bible College, and other area schools, students whose names would become legendary, including Diane Nash, James Bevel, John Lewis, and Marion Barry. In February of that year, the students staged nonviolent sit-ins at Nashville's segregated department-store lunch counters. Though angry whites beat them, poured coffee on them, and burned cigarettes into their flesh, and though they were arrested, these students remained true to Lawson's teachings on nonviolence, appealing to the moral conscience of white Nashville.

For Wallace it was the beginning of an education unlike anything he had ever imagined. His teachers talked about the demonstrations, and a classmate raised the question, "Why do we have to sit in the back of the bus?" This was something Wallace had never thought about before. That was just the way it was: you went to the back of the bus. Suddenly, these teachers and classmates were opening his eyes. Why *did* he have to use a different water fountain downtown? And the more curious he became about these questions, the more he had to see what these older students were doing at the protests. He and some friends would sneak downtown—their parents would *kill* them if they knew what they were up to—sometimes by bus, sometimes by darting in and out among the marchers, and watch the action at the department stores and cafeterias from a safe distance.

His thirst for knowledge was intense. After school and on weekends, he walked a few miles to the Hadley Park library and flipped through the pages of *Ebony* and *Jet*, buried himself in the works of W. E. B. DuBois, and absorbed Walter White's accounts of southern lynchings. While he was fascinated to discover these black writers, his interests were broad. A self-described "Sputnik-affected kid," Wallace was influenced by teachers who were determined to improve the math and science skills of their students, lest the country fall further behind the Russians. He began to take a genuine liking to those subjects, checking out college-level math and science books and sitting for hours at the library trying to make sense of it all.

When the bystanders at Hadley Park didn't see the Wallace kid trudging over to the library to read DuBois, they may have seen him lugging his trumpet to private lessons on the Tennessee A&I campus. Though bouts with asthma had occasionally interfered with his trumpet playing (his band teacher at Wharton, Mr. Howell, grew upset with him when he botched a solo in the *Carnival of Venice* because he simply couldn't breathe), he had a desire to get better. Howell respected his young pupil's determination and set him up with the university's assistant band director for private lessons in the summer. A few days a week, Wallace carried his trumpet three or four miles to the offices of Edward Louis Smith, a demanding teacher who later became a jazz trumpet player of note. The lessons lasted an hour, and Smith had Perry practice four hours a day, five days a week, using the classic method books of the legendary French trumpeter Jean-Baptiste Arban, which were printed with instructions in English, French, and German. "It was exactly four hours a day," Wallace recalled. "I would time it, because I didn't want to practice that long. I would read the English and then see if I could understand the French and German. I spent a long time with those melodies and rhythms, and I came to really appreciate the notion of clear, pristine, very good music."

Even with its racial discord, there were obvious signs that Nashville was proving to be a good place for the Wallaces to raise their children. The music, the exposure to role models, the educational opportunities, and the job prospects were simply better than they were back in rural Rutherford County. And yet it was important to the parents that their children retain some of the country spirit, a closeness to nature and a measured outlook on an increasingly fast-paced life. For Perry Sr. and Hattie, there was a value to being "out in the country, sitting on the front porch, walking through the fields, and walking the country roads where nature is really in charge," Wallace recalled. "It's not like in the city, where if it's dark or if it's light it has to do with the switch on the wall. Out there, it has to do with the forces of nature. There's a different tempo, a different feel, and when it all comes together right, there's a sense of the world and your place in it."

During the summer and on Sundays after church, Perry rode out to the country with his father, visiting cousins at the Wallace family farm. For the perceptive youngster, the trips were full of lessons on social status, especially divisions within the black community. First there was the exotic drive itself, which marked the distance between the branches of the family in the very roads it required to travel from Nashville to the farm near Murfreesboro.

"You'd start in poor North Nashville, and take Lafayette out to Murfreesboro Pike, and eventually the road would become more gravelly than paved," Wallace recalled. "And then you'd get to roads where you'd have bridges where you'd have to wait, because only one car could pass at a time. And then the roads would get unpaved and ungravelly, and there you'd have big limestone rocks in the road. There would be brush scraping against the car because it hadn't been trimmed, and you'd see little creeks off to the side. And, finally, you'd come to a clearing, which was Alford Wallace's farm."

Somewhat bewildered, somewhat enchanted by the trip, Perry felt like quite the pampered city boy in the presence of his country cousins. These kids were bigger and stronger, their hands were rougher, they knew how to run around on the limestone rocks and the gravel without cutting their feet. Perry, meanwhile, used a lot of big words and did a lot of talking—talking about what, the cousins didn't always know. Education was making this boy *crazy*. By the standards of young rural boys, it was the country kids who were on top. They were more "down to earth," and that was a good thing. And yet Perry sensed that these cousins were aware of their disadvantage, knew that he had opportunities in the city that they would never have, and there was a bit of envy. While still trying to hold on to their rural culture in as many ways as possible, Perry's parents, like so many others, had made a break from their own families in pursuit of a better life. And so what did that say about those who chose to stay behind? The dynamic created a bit of tension.

What the country cousins did not know was that Perry, the one they thought was a little too citified, was equally marginalized by many of his peers back in Nashville. The city kids would "give me hell, and my sisters, too, because they thought we weren't street smart," he recalled. Every member of the Wallace family knew exactly why they were catching hell, and they chose to endure the insults, accepted being called *different*, sacrificed some ephemeral pleasures, because they believed that someday, it would all pay off.

"My father talked a lot about what it takes to make it in America now," Wallace recalled, "what skills you needed, what ways you need to be, what was the *worthless* way. Not that people were worthless, he wasn't someone who condemned people, but he did understand unintelligent behavior and approaches to life. He had seen a lot of it." It was his passionate desire for black people to do well, Wallace said, that often made his father concerned about their well-being and critical of bad habits and behavior: "Probably the best proof of this was his willingness to let people work for him in his business. The only 'catch' was that he was a tough boss—not a mean one, but a tough one—in the sense that you had to be punctual, work as hard as he did, and conduct yourself in a respectable manner."

To keep the kids out of trouble, like other families trying to prevent their children from making bad choices, the Wallace parents kept their kids in the house. There was no hanging out at the fast food joint after school, no detours on the way home from band practice. While other guys in the neighborhood developed their own signature struts, that wasn't an option for Perry: "Daddy said, 'You can't have a cool walk. Cool walk? That's out.'" The Wallace kids even *sounded* different from their peers, and that was no accident. They were taunted for this, too, told they were trying to sound white.

"The notion was not trying to be white; that was the last thing you wanted to be," Wallace recalled. "It was what works in America now, and what is going to work in the future? The idea was to look at television, listen to the radio, and listen to the basic way that these people expressed themselves. We were living in a very humble place where people up and down the street talked and acted a whole different way. And what we understood was that these people were locking themselves in, potentially in a perilous and maybe even tragic way. So you understood what you needed to do, and you took the hits. People would give you hell, and you always would have doubts. But this was a decision I thought made a lot of sense and would pay off."

In countless circumstances, Wallace made a conscious effort to be different from the people around him. He was shy, he was smart, and he "tended to have a more limited social life; I wasn't going to have a bunch of friends." But in one very important way, he fit in just fine.

When Perry Wallace stepped onto a basketball court, he was just one of the guys.

Woomp Show

D o you know how to dribble a basketball?"

In the chain of events that would come to define Perry Wallace's life, all the tragic and heroic moments, it was this simple question from his cousin Clarence, son of his father's brother Dewey, that set everything in motion.

Around ten years old at the time, Perry answered, "no," he never had dribbled a basketball. He didn't even *have* a basketball.

Clarence, one of the cousins from the farm, moved up to Nashville and lived with the Wallaces after graduating from high school, earning some money working for Perry Sr. He hung out with some of the guys in the neighborhood, young men whose fathers had brought them up on the pastoral game of baseball, but who were drifting toward the more modern, more lively sports of football and basketball. With his brother James off in the air force, Perry found his charismatic cousin an intriguing role model. If Clarence, so athletic and smart and handsome and nice, thought playing basketball was a good thing, then it must be true.

Hattie and Perry Sr., the protective parents, allowed Clarence to take Perry across the street to the playground at North High School—when the white kids weren't around—to teach him how to play. On long summer nights, Clarence taught his younger cousin the fundamentals of the game. Dribbling. Shooting. Passing. Rebounding. His pupil—the trumpet-playing, Sunday-School-teaching, mama-obeying, voracious reader—loved every minute of it.

"I caught the bug," Wallace recalled, "and things took off from there."

Perry began spending more and more time at the North High hoops, learning the game from older kids who cut him no slack. The late bloomer excelled.

It was at this same time that Perry—fascinated by the people and lifestyles that appeared unbound by the narrow walls of segregation that confined his own existence—found a new outlet for his imagination. He could look around town and admire the basketball players at Pearl High and Tennessee A&I, young black men who not only were succeeding in a segregated society, but whose talents were recognized and even celebrated. And he could turn on the television and see black role models of a different sort, stars like Wilt Chamberlain, Bill Russell, and Oscar Robertson out there on the biggest stages of the North, East, and West, playing alongside whites and succeeding in the America he had read about in the magazines.

"You didn't see many blacks on television back then other than in subservient roles," Wallace recalled. "But guys like Chamberlain and Russell were actually getting a chance to look like real-life, dignified figures. It was so spectacular to see them out in a world where they were in the mainstream. And what we knew about the mainstream at the time was that we weren't allowed to be in it. To see these guys have their strength and artistry respected in the larger world was huge. They were the ones you tried to be like."

And then, nirvana. Wilt Chamberlain and his Philadelphia Warriors came to Nashville to play an exhibition game at Tennessee A&I's gym. Somehow, Perry got permission from his parents to go to the game. There, decked out in the blue and gold of the Warriors, was the Big Dipper: huge (seven foot one), charismatic, and dunking like crazy.

"To actually see Chamberlain, this had such an impact on me it's hard to describe," Wallace recalled. "I decided right then that I was going to learn how to jump so I could dunk the ball like Wilt."

Some kids in the neighborhood wished they could fly through the air. Others dreamed of making themselves invisible or as fast as lightning. The only superpower Perry Wallace wanted was to dunk a basketball like Wilt Chamberlain. Never mind that Wilt was virtually without peer in those days, as rare a sight as any caped crusader. Perry had a plan.

Every night, after finishing dinner and his homework, he made his way to the living room, took a spot in front of the family's black-and-white television, turned the channel to *Leave It to Beaver* or *The Three Stooges*, and got down to business. He knew he had to strengthen his skinny legs if he wanted to jump high enough to dunk a basketball, so he improvised a workout regimen. One. Ten. Fifty. One hundred. Who knows how many squats he did in that living room, bending at the knees over and over and over again, his eyes on Lumpy and the Beave and Curly and Moe and his sights on the prize, that rim that loomed ten feet off the ground on every backboard in town. To see how he was progressing, he'd leap at anything in sight, his random lurches at door frames, ceilings, and window sills not exactly a crowd-pleasing routine for his captive audience of Perry Sr. and Hattie, who preferred a quiet home.

Certain athletic skills, like speed or leaping ability, are often diminished as simply "God-given" traits, implying that the athlete in question didn't have to work as hard as the teammate who succeeds on heart or hustle. But Perry Wallace wasn't born with springs in his legs. Dunking was a goal he set for himself, something he worked at for years without success. There were the squats, night after night on Cass Street. He even looked for a silver lining in those "fight or flight" moments on his journeys to Elliott School and the long walks to trumpet practice, believing that whether he was running from danger or trudging miles to a music lesson, at least he was strengthening his legs in the process.

As his legs grew stronger, he tested himself on the baskets at North High. From age ten to age twelve, he was a fixture on those courts.

"The dog's baying at the moon, I'm jumping at the goal," he recalled.

For Perry and the other neighborhood kids, the progression toward the rim proceeded at a methodical pace. At first, they grabbed a ball and backed up all the way to the baseline at the far end of the concrete and ran as fast as they could toward the basket—like a plane hurtling down a runway—and then there was liftoff.

Plop.

Their flights were as brief as they were earthbound.

Little by little, the puddle jumpers transformed into jets. First the contest was to see who could run down the court, leap, and touch the rim with his fingertips. For months, Perry and crew worked at this. Finally, success. And then, if you were good enough, you didn't need the running start anymore, you could just stand under the basket and jump up and touch the rim. For months they worked at this. And when you could do that, then you'd back up again, and get a running start and soar through the air and actually try to dunk the basketball.

"I tried and tried and tried, and then one summer, I had to be twelve years old, I finally dunked the ball," Wallace recalled. Literally and figuratively, he had reached a goal. And with that fulfillment came success on two important fronts.

One, he gained a measure of respect from the same neighborhood kids who mocked his studiousness. "In some respects, our enthusiasm for the game was what we had in common, and the dunk was the high point of that," Wallace recalled. "Otherwise, I would have been a very different, strange little kid playing the trumpet four or five hours a day and listening to classical music when everybody else was listening to Motown. On the court, we all came together and we were just the same."

Two, he found in basketball a passage to freedom and accomplishment in a society engineered to limit both. "Playground basketball allowed a sense of expression in a world that was dark and uncertain and in which there were a lot of ways that you were weak," he said. "This, on the other hand, was bright. You could express all these different things, this artistry. It was like a big lift, and the dunk was like a freedom song."

A youngster like Wallace couldn't have fully comprehended it, but his game was blossoming at the very moment in time when Nashville was at the center of black basketball in the South.

In the days before integration siphoned off its best athletes, Tennessee A&I was a powerhouse. Coach Ed Temple and his Tigerbelles (including the legendary Wilma Rudolph) dominated not just collegiate track but the entire world, winning Olympic medals in 1952 and 1956 and dominating the 1960 games in Rome. Football teams coached by Henry Kean, Howard Gentry, and John Merritt won seven black college national championships between 1946 and 1970. And on the hardwood the pioneering coach John McClendon built one of the winningest basketball programs in the country.

McClendon would go on to be considered one of the game's true innovators, credited with developing both the fine points of the full-court press and the fast break as well as the four-corners stall game that is most often attributed to Dean Smith. If McClendon is a father of the game in some ways, it's no wonder: he learned it from *the* father, James Naismith, the inventor of basketball, while a student at the University of Kansas.

After successful runs as head coach at North Carolina College for Negroes and Hampton University, McClendon arrived at Tennessee A&I as an assistant coach in 1954 and took control of the program for the 1954–55 season. Along with the coaches at other black programs, he unsuccessfully lobbied the National Collegiate Athletic Association (NCAA) for years to allow black schools into the organization's tournament. In 1953 a small-school counterpart to the NCAA, the National Association of Intercollegiate Athletics (NAIA), allowed the black colleges to participate in their tournament. By the time McClendon took the reins at Tennessee A&I, a national platform awaited if he could get his Tigers to the NAIA's big dance.

And that's just what he did. After recruiting a flashy, sharpshooting guard from Gary, Indiana, named Dick "Skull" Barnett, McClendon led the high-scoring "Skull and the Whiz Kids" on an unprecedented run, winning the NAIA title in 1957 to become the first black college team to win a national championship against white competition in any sport. And then they did it again in 1958. And again in 1959.

Meanwhile, black high school basketball had flourished in Nashville since before Wallace was born. In 1945 Tennessee A&I president Walter Davis and athletic director Henry Kean saw an opportunity to raise the profile of the game—not to mention their university and athletic program—by reviving a national high school basketball tournament that had previously been held at Hampton before World War II.

For the next two decades, the National High School Athletic Association tournament was held on the A&I campus and at Pearl High, and it became the place not only to spot the South's finest black basketball players, but also

Nashville's most enterprising young gym rats, who discovered countless ways to sneak into the gyms to watch some of the best basketball being played anywhere. Teams from sixteen states traveled to Nashville for the tournament each year, with the city's own Pearl High winning three consecutive national championships between 1958 and 1960, just as Perry Wallace was teaching himself to dunk.

"I'll never forget watching those teams who came from all over the South," Wallace recalled. "You had all of these teams coming from all these places, and all this drama and all this talent and the movement and the shooting and the dunking. It was magnificent, just a super high."

Coached first by William Gupton and then by Cornelius Ridley, the Pearl Tigers were big men on campus and all across North Nashville. Adults jammed Pearl's old gym for Tiger games, whether they had children in the school or not, and neighborhood boys dreamed of one day wearing their own red letter jackets with the big white "P."

Pearl's star players usually went on to play their college ball at black colleges like A&I and Fisk; the recruiting trail was only a few blocks long. White schools in the South still hadn't integrated their teams (or even their universities, in many cases), and most colleges outside the South recruited only a limited number of blacks. But three standouts from those national championship teams were recruited out of state and challenged longstanding stereotypes about black ballplayers. Ron Lawson headed west to join John Wooden's team at UCLA in 1960, and Les Hunter and Vic Rouse were lured to Loyola of Chicago by Coach George Ireland, where they led the Ramblers to an NCAA title in 1963 on the same night Pearl High won its fourth national high school championship. Nashville's budding black stars, hiding in plain sight for so many years, were no longer ignored.

"I was the only white coach in the stands at the tournament at Tennessee A&I in Nashville when Hunter and Rouse were seniors in high school," Ireland once said. "The year after we won the [national] championship there were so many scouts there that you couldn't get tickets."

In this context of excellence emerged the twelve-year-old kid who could dunk. Harold Hunter, who had taken over the Tennessee A&I program from McClendon before the 1959–60 season, made sure to take care of the boy, inviting Wallace to the A&I gym in the summer to play pickup games with his own players and other local kids with talent. "The older guys were amazed," Wallace recalled. "I was running around playing full-court basketball. They'd say, 'Look at this young boy dunk!'"

Wallace continued playing in pickup games at A&I all the way through junior high. He was never the best player running the court; the bigger and older kids made sure he knew that. But he was something of a curiosity, especially early on—the young kid who could dunk. Just as he had done on the playground at North High, he was playing ball against older kids. They were a big influence.

And then one day Big Daddy D strolled into the gym.

Bye-bye, old influences. Hello, David Lattin.

In three years, Lattin would lead an unheard-of school named Texas Western to the NCAA championship, part of an all-black starting five that would startle Adolph Rupp's Kentucky Wildcats in the 1966 title game and serve notice to a national television audience that the days of all-white basketball were over. But for now, Lattin was about to enroll at A&I, a school that had already sent the same message, with far less fanfare, with those three consecutive NAIA championships. Lattin wouldn't last a semester in Nashville before transferring to El Paso and making history, but none of that mattered now. He was "big, strong, and menacing," Wallace recalled, the baddest man in the gym.

Wallace, of course, could dunk. The guys he played with at A&I could dunk. He had watched Chamberlain and Russell dunk. All these guys would pull out the occasional in-your-face slam, but in that era most dunks were still quick little stuffs, more about efficiency than theater. For Wallace, still looking for cues on how to play the game, Lattin took the dunk to another level of possibility. Wilt had made the first major impression; Big Daddy D made the gym shake.

"David Lattin was like if you had a cross between Michael Jordan and a gorilla, and obviously I am not insulting the guy racially," Wallace recalled. "Guys played very serious ball, everybody's sweating and going after it, but he would get the ball and go down the floor and he would do the Michael Jordan dunk—his legs were spread apart the same way—and he'd be flying through the air and everybody under the basket went, 'Oooooooh shit, time to leave, time to go, don't even mess with this, get out of the way!' He's so far in another league, it had a big impression on me."

Between his private trumpet lessons and the pickup basketball games, Wallace had already accomplished quite a bit on the A&I campus before he had even enrolled at Wharton Junior High School, a fact that eluded neither the band instructor nor the basketball coach at Wharton. They both wanted the protégé all to themselves. That he was able to engage in both pursuits came only after significant "pain and diplomacy," he recalled.

The uneasiness caused by this tug-of-war was compounded by Wallace's asthma, which made both of his loves more difficult. As hard as it was to get through the *Carnival of Venice*, it was equally difficult to run up and down the court while regulating his breathing enough to maintain a steady hand. Wallace later concluded that his asthma was worsened by fear, nerves, and excitement, all of which were heightened in concerts or games. On the basketball court, he was often unsteady and short of breath, and he developed a reputation as a poor shooter, the one knock against his game that would linger for years. As the minutes ticked closer to tip-off time before games, he felt an uneasiness in his chest, a mounting nervousness, an inability to breathe. This could have been the end, the wind knocked out of a promising basketball career.

But Wallace improvised. He called upon deep breathing exercises he had learned in his musical training to build his lung capacity. He called upon the hearty and hale tradition of the Rutherford County Wallaces to improve his physical condition through more strenuous drills. And most important, he called upon his mother. In what he would recall nearly a half century later as "a pivotal point" in his youth, Wallace asked his mom for advice on conquering fear, fear that wasn't just confined to the basketball court but pervaded nearly every aspect of his life. "Put on the full armor of God," Hattie advised, and Wallace gradually came upon a way of living that relieved his anxiety and became a core part of his being: prayer and preparation.

The self-help regimen worked, and it became irrelevant to Wharton's opponents whether Perry Wallace was breathing easy. All they knew was that the boy could jump.

"I first learned about Perry when he was in ninth grade at Wharton and I was playing at Washington," said Walter Fisher, who would become a high school teammate of Wallace's. "We had to play Wharton, and I remember this guy who could jump so high. It kind of intimidated me. I said, 'Jesus, is he going to go to Pearl when I get there?'"

The truth was, yes, the guy who could dunk since the time he was twelve, who wanted to be just like Wilt Chamberlain, who held his own in pickup games against college players, yes, that kid would be going to Pearl.

With the full intention of trying out for the band.

And not the basketball team.

Hard as it is to believe now, when basketball phenoms seemingly have signed lifetime sneaker contracts and reality-show TV deals by the time they reach puberty, Wallace had not yet been contacted by Coach Ridley. Without the experience of a basketball-playing older brother to draw on, or parents who were particularly interested in basketball, Wallace wasn't surprised. He wasn't angry. He just thought he wasn't going to be on the team. His junior high band teacher had already made a connection with the Pearl band director. The road to the Marching 100 was paved. But there was no clear path to the basketball team.

"Unfortunately, that's how a lot of things happen in life," Wallace would say of his basketball career that nearly never was. "I was just going to go in the band, and that seemed fine. I was just going to move along and be a student. After I finished the season [at Wharton in ninth grade; Pearl started with tenth grade], I figured I would play on in the playground, with no future in mind. I liked basketball, I loved it, but I didn't have the sense that I could do any more with it. I didn't have a sense of how you make that connection to the team at Pearl. Do they talk to you? Do you talk to them? What do you do? It was clearer with the band."

Coming off the 1963 national championship, Ridley had lost a number of key players and was looking to reload his team. Coach John Tisdale's high-scoring Washington Junior High team had been more of the feeder program for Pearl, producing far more Tiger players than Wharton. Ridley had seen Wallace play, but Perry wasn't at the top of his mind when he paid a visit to Coach Hunter early in the fall. "Have you seen the Wallace kid?" Hunter asked.

"You mean the big kid in the band?" Ridley replied.

"The band?! Have you seen the boy dunk?!"

One can only surmise that it was with Roadrunner-like speed that Ridley vacated Coach Hunter's office and emerged at Hattie Wallace's dinner table. Whether it was a matter of minutes, hours, or days, the coach knocked on the door at Cass Street, intent on pulling the six-foot-five incoming sophomore out of the trumpet section and onto his basketball team.

As Ridley put on his best recruiting pitch, Mr. and Mrs. Wallace worried about Perry's schoolwork, about bad influences, about the lessons they had worked so hard to teach him.

Perry thought about actually being one of those Tigers he looked up to, about playing ball in the old gym, which was so raucous on game nights. He had thought he just wanted to be in the band, but the more Coach Ridley talked, the more he realized what he really wanted to do. Perry Sr. could sense it.

"You've got to keep your grades up," father told son. "You've got to act like you have some sense, you've got to respect people, and you've got to keep going to church. If you do all those, all the time, you can play. Otherwise, come back home."

One of the proudest days of his life, Wallace recalled years later, was the bright, sunny morning in September 1963 when he walked down 17th Avenue and through the doors of Pearl High School on his first day as a Pearl student.

It was, he said, a powerful moment for many reasons. His brother and sisters had gone to Pearl. He was fascinated by the basketball team, and the band. He admired the Pearl students he saw around the neighborhood: They seemed smart and confident. They looked the way he wanted to look. He loved Pearl long before he ever experienced it for himself, as if the school were already a part of his very being.

In a way, it was. When he walked through those doors, he followed in the footsteps of generations. A Pearl education was something just about every black person who grew up in Nashville had in common. Class pictures dating back to the 1890s lined the walls of each corridor, and it seemed as if the eyes in the photos were staring right through the souls of the students who walked down the halls, encouraging them to make the most of their brief time at Pearl and to build on the sacrifices of preceding generations. The school wasn't just the pride of the neighborhood in the 1960s; it had been that centerpiece for more than eighty years.

Like Dunbar High School in Washington, DC, Melrose High School in Memphis, and L. C. Anderson High in Austin, Texas, Pearl was a classic example of one of the ironies of segregation. The same forces designed to limit blacks—most significantly in terms of jobs and neighborhoods—created just the environment necessary for these jewels of education to emerge. With limited job opportunities, many of the most talented black college graduates became teachers. With only a few high schools—or in many cases, just one—available to black students, the best and brightest kids weren't scattered across many schools; they shared the same classrooms. With blacks confined to tightly defined neighborhoods—the cocoon—these schools naturally became hugely important community institutions, an extension of church and family.

Pearl traced its roots all the way back to 1883, when it opened as a grammar school for blacks. Named after Nashville's first superintendent of schools, a northerner named Joshua Pearl who left town to fight for the Union army during the Civil War and later returned to Nashville, the school was converted into a high school and graduated its first class in 1898. One of its first principals was G. E. Washington, whose grandson, Julian Bond, would become one of the key civil rights figures of the 1960s. The school bounced around to a few locations before settling in at the corner of 17th Avenue North and Jo Johnston Avenue in 1937. The building was a masterpiece of art deco craftsmanship designed by Nashville's McKissack and McKissack, a black-owned architectural firm. When the school added a vocational wing in 1945, it began to tout itself as a comprehensive high school, preparing students for college and work. Until Cameron High School opened in 1955, Pearl was the only high school available to blacks in Nashville. Its graduates included doctors, lawyers, and domestics; musicians, pharmacists, and porters.

"When you put the beginning of Pearl into its historical context—at that time segregation had been legally sanctioned from crib to grave, and before Pearl there was no chance of a black even receiving a high school education," historian and Pearl graduate Linda Wynn once told journalist Patrick Connolly, "you can begin to understand how there was so much pride and history mixed together for the African-Americans of Nashville from the very beginning."

The pride and history were palpable as students walked the halls, and so was the discipline. When Perry and his classmates entered the lobby of the brown-brick building each day, there to greet them in his brown suit was a brick house of a man, Principal J. C. Hull. Tony Moorman, a six-foot-four forward on the Pearl basketball team, thought the average-sized principal was one of the most intimidating men he'd ever encountered. "He carried a big stick," Moorman said, "without carrying anything at all."

"Good morning, good morning, good morning," Hull would say in a monotone voice as student after student walked by, hands behind his back, and then, as if by secret elevator or by levitation, there he was again upstairs outside a classroom, checking to be sure everyone made it in by the bell.

Principal Hull, a 1926 Pearl graduate, didn't just know everything about his students—their names, their class schedules, the stipulations of their suspensions ("He would have three hundred people on detention, and he would remember exactly when each one was supposed to report back to school," one alum recalled)—he knew everything about his students' *families*, which made the consequences of any misstep problematic. Get into trouble at school and you embarrassed the whole family.

"A lot of our parents were not educated people, but they knew the value of education and the doors it could open for you," said Pearl alum Lee Hayden. "Going to Pearl was a great opportunity and we shouldn't be squandering it whatsoever. Not graduating from high school was not an option, even if it took you four hundred years."

What made this discipline different, what allowed the students to appreciate it as much then as they did later in life, was that it was so clearly administered with love. The teachers were highly educated men and women—more than half held master's degrees—who had been denied most of the career possibilities available to their white counterparts. They knew the odds were stacked against their students, but they also understood that the world was changing, that opportunities would be available to these kids that they never enjoyed themselves. Wallace's Class of '66 entered Pearl as sophomores just a week after Martin Luther King's "I Have a Dream" speech in 1963. Before he and his classmates earned their diplomas, they'd see the passage of the 1964 Civil Rights Act and the 1965 Voting Rights Act. America, it seemed, was opening its doors, and this generation of students would enter adulthood at just the right time. "There was something special in the air," Wallace recalled. "Perhaps it was hope, maybe it was just a sense of excitement. But by then even those of us who were not directly involved in civil rights activity could tell there was movement and change on the racial front."

Embracing their roles as mentors at this critical point in history, Pearl's teachers threw themselves into their jobs with uncommon enthusiasm and dedication, and in the process created a rich, nurturing, and intellectual environment that made up for the deficits of a separate and unequal system.

Decades later, Perry Wallace coined a term for it: Pearl had become separate but *equalized*.

The special danger of separate but unequal—as damaging and dangerous as the lack of opportunities and resources—was the message sent to black kids that they were inferior. *Separate but equalized*, Wallace came to believe, was the most positive response possible to the discriminatory practices of a separate and unequal world.

To create an *equalized* environment, the teachers at Pearl sometimes spent their own money to buy new textbooks to replace the tattered ones sent over from white high schools. They made sure that black entertainers and other celebrities passing through Nashville took some time to encourage and inspire the students. They talked about ideals like equality and opportunity, and they taught lessons about black history that could be found in no textbook. They shared lessons they had learned from their own teachers—teachers, in several cases, named Booker T. Washington and W. E. B. DuBois. In the vernacular of the day, the teachers at Pearl were "race people," dedicated to improving the lives of their black students.

"It was the old style, but our teachers invested in us day after day, made us set high standards, and held us to them," Wallace said. "Opportunity seemed so close at hand. Things were happening right before our eyes, and there seemed to be such a good possibility of people living really good lives."

Students gravitated toward Minerva Hawkins, a history teacher who had once studied under DuBois. Hawkins, who was so light-skinned that many students initially thought she was white, was such a captivating speaker that some students spent their free periods or homeroom hours sitting in on extra lectures. An expert on African American history, not a field of study taught in the schools at the time, Hawkins made sure her students were aware of the contributions of blacks that were so often ignored. "That's what the textbooks tell us," Hawkins would say, closing her book. "Now let me tell you what really happened."

Wallace, the math and science scholar who had been studying college texts at the Hadley Park library for years, was especially influenced by trigonometry teacher Dorothy Crippens. Short, petite, prim, and proper ("She spoke the King's English and she expected you to, also," one student remembered), Crippens was the wife of a prominent doctor and the embodiment of Nashville's strong black middle class. She had taught Perry's sisters years earlier, and because she saw such promise in their younger brother, she pushed Wallace hard. He loved the challenge.

To be sure, there were students at Pearl who were more interested in sports or dating or cutting class down at Jake's Barber Shop, doing who knows what, than they were in academics. The kids weren't all saintly bookworms; Principal Hull did have that suspension list memorized. But for most students,

Pearl was a warm, nurturing, inspirational place, free of the kind of peer pressure that made it uncool to take school seriously.

"You didn't have to hide being smart," said Pearl graduate Donna Murray, whose only C came in driver's education when she couldn't master the stick shift. "Our teachers made us feel special, and in an unspoken way they made us know that we were somebody, that nobody could tell us we were less than that."

Years later, Wallace came to better understand the poignancy of those student-teacher relationships. He thought about the battles his teachers must have fought to earn their degrees, the way they overcame fear and self-hatred living in the Jim Crow South, the pain and frustration of emerging educated into a world of closed doors and scarce opportunities.

"Our teachers somehow took all this insult, this institutionalized, nationalized insult called segregation and turned it into a force to make the world better, and particularly to do it through all these young students," Wallace said. "Sometimes they seemed a little mean and to have an edge. I guess I can understand that now. This was the America they lived in; for all the good, there was all this madness."

Standards were high when it came to academic achievement, but they were high in other ways, too. In the days before business-casual at the office and jeans and T-shirts at school, when suits and ties and fedoras and dresses and heels were still the norm at all levels of society, an education in social conventions was all part of the package at Pearl. Students dressed up for school every day; the "best-dressed" superlative award was highly coveted. No pants for girls, no untucked shirt-tails for boys.

And then there were Fridays.

Step inside the Pearl High gym on a Friday afternoon in the mid-1960s. Boys in coat and tie, girls in their Sunday best. Gym class is canceled, as it is every Friday, and in its place is Co-Recreation, co-rec. The smell of sweat has been replaced by whiffs of perfume and cologne. The shrill sound of a gym teacher's whistle silenced in favor of the grooves of the Temptations, the Supremes, and the Four Tops. There's no running or rope climbing on Fridays. Instead, boys and girls are dancing. The kids are having fun, but they're also learning how to socialize, how to treat each other with respect, how to practice good manners. The Friday co-rec dances were a blast, even for those students sitting on the bleachers, just listening to the music and talking to friends, the shy ones who did not dance, the ones who could not dance because they were Church of Christ, the ones like Perry Wallace.

WOOOOOOOOMP! WOOOOOOMP! WOOOOOOOOOMP!
Sometimes being a student at Pearl was just plain fun. There was nothing more raucous, nothing more exhilarating, than the "woomp show" before a basketball game in the old gym.

Here came the Pearl High cagers in their satin warm-up suits, red and white pinstripes and Tigers ablaze. The gym was already packed, and it was only halftime of the JV game when the varsity came running out on the court for their early warm-ups, accompanied by the bones and whistles of "Sweet Georgia Brown," theme song of the Harlem Globetrotters.

Balls bouncing, sneakers squeaking, girls shrieking.

First some layups, Tiger after Tiger rolling to the hoop and laying the ball off the glass.

The repetition was hypnotic, Tiger after Tiger, but then there was a wink, and "woooomp!"—there it was, Willie Fisher flew through the air and dunked the ball. And then another guard, Joe Herbert, dunked it, and then came Hound McClain, and the crowd yelled, "woooomp!"—another dunk. And then came Walter Fisher and the rest of the big sticks, the forwards and centers, and the dunks got more powerful and the wooomps! got louder. Wooomp! Wooomp! Woooomp!

And then to finish it all off, to make the walls shake and the gym cave in, came the high-flyingest dunker of them all, the kid who idolized Wilt Chamberlain and Big Daddy D: here came Perry Wallace with a swish-swash reverse slam or a tomahawk or a rock-the-cradle or a one-handed windmill to top it all off, and the gym erupted with one final woooomp!

The dunk was Perry's "freedom song" and his connection to his class-mates, and it was also the end—before the game had even begun, before the JV game was even complete—for more than a few Pearl opponents, who stood on the other end of the court, slack-jawed, watching an entire team slam dunk the ball in warm-ups. Woooomp! Game over.

Some coaches may have frowned upon such displays of individual flair, but not Cornelius Ridley. The Pearl coach knew the demoralizing effect the dunks had on his team's opponents, and he encouraged his charges to throw it down with authority.

Pearl had won its first Tennessee High School Athletic Association (THSAA) basketball title in 1942 under legendary coach William Gupton, whose teams won more than 80 percent of their games during his tenure from 1939 to 1960. By the time Wallace enrolled in the fall of 1963, the school had won twelve state championships, far more (Knoxville's Austin High was second, with three titles) than any other black high school in the Volunteer State.

Ridley, a former Pearl football and basketball player, had been named head coach at Pearl prior to the 1960–61 season at age twenty-eight. Known as Pra' (short for "professor") Ridley to his players, he was every bit as tough, demanding, passionate, and caring to his ballplayers as any of the school's teachers were to their students.

As a biology teacher, Ridley intimidated some of his students, never allowing any joking or horseplay in his classroom. On the practice court, he demanded complete respect for authority. Many Pearl players believed that their practices were harder than their games, but because they knew the success Ridley had achieved, they bought into his hard-driving style without complaint. Mainly that meant running. As Walter Fisher once put it, "Ridley ran us to death."

Mostly, the running was for conditioning's sake. Nobody was in better shape than the Pearl Tigers. By the time the fourth quarter rolled around, Fisher recalled, the Pearl players were "getting [their] second wind before our opponent even got their first."

Occasionally there was another message behind all the running, which was never more evident than the day one of the Pearl players got caught smoking. When a cigarette fell out of his pocket. Before practice. In front of Coach Ridley.

"Whose cigarettes are those?!" the coach demanded.

"Their yours, Pra," the offender offered.

"No they're not, they're not my brand!" Ridley bellowed, deciding that group punishment was the best way to teach his team a lesson, even though he himself chain-smoked Winstons. And with that, the entire team was made to run up and down the gym stairs, across and around the length of the court, again and again, for an hour before the regular practice started. As the players ran, not daring to throw up, Ridley kept up a drumbeat of admonishment.

"Marlboro . . . Camel . . . Kool . . . Which one do you smoke? Viceroy! I'm a coach, I'm not a basketball player . . . I don't need endurance . . . I don't need wind."

Ridley's practices were as methodical as they were lively. He began each session with individual drills, designed to improve skills such as ball handling. The players worked against each other two-on-two or three-on-three before the whole team practiced together, running through specific plays five-on-five. He ran the same sets over and over until his guys got it right. All the while, Ridley was thoroughly engaged, pouring his soul into the workouts.

"I can still hear him to this day," recalled Moorman. "We'd be working on a one-three-one half-court trap in practice and he'd be hollering out, 'You got him, you got him, you got him, don't let him out!'"

Ridley's zeal in practice, however, was nothing compared to his demeanor in games. In particularly intense games, one of the primary duties for Assistant Coach James Armstrong (who was also the head football coach) was to pull on Coach Ridley, holding him back from the referees while shouting, "Calm down, Ridley, calm down!"

Ridley, Wallace recalled, "was a show to himself" during games, up and off his seat, hollering at the refs, collar loosened, shirttail untucked, game program rolled up in his hand, necktie flying this way and that, Armstrong and some of the guys on the bench pulling and yanking on him like deckhands trying to keep a man from falling overboard in a heavy sea.

Ridley's antics made him no referee favorite, often sending the refs so close to the brink over the course of a game that the slightest peep out of Ridley's mouth would result in a technical foul. Briefly, he came up with a plan to get around this problem, writing the team's plays on big cards so he could hold them up and call a defense without saying a word. The experiment didn't last long; it just wasn't Pra Ridley's style.

The fact was that Ridley's demeanor obscured his basketball IQ. He was a student of the game and an insightful reader of people, knowing exactly which buttons to push at any given time. There were times when his players could see him out of the corners of their eyes, going ballistic over on the sideline, screaming and hollering and all disheveled, and they'd be a little afraid of what he might say at the next timeout. But when they arrived in the huddle, it was as if the storm had passed. "Now listen," Ridley would say calmly, "this is what we're going to do."

There were times, when the team was rolling, when he wouldn't say much at all at halftime. He and Assistant Coach Melvin Black would fire up their Winstons, taking such long and slow drags that Fisher found it soothing just to watch. And there were times when the Tigers needed nothing more than a butt chewing, and Ridley would tell his men that they better get their heads out of their butts and get their butts back on defense, or they were going to get their butts run out of the gym—*and nobody runs better than we do!*

Ridley's style was unlike anything Wallace had ever experienced. His junior high band instructor had been tough, but this was different. Ridley was demanding and he was out of control at times, but Wallace loved his coach. He admired the way he approached basketball with not one bit of self-consciousness. Ridley was all the way in, every second of every game and every practice. His intensity had a profound effect on Wallace, helping draw the naïve kid out of the shell that had developed over his ever-so-protected childhood.

Many times, Pra Ridley and his wife would drive Perry home after games. After the obligatory admonishment from his wife—"Ridley," she'd say, "you're going to have a heart attack out there jumping up and down like that"—the coach would engage his young ballplayer in conversations on all sorts of subjects, sharing his thoughts on people, on the times, and on the ways of the world. Driving through the streets of North Nashville on those dark winter nights, a deep friendship developed between the dynamic coach and the "shy little boy who was afraid of [his] own shadow." It was as if Ridley were injecting the book-smart Wallace with booster shots of street smarts and perspective.

"What I learned from him were things that were just not a part of me at the time," Wallace recalled. "He knew people and he knew the world so very well, and I didn't. I was the good little boy who was naïve and didn't hang out on the streets or go to parties, so I didn't know a lot of 'grown-up' stuff. I was the kind of kid who was like, 'Brooklyn Bridge? Great, how much? Five dollars? That's a bargain, where is it? Bring it to my backyard!' But Ridley had so much savvy and he helped me develop a deeper knowledge of people and life."

Over the years Wallace would build on the lessons taught by Pra Ridley and become known as someone with an uncommonly insightful perspective on people and events—a fact, he said, that would have shocked the people who grew up around him.

Together this duo, the wise young coach and the willing young student, made a dynamic pair. Along with a roster full of players who would go on to play college ball, Wallace would be a part of a state championship team in the all-black THSAA in the 1964 season, his first at Pearl.

By this time, there were signs that segregation's hold in Tennessee was unraveling, even in the highly politicized and tradition-soaked area of high school athletics. The first stitch had come undone a decade earlier, when just months after the *Brown* ruling Nashville's private Catholic high school for boys, Father Ryan, became the first white school in the state to admit black students.

By 1964 the state's white and black teachers' associations began to discuss a merger, as did the all-white Tennessee Secondary School Athletic Association (TSSAA) and the THSAA. For centuries, custom in the South had accepted some amount of interaction between young white and black children, but as puberty neared, those playground friendships were squashed in the name of the Southern Way of Life. But now, not only would blacks and whites attend some of the same schools, but they'd sweat on each other on the basketball court, bleed on each other on the football field. Perky white female cheerleaders in their skirts and sweaters would jump and kick just inches away from muscular black boys in shorts and sleeveless jerseys. Changes this jarring to the old guard would not come easily in the South. In fact, the voluntary merger between the white and black athletic associations in the spring of 1964 in Tennessee represented the only "peaceful" transition; every other state in the region allowed blacks and whites to compete against each other at the high school level only after state order.

Even in Tennessee, the merger was implemented gradually. Black schools would participate only as "affiliate members" of the TSSAA for one year, meaning they would compete in an all-black subset of the association in 1965 before becoming eligible for unified state championships in 1966.

While the public schools plodded along, Father Ryan High School, in the tradition of many Catholic schools around the country that were relatively progressive on race, continued to strike its own blows against segregation. First, the school, which occupied a revered place among Nashville's small Catholic population much as Pearl stood at the center of the city's black community, scheduled football games against integrated squads from Kentucky. Then, nearly a decade after admitting its first black students, Father Ryan finally allowed some of those boys to participate on its athletic teams beginning in the 1963–64 school year, coming to the conclusion that the threats it had received from other members of the Nashville Interscholastic League— *We won't take the court if you play those black boys*—were nothing but hot air. When the Irish team picture was taken that year, there were two black faces in it, belonging to Willie Brown and Jesse Porter.

And then Ryan coach Bill Derrick got an idea. It was one thing for his integrated team to play against Nashville's all-white competition. How about taking the next natural step in his school's stand against the status quo? How about testing his talented team against the very best? How about playing Pearl?

So many turning points in history seem inevitable in hindsight, though they never were at the time. In the lore of Tennessee high school basketball, the transformation from unfathomable to inevitable began the moment Derrick picked up the phone and called Cornelius Ridley.

That Ridley's answer would be "Yes, we'll play you" was a foregone conclusion for two reasons. Segregation was the white man's idea, his burden. Ridley hadn't *preferred* to drive all the way to Memphis and Clarksville and Chattanooga just to find black schools to play. Second, he knew he had a great team returning for the 1964–65 season. If he was going to get his opportunity to play against a white team, it might as well be now, with so many key players returning from the 1964 black state champions.

No sooner had the first game between a black and a predominantly white school been scheduled—for January 4, 1965—than it became the most highly anticipated schoolboy basketball game in Nashville history. As players and coaches from both teams enjoyed some time off from school over the Christmas holiday, they were bombarded with questions from friends and neighbors about the historic game. Tony Moorman, the Pearl forward, couldn't escape the hype anywhere. Even at church, he said, all anyone wanted to talk about was the Ryan game. Even the sermons touched on the game.

All this was taking place during one of the most intense periods of the civil rights movement. Just a year and a half earlier, the 16th Street Baptist Church in Birmingham had been bombed, killing four young black girls; six months earlier, President Johnson had signed the Civil Rights Act; five months earlier, civil rights workers James Chaney, Andrew Goodman, and Michael Schwerner—one black, two white—were killed by Klan members in Neshoba County, Mississippi. One month after the game, Malcolm X would be shot down in New York; two months later, the Edmund Pettus Bridge in Selma, Alabama, would be the site of the "Bloody Sunday" attacks on peaceful protestors; seven months later, President Johnson would sign the Voting Rights Act, and riots in the Watts section of Los Angeles would set the city ablaze.

Interest in the game was so overwhelming that both schools realized that neither of their own gyms would be large enough to accommodate the expected crowd. Neither would Vanderbilt's Memorial Gym, which had a capacity of 7,229. The game, then, would be played downtown at the city's modern Municipal Auditorium, a locale that reflected the conflicting forces pulling on the city. The fact that the 10,000-seat arena even existed was evidence of the city's aspirations to be something more than a parochial hamlet; with a new auditorium, traveling shows and events from around the country could be brought to the capital city. The site of this game that would bring blacks and whites together like never before had opened in 1962 with an old-fashioned Church of Christ revival and was the site of more than a few rodeos. "Municipal," as locals called it, was also home to an unlikely source of pride in the South: a professional hockey team. The Nashville Dixie Flyers were drawing huge crowds and sitting atop the standings of the East Coast Hockey League in January 1965, so popular that on the day of the Pearl-Ryan game, the *Tennessean*, a newspaper known for its perceptive coverage of the civil rights movement, editorialized not about the historic basketball matchup but about the success of the Dixie Flyers, calling the team's eight-game winning streak "one of the most unbelievable performances in Nashville sports history." Perhaps the most telling example of the competing ideologies in Nashville came a week after the Pearl-Ryan game when Alabama's segregationist governor, George Wallace, appeared at Municipal Auditorium as the keynote speaker at a state teachers' convention. On the one hand, he had been invited to speak; on the other, according to Metro police detective R. B. Owen, who did the counting, only 369 people bothered to show up, leaving 9,631 empty seats.

As good as they were, the Pearl Tigers rarely received coverage that wasn't relegated to the back page of the sports section. Even the white schools were accustomed only to postgame accounts of their games. Rare was the preview article. But as soon as the calendar turned from 1964 to 1965, coverage of the upcoming Pearl-Ryan game dominated the sports pages.

Both Ridley and Derrick engaged in coach-speak familiar to sports fans decades later. Ridley warned that his current Tiger team wasn't "as good as the club that won the national tournament." Derrick bemoaned his squad's poor free-throw shooting, saying, "We are expecting the worst if we play like we have been playing."

Not that anyone bought into the poor-mouthing. Pearl entered the game with a 6–1 record, its only loss coming in an unofficial season-opening contest against a collection of Pearl alums. The Tigers averaged seventy-nine points per game, boasted four players scoring in double figures, and had blown out Memphis' Lester High School 105–49. Ryan also was 6–1, on its way to a 27–2 record that still stands as the best in school history, its suffocating zone press limiting opponents to just forty-eight points per game.

As game day approached, Coach Ridley issued a subtle rejoinder against the common stereotypes of the day. His Tigers, Ridley told *Tennessean* reporter Jimmy Davy, "will surprise some people who believe all we do is run and shoot. We like to shoot, all right, but we do some other things, too." It was just the kind of perceptive statement that the ever-more clued-in Wallace was beginning to appreciate. On the eve of the most important game of his career, Ridley was thinking not only about the game at hand but about the larger issues at play. He didn't just roll out the basketballs and let his Tigers loose, a common stereotype whites ascribed to black teams then and for decades to come. He had a system, his practices were tough, his players were smart.

"We understood," Wallace recalled, "that this was not just another game."

January 4, 1965. Game day.

In Washington, DC, President Johnson delivered his State of the Union address, talking to the nation about a "Great Society," the iconic agenda that spawned programs to improve public health, protect the environment, fight poverty, support the arts, and combat institutionalized racism.

In downtown Nashville, Memphis attorney A. W. Willis Jr. walked into the state capitol and took his seat at a rickety old desk, becoming the first black since Reconstruction to serve in the Tennessee General Assembly.

And just a few blocks away at Municipal Auditorium, the gates to history opened at 6:00 p.m., fans from both schools flooding into the arena with their $1.25 general admission tickets, so many of them coming in so fast that the doors would have to be locked before tip-off.

It was the junior varsity players from Pearl and Ryan who actually made history first on this night, since their 6:30 p.m. game preceded the main attraction. As fans by the thousands scrambled to find the best seats, the kids who weren't yet good enough to make the varsity suddenly found themselves playing ball in front of more than eight thousand people.

"I remember coming out onto the court for the fourth quarter of our game," Pearl JV forward Tony Moorman recalled, "and it seemed like there were two million people in there. We'd make a basket and our fans would erupt so loud you'd hear ringing in your ears. Then they'd make a basket and their side would erupt. It was a first for both teams to see that many people at a game."

As usual, Pearl's varsity squad put on its high-flying "woomp show" dunkathon during halftime of the JV game, bringing the Tiger partisans to their feet and nearly sending Ryan varsity center Robert Forte, who had poked his head out of the locker room to see what the noise was all about, into cardiac arrest when he mistook the Pearl varsity for the JV.

"I thought if this is the B-team, we don't have a chance," Forte later told journalist Andy Telli.

Both junior varsity teams played tight with so many eyes watching their every move, Moorman felt, but the Pearl JVs ended up winning the game handily.

After brief remarks by the principals of both schools, it was time for the main event, the first of sixty-three high school basketball games in Nashville that week but the only one that mattered.

Once again, Wallace and his teammates went through their dunking show in pregame warm-ups. Dunk. woomp! Dunk. woomp! There seemed to be more Pearl fans than Father Ryan supporters in the gym, and, at least in pregame, they had more cause to cheer.

Irish guard Pat Sanders found himself momentarily mesmerized by a sight he'd never seen on a basketball court, as the Pearl players (every single one of them!) rolled to the basket and threw down dunk after dunk. Coach Derrick saw that the Tiger routine was having its desired effect, yelling at Sanders to either quit staring or head back to the locker room.

The game started and most fans remained standing, as they would for the entire game. The crowd was so loud that at one point in the first quarter, Father Ryan was issued a technical foul when Coach Derrick couldn't hear the buzzer summoning the team back to the court after a timeout.

Though his team held a slight height advantage over Pearl, Derrick believed the Tigers' strength and leaping ability would prevent his team from collecting many rebounds, especially on the offensive end. *We're only going to get one shot each time down the court*, he thought, *so we better make it count.* Ryan took its time, working the ball around and waiting for the perfect shot.

The deliberate style worked early on, with Ryan holding a 15–11 lead after the first period. In the second quarter, however, Pearl's speed and pressure altered the flow of the game, and Wallace began to dominate. He hit five of seven shots in the second quarter alone, sending the Pearl crowd into pandemonium with two dunks, one off a fast break and the other following a missed free throw.

Pearl led 31–29 at halftime and scored the first six points of the third quarter to take an eight-point advantage.

Cue Willie Brown.

One of three blacks on the Father Ryan roster but the only one to see playing time in the game, Brown grew up in the same neighborhood as many of the Pearl players. All the Tigers knew him; they had played with him in summer pickup games for years. One Pearl fan had brought her thirteen-year-old nephew with her to the game. As she cheered for the Tigers, the young boy rooted for Willie Brown and Father Ryan. In many ways, for the one time in his career, Brown was the most comfortable guy on the court. Half the crowd was rooting for his team; the other half—and all of his opponents—knew him, admired him, and looked like him.

"I had a very special place in my heart for Willie Brown," Wallace said years later. "He was as warm and good as he was a fierce competitor."

Brown hit a shot. And another. And another. And another. He added a free throw. As the fourth quarter began, he had pulled the Irish to within one point, 44–43. The pace of the game slowed considerably, both teams trading a handful of baskets until Ron Parham put Pearl up 51–50 with just thirty-six seconds remaining.

And then, a blur.

After Parham's basket, Pearl gets the ball back five seconds later, but almost immediately turns it right back over to Ryan. The final seconds tick away, all the fans standing and cheering, everyone knowing the ball is headed in Willie Brown's direction, and it is, and he shoots from the right corner, but the ball caroms off the rim, and it looks as if Pearl has won, but there is Ryan's Lyn Dempsey, the backup guard who hasn't scored a point or grabbed a rebound all game, and the ball lands in his hands, and he takes a step back, and Wallace lunges toward him, and Dempsey launches the ball high over the defender's arms, and the buzzer sounds, and the ball soars fifteen feet before it rips through the net, and Ryan has won 52–51.

Dempsey was the hero, but the star of the game, this first-ever contest between black and white, was the black player named Brown on the white team who would celebrate his birthday the following day, Willie Brown, whose twenty-one points led all scorers.

Ryan's players and fans celebrated on the court, and the whoops and hollers continued all the way back to the locker room. Amid the chaos, Derrick told *Banner* reporter C. B. Fletcher that "this could have well been the finest victory in Ryan's long athletic history. I'm sure no other was more hard-fought or richly deserved. . . . Willie was just great. You can't ask for much more."

Those hoping the game would strike a blow for racial reconciliation couldn't have asked for more, either. Though there was a heavy police presence at the game and much consternation about potential fights on or off the court, there were no incidents. Far from being awkward or unnatural or unfair or whatever else segregationists thought might happen if white kids and black kids stepped on the court together, this game had been so well played that one fan leaving the arena was heard to say that fans should have to pay another $1.25 to get out. A black player had excelled on an integrated team, one of the most high-profile examples in Nashville's history of blacks and whites working together to achieve a common goal. All this was a step in the right direction, something many of the Pearl players would admit decades later.

But for now, as they trudged off the court, the Tigers just felt numb.

Ever since this game had been announced, folks had approached these players in the barbershops and on the street corners and in church and told them that this was the opportunity everyone in Nashville's black community had been waiting for, the first—and maybe *only*; who knew?—chance to compete on the same basketball court as whites and prove that blacks were just as good, if not better. You get that opportunity, the older folks told the Pearl players, and you play like there's no tomorrow.

They had done just that, but all that mattered was that they had lost. Perry Wallace, Walter Fisher, and Ted McClain walked off that court together, heads hanging low. And then, determined that he'd never feel this pain again as long as he wore a Pearl High uniform, McClain broke the silence.

"Walt," he said to Fisher, "you know, we ain't going to lose any more games."

They walked on, and Wallace lifted his head. "I don't think we will, either."

4

They Had the Wrong Guy

She wasn't the kind of person fans were accustomed to seeing on the basketball court. Pearl High School's "Sweetheart of the Week" was usually one of the popular girls, someone a little more glamorous, more outgoing. But there stood Jackie Akins in her best dress, alone at the center of the gymnasium, all eyes on her, and nobody could believe what they were seeing.

Jackie Akins was the kind of girl who felt most at home at the library, more likely to be found studying for a math contest than hanging out with friends. She was six feet tall and intensely thoughtful—a self-described nerd. She was attractive, but she wasn't the type of girl who swooned at the mere sight of a Tiger basketball player.

But here she was at halftime of the ballgame, Sweetheart of the Week, and her parents could not have been more proud. Their little girl, who had "never done anything desirable in terms of social things," was suddenly the center of everyone's attention. Jackie Akins soaked it all in. As her date walked slowly toward her, she realized that for this one brief moment in time, she existed "in the same realm as all the hot chicks."

Her boyfriend drew closer, clutching a corsage. He looked slightly out of place, holding that flower while dressed in his Pearl Tiger uniform, but he was confident out there on the basketball court, and that was reassuring.

As Jackie Akins watched Perry Wallace pin the corsage to her dress, she knew that it was only by the sheer force of his persona that she had been named Sweetheart of the Week, a bookworm in the land of the foxes. Just because she didn't fit the mold, he told her, didn't mean she didn't deserve to be there.

Perry and Jackie had met at Pearl, grouped into many of the same courses with the other exceptionally smart kids. She was Perry's first girlfriend, and he was attracted to her mind as much as anything else. Though Perry would be named the valedictorian of their graduating class, he believed that Jackie was the smartest kid in the school.

"You always felt like, 'There's a whole lot of stuff that she knows that I don't know, and I don't even know what it is!'" Wallace recalled. "She was that much smarter than the rest of us. But it was a really nice relationship because it laid the groundwork for being interested in intelligent women who had a broad interest in the world."

Well-mannered and comfortable with adults, Perry was at ease with Jackie's parents. Her boyfriend, Jackie realized, wasn't just the kind of guy *mothers* liked; he was the sort, more impressively, that *fathers* liked. Her own dad, a railroad worker, was the type who thought nobody was good enough for his girl, but even he accepted Perry without hesitation.

"Most of the basketball players were ladies' men, but Perry was not that kind of guy. He was not scary to someone like me," Akins recalled. "I remember the first time he came to my house and he talked to my parents in a way that was both respectful and engaging. After he left, they were both impressed by this guy—who was already becoming famous for his athletic ability—who was also a genuinely respectful and interesting human being. And of course they thought it was pretty cool that *Perry Wallace* was at all interested in their daughter. It gave them some cachet, too."

Perry and Jackie found their own niche. There were the barbershop boys who cut class and partied, there were the guys in the band who snuck liquor into their instrument cases and were popular with the girls, the athletes who ruled the school cafeteria, the kids who smoked and drank and did all the other things expected of a cool teenager in the mid-1960s. Perry and Jackie were content to be different.

At a party, Wallace recalled, they would find a quiet corner and just talk, the conversation inevitably turning to their hopes and fears about life beyond high school—outside Nashville, outside the South—about how they felt "pretty unsuited for the narrow world that had birthed us and raised us."

They went to movies and on picnics, even horseback riding ("such a Nashville thing to do," Akins recalled). Eventually, they attended the senior prom together ("He couldn't dance because he was Church of Christ, and I couldn't dance because I didn't know how," she remembered). They teamed up on projects at school and on extracurricular activities, including a memorable Junior Achievement project one winter.

The assignment was to come up with an idea for a small business and then put the idea into action. Not surprisingly, their concept wasn't particularly cutting edge. They didn't come up with an idea for a record company or a line of clothing or accessories for a car. No, their idea was perfectly sensible, practical, and parent approved.

"We had this little machine and we made these little bows that go on

Christmas gifts," Akins recalled. "It was a very narrow niche and we only had about three weeks to sell them. I'll never forget making those darn bows. To top it off, our sponsor was the Neuhoff meat packing plant. They took us on a tour, and after that you didn't want to eat meat ever again."

Perry and Jackie were drawn together by their similar personalities, but there was also something else—*someone else*—at work. He was a fellow Christmas-bow salesman, and his name was Walter Murray.

Perry had known Walter since their days together in the All-City Band in elementary school, while Jackie had known the preacher's son since she was nine years old. Along with Walter's girlfriend, Donna, who was a year ahead of them in school, the group became tight friends at Pearl, and it was Walter, more socially confident and outgoing than the rest, who most easily bridged the gaps between the band members, the basketball players, the smart kids, the partiers, the teachers and administrators, and the parents. Everyone, it seemed, admired Walter Murray, who was voted Pearl's student council president as a senior. From an early age, he was a natural politician in the best sense, Akins recalled, with an uncanny ability to relate to people on both sides of an issue—big or small—in a way that inspired both camps to have confidence in him. "We were the same age but he always seemed to be not just a confidant but an advisor to me and to others," she said.

While Akins and Wallace lacked some social skills, Murray was a natural, no matter the circumstance. Donna remembered laying eyes on him for the first time at a party the summer before her first year at Pearl. A record player blared, and everyone was doing a dance called the Pony; Murray, the youngest kid in the room, confidently led the other students across the floor in the Pony line.

Donna and Walter didn't officially meet until a year later, as she was walking out of school after a chorus practice. Carrying a stack of 45-rpm records, she was ready for her mom to pick her up and drive her home to get ready for a party. But as she stepped outside, she lost her grip on the records, and they all went flying to the ground, some cracking, some rolling down the stairs. Total heartbreak for the would-be party hostess. Almost immediately, there was Walter Murray, the boy she remembered from the Pony line, down on his knees helping scoop up all the discs. That would have been enough, a generous gesture for a tenth grader, but Donna was won over by what came next. Walter sensed how flustered and saddened Donna was over breaking the records she had collected for her party, so he sat down beside her and helped pass the time before her mother arrived to pick her up. He told funny stories to take her mind off the accident, and she found herself feeling better. Donna's mom pulled up and drove her home, but within days it was Walter who was walking Donna home from school every day, the beginning of a relationship that would lead to marriage.

Murray's uncanny ability not only to empathize with others but also to actively help people manage their circumstances made him a particularly helpful best friend to Perry Wallace. While they shared a love for music and an intellectual curiosity, they both possessed something the other did not. Walter knew people and what motivated them; Perry's basketball skills had him on the verge of becoming a community hero to blacks and a highly coveted commodity by whites. Walter picked up on this more quickly than most, sensing how much pressure his friend would be facing as he prepared to make a choice about college and how much support he would need.

There were lots of smart, ambitious students at Pearl, and plenty of the 441 graduates would continue their education after graduation. The question for many of them wasn't whether they were going to college, but where. For the college-bound Pearl graduate, the choices had always been black colleges like Fisk, Tennessee A&I, Howard, and Spelman, or, for a few, white schools in the North or East. Murray had his heart set on Brown University in Providence, Rhode Island, while Akins was drawn to Bryn Mawr College in Pennsylvania. Wallace thought about getting away to a school in the Midwest.

What Murray understood was that to the outside world, the future plans for 440 Pearl students were irrelevant.

The other kid? That was a whole other story.

Walking off the court after losing to Father Ryan in 1965, Wallace, McClain, and Fisher predicted they would never lose again. They were proven wrong almost immediately, losing another game eleven days later. But following that loss to Clarksville's Burt High School, the Tigers completed the rest of Wallace's junior season without another defeat, earning a reputation around North Nashville as "The Fabulous Five," as they outclassed one opponent after another en route to the final all-black state tournament championship (as "Affiliate Members" of the state athletic association) in Tennessee history.

Wallace was not the best player on that team—that honor belonged to McClain—but he had size, phenomenal leaping ability, and an overall game that was improving each week as he battled in practice with senior Jesse Rucker, a tough player who ferociously fought for every rebound. It was around this time that Rucker and his teammates started calling Wallace by a nickname that would have a derogatory connotation if it had been used outside the black community, but was just fine within it: Ape Baby.

Like any good nickname, it caught on so fast that nobody knew how it started. Take one look at Walter Fisher and you knew why everybody called him Slim. But Ape Baby? Fisher believed it was Rucker who came up with the name "because Perry was so monstrous on the backboard, like an ape. And when apes grab something, they don't give it back." Moorman thought one of the team trainers gave him the name because "that's what Perry did on the court. He just took stuff and there's nothing you could do about it."

The truth is, the nickname wasn't coined by anyone as tough as Jesse Rucker, and it had more to do with "baby" than "ape." Decades later, Wallace remembered exactly when, where, and why he was given the name. It was just a girl trying to flirt with him.

"We were playing against Merry High School in Jackson, Tennessee," he recalled. "As we played, the crowd was very lively, and then after the game a group of girls was teasing with us, and one of them called me Ape Baby. She said, 'Look at this cute little baby-faced boy with these long arms.' And so for that reason, Ape Baby became my name. Also, 'Duck,' because I had big feet. Ape Baby was one I didn't share with people later on for obvious reasons."

Whether you called them Slim, Ape, and Hound, or Walter, Perry, and Ted, the Tigers were dominant for the rest of that 1965 season. They saved their most impressive performance for the Affiliate State Tournament on the campus of Tennessee A&I, dunking the ball with such power that the backboard finally gave way, delaying the games for five hours before a replacement was found at Vanderbilt. When Pearl beat Gallatin Union for the title (with Wallace named to the All-Tournament team), it was the end of an era in Tennessee. The following season, as every Pearl player knew, they would compete against white schools as full members of the TSSAA. When they lost to Father Ryan, it seemed as though they'd let their one and only opportunity to prove themselves slip by. Now they'd have another chance, but it wouldn't be as simple as just winning one game against an integrated team. To make a statement that mattered, they would have to win the state championship.

"Our senior season was going to be the culmination of everything we had worked for all our lives," Wallace recalled. "You didn't have to convince us. Coach Ridley talked about it—not too much, but enough. But apart from that, we knew. Even though there was turmoil in America, there were coming to be more openings and opportunities for blacks, and we felt the energy of that. Here was the opportunity to go to *the* big dance if we got it right throughout the season."

Losing to Father Ryan, Wallace came to believe, was the best thing that ever happened to Pearl. The players felt they not only had let themselves down, but also the entire black community. In practice sessions during the ramp-up to their senior year and throughout that season, Wallace said, the Tigers played with a ferocity that was "even greater than it would have been otherwise. We were good—we played hard and we played tough—but there was even more to it."

Picture the Hollywood montage: A school bus pulls up outside a gymnasium somewhere in Middle Tennessee. Here come the 1966 Pearl High School Tigers, dressed to kill in red blazers, black ties, and black slacks, and the camera freezes on each player as he steps off the bus.

Here's Ted McClain, known as "Hound," the prodigious scorer, born to play basketball, so stingy with money that his teammates tease him that he'd hang on to a dollar for a whole year. Here's Tyrone Fizer, T-Y, a team comic and second-teamer who does the dirty work under the boards. Here's "Doug," James Douglas, the kind of intimidator who'd give you an elbow or shoulder to the face if you got too close, or would whisper, "Don't make that damn shot," as you lined up for a free throw. Here's Ervin Williams, "The Big Turkey," the big ol' football player who hardly said a word. Here comes "Still," Willie Fisher, known to drink a little whiskey and drain jump shots from midrange. Here's Melvin Smith, better known as Spider for his long arms and legs, a fundamentally sound player whose form was *perfect* when he went up for a layup or shot a jumper. Finally, here came Joe Herbert, the quick defensive specialist; Walter "Slim" Fisher, the long-range jump-shooting, chain-smoking team leader who could get everybody to shut up and listen; Tony Moorman, the second-teamer who'd join Fisher for a smoke; and Perry Wallace, the dunker and the preacher, ready to lead the team in a pregame prayer.

Cut to the pregame layup line: Tiger after Tiger dunking in their pin-striped warm-up suits, opponents mesmerized. And now cut to the newspaper headlines, spinning on and off the screen: Pearl 53, Father Ryan 41 . . . Pearl 101, Memphis Lester 61 . . . Pearl 102, Clarksville Burt 59 . . . Pearl 76, Jackson Merry 29.

The winning streak dating back to the 1965 season kept growing: thirteen, twenty-three, thirty-three games in a row overall; twenty-one wins and no losses for the 1966 regular season. The Tigers were so good that virtually every player attracted interest from college recruiters, with eight members of the team going on to play college ball. But in an era when most white schools were looking for just the right black player—and only just the right black player—to join their program, it was Perry Wallace, surely one of the only valedictorians in the country who could also dunk and average nineteen rebounds a game, who received the most attention.

By this time, Perry Sr.'s brick-cleaning business was doing well enough that the family had purchased their own home for the first time, and the mailbox at the white house at 1908 10th Avenue became flooded with hundreds of letters from college coaches from all over the country. Soon the coaches themselves started arriving at the doorstep to talk to Perry and his parents, so many coming so often with such great things to say about their son that Mrs. Wallace told her daughter Jessie, "I do believe that President Lyndon B. Johnson will step on this porch one day, because everybody wants our boy!"

Just a few years earlier, the Wallaces had been excluded from white restaurants downtown; now they were the guests of honor every time a college coach wanted to take them out for dinner. "They were suddenly in a lot of situations with whites they had never been in before," Jessie recalled. "Everybody is coming to see them, they're being courted and treated royally, and they were dressing up to go to all these restaurants all over town. It put a lot of pressure on them even though it also involved a lot of pride and attention."

Especially frustrating for the Wallaces was the fact that the mounting news coverage of Perry's recruitment frequently expressed some measure of surprise that a kid "from the ghetto" was not only a good basketball player but also a great student. "What is this ghetto they keep talking about?" Hattie asked Jessie during the height of the recruiting period. "He didn't grow up in an alley! We may have been poor on Short 26th but that wasn't an alley!"

Any recruiter interested in Perry Wallace wouldn't just have to go through his parents; they'd have to deal with Cornelius Ridley, too.

Every day, it seemed, came the long-distance calls to Ridley's office, another coach from another school inquiring about Perry's intentions. The calls didn't stop when Ridley went home: they came when he was trying to eat dinner, they came when he was trying to watch TV, they came when he was headed to bed, and they came when he was asleep, as late as midnight on some nights. And it wasn't just phone calls. Folks Ridley saw around town, salesmen stopping by the school, *everybody* was putting in a good word for their alma mater. And most of all, it was as if another dump truck full of letters arrived at Ridley's office each afternoon.

"I remember hearing Pra Ridley, at the end of practice, telling Perry to come by his office, which was in the locker room," Moorman recalled. "We would be dressing after practice, and I would listen to Ridley. 'Iowa came in today, Iowa State came in, two or three others came in.' And then I'd turn to the others and say, 'Man, Perry got four more offers!'"

From the time that Perry first began to understand that he might be able to earn a college basketball scholarship (he had been offered a scholarship by Loyola coach George Ireland as a tenth-grader when the coach mistakenly thought he was a senior), he told his coach exactly what he was looking for.

"I told him I loved the game and what I wanted to do was to get a scholarship to a good university," Wallace recalled. "He would let me know who all was interested and give whatever insights he could on how to talk to these recruiters and how to do it so that it didn't disrupt our season." All through the process, Ridley repeated a simple phrase to his young star. "Make the right choice," he implored Perry, "make the right choice."

Initially, Wallace was certain that the right choice would mean leaving the stifling segregation of the South. A basketball scholarship would provide the opportunity to realize a dream. From the time he started reading those magazines his mother brought home from work, Wallace dedicated his life not only to preparing for the future but to getting out of Nashville.

"You had this feeling that you could be part of the larger world if you were in the North. The image was that you would have more opportunities and not the harsh prejudices," Wallace recalled. "I saw myself moving up north, moving into the American middle class, getting a job maybe as an engineer, living in an integrated setting with a nice house and a nice family. I didn't throw in the dog, but it was the whole American Dream. I had been dreaming at a distance, through magazines and television, and here was my opportunity to make it come true."

When letters arrived from Big Ten universities in the Midwest—schools such as Iowa, Wisconsin, Michigan, Northwestern, and Purdue—Wallace took notice. He would begin taking trips to visit some of the schools during the basketball season, others as soon as it ended. These were the first airplane flights of his life—heady stuff for a teenager, being flown all over the country and treated like the most important person in the world. On his recruiting visit to Iowa, Wallace arrived at the airport along with another basketball recruit and a football player. There to greet the trio was a marching band, which promptly whisked them away on a parade through Iowa City, culminating with a photo op with the governor.

Perry's visit to Northwestern was especially meaningful since his brother, James, was then living with his wife in the Chicago suburb of Evanston, where the school was located. Because of their age difference, Perry had never really gotten to know his older brother, but he could still recall the scent of Old Spice cologne on James' blue air force uniform from the times he'd hug him goodbye back in his youth. Now, here was one small way for Perry to repay his brother for the sacrifices James had made for the family. When Perry visited the Northwestern campus, he brought James along, the younger brother feeling an immense satisfaction in seeing his older brother treated well by the people they encountered on campus. "We got a chance to talk at length, the first time we really had a dialogue as grown men," Wallace recalled. "It was really a wonderful thing."

I n some respects, Perry was thoroughly enjoying the recruiting process. He was experiencing new things, seeing new parts of the country, reconnecting with his brother. But he also began to pick up on the unsavory side of the recruiting game, a process that was just as dirty in 1966—perhaps more so— as it would be nearly a half-century later. The enticements that would be quite attractive to the typical wide-eyed recruit were wasted on Wallace.

"He was being courted by all these places, and the people were gracious. A little more than gracious," Akins recalled. "They were trying to show him a very good time—the whole wine, women, and song thing—and that just wasn't who he was. It was a wasted effort, because they had misjudged him. He was an athlete, but he was also a genuine intellectual and I think it was hard for folks to understand that there were two sides to him. The people who saw him as just a jock didn't get him in a fundamental sort of way."

There was the cash—sometimes a promise of money if he signed with the school, sometimes a straight-out roll of two or three hundred dollars to "tide him over" for the weekend. There were even bigger inducements—"Here's a car, you ride around in it," he was told—and there were promises of bigger, better cars upon his arrival, maybe even a nice townhouse to live in.

"All of that was great, it was just that they had the wrong guy," Wallace recalled. "I really didn't care about that stuff. I had no interest in that and it really turned me off to the places that tried to make a deal with me, either indirectly or outright. It seemed to me that there were a lot of good possibilities in life just by playing by the rules."

In their recruiting pitches, many coaches would throw in a bit of negative talk about schools in the South that were showing interest in Wallace, stressing the hardships he'd surely endure playing in Dixie while extolling the virtues of their more tolerant environs. It wasn't a point Wallace needed to be sold on: his whole goal was to get out of the South. The problem was, as great as that urge remained, it wasn't enough to blind him to the lives he saw many of the black student-athletes living on northern campuses.

He wasn't going to trade one plantation for another.

Wallace approached each recruiting trip with a skeptical eye, eager to learn as much as he could about the daily routines of the athletes, especially the black ones. Did they go to class? Were they encouraged to take meaningful courses, or were they mostly physical education majors, doing just enough to remain eligible? It was a line of questioning appropriate for a gifted student like Wallace, but it was also consistent with the messages Wallace heard from some of the first black athletes to make it big at white schools—men like Bill Russell of the Boston Celtics, who in 1963 was the subject of a widely discussed article in *Sports Illustrated*.

In the story, Russell talked about the obligations of the African American athlete in the tumultuous 1960s, struggling with the relative unimportance of athletics. He said he had "not made any worthy contributions to society" and that playing professional basketball was "the most shallow thing in the world." What was required of a "Negro in American society today," Russell concluded, "cannot be met on the floor of the Boston Garden."

Wallace echoed those thoughts, saying that his goal was not to prepare for a career in the NBA but to get the best education possible. The deeper he looked, the less he liked what he saw from the athletic factories up north, even schools with strong academic reputations. As he saw it, the big, strong, talented black athletes—many nearly illiterate—were being asked to produce on the athletic fields and then retreat to their dorms until called upon again. It was pure exploitation.

"What I saw was that at a lot of these places, the black athletes weren't necessarily getting the best education. Too many of them were not integrated into the life of the university, and too many of them were not pursuing serious academics. That rattled me. It scared me," Wallace recalled. "I'd talk to players and it was obvious that they weren't getting a chance to think and develop socially and to take advantage of a great university and a rich social environment. My attitude was 'Wait a minute, what else is left? You're getting great basketball, but you're not doing great academics, and you're not really integrating and participating in this microcosm of American society, so why should I go there?'"

Wallace had entered the recruiting process full of hope, certain he was soon to find his ticket out of the racism of the South, out of what he called the bullshit. "My attitude was if there's anywhere where there is no bullshit or less bullshit, then get ready for me."

What he discovered was that while the grass appeared greener at some of those universities up north, it was only because it was well fertilized.

It was a mature—and disheartening—realization, but it opened the door for a school that was one of the unlikeliest destinations of all for a black kid from Short 26th: Vanderbilt University.

5

Harvard of the South

The three pillars of old-money Nashville, they used to say, were the Belle Meade Country Club, the Chamber of Commerce, and Vanderbilt University. There was a good deal of truth to this, and more than a few of the city's powerbrokers pledged allegiance to not just one of these institutions but all three. It was an uncomfortable distinction for Vanderbilt at times, considering the school had—to varying degrees and with a few notable false starts along the way—been a bit more cosmopolitan and forward thinking than its neighbors.

The university had been financed, not by any southern icon, but by New York shipping tycoon Cornelius Vanderbilt, a Yankee who achieved the distinction of being "America's richest man" and never set foot on the campus. Besides lending his name to the institution, the closest the old Commodore came to the university was in the form of a statue that stood in front of the main administration building, Kirkland Hall. As the joke went in the 1960s, the statue faced north, "toward the Ford Foundation."

There were great expectations for Vanderbilt ever since its founding in 1873, with one generation of professors and administrators after another seeing it as their duty to lift the private university to greater heights, first as one of the leading universities in the South, then as a competitor to the Ivies.

The school was located just west of the city's downtown, situated on a patch of lush, leafy land that had once been the site of a Civil War battle. According to author Bill Carey, the school's first chancellor had intended that Vanderbilt become such a good school that "our sons need not go to England or Germany or France" to get an excellent education. In effect, Carey wrote, Chancellor Landon Garland envisioned a "Harvard of the South." From 1896 to 1938, the next chancellor, James Kirkland, led the university closer to that distinction. It was Kirkland, historian Don Doyle wrote, who took Vanderbilt, which was church affiliated until 1914, "from a struggling, obscure Methodist college to a regionally powerful university."

The succeeding chancellor, Harvie Branscomb, wrote Doyle, "saw Vanderbilt's domain as the only noteworthy private university south of the University of Chicago and north of Tulane." Still, despite the academic excellence it cultivated, the university remained provincial, with more than half its students hailing from Tennessee as late as 1950. The student body wasn't particularly activist: In 1954, when president Dwight Eisenhower proposed lowering the voting age from twenty-one to eighteen, a college-aged columnist's pet cause if there ever was one, Vanderbilt student Doug Lipton wrote an editorial claiming it was a *bad* idea because kids that age weren't mature enough to vote. In 1959 students mounted the largest protest in the school's history when they took exception to what they perceived as Branscomb's anti-Greek stance, carrying banners with such incendiary messages as "Save Our Frat Houses."

On campus to witness that demonstration was a Vanderbilt divinity student named James Lawson, a Korean War objector who had spent time in India studying Mahatma Gandhi's philosophy on nonviolent protest.

That Lawson was at Vanderbilt at all was a rarity—not because he had spent eleven months in prison for refusing induction into the army but because he was black. The university had approached integration with extreme caution, initiating a policy in 1953 to admit blacks only to graduate programs (such as the Divinity School and the Law School) for which there were no counterparts at Nashville's black universities. Even this limited concession to progress was carried out grudgingly; the handful of black graduate students were not permitted to live in campus dorms or eat in the student cafeteria, and Branscomb attempted to reassure anxious alums by telling them that "the university was not so much taking the lead in this area as being carried along by events."

In addition to completing work toward his degree as the second black admitted to the Divinity School, Lawson was involved in groundbreaking work outside the classroom. He may have been the first "black athlete" at Vanderbilt, participating in intramural football. More significant, he served as regional director for a civil rights organization known as the Fellowship of Reconciliation and was a member of the Christian Leadership Council. One of his chief responsibilities was to conduct a series of intense workshops on nonviolent protest for students from Nashville's many black colleges.

By early 1960, black students in Nashville and elsewhere in the South were prepared—thanks to the guidance of mentors such as Lawson—to mount nonviolent challenges to segregationist practices by staging sit-ins at whites-only lunch counters. After the first demonstration took place in Greensboro, North Carolina, on February 1, 1960, Lawson helped organize larger protests in Nashville on the thirteenth and twenty-seventh of that month. At the second demonstration, dubbed "Big Saturday," eighty-one students were arrested, and though they were attacked by angry white bystanders, they remained true to Lawson's teachings on passive resistance.

Suddenly, Nashville was at the center of the civil rights storm. When Mayor Ben West met with a group of black ministers two days later to discuss the protests, Lawson's leading role became known to Vanderbilt administrators, who had been unaware of his off-campus activities. Given the institution's attitude toward issues of race and the personal philosophies of the two leading decision-makers—Chancellor Branscomb and Board of Trust president Jimmy Stahlman—Vanderbilt's response was predictably reactionary. For, at the time of the sit-ins, David Halberstam wrote, "Vanderbilt was a school which did not so much want to live in the past as it wanted to perpetuate the past."

It was Stahlman, publisher of the conservative *Nashville Banner* afternoon newspaper, who had been quoted in a national newsmagazine in 1956 spouting off against integration, warning that "a lot of us [are] determined that it isn't going to happen so long as we can do anything about it, legally." And it was Branscomb who had already lodged one complaint against Lawson, imploring (without success) the dean of the Divinity School to prevent his black student from playing intramural football.

Stahlman, whose bombastic front-page editorials railing against the civil rights movement are nearly comical in retrospect, plunged into the fray. First, fearing that the Gandhian protestors might turn their attention to his newsroom armed with weapons, he ordered loyal staff members to purchase a stockpile of munitions, including reconditioned World War II rifles, bullets, helmets, bulletproof vests, and Mace. Then he put down his sword long enough to raise his pen. "To plead his [Lawson's] cause in the name of 'Christian reconciliation' as a 'Christian missionary' is so much hogwash," he editorialized. "And his use of the Divinity School of Vanderbilt University as a base and screen for his nefarious operations is as detestable as his effort to cloak his racial deviltry in clerical garb."

When the Board of Trust's executive committee met days later (a committee that included among its members Branscomb, Stahlman, and the owner of one of the downtown department stores that had been targeted by the demonstrators), the group acted swiftly to distance Vanderbilt from its troublemaking grad student. Decades later, Vanderbilt would make amends with a forgiving Lawson, by then considered one of the great unsung heroes of the civil rights movement. He'd even return to Nashville to teach a new generation of Vanderbilt divinity students. But in the spring of 1960, the old guard simply did not see the righteousness of his cause, choosing to focus on the arrests rather than the larger issues at hand.

"There are, in all social crises, moments when the forces of the past collide

Nashville Banner publisher Jimmy Stahlman was a prolific and colorful—but reactionary—voice who presented constant challenges for Vanderbilt chancellor Alexander Heard. Despite his ideological differences with Heard, Stahlman was a loyal Vanderbilt supporter, chairman of the Board of Trust, and the pivotal figure behind the creation of Memorial Gymnasium, Vanderbilt's quirky basketball arena. *Nashville Banner* Archives, Nashville Public Library, Special Collections.

head-on with the forces of the future," Halberstam wrote in *The Children*. "What makes them particularly interesting is that those who are summoned to make critical decisions rarely understand on the eve of the collision that they are dealing with something epic; rather for them it tends to be bureaucratic business as usual."

The Board of Trust vote was unanimous: Lawson could either withdraw from the Divinity School or be expelled.

He didn't quit.

In the aftermath of his expulsion, campus reaction was mixed. As a whole, the student body agreed with the decision. The undergraduate senate, which included future Tennessee governor and US senator Lamar Alexander, unanimously supported the board's action. The editorial staff at the school newspaper, the *Vanderbilt Hustler*, concurred, reminding readers that students who had recently been expelled for participating in panty raids hadn't done anything nearly as disruptive as Lawson.

Many faculty members, however, were outraged. The day after Lawson's expulsion, eleven of the fifteen Divinity School faculty members released a statement saying they disagreed with the decision, and a small group picketed in front of Kirkland Hall. Within days, more than one hundred of the university's faculty had published a statement supporting Lawson.

In the end, reaction to the sit-ins helped move Nashville forward and set Vanderbilt back, at least in the short term. Mayor West appointed an integrated citizens committee to "seek a solution to the racial problem." In April black college students led a group of three thousand marchers on a trek from Tennessee A&I to the steps of the courthouse. In front of the throng and the media, one of Lawson's protégés, Fisk student Diane Nash, asked the mayor if he agreed that it was wrong to discriminate at the lunch counters based on a person's color. West saw it as a question of morality for which there was only one answer. Yes, he said, it was wrong, and with that, Nashville's walls of segregation began to tumble. The Nashville campaign—led in such large part by Lawson—achieved its goals so peacefully that Martin Luther King Jr. later referred to it as "a model movement" and to Nashville as a place from which he drew inspiration.

Given the moral high ground Lawson had claimed, his supporters called on the university to readmit him. Lawson applied, but, to the great shame of a number of faculty members who later threatened to resign, his application was denied. In his history of the university, Carey tells the story of Divinity School professor Langdon Gilkey and Medical School professor Rollow Park, who called on three Board of Trust members at a home in Nashville's patrician Belle Meade neighborhood.

"We hope that you realize that with this, Vanderbilt ceases to be a major university in America. You will not be able to get an appointment from anybody from MIT or Cal Tech or the University of Chicago or any other place," Park said. "No one will consider coming here, and you will become a Southern finishing school."

"Well, sir," came the response, "we'll take the Southern finishing school."

Vanderbilt's image was nearing rock bottom. The national media pounced, and the school, Carey wrote, "received more negative national press than at any other time in its history."

With nowhere to go but up, the university began to take its first steps toward racial reconciliation. Lamar Alexander, by then editor of the *Hustler*, used his first column of 1962 to outline four issues the chancellor should address that year. Three were typical student concerns: the rising cost of tuition, the high cost of fraternity housing, and the poor overall performance of the athletic program. The senior from East Tennessee then challenged the administration to examine its policy of only admitting blacks to programs unavailable at other Nashville colleges.

"This is a cowardly policy. At best it is avoiding the issue," he wrote. "How consistent is it to say that Vanderbilt is one of the nation's best universities but that Negroes may find equal educational opportunities at other Nashville schools? Vanderbilt has fallen behind every other southern school in announcing an intelligent and well-founded policy on this touchy subject. It will be a blot upon the university's reputation if the administration continues to avoid the issue."

Student senator John Sergent also took up the cause, urging his fellow senators to adopt a resolution calling on the Board of Trust to begin integrating Vanderbilt's undergraduate schools. Roy Blount, a *Hustler* columnist who would go on to national fame as an author and humorist, wrote in defense of Sergent's proposal, arguing that "such an assimilation is both necessary and proper on the grounds of basic decency and human equality before the law." Nonetheless, the future US senator, the future bestselling author, and the future Dr. Sergent were unable to sway campus opinion. After a tense three-hour debate at "hot and sticky Alumni Hall," Sergent's measure was defeated 14–13.

A week later, on Valentine's Day of 1962, the entire student body voted on the issue in a special referendum. With 60 percent of students turning out to vote, the measure was defeated 862–661. Students in the College of Arts and Science and the Nursing School voted in favor of integration, but a segregationist landslide (239–93) in the School of Engineering shifted the balance in favor of the status quo.

"I had confidence in Vanderbilt students as a body of thinking people," Bill Brooks, the student senator who had led the opposition to Sergent's bill, told the *Hustler*. "I expected a majority to vote against integration. I do not feel that integration is the right thing for Vanderbilt at this time, and I hope that for now, the issue is dead."

In truth, the issue was gaining new life. Later that spring, the Graduate School student council voted unanimously to recommend an open admissions policy, and by an overwhelming majority the university's faculty voted to recommend an official policy of racial integration. Finally, at the Board of Trust's annual meeting in May, the board recorded a historic 28–6 vote approving a measure to allow blacks into all programs of the university—graduate and undergraduate. Chancellor Branscomb retired soon after, with integration approved under his watch.

Still, Vanderbilt had much work to do, not only to improve its reputation—particularly among the foundations that played such an important role in fundraising and were looking for signs of racial progress—but also to live up to its vision of being a truly great national university. To begin to put the fallout from the Lawson episode in the past, to ensure that integration at Vanderbilt worked, Branscomb's heir would need to be a man of the New South, not the Old. The best interests of the university called for a new brand of leadership.

Into the chancellorship in 1963 stepped a man with the most pronounced Savannah drawl anyone at Vanderbilt had ever heard. He may have sounded like a southern aristocrat, but Alexander Heard was an academic pluralist with liberal politics, and he was just what Vanderbilt needed.

Such a good fit, it turned out, that the only person the search committee feared might sour the deal to land the University of North Carolina administrator was Jimmy Stahlman. In the latter stages of the search process, John Seigenthaler, editor of Stahlman's rival newspaper, the *Tennessean*, received an unexpected visit from Edwin Craig, chairman of the board of one of Nashville's largest corporations, National Life Insurance. Craig, who chaired the search committee, had followed the *Tennessean*'s coverage of the nationwide search and wanted to ask a favor.

"John, we have a good chance here to get a great chancellor, and I know you well enough to know that you want that," he told Seigenthaler. "But every time that you write in the paper that [Heard is] a liberal, it just gets Jimmy's back up and it makes it a helluva lot more difficult for me. Would you please just eliminate calling him a liberal? I mean you've already identified him and everybody knows it, just don't say it anymore."

A journalist's journalist, Seigenthaler wasn't the type to accept any form of censorship, but in this case, perhaps out of a respect for Vanderbilt, out of a desire to see Heard land the job, or merely to help further a cause he knew would rile up his rival over at the *Banner*, he didn't take long to consider the request.

"OK," he told Craig. "We can handle that."

Decades later, he knew he made the right decision.

"Alec came and he was the right choice for the time," Seigenthaler recalled. "I think his selection was an effort to atone [for the Lawson controversy]. The university knew it had to get its credibility back. Obviously, they wanted a southerner, but they wanted a southerner who was on the cutting edge of change."

From his first days on campus, Heard set out to strike a new tone and to chart a new course for the university. He understood that Vanderbilt could only stake a legitimate claim as a national academic power if it dealt head-on with the peculiarities that festered in its own backyard. At a ceremony on the university's sloping library lawn to officially install him as chancellor

on October 4, 1963, Heard used the occasion to address the controversial issue of race, the most high-profile discussion of the subject in the university's
history.

"For our country," he said, "the most tenacious and important issue of our
time is the struggle of American Negroes for a fuller freedom." He lauded the
Board of Trust's decision to admit students of all races, but warned that a
university's role in such an important matter called for greater action. "By
definition," he said, "a university must be a place where anybody's plea for
a fuller freedom can be calmly heard, fairly debated, and conclusions about
it stated freely. The more perplexing a public issue is, the more significant to
society is this inherent responsibility of a university."

It was clear from Heard's statements that he brought with him from North
Carolina a more nuanced sensitivity to racial issues than Vanderbilt had ever
seen. Under his watch, the university would no longer look to distance itself
from the central issue of the time. Just the opposite—it would occasionally
seek opportunities to stir things up.

Alexander Heard was of a mixed mind when it came to athletics. He was
a sports fan, a walking baseball encyclopedia who enjoyed regaling his
children with stories about Shoeless Joe Jackson and the infamous 1919 Black
Sox scandal, and who had been a devotee of Connie Mack's Philadelphia
Athletics. When it came to the role of athletics within a university, however,
he was adamant that Vanderbilt not succumb to the pressures that had
overcome many fellow members of the Southeastern Conference. Never one
to shy away from delivering uncomfortable news to partisan audiences, he
shared his philosophy with members of Vanderbilt's athletic booster club
even before his official installation address.

"On some campuses, preoccupation with intercollegiate athletics has at
times become so pervasive that it has deflected the attention of students,
faculty, trustees, and friends from the principal purposes for which the institution was created in the first place," he told members of the Vanderbilt
Quarterback Club on September 23, 1963, at their gathering at Nashville's
Noel Hotel. "This will not happen at Vanderbilt."

Within the course of eleven days, then, Heard had delivered speeches
drawing attention to the critical role universities could play in blacks' struggle
for freedom and acknowledging the outsized influence that athletics exerted
in American life. With black undergraduates now eligible for admission to
the school, it must have been obvious to Heard that if he wanted to make a
bold statement about Vanderbilt's evolving approach to race relations, the
athletic realm would be an effective place to do it.

He wasn't the first Vanderbilt administrator to consider the possibility
of black athletes competing at Memorial Gym or Vanderbilt Stadium. In a
confidential report supplied to the Board of Trust by the university senate

before the 1962 board meeting at which Vanderbilt's open-admissions policy was approved, the subject of integrated athletics was broached. Apparently the idea of a black athlete in a Commodore uniform was still farfetched; the memo dealt only with the possibility of an *opponent* of color.

"Audience segregation has been discontinued without incident," the memo reported. "Vanderbilt's varsity teams [have] played against Negroes while away from home, and it is only a matter of time until a Negro appears on a visiting team, even within our own conference."

For years, a common "out" for segregationists was to claim that they would have no problem with integration—they just didn't want to go first. Heard was about to change that mindset at Vanderbilt.

When Coach Roy Skinner climbed the twenty-four cement steps outside Kirkland Hall on his way to Heard's office sometime in late 1963 or early 1964, he knew the conversation was going to have enormous ramifications for his basketball program and would send an unmistakable signal throughout the country that Vanderbilt was serious about basketball. It wasn't every day that he was invited to the chancellor's office; in fact, this was the first time. Yes, Skinner thought, the conversation was going to be important: he and the new chancellor would be talking about the merits of expanding the capacity of Memorial Gym to accommodate the growing demand for tickets. Even Heard, so leery of the public's insatiable appetite for college athletics, had a soft spot for Commodore basketball.

The chancellor and the coach discussed plans to add balconies to the north end of the gym, and then, almost casually, Heard floated an idea by his Kentucky-born coach.

"He told me that Vanderbilt was open to blacks," Skinner recalled more than forty years later, "and he told me that I could recruit a black player, and, in fact, that he would like for me to."

In his trademark low-key way, Skinner's reaction proved that changing the course of history need not require a particularly confrontational first act. When challenged to do something that had never been done before in a conference whose member institutions spanned the former states of the Confederacy, he didn't come up with excuses, he didn't threaten to quit, he didn't appeal to an influential alum to try to change the chancellor's mind.

He simply said OK.

Skinner was an unlikely integrationist. He had grown up in the western Kentucky town of Paducah, where his father earned a living collecting milk from area farmers and delivering it to dairies. As a boy, Roy loved Adolph Rupp's Kentucky Wildcats as much as he loved listening to St. Louis Cardinals games on the radio; he counted as one of the biggest thrills of his life the time he traveled to Sportsman's Park to see Stan Musial in person. A five-foot-nine guard, Skinner was the captain of his high school basketball team and then attended Paducah Junior College before transferring to Presbyterian College in Clinton, South Carolina, where he helped lead the Blue Hose to a conference championship in 1951. Upon graduating, he found work as the athletic director and basketball coach at a boys club in Portsmouth, Virginia, and success there earned him the head coaching position at the town's Craddock Junior High. An 18–1 season earned him a promotion to Craddock High School (as head basketball and tennis coach and assistant football coach), and by 1956 he was back at Paducah Junior College, this time as the head coach, at the age of twenty-six. The following year, Skinner's junior college squad beat Vanderbilt's freshman team, the only game the VU frosh lost all year, making such an impression on Commodore coach Bob Polk that he hired Skinner as his only assistant. When Polk suffered a nonfatal heart attack on a recruiting trip in the fall of 1958, Skinner stepped in as acting head coach for one season. To the surprise and delight of the Commodore faithful, he led Vanderbilt to a 75–66 win over Rupp's undefeated and Number 1–ranked Wildcats in Polk's absence, all but assuring himself the head job when Polk called it quits. Indeed, that's what happened in 1962. The man Heard asked to take the historic step of integrating the Southeastern Conference a couple of years later was a salt-of-the-earth, chain-smoking, beer-drinking Kentucky farm boy, only about a decade removed from running a Virginia youth center and coaching a high school tennis team, a man who had never played alongside or coached a black player at any level.

For all those reasons, Skinner was the unlikeliest of trailblazers. But in another respect, it made all the sense in the world. He was chasing the Number 1 spot, willing to do whatever it took to knock his home-state Wildcats from their perpetual perch atop the SEC. While Rupp may have had no interest in breaking the league's color line, there was more motivation for an underdog to shake up the status quo.

"I didn't care what color they were if they could win," Skinner recalled. "That's the name of the game."

That winning basketball games mattered at Vanderbilt was a sentiment that had its own creation story, traceable to an exact place, date, and time.

Louisville, Kentucky.

February 27, 1947.

Around 11:00 p.m.

It was at that fateful hour that Vanderbilt athletic director and football coach Red Sanders slumped into the hospitality room at the Louisville Armory, having just watched Kentucky humiliate the Commodores, 98–29, in the first round of the SEC Tournament. Sanders threw back a few drinks to

A native of Paducah, Kentucky, Roy Skinner, left, loved nothing better
than to beat legendary Kentucky coach Adolph Rupp. He believed
recruiting a player of Wallace's talents could give him the edge he
desperately wanted in the rivalry with UK. Rupp, meanwhile, resisted
repeated requests from Kentucky president John Oswald to become
more active in recruiting black players. Vanderbilt University Special
Collections and University Archives.

ease the pain, and as he departed, he acknowledged that the days of assistant
football coaches moonlighting as Vanderbilt basketball coaches were over.

"If we're going to lose basketball games," he told the assembled sportswriters and school officials, "we are going to lose with a coach."

Not exactly the most inspirational words ever spoken, but they set in motion a chain of events that within five years would see the Commodores playing in one of the nation's finest gymnasiums and competing for tournament
championships.

Vanderbilt actually had been one of the first universities in the country—
some historians say *the* first—to field a basketball team. James Naismith famously invented the game in Springfield, Massachusetts, in December 1891,
and by 1893 a group of Vanderbilt students had organized a team to challenge
a squad from the Nashville YMCA. Nine players took a trolley downtown to
the Y and proceeded to win that historic first game, playing with a soccer

ball, by a score of 9–6. The first unofficial season of Vanderbilt basketball thus ended the same day it began, with a perfect 1–0 record.

A varsity team was formed in 1900, and by 1907 the team played its home games at the Hippodrome roller skating rink, a decent enough place but for the fact that the crepe paper hanging from the ceiling interfered with shots arcing toward the basket, and the oil-slick floor, so useful for skates, wreaked havoc on gym shoes.

Vanderbilt won its first basketball championship in 1920, capturing the Southern Intercollegiate Athletic Association title a year before joining fifteen other SIAA schools to form the Southern Conference. There was another split in 1933, with Vanderbilt becoming a charter member of the Southeastern Conference.

Despite occasional success, Vanderbilt's basketball program remained second fiddle behind what was a successful football program in the first half of the twentieth century; the job of coaching the basketball team annually fell to an unlucky assistant football coach. Among those early hoops coaches were Wallace Wade, who would go on to win three national championships as head football coach at Alabama, and Norm Cooper, who had succeeded a one-time Vanderbilt assistant named Paul "Bear" Bryant as the VU football team's line coach.

"You want to know how we decided who would be basketball coach?" Cooper once asked Vanderbilt basketball historian Roy Neel. "Jim Scoggins [another football assistant] and I would flip a coin before the season; the man that lost got to coach basketball."

By the 1947 season, the Vanderbilt basketball program remained a second-rate outfit, with no full-time coach and no players on scholarship, despite the fact that other SEC schools had become the first in the country to begin awarding athletic grants-in-aid in 1936. The SEC tournament drubbing at the hands of Kentucky was no surprise, given that the Wildcats had beaten the Commodores 80–30 in the regular season, a game so lopsided that Rupp ordered his starters to change out of their uniforms at halftime.

Following the tournament lambasting, Sanders set to work solving the three biggest problems hindering the basketball team's success: no full-time coach, no scholarship players, and no place to play. Other than those minor issues, the program was in great shape.

After considering Georgia Tech assistant Bob Polk and a young coach who had just completed his first season at Indiana State, John Wooden, Sanders hired Ted Hornback, an assistant at nearby Western Kentucky University. A sudden change of heart by a new coach is something sports fans have grown accustomed to over the years, but Hornback's excuse for heading back to Kentucky before his first season ever began was original: he claimed he couldn't find a place in Nashville to live. Sanders then turned his attention back to Polk, and the Commodores began the 1947–48 season with their first-ever full-time head coach and first-ever scholarship player, Billy Joe Adcock. Looking to drum up support for his squad, Polk personally sold all sixteen season tickets to his team's games, a tough sell considering the games were played in a Quonset hut at Nashville's navy classification center.

A year later, things were starting to look up. Plans for an on-campus basketball gymnasium generated buzz around town, and in the meantime the team's games at East High School were carried on a delayed basis on WKDA radio, with listeners captivated by the energetic style of one Larry Munson, a future broadcasting legend who would continue to call college games for more than a half century. By the 1950 season, Polk had recruited his first full-scholarship class with the promise, ultimately unfulfilled, that the new gym would be completed by the time they graduated. In the meantime, though Polk's team played at yet another home court (Nashville's David Lipscomb College), it began to find some success, beating New York University at Madison Square Garden and finishing second in the SEC.

In the spring of 1951, the Vanderbilt basketball program completed the march to respectability that had begun four years earlier, achieving a feat that more than fifty years later still stood as perhaps the greatest victory in school history.

The Commodores again found themselves playing Kentucky at the SEC Tournament in Louisville, this time in the event's championship game. Vanderbilt was a decided underdog that evening, having lost to Kentucky twice in the regular season by a combined fifty-seven points, and having just played Louisiana State University in the tournament semifinals earlier that same afternoon. Looking to conserve his squad's energy, Polk instructed team trainer Joe Worden to serve the players their pregame meals in their beds as they rested between games.

The Wildcats entered the game ranked Number 1 in the country, their only loss an overtime defeat at the hands of the Saint Louis Billikens. But this night belonged to Vanderbilt, with the Commodores overcoming a ten-point deficit to mount a stunning second-half comeback, winning 61–57. Vanderbilt's first televised game was a shocking upset, so improbable that it was as if, wrote Walter Stewart of the *Memphis Commercial Appeal*, "the calf killed the butcher."

Again, the Armory's hospitality room was the site of a memorable exchange of words, with a visibly agitated Rupp confronting Polk in front of a gathering of reporters and coaches. "Bobby, you made a grave mistake tonight," Rupp hissed, an imposing figure more menacing than ever with his injured right eye covered up by a patch. "I want you to make the most of it. It is not going to happen again."

Polk and his boys were too giddy to pay much attention to Rupp's sour grapes. They walked back over to the team hotel, encountering a group of silent and stunned Kentucky fans whose planned victory celebration, complete with a trophy already engraved with Kentucky as champion, had been ruined by the upstart Commodores.

Kentucky players later claimed the game hadn't meant all that much to them, and that may have been the case. It was the regular-season SEC champion, not the tournament champion, that earned a bid to the NCAA Tournament, and the Wildcats, led by seven-foot-one center Bill Spivey, went on to win the national championship. But for Vanderbilt, the victory reverberated back in time—atoning for the sixty-nine-point loss four years earlier—and well into the future; until 2012 it remained the only SEC Tournament championship in school history. More than fifteen hundred raucous fans met the team's DC-3 when it arrived at the Nashville airport the next day; in more ways than one, Vanderbilt basketball had arrived.

"Without question," Polk said, "it was the most important step in the growth of the program."

When Memorial Gymnasium opened in December 1952, the Commodores finally had a home of their own, and it became the place to see and be seen among Vanderbilt alumni and Nashville's social elite. Over the next decade, there were just enough victories to keep the fans excited, more than enough losses to keep them hungering for greater success. By the time Skinner took control of the program before the 1962 season, Vanderbilt had lost five of its last six games to Kentucky, the program that stood as the standard against which all other SEC teams were judged. The Commodores limped to a 12–12 finish in Skinner's first year as head coach, losing to the Wildcats two more times. Then Clyde Lee arrived on campus, and with him came steady progress: 16–7 in 1963, 19–6 in 1964, 24–4 and the Mideast regional finals in 1965. In that last year a heartbreaking, controversial loss to Cazzie Russell's Michigan Wolverines was all that had come between a beloved Vanderbilt team and the Final Four. Skinner's program had closed the gap on Kentucky and achieved national prominence; dreams of a national championship, he believed, were realistic.

If a black player could help him get there, he was all for it.

In the immediate aftermath of Heard's invitation, Skinner tried to recruit a few black players but found no success. Decades later, he attributed his early failures to two factors: he said he had a hard time finding southern blacks with the necessary high school coursework and an even harder time convincing blacks from the North to come down to Nashville to integrate the SEC.

No doubt it was a tough sell, one that for many prospects might have been compounded by Skinner's legendary low-key recruiting style. While coaches at many other schools, including some of those in pursuit of Perry Wallace, led their pitches with promises of cash or other inducements, Skinner's approach was plain vanilla.

He would plop down on a family's sofa, wedge himself between a recruit and his mother, and open up a simple scrapbook full of photos of the campus.

This is the dining hall. Pause.

This is a picture of the gym. Pause.

These are the dorms. Pause.

We play in a good league. Pause.

We have very enthusiastic fans, we travel all over the place, and you're going to get a fine education.

For prospects turned off by high-pressure sales tactics, Skinner's manner was a refreshing change of pace. "He came into the house and made you feel comfortable with the Vanderbilt program right away; that soft-sell approach left you with a tingle," Clyde Lee once said. "As a high school player, it was an honor just to have him in your home. The parents loved him. You knew you were talking to an honest man."

Skinner's style was so laid-back it left some would-be Commodores feeling somewhere between sympathetic and dumbstruck. Skinner showed up at the home of Indiana high school star Rod Freeman in the late 1960s so relaxed that Freeman couldn't believe the man who'd driven up from Nashville was in fact a major college basketball coach.

"He sits down and starts talking to me, and had not a lot to say, to be honest with you," Freeman recalled. "And then he says, 'Would you like to look at a highlight film?'"

Having nothing better to do, Freeman said "sure," and the coach was off to his car to retrieve a bulky projector and roll of film. After a minute or two fumbling around with the film trying to thread it into the projector, Skinner took a seat beside Freeman. The film flickered on, a bunch of guys playing ball, Freeman having no idea who they are, no words coming out of the coach's mouth for a full five minutes. Finally, Skinner leaned forward in his chair and spoke.

"I think this is the wrong film."

"And then," Freeman recalled, "he leans back in his chair and says, 'Aw, it doesn't matter, we'll watch it anyway.' Evidently, we had just watched a game film from two years prior that didn't have any bearing on anything."

Finally, the movie ended, and Skinner asked Freeman if he was hungry. He was, so they went off to a nearby restaurant for a quick bite, and with that the coach was on his way back to Nashville. Freeman's initial reaction was that he was less than impressed by the coach from Vanderbilt, but eventually he came to the conclusion that a man that genuine was the kind of guy he wanted to play for. He decided to attend Vanderbilt and came to love Coach Skinner.

Growing up, Perry Wallace had never thought much about Vanderbilt University. He wouldn't be welcome there as a student, and as a basketball fan, he was far more interested in the teams at Pearl and Tennessee A&I than in the Commodores. But as the choice of a college became an important consideration, Vanderbilt entered the picture. First, the school began admitting blacks, including a friend from the neighborhood named Moses Taylor. Then, as Wallace began to earn notice on the court and in the classroom, folks from Vanderbilt started to show up at the Pearl High gym. Clyde Lee was in the bleachers at one game, Roy Skinner at the next. All his life, the message Wallace heard from white Nashville was, "You stay over there." Now, suddenly, people were coming over to his side of town to see him, and they were saying, "Come on and join us."

By the time Roy Skinner arrived at the Wallace home to pay a visit in the midst of what remained an undefeated season for Pearl, Perry had winnowed offers from more than one hundred schools down to a handful. He'd even turned down a scholarship offer from UCLA, a program in the early stages of its historic run of ten NCAA championships in twelve years, because he felt he would have trouble earning significant playing time as a Bruin. Here was Skinner, knocking on the door on 10th Avenue, about to try to convince Wallace to integrate the Southeastern Conference, a kid smart enough to see what was going on at the basketball factories up North and grounded enough to know he wasn't quite good enough to play at UCLA. It should have been a tough sell.

But from the moment Skinner walked in the door, there was something all the Wallaces liked about the man. His reserved, country style fit in quite well in this home.

"My parents knew people, and they knew life," Wallace told author Frye Gaillard years later. "And they had a feeling about Coach Skinner. When he came over that day and sat down in our house, he had a certain manner about him, a certain honesty and decency, a rhythm and a style that seemed easygoing. My parents, of course, were looking at him hard. They were asking themselves, 'Who is this man who wants to take our son into dangerous territory?'"

Perry was listening to the coach through ears as skeptical as those of his parents. He heard something, however, that meant a lot back in 1966 and led him to take a closer look at Vanderbilt. When Skinner talked to his parents, he addressed them not by their first names, as would have been the convention of the day for a white man addressing blacks, but rather as Mr. and Mrs. Wallace. For Perry, eager for his aging parents to be treated with respect and looking for signals on how this southern white coach might treat a black player, Skinner's choice of words spoke volumes.

"Coach Skinner treated me and my parents in a way that a lot of people back then would not have," Wallace recalled. "When he called my parents Mr. and Mrs. Wallace, that was a very, very big deal. For them, born in 1906 on farms in Rutherford County, Tennessee, and traveling along that whole rough, difficult path in the South, how often are they going to be called Mr. and Mrs. Wallace? And this is not the big-eyed, dumb, naïve person reaction to that; this is the 'I know people and I don't expect them to be perfect, but this is sincere enough to work with' version. At that point, along with the comparison to those other schools that were recruiting me, I began to take Vanderbilt seriously."

For his part, Skinner's demeanor with the Wallaces was genuine; he was the same man in their home as he was in the company of any white family, a fact that was significant in its own right in 1966 Nashville. "I just called *all* parents Mr. and Mrs.," he recalled, "especially since most of them were older than I was."

Even as the Pearl basketball season rolled along, Wallace attended games at Memorial Gym, spending time with the Commodore players to get a better sense of his potential future teammates and the lives they lived on campus. He was impressed by what he saw. Here was a place that offered the best of both worlds: big-time basketball and first-rate academics. There was no P.E. major at Vanderbilt, and the players appeared to take their schoolwork seriously. Vanderbilt's engineering school had a fine reputation, a fact that also remained one of Purdue University's biggest selling points for Wallace. There was little talk of the social life on campus, but Wallace wasn't much of a partier anyway. Clyde Lee walked him around the perimeter of the campus and showed him where the closest Church of Christ chapel was located, a church Lee himself attended. There was not even a hint of scandal, no wads of cash to tide him over on his drive back to North Nashville, no loaner cars to get him there.

Everything about Vanderbilt was turning out to be appealing, except for one thing.

Perry Wallace did not want to be the first black basketball player in the Southeastern Conference; he had absolutely no interest in being a pioneer. If progress was going to happen, that was great, but not on his back.

What kind of masochist would choose to step into the fire alone? With numbers came strength. There had been dozens of students at the sit-ins and Freedom Rides, thousands at the March on Washington, and millions watching it all on television. But to desegregate the SEC meant going it alone in backwater southern towns like Starkville, Mississippi, and Auburn, Alabama, a teenage black male sweeping through the South like a magnet, attracting all the scattered hatred left behind by the tumultuous events of the mid-1960s.

As Wallace began to think deeply about whether this was a mission he wanted to accept, pressure mounted from all sides. His decision was entering the public realm; everyone in Nashville, it seemed, had a stake in where Perry Wallace decided to attend college. What made a difficult calculation even more complex were the mixed messages he received from both blacks and whites. Members of both camps urged him to make history at Vanderbilt; others from both sides were equally adamant that he go elsewhere.

The socially progressive Vanderbilt alums Wallace encountered expressed hope that he would break the color line at their school. Many blacks who believed in the promise of integration and the "progress of the race" were also eager to see Wallace choose Vanderbilt. Positive as they were, these messages were accompanied by a corresponding pressure: the obligation to live up to high expectations.

And then there was the hate.

Perry Sr. and Hattie did their best to hide the mail that arrived at their home, and indeed their son didn't see most of the letters until years later. But some did slip past his parents' protective eyes, handwritten notes threatening Wallace's life if he made the choice to attend Vanderbilt.

Interestingly, Wallace suspects that not all of the hands that wrote those letters were white. Take, for example, a letter that read, "Don't go to Vanderbilt because it could cause a lot of problems and it could endanger your life."

"Just think of the different people who could write that," he said. "You could have a person who was against integration, of whom there were many, and their attitude was that you just don't mix the races. You could have a black person who had a sense of what pioneers go through, and they thought well of me and were concerned about me. Then you could have people who wanted to protect black institutions, including historically black universities, who saw this pioneering as the beginning of the end."

On this last point, many whites may have been surprised that all blacks didn't necessarily see integration as a good thing. In sports, especially, blacks had seen the downside before. As William Rhoden wrote in *Forty Million Dollar Slaves*, for all the good feelings engendered by Jackie Robinson's breaking of Major League Baseball's color line, one of the consequences was the demise of a strong black-owned operation, the Negro Leagues. "A black institution was dead," Rhoden wrote, "while a white institution grew richer and stronger. This was the end result of integration."

Wallace's Pearl High classmates were of mixed opinions. Many were impressed by the opportunities Vanderbilt afforded: to attend a good school, to play major college ball, to be a pioneer, to succeed in Nashville. Others worried that he would be embarking on a dangerous journey that would not be worth the pain. Still others were dismissive of Vanderbilt's motives: they've never wanted us as students before, but now that we have a great athlete, *now* they come calling.

Throughout it all, there was another source of information for Wallace. The most insightful people he heard from were the neighbors, church parishioners, and family friends who held jobs as maids, waiters, shoe shiners, and cooks in the white community, people who were often invisible to those they served on the other side of town.

"Listen to what I heard," they'd confide to Perry.

Some of them want you, some of them don't.

They're saying the team is doing just fine and they don't need *to bring in a nigger.*

They're saying a lot of Vanderbilt alums are rolling over in their graves right now, and some who are alive feel the same way.

Throughout the winter and early spring of 1966, Perry Wallace had a lot on his mind. So many people with opinions, so many big questions for a teenager to answer, so much pressure to make a decision.

The thing was, he really wasn't in any big hurry.

The Pearl Tigers still had a championship to win.

6

These Boys Never Faltered

The challenge facing *Nashville Banner* cartoonist Bill Duke as the 1966 TSSAA basketball tournament began was emblematic of the recalculations taking place in the minds of white fans across the state. The notion of black teams and white teams playing in the same tournament was a bit slow to take hold.

Duke's cartoon on the front of the *Banner* sports page the afternoon of March 14 was brilliant in many ways. A tall, young basketball player stands in front of a mirror, surrounded by shelves full of crowns, each emblazoned with the name of one of the high schools in the tournament. The back of the player's jersey reads "TSSAA STATE BASKETBALL CHAMPIONS 1966," and the white-haired tailor at his side is about to hand him a crown that reads "PEARL." The drawing captured the anticipatory mood in Nashville as the tournament got underway that day, eighteen teams in town for the tournament and Pearl the favorite to win it all. But the sketch was also an instant anachronism.

The tall young man peering into the mirror, about to be fitted with the PEARL crown, was depicted as white.

Ever since the loss to Father Ryan a year earlier, Pearl had been on a mission to win what would be the first-ever TSSAA state tournament to include black schools, and pity the teams that stood in their way. Dating back to the loss to Clarksville Burt two weeks after the Father Ryan game, the Tigers had won thirty-three games in a row as the postseason dawned, including a perfect 21–0 record during the 1965–66 regular season. A 53–41 victory in a rematch against Ryan was as tense as things had gotten all year for the state's Number 1–ranked team.

But even this desegregated tournament began its march toward progress with baby steps: Pearl's postseason run began with the District 17 tournament, a field that grouped together the Nashville area's black high schools. Pearl easily handled Gallatin Union, Haynes, and Cameron, and Wallace dominated near the basket, notching eleven points and sixteen rebounds against Union and eighteen points, thirteen rebounds versus Cameron.

Next up came the Region V tournament (the jump from district to regional competition brought with it a corresponding switch to roman numerals), to be played at Vanderbilt's Memorial Gym, which would also be the site of the state tournament games the following week. Here in Region V, Pearl was matched against the top white Nashville high schools, including Nashville Interscholastic League champion Stratford.

Respectful of the competition, especially Stratford, skeptical of the reception his team would receive from the mostly white fans at Memorial, and unconvinced that the tournament's power structure—including the referees—wanted the Tigers to represent Nashville in the state tournament, Coach Ridley figured that advancing out of the regionals would be the stiffest challenge his team would face all year. "I think the region will be tougher than the state, that's the problem," Ridley said the day before Pearl's game against Glencliff High. "If we can get out of Region V, we'll be rolling."

In the final minutes before tip-off against Glencliff, Pearl ran through its pregame dunkathon, the first time many white fans in Nashville had ever seen the woomp show. Ridley challenged his players to dunk in warm-ups harder than ever before. "We wanted to go for some big intimidation early in the tournament," Wallace recalled, "because we knew that would have reverberations not only throughout that game, but throughout the rest of the tournament." Beloved *Banner* sports editor Fred Russell, an old-school baseball, golf, and football man not quite sold on basketball, was so impressed that he urged his readers to arrive early at future Pearl games so as not to miss the "dunky-dunk-dunk-dunk-dunk pregame warm-up," wondering if the "bouncy Tigers" should be inspected for "hidden springs attached to ankles or calves."

In case the pregame theatrics had not sufficiently intimidated the Colts, the Tigers knocked any thoughts of an upset right out of the gym immediately after tip-off, blocking not one, not two, not three, not four, not five, not six, not seven, but eight Glencliff shots in the first quarter alone. And then came the exclamation point. To erase any doubt that a new brand of basketball had arrived along with these Pearl High Tigers, they nearly tore the rim off the backboard.

Walter Fisher, Perry Wallace, and James Douglas trailed teammate Joe Herbert as he sailed down the court for a breakaway layup, and they all had one thing on their minds: *Joe might miss.* They'd seen it happen. Herbert was so fast that his momentum occasionally got the better of him, and maybe two out of ten times he'd bounce the ball too hard off the backboard. If one of the big guys was close enough to the play, it was an easy opportunity for a rebound and a slam dunk.

There went Joe, and right behind him, fanned across the court, barreled Slim, Ape Baby, and Doug, each prepared, Wallace remembered, "to knock everybody out of the way and jam it as hard as we could, because if you do that, it will scare the hell out of everybody and that will help us win this tournament."

As if on cue, Herbert laid the ball off the glass a little too hard, and it rolled off the rim, hanging in the air long enough for Fisher, Wallace, and Douglas each to see their opportunity for the slam dunk unfold in what felt to Fisher like slow motion.

"And I can remember like it was yesterday," he recalled, "all three of us up there at one time to slam it back in. We were up there on the rim and we kind of looked around at each other like, 'What the hell are *you* doing up here?'"

In the era before break-away rims (who needed such a thing?), the combined weight of the three big men attacking the basket was more than it could handle. Fisher could hear the sound of the rim bending, and as he floated back down to earth, he thought, "Oh, Lord, we are out to Vanderbilt and we tore up their rim. Are they going to put us out of the tournament?"

Wallace, meanwhile, was disappointed that the show of force had only gone so far.

"I was trying to tear the backboard down," he recalled. "I was really pissed because we only bent the rim."

For Wallace and his teammates, indeed for many Pearl students, the spectacle had an impact much greater than the nine-minute delay it caused in the game. The rim itself would be carried back to Pearl, and a picture of it was used as a recurring icon throughout the school's 1966 yearbook. Out there on the big stage for the first time, Pearl High announced its presence with a style that could not be matched. For the Class of '66, the bent rim symbolized the strength, will, determination, and pride of the entire black Nashville community.

Back on press row, the whole episode was nearly incomprehensible to sportswriters who had never seen such a thing. Russell found local sporting goods dealer Dan McAlpine and asked how it was possible for the rim to just warp like that.

"The rims at Vanderbilt are steel five-eighths of an inch thick," McAlpine told him. "It's impossible for a ball alone to bend them." Like the *Banner* cartoonist, it was as if the salesman were blind to the changes taking place before his eyes. In this new era, it wasn't just basketballs that were colliding with rims.

Pearl went on to demolish Glencliff 73–46, then toppled Overton High School 59–43 in the regional semifinal. That victory assured the Tigers a berth in the state tournament, since the top two seeds from the region advanced on to state play. As the favorite to emerge as the top seed out of District V and to go on to win the championship, Pearl's performance in the first two games was so impressive that sportswriters debated where this team ranked among Tennessee's all-time best. *Banner* scribe Edgar Allen, who had covered Nashville prep sports since the early 1940s, had little doubt. "They are probably the best high school team ever assembled here," he remarked. "They combine tremendous size with great ability. They can do more things better than any club I can recall."

Now standing 26–0 for the 1966 season and winners of thirty-eight straight games overall, Ridley and his Tigers were prepared for their biggest test, the regional final game against NIL champion Stratford. Since both teams had already clinched berths in the state tournament, the game wouldn't determine who advanced and who stayed home, but a victory would assure Pearl the Number 1 overall seed. And as the stakes got higher, Ridley believed, any forces conspiring against his team would grow more pronounced.

With the high-scoring McClain in foul trouble and relegated to the bench for much of the game, Pearl's offense came from a pair of unexpected sources, the defensive-minded Wallace and substitute Tony Moorman. Moorman's parents listened on the radio as he came off the bench to score seven points and as Wallace jammed in two dunks to give Pearl a narrow 29–26 halftime lead over Stratford. The seventy-five hundred spectators in the gym were treated to a game that remained close throughout, by far the Tigers' tightest game of the season. Pearl held on for a 53–49 win, but the air of invincibility that had surrounded the team was deflated, causing sportswriter Allen, who had been so high on the Tigers, to remark that the "odds of Pearl losing appear greatly enhanced."

Still, when TSSAA executive secretary A. F. Bridges presented the Region V trophy to the Tigers after the game, it meant their mission was still on track. If anybody had a legitimate shot to upend top-ranked Pearl, it was Treadwell High School of Memphis. Coach Bill "Bear" McClain's all-white team was in the midst of its own impressive winning streak, having won twenty-four consecutive games; the lone blemish in a 32–1 season to that point had been a two-point defeat to Memphis University School. Making its sixth trip to the state tournament in the last eight years, Treadwell was led by All-State pick Darrell Garrett and second-team All-State selection Curry Todd. Pearl and Treadwell were placed atop the pairings on opposites sides of the tournament bracket; if they were to meet, it would not be until the championship game on March 19.

In the decades that followed the 1966 state tournament, it was often implied that Pearl made history just by advancing to the tournament, but this measure of history would have been made even without them. Two black high schools, Jackson Merry (Pearl's first-round opponent) and Weakley County Training, had advanced to the tournament, and four other teams—Oak Ridge, Alcoa, Bradley Central, and McMinnville City—each had at least two black players on their rosters. And while this was the first TSSAA basketball tournament to include teams from the state's all-black high schools, none of these kids were the first blacks ever to play in the tournament: Oak Ridge, Alcoa, and Father Ryan all competed with at least one black player in the 1965 event.

Nor would Pearl, Merry, or Weakley County become the first black school to win a TSSAA title should any of them advance that far. In the spring of 1965, the state track meet was the association's first championship to include black high schools, and, in front of three thousand spectators at the Memphis Fairgrounds, the city's all-black Melrose High School ran away with a championship.

Still, this was different. The stakes were higher, the spotlight was more intense, and basketball was becoming the black national pastime. Pearl had dominated the state's black high school circuit, winning thirteen state titles, but nobody knew how they would fare against Tennessee's top white teams. The only undefeated team in the tournament, the Tigers felt enormous pressure to complete their unbeaten season and to deliver a championship to Nashville's black community, their own small contribution to the civil rights gains taking place across the South. But even among Pearl's followers, there were those who felt the Tigers would not seal the deal. Coach Ridley and several Tiger players had friends and neighbors tell them they would choke once they squared off against white competition. This knock against black athletes—that they were mentally inferior and would crack under pressure—was a stereotype as old as sports itself in America. There was some determination to prove the doubters—black and white—wrong. But, more than anything, Coach Ridley and his kids could feel just how deeply the majority of their supporters had invested themselves in this team. So much hope to fulfill.

"We had a great sense that we had made it to the big dance, and it was the biggest dance that colored people had ever been invited to in basketball before," Wallace recalled. "So there was a certain amount of savoring the moment, but at the same time there was work to do. It became more intense because we were so close to the goal."

With big league sports in the state still more than thirty years away and the college basketball season complete by this time of year for top-tier programs Vanderbilt, Tennessee, and Memphis State, the tournament in 1966 remained one of the biggest annual sporting events in Tennessee. Nearly every newspaper in the state sent at least one reporter to cover the action and devoted front-of-the-sports-page coverage to the games, while Nashville radio listeners could turn the dial to any of three stations—WENO, WSIX, or WNFO—to hear live play-by-play commentary. Memorial Gym was the place to be even for coaches whose teams had not advanced to the tournament, with three sections of the gym crammed with high school coaches from across the state. Even football coaches showed up, taking advantage of the convention-like atmosphere to find other schools looking to schedule games. Between games, reporters and school officials jockeyed for position in the hospitality room. Cub reporter Bob Baldridge of the *Tennessean* documented their eating habits in his columns, ranking and reranking the top press room eaters from one to ten over the course of the tournament while noting, for example, which freeloader had a particular affinity for ice cream sandwiches. With many of the state's top individual players showcasing their skills, the tournament was an easy one-stop recruiting opportunity for area colleges. Roy Skinner from Vanderbilt, Kentucky assistant Harry Lancaster, Dean Ehlers from Memphis State, and Jimmy Earle from Middle Tennessee State were among a dozen coaches on hand for the tournament's opening games. Fans descended on Nashville from every corner of a state that stretches 440 miles from west to east, filling the restaurants on West End Avenue near the Vanderbilt campus and booking rooms at places like the Anchor Hotel, where the Alcoa fans slept and held their pep rallies. Just to be part of the spectacle, Nashville's Coca-Cola bottling company provided free Cokes to all the participating teams, and just to be even *closer* to the spectacle, eager members of the Junior Chamber of Commerce volunteered to hand out the bottles to the players. Nashville didn't host the tournament every year; it was an honor that also rotated to Memphis and Knoxville, representing a regionalism—Tennessee's three "grand divisions" of West, Middle, and East—and a rivalry that had existed since before the Civil War. As if to underscore the importance of those rivalries, a huge board above the bleachers on the south end of Memorial Gym burned brightly for the duration of the event, each team identified in lights not by the name of their school, but by the region it represented. When a team was eliminated, its lights were extinguished, a region gone dark. Pearl entered the tournament not only playing for themselves and for the black community, but also for Middle Tennessee, looking to become the third consecutive team from the area to win the state championship. Treadwell, meanwhile, sought respect for the West, as West-State teams had lost eleven consecutive state tournament games by the time the Eagles took the court. All of this—the Cokes, the hotels, the backslapping, the rivalries, the media spotlight—added up to a tournament with its own rhythm, its own familiar cast of characters, its own lore. For those who had always been a part of it, it was all quite comfortable.

Then Pearl comes in and busts the rim and now they're probably going to win the whole damn thing.

In the dressing room just before tip-off of Pearl's opening game with Merry, Ridley had a bad feeling. Colds were circulating among his players. Perry Wallace chugged orange juice as fast as he could, but his temperature

The rim that James Douglas, Perry Wallace, and Walter Fisher and broke in their game against Glencliff served as a symbol of strength and determination to the Pearl High Class of '66. Photo by Joe Rudis, *The Tennessean*.

still read 103 degrees and he felt faint. The guys who weren't sick didn't seem especially energized, either; how could they get fired up to play a team they had beaten twice by a combined seventy-five points?

The game started and to Ridley, it was like his team was sleepwalking. Only Ted McClain was on top of his game, scoring eighteen of the Tigers' thirty-three points in the first half. There was no way, Ridley thought, that Merry should be hanging around like this, closing to within five points early in the third quarter. But then the crowd of fifty-five hundred got a taste of what this Pearl team could do—outscoring Merry 13–0 in one spurt—and the game was suddenly close no more. Pearl wound up cruising to a 74–52 win, but Ridley wasn't impressed. Too many fouls, too many turnovers.

"If we keep playing like this," he told the reporters who followed him back to the locker room after the game, "we can put our suits in mothballs."

And he said one more thing, something a future opponent would not forget. When asked whom he would prefer to play in the semifinals should Pearl beat Kingston in its next game, he didn't hesitate. "Hampton," he said. "I don't want any part of Alcoa."

It didn't take long for Ridley to get his wish. The next day, Hampton pulled off the biggest upset of the tournament, capitalizing on an 18–4 run in the second period to shock the heavily favored Alcoa Tornadoes. Along the

Pearl High Coach Cornelius Ridley gathers his thoughts in the minutes before the Tigers faced Memphis's Treadwell High for the 1966 Tennessee state championship. Ridley told his players they were representing every black household in the state of Tennessee that night. Photo by Jimmy Ellis, *The Tennessean.*

way, the Hampton team won over the fans in Memorial Gym, which, like any tournament crowd, adopted the underdog as its team.

With the crowd of seven thousand still roaring its approval after Hampton's stunner, Coach Buck Van Huss and his boys ran off the court and through a doorway that led to their locker room. Standing off to the side, waiting to take the court for their game against Kingston, were Ridley and his Tigers, the team that apparently had such little regard for Hampton.

"Do you hear them?! Do you hear them?!" Van Huss shouted rhetorically to his players as they ran past the Tigers. "Pearl *wants* you tomorrow!"

Ridley hadn't meant any disrespect to Hampton when he was asked his opinion about the Alcoa game; he honestly felt Alcoa was the better team. Regardless, he had provided the juiciest bulletin-board material possible to a team that was now the crowd favorite. As if his Tigers needed another challenge to overcome, he had created a doozy.

When Baldridge, the young *Tennessean* reporter, shook Ridley's hand just before tip-off a few minutes later, he thought the Pearl coach's grip wasn't as steady as usual. "I don't know if the boys are worried or not," Ridley had told him, "but I sure am."

Ridley's butterflies subsided in the early going. The Tigers had performed their pregame dunk show to perfection, and to their delight they saw the Kingston players just standing there, watching the dunks. The routine had its desired effect: Kingston started off fidgety and Pearl jumped out to an early lead. Little by little, however, the Yellow Jackets made their comeback. The crowd, which had already lifted Hampton to its surprise victory just a couple of hours earlier, was in full-throat, sensing a possible upset of the tournament's prohibitive favorite. With just under seven minutes to play, Vic Young's driving layup cut Pearl's lead to 46–44. Was this how the dream was going to end?

No. Moorman came off the bench and made a basket, then another. Then McClain took over, driving in for a layup on one possession, popping in a jumper on the next. Wallace soared above the rim for rebound after rebound, collecting fifteen in all. Suddenly, Pearl's lead had ballooned to eight points; within minutes, the game was over, Pearl winning 62–54. Ridley would get his wish: Hampton in the semifinals. But the Pearl locker room was subdued. Many of the players were still sick, and Ridley's nerves were eating at him like never before. He looked down at his waistband and told reporters he felt like he had lost two inches in the two weeks since district play had begun. He wondered, too, if the pressure was getting to his players. Crowds may have always pulled for underdogs in the TSSAA tournament, but this was the first time the favorite had also been black. Though there were no accounts of any outright hostility, he sensed there was an extra edge to the crowd's cheers for Pearl's opponents.

"I think it's the pressure that's making [us] not play up to [our] capabilities," he told reporters in the locker room. "It takes a lot from a kid when he knows the majority of the spectators are pulling against him."

Friday, March 18, 1966, was an unseasonably warm day. State tournament fans woke up to strong winds outside their doors and temperatures in the seventies, and the cinder block walls inside Memorial Gym shook with the thunderstorms that rolled through Nashville.

Any Pearl fans looking for bad omens didn't have to look far to find them. The gym was sweltering, the skies were menacing, the wind was whipping, many of the Tigers were still woozy with fever, their opponent felt disrespected, and the majority of the fans jam-packed into Memorial Gym had adopted the Hampton Bulldogs as their team for the day. And while Hampton may have been an underdog, it was no mutt: with thirty-eight victories in the season, the Bulldogs were in fact the winningest team in the state.

Pearl started the semifinal game slowly, trailing by as many as five points in the first quarter. Gradually, however, the Tigers' talent advantage began to show. McClain clamped down defensively on Bud Winters, hero of Hampton's win over Alcoa, limiting him to just six points. Wallace was determined not to let his fever hold him down, collecting nineteen rebounds. McClain and Walter Fisher drained jumpers from all over the court, scoring twenty-eight and twenty-one points respectively. The five-point deficit became a two-point Pearl lead at halftime, a seven-point lead after three quarters, and a blowout in the fourth, Pearl winning 74–51. Finally, Ridley believed, his team overcame its jitters, learned to deal with the crowd, and played up to its capabilities. The locker room scene this time was jubilant, players chugging down the Cokes handed out by the Jaycees. The sense of relief in the room was palpable. An exhausted Ridley was content to know that the journey was nearly complete.

"Just one more to go, and the season will be over, anyhow," he told reporters. "It's been a long one."

The only question now was who Pearl's opponent would be in the championship. The day's second semifinal would match up Treadwell, the other pretournament favorite, and Oak Ridge. Passing by the Pearl team between games, Treadwell coach McClain remarked to a collection of Tigers that he would be seeing them tomorrow; he saw one of the Pearl players pat Darrell Garrett on the backside and tell him to "go out there and get with it." The two heavyweights wanted nothing more than to face each other in the title game.

Paced by senior big man Randy Pool and black point guard Willie Golden, Oak Ridge dominated Treadwell in the early stages of the game, Pool turning heads with twenty-nine points and twelve rebounds. When Oak Ridge took a fourteen-point lead in the second half, Ridley, who had found a seat at courtside to scout the game, decided to stop taking notes on Treadwell, figuring his next opponent surely would be Oak Ridge. At that very moment, Treadwell coach McClain called a timeout, offering one last-gasp bit of encouragement to his boys. It was never too late to win, he said. It was up to them. How bad did they want it?

Inspirational pep talks go only so far. With 4:23 left in the game, Treadwell had managed to shave just four points off the deficit, still trailing by ten. More important than words were whistles; so many of them blown in the direction of Golden that he fouled out. Oak Ridge suddenly seemed lost, falling prey to Treadwell's press defense for the first time. The Ridgers started turning the ball over and Todd began pouring in the points, and Treadwell mounted a ferocious comeback. With thirty-nine seconds to play, Todd made two free throws to put Treadwell ahead 54–53. Somehow, teammate Garrett misread the scoreboard, believing his team was still trailing by a point. When the final buzzer sounded with the score still 54–53, Todd and all but one of his teammates celebrated wildly. Garrett, thinking Treadwell had lost, was inconsolable, his dreams crushed, tears streaming down his face. But with Treadwell fans rushing to the side of the court shouting, "We're number one! We're number one!" Garrett, to his great joy, finally realized his mistake. Heartbreak to elation in a split second. Rushing off the court, McClain shouted to reporters, "I told you we could play, didn't I? Turn out those East Tennessee lights! Bring on Pearl! That Region IX light'll still be burnin' when we finish."

The championship game would be the one everyone wanted, after all.

Pearl against Treadwell.

Mid-State against West-State.

Black against white.

Pearl student Lee Hayden had walked from North Nashville over toward the Vanderbilt campus many times before on his way to one job or another across town. On the afternoon of the title game, he left his home three hours early not because it was a long or unfamiliar walk, but because he was so excited to get to the game. It wasn't all that far geographically from the heart of black Nashville to the epicenter of white Nashville wealth and power, less than two miles, but metaphorically, the neighborhoods were worlds apart. With Pearl putting on such a show at Memorial Gym the last two weeks, the many Vanderbilt fans who turned out for the state tournament were getting their first extended glimpse of one of their own city's true jewels. Hayden sensed what was happening, and he paid extra attention to what the white fans said about his school.

Climbing the stairs to the gym entrance for the state championship game, he smiled to himself as he overheard a conversation between two young, white female ticket-takers.

"Have you seen Pearl of Nashville?" one girl asked the other. "They are *phenomenal!*"

With that, Hayden presented his ticket, walked to his seat with hours to go until tip-off, and thought about what the Pearl teachers had told all their students: *Number one, don't go cutting up. Represent the school with pride. We're going to make history.*

Not if Bear McClain had anything to say about it.

Shaky tournament performances aside, McClain's Treadwell Eagles were formidable. Pearl's forty-two-game winning streak was impressive, but so, too, was Treadwell's twenty-eight-game streak. Pearl's players felt part of a cause greater than themselves, but so did the Eagles: five times in the previous seven years Treadwell had advanced to the state tournament, and five times they'd returned home without a trophy. A championship in 1966 would provide some measure of redemption for all those teams that had come home empty-handed.

Just like Coach Ridley, McClain was the kind of mentor who invested every ounce of his being into his basketball program. When Curry Todd was an eighth grader not even yet on the high school varsity, McClain would show up at his parents' home and take him across the street to a gymnasium, where the coach worked with the up-and-coming ballplayer on his shooting form. During summers when official practices were off-limits, the entire team would just happen to show up in the front yard of a player with a particularly wide driveway, McClain running the team through set plays on the hot asphalt. Like their opponent, the Treadwell Eagles were a bunch of well-coached gym rats, and in the final minutes before the tip-off of the championship game, they wanted to win this game so bad they could taste it.

Across the hallway, alone in the Pearl locker room as his players ran through their pregame dunkathon, Coach Ridley sat down on a bench and took a moment to gather his thoughts. Here it was, the opportunity he'd waited for his entire life.

But it wasn't enough just to win; the tenor of the times, Ridley believed, demanded that the Tigers win in just the right way. Ever since Wallace, Fisher, and Douglas had busted the rim in the game against Glencliff, Wallace recalled, Ridley had been more conscious than ever that his Tigers could make their greatest statement if they managed to win ball games while playing with a style that white fans could not possibly disparage as "wild black basketball." Ridley told his players that they didn't want to play out of control both for appearances' sake—everything they did reflected on the race—but also for the simple fact that if they slowed things down and minimized the chances to make mistakes, they could prove that blacks didn't choke when the stakes were high.

"People who only see you in terms of stereotypes have no idea that you're sitting down saying, 'We know what people think, so how are we going to proceed so that we can be effective *and* disabuse them of those thoughts?'" Wallace recalled. "They never stop and think that the people they're watching out on the court might have thought really, really hard about all that."

When his players returned to the locker room after their warm-up act, Ridley was ready to speak. All eyes were on him.

"You're not only representing Pearl High School," he told his players, "you're representing North Nashville, you're representing your household, and just about every black face in the state of Tennessee—you're representing them, too. You need to go out there and do what's necessary to win in a very controlled manner, with personality and with sportsmanship. Maintain your poise and character at all times."

At this crucial, frenzied time, just minutes before his players took the court in the most socially significant athletic contest in Tennessee history, Ridley saw the big picture, calmly conveying thoughts that would ring true to black historians for decades to come.

"Black athletes have symbolically carried the weight of a race's eternal burden of proof; their performances were among the most visible evidences that blacks, as a community, were good enough, smart enough, strong enough, brave enough—indeed, human enough—to share in the fruits of this nation with full citizenship and humanity," William Rhoden wrote in *Forty Million Dollar Slaves*. "This was a heavy burden on one hand, but on the other it represented a noble, time-worn responsibility. You always represented."

This was it. The big dance. Pearl's chance to shake things up.

The Tigers wasted no time; even the way they approached pregame introductions was unlike anything the fans at Memorial Gym had ever seen before. Rather than returning to the team bench or heading out to midcourt after the starting lineup had been introduced, the entire Tiger team—players and coaches alike—formed a tight circle, waists bent, hands clasped together down low in the middle of it all, the group linked as one, pulsing in and out, back and forth, up and down, like a beating heart about to explode. With the Tiger cheerleaders in their pleated skirts shrieking at the top of their lungs just a few feet away, Walter Fisher had to shout to be heard. He called out, and his teammates, still pulsing, pulsing, pulsing, repeated: "Team! *Team!* Can't be beat! *Can't be beat!* Won't be beat! *Won't be beat!* All for one! *All for one!* One for all! *One for all!* All for Pearl! *All for Pearl!* Pearl High! *Pearl High!*"

With that, the Tigers took the court, Perry Wallace walking to the center jump circle and exchanging a quick handshake with Darrell Garrett. Seeing the Pearl players up close for the first time, the Treadwell players were reminded of some of the rumors they'd heard about the Tigers.

Did you hear that some of their players are twenty-five years old?

All of them can dunk the ball and all of them are married!

If we were that old, we could probably dunk, too!

There was the tiniest sliver of truth to one of the accusations: Ted McClain had repeated a grade in elementary school, and though he was just a junior, he would be too old to play another year of high school ball the following season. Still, he was nineteen years old, perfectly legal in this tournament, and the rest of Pearl's players were no older than the Treadwell group. Wallace, in fact, was likely the youngest senior on the floor, having just turned eighteen less than a month earlier. The rumors were nothing more than well-worn stereotypes, a frequent charge leveled against the oncoming flood of talented black athletes who, as author Nelson George wrote, were "elevating the game" at all levels.

To the modern eye, the black-and-white footage of the 1966 Tennessee high school championship game looks positively ancient. The Chuck Taylor hightops, the short-shorts, the straight-up-and-down dribbling style, the lack of contact between players, the unorthodox free-throw shooting. But every now and then, a flash of the contemporary from both sides: Ted McClain's legs kicked up behind him on a jumper, Curry Todd's picture-perfect shot from the corner, Perry Wallace skying for a rebound and making an outlet pass to start a fast break. The next generation of basketball was breaking through.

Ted McClain opened the game's scoring with his patented jumper, and throughout the early going he and Walter Fisher were as hot as ever from the outside. By the end of the first quarter, Pearl led 16–10. By halftime the Pearl lead had grown to 31–18. There had been no dunks, only a couple of fast breaks. Just a few days earlier, Pearl made a statement with its show of force; the beauty of this effort was in how methodical it was. All that remained now were two eight-minute quarters, sixteen minutes to history.

But Garrett began to heat up in the third quarter and Todd's jumper was true. When Todd took the fourth quarter's opening tip and scampered all the way down the court for a layup, the lead was cut to five. The Treadwell faithful were up and out of their seats, Pearl seemingly on the ropes. The teams traded baskets for nearly five minutes, and when Wallace fouled Todd with 3:23 remaining, the Treadwell junior hit both free throws to cut Pearl's lead back down to five at 53–48. A McClain layup and another Todd jumper, and the lead was 55–50 with 2:39 left.

After the game, Wallace told *Tennessean* reporter Jimmy Davy that it was at this moment that he realized that if he wanted this victory bad enough, he could make it happen.

"I knew we had to have the ball," Wallace told Davy, "and I knew who could get it. Me."

Todd misses a jumper, Wallace skies for the rebound, tosses a quick outlet pass downcourt to lead the break, and Fisher lays it in for two. The Pearl fans leap to their feet.

Garrett misses, Wallace grabs another rebound, passes downcourt, and Fisher lays it in again. Tiger fans grow louder, a cascading crescendo reverberating off the cinderblock walls, the gym taking on the supercharged air that only comes when the partisans know a victory is at hand.

The Pearl players know it, too, and they finally begin to loosen up, Wallace leaping high again to grab another missed shot, his seventeenth rebound of the game, one less than the entire Treadwell team had collected, this time his legs kicked out to the side, his body forming a giant X as he snatches the ball in midair. His toss downcourt this time is straight over the top, like a baseball pitcher's, a rare flourish from the straight arrow. Next time down the court, McClain whips a perfect behind-the-back pass to Douglas for an easy layup, and the rout is on and the game is over, the final score 63–54.

One moment in time, so many different reactions:

Over there, behind the bench, those are the Pearl cheerleaders, leaping high into the air and screaming with joy for their school.

Across the way, there goes Curry Todd, running toward his coach, for the

Pearl High School fans and cheerleaders celebrate after the Tigers beat Treadwell to complete an undefeated 1966 season and win Tennessee's first-ever integrated state basketball tournament. *Nashville Banner* Archives, Nashville Public Library, Special Collections.

very first time thinking a thought that would still echo in his mind four decades later: *We beat ourselves. This was our chance to do it, and it just wasn't meant to be.*

Down there, in the Pearl cheering section, that's Lee Hayden, bursting with pride. He loved being young and alive at this moment, so much happening around the world in the 1960s, people confronting issues, progress coming every day. He could read about 1776 in a textbook, but this was real. His team had made history, and he was there to see it.

Right on the court, there are Perry Wallace and all but one of his teammates, grabbing Coach Ridley and hoisting him to their shoulders, playing to the newspaper photographers, all smiles and hugs, leaning in and holding their index fingers up in the air. *Pearl's number one!*

And there goes a solitary teammate, Walter Fisher, walking slowly past his celebrating teammates, exhausted from playing every minute of the game, head down, taking a seat on the Pearl bench, towel over his head, head in his hands. *Thank you, Jesus, we pulled this one off. Nobody got hurt, there were no mishaps. We made it through the entire season undefeated. We've got so much to be thankful for, Lord.* Forty years later, the emotions of that moment would come flooding back to Fisher when asked about it, tears welling in his eyes, his voice breaking.

And here comes Richard Baker, Memorial Gym custodian, a Vanderbilt

Pearl's players receive the championship trophy from Governor Frank Clement. Minutes earlier, Walter Fisher was overcome with emotion: "We've got so much to be thankful for, Lord." Photo by Frank Empson, *The Tennessean*.

employee since before Pearl Harbor, the only black man associated with the Commodore Athletic Department; here he comes with a ladder straight to the hoop next to the Pearl bench, just as he's done so many times before, setting up that ladder so the championship team can cut down the nets, only this time with an extra measure of pride.

After Governor Frank Clement presented the Tigers with a four-and-a-half-foot-tall championship trophy, coach and players made their way back to their lockers in the bowels of the gym, where they were surrounded by reporters eager for quotes from the champs. "We weren't leaving without that trophy," James Douglas said amid the whoops and hollers of a jubilant locker room. "We've done a lot of things together and we knew we could do this."

As usual, Ridley looked at the big picture.

"I'm especially happy for the other 80 Negro schools in the TSSAA who came in with us," he said. "We proved it could be done. A lot of folks thought we'd choke and get beat somewhere along the line, but these boys never faltered. I guess I was proudest of the fact that in all of our tournament games, regardless of what happened, our boys never seemed to lose their poise."

Throughout the tournament, the Pearl players tried to earn respect for themselves and for the black community. And yet, for many players, the

Vanderbilt custodian Richard Baker, the only black employee of the Athletic Department in 1966, hands Wallace a net after Pearl defeated Treadwell at Memorial Gymnasium to win the first integrated state tournament in Tennessee history. Photo by Jimmy Ellis, *The Tennessean.*

Pearl players celebrate their state championship. After showering and dressing, most of the team partied in East Nashville, where they watched on television as Texas Western beat Kentucky for the NCAA title. *Nashville Banner* Archives, Nashville Public Library, Special Collections.

locker room celebration was marred by the realization that their excellence could be dismissed by some whites who chose not to see it. Ted McClain had not been named the tournament's MVP. The honor, voted on by sportswriters, had instead gone to Randy Pool of *third-place* finisher Oak Ridge. Pool had played exceptionally well, no one disputed that, but McClain was the best player on a squad that easily won the tournament and was being called the greatest team in state history. McClain had been the high scorer on a team loaded with college prospects, and had nearly set a tournament record for field goal percentage (hitting ten of fifteen shots in the championship game alone). "There's no question," Jimmy Davy said forty years later, "that McClain got jobbed for MVP." Fellow *Tennessean* columnist Jim Andrews called out his press-box brethren in a column two days after the championship game, stating McClain's case by simply asking "What more does a guy have to do?" Disappointing as it was to the Tigers, these kinds of slights were all too common. Wallace saw it as the perfect illustration of a mentality that saw desegregation not as a long-overdue redress of a grievous inequity but as a gift from whites to blacks. Pool's award was a sort of jury nullification of Pearl's title, a righting of the ship for those threatened by the departure from the old "normal." *We* let *you in the tournament this year, but you're not going to claim it* all *for yourselves.*

Still, Pearl had come away with the only trophy that mattered. Showered and dressed, most of the Tigers had one thing on their mind: the postgame party. In the days leading up to the tournament, Tony Moorman had gone to the barbershop to get an "edge up," and his barber, who happened to be teammate Melvin Smith's brother, told him that if the Tigers won the title, they could party at his apartment in East Nashville. Eight people piled into the Corvair Moorman's aunt had let him borrow, and the rest of the team followed close behind. Girlfriends showed up and the whole crew partied late into the night and early the next morning. All but one guy.

Elated over the victory but still weary from the cold and fever that had dragged him down throughout the tournament, Perry Wallace rode home to 10th Avenue with his parents, picked up a burger and milkshake along the way, and settled in for a late night of television. He fell asleep watching a horror movie, but before the flick had come on, he had watched a little basketball.

March 19, 1966, wasn't a date that would go down only in Tennessee high school basketball history.

That very same night, in College Park, Maryland, Texas Western was taking on Adolph Rupp's Kentucky Wildcats for the NCAA men's basketball championship.

Perry Wallace drank his chocolate shake while watching the single most important college basketball game ever played.

7

Somewhere Like Xanadu

Even as the Tigers were revolutionizing high school basketball in Tennessee, dozens of fans at Memorial Gym had brought along portable televisions to watch the beginning of the Kentucky-Texas Western national championship game, which started just as Pearl's victory was winding down.

John Oldham, the head coach at Western Kentucky University, had driven sixty-five miles from Bowling Green to catch the Pearl-Treadwell game. Before heading back home that evening, he stopped by the Memorial Gym hospitality room. Nashville's WSM-TV, Channel 4, boasted that it was carrying the NCAA title game *in color*, and he wanted to take a look.

Lee Hayden walked home from the gym, flipped on his black-and-white TV, and thought they must be airing a replay of the Pearl-Treadwell game, what with five black kids playing against five white kids. But the uniforms were wrong—Pearl had worn white uniforms in their game, not dark ones. It took him a minute before he realized he was watching Miners and Wildcats, not Tigers and Eagles. All seven players Texas Western coach Dan Haskins put on the court were black; Rupp's Wildcats were all white.

Throughout Pearl's championship run, Wallace heard rumblings about Texas Western's improbable march through the NCAA Tournament. Older guys in the neighborhood talked about how well the Miners were playing, wondering aloud if they weren't in fact *too* good, and if somehow, some way, a team that featured so many blacks would be booted from the tournament. "The feeling was, 'Are they going to let them play, or if they win enough games, will they tell them go home, we can't let you win the championship?'" Wallace recalled. "It's not like that was out of the question."

While blacks across the country had a special rooting interest, Wallace had more personal reasons to stay glued to the set. For one thing, David Lattin, Big Daddy D, the gym-rattling dunker who had been such a big influence on a young Wallace and had briefly attended Tennessee A&I, was now

Texas Western's biggest star. In El Paso, Lattin was still the intimidator that he had been in those pickup games in Nashville. Haskins liked to recall the time Daddy D dunked the ball so ferociously that he tore the rim off the backboard, sliced a gash in his arm, and knocked a teammate out cold in the process—at practice. Wallace was struck by the obvious similarities between the game he was watching and the game he had just played, right down to the fact that he had become Lattin's Pearl High counterpart. Just as Wallace had ushered in the new era of high school hoops in Tennessee when he helped bend the rim at Memorial Gym in Pearl's win over Glencliff, Lattin had commanded the attention of the Wildcats—and the nation—on Texas Western's second possession of the championship game. "Just dunk it like they ain't never seen it dunked," Haskins had instructed, and Big Daddy D obliged, slamming the ball over Pat Riley's outstretched arms and off the future NBA coaching legend's head. Physical statement complete, verbal one on the way to the free throw line: "Take that, you white honky," Lattin reportedly yelled in Riley's direction.

Lattin's theatrics aside, Wallace had another reason to pay close attention to the game: Kentucky was recruiting him. Conventional wisdom holds that it was only in the aftermath of the Miner-Wildcat game that SEC schools began to recruit blacks, and while that is true in some respects—at some schools, there was an added urgency—the fact is that Kentucky and Vanderbilt had already been making an effort, albeit an ineffective one, for two years.

Though Wallace was pulling for Texas Western to hold on to a lead it had held since midway through the first half, there were aspects to Kentucky's program that appealed to him. Most obvious was the winning tradition. In his lifetime, the Wildcats had won four national championships. Wallace also admired the Kentucky assistant coaches who were recruiting him: Harry Lancaster, who was known for playing the role of "good cop" to Rupp's "bad cop," and Joe B. Hall, who had prior experience coaching blacks. "They were just great," Wallace recalled. "I really liked them."

If any team was the logical choice to become the first to integrate SEC basketball, it was Kentucky.

Here was the northernmost SEC state, the only one that had not been a part of the Confederacy. In 1949 the university became the first in the league to admit black undergraduates, and by the early 1960s the school's president, John W. Oswald, and the Kentucky governor, Ned Breathitt, both had spoken publicly about their desire to see the university's athletic programs, and particularly the basketball team, recruit black players.

If breaking the color line was an unpopular proposition among some Kentucky fans, certainly a living legend like Rupp, head coach since 1930–31, had the political capital to withstand any pushback. The Wildcats won so many games and had become so popular under Rupp's watch that when the team moved out of the twenty-eight-hundred-seat Alumni Gym in 1950, the new Memorial Coliseum was more than quadruple the size of the old gym and immediately considered too small. "When a Kentucky baby is born, his mother naturally wants him to be President, like another Kentuckian, Abraham Lincoln," Rupp once said. "If not President, she wants him to play basketball for the University of Kentucky."

Rupp had even survived a major scandal that would have brought down less imposing coaches. A point-shaving scheme involving three of his players in the late 1940s and revealed in the early 1950s led the NCAA to ban the Wildcats from participating in the entire 1952–53 season, and in the course of receiving sworn testimony from UK players and administrators, Judge Saul Streit said that he found "undeniable evidence of covert subsidization of players, ruthless exploitation of athletes, cribbing on examinations, illegal recruiting, a reckless disregard for the players' physical welfare, matriculation of unqualified students, [and] demoralization of the athletes by the coach, the alumni and townspeople." Rupp had survived all that, emerged stronger. Certainly he would have survived the recruitment of a black high school star.

To his credit, unlike SEC coaches who refused to even let their teams take the court against teams with black players, Rupp took on all comers, traveling north, west, and east to play the best squads in the country, many of which fielded blacks, and bringing teams with black players to Lexington. "We play teams from the Big Ten and Missouri Valley Conference who have Negro boys who can jump a mile and we hold our own," Rupp said, a statement that was at once both a defiant defense of the status quo and a considerably more liberal position than that at, say, Mississippi State, which had routinely turned down NCAA tournament bids lest the Maroons be forced to play against blacks. If Rupp had no problem playing *against* blacks, why not let them play *for* him?

Had Rupp decided to send a message to his fellow SEC coaches, it would not have been the first time. From the moment he arrived in Lexington, he considered it his personal mission to raise basketball's profile below the Mason-Dixon line and to implore his competitors to take the game more seriously. "Rupp was brash, arrogant and antagonistic in his drive to make basketball matter as much as football in the South," wrote his biographer Russell Rice. "By the 1934–35 season, writers were calling Rupp the most hated person in Dixie. He earned that distinction the hard way, criticizing practically everything about basketball in the South: the schools and their untrained coaches, who were mostly assistants in football; the red-neck fans, incompetent officials, substandard arenas and slow-down basketball." If SEC basketball was still backward by the 1960s, it was in the most obvious of ways: while teams from Chicago to Cincinnati to San Francisco to Pittsburgh were more than happy to recruit black players from the South, white universities in the region continued to exclude them. Still, this was one aspect of southern basketball Rupp chose not to disparage.

While Rupp was already an unpopular figure among blacks in Kentucky by the 1960s, Wallace was only vaguely aware of the coach's reputation. As he sat and watched the championship game, his opinion of the Wildcats was shaped more by his own personal experiences—namely, a recent encounter with two blacks Rupp had failed to sign and the encounters he had *not* had with the coach himself.

In late February 1966, a white Nashville businessman who was a fan of both Vanderbilt and the University of Louisville offered to drive the entire Pearl starting five up to Louisville for a Cardinal basketball game against Wichita State, which was to be preceded by a freshman game against Kentucky Wesleyan. Wallace and his teammates eagerly accepted the chance for a road trip and the opportunity to see Louisville's two black superstars, freshman Butch Beard and sophomore Wes Unseld, and meet them after the game. Wallace was mesmerized by the pace of the freshman game, with Beard engaged in a back-and-forth battle with former Kentucky high school legend Mike Redd. Unseld made a big impression as well, but for a different reason. "Wes was a great player, but most important, he made a huge impression on me as a role model," Wallace recalled. "He was quiet, polite, and yet ferocious on the court."

Both Beard and Unseld had been recruited by Rupp, and neither emerged from the experience with positive feelings toward UK. Beard and his family got the impression that Rupp was under pressure to recruit a black player but wasn't himself sold on the merits of the idea. Unseld felt much the same way. At one point in the recruiting process, Rupp refused to visit Unseld's home, so Kentucky president Oswald accompanied Lancaster on the visit. By this point, Unseld had already received several death threats from Kentucky fans, and though he led his Seneca High School team to consecutive state championships and earned the state's Mr. Basketball honors, a group of fifteen Lexington residents sent him a letter urging him to play basketball out of state. "[Unseld] had an opportunity to say some nasty things about Rupp or Kentucky," Oswald said of that visit, "but he did not say them. I was halfway expecting him to say, 'I wouldn't play under Rupp.'"

Beard and Unseld continued to take the high road when Wallace asked for their opinions of Kentucky. "They were measured," Wallace recalled. "They didn't talk down Kentucky, but they didn't have a lot of good stuff to say, either. What they did say was that just in general, you'd want to be careful going in there integrating, being a guinea pig."

Wallace remembered those words as he watched the NCAA title game, and though he personally had not developed negative feelings toward Rupp, he was struck by the fact that he had very little feeling for the man at all. He

Wallace and a group of Pearl High teammates traveled to Louisville, Kentucky, in February 1966 to watch Cardinal freshman and varsity basketball games. Here, Wallace, right, visits with Louisville's Butch Beard and Wes Unseld, both of whom had been recruited by Kentucky and tactfully recommended that Wallace steer clear of Rupp's program. Photo by Russ Glass, courtesy of Perry Wallace.

hadn't even met him. Lancaster and Hall had done all the recruiting. Given the enormity of the decision facing Wallace, the hardships he'd endure as a pioneer, he determined that he couldn't put his fate in the hands of a man who hadn't bothered to visit him.

"It wasn't that I wanted special treatment," Wallace recalled, "it was that this was a special situation. Anybody that wouldn't lend that personal touch, I couldn't go there. I liked Coach Lancaster and Coach Hall. If Coach Rupp had shown a little bit of that, I might have gone to Kentucky. But to have the top guy say nary a word, that was a very important consideration."

Wallace was operating partly on gut feeling and partly on the reflected wisdom of mentors such as his parents and Coach Ridley, people who were good judges of character. He made the decision to cross Kentucky off his list, but he never could have known the extent of Rupp's reluctance to break the SEC's color line.

Rupp had missed an easy opportunity to take a symbolic stand for racial equality back in 1956 when three of the other four teams slated to join Kentucky at the annual Sugar Bowl basketball tournament in New Orleans pulled out in protest of a Louisiana law that prohibited blacks and whites from mixing at social events, including basketball games. Rather than take the relatively painless step of joining Notre Dame, Saint Louis, and Dayton in withdrawing from the event, Rupp chose the opposite approach, finding three willing participants—Alabama, Houston, and Georgia Tech—to take their place.

Around the same time that Alexander Heard arrived at Vanderbilt and attempted to usher the school into the modern era, Oswald took command at Kentucky with much the same mission. And almost from the day he arrived, as author Frank Fitzpatrick wrote in his profile of the 1966 NCAA title game, he sought to integrate the Wildcat basketball team. Put another way, as Lancaster said of Oswald, "He drove Adolph crazy telling him to recruit blacks."

While Heard found Skinner amenable to the idea of recruiting black players, Oswald knew he was fighting an uphill battle with Rupp. He later recalled that from his first encounter with the coach, he felt that Rupp "sounded like a bigot. I guess primarily it was his language and expressions. He tended to refer to blacks in terms which are now considered derogatory."

Even as Oswald failed to sway the opinion of his coach, Kentucky governor Breathitt got in on the act, vowing in December 1965 to begin an "immediate all-out effort" to integrate Wildcat athletics.

Rupp, who had such total control of his program that he didn't even allow his players to speak during practice, wasn't about to let anyone—even a governor or university president—tell him whom he should recruit. Speaking of his contentious conversations with Oswald, he confided in Lancaster: "Harry, that son of a bitch is ordering me to get some niggers in here. What am I going to do?"

What he did was make half-hearted attempts to land Beard and Unseld and justify his general reluctance to recruit blacks by claiming that he could not guarantee their safety on the road. He pointed to the treatment he and his white players received at Mississippi State, where Rupp once found a dead skunk under his seat on the bench and where players would have the hairs on their legs plucked by students seated near the playing floor.

"If they treat me and my boys like that now, what do you think they would do if I brought a Negro to town?" Rupp said. "I've had many fine black prospects tell me they did not want to be the first to go to Mississippi to play, and I don't blame them."

The fact remained that some coach was going to have to make the first move, and Rupp had the clout to ease the transition better than anyone if he had chosen to use his bully pulpit for this cause. "He apparently didn't want to be the first to set a trend of recruiting a black in the conference," black Lexington high school basketball coach S. T. Roach once said. "With his stature, he could have made all the difference in the world."

In the end, had Rupp been just a little more convincing in his dealings with Beard, Unseld, or Wallace, he would have been the man who broke the SEC color line, another plaudit to add to the dozens that grace a biography that includes more accomplishments than just about any coach in history. What a difference one recruit might have made to the complicated legacy he left behind. Adolph Rupp would have been considered a trailblazer. Instead, it was Haskins and the Miners who would bask in history's glow.

Though the Miner roster was not all black—white forward Jerry Armstrong had played a pivotal defensive role in Texas Western's semifinal win over Utah—Haskins chose to stick with a smaller lineup in the championship game against "Rupp's Runts" (no Kentucky starter stood over six foot five), and that meant going with five black starters and two black reserves. While Kentucky hung close to the Miners for much of the game, Texas Western's suffocating defense was more than the Wildcats could handle. Bobby Joe Hill's back-to-back steals midway through the first half set the tone, and Kentucky never recovered. Final score: Texas Western 72–65. Lasting impact, just beginning.

In the days that followed the Pearl and Miner victories, some whites in Tennessee complained that the TSSAA had acted too quickly in desegregating the state tournament, arguing that the association should have waited until Tennessee high schools had become more fully integrated so that the black talent would be more evenly distributed (one of the more convoluted and self-serving arguments in favor of school desegregation ever put forward). Others throughout the South who had watched an all-white Kentucky team fall flat reached a similar conclusion. "It was quite clear after March 1966," wrote sports historian Charles Martin, "that Southern basketball teams would have to change or become increasingly noncompetitive nationally."

Decades later, a Disney movie would be made about Texas Western's march to the championship; *Glory Road* was a feel-good flick that gave the Miners their due. Anyone could watch that movie and be proud of the progress that has taken place in American sports since that watershed game. Reality was far more complicated.

While the sight of an all-black Texas Western lineup may have been jarring for some white viewers, the black players who cut down the nets that night weren't the first to win an NCAA basketball championship. In fact, in each of the previous five years, the tournament champion had included anywhere from two to four black starters. White teams weren't rendered immediately irrelevant; the very next year, an all-white North Carolina team advanced to the Final Four. Many Kentucky fans wouldn't even point to the Texas Western game as the first that convinced them they could not win with an all-white lineup. They'd look back instead to the 1964 tournament, when Kentucky lost a Mideast regional final to Ohio University, a team with three black stars, and a third-place game to Loyola of Chicago, which featured black Nashvillians Les Hunter and Vic Rouse. SEC schools didn't immediately rush out and sign black players: as late as four years later, only two blacks were on varsity SEC rosters. Rupp would eventually sign just one black player before he retired, center Tom Payne, who played on Rupp's penultimate team in 1970–71. The game did mark the beginning of the end for the Baron of the Bluegrass; after Texas Western, none of his teams advanced beyond the second round of the NCAA tournament.

While Haskins was a hero in the black community in the short term, it was only a matter of a few years before many observers branded *him* a racist for "exploiting" black players that championship season, claiming he cared only about what his players could do for him on the court and nothing about their academics or social lives. It was an ironic turn of events for Haskins, who received forty thousand letters in the immediate aftermath of the title game, "most of them from the South and a lot of them from Kentucky," he recalled, many of them attacking him as a "nigger lover."

"Anybody who tells you that our 1966 team was celebrated across the country for what we accomplished is lying," Haskins wrote in his biography, *Glory Road*. "We were loved in El Paso. And certainly there were blacks who saw us on television and couldn't believe their eyes and loved what we did. But the establishment and the media it controls were completely against us. We were pariahs. We were villains. We were 'wretched.' We were not being held up as heroes."

The Wildcats traveled back to Lexington with their second-place trophy and held their annual postseason banquet five days after the championship game. Despite the disappointing loss, President Oswald was eager to attend the dinner. Rupp had assured him that all the high school seniors he was recruiting would be in attendance at the Lexington hotel where the banquet was held, including two black players. Including Perry Wallace.

Oswald scanned the ballroom. All the white recruits were there. Neither of the blacks was. Had Rupp been misleading him all along? Billy Thompson, sports editor of the *Lexington Herald* and the evening's master of ceremonies, took the podium. The Wildcats, he said, should not be ashamed. "At least we're still America's number one white team."

Oswald was livid.

Wallace was home in Nashville. If he had been invited to the banquet, it was not something he remembered.

He may not have dined with the Wildcats, but Wallace was busy. In the days following Pearl's victory, the team was paraded around town from one photo opportunity to another, black Nashvillians proud of their team and white elected officials and business leaders taking advantage of the chance to put their fair-mindedness on public display. There was a visit to the *Tennessean* newsroom, where a group of coat-and-tie-clad Tigers posed for photos alongside the Associated Press wire-photo machine. There was a visit to City Hall, where Mayor Briley presented each Tiger with a special award of achievement. There was a luncheon at a community center hosted by the Nashville chapter of the black service organization Frontiers International. In the midst of a week that had seen a wave of black church burnings in the South, Frontiers president William Harper lauded the Tigers as "a group that has certainly contributed to better race relations in Tennessee."

"Your sportsmanship," Harper told the players, "created an image of our people that no other group has had the opportunity or privilege to do."

There was an appearance at a Metro school board meeting at the invitation of schools director Dr. John Harris, an invitation extended, Harris said, because "not once have I had a negative call about these boys. They are a group of clean sportsmen who did a magnificent job."

Wallace was quick to return the compliment, extending characteristically diplomatic words to a group that still oversaw an almost entirely segregated network of schools. "On behalf of the team," he said, "I'd like to express appreciation to a school system which makes us proud to bring the state championship trophy to Nashville."

The school board members then engaged in some playful and hypocritical banter, wondering aloud whether now that the "boys" had gotten the opportunity to play at Memorial Gym, might some of them like to continue their basketball careers there. The Tigers must have been incredulous at the sudden color blindness of the backslappers; for forty-five years the TSSAA had excluded blacks. The SEC still did. Suddenly Pearl dominates the tournament and race is no factor? Wallace stuck to the facts and gave away no hints, telling the board members about his upcoming official visits to Iowa and Vanderbilt and indicating that he'd be taking another six trips on top of those. To *Tennessean* reporter Jimmy Davy, he added, "I'll be perfectly honest, I have no leaning whatsoever. The visits will help me decide. When that will be, I don't know. I've set no deadline."

Davy had taken a keen interest in Wallace's plans, an unusual circumstance even in an era of chummy relationships between sportswriters and the subjects they covered. Davy had covered high school sports for the *Tennessean* for a decade, and in the early years, like every other reporter in town, he concentrated only on Nashville's white schools. Then James Watkins, the Pearl athletic director, approached him with a proposition: if Watkins supplied Davy with information on Pearl and other black schools in the area, would he run some blurbs in the paper? While Davy liked Watkins and agreed to the deal, his editors were reluctant to give him much space for the notes. *Spend more time on your real job*, they'd tell him.

Davy pressed on, covering Nashville's black circuit and the black national high school tournament at Tennessee A&I—witnessing a slam dunk for the first time in his life—in addition to his duties assisting the paper's

Vanderbilt beat writers. It was not too much of a surprise, then, when Watkins approached Davy in the spring of 1966 with another proposition. Perry Wallace was considering Vanderbilt. Watkins knew that Davy was familiar with the school and the Southeastern Conference. Would he be willing to talk to Watkins, Ridley, and Wallace about what Perry might expect if he chose to become a Commodore? They knew he couldn't speak for Vanderbilt or for the rest of the league, but any information was valuable in Wallace's decision-making process.

Davy was happy to oblige, and he soon found himself walking through the hallowed halls at Pearl High and into a classroom with the athletic director, coach, and prospect. His immediate impression was that Watkins and Ridley wanted Wallace to choose Vanderbilt, even though they wouldn't come out and say it. He knew how hard Ridley had been fighting for integration, how much he wanted to be a part of the changes taking place in society. He also knew that Wallace was aware of the enormous responsibility he'd be taking on if he chose to become a pioneer. Despite some overtures to the contrary, Davy was convinced that many longtime Vanderbilt fans were not receptive to the idea of Wallace enrolling at the school. He decided to paint as bleak a picture as he could about the difficulties Wallace might run into, not only on the road but also in Nashville. Still, Davy was personally excited about the opportunity that lay before Wallace, so he also told him what a historic thing it would be if he signed. He'd be another Jackie Robinson.

Wallace was warm, gracious, talkative, and inquisitive, Davy felt, the kind of guy who made you feel as if you'd known him forever. But he gave no hint as to the conclusions he was drawing about Vanderbilt. Davy walked back to his car uncertain whether he'd made any kind of impression on Wallace. He was absolutely sure, however, that Wallace had made an impression on *him*.

"I left that meeting convinced of one thing, and that wasn't that he was going to Vanderbilt or any other place," Davy recalled. "I left convinced that this is the kid who can do it if he wants to. He had everything. He was beyond bright. He was athletic. He never met a stranger. He had a presence. I felt like if he wanted to go to Vanderbilt, he was going to be a guy who would stick it out. No matter what happened to him, he could handle it."

Though many in Nashville felt it was only a matter of time until Wallace chose Vanderbilt—Vanderbilt wanted *him*, after all—that belief reflected a sense of inevitability that simply didn't exist within Wallace's own mind. When he told Davy that he still had no leaning, he was telling the truth. At that point, he still had not visited many of the Big Ten schools that ultimately would turn him off, and he still had fond memories of one Big Ten trip he had already made: an experience he enjoyed so much that if not for the hint of a scandal, he likely would have ended up wearing the black and gold of the Purdue Boilermakers rather than that of the Commodores.

Wallace had made the trip to Indiana to visit Purdue's West Lafayette campus earlier that spring. Because the school had a history of recruiting black athletes, Purdue was a name that carried some cachet for Wallace. He was impressed with Coach George King and with a budding black Boilermaker star named Herm Gilliam, who unlike some of the players Wallace encountered at other big-time programs, relished the academic side of campus life. Purdue's engineering school had an outstanding reputation, the basketball team was successful and about to move into a brand-new arena, and because the Big Ten had been desegregated way back in 1947–48 by Bill Garrett at Indiana University, Wallace wouldn't be cast in the role of trailblazer.

During his visit to Purdue, Wallace at one point found himself being driven past the farms and rusting barns along US Route 52, headed southeast to Lebanon, Indiana, home of prize recruit Rick Mount, whom *Sports Illustrated*'s Frank Deford labeled "as good a high school basketball player as there ever was." In the gym at Lebanon High, Wallace participated in pickup games alongside Mount, other ballplayers from Indiana and Chicago, and seven-foot Purdue freshman Chuck Bavis. Initially, Wallace didn't think anything of the sojourn to Lebanon; it was a chance to play ball and strike up a friendship with Mount. There didn't seem to be anything clandestine about the trip. Soon, however, people started asking questions: How is it that Perry Wallace from Nashville, Tennessee, ended up in Lebanon, Indiana, playing in pickup games at Rick Mount's high school gym? Wallace, who was turned off by the cash, cars, and promises made at some schools, hadn't considered the games unusual. He had played informally against collegiate players in Nashville for years. But the NCAA began investigating, looking into whether Purdue was violating recruiting rules. There was still a lot to like about Purdue, but the taint cast on his visit weighed heavily on Wallace's mind.

By mid-April, Wallace still had not made a decision. Skinner was working him hard, receiving indications from Ridley and others that Wallace had Vandy high on his list. A segment of Vanderbilt's student body, namely those who had walked across campus to catch some of the TSSAA tournament, were especially curious about Wallace's plans. Eager to win games and build on the successes of the Clyde Lee era, they wanted nothing more than to land the prize recruit.

One such student was senior Van Magers, a *Vanderbilt Hustler* sports editor from the Jackson, Mississippi, suburb of Raymond. Though he would be off to law school at Ole Miss by the time Wallace made it to Vanderbilt—*if* he chose Vanderbilt—Magers was passionately interested in the Commodores' future. His little school, he believed, was on the cusp of greatness, and a talent like Wallace could put it over the top. Whether Wallace selects Vanderbilt or not, he told his friends, the fact that he's even considering the school, and that Vanderbilt is considering him, is a big story. Magers set out to tell it.

First he called on Coach Skinner and told him he planned to write a column on Wallace's state of mind and what kind of chance Vanderbilt stood to get him.

"I wish you wouldn't," the coach said.

Magers protested, "Why not? It's a great story."

"Well," Skinner requested, "just don't talk about race."

Magers was dumbfounded. Vanderbilt was this close to breaking the color line, a local player was this close to making history, the SEC was about to break thirty years of segregationist tradition, and Skinner asked him to write about Perry Wallace but not to discuss race?

Magers changed the subject, asking Skinner for a quote on Wallace's playing ability.

"He's probably the best rebounding prospect we've ever tried to get at Vanderbilt," Skinner said. "We want him badly."

Next, Magers went back to the *Hustler* office and called Coach Ridley. He arranged a time to interview Perry and the coach, and soon he was driving over to Pearl's North Nashville campus. Walking into Ridley's office, he felt self-conscious as a white kid in an all-black school. Ridley put him at ease.

"Where do you think Perry will end up?" Magers asked.

"I think there is a really good chance that Perry will go to Vanderbilt," Ridley said. "It would be a sin and a shame if Perry went somewhere else. Besides," he smiled, "I want to see him play."

Next, Magers walked over to the school cafeteria, where he met Wallace for the first time. Magers plopped down his reporter's notebook on the cafeteria table and took notes as Wallace talked, listening to stories about the recruiting trips he'd made, the tours and routines that seemed so similar at each school. As he listened, Magers was impressed by the maturity and wisdom of the eighteen-year-old basketball phenom.

"I remember nice rooms and good meals," Wallace told him, "but I know they aren't what I would have as a student. I try to see an ordinary dorm room and talk to a random sample of students. I talk to the players, Negro players if there are any, and get their impressions of the school; then I try to judge the persons themselves, so I can know how to evaluate their opinions. What the players are studying is important to me. If they're all PE majors, I know that they're at school just to play basketball."

Magers asked him to list the pros and cons of choosing Vanderbilt.

First, the pros.

"I like Coach Skinner and his basketball program," Wallace said, "and I appreciate the scholastic reputation at Vanderbilt. I don't foresee a great future in pro basketball, so I'm thinking more of Vandy's academic advantages. Vanderbilt is a good school in a well-known conference, and it's in a city. There are certainly advantages."

Beaming with excitement after what he considered to be two great interviews at Pearl, Magers drove over to his apartment up on a hill just south of campus. He pulled out his portable Smith-Corona typewriter and began to type. It wasn't until the twenty-third paragraph of the column, in a section subtitled "To Be or Not to Be the First" that the dutiful columnist broke Coach Skinner's request. He finally broached the issue of race.

"Why not Vandy?" he wrote, setting up the "con" side of the Vanderbilt proposition.

"I'd be the first Negro in SEC basketball. That has to have some consideration on my decision—but it won't have a lot," he quoted Wallace as saying. "I don't think I'd really be concerned. I'd feel more obligation here than somewhere else, away from home. There would be some pressure from the Negro community here. They would be behind me, wanting me to do well. That would give me a lot to live up to."

Magers concluded his column by admitting that Wallace would not provide any hints as to which way he was leaning. The fact that Wallace thought so highly of Vanderbilt, Magers wrote, was "quite a compliment to a school that wouldn't have considered him five years ago."

And then he ended with a perspective that was both gracious and naïve, perhaps only fitting for an idealistic, starstruck young columnist.

"On talking with Perry, the valedictorian of his class of four hundred," he wrote, "you feel that he would be a better man because of the advantages Vanderbilt offers him. And you know that Vandy would be better for his coming."

There it was, he said it. A few years earlier, students in his position had voted against integrating the school, and now he was advocating that Vanderbilt integrate an entire conference. Coach Skinner, a man he admired, had asked him not to mention race, and Magers had made it the crux of his piece. Would it scare Wallace away? When the printed newspapers arrived on campus a few days later, Magers drove back over to Pearl and dropped off a few copies for Wallace and Ridley. And then he went back to his apartment and hid, not daring to show his face around the Vanderbilt Athletic Department, where he was a regular fixture. Afraid of what Skinner might say, he steered clear of the coach for weeks.

While Magers' article reached a limited audience of Vanderbilt students and staff, two weeks later in its Sunday magazine the *Tennessean* devoted a two-page spread to the hometown prospect who was attracting so much national attention. It was in this article, written by Max York, that the major themes in the commonly accepted narrative of Wallace's early life began to take form. A few thousand white Nashvillians had seen Wallace from a distance at the state tournament. Here, for tens of thousands, was a more detailed introduction, the necessary framework to begin constructing a mental picture of the young man. Bits of the emerging portrait turned out to be accurate and would still help define Wallace nearly fifty years later; readers misinterpreted other aspects to satisfy their own biases.

Here, in black and white, was evidence that Wallace was as wholesome as they came: one photo shows him eating breakfast in the Pearl cafeteria with three cartons of milk spread out before him; in another photo his girlfriend, Jackie Akins, gently strokes his chin with a dandelion; in still another, dressed in coat and tie, he sits in the front row of class, eyes fixed on his teacher.

Here was confirmation that he was smart: *He'll be the valedictorian of his class, he's made nothing but A's, he takes hard classes like trigonometry, physics, and chemistry.*

His work ethic was second to none: *He developed his own off-season weight-training program, he once did 450 sit-ups between classes, and when the chips are down, you can count on him to come through.*

He was humble: *"I'm lazy. I don't do half what I could."*

He could leap: *"I can jump high enough to get my elbow up to the rim of the basket."*

He was mature: *He has good perspective. He has a strong will. He could have been president of his class, but he decided to let someone else have the post.*

And for white readers, as if all of the above weren't enough, there were more than a few code words to convince them that for a black teenager, Wallace was nonthreatening: *He's old-fashioned. He thinks college recruiters are kind men. He believes in prayer when things get rough.*

In every possible way, Wallace was portrayed as the All-American boy. Within a day or two, Coach Skinner was deluged with letters from Vanderbilt fans and alums.

They had seen Wallace play.

They had read about him in the paper.

And if Skinner signed him to a scholarship, they'd never attend another Vanderbilt basketball game again.

"I got an awful lot of petitions with an awful lot of signatures," Skinner recalled. "I got some, the school got some. It was a little uproar. They would say they didn't want me to recruit black players."

Skinner threw out the petitions as quickly as they arrived. The letters represented only a minority of the Vanderbilt community, he believed. Plus, he knew Heard and the university were with him on this one, "and they were the ones who paid my check. I wanted to recruit Perry Wallace and there wasn't anything those alums could do about it."

As the calendar turned from April to May, Wallace began to feel mounting pressure to make a decision. Akins knew where she was going to college. Though she had been admitted to Vanderbilt, she was headed to Bryn Mawr. It was not a popular decision with family or friends. Her mother desperately wanted her to stay in town. Everybody knew Vanderbilt; everybody knew what an accomplishment it would be to attend Vandy. Bryn Mawr? *What a strange name. Where is it?* But Akins felt strongly that she had to get out of the South. Her entire family had lived within fifty miles of Nashville since emancipation. She was ready to see the world. She had studied hard and earned the opportunity to get away. She didn't relish disappointing her mother, but otherwise it wasn't a hard choice.

Walter Murray also had made a decision. Like Wallace and Akins, he had dreamed of breaking free of the confines of the South. His sights were set on Brown University, an Ivy League school with a liberal reputation, where he figured he would be free to study and explore new ideas without the social restrictions he'd endured his entire life.

His application to Brown was rejected.

Devastated by the news, Murray accepted a scholarship to Vanderbilt. Though he'd hardly be breaking free at all, he could take solace in having earned a grant-in-aid to a fine university. He would make the most of it. His father, the Baptist preacher who had passed away when Walter was just a young boy, would have been proud.

Now it was Perry's turn to decide. His parents thought it was time he quit taking so many recruiting trips; he'd get to do more traveling once he started playing. "It's beginning to be clear what you want to do," Perry Sr. told him. "You should go ahead and make your choice."

High school coaches, teammates, friends, college recruiters, sportswriters—everyone had an opinion, but this was a decision Perry wanted to make on his own. Those other people weren't going to have to live with the consequences. Before he decided where to spend the next four years of his life, he knew exactly where he needed to spend the next hour: down in a clearing among the cliffs and trees over by White City Park.

For years Perry had worked to strengthen his legs and his stamina by jogging around the neighborhood, winding his way up and down the same steep hills he had sped down on makeshift wagons as a kid. On one of these jogs he discovered a hidden thicket of trees and rocks about fifty yards off to the side of 9th Avenue as the road meandered toward the Cumberland River. When he was stressed out by school, by racial tensions, by the everyday troubles of a teenager, this is where he came to sit and think in peace. Surrounded by nature in the heart of the city, he felt far from the troubling and hurried aspects of the world, closer to the rhythms of the country, closer to his grandfather's farm out in Rutherford County. But, even beyond that, when he sat atop a rock in the clearing, he felt transported to a "mystical place," no longer confined to North Nashville, but ascended to one of the magical places he was reading about in poetry class, "somewhere like Xanadu."

"And this," he said on a tour of his old neighborhood more than forty years later, looking at the very spot, "is where I went to do my last thinking about whether I would go to Vanderbilt."

It was an especially hard question for the eighteen-year-old Wallace to answer because he could hardly believe it was one that had presented itself. He had grown accustomed to segregation; for most of his life, it was all he knew. Yesterday, white Nashville slammed its doors shut; today it was swinging them wide open?

He felt pressure from people whose opinions he respected. Coach Ridley had told him to remember that he'd have a harder time finding a Church of Christ up north, and that he'd love to be able to watch him play ball in college. Ridley had even told that kid from the *Hustler* that it would be a *sin* if he didn't go to Vanderbilt.

Though his parents had never come out and expressed a preference, as he sat on that rock, Wallace knew that deep down they wanted him to stay. He understood how much pride it would give them to see their son "go across town to the big white folks' school."

As he sat and meditated among the trees, Wallace allowed the opinions of others to float away, determined to make this critical decision on his own. There was a lot to like about Vanderbilt. He had been impressed by the small campus and the engineering curriculum and was pleased to see that the basketball players took their schoolwork seriously. The Commodore team had a winning tradition and played in a major conference. Coach Skinner had treated him and his parents with respect. But more than anything, he was attracted by the promise. The promise that the world was changing, that the playing field was being leveled, that if you worked hard and played fair and made the right decisions, you could participate in the full measure of society whether you were white or black. With segregation dying, the America in which he'd live the rest of his life would require that he learn to interact with all different kinds of people. His teachers had prepared him for this moment, and he was ready to seize it.

Still, it was one thing to steel himself for the journey across town, another to ponder road trips to Alabama, Georgia, and Mississippi, going it alone deep in the heart of Dixie. He'd heard over and over again what a special opportunity it would be to become a pioneer in the Southeastern Conference, but what he was beginning to understand better than anyone was how easy it was to talk about such a thing and how difficult it would be to actually live through it. As he climbed down from the rock and began to run back home, he knew that he had just made the decision to attend Vanderbilt University not because of the fact that he would be a trailblazer, but in spite of it.

Over in the *Nashville Banner* newsroom in the building the paper shared with the rival *Tennessean* at 1100 Broadway downtown, Sports Editor Fred Russell was getting anxious. If there was anything he hated, it was to get scooped by the *Tennessean*, especially on any story related to Vanderbilt. A 1927 Vanderbilt alum, Russell was a beloved figure in town and a virtual adjunct of the Commodore Athletic Department. More than a few coaches over the years owed their jobs to the man. He was the kind of walking Commodore encyclopedia who could tell you every detail of the Vanderbilt football team's train ride up to New York to play Fordham in 1935, whose institutional memory and network of friends was so great that he often lunched with the men whose names were already affixed to buildings on campus. Russell had read the Sunday feature in the *Tennessean* and figured Wallace was close to making a decision. Speculation around town had reached a fever pitch, and Russell's gut told him an announcement was coming soon. This was a story he would not get beaten on.

Russell walked into the *Banner* on the morning of Monday, May 2, the day after York's article had run, knowing that he had to get the lowdown on Wallace fast. But Wallace was somewhere out of town, and nobody knew how to reach him. More troubling, the reporter he needed to turn to on this story was just a kid himself, Roy Neel, a former Vanderbilt basketball student manager who had covered Pearl's run through the state tournament.

The legendary sports editor asked his twenty-one-year-old cub reporter whether he thought Perry would announce his decision soon. Yes, Neel said, he did think so; some people at Vanderbilt thought it could be as soon as tonight. *Tonight?!* If that was the case, the *Banner* was in trouble. As an afternoon paper, it went to press around 10:00 a.m. The story would hit the streets first in the next morning's *Tennessean*. There was only one solution—they still had an hour to get the story in that day's paper.

Where, Russell asked, do you think Wallace is headed to school?

Neel quickly ran through everything he knew about Perry and his family. He figured his parents would want to watch him play. His church was here; his friends were here. Neel also knew how badly Coach Skinner wanted Wallace. And that was about it. With nothing more to go on, no inside information, nothing substantial from Coach Skinner or Coach Ridley to tip him off, Neel blurted out his answer.

"I think he's going to go to Vanderbilt."

"OK," Russell said, playing a hunch, "we're going to write that story."

A few hours later, the *Banner* came rolling off the presses, copies loaded into trucks and delivered to front porches and mailboxes all over town. On page 27, above an ad for Kermit C. Stengel–Realtor and another promoting a $13.95 special on straw fedoras, there it was in big, bold type: WALLACE TO SIGN VANDERBILT GRANT TONIGHT.

Across town, Van Magers was still holed up in his apartment, hoping to avoid Roy Skinner at all costs. And now all Neel could do was sweat it out and hope his prediction came true. Truth be told, if he was wrong, he was wrong. He had bigger things on his mind. Within a matter of days, he'd ship out for the navy and Vietnam, having lost his student deferment after flunking out at Vandy.

Wallace, meanwhile, was two hundred miles away in Memphis, running through the pros and cons one last time and eventually breaking the news to his sister Jessie and her husband, Charles.

"I've made a decision," Wallace said, "and I'm going to Vanderbilt."

For Jessie, it was the worst news possible. She was so distraught she wanted to get up and run, but instead she found herself pressed up against the couch, unable to breathe. Her brother went on and on about Vanderbilt's fine engineering department, about how their parents had enjoyed watching him play at Pearl, how they were growing old, how he could give them more enjoyment if he stayed in Nashville. Jessie was struck by her younger brother's compassion, but more than anything, her protective instincts kicked in. Storm clouds were gathering over civil rights, she believed, and her brother was placing himself right in the eye of the hurricane. "I didn't want my brother to be mistreated by white people, plain and simple," she recalled decades later. "I would have been comfortable if he had gone to Fisk or TSU, but not Vanderbilt. But I didn't say anything—he made the point that the decision was made and I was not going to tamper with his decision."

Jessie's husband, Charles, broke the silence. He could see dark days ahead, too, but he also understood that the family needed to gather its strength and support the decision. "There are some advantages to Vanderbilt," he said, proceeding to build up the school and express confidence in Perry's choice.

At 4:00 p.m., Wallace picked up his sister's phone and delivered the good news to Skinner. He wanted to be a Commodore. Within hours, he was back home on 10th Avenue, sharing the news with his parents, comforted by the hug of his mother, who told him that she had secretly hoped all along that he would choose Vanderbilt. He returned the phone calls from reporters who had been after the story.

"In the final analysis, I thought a long time about being the first Negro boy in the SEC," he told Davy of the *Tennessean*. "But Coach Roy Skinner is a very sincere person and the fellows on the Vanderbilt team are the nicest I met during all my trips. I'm willing to work hard and give it a try with these kind of people."

Skinner had never been so relieved as when he got the call from Wallace, and he quickly arranged for a signing ceremony to take place in the lobby of Memorial Gym the next day. The coach woke up on Tuesday, May 3, with plenty to do to get ready to meet the Wallaces, but first, he had a phone call to make.

"Van Magers? This is Roy Skinner, I've got something to tell you."

Magers' heart sank. This was the call he had been dreading for weeks.

"Van, Perry Wallace is going to make his decision today, and he said your article played a part in it."

Magers felt his stomach drop. Had he actually cost his school its top prospect?

Wallace is joined by his parents, Perry Sr. and Hattie, as he appears with Vanderbilt coach Roy Skinner to officially announce his commitment to Vanderbilt. A photo of former Commodore star Clyde Lee hangs in the background. Photo by Eldred Reaney, *The Tennessean.*

"He's coming to Vanderbilt."

Having gone from "fear and trembling" to instant elation, Magers felt as if he were walking on a cloud the rest of the day.

The air was hot and stale in the unair-conditioned gym that afternoon. As a slew of photographers scurried around to get the best angles for their shots, Wallace officially signed his scholarship papers, flanked on one side by his parents and on the other by Skinner. Hovering above the crowd was a not-so-subtle reminder of the world Wallace was entering: nailed to the wall behind him was a large photo of Commodore hero Clyde Lee, left foot planted firmly on the ground in mid–hook shot, white shoes, white socks, white shorts, white jersey, square jaw, and crew cut.

Here, in one frame, the photographers captured a turning point in history.

One era fading fast, relegated to two dimensions, to black and white.

The new face of southern basketball just coming into view, in full color, in flesh and blood.

8

Reverse Migration

Historic Stay-at-Home

Perry Wallace is a Nashville high school senior (6 feet 5 inches tall, 217 pounds), with an intriguing tendency to bruise his elbows on the rim of a basketball hoop. Wallace is also a Negro. Heretofore, Nashville's outstanding Negro athletes have headed north for college varsity sport. Vic Rouse and Leslie Hunter, for instance, hopped a bus for Chicago and eventually won a national basketball championship for Loyola in 1963. Now Wallace has become the first Negro to sign a basketball grant-in-aid in the Southeastern Conference—at hometown Vanderbilt University. The exodus, it appears, is beginning to end.

—"Scorecard," *Sports Illustrated*

Vanderbilt Signs Second Negro Star

—*Nashville Banner*

One week after signing his scholarship papers, Perry Wallace, like most Nashvillians, was shocked by the *Banner* headline. In his talks with Coach Skinner, Wallace had never heard the coach mention that he was close to landing another black player. In Wallace's discussions with friends, in his quiet meditative sessions, he always envisioned himself as a solitary pioneer. Now, just seven days after taking the first step to end the great migration of southern black athletes to northern campuses, Wallace was surprised but heartened to discover that he had already paved the way for a high-scoring black guard named Godfrey Dillard. The irony was that Wallace had cleared Dillard's path to Vanderbilt not from another segregated public high school in the South but from an integrated Catholic school up North, in Detroit.

And while Wallace had selected Vanderbilt only after reluctantly accepting the idea of becoming the SEC's first black ballplayer, that notion was the only reason Dillard wanted to head south. Dillard wasn't particularly impressed by Coach Skinner, didn't put much stock in Vanderbilt's academic reputation, and sensed that the university was recruiting him as much for political reasons as for basketball ones. Still, for Dillard, the opportunity to break a color line was irresistible: aligning with Vanderbilt and Skinner offered him the chance to contribute to the civil rights movement in a way that he felt wasn't possible in Michigan.

Dillard's "reverse migration" from the North was unusual enough but was especially ironic given his departure point. Detroit had attracted southern blacks for more than a century, its proximity to Canada making it one of the key last stops along the underground railroad, its thriving munitions and automobile factories making it a magnet for black laborers throughout the first half of the twentieth century. His parents had been a part of the migration, and for a brief time, their experience had been a classic example of the opportunities the city afforded black families. Earl Dillard, from rural Stamps, Arkansas, and Vera Norman, from Taylortown, Louisiana, had first met in Marshall, Texas, when Earl was a student at Bishop College. Not long after they married, he became one of the original Tuskegee Airmen during World War II, serving as a mechanic for the 99th Fighter Squadron in Morocco, Italy, Sicily, Greece, and France. The Airmen's stateside home during the war was Selfridge Field in Detroit, and following the war and Staff Sergeant Dillard's discharge at Selfridge, Earl and Vera chose to settle in Detroit. The Republican, entrepreneurial veteran used funds from the GI Bill to open his own small business in the lower west side of the thriving city.

With five young children, their own home, and a ringing cash register at Dillard's Market on Buchanan Street, Earl and Vera were living the American Dream.

Then Earl, at age thirty-six, died in his sleep of a heart attack.

Elvera, Kenneth, Eric, Chad, and Godfrey, just five years old, were left fatherless but, thanks to several shrewd decisions by their mother, not without hope. First, Vera sold the grocery store and called on her mother to move up from Texas to help raise the children. Then, pooling the proceeds from the sale and from her husband's life insurance policy, she bought a modest new home for the family in the integrated Boston-Edison neighborhood of downtown Detroit. Finally, she purchased several rental properties as a way to generate ongoing income. In the most difficult of circumstances, Vera had acted wisely to give her kids a chance to live the kind of lives she and Earl had always imagined for them. "My mother," Dillard recalled, "was totally committed to her children and totally committed to making sure we made it."

Dillard's grandmother, Carrie Norman, had worked as a cleaning lady at a hotel in Marshall, and she helped Vera run the home at 2305 West Boston

Boulevard like a cross between a five-star establishment and an army bar-racks. Every inch of the home was spotless, everything had its place, the rules were clear, each child had their chores. "They would tell us what to do, and we would do it," Dillard recalled. "We were in awe of them."

From the time he was seven years old, Godfrey was up at five o'clock each morning to begin his paper route, hurling newsprint into the front yards of the stately homes in Boston-Edison. The thirty-six-block neighborhood had come alive in the early 1900s, counting among its first residents the very model of Detroit ingenuity, Henry Ford. As he traversed the wide, elm-shaded boulevards with his sack of papers, Godfrey saw accomplished blacks and whites living side by side in what was increasingly becoming "a very inte-grated, progressive neighborhood." Along with wealthy white businessmen, Boston-Edison was the home of many of Detroit's most successful blacks; the Dillards' neighbors included the likes of the heavyweight champion of the world, Joe Louis, Motown Records founder Berry Gordy Jr., and attorney Ho-bart Taylor Jr., who, as an associate counsel for Lyndon Baines Johnson and later head of the Equal Employment Opportunity Commission, became one of the first blacks to hold a prominent White House position and is credited with coining the term "affirmative action."

"In my neighborhood, I saw examples of black men who could succeed," Dillard recalled. "I saw a black lawyer who was successful. My next-door neighbor was a dentist; he was successful. There were a couple of black doc-tors who lived down the street. They had clean homes. They had nice cars. So as a young person, the idea that the Afro American could not succeed was not an issue to me."

Young Godfrey learned similar lessons about equality and opportunity each day at school. A lifelong Catholic, Vera enrolled her children in Detroit's church-aligned Visitation School, a small, diverse K–12 school at 12th and Webb that welcomed not only blacks and whites but also a significant number of Chaldeans, Christians who had been exiled from Iraq. A smart, gregarious kid with a quick smile and an easy way with people, Godfrey became one of the most popular students in the school. After finishing his paper route each morning, the altar boy would walk to eight o'clock mass at Visitation, in a hurry to get to school, say hello to the Dominican nuns, and enter what he considered a "very loving, very nurturing environment."

Following in his older brothers' footsteps, who had each achieved some level of fame on the basketball court, Godfrey built a reputation as the school's best athlete, earning All-State honors in football and basketball and playing some baseball, too. While Godfrey's mother wanted him to become a doctor or lawyer like the men along his paper route, he dreamed of becoming a professional athlete, which wasn't much of a surprise considering the sheer quantity of bats, balls, sticks, hoops, and pucks he'd been surrounded by his entire life. In an attempt to give her sons what their father might have pro-

Godfrey Dillard grew up in the Boston-Edison neighborhood of Detroit, delivering newspapers each morning before Mass at Catholic school. Courtesy of Godfrey Dillard.

vided and to tire them out so they wouldn't be too rambunctious in the house at night, Vera bought her boys every piece of sports equipment they ever wanted. Need a football? Here you go. A new baseball? Sure thing. Basketball hoop in the back yard? Of course. Equipped like a sporting goods store, the Dillard home became one of the hubs of the neighborhood; all the kids, black and white, loved to come over and play. "You think black kids don't play hockey, but yes we did," Dillard recalled. "We used to freeze the backyard or the alley, my mother would go buy us hockey sticks, and we'd play against the Canadian kids." Basketball and hockey in the backyard, football in the grassy island that ran down the middle of West Boston Boulevard—the Dillards' corner of Boston-Edison was becoming a sort of mini–Olympic village. Exhausted from a full day of paper deliveries, early mass, school, and sports, the boys were sound asleep soon after dinner and homework.

By the time he reached his senior year of high school in 1966, Godfrey's popularity at Visitation was rising: His teammates named him captain of the football team, he could swim the butterfly like nobody in Detroit, his classmates voted him the school's first black student council president, and his exploits on the basketball court were becoming legendary. Taking the court in the city tournament against many of his black public school friends with whom he'd played rec center ball his whole life, Dillard was dominant, leading the fast break from his guard spot and averaging twenty-eight points per game.

With ever-blossoming basketball skills and a transcript that included strong grades earned at a well-respected, integrated school, Dillard began to attract interest from college recruiters; Cornell and Vanderbilt rose to the top of his list.

Invited to take a look at Vanderbilt on a weekend recruiting visit, Dillard was eager to check out the campus and to see Nashville, a city he had heard about from a friend in the neighborhood who was then attending Fisk University. His host on the trip was Commodore center Hal Bartch, a "big, muscular guy" from St. Louis who reminded Dillard more of one of his football teammates in Detroit than of a basketball player. Bartch took his guest on a tour of the campus, and Dillard was impressed by the athletic facilities, especially Memorial Gymnasium and its wide, raised court, which appeared more forgiving than the tiny gym at Visitation with its hard walls so close to the sidelines. The campus itself seemed small to Dillard, who had spent time walking around the sprawling grounds at Michigan and Michigan State. He was unfamiliar with Vanderbilt's academic reputation—"I was not all caught up in the 'Harvard of the South' or anything like that," he'd recall—and he felt neither impressed nor oppressed by the university's steeped southern tradition. His mother and grandmother, both born and raised in the South, were strongly opposed to Godfrey's interest in Vanderbilt, wanting to protect him from the degradation they were certain he would encounter, a racism unlike anything he had ever experienced in Detroit. But if his visit to Nashville was any indication of what it would be like to live there, Dillard believed, the women were being overprotective. Bartch took Godfrey out for steaks in Nashville's famed downtown Printers Alley entertainment district, and nobody gave the guys a second look. On campus, Dillard found himself surrounded by white students, but he was used to that. While Visitation had a diverse student body, it was still mostly white. Besides, with his buddy Wilson Copeland enrolled at Fisk, Dillard figured there would be opportunities for socializing across town. On his flight back to Detroit, Dillard had a good feeling about Vanderbilt.

"At first blush, it didn't appear to be that challenging of an environment," he recalled. "I didn't sense any discrimination on that visit. I liked the facilities and I knew that with the historically black colleges in town, they would be available to me socially. I figured I could move back and forth between the two cultures relatively easily."

Back home in Detroit as the NCAA Tournament unfolded, Dillard watched with much the same mindset as Perry Wallace; he was thrilled by Texas Western's accomplishments and suspected that a Kentucky loss in the finals would be the catalyst for change in the Southeastern Conference.

"We all watched it and everybody knew the significance of it," he recalled. "We understood that the times were changing and that teams like Kentucky were in trouble. At that point, being recruited by Vanderbilt, you understood that part of the reason why was that the SEC was going to have to change in order to keep up. When Texas Western defeated Kentucky, it was like the doors were opening up. If I had the chance to come in and integrate the SEC, it was going to be a whole new day."

Skinner had never seen Dillard play in person, but he'd watched enough film to see that he was the kind of guard who might thrive in his fast-paced offense. He also knew that Dillard was a good student and figured that Wallace might like to have a black roommate on road trips.

On May 10, accompanied by a newspaper photographer, Skinner paid a visit to West Boston Boulevard. Dillard's mother and grandmother were cordial to the coach but still squarely against the idea of Godfrey moving down South. Black people were still getting lynched down there, they told him. Grandma Norman's pleadings carried an extra poignancy; her daughter, Godfrey's mother, Vera, was half white. Godfrey didn't know the details; all he knew was that his grandmother's relationship with some unknown white man in Louisiana "wasn't all voluntary." Despite the protests of the women who had raised him, Dillard would not be swayed. He had succeeded in school. He had excelled in sports. He was his own man. Skinner took a seat at the dining room table. He and Godfrey were all smiles; Mrs. Dillard and Grandma Norman all fears. Skinner was certain he'd found a capable ball handler, a guard who could lead the Vanderbilt fast break. Dillard was overcome with excitement as he thought about signing the scholarship papers the coach had brought with him from Nashville, an act that would put him squarely in the vanguard of the movement. He had considered himself a political figure at Visitation High School, the first black student council president, the leader of a small black community at a small school. He had followed the news accounts of what was happening in places like Birmingham and Montgomery and Nashville, and he knew deep down that he really hadn't done anything yet. But those papers Skinner pushed across the table, those would allow him "to move the race forward."

This is what the 1960s were all about, he told himself, breaking barriers in all facets of American life.

He signed the papers and smiled for the camera.

When it came to Godfrey Dillard and Vanderbilt University, he believed, "the sky was the limit."

9

Growing Pains

W*e're* not prejudiced," the men told him, "but we think you'll understand why we have to do this."

It was all quite civil. A peaceful August Sunday morning, the men dressed conservatively in dark suits, speaking quietly but firmly, standing in a small room just inside the entrance to the University Church of Christ.

Perry Wallace had arrived on campus several weeks early, before most of his classmates, to get a few math and science courses out of the way in a special summer Engineering School program before his schedule became crowded with basketball practices. He wanted to get a feel for the campus, to slowly test the waters of integration. New faces, new sounds, new smells, new surroundings. And new twists on the familiar. Perry had been a devout churchgoer each Sunday ever since he had been baptized in the tiny pool at the 15th Avenue Church of Christ. He had taught Sunday School classes, endured the taunts of the tough kids who hung out on the porches of the shotgun houses in the Bottoms as he walked by with his Bible. Attending a weekly sermon was as important a routine in his life as any.

That summer, when Sundays came around, Perry had woken up early, put on a coat and tie, and walked over to the church that Clyde Lee had recommended on one of Wallace's first recruiting visits. The University Church of Christ was not affiliated with Vanderbilt but sat across the street from campus on the school's southeast side, a few blocks away from Wallace's dorm room in the Kissam Quadrangle.

Three or four Sundays, Wallace made the short walk to the chapel, quietly taking a seat in the back, the only black person in the place. A few folks would come by and say hello.

I know who you are.

I saw you play at Pearl.

Good luck at Vanderbilt.

Still, the room seemed cold to Wallace, as if the religion had been sucked out. Church of Christ was a conservative denomination whether the congregants were black or white, no instrumental music allowed, but over on the north side of town at least there had been a little more emotion, the teenage Wallace thought, even singing. Here, it seemed, people were just going through the motions. He sat in the back pews and asked himself the same questions over and over: What are these people *doing* in here? Where was the spirituality? They might as well be across the street at Burger King.

Uncomfortable as he may have been, Wallace knew this was the first of many tests he would be confronted with as a pioneer. He'd give it a go.

"Just a few years earlier, it would have been very clear to me not to go into that white church, because I was a child of segregation. I knew the rules. But in coming to Vanderbilt, part of the idea was that this was a new day," Wallace recalled. "This was a new set of relations. They let me move onto the campus. [Alabama governor] George Wallace wasn't standing at the door. So much seemed to be opening, so I went ahead and went to the church. And it was a lot easier to walk across the street to church than to find a way back to my old neighborhood without a car."

Wallace made the short walk for the fourth or fifth Sunday, prepared to sit quietly in the back, prepared, once again, to try and figure out how these congregants practiced their religion.

Then they stopped him at the door.

Perry, come with us.

He followed a group of church elders into a side room.

We're not prejudiced.

We think you'll understand.

Some people in the church don't like you being here.

They say they'll write the church out of their wills if you keep coming.

We can't have that.

You can't keep coming.

Do you understand?

You need to go.

Now.

"OK," Wallace said, "I understand."

He walked out the door, past the worshippers on their way in, and continued back to his dorm room, largely emotionless. The old survival mechanisms handed down through generations of segregation kicked in: at once, he later concluded, he was denying his feelings and accepting the cold reality of the situation.

"There was a dangerous automaticity about the responses to exclusion and segregation," he recalled. "You would try to suppress it or hide from it even as it was happening. Most of us at that point were not brave heroes, so we just said 'OK' in those situations. It was a lot easier to do that."

He entered his dorm room much earlier than planned, loosened his tie, and sat down on his bed, coming to the realization that maybe America wasn't changing as quickly as he had been led to believe. He was reminded of the first time he had learned about segregation, as a five-year-old boy stepping onto a city bus with his mom. While his mother paid, he took a seat next to a white man. Immediately, Hattie rushed over and lifted Perry up, ushering him to the back of the bus. "While I still didn't understand what was going on, and it all seemed quite strange," Wallace recalled, "I did what Mama said. I played by the rules and, in effect, sang the 'Song of the South.'"

Wallace's experience at the University Church of Christ was one small episode that reflected an increasingly uneasy national mood in the late summer of 1966. Old assumptions were being challenged, boundaries pushed, and the resistance was fierce. At the same time Wallace took his first steps as a trailblazer, a near-daily barrage of national news reports placed his own delicate struggle in context. Confrontation, violence, protest, change, and suspicion were everywhere.

July 31   In Chicago, nearly three thousand whites confront a much smaller integrated group of citizens marching for fair housing by shouting epithets, turning over and burning thirty of the demonstrators' cars, and hurling rocks, bottles, and firecrackers. "I wish I were an Alabama trooper," chant the white youths, "that is really what I want to be; for if I was an Alabama trooper, then I could kill a nigger legally!"

August 1   In Austin, Charles Whitman ascends to the top of the University of Texas' landmark Texas Tower with a small arsenal of guns, where he opens fire on the campus below, killing thirteen and wounding dozens more.

August 5   Brenda Beaty, an eighteen-year-old from the Nashville suburb of Hermitage, writes a letter to the *Tennessean* questioning the impact of domestic strife on the morale of troops in Vietnam: "I bet it must be a horrible feeling," she writes, "to be so far away from home and see nothing but hatred and killing and hear that the same thing is happening at home, and for no reason. We're taking away their reason for being there. We can't even get along among ourselves."

August 10   Congressman Roman Pucinski of Illinois calls on President Johnson to beseech civil rights leaders to "restore law and order in America," while a KKK spokesman, having been denied a permit for a rally at Chicago's Soldier Field, asserts he'll nevertheless "demand the arrest of Martin Luther King."

August 18   Alabama governor George Wallace urges the state legislature to resist federal school integration guidelines, calling the standards "a blueprint devised by Socialists" with the "100 per cent, unqualified support of the Communist Party USA."

August 22   Pittsburgh Pirates outfielder Roberto Clemente tells sportswriters in New York that black and Hispanic stars are not treated with the same respect as their white counterparts. "I am an American citizen . . . but some people act like they think I live in a jungle someplace. To the people here we are outsiders, foreigners. This is a matter of sports . . . of a man's ability and his accomplishments. What [does it] matter what language he speaks best?"

August 23   In Louisville, heavyweight boxing champion Cassius Clay, clutching a Koran, appears at a federal courthouse to appeal his 1-A draft status. His attorney claims that Clay spends 90 percent of his time on religious work and thus, as a Muslim minister, should be exempt from the draft.

August 31   Just outside New Orleans, not a single white student shows up for the first day of school at Woodlawn High School, where five boys become the first blacks to attend the formerly all-white school. White parents say they'll establish "private schools as an answer to desegregation."

September 4   "VU Avoids Guerillas." Vanderbilt basketball fans are startled by a headline in their morning *Tennessean*. The team's summer trip to Peru (which did not include incoming freshmen such as Wallace) was cut short due to fears of "possible anti-American demonstrations by Communist sympathizers."

September 7   In New York, black congressman Adam Clayton Powell endorses the concept of Black Power, questioning the relevance of Martin Luther King Jr. An organizer of an upcoming Black Power conference goes a step further. "Up to now the movement has been saddled with Uncle Toms and black lackeys of the whites," says Julius Hobson. "If we do nothing else we're going to get rid of them."

In Oxford, Mississippi, Ole Miss football coach John Vaught jokes with reporters that he is recruiting black players. "We're recruiting them, but we haven't got any yet," Vaught tells a group of sportswriters, before adding that he was only kidding. Vaught says that his staff has gone through the motions of recruiting blacks because "we have to comply with some sort of act to get federal funds. We fill out a form to show we have looked at one. We have not found one good enough yet. By the time we find one good enough, I'll be gone."

September 8   In Atlanta, black activist Stokely Carmichael is arrested on charges of inciting a riot in which "1,000 rock- and bottle-throwing Negroes attacked police and toppled Mayor Ivan Allen from atop a car when he tried to reason with them," the UPI reports. "Carmichael and his anarchist group belong behind bars and the quicker we get him there the better off this country will be," says US representative Wayne Hays of Ohio.

September 13   In Chalmette, Louisiana, whites throw rocks at—and attempt to overturn—a car carrying black students away from newly integrated St. Bernard High School. In Grenada, Mississippi, a group of 150 black marchers is attacked by whites when nearby state troopers are slow to react. "Either nobody has trained the troopers to protect demonstrators, or they just don't want to," says the Reverend Andrew Young.

September 14   In Nashville, 1,015 freshmen arrive on the Vanderbilt campus for a week-long orientation session prior to the start of classes.

Cars from the Peach State, the Lone Star State, Sportsman's Paradise, the Land of Lincoln—and cabs from the Greyhound bus station—arrive on campus throughout the day. As dads lug trunks and suitcases to dorm rooms and moms make beds and hang clothes, many of the 711 men and 304 women in the Class of '70 march over to the Athletic Department to pick up their tickets to the Commodores' football season opener against The Citadel.

These Vanderbilt freshmen are smart kids: Perry Wallace is one of 55 valedictorians, and about half of the new arrivals earned straight-A averages in high school. For many of the freshmen, arriving on the West End campus is a dream fulfilled. Of the 78 high school seniors who had been accepted by both Vanderbilt and the University of Tennessee, for example, 71 had chosen Vanderbilt. Vanderbilt had also won over 36 of the 48 students also accepted at Georgia Tech, and 71 of the 89 also admitted to Emory. Conversely, Vanderbilt was the "safety school" choice for some—enrolling only 46 of 116 frosh also accepted by Duke. And of the 27 high school seniors who were accepted by Vanderbilt and either Harvard, Princeton, or Yale, all but 3 went Ivy League. For Vanderbilt's admissions director, David E. Wood, the statistics are telling. "The theory that students are picking easier schools to compile better grades to beat the [military] draft just doesn't hold up," he tells a *Hustler* reporter.

The freshmen are greeted by student volunteers (known as VUceptors) who help carry boxes, dispense advice on classes, point out directions around campus, and view the newcomers with a mix of envy and skepticism. One freshman tells a *Tennessean* reporter that "once you get off the Nashville streets, you don't even know you're in Nashville." For better or worse, the student is right. The world outside the campus bubble is changing so fast; will these freshmen, some of the older students wonder aloud, change Vanderbilt?

"In the coming month, you will become familiar with the complexity and contradiction that is Vanderbilt University," reads a September 16 *Hustler* editorial. "We hope you will like Vanderbilt, but we also hope you will not be satisfied with it. Vanderbilt is a university in transition. A school that was once content to be an educational leader in a limited geographical area is now struggling to win a national reputation. But it will be a long, slow process and if you watch the University carefully you can see growing pains."

One such growing pain that wasn't hard to spot was the university's awkward attempt to welcome its black students. The first black undergraduates arrived in the fall of 1964, and administrators held a series of meetings throughout that spring and summer attempting to prepare for the various scenarios that might occur upon the students' arrival. How would VUceptors react if a white father objected to his son living on the same hall as a Negro? How could Negro parents be made to feel at ease on move-in day? Should Negro moms be handed a cup of coffee and invited to sit down? The administrators' questions may have been well intentioned, but these people had a long way to go. "We discussed, among other things, the manner in which a Negro should be addressed," Dean Sidney Boutwell later reported to the Arts and Science faculty. "It was pointed out that the term 'colored boy' should not be used." By the time Wallace arrived in the fall of 1966, the only administrator who had much experience dealing with black students was Assistant Dean of Men K. C. Potter, who, though only in his mid-twenties, became the go-to staffer for advice by virtue of his having attended the integrated Berea College as an undergraduate.

There were blacks on the Vanderbilt campus from the school's very beginning, but they had been there only to serve whites. John Fulton, known to students as "Uncle Remus," toiled as a butler for a few faculty members around the turn of the century, and in retirement he lived in a campus basement where he greeted returning alumni with sweets and lemonade. Bowling Fitzgerald lived for years in a campus dormitory and was a respected, if unofficial, athletic trainer during the football team's glory days in the early 1900s. In succeeding decades, blacks were hired to cook meals, clean rooms, and mow lawns. There they were, on campus every day, practically invisible.

But with the Board of Trust's decision to admit black undergraduates, coupled with incentives to integrate the school from influential national funders such as the Rockefeller Foundation, university officials found themselves in the unusual position of actively seeking out black students. "It used to be that to have it made with scholarship offers you needed brains and brawn," Vanderbilt's assistant director of admissions Dyer Moss told *New York Times* reporter Gene Roberts. "Now you have it made if you have brains and are brown—and personally I'm glad."

In Roberts' article, he noted that the brightest black high school students in the South were busy accepting scholarships to predominantly white southern colleges, the same schools that had actively barred these students just years earlier. While it was on the whole a positive development, there were those who were quick to notice the consequences for historically black colleges and the double standard inherent in the white schools' penchant for accepting only the most elite black students.

"If you're a Negro, you still have to be better than the best to be admitted to the white schools," Dr. James Cheek, president of predominantly black Shaw University, told Roberts. "And that leaves the Negro schools with all of the risk students—all of those who need some type of remedial work. . . . We're having to take students we wouldn't have been interested in five or 10 years ago."

So it was that in late September 1966, some of the best and the brightest young black scholars began arriving on the Vanderbilt campus.

From the tiny Appalachian town of Red Fox, Kentucky, came Bobbie Jean Perdue, the first black valedictorian at integrated Carr Creek High School. Her mother had died when Bobbie Jean was a junior in high school, and her father, a coal miner, was battling a brain tumor. Before their illnesses, both parents told all eight of their children that they were smart and they could do anything they wanted to do. Bobbie Jean wanted to go to Vanderbilt. The town's superintendent had been a law student there, and the minister's son was a physics major there. Both men had told young Bobbie Jean that "the smart people go to Vandy." And then there was Clyde Lee. A self-described "sports maniac," Perdue kept the family radio tuned to broadcasts of SEC basketball, and she was drawn to the way Lee's Commodores didn't back down against the Kentucky Wildcats. When the Carr Creek principal told his valedictorian that he'd help her get into any college she wanted, she told him she wanted to enroll in nursing school at Vanderbilt. When she couldn't afford the one-hundred-dollar application fee, the principal paid it. When she was accepted, the white minister drove her to Nashville to start school. A country girl in the big city, she was startled by the wealth of her new classmates.

"Here I was seeing girls come in with trailers attached to the family car with their belongings," Perdue recalled. "I arrived with a suitcase, and it was an old suitcase. And then I went to the bus station and got the wood trunk I had sent ahead."

Bedford Waters arrived from Knoxville, Tennessee, where as a child he drank from the "colored" water fountains and sat behind a white line that marked the back of the bus. His mother, a college graduate, worked for an insurance company, and his father was a pastry chef with an eighth-grade education. From the time he was five years old, Bedford proclaimed that he wanted to grow up to be a doctor, and each Christmas he received a larger and fancier doctor's kit. "Go to college and better yourself," his parents stressed to their only child. As part of the first integrated class at Knoxville West High School, Waters joined the marching band and became the first black in the school's National Honor Society. When it was time to choose a college, Bedford considered out-of-state schools until his guidance counselor told him she'd talked to the folks at Vanderbilt and that he should consider heading to Nashville. He earned a National Merit Scholarship, and arrived at Vanderbilt with a can-do mindset: "I'm going to do my best, get involved, not isolate myself, and compete with the best students because I'm good enough."

Carolyn Bradshaw came to Nashville from Winston-Salem, North Carolina. Growing up with two little brothers and a single mom, Carolyn had always known that if she wanted to go to college, she'd have to earn a full scholarship. Attending segregated schools, she gained a comfort level with whites while participating in integrated advanced-placement classes and summer camps. She worked so hard in school that she was named valedictorian and earned a Rockefeller scholarship to Vanderbilt.

Morris Morgan, from Cedartown, Georgia, devised an ingenious plan to get to Vanderbilt. Because none of the historically black colleges in Georgia offered a chemical engineering major, and because Georgia Tech had yet to integrate, he declared his interest in chemical engineering and took advantage of Georgia's "out-of-state aid" program that essentially paid for blacks to study elsewhere. The son of an elementary school principal and seventh-grade teacher, Morgan's parents valued education so much that they arranged his summers around National Science Foundation programs in places like Worcester, Massachusetts, and Frankfort, Kentucky. Their child prodigy entered Vanderbilt at the age of fifteen.

For those who bothered to pay attention, it was obvious that these pioneering students were no ordinary people.

Frye Gaillard was raised in what he considered a typical, white Old South family, very much, he recalled, "a part of the racial status quo." How Old South? His ancestors arrived in Charleston, South Carolina, in 1680, and settled in Mobile, Alabama, in 1850. His father was a circuit judge in Alabama, a contemporary of another onetime Alabama judge, George Wallace. Like Wallace, his father was, by 1950s Alabama standards, considered a racial moderate, and his parents always told their son to treat everyone with respect, whether they were white or black, rich or poor. Still, Gaillard attended white-only schools and was surrounded by classmates, friends, and relatives who were "raised to believe that white people were better than black people," growing up in an environment where "segregation was the natural order of things."

When he arrived at Vanderbilt in the fall of 1964 along with the first black undergraduates, he was just beginning to question the assumptions of the Old South. Soon enough, his worldview was completely turned upside down.

"These brilliant young black people were so far ahead of me academically that the foolishness of that sort of southern white assumption of superiority became immediately obvious," he recalled. "My black classmates were the living refutation of it. A black guy down the hall began to tutor me in calculus, because I was making an F and he was making an A. That's when it all clicked for me, understanding the society I had come from. It was like, 'Oh, shit, we've really been a part of something bad.'"

Having returned home to 10th Avenue for a few days when the summer engineering program ended, Perry Wallace moved back to campus with the rest of the incoming freshmen on September 14. Perry Sr. drove him in his Chevy and helped his son unpack a few suitcases and arrange his single room at Vanderbilt Hall. There would be no roommate, affording a level of privacy that suited Wallace just fine. Perry set out his favorite graduation present, a record player his sisters had bought for him. He lined up his records, a collection that included lots of jazz, some big band, some classical, and some Motown.

Godfrey Dillard arrived on campus later that same day, flying from Detroit along with his neighbor, Wilson Copeland, who was attending Fisk University. A delegation from Fisk met Copeland at the airport and offered a cheap ride to campus, and Dillard paid a little extra for a detour over to Vanderbilt. He found his dorm room—also in Vanderbilt Hall—and began to unpack his clothes. Not five minutes later, there was a knock on the door.

It was Perry Wallace, there to welcome his new teammate and fellow trailblazer. It was the first time they ever met.

Conversation came easily to these two. They talked for an hour before there was another knock on the door. And another. And another. The few black students on campus were finding each other, and Dillard's room, one he hadn't even slept in yet, became the hub. The other students eventually drifted off to dinner or back to their own rooms, but Wallace remained. He and Dillard were getting along great, but they were also feeling one another out, discovering their similarities and differences.

They both immediately felt that the other represented a certain stereotype. Dillard had traits of the "typical" northern black of the day: he was louder, more assertive, more outwardly confident, carried himself with a swagger, acted as if he were in control of his own destiny. Wallace, the southerner, was more reserved, more diplomatic, seemingly less self-assured, more consciously aware of the hazards of the world they were entering.

Perry talked to Godfrey about growing up in Nashville, about his love for music, about the state championship he had won at Pearl, about what little he knew about the Vanderbilt campus. He told Godfrey about the state of race relations in Nashville, some of the obstacles they were sure to encounter.

Godfrey told Perry that he wasn't much on music, at least not playing it. His mother had tried to make him play the violin, and that was the end of that. He talked to Perry about Detroit's own racial tensions, death threats during the state tournament, harassment by "The Big Four," a group of Detroit plainclothes cops who drove around town in a menacing big, black Mercury. Godfrey asked Perry where the best places were to meet girls, and what he thought about Coach Skinner. They talked with excitement about being pioneers in the Southeastern Conference, the history they would make, the energy they felt on the precipice of change. As their conversation extended deep into the night, Godfrey got the sense that his new teammate appreciated his northern sensibilities.

"I knew we were going to be very good friends right off the bat, and I knew I was much more outgoing than he was," Dillard recalled. "I sensed that I could influence him, because I had been a student leader in high school and could tell when someone was attracted to me and could pull them into my environment and we could work as a team. Not to dominate, but we could move in directions that I wanted to. So I sensed that he was excited about me; it was almost like we were very good complements. Perry had a sense of knowing the landscape that I didn't have."

Which, in Wallace's mind, was everything. He may have been intrigued by Dillard's bravado and impressed by his intellect, but that didn't mean he was ready to follow. For Dillard, the sky was the limit; Wallace, for all his naïveté, knew it wasn't that easy, not for a young black male in the South in 1966. In the wee hours of this, the very first night they met, Wallace sensed that Dillard was headed into dangerous territory. He'd put his finger on the feeling years later, drawing a parallel to another northern black teenager— one who met tragedy in the South.

Godfrey Dillard, he came to believe, was "our Emmett Till."

10

Icicles in Raincoats

The problem with controversy on the Vanderbilt campus is that there isn't any. It is a dead issue."

So began an article that filled the entire front page of a special 1967 edition of the *Hustler*, an issue devoted to explaining "Why The Campus Sleeps." As Dillard and Wallace prepared to make history, the irony was that they were doing so at a place that was not just highly resistant to change but seemed to repel even the very thought of it.

Associate Editor Tom Lawrence detailed the frustration felt by leaders of both liberal and conservative student groups, campus organizations that found themselves with few members and even less energy. In a country experiencing polarizing social upheaval, how was it possible that vigorous debate was virtually nonexistent at Vanderbilt?

"Both groups," Lawrence wrote, "point their accusing finger at the student stereotype," a portrait that would-be campus activists on both the left and right could sketch in an instant: the stereotypical Vanderbilt undergraduate was southern, wealthy, status conscious, career oriented, and intellectually uncurious.

Apathy was so rampant that *Hustler* reporter Frye Gaillard felt compelled to educate his fellow student readers in the most basic of terms. His article, headlined "Issues of Controversy," began as if he were addressing a Rip Van Winkle type seeking a primer on current events after decades of slumber. "On campuses where there is controversy," he wrote, "debate centers generally on three topics: the civil rights movement, the Vietnam War, and intellectual freedom on campus."

Elsewhere in the special issue, Lew Coddington wrote that "Vanderbilt political organizations of the Right and Left are either dead or barely breathing," left to "choke and die on a campus that will not support them."

Activity on the left had its moments, Coddington wrote. In 1963 a group of students picketed a popular off-campus restaurant to protest its whites-only policies. In 1965 eight students and faculty participated in the Selma-to-Montgomery civil rights march. A small Students for a Democratic Society (SDS) chapter existed for less than a year, disbanding after attempts to engage the campus community on issues of race, free speech, and Vietnam failed to stir up any meaningful dialogue, managing only to attract a bit of harassment from the *Nashville Banner*. On the right there was just one active student group, the Conservative Club. Its leaders, having grown accustomed to empty seats, were reluctant to invite speakers to campus, an unfortunate circumstance considering that the group's charter mandated that the club do one and only one thing: bring in outside speakers. "It's a bit embarrassing," a club member told Coddington.

If the stereotypical characteristics of Vanderbilt students were to blame for the lack of intellectual vitality on campus, so was the very nature of the campus itself. There was no central meeting place, no student union or activity center where students could meet to relax or debate the issues of the day. Plans for the construction of such a building—with promises of a bowling alley, billiards room, and Laundromat—were met with a measure of excitement but also the realization that only future students would reap the benefits.

In the meantime, whether it was cause or effect, social life at Vanderbilt revolved around its Greek system, just as it had since the school's first fraternity was chartered in 1883. One week, there were classes, exams, and frat parties, and then the next week there were classes, exams, and frat parties. And that was it. "Pretty much the entire social scene revolved around the fraternities and sororities," recalled Sara Hume, a Tri-Delt from Nashville. "If you weren't in a frat or a sorority, you were *independent* in a bad way."

Conformity was so prized that even national magazines were aware of the term "Typical Vanderbilt Coed," describing the TVC as "an icicle wrapped inside a raincoat." Sexist as the label may have been, the TVC moniker became common parlance among several waves of Vanderbilt students in the 1960s. Four decades later, Vanderbilt alums, without fail and without deviation, could detail the standard TVC look from head to toe: Leather Pappagallo loafers or Bass Weejuns. Knee socks. Plaid Villager skirt. McMullen blouse with a round collar, complemented with a sweater in the fall. Circle pin. Topped off with the signature flip hairdo, which coed Marshall Chapman dubbed a "'banana roll,' because you could set a banana in there and it wouldn't go anywhere." Whether it was fair to compare Vanderbilt women to icicles, the magazines had at least been accurate about the raincoats: dorm mothers prohibited female students from wearing slacks or shorts on campus, so on their way to the tennis courts, girls wore trench coats to cover their legs. Facing increasing resistance on this particular issue from students in the winter of 1966, Dean of Women Margaret Cuninggim attempted to convey an open-minded attitude. "Of course we try to have flexibility," she assured a *Hustler* reporter. "We would not look harshly on a girl wearing pants during a blizzard."

The 948 TVCs on campus for the 1966–67 school year didn't just tend to dress alike; by and large, they had pretty much the same story. They came to Vanderbilt from Tennessee, Georgia, Kentucky, Texas, or Alabama. They majored in English, nursing, psychology, or history. They studied to become teachers and nurses. They came across as a bit snobby or prudish to the frat boys—hence the icicle comparison—a far cry from the more approachable and less bookish girls at the Peabody College for Teachers across the street. Even if you found a Vandy girl willing to let her guard down, the opportunities for much interaction were limited. Strict visiting hours in the campus dorms were enforced with such precision that the same scene played itself out in the lobbies of the girls' dormitories virtually every weekend, Chapman recalled.

"Dean Cuninggim or some dorm mother would come out and tell everybody they had to leave, and there would be this great protest," she said, recalling the make-out scene on the Branscomb lobby couches, where three out of a couple's four feet had to remain on the ground at all times. "It was kind of like last call for sex. Then the girls would head back up to their rooms, and the guys were all horny and everything and they were not ready to leave. So, on their way out, one of the guys would throw a brick through a window or break it with their fist. And every Monday, you'd see these big glass windows being carried into the lobby at Branscomb Quad, replacing the ones that had been broken over the weekend."

While protests over Vietnam gained steam on campuses from coast to coast, while racial violence erupted from Illinois to Mississippi, this was where Perry Wallace and Godfrey Dillard came to challenge a legacy of segregation: a campus so sedate that a girl could cause a stir by walking across campus in pants, where a guy couldn't make out with his date after 11:00 p.m., where frat parties were the only form of entertainment, and where campus political groups didn't invite speakers because they were afraid nobody would show up.

Wallace and Dillard asked themselves fundamental questions about their mission at Vanderbilt. Who, other than the handful of other black students, would have any sensitivity to the dangers they were about to confront? Who would even have the slightest appreciation for the audacity of their mission? While change agents on other campuses could gain inspiration and protection from kindred spirits, even those focusing on other issues, Wallace and Dillard operated in no such atmosphere. At Vanderbilt, which zigged as other campuses zagged, the catalyst for changing the campus culture was not some shaggy-haired undergrad but a middle-aged man in a suit with the best office in Kirkland Hall.

What Vanderbilt needed most, Chancellor Alexander Heard decided, was a little controversy.

The fact that Alexander Heard would be leading the charge for change might have taken some casual observers by surprise. The chancellor's own life was quite conventional. The Heard home at 211 Deer Park Drive in the heart of aristocratic Belle Meade was full of both the soothing sounds of classical music (his wife, Jean, was an accomplished violinist who played for a time with the Nashville Symphony and occasionally joined Music Row recording sessions) and the cacophony of four young kids: sons Stephen, Frank, and Kit, and the youngest, daughter Cornelia.

The children played Ping-Pong in the basement and loved wandering through a tall bamboo forest in front of the house. There were pets galore—cats, ducks, hamsters, guinea pigs, fish, and always a dog—George Washington Branscomb Heard, Jigger, Wetska. One summer, Kit found thirteen snapping turtles in the creek that ran through the enormous front yard. When the creek froze over in the winter, the young Heards skated all day long.

Mealtime was family time, the entire gang gathering at the dining room table for both breakfast and dinner every day. Before dinner came Happy Hour. The kids would come home from school and do their homework or practice their instruments, and around 5:30 or 6:00, the call would come from Papa: "Come on, it's Happy Hour!" Mom and Dad with their cocktails, Stephen, Frank, Kit, and Connie with their kiddie drinks, all gathered in the cozy walnut-paneled library to discuss the issues of the day for an hour before supper.

There was a TV in the basement, but nobody watched it much. The day Papa brought it home, Connie sat and stared at the "snow" on the screen, spellbound because there was *color* in the static. Heard watched the occasional baseball game or documentary but spent more time polishing his brass antiques and admiring his collections of Christmas tree ornaments, crèches, stamps, and coins. He was a voracious and eclectic reader, enjoying everything from the *Chronicle of Higher Education* to Agatha Christie novels to *The Autobiography of Malcolm X*. Unlike many families in traditional Belle Meade, it was Mom who enforced the rules, while Papa was the soft touch.

"We had friends who had real stern disciplinarian fathers, but that just wasn't true with him," Connie recalled. "He always seemed fair, thoughtful, and smart. He was the go-to guy if you were in trouble. When my mom would say, 'We're going to talk to your father about this!' we thought, 'Whew, we're safe.'"

When Connie was discovered cheating on an assignment in fourth grade, her mother was summoned to school to talk to the teacher. Young Connie considered it the worst day of her life until she came home to talk the incident over with her father. "He would talk to you in such a way that wasn't scary," she recalled. "He made you think, and made you want to do what he thought was honorable or good."

Heard kept a study on the home's third floor, and each morning he woke before sunrise and took a seat at his desk. No barking dogs, no snapping turtles, no whizzing Ping-Pong balls. In the hushed study, under lamplight, the chancellor enjoyed what he called his "precious time," an opportunity to write letters and memos so that by the time he arrived at Kirkland Hall, he was free to do what he liked best—meet with people.

Heard's workday was as regimented as his home life. He'd arrive on campus at 8:00 a.m. in his long black Cadillac, careening through the gravel toward his reserved parking space, and before the door had slammed shut, he was off and running up the stairs to his corner office. Quick hellos for the security guard and the secretary, a briefcase in one arm and a pile of manila folders in the other. Into his office, where his yellow pencils were arranged in a row. He'd sharpen one if its point didn't look quite right. Then, he'd look at the day's work laid out before him—folders marked in red grease pencil: "Instant Action," "Board of Trust," "Decisions," "To Be Noted—Priority," and "Routine." He disposed of these tasks quickly, jotting notes with the thick, China-red fountain pen his sister had given him for his thirteenth birthday, and returned a series of phone calls. He'd meet with students, or a disgruntled alum, or a PR man working to shape the university's image, and then it was time for lunch—peanut butter and jelly on white bread.

From the moment Heard arrived at Vanderbilt from Chapel Hill, he immersed himself in the history of the university, studying decisions made by preceding chancellors, familiarizing himself with the stories of legendary professors, seeking to understand the reasoning for precedents. "Each university, on the Charles or on the Cumberland," he later said, "has its unique bundle of qualities—its heritage, its resources, its special opportunities and obligations, its hopes—a unique bundle of qualities that defines its own role."

As he looked back at Vanderbilt's history, he also looked deep into its future, commissioning a Vanderbilt Planning Study that brought together three hundred staff and faculty members and outside consultants, divided into forty-six committees, to examine every aspect of the school. Vanderbilt, he told committee members, "should be taking a reasonable look 50 years into the future." It may have taken that long just to read the thing: when completed, the forty-four-hundred-page report weighed thirty-six pounds.

Planning Study or not, Heard understood intuitively that Vanderbilt had sold itself short when it took pride in being known as the Harvard of the South. A more worthy ambition, he said, was to be known as the "Vanderbilt of the Nation." National, not regional, prominence was the goal. To get there,

Heard believed, meant opening up the campus, both in terms of recruiting a more diverse student body and promoting academic freedom of expression.

"Alec knew that the more diverse [Vanderbilt] was," recalled *Tennessean* editor John Seigenthaler, "the more prestigious the school was going to be."

In his first speech on campus after being named chancellor, Heard told the faculty members assembled at Underwood Auditorium that his goal was to make Vanderbilt "an increasingly significant American university. . . . [Vanderbilt] will view the nation as its campus and the world as its proper concern." A few weeks later, in an address to the business-minded Rotary Club, he laid out the case for the "open forum," attempting to preempt any complaints from the old guard as his plan to encourage campus dialogue unfolded in the years to come.

"A university campus is a lively place hospitable to debate and controversy," he told the group. "It will hear many points of view (some of them strange), from many sources (some of them odd), on many topics (some of them major, many of them minor). Most of these points of view will never reach your ears or mine. Occasionally some do. The peculiar ones that we agree with we usually let go without notice. Occasionally some of the peculiar ones startle us. When they do, we need to remember that differing points of view are inevitable and desirable in a university at work."

If Heard was passionate about this aspect of university life, it was because it had been one of the most enjoyable parts of his own education. His parents had attended elite northern universities—his mother had studied at Vassar, his father, Lehigh—and by the time Heard arrived at UNC in the mid-1930s, it was enjoying what one writer called "a surge of intellectual activity."

As president of the school's Carolina Political Union, Heard was responsible for inviting speakers to campus. He loved the assignment, loved the clash of ideas, and he made it his mission to invite wildly divergent voices to Chapel Hill. He brought in Norman Thomas, the perennial Socialist Party candidate for president, and James Roosevelt, son and advisor to FDR. He hosted Earl Browder, general secretary of the Communist Party USA, and Hiram Wesley Evans, Imperial Wizard of the Ku Klux Klan. With world tensions rising, he invited the German ambassador to campus, and a consul from Japan. He worked tenaciously to get President Roosevelt to North Carolina, persisting—and ultimately succeeding—even after Heard had graduated and gone on to graduate school at Columbia.

Heard continued to soak in diverse perspectives outside school, in stints with the Interior Department in Albuquerque, the State Department in Quito, Ecuador, and as an ensign and lieutenant in the wartime navy. He sharpened his political insights as an apprentice to noted political scientist V. O. Key, collaborating on the landmark book *Southern Politics in State and Nation*. In his remarks after being officially installed as Vanderbilt chancellor on October 4, 1963, one line was as heartfelt as any he'd ever deliver. "You can be sure," he told students and faculty, "that while I'm your chancellor, this campus will be a place of intellectual freedom."

Beyond the rhetoric, Heard made a series of moves to surround himself with like-minded people. He placed his stamp on the school's Board of Trust by lobbying for the installation of its first woman—a Jewish woman, no less. Mary Jane Werthan came from a wealthy, liberal Nashville family and was known to drive a Mercedes convertible to board meetings. Over the years, it was Werthan who argued most strenuously for more divergent voices on the board and, it was believed, anonymously provided scholarship money for low-income students, especially blacks.

Another of Heard's significant early moves was to hire the university's first chaplain, which may have sounded like an unusual way to jump-start the open forum concept—until one actually met the Reverend Beverly Asbury.

Asbury was born in Elberton, Georgia, in February 1929, or as he liked to put it, "one month, 100 miles and worlds apart from Martin Luther King Jr." Growing up white in segregated Elberton, Asbury had little contact with "40 percent of the town's population," but he entered the University of Georgia interested in exploring racial issues. His life was transformed, he'd later say, when he attended an integrated Christian student conference hosted by Atlanta's black colleges. First, on a field trip to Ebenezer Baptist Church to meet Martin Luther King Sr., he was introduced to the preacher's charismatic teenage son, already by then a Morehouse College graduate. Later during that conference, black and white students were socializing at a party in the gymnasium at Morris Brown College when the room went dark. This was no accident: Klan members had cut off electricity to the room and left a burning cross in the lawn out front. As Asbury and the other students sat in the dark waiting for the slow-footed Atlanta police to arrive, he knew he had just been handed his reason for being. "I look back on my career and my life as having been formed in that particular crucible," he recalled.

After graduating from Georgia and earning his divinity degree from Yale University, Asbury took his first job as the preacher at Zebulon Baptist Church in Wake County, North Carolina, a state, he said, whose moderate tendencies on race issues were shifting in reaction to the *Brown* Supreme Court case. What at first had been an ideal fit turned dangerous. Asbury's statements on racial equality, coupled with his efforts to help establish a workers' union at a Westinghouse plant in Raleigh, earned him death threats, one of which was delivered in the form of a pistol-wielding man standing on his door-step in the middle of the night. Eventually, he said, a combination of town heavyweights, including members of the Chamber of Commerce and White Citizens' Council, succeeded in running him out of town.

Though the ugliness of the situation compelled him to drop his Baptist affiliation, Asbury's passion for racial justice only intensified in his subsequent jobs. As a Presbyterian minister outside St. Louis, he led a successful clergy-driven effort to desegregate the town of Webster Groves, Missouri. As the university chaplain at the College of Wooster in Ohio, he not only encouraged students to participate in the Freedom Summer activities of 1964, but he himself traveled to Hattiesburg, Mississippi, where he was arrested while helping register blacks to vote. The next year, he traveled southward again, this time joining Martin Luther King Jr. on his march in Alabama. By the time a search committee from Vanderbilt came calling, he suspected it was time to return to the South for good.

Heard knew exactly what he was getting in Asbury, calling on none other than Yale chaplain William Sloane Coffin for advice during the search process. Well known for his liberal positions on civil rights, nuclear proliferation, and Vietnam, Coffin heartily endorsed Asbury.

Asbury, an admirer of Heard's contribution to *Southern Politics*, was intrigued by the Vanderbilt job as long as he "wasn't walking into some ultra-conservative trap," as he felt he had done in North Carolina. In discussions with Vanderbilt's search committee, Asbury's concerns were put to rest. As Potter, the assistant dean of men (who was not a part of that committee), later recalled, it was clear to some in the Vanderbilt administration that "there had been no one speaking from the point of view of the religious community about the moral position of the university." With the Rockefeller scholarships sending blacks to Vanderbilt, Heard realized the school needed help integrating them into the student body. But Vanderbilt was so parochial it also needed help doing the same with Jews and Roman Catholics. Asbury's marching orders were clear.

"I was brought in," Asbury said four decades later, "to open up the university socially, religiously, and racially. Vanderbilt had been a very good southern, provincial university. It was the best university in Georgia, Tennessee, Alabama, and Florida, and that's about all you could say for it. But [Heard] wanted it to be a national university. A more open agenda on the issues of segregation and the admission of blacks was all part of that."

Before assuming his duties, Asbury told the *Hustler* that students would find his sermons relevant to the world around them. "I expect to deal with things in the pulpit that are significant to human life," he said. "For example, I don't think you can work out questions of personal morality and ignore the broader problems of society such as poverty, racial justice and housing."

While Asbury became an unpopular figure in conservative circles on campus and around town, he succeeded in changing the tone of campus discourse in just the way Heard had imagined. One of Heard's greatest gifts as a leader was his ability to set in motion a chain of events that suited him, all the while staying largely above the fray and maintaining a distance, or, some might argue, the appearance of distance, between his personal beliefs and his professional actions. Heard backed Asbury unconditionally; in turn, Asbury spoke out in ways the chancellor could not.

Though he had been active in the Democratic Party in North Carolina, Heard steadfastly resisted overtures to get involved in partisan political issues in Nashville, believing such activity was unbecoming of a chancellor representing a broad constituency. Asbury considered the chancellor "the very epitome of a diplomat. For all his liberalism, he was able to build bridges between liberals and southern conservatives."

While Heard's ability to work with conservative factions was critical in his efforts to change the culture at Vanderbilt, his idealistic rhetoric may have also blinded his liberal followers to a quite practical reason for recruiting black students, encouraging free speech, and generally opening up the campus. Heard once told attendees at a Methodist training academy that "a university is not a university unless it keeps itself relevant to the society it serves." In an interview with the *Tennessean*, he said that "the university's obligation is not to protect students from ideas, but rather to expose them to ideas, and to help make them capable of handling, and hopefully, having ideas." In the turbulent mid-1960s, these statements were sweet music to the ears of progressive students and faculty. But the young chancellor also had another important audience in mind, one that wanted to hear that sleepy Vanderbilt was coming out of its shell—the major national foundations on the East Coast.

Alexander Heard, it so happened, had just launched a $55 million fundraising drive, the most ambitious in Vanderbilt's history.

11

Articulate Messengers

So," the professor smirked, "they've let the niggers in after all."

Thus goes the story of how Walter Murray was welcomed to English class on the first day of his freshman year. Chancellor Heard and Chaplain Asbury may have been saying all the right things about Vanderbilt's newfound commitment to its black students, but they weren't the only ones talking. In large measure, Wallace, Dillard, Murray, and their fellow black classmates were on their own, their lives influenced not so much by distant proclamations but rather by the personal interactions they experienced each day.

The professor chose to greet Murray in a manner that provided an ugly counterpoint to the poignant way the freshman had been sent off to college just weeks earlier. One Sunday in the summer of 1966, the preacher at Murray's church announced that the young man would be attending Vanderbilt. After the sermon, parishioners celebrated the achievement, and many came up to Murray to shake his hand and offer their congratulations. An elderly woman shuffled up to him, grabbed Murray's right hand, and put something in it. He opened the palm of his hand to discover a solitary quarter. "Son," the old woman said, "it ain't much, but it's all I can spare. And I want to give you something to speed you on your way."

More than forty years later, Wallace remembered this story vividly, saying that it served as a constant source of inspiration both to him and to Murray during their four years at Vanderbilt. "It was the symbol and the substance of the humble but dogged struggling spirit that had brought us, and those like us, that far," he said. "We would soon come to know that we needed that inspiration—and then some."

The cold dose of reality that Murray encountered on his first day of college was not unique. K. C. Potter recalled the story of one black student who came to Vanderbilt full of an optimism and energy that was uncommon for any freshman, black or white. By the time he graduated, Potter said, the young man was as bitter and disillusioned as any he had ever seen.

For Eileen Carpenter, who grew up in an upper-middle-class black family in Nashville, attending both segregated and integrated Catholic schools, race had never been much of an issue. Her father was a professor at Tennessee State, and her mother was a secretary there. She lived in a nice home in the Haynes Meade subdivision, vacationed in Chicago each summer, attended cotillions, and gazed at the stars through the big telescope her parents bought for their budding astronomer. "We had our own little world, and it didn't seem like we were missing out," Carpenter recalled. "It was not until I got to Vanderbilt that my world came crashing down."

The crash came gradually, and at first Carpenter couldn't put her finger on what was happening. In the summer following her senior year of high school, a puzzling pattern repeated itself when she attended parties for incoming Vanderbilt freshmen.

Carpenter arrived at the parties, held in the homes of wealthy alums, excited and happy, only to find herself standing alone with her plate of food while others in the room laughed and talked as if they all knew each other. "People were not mean or anything, and if they caught your eye, they'd smile, but I started having this sense that I was just kind of there, just being politely ignored," she recalled. "At the time, it did not occur to me that maybe it was because I was black. I was making mental notes, but things weren't clicking." Carpenter lived at home that freshman year, and her proud parents drove her from 1603 Whites Creek Pike to the West End campus for her first 8:00 a.m. English class. As she stepped from the car and through the campus gates, she later recalled, it was as if she'd walked into an episode of *The Twilight Zone*, theme music and all. "I don't think this is going to be good," she thought to herself. She walked into the classroom and sat next to another black woman. A white boy joined them in the second row, several seats to their right, and the rest of the class sat two or three rows behind, leaving a virtual buffer zone around the two black freshmen. "I remember thinking, 'This is really strange,'" Carpenter recalled. But again, it wasn't until later in the semester that she asked herself whether this was happening because she was black.

"For me, not having been exposed to in-your-face racism, I guess I didn't understand the very subtle forms of racism where you just don't exist, where you're just kind of ignored. That's what was happening, but I didn't understand it," she said. "I just knew I was very unhappy and something was wrong. Nobody called me nigger, nobody spat on me. In fact, it was just the opposite. Everyone was polite."

It wasn't until Carpenter sat alone in the Rand Hall dining room that everything began to click. A cat darted through the cafeteria, but nobody seemed to notice. "I remember thinking to myself, 'I'm just like that cat. I don't make any difference.' Nobody paid any attention. Nobody looked up. It was then that I started understanding what I was feeling and what was going on. It was Ralph Ellison's *Invisible Man*. You were not there. You didn't impact anyone's life. You could be totally ignored, and if you disappeared, nobody would notice." Frustrated by these experiences, Carpenter would come home from school, throw her books in the corner of her room, and crawl into bed. "My parents couldn't understand," she recalled, "because nobody was being mean to me."

These periods of isolation only told half the story. When not completely ignored, many black students felt that they were on the receiving end of piercing stares from their white classmates. They could experience both extremes in a matter of minutes, creating a chronic self-consciousness that made even the most mundane of activities unpleasant. Wallace accompanied a small group of white classmates to dinner one evening in the cafeteria at the women's quadrangle. As he waited in line to choose his food, he looked up, and realized that every pair of female eyes in the room was focused right on him, the coeds' pinched faces betraying feelings of fear, hatred, or maybe both, he couldn't be sure. Wallace's mother had warned him to "stay away from the white girls," and now, before he could even take a bite to eat, it seemed to him that the smartest solution might be to just leave the room.

Accustomed to being a big man on campus in high school, Dillard was disturbed by the eerie silence as he walked to his classes at Vanderbilt, nobody saying a word to him. Back in his dorm, the opposite extreme: cries of "nigger on the floor" accompanied by slammed doors. In the classroom, he bounced between two opposing forms of isolation. In one lecture, his professor never called on him, as if he weren't even in the room. The next class, he was in the center of a harsh spotlight. "You're the only black in the class, and everybody *knows* you're the only black in the class," he recalled. "They start talking about slavery or something, and the focus was on you. You were the representative of your race. If you raise your hand, you better damn well know the answer. Or if you raise your hand and your professor criticizes your answer, you internalized the criticism in a personal way, much more than you normally would have, because you're the only black and you don't want to sound stupid. That kind of isolation was depressing."

The dichotomy was especially pronounced on weekends: with few social options, many black students spent quiet, lonely nights in their dorm rooms, listening to the shrieks and beats of beer-soaked frat parties outside. Dillard was struck by a conspicuous hypocrisy: while the frats would not accept black members, they frequently hired black bands to perform at their parties. "One thing about Vanderbilt, those students went crazy on weekends," he recalled. "They would get drunk as hell. And they loved black music. The only blacks you saw on campus all week were maintenance workers, and then on weekends, every fraternity had black entertainers. We could walk by and see what was going on." But just walking past a frat house late on a

Friday or Saturday night could be a distressing experience, Bedford Waters recalled. "When people were drunk, they'd holler things as you were walking back to your dorm," he said. "'Nigger, what are you doing here?! Go home, go back, you're not wanted here!'" Arriving back at the dorm on a weekend night wasn't without its tense moments, either. For Dillard, there was nothing worse than finding himself riding on an elevator with an inebriated white couple. The door would close, white guy, white girl, black guy stuck together in a confined space. The couple reeking of alcohol, the white guy suddenly super-protective of his date, shooting daggers at Dillard. "You'd just get off the elevator as quick as you could," he recalled.

Whether it was naïveté or just the fact that they hadn't really thought about it before arriving at Vanderbilt, the degree of seclusion they felt on campus initially came as a surprise to the black students. "I came to Vandy for the same reason everybody else did—to get a good education, to have a good college experience, and to party like everybody else," Carolyn Bradshaw recalled. "Little did I realize we would have so much more to do there in terms of integration." Wallace said he and his black classmates gradually began to develop "parallel lives." They would do the best they could to make the most of their days at Vanderbilt, but they would also seek alternative social outlets. While the grand social experiment of integration might take decades to sort itself out, these students only had one college experience, just four years to determine what worked best for them as individuals.

For some, this meant approaching student life at face value—attempting to do the same things white students took for granted. Unaware that none of the Vanderbilt sororities admitted blacks, Eileen Carpenter arrived on campus thinking she was going to "have a great time and join a sorority like the college days you saw on TV." Decades later, Carpenter said that as a freshman, she was equal parts naïve, hopeful, and ignorant—believing that the passage of the civil rights bill meant the end of racism. She walked past all the sorority houses and picked the one she liked best—Kappa Alpha Theta. Her VUceptor was a Theta, and Carpenter attended the sorority's first rush party. Everything seemed to be going just fine, and when Carpenter's aunt came to visit one day, Eileen told her all about her plans to join the sorority. "She looked at me like my head had just dropped off my body," Carpenter recalled. "She said, 'You can't join a sorority there, they won't allow Negroes.' I couldn't quite believe her, so I called my VUceptor, and I immediately knew by the way she started sputtering that it was true." Still, because most of the Vanderbilt frat parties during the fall semester were ostensibly open to all students, not just frat members and their dates, Carpenter found the courage to walk in and try to have some fun from time to time. By the time her junior year rolled around, she noticed that as the night grew later and the alcohol lowered inhibitions, nobody seemed to care what color she was. Bradshaw noticed the same thing, more than once dancing the night away underneath a Confederate flag in the KA house. "It wasn't like you walked around the campus in fear," she recalled. Henry Robinson, a black student from Raleigh, North Carolina, became a regular in the white football players' poker games. As many painful racial slights as she endured, Bobbie Jean Perdue said there was also always a group of white students who were helpful, who made sure she wouldn't have to eat alone.

Bedford Waters made it further through the rush process than Carpenter, what he later called "an enlightening experience." He visited all the frat houses just like all the white freshmen, enduring some "What are you doing here?" taunts along the way, but also catching flak from other black students, who questioned his motivation for attempting to join a white fraternity. Waters was pleasantly surprised by some of what he encountered, discovering that some of the Kappa Alpha brothers—the same guys who paraded through campus in their Confederate uniforms once a year—were "very open-minded and very gracious, which wasn't the image of the fraternity." Over the next four years, he often returned to the KA house to eat lunch with some of the brothers he met there during rush. Eventually, Waters felt like he hit it off best with members of Zeta Beta Tau, one of two Jewish fraternities on campus. All was going well and the chapter even offered him a bid, only to have it rescinded by the fraternity's national office. Undeterred, Waters threw himself into other campus pursuits, joining the men's residence hall executive board and eventually becoming the organization's first black president— a feat that earned him ridicule, not so much from whites but from blacks who accused him of selling out. "Some of the other African American students thought that I was being an Uncle Tom by doing that, and they said that to me," Waters said. "But I am who I am and I was not going to let that stop me." Waters felt he was constantly engaged in a game of tug-of-war, trying his best to enjoy his college experience by participating in the pursuits that interested him, all while catching hell from some whites who didn't want him around and some blacks who thought he was betraying them. "You want to be accepted among all your peers, but there was this perception that if you're doing anything outside of what was considered to be the norm for African Americans at the time, that you were being disloyal and you were trying to act white," Waters recalled. "How the hell do you come out of that with some kind of sanity? Obviously I did, but it was a very, very difficult time."

When it was announced that students would have the opportunity to participate in a computer-based matchmaking project, Bradshaw and Perdue eagerly signed up. Much like a modern online dating service, the idea was that students would fill out information about themselves that would be used, with the aid of a primitive computer program, to match them with a date for an on-campus dance. Organizers found themselves in an uncomfortable bind when none of the black male students filled out a form. Who would they match up with Bradshaw and Perdue? After dubious excuses were given as to why a match just didn't emerge, eventually a French exchange student and another white student invited the two black women to the dance. "It was our first rebellious act on campus," Bradshaw recalled.

Increasingly, the black Vanderbilt students began to look off campus for extracurricular fun. If breaking into the social scene at Vanderbilt was difficult, thousands of black students were across town at Fisk and Tennessee A&I.

"Fortunately, the people at those universities were welcoming and they understood what the situation was, and it allowed us to forge our own social world," Wallace recalled. "What was unfortunate about that is that it was a statement that America was still in transition." The fact that a segment of Vanderbilt's student body had to get off campus to relax like any other college student, Wallace believed, was a statement about how far the country had not come. But just as black businesses and institutions thrived during the days of segregation, Wallace said he and his classmates ultimately benefited from the exclusion in significant ways. If they wanted a rewarding social life, they were forced to be creative, energetic, and resourceful. They found open-minded classmates at Vanderbilt with whom they could talk or drink a beer. They found students at A&I who admired the pioneering they were doing at Vanderbilt. They ventured out to listen to prominent black speakers and celebrities who passed through town, people like Harry Belafonte and Ossie Davis. The irony, Wallace concluded, was that as outsiders on their own campus, many black students wove a tapestry of experiences and contacts much more vibrant than the norm for the "in crowd" at Vanderbilt. "By not being an insider, but by reacting positively," he said, "we created a rich set of social opportunities that we cherish even to this day."

While Dillard was ignored walking across the Vanderbilt campus, he found the opposite to be true at Fisk. "They loved me there, they embraced me," he recalled. "It was like, 'You're playing at Vanderbilt, man, you're a star.' They were proud of me and they accepted me. It was like my family away from home." Dillard also found the girls at TSU and Fisk to be more his style than the more straitlaced black girls at Vanderbilt. "I love Eileen, I love them all, but they were southern girls and I was a big-time northern guy, and I was looking for a little bit more excitement," Dillard recalled. Given the paucity of black men on the Vanderbilt campus, the girls didn't appreciate Dillard and others looking elsewhere for dates, but sometimes, they returned the favor. Because Vanderbilt freshmen were prohibited from bringing cars to school, Bradshaw said TSU boys were in demand because they often had cars and could drive girls places on dates. And even for the black Vanderbilt men looking for dates over at Fisk or TSU, things did not always go as planned. Constantly engaged in the pull between the white and black worlds at Vanderbilt, Waters found that the tensions followed him across Nashville. With social opportunities limited on West End, he'd cross over to the black side of town, only to be rejected by a girl for having come from Vanderbilt. *You're not one of us. You're not black enough.* "You couldn't win for trying," he said.

Perry Wallace has long remembered a pearl of wisdom once delivered to him by an old man in the ghetto. "Necessity," the man told him, "is a motherfucker for invention." Wallace believes that this approximation might just be a more cogent statement than the standard cliché, especially when he remembers those early days at Vanderbilt, when black and white students were inelegantly trying to figure each other out—succeeding and failing, improvising, accepting and rejecting. Two worldviews were colliding, he said, one that saw society advancing by placing its trust in movements and causes and legislation, the other rejecting such things, believing that what really mattered were one-on-one relationships. In the end, Wallace concluded, both ideologies were necessary. Without the civil rights movement, much progress would not have taken place. But even with a strong movement, what ultimately mattered to the people living through it were their daily interactions and experiences with individual human beings. Integration was a new exercise for everybody, black and white. For every white student who cursed a black kid just trying to walk back to his dorm, there was another who hadn't spent any time around blacks and didn't quite know what to say.

"People talked about, 'Let's all come together and we'll all get along.' Nope, we had too much practice *not* getting along," Wallace says. "A lot of us blacks had to practice not feeling inferior after all of that segregation bull. There were a lot of whites who had to practice not feeling superior. We had a chance to practice at Vanderbilt, and some of us did. Some blacks and whites practiced and got better and better. The people who decided that 'Oh, blacks don't have anything to offer, and I don't need to be around them, and in fact I can do better not being around them, and the world is my father's world and my grandfather's world,' they may have been right *then*. But history made them wrong, progress made them wrong. They were eventually going to have to get along with blacks and with Hispanics and Asians and Middle Easterners, but they didn't engage in the practice. They turned down the opportunity."

Segregation doesn't need any extra condemnation, Wallace says. Its evils speak for themselves. There's a certain level of decency everyone should be afforded. But look at who was being ignored at Vanderbilt in 1966: the best and brightest black students from North and South, the class presidents, the valedictorians, the salutatorians. "Just think about the stories we had to tell," Wallace said. "The students on campus who rejected us, who ignored us, who isolated us—we brought the opportunity for them to 'practice being equal.' The irony is that we were just who they needed to know. We brought with us insights into the world that they lived in that they did not have because segregation had set people apart. We had the other half of the story about race. And we were articulate messengers."

12

A Hit or Miss Thing

"It's always a little humorous to watch a freshman's face when things first start each fall," the coach told the businessmen. "He's looking for the pass that he's used to getting in high school, and all of a sudden somebody else shoots." Roy Skinner was relaxed—likely for the last time until March. There were still two days until his varsity team squared off against the freshmen in the annual intrasquad scrimmage that marked the beginning of another Vanderbilt basketball season.

With stars Keith Thomas and Clyde Lee gone, not much was expected from the 1966–67 varsity. Lee would be back in town for an NBA exhibition game in four days when his San Francisco Warriors played the St. Louis Hawks at Municipal Auditorium, but little good that would do the Commodores. Point guard Jerry Southwood was a dependable leader, and Bo Wyenandt, Bob "Chicken Man" Warren, and Tom Hagan could score, but without Clyde, most fans anticipated a down year.

When Skinner addressed the Downtown Optimist Club on November 17, he focused his remarks on what everybody was curious about anyway: the freshmen, the future, the players who wouldn't even be eligible for the varsity for another season. "Our freshmen have really been making progress in the last week or 10 days," he said. "[This is] potentially an outstanding group." There was some truth in what Skinner was saying—the freshman had given the varsity decent competition in practice—but he was also trying to sell tickets. The previous year, an enormous line had formed outside Memorial Gym for the varsity-freshman game, but that had been the start of Lee's final season, and there had never been a greater fan favorite. Tickets for this game weren't included in the season ticket package, so hyping the potential for a competitive scrimmage could help build another big crowd.

Commodore boosters were always curious about the newcomers, but there was special interest in this freshman class, especially the two young players breaking the color line. Skinner had already said that Wallace might become the best rebounder in the history of the program, and he predicted that Dillard's quickness would allow him to score points in bunches. But the coach was also intrigued by the other freshmen. Art Welhoelter, a six-foot-five forward from the same town of Webster Groves, Missouri, where Reverend Asbury had made his mark, was scorching the nets in practice. Dan Due, a sharpshooting guard from Indiana who had broken all of the high school scoring records of University of Kentucky star Louie Dampier, was just beginning to shake off some freshman nerves. Alex Beavers, a homegrown star from Nashville, and Pat Toomay, a Commodore football player, were banging heads in the paint. While the team also included some grateful walk-ons who had no chance of ever advancing to the varsity, no one was happier to suit up for the freshman squad than Toomay. Happily slipping away from the misery that was Vanderbilt football to the heavenly aura that surrounded the basketball program, Toomay appreciated every second away from the gridiron. "As football players, we were hated on campus," Toomay recalled, the disgust building over the course of the previous five seasons, in which the Commodores had won all of nine games. "There was tremendous animosity between the football players and the regular students. Football was still going on when basketball practice started, so I got out of that horror and went to [Memorial] Gym. There was tremendous prestige around the basketball program, tremendous community approval."

While Skinner gave the downtown boosters the scouting report they wanted to hear, the truth was that once the season began, he wouldn't pay much attention to what the press called the "baby Commodores"; the varsity squad was all that really mattered. A St. Louis Cardinals baseball fan, Skinner's philosophy was to treat the freshman team like one of the Redbirds' minor league clubs: wins and losses didn't matter so much as developing talent for the future. And though he saw enough flashes of competence from the freshmen to say a few optimistic words to the Optimists, this group of recruits, he believed, was a lot like the ones that had preceded them: they had a lot to prove. "They weren't that good," he recalled forty years later. "I wasn't excited about them. Just like all the others, you hope they improve with age and practice and keep getting better."

Charged with developing these players was a new freshman coach named Homer Garr, a Virginia gentleman who came to Nashville with a flat-top haircut and a successful coaching résumé at Manchester High School in Richmond. This was Garr's first crack at collegiate coaching, and there were whispers that he landed the job because one of his former players, Bob Bundy, had signed a scholarship with Vanderbilt a year earlier. "Homer," Jerry Southwood later concluded, "was not ready for college basketball."

Back in high school, Garr was highly respected by his boys, demanding as much of them in the classroom as on the court. "He had a very strong set of dos and don'ts for his players, and he expected us to dedicate our lives to schoolwork and basketball," Bundy recalled. "It was a father-figure approach with the appropriate discipline." Which is where the difficulties began in his adjustment to the college game—at least the way it was practiced at Vanderbilt. Skinner's style was decidedly laissez-faire, more akin to that of present-day professional coaches (who make no pretense of controlling their players' off-court behavior) than their autocratic college counterparts. Skinner believed in recruiting mature, solid citizens who loved the game, the types of guys who, more often than not, were inclined to make the right decisions. That they did not always live up to the responsibility he entrusted in them was no cause for micromanagement. Skinner knew that occasionally his players smoked and drank and stayed out late, but as long as they had the big things covered—showing up on time for practice, playing their hearts out, going to class—he didn't mind the indiscretions. He called his players "men," not "boys," and that's how he treated them. For a coach like Garr, who had dictated virtually every minute of his high school players' daily routines, not only was it a tough adjustment, it was a less rewarding experience. "His ability to get involved with the kids was a little bit different in college, and I think that's probably where he struggled a little bit," Bundy said. "After practice, the kids go off on their own [in college]. It was not what he expected it to be."

Because schools in Richmond were segregated, Garr, like Skinner, had never before coached a black player when he came to Vanderbilt. He had, however, recognized the talent level at the former Confederate capital's two black high schools, and he encouraged his Manchester players to schedule pickup games against players from Armstrong and Maggie Walker high schools. One of the black players Bundy matched up against on the playground was Maggie Walker star Bobby Dandridge, a six-foot-six forward who went on to win two NBA titles in a thirteen-year pro career. "It was never about black and white with Coach Garr," said Bundy. "It was always about being better basketball players, and that's where the competition was." As they experienced their first taste of basketball at the collegiate level, neither Wallace nor Dillard felt that Garr treated them any differently from their white teammates. Which is where the compliments from Dillard end. "He was glad to be there," Dillard recalled. "He was glad to be an assistant coach at Vanderbilt, and anything Coach Skinner told him to do, he did. I can't remember an original thought or idea that came out of his mouth. None. It was a total letdown." For his part, Wallace felt that what Garr may have lacked in sophistication, he made up for in what Wallace needed most at the time: simple human decency. "I thought he was good with me, and it was helpful having someone like Coach Garr," Wallace recalled. "He was a sincere man who did the best he could under the circumstances. He treated me just fine."

The squeaks of the Chuck Taylors and the thud of the bouncing ball were always amplified in Memorial Gym, caroming off the cinderblock walls in the cavernous building. Those sounds were familiar to the "railbirds," a small group of hard-core Commodore fans who skipped out of work to watch practice every day. But there was a new, unfamiliar sound in November 1966, one that took everybody by surprise: it was the voice of the freshman guard from Detroit, confident Godfrey Dillard, full of energy and yammering to anybody who'd listen as he high-dribbled the ball down the court. *Come out and get me! Come out and get me! Ahhh, get back, you need to move away, I'm taking it to the basket!* Dillard brought a lot of the Motor City style to Commodore practice sessions, which some of his teammates found to be a welcome diversion. "He felt like he was a good player, he was sure of himself, he was aggressive, and he wasn't fazed at all that he was with a bunch of white guys," recalled Tom Hagan, the Commodore varsity's leading scorer in 1967. "He talked a lot, but often it was just an observation, not trash." One time in practice, Hagan backed Dillard down further and further underneath the basket, until finally, about five feet from the goal, he surprised the freshman by making a shot he'd been working on during the off-season. "Whoa!" Dillard yelled to Hagan as they ran down to the other end of the court, "I knew you were going to shoot it, but I never would have expected a *hook* shot." To Hagan, Dillard's constant chatter made the game more fun. Dillard's energy may have started with his mouth, but it extended to his legs. He relished participating in a fast-break drill where he stood back in the paint as the lone defender, attempting to stop a pair of fast-charging offensive players from scoring. "I was a very good jumper as a freshman, and two guys would come down and I'd jump up and pin the ball against the backboard, because I was so quick and they were so slow with their layups," Dillard said. "After a while, they stopped letting me do that because they couldn't get the ball up to the basket against me."

Dillard had more confidence in his own game than in the abilities of his new teammates. The level of talent was low, he believed, not nearly what he expected from a major college basketball program. Not only that, but the style of play was boring: all they did was set picks for Hagan. *Anybody could hit a shot if you set three picks for him. Put him alone on the wing and see what he could do then.* And the way Coach Garr liked to walk the ball up the court—so slow, and so ineffective, Dillard thought. Nobody seemed to appreciate his up-tempo game; in fact, they tried to stifle it. Had they not seen the way he could snatch a rebound off the boards and run coast to coast, blowing right past everybody? Had they not seen the way he and Perry could run the break together? "Perry could take the house down running the floor," Dillard recalled. "He could run. The. Floor." But that was the beginning and end to Wallace's offensive game, Dillard thought; for a player who had received such attention, Wallace, he believed, was one-dimensional on the court. "Initially, that was the striking thing," Dillard recalled. "He was a fast-break player, but that was about all."

Dillard's big-city style rubbed some teammates the wrong way. To them, the young guard wasn't nearly as good as he thought he was. "He took a lot of shots, let me put it that way," Due recalled decades later. "I have nothing against Godfrey, he was a nice, fun-loving guy, but I just wish he had passed me the ball a little more. If the other team would score, he'd run away so I had to take the ball out of bounds and pass it to him, and then I'd never see it again."

Wallace and Dillard displayed a contrast in styles. While Godfrey yammered nonstop, Perry barely said a word. "He was unbelievably quiet," remembered reserve center Bill LaFevor. Wallace was the kind of player who showed up early for practice, nodded his head when asked to do something, and then stayed late to work on an aspect of his game—alone. In some ways, Wallace was merely exhibiting the same work ethic and respect for authority that had always been fundamental to his personality: he did what the coaches asked, didn't pick fights with his teammates or opponents, didn't talk trash. This is who he was, in any setting, but it was also a personality that was shaped by, and consciously developed to manage, the realities of segregation. Wallace arrived at Vanderbilt barely accustomed to looking a white man in the eye, he recalled, let alone talking back to a white coach. He believed that everything he said or did on the court reflected not only on him, but on an entire race. In his behavior, he believed, he could either confirm or refute stereotypes and, in the end, earn respect for himself and for blacks through hard work and unquestionable character. There was also a survival instinct at play: by keeping his head down, not making waves, he believed he could avoid misunderstandings that often did not end well for blacks in white settings. All told, it was a traditional, conservative approach to integration that reflected Wallace's experiences growing up in the South. He could see that while Dillard was expressing himself in an entirely different way, they were both trying to make the same point: "I belong." While Wallace made his case gradually, virtually nonverbally, Dillard shouted it loud and clear. "That was the northern thing, more unapologetic, more in your face," Wallace said of Dillard's style. "I came from a southern environment and you just didn't think a lot of thoughts like that—not out loud."

Most of the other freshmen had played with or against blacks before; Skinner's most fertile recruiting grounds were Kentucky, Missouri, and Indiana, states that were ahead of Tennessee in terms of high school integration. Still, there was some curiosity among the freshmen and returning Commodore players when Wallace and Dillard joined the team, including that of the locker room variety. LaFevor said he and his teammates peeked at their new black cohorts in the shower to see if the rumors they'd heard about a certain part of the black male anatomy were true. Centuries-old white stereotypes about black sexuality were a constant source of frustration to Wallace. Basketball teammates and acquaintances from the football team made lewd comments about his dates, Wallace said, and one hoops teammate suggested that Wallace surely would have enjoyed "picking cotton" and spending time "at slave breeding camps," where the sex must have been plentiful for male slaves. "He honestly thought that was funny," Wallace recalled. "The same guy said to me, 'I think those guys on the *Amos 'n' Andy* show are just pretty funny.' He was just foolish, and came from a world where there was a lot of prejudice." At the same time, Wallace said, there were always inconsistencies. In other circumstances, he and this teammate, whom Wallace declines to name publicly, worked quite well together. They talked about issues of race and played ball together with no problems. "You just knew that at any given time, that [racist] stuff was going to come down the pipe and hit you," Wallace recalled, "but the rest of the time, it made sense for you to try to get along as well as possible."

Denigrating comments from teammates were more the exception than the rule. No Vanderbilt players protested Wallace's recruitment, there was no mean-spirited hazing, nobody transferred or threatened to quit when he and Dillard joined the team. Benign neglect was the most serious offense for most of the guys: we'll go our way, Perry will go his. Many chose to leave Wallace alone—no special treatment, the way he'd want it, they told themselves—at a time when he needed them most. "I remember vaguely having the feeling that Perry was introverted, just like I was," recalled student manager Gene Smitherman. "He was not the kind of person who needed to go out and be your best buddy. This is what bothers me, forty years later, is that it was almost like, 'Let Perry be.' I'm wondering if Perry needed more than he got from me and from others as well."

One white teammate who made an effort to spend time off the court with Wallace and Dillard was Toomay. Growing up in a military family, the future NFL star moved around several times, bouncing from one air force base to another, all of which were integrated. Having spent time around blacks, he had no hang-ups with the style of ball that Perry and Godfrey played. He loved Dillard's ear-high dribble, got a kick out of the way he talked trash. He stood back in awe of Wallace's leaping ability, the way he could touch the top of the square on the backboard above the rim, the way he could dunk from a standing start. "You just couldn't fathom how this guy could be doing what he was doing, and then the ball was smashing you in the face," Toomay recalled of his attempts to guard Wallace in practice. "It was like explosions raining down from Zeus or something. It was really amazing." Feeling like an outsider on the Vanderbilt campus himself, he identified with his black teammates and began to hang out with them. "We hit it off immediately," he recalled. After a long practice, Toomay would walk back to Wallace's dorm room at Vanderbilt Hall, sit on the edge of the bed, and soak up an impromptu lesson in jazz appreciation. "Perry was intelligent, sensitive, quiet, deep-thinking," Toomay recalled. "And he turned me on to jazz. I didn't know who Jimmy Smith was, who Wes Montgomery was. I learned jazz from hanging out with Perry and Godfrey."

For Wallace and Dillard, spending time with Toomay and Southwood, who occasionally drove them over to parties in North Nashville (and stuck around to socialize), made a tense existence more bearable. Wallace could let his guard down, just be himself. Jazz represented one expression of the new world Wallace wanted to live in—modern, urban, intelligent—but still connected to his roots. That Toomay wanted to learn more about that world was meaningful. People who were open-minded about appreciating different kinds of music, Wallace believed, usually were equally open-minded about appreciating different kinds of people.

"There were a core group of people who were mainly great guys, and Pat was one of them," Wallace recalled. "We got together and acted like normal, civilized people, and that was great. Godfrey and Walter [Murray] and all of us would get together with these guys and it would be a very, very nice time. Pat was special—he was intelligent and he was an excellent athlete. That's the reason I came to Vanderbilt—for people like that. Here you had a big, strong, tough football player with subtleties and nuances."

Toomay's friendship and understanding carried a more profound meaning for Wallace than one might imagine. Even something as seemingly benign as enjoying music could be fraught with racial stereotypes. "To appreciate people like Pat, you have to know that some whites would see or hear us listening to jazz and they would somehow conjure up images of wide-eyed, crazed blacks who could only express crude, base emotions—jungle bunny natives, in other words," Wallace recalled. "This view was not only more wrong than they could have imagined, it was bigoted and insulting. Pat was a real pleasure because he could appreciate the complete range of thought and being of black people. And because he could, we all felt free enough to express ourselves more fully in music and to include him, also."

When exactly was history made? When Perry Wallace became the first African American to sign a basketball scholarship with an SEC school? When he and Dillard stepped onto the practice floor for the first time? Was it this night, when they took the court in Commodore uniforms for the scrimmage against the varsity? Would it be in a few weeks, when Vanderbilt traveled to Bowling Green for the season opener against Western Kentucky? Would it not be until the next season, when Wallace became the first black to play in a varsity SEC basketball game? Would it be the spring of 1970, when Wallace completed his basketball career and earned his degree? Take your pick; there's an argument to be made for each of these milestones. Regardless, it's safe to say that when Nashvillians took stock of their world on November 19, 1966, few of them considered the significance of what was about to happen at Memorial Gym. Images from the war in Vietnam grew more troublesome by the day: a photo of a blindfolded Viet Cong prisoner on his way to an interrogation cell dominated the front page of the morning's *Tennessean*. Traditions that had stood the test of time seemingly were discarded at every turn. The day's news brought word that even the Catholic Church was succumbing to modernity: there would be no more prohibition against eating meat on Fridays. Reactionary measures were finding favor in some circles, too. In rural Mt. Juliet, east of Nashville, the school board upheld its decision to ban the high school prom, denying that there was any racial motivation behind the decision, or that their actions should be seen as a referendum on the sinfulness of dancing. No prom in Mt. Juliet, but plenty of entertainment options elsewhere. Down at Printers Alley, Suzette Dupree ("Canada's sizzling dish to the United States") was dancing at the Rainbow Room. Next door, "those singin', swingin', stompin' sensational Stonemans" were performing at the Black Poodle. Young Michael Caine was starring in *Alfie* at the Green Hills Theater, and over at the Crescent Drive-In, the big screen was showing *The Plague of the Zombies*. For those inclined to spend the evening at home, WSM-AM was carrying the Grand Ole Opry, as usual, and on television it was quite a night: Gina Lollobrigida on Channel 4, *Mission: Impossible* on Channel 5, and Lawrence Welk on Channel 8. Options galore, and yet fifty-five hundred people, including Ray Mears, coach of archrival Tennessee, and the coaching staff from Western Kentucky, decided that there was no place they'd rather be than Memorial Gym for a night of Commodore basketball. These thousands were the first to see black men suit up in SEC basketball uniforms.

The varsity turned a close game at halftime into a blowout, outscoring the freshmen 16–3 in the first minutes of the second half before eventually winning 92–82. The star of the night, however, was Wallace, who scored seventeen points and grabbed seventeen rebounds, the most of any player on either side. It was as if he'd been dropped into the game from the future, discombobulating animate and inanimate objects alike. The rims weren't ready for him—one of the goals had to be replaced at halftime after he bent it with a dunk that drove the crowd wild—and the sportswriters weren't ready for him either. The *Banner*'s Waxo Green struggled so mightily to describe Wallace's uncommon scoring method that he veered into the parenthetical. Wallace, he wrote, "brought the fans to their feet cheering with a 'spiking tip' (driving the ball down through the goal with his hand and/or fist)."

It may have been a scrimmage, a glorified practice, but thousands of Commodore fans went home happy. The game was entertaining, the freshman Wallace was spectacular, but most of all, it was basketball season, and that alone was reason to smile. Earlier that afternoon, the Vanderbilt football team had played Ole Miss down in rain-soaked Jackson, Mississippi. The

Godfrey Dillard's Detroit style took some Commodore teammates by surprise. "He talked a lot, but it was often just an observation, not trash," said Tom Hagan. Dillard wore Jackie Robinson's number 42. Vanderbilt University Athletic Department.

(*Opposite*): Wallace fights for a rebound in the 1966 freshman-varsity game, his first game action as a collegiate player. Wallace and Dillard were the first African Americans to suit up in SEC basketball uniforms. Photo by Bill Preston, *The Tennessean*.

Rebels took pity on the Commodores, keeping their offensive starters on the bench for the entire second half.

Vanderbilt still lost 34–0.

Not only were Perry Wallace and Godfrey Dillard breaking ground on a campus that was highly resistant to change, but they also were making Southeastern Conference history at a school that was giving serious consideration to leaving the league, largely due to its inability—or unwillingness—to compete in football. The blowout against Ole Miss was no aberration: Coach Jack Green's Commodores were outscored 237–72 over the course of the 1966 season, held scoreless four times, while losing their final nine games of the year. The football Commodores hadn't posted a winning record since 1959; things were so bad before Green's arrival in 1963 that the team's 1–7–2 record in his first year was an *improvement* over the previous season, when the Commodores limped to a 1–9 finish.

It hadn't always been this way. Just as Vanderbilt had been one of the first universities to field a basketball team, it had also been one of the early powers in college football. As respected as any program in the country in the early decades of the twentieth century, Vanderbilt produced eight All-Americans and eighty-six All-Southern selections between 1903 and 1937. If football was becoming a religion in the South, Vanderbilt was one of the first devoted congregations.

Dan McGugin, Vanderbilt coach from 1904 to 1934, was the son of a Union Civil War veteran and the brother-in-law of legendary Michigan coach Fielding Yost. Under McGugin, the Commodores compiled a record of 197–55, outscored opponents 452–4 in his inaugural season, and averaged more than a point per minute over the course of the 1915 season. The football team was so popular in the years just after World War I that McGugin began pushing for a new stadium to replace old Dudley Field (named for William Dudley, a Vanderbilt chemistry professor who had helped form the Southern Intercollegiate Athletic Association, predecessor of the SEC), which had been the South's first football stadium. Yost, who lived in Nashville during the off-season, spread the word around town that if the university built a large new stadium similar to the Big House in Ann Arbor, fans would fill it. When Yost brought his Wolverines to Nashville for the new stadium's dedication game in 1922, an Atlanta sportswriter called the stadium "a stunning affair," and others predicted that more southern schools would follow suit.

Indeed, that's what happened, and as the state schools in the region began to pour more resources into their football programs in the 1930s, and then more purposefully after World War II, Vanderbilt administrators grew weary of the monster their institution had helped create. The rise of big-time college football in the South brought with it the sort of excesses, corruption, and erosion of academic standards that made a university with elite academic aspirations uneasy. After becoming chancellor in 1946, Harvie Branscomb was adamant that Vanderbilt not emulate its SEC peers. "Football had become big business, with large professional staffs, astronomical budgets, and enormous public following," he wrote in his memoirs. "Unfortunately, the gladiators in these titanic struggles were college students who presumably had come to the institution to secure the education essential to their future careers." College athletics, he believed, were "like sin. We all have it, and we have to make the best of it." By the time Heard arrived at Vanderbilt, the school had adopted a philosophy that some called "representative football," meaning that the university would not compromise its academic mission on behalf of its football program, fully aware that this meant the team would take its lumps on the gridiron. Essentially, Vanderbilt, a charter member of the league, would continue to be represented on the field each Saturday, while consciously trying to remain as different from its competition as possible. No P.E. majors. No special dorms just for athletes. No rescheduling labs to make practice more convenient. In many ways, the position was admirable: from the earliest stages, Vanderbilt saw the big state schools in the South become mere adjuncts to their football programs and chose not to fully participate in the charade. In other respects, however, the school's stance was hypocritical at best and exploitive at worst, participating in a system it didn't fully respect while sending its young men into slaughter week after week—on the field and in the classroom. "The football program was a nightmare," Toomay recalled. "Really, a nightmare."

While at other schools football players were singled out by their professors for preferential treatment, at Vanderbilt it was the opposite. Jim Combs arrived from Detroit and felt out of place with his northern accent, white T-shirts, and blue jeans, a have-not in a sea of haves. Professors, he recalled, would start the first lecture of a new semester by asking all the athletes to raise their hands. "Then they would dress you down in front of the entire class," he recalled. "It was reinforced that we were getting no free rides."

Even Chancellor Heard wasn't above a joke at the football team's expense. When in public with his right-hand man, Vice Chancellor Rob Roy Purdy, a Chaucer scholar who oversaw the Athletic Department, one of Heard's favorite jabs was to say that he, the chancellor, was in charge of basketball, which was faring quite well, while Purdy was in charge of football. *And how was that going, Mr. Purdy?*

By the fall of 1966, things were going so badly that even the mascot was killed. Run over, actually. George, a basset hound that served as an unofficial team mascot for three years, was hit by a delivery truck near Kirkland Hall. George's passing was just one bit of somber news. Effigy hanging became such a popular pastime among students that one *Hustler* columnist joked that it should become a varsity sport. Coach Green or unnamed Athletic Department officials were the usual targets of the gallows humor. As loss piled upon loss, phrases used by the local media to describe the state of the football program and student support for it included sports-marketing gems such as "rampant apathy," "indifference," "devastatingly weak," "depressing," "admission of failure," and "drifting half-heartedness." And it wasn't just football. *Hustler* sports editor Paul Kurtz described the golf program as "dismal" and the baseball team as "even more depressing." Take basketball out of the equation, and Vanderbilt's athletic teams had posted a pathetic winning percentage of just .353 over the previous year. With campus-wide malaise reaching a crisis point, on November 10 Heard announced the formation of a blue-ribbon committee to explore ways Vanderbilt might strengthen its athletics program and to nominate candidates for the vacant athletics director position. Former football team captains Willy Geny and Vernon Sharp were among the eleven men named to the committee, and some saw the effort as a step toward making the Vanderbilt athletic program more competitive in the SEC. Others, noting that the committee's charge included the study of intramurals and club sports, worried that the group might produce a report urging the de-emphasis of varsity sports. Especially troubling to the pro-SEC crowd were the three pairs of universities the chancellor specifically asked the committee to examine: Harvard and Princeton, Rice and Duke, and Johns Hopkins and Washington University in St. Louis. Not a football power among them.

Against this backdrop, *Tennessean* sportswriter John Bibb wrote in mid-November that the Vanderbilt football program was entering the most important period in its seventy-year history. Questions of competitiveness would be answered, Green would be fired, a new coach hired, and a full-time athletic director would be brought aboard.

What Bibb and others who obsessed over the sorry state of Commodore athletics missed was that out of this crucible of failure, from this school that existed as an outsider within its own conference, came change that forever altered the landscape not only on a small campus in Nashville but of sports in America. November 1966 carries no lasting significance in the history of Vanderbilt football, but the echoes of Godfrey Dillard's high dribble and Perry Wallace's thunder dunks—first heard then—reverberate still today.

The chartered bus rolled north along US Highway 31, bound from Nashville to Bowling Green, carrying the Commodores' traveling contingent to the campus of Western Kentucky University for the 1966–67 season-opener. Seated up front were the coaches: Coach Skinner and Coach Garr joined by assistants Bobby Bland and Snake Grace. Chattering away in the next few rows were the student managers, the team trainer, Joe Worden, and the sportswriters—Dudley "Waxo" Green from the *Nashville Banner* and John Bibb from the *Tennessean*. Players from the varsity and the freshman teams settled into the remaining seats for the sixty-five-mile trip across the border into Kentucky. A few minutes earlier, as they boarded the bus at Memorial Gym, a teammate loudly questioned why Wallace passed by empty seats and headed straight to the back. *Not a battle worth fighting.* Wallace played along with the bad joke. "Instinct, man. Instinct."

The sportswriters passed the time by discussing the season outlook for the varsity squad. Skinner had enjoyed a fine run with Clyde Lee and the boys, winning the SEC title in 1965 and going 22–4 in '66, but with Lee and fellow starters Keith Thomas and Ron Green gone, along with top assistant Don Knodel, who had taken the head coaching job at Rice, a consensus emerged as the scribes predicted the Commodores' likely final record: 13–13. This would be a rebuilding year, they figured, and treading water was all that was realistic. On top of having to replace key players and his most valuable assistant, Skinner had pieced together a rugged schedule. Vanderbilt had not lost a season opener in a decade, but the writers suspected that a poor start on the road against the Number 8–ranked Hilltoppers could send the Commodores into a tailspin from which they might never recover. Up next was the home opener against a Southern Methodist team that had reached the NCAA tournament in 1966. Road games against traditional Atlantic Coast Conference powers Wake Forest and Duke beckoned, as did the rigorous eighteen-game SEC schedule.

The Vanderbilt–Western Kentucky game would literally be the biggest thing that had ever happened on campus at WKU, defending champions of the Ohio Valley Conference. The game had been sold out for so long that Athletic Department officials announced that the ticket windows at Diddle Arena would be locked shut on game day. A crowd of more than thirteen thousand would jam the building, ensuring the Arena's first sellout and the largest gathering of people for any campus event, athletic or otherwise, in the school's sixty-year history. With four returning starters, including Clem "The Gem" Haskins and the Smith brothers, Dwight and Greg, Coach John Oldham's team was expected to achieve even greater things than the 1966 team, which had placed third in the NCAA Mideast regionals. Oddsmakers made Western a twelve-point favorite over Vanderbilt. The game was so hyped that even Jack Green, the embattled Commodore football coach who had resigned just days earlier, drove up to watch.

This was supposed to be Western's night, but from the moment the Commodores walked into their locker room, they began to feel a mounting sense of self-confidence. Tacked to a bulletin board next to the lockers was a telegram from Coach Knodel. About to begin his first season as a head coach down in Houston, Knodel had taken the time to wire good wishes to his former players. "Good luck tonight and the rest of the season," the telegram read. "My thoughts are with you." It was a touching gesture from their beloved former coach, a surprise that provided an extra jolt of energy to the underdogs.

By 5:30 p.m., it was time for the Commodore freshmen to take the court. As the ball was tipped into action, Wallace and Dillard became the first blacks to play for a Southeastern Conference basketball team in an official game, freshman or varsity. Despite the fact that the gym was filling beyond capacity, eventually surging to a standing-room total of 13,720 jacked-up Hilltoppers, Diddle Arena was an ideal spot for Wallace and Dillard to begin their careers. With black stars such as Haskins and the Smiths suiting up for the Western varsity that night, the crowd was accustomed to the sight of black players; and with such high expectations for the Hilltoppers, all the focus was on the home team. Two blacks on the opponents' freshman squad were of little consequence. But to the Vanderbilt fans who made the trip north, and to the Commodore varsity players who watched the first half from the bleachers, the game was transformational: the new look of SEC basketball unfolded before their eyes. Dillard pushed the ball quickly up the court, alternately feeding the ball to Welhoelter for long, open jumpers or taking the ball to the rim himself. Wallace owned the paint, leaping high for rebounds and running the floor for dunks. On one possession, an errant Commodore shot bounced high off the back rim, and before they could wince at each other over the missed opportunity, Vanderbilt diehards Bob Calton and John Thorpe were dumbfounded to see Wallace shoot straight up in the air like a rocket, catch the ball, and slam it through the basket in one motion. "Obviously nobody at Vanderbilt had ever been able to do that before," Calton recalled. "That was an eye-opener." In the end, Welhoelter poured in twenty-five points, Dillard sixteen, and Wallace capped off an eighteen-point, twenty-one-rebound effort with a left-handed slam dunk in the final minutes that sealed a 73–65 win for Vanderbilt.

With the evening's sour appetizer complete, the Hilltopper crowd was back in full throat as the varsity teams began their pregame warm-ups, retired Coach Diddle leading the fans in cheers. As Wallace passed by Coach Skinner, one man having made history, the other about to step out into the frenzied crowd, the youngster assured his coach that the varsity would "do OK." They both smiled.

Southwood watched most of the freshman game from the bleachers, drawing inspiration from the newcomers in black and gold. "It was exciting. Perry and Godfrey and the whole team were fun to watch," he recalled. "It helped us get started." There was one black-versus-white incident in the varsity game that sent the crowd howling—with laughter. As Commodore center Bob Bundy ran down the court after a missed shot, he collided with Haskins, who had stopped in his tracks. Bundy was unable to halt his momentum, and he ended up bear-hugging Haskins and carrying him five feet down the court before he was able to stop. "The crowd went crazy, they were laughing so hard," Bundy recalled. By game's end, however, it was the Commodores who had the last laugh, Southwood sealing the 76–70 upset with twelve consecutive free throws in the second half, including ten in the last two minutes.

In the decades that followed, members of the 1966–67 Commodore varsity credited Wallace, Dillard, and the Vanderbilt freshmen with inspiring them to victory that night in Bowling Green, and setting the tone for a surprisingly successful season. The mediocrity the sportswriters predicted never materialized; instead, the Commodores' first season without Clyde Lee was about as good as any in school history. Over the next four months, the varsity would compile a 21–5 overall record, 14–4 and second place in the SEC. On the bus ride back to Nashville, there were smiles all around. Southwood knew something special was possible. Wallace and Dillard had broken a color barrier without incident. All was good.

In his book *Forty Million Dollar Slaves*, William Rhoden describes a litany of attempts by whites to thwart the ascendance of blacks in American sports. Whether by changing the rules of a game to minimize the contributions of blacks, straight-out exclusion based on race, or other means of tilting the supposedly level playing fields of athletics, the pattern has repeated itself since the days of slavery, Rhoden writes.

Which, in retrospect, is why the news that came out of Mississippi the very next day after Wallace and Dillard's triumphant debut was utterly predictable: the University of Mississippi, just four years removed from James Meredith's tumultuous desegregation of the school, canceled both of its freshman games against Vanderbilt. What better way to limit opportunities for blacks in the SEC than to deny their very existence?

Ole Miss coach Eddie Crawford announced that he had suddenly discovered two glitches in the Rebels' freshman schedule, and the Rebs would be nixing both of their games against the Commodores, one scheduled for January 14 in Oxford and the other for February 11 in Nashville. Crawford claimed that he had double-booked his squad on January 14, and instead of hosting Vanderbilt, the Rebel freshmen would instead be taking on John C. Calhoun State Junior College. As for the February 11 game, Crawford told *Sports Illustrated*, the Rebels would not make the 240-mile trip to Nashville "on account of school work." The magazine noted that in place of the supposedly too-taxing trip to Vandy, the Rebels would instead make a 175-mile trip to Newton, Mississippi, to take on Clarke Memorial College. Crawford and Ole Miss athletic director Tad Smith, whom *Sports Illustrated* hinted may have been the actual decision maker behind the cancellations ("[Crawford] may only have been doing what he was told"), denied that the presence of Wallace and Dillard had anything to do with the announcement. "You newspaper people are always trying to make something out of nothing," the coach told a caller from the *Vanderbilt Hustler*. If it was all a coincidence, that was nearly impossible to believe anywhere outside Mississippi. "Everybody,"

Wallace said, "knew that wasn't true." A *Hustler* cartoon aptly captured the sentiment in Nashville: an Ole Miss basketball coach is pictured reading a newspaper with the headline, "First Negro Basketball Players in S.E.C. Spark Vandy Frosh." The coach smacks his head, exclaiming, "Oh my . . . I just remembered a schedule conflict."

More than forty years later, Crawford continued to deny there was any racial motivation behind the decision, claiming he didn't remember the controversy and that it sounded more like something that would have happened at Mississippi State. That it does indeed sound like something that would have happened at the state's other major public university merely strengthens the case against the Rebels: the Vanderbilt cancellations marked the latest chapter in a well-chronicled history of Magnolia State universities going to great lengths to avoid playing basketball against blacks. In 1956 Mississippi State president Ben Hilburn and athletic director Dudy Noble (for whom the Bulldogs' football stadium is now named) demanded that their basketball team return home to Starkville rather than play a holiday tournament championship game against host school Evansville, which had one black player on its squad. "I believe in what the people of the state stand for," Hilburn wrote to a fan who had applauded the president's defense of segregation. "I will not, in my official actions, deviate from long-established policies and cherished traditions." In 1959, 1961, and 1962, MSU won the SEC regular season championship and earned invitations to the NCAA Tournament, but the university declined the coveted bids in each instance rather than allow its white players to play against blacks. When Crawford canceled the games against Vanderbilt, he upheld another "cherished tradition" in Mississippi: no black opponents had ever suited up against the Rebel or Bulldog basketball teams on their home courts. A month and a half later, when the varsity Commodores traveled to Mississippi without the freshman team, a group of Oxford citizens extended their finest southern hospitality, meeting the Vanderbilt team at the airport and driving their guests through the fog to the school's brand-new Coliseum. These Commodores were more than welcome.

Despite the discouraging news out of Oxford, the vibe around the Commodore program was overwhelmingly positive in the aftermath of the win at Western Kentucky. Vanderbilt's home opener against SMU at Memorial Gym on December 3 was attended by a sellout crowd of 9,222, and just before the game, it was announced that the university would be adding twenty-four hundred seats to the Gym prior to the following season. Commodore basketball tickets remained the hottest thing in town, and with Wallace on the way up to the varsity in a year, demand was expected to intensify. Prior to the varsity's game against SMU, the freshman team played Pensacola Junior College, and Wallace dominated the action, scoring twenty-three points while making eleven of fifteen shots from the field and grabbing twenty-four rebounds, just three shy of Clyde Lee's freshman record and seven short of the total rebounds collected by the entire Pensacola team. Wallace's playing career would come to be marked by near constant stress, but for now, he was having fun. When Middle Tennessee State University came to Memorial, it provided a chance for Wallace to square off against one of his old black high school rivals. MTSU's Ken Riley was a six-foot-six leaper whom Wallace described as a "savage dunker." Back on the playgrounds of North Nashville, the powerful Riley had earned the nickname "Khrushchev," the Cold War comparison to the Soviet leader validating Riley's reputation as one bad dude. The freshman game took on the air of one of those rollicking dunkathons back at Pearl High, with Wallace and Riley exchanging thunderous jams to the delight of the crowd. By game's end, Wallace had produced six dunks and nineteen rebounds, but on three occasions he had blocked Blue Raider shots only to see his opponents scoop up the rebound and score, and Vanderbilt lost the game 68–64 in overtime. The loss to his old rival was disappointing, but the biggest blow came in the pregame warm-ups when Pat Toomay, the team's second-leading rebounder, tore cartilage in his knee, an injury that spelled the end of his days on the Commodore basketball team. Wallace would lose another ally two years later, but for now Toomay's departure carried significant ramifications for both black freshmen. "He was the only white guy who could really relate to us," Dillard recalled, "and it created a big void when he left."

Wallace suffered an injury of his own around this time, a groin pull that limited his mobility, leaping ability, and productivity for the entire second half of the season. Wallace played through the pain, a suffering that was intensified, he said, because nobody seemed too concerned about his well-being, especially a vocal few of the diehards who attended practices and sat close to the court at games. He could hear them hollering. *You're just like a horse, you get out there and play! You play until we're finished with you! You just play through it!* "I felt really abused by that," Wallace recalled. "I wanted more treatment for the pain, not to be treated like an animal." With the freshman team now losing more often than not (the squad was 6–2 before Toomay's injury, 2–5 after it), his hamstring hurting, his mother increasingly showing signs of a serious illness, and feelings of isolation on campus intensifying, Wallace grew painfully lonely and discontent. He spent long nights alone in his dormitory, thinking about what lay ahead of him in the classroom and on the basketball court, praying to God for the support he wasn't finding anywhere else.

He found a brief reprieve at Memorial Coliseum in Lexington, Kentucky, home of Adolph Rupp's Wildcats, the team that to some had symbolized the old, white, establishment brand of basketball in the previous season's title game against Texas Western. Still, it was Kentucky that gladly stepped into the void when Mississippi State turned down its NCAA tournament bids, and

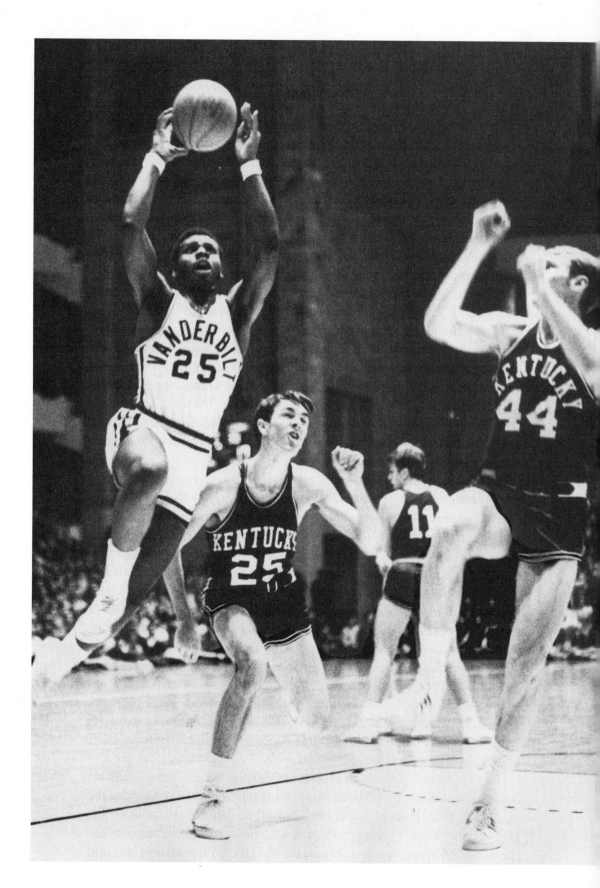

Rupp routinely scheduled games against teams with black players, home and away. UK fans, Wallace concluded over his four years at Vanderbilt, cared only about winning games and watching good basketball. In an atmosphere like this he could relax, play his game, not worry about inciting a riot with an accidental elbow, not be subjected to a barrage of epithets. Best of all, he could test his skills against elite competition. Playing against Kentucky, he believed, was as close as it came in the SEC to what he imagined it would have been like if he had left the South and gone to a school in the Big Ten: basketball for basketball's sake, no extra baggage.

Almost.
After more than four decades, the particulars of individual plays within specific games have faded from the memories of the men associated with the 1966–67 Vanderbilt freshman basketball team, but many of them vividly remember this: Perry Wallace leaping high in the air for an offensive rebound, grabbing the ball, and slamming it through the basket over the defenseless arms of Kentucky prize recruit and future NBA star Dan Issel. It was a dramatic scene in its own right, but what came next is what everyone remembers most: an old man on the side of the court, watching the dunk and going ballistic, yelling and complaining about the affront to fundamental basketball.

It was Adolph Rupp.

"It was just a flash; I saw him as I was running back down the floor," Wallace recalled. "He was upset and I saw him over on the side complaining about the dunking." Years later, Wallace suspected that it wasn't this one dunk alone that caused Rupp to throw a fit; it was the context of it. Big Daddy Lattin's dunk over Pat Riley had set the tone for UK's loss in the NCAA title game. "And now, I was right there in the conference," Wallace recalled, "ready to dunk on his team. It must have been an exclamation point on a terrible sentence in Rupp's mind."

In addition to the dunk, Wallace scored fourteen points, grabbed twenty-one rebounds, and blocked several shots, but UK still blew out Vanderbilt 85–64. After the loss, Wallace took a seat in the stands to watch the varsity game, where he was approached by *Louisville Courier-Journal* sportswriter Billy Reed. "Life isn't one big holiday right now," Wallace told Reed, a young reporter who would go on to a distinguished career with *Sports Illu-*

(*Opposite*): Though Wallace has long remembered angering legendary Kentucky coach Adolph Rupp with a slam dunk during a freshman game during the 1966–67 season, he also recalled his games against UK, a true "basketball school" in the midst of a football conference, as the most enjoyable of his SEC career. Vanderbilt University Athletic Department.

strated. "I know it's going to be rough, and I wonder if I'll make it, but that's when I get support from God." Reed asked Wallace about the trailblazing aspect of his budding career. "Honestly, I don't have the pioneering spirit," Wallace told him. "I'm not mature enough to be a Martin Luther King or a James Meredith. I've got my hands full being a player-student without leading any civil rights movements." With Rupp's angry display fresh on his mind and an ominous road trip to Starkville, Mississippi, on the horizon, a sense of foreboding was growing in Wallace's gut. He was steeling himself for the crises he knew lay ahead. "I've got to adapt and look at things not as pressures but as challenges," the eighteen-year-old confessed to the sportswriter. "Life has been a series of challenges for me. I've just tried to meet them as they come along. If I come through now, I'll be a better man for it. It's a hit or miss thing. Either I'll make it or I won't."

13

Inferno

Some six hundred years after Dante stamped an image of the underworld firmly in the consciousness of Western civilization, in February 1967, Perry Wallace and Godfrey Dillard ventured south to a place they'd later describe as their own version of hell on earth: Starkville, Mississippi.

While Ole Miss had canceled its games against the Commodores, Mississippi State did not. In the bizarre hierarchy that defined Mississippi segregation, it was MSU, the "cow college" that turned down those three NCAA tournament bids, that had finally broken through a barrier and had set precedent by allowing its basketball team to face opponents with black players.

But to reach the point where a Vanderbilt team with two blacks could come to Starkville for a basketball game first required a surreptitious 1963 escape, a plot worthy of a Cold War spy novel.

By 1963 Ben Hilburn had been replaced as the school's president by the more moderate Dean W. Colvard, who, like Heard, had roots in North Carolina, and who, like the Vanderbilt administrator K. C. Potter, had attended the integrated Berea College in Kentucky. With the Bulldogs on the verge of winning another SEC title, Colvard announced that this time the team would participate in the NCAA Tournament unless "hindered by competent authority." This challenge to the state's power brokers ignited a firestorm of controversy just a few months after Mississippi's racial order had been shaken when James Meredith enrolled at Ole Miss. While the majority of students and citizens came out in support of Colvard, the outsider was fully aware of how divisive his position was in what still amounted, essentially, to an apartheid state. "As one who has lived in the midst of Mississippians for less than three years," he said, "I am cognizant of the hazard of this action and am fully reconciled to the possible consequences of it upon my professional career."

The state's major newspapers editorialized against this threat to the

"Southern way of life," which, the *Meridian Star* wrote, was "infinitely more precious" than athletic glory. "A crack at the mythical national championship," read a column in the *Jackson Daily News*, "isn't worth subjecting young Mississippians to the switchblade knife society that integration inevitably spawns." The media chorus was amplified by comments from some state legislators and ordinary citizens. Former Bulldog cheerleader and student body president Billy Mitts, by then a state senator, said Colvard's decision was a "low blow to the people of Mississippi." A woman from Ashland, Mississippi, wrote to Colvard that "for a coach to insult those white boys by asking them to play against Negros [*sic*] is most disgusting."

The state's college board took up the issue; one member called Colvard's decision "the greatest challenge to our way of life since Reconstruction." Another member, who supported the university president, later had a cross burned on his lawn. In the end, the board voted 8–3 in support of Colvard, but Mitts and his cronies pressed the case. Just a day before the SEC champion Bulldogs were scheduled to depart Starkville for East Lansing, Michigan, for their first-round NCAA tournament game, the ex-cheerleader convinced a like-minded judge to issue an injunction preventing the team from participating and violating the "public policies of the State of Mississippi."

Colvard figured that if he, Coach Babe McCarthy, and other high-ranking Athletic Department officials could get out of town before the court order was served, the game would go on. In one of the more bizarre scenes in the long American struggle against segregation, McCarthy, coach of an all-white team at an all-white university, was pressed against the floorboards of a booster's car and secretly driven to a dairy farm on the outskirts of town while a group of Mississippi State students hanged a segregationist—Mitts—in effigy. President Colvard was chauffeured out of state, and McCarthy and one of his assistants then drove to Memphis under the cover of darkness, where they caught a flight to Nashville. The next morning, the team's bench players arrived at Starkville's tiny airfield; if the injunction were served to them, the starters would be whisked away by private plane from another airport. When the deputy sheriff carrying the injunction never materialized, the starters were rushed to the airport, and as *Sports Illustrated*'s Alexander Wolff wrote in a detailed account of the episode, "by 9:45 a.m., the chartered Southern Airways Martin 404 Aristocrat was bound for Nashville, where it would fetch McCarthy, [Athletic Director Wade] Walker and [Assistant A.D. Ralph] Brown before continuing on to East Lansing. The passengers let out a yell when the plane went wheels up. One said, 'Now I know how those East Berliners feel when they make it past the wall.'"

In East Lansing the Bulldogs took the court against none other than George Ireland's Loyola University Ramblers—a team that started four blacks, including the two stars he had recruited from Pearl High School when no other white coaches would visit the place, Wallace's predecessors

Vic Rouse and Les Hunter. Loyola won the game 61–51 and went on to win the national championship, but McCarthy's team received a hero's welcome upon its return to Starkville: seven hundred people mobbed the airstrip to gleefully meet the team's plane. Even the Ramblers' black players respected what the Bulldogs had accomplished. "After we heard what they'd done to get there, all of us had our hats off to them," Loyola captain Jerry Harkness told Wolff.

Four years after McCarthy's team made a soaring bid for freedom by flying from Starkville to Nashville, Wallace and Dillard made the same trip in reverse, literally and figuratively. From the very moment their Southern Airways charter from Nashville landed at Bryan Field, it was obvious that any goodwill that may have been generated by the peaceful MSU-Loyola game had long since evaporated; their flight led the black freshmen straight into the heart of intolerance. None of the Vanderbilt freshman team's previous road games had taken place any farther south than Nashville, so this was Dillard's first foray into the Deep South his mother and grandmother had worried about. In Knoxville, orange-clad fans shouted racial epithets at Wallace and Dillard during the game against Tennessee, but Dillard knew this trip to Mississippi was different even before the plane had rolled to a stop on the tarmac.

"I remember landing at Mississippi State in our little prop plane on what appeared to be a gravel runway, and I looked out the window and said, 'This is backwoods,'" Dillard recalled. "And then we get to the hotel and there are students milling around yelling at us and banging on the bus. We go inside the hotel and they had a little eating place roped off for our team. I remember seeing the white folks turning around and looking at us. We knew we were in trouble."

Sleep did not come easily for Wallace and Dillard at the Holiday Inn that night, as equal parts anticipation, fear, adrenaline, and curiosity formed a potent stimulant. Prior to the trip, Wallace told the *Tennessean*'s Bibb that he hadn't thought much about what might lay ahead in Starkville. "Schoolwork and basketball practice keep a man's mind on other things," he said. "However, I certainly do wonder just what sort of reception we'll get." In truth, Wallace had thought quite a bit about the trip, bracing himself for the hatred he suspected he and Dillard would encounter. Years later, he described road trips to Mississippi as a form of Russian roulette where there was no hope of avoiding the bullet. "You knew you were going to get hit in some way," he recalled. "It was just a question of how bad was it going to be."

On game day, as the Commodores prepared to head over to Mississippi State's five-thousand-seat "New Gym," which had replaced the "Tin Gym" back in 1950, Wallace contemplated his surroundings. He was troubled by what he knew of Mississippi: less than three years had passed since Chaney,

Goodman, and Schwerner had been murdered only about sixty miles from Starkville, and less than a year had passed since James Meredith had been shot in broad daylight, even while surrounded by FBI agents, in Hernando, Mississippi, on his "March Against Fear." Because Wallace knew all this, he was most troubled by the *unknown*. "That's the problem for pioneers," he recalled. "You don't know what could possibly happen to you. When you don't know what's going to happen, the sky is the limit."

It is possible that the cramped visitors' locker room in the bowels of the New Gym was *always* a stinking hellhole, but when Godfrey Dillard and Perry Wallace walked into it on February 27, 1967, they took stock of their surroundings and believed that what they saw and what they smelled were directed squarely at them, a pair of unwanted guests: toilets overflowing with excrement, towels scattered everywhere across a dirty floor. "By this time, we had been to a few other SEC schools so we had some reference, and this was just filthy and it was shocking," Dillard recalled. "To me and Perry, we immediately felt like it was an attack on us."

Game time approached, and the Commodores made their way from the locker room to the portal that led to the court, most of the players mentally preparing for a basketball game, Dillard and Wallace bracing themselves for the unknown, feeling like they were at the very apex of a roller coaster, their stomachs briefly suspended as if at zero gravity.

And then out of the tunnel and onto the court and *boom*, the sensation of the rapid drop, the too-bright arena lights searing their eyes, the cacophony of cowbells, the piercing screams from the fans jammed so close to the court, flashes of light and sound, and eruptions of hate from every direction. Two young black kids exposed and surrounded in the heart of Mississippi, there for the taking.

Go home, niggers! We're going to kill you, coons! Why didn't you go to Jackson State where you belong?! We're gonna lynch you! Shoe polish! Leroy! Forty years later, the scene stood out in Bob Bundy's mind; in his memory, as the Commodore freshmen warmed up under one basket, "the whole bleachers were full of football players," "verbally harassing" Perry and Godfrey. When Vanderbilt switched baskets, the football players followed them across the gym, continuing the barrage. Wallace's blood ran cold; he had trouble gripping the basketball, his fingers gone stiff and numb. His mind raced to scenes from his childhood: the carload of thugs who pointed the gun at him as he waited for the bus, the bullies who harassed him as he walked to school, the skirmishes he witnessed outside the lunch-counter sit-ins. He had seen racism bring out the worst in people. But this was entirely different.

"Not that high-class bigotry is worthy of praise, but these guys at Mississippi State were just low-class, crude, ignorant rednecks," Wallace recalled. "And they were screaming and hollering and insulting us, calling us names, saying they were going to kill us, and as the game started, it got worse. You had a whole gym full of people just raining down on you. Here they were, all these Mississippi bigots, so loud and so close, and it was harsh. It was just awful, and it was the first time I'd ever dealt with this kind of stuff." Mack Finley, a white graduate student at Mississippi State who had grown up in West Tennessee, was shocked by the epithets directed at Wallace. "It was the ugliest thing I have ever seen in my life, the way they treated that man," Finley recalled. "I was ashamed to be from [the South]. I have seen a lot of ugly things, but nothing like that."

Dillard's uniform grew cold and wet as the first half wore on, soaked with his own sweat, but also from spit flying out of the stands, and from Cokes dumped on him when he ventured too close to the sideline. "These people are crazy," he whispered to Wallace at one point. The game clock ticked down under five seconds before halftime, Vanderbilt trailing 43–39. Wallace found himself with the ball sixty feet from the basket, and he threw it downcourt in desperation. Team manager Paul Wilson watched Wallace launch the errant heave, simultaneously hearing a shriek from the crowd he'd remember four decades later. *Shoooot, nigggggggerrrrrrr!*

At halftime, the Commodores filed back into the decrepit locker room, which now, given the added context of what he'd just experienced out on the court, felt to Wallace like the dungeon of a medieval castle. "Bear in mind the dramatic effect of that," Wallace recalled. "It's not like if we were at the Ritz we would have felt a whole lot better, but in some ways, we actually would have. At least you'd have felt like you had made it to the big time. But this dirty, rinky-dink place just accentuated how horrible the situation was. You're in this dump, and you have all this hell breaking loose. We knew we were going to have to go out into this madness for another half, and you don't know if anything worse is a possibility."

Before Jackie Robinson broke Major League Baseball's color line, Brooklyn Dodgers general manager Branch Rickey sat Robinson down to talk about the heckling and threats he was about to encounter. Rickey consulted with a sociologist to discuss ways to approach skeptical white fans on the topic of integration. Robinson's managers repeatedly stood firm against white players on the Dodgers' and opponents' rosters who protested Robinson's presence. Black fans by the tens of thousands showed up in Chicago and Cincinnati and other National League outposts to support Robinson during his rookie season of 1947. Here in the madness of Starkville, Wallace and Dillard received no such show of support: they scanned the crowd and found no black faces. And not here in Mississippi nor back in Nashville nor anywhere else did Coach Skinner or Coach Garr ever sit the Commodores down and talk about the unique nature of their teammates' situation, the need to show support on the road, to be sensitive to the catcalls, to do their parts to defuse tense situations, to have their teammates' backs.

As Coach Garr delivered his halftime pep talk, the white players listened intently to his instructions, absorbing direction on which offense to run, the adjustments the Commodores would make on defense, oblivious to the torment Wallace and Dillard were experiencing. Expected to be listening to the exhortations of their coach, the black freshmen turned their focus inward. "We were trying to be in denial," Wallace later told Gaillard. "We didn't want it to be this bad. But it was such an outrageous display of racism, like the blaring of trombones. The crowd was starting to shatter our denial."

At that moment, Wallace recalled, there were "two dramas" taking place. There was the game itself, which, though wholly insignificant in any larger sense, was what mattered most to the coach and the other Commodores. The subplot, far more meaningful, was the centuries-in-the-making hatred directed at Wallace and Dillard and the acute pain they felt as they were supposed to be listening to the banalities of a freshman basketball halftime speech. The fact that no one acknowledged that aspect of the plot made a grotesque scene all the more bizarre, Wallace recalled.

"Nobody was saying anything about it, and that was always part of the insanity," Wallace said. "I later wondered, what would Kafka have said about this? And he would have said, 'This is too crazy for me.' Because it was that wild. Only the most far out, progressive literary and dramatic fiction could rival the insanity, the insane drama, the wild parallel themes that were going on."

Seated next to each other in the dungeon of a house of horrors as Garr continued to deliver his halftime instructions, looking for support and finding none, the powerful forward from Nashville and the cocky guard from Detroit, determined not to sink, found strength in each other. Quietly, secretly, subconsciously, the teenagers clasped hands and held tight. No words were spoken, but the message was clear: *We're going to survive this.*

The survival instinct played out in entirely different, but characteristic, ways in the second half. Wallace remained cautious, ever aware of the looming powder keg. "You needed to make sure that there wasn't some kind of incident," he said. "You bump into another player or there's a collision, and the crowd gets fired up and they decide to do something during the game or after the game. If people are threatening to kill you, saying they're going to lynch you, then you don't know whether these are just empty threats or not."

Dillard's approach could not have been more different. A foul is called, the action stops, Dillard lines up to shoot a free throw, all eyes on him, all the taunts directed at him, *nigger* this, *coon* that, and what does he do? He stops, smiles, and waves to the crowd. "I was thinking, 'Godfrey, please don't do that!'" Wallace recalled. "It worked out OK, but this was a world that I had a better sense of than he did, and my approach was that you acted like nothing was going on. Don't give them anything that can escalate the situation to another level."

Later, dribbling the ball down the court, Dillard taunted his defender all the way. *Uh oh, here I come!* "You *know* I was talking trash during the Mississippi State game," he recalled. "It became an us-against-them kind of thing. We were in the lion's den, but I was too young or too stupid or whatever to realize how dangerous the situation was. I decided that this was why we came to Vanderbilt. It wasn't about going to places like Kentucky or Knoxville. When you start talking about Alabama, Mississippi, Mississippi State, that's what it was all about."

Bravado aside, Dillard, like Wallace, remembers the game as one of the most profoundly troublesome and bizarre experiences of his life. So strange, in fact, that his mind's eye conjures up hallucinatory imagery when he thinks back on that night in Starkville. "I don't know if I'm just dreaming or what, but in my mind, when I think about that game, I see a damn chicken running across the floor. That sort of symbolizes how crazy it was."

Wallace and Dillard may have handled the pressure in entirely different ways, but each got results: keeping one eye out for trouble and another on the ball, Wallace led both teams with nineteen rebounds. Dillard was Vanderbilt's second-leading scorer, with sixteen points. Though Mississippi State won the game, 84–70, if ever two basketball players deserved a "mission accomplished, now let's get the hell out of here" moment, this was it. But with the varsity game still to come, not only would Wallace and Dillard have to stick around for that game to end before they could fly back to Nashville, they'd have to live out a cliché, jumping from the frying pan into the fire by having to watch the varsity game from the bleachers behind the Vanderbilt bench, right in the midst of the crowd. Dillard was pelted with wads of paper, but curiously enough, the crowd quickly grew tired of harassing the black players from Nashville. "Once we left the floor and took a seat in the stands, everything converted to an ordinary college basketball game, because you had white players playing against white players," Wallace said. "Godfrey and I were just sitting in the stands, and I guess they were finished with us anyway. They didn't choose to continue the taunting. That was it."

As Vanderbilt's Southern Airways charter soared back through the cold February sky from Starkville to Nashville, Wallace gazed out at the stars, thinking back to nine months earlier, when he had accepted a scholarship to Vanderbilt aware that there would be difficulties but still full of hope. That hope had been dashed in many ways and places—in the lobby of the University Church of Christ, in the girls' dormitory cafeteria, in his own lonely room—and now here in Starkville, Mississippi, came the most painful proof, he believed, that his hope had been misplaced. What could he really expect from America?

Most painful of all, he thought about his mother, had been thinking about her all day. Wallace hadn't told any of his teammates the news, but just before the game, he had learned that Hattie was on her way to Vanderbilt Hospital for emergency surgery to treat the colon cancer that would eventually take her life. Not only had he feared for his own life that day in Starkville, he had feared for that of his mother. Lying in pain in her hospital bed, Mrs. Wallace listened to her son's game on the radio.

She could hear the crowd.

14

Subversion's Circuit Rider

The bearded man attracted so much attention that nobody even noticed Little Miss Dynamite.

Brenda Lee stepped off an American Airlines flight and quietly made her way through the Nashville airport, greeted in her hometown on April 7, 1967, by an indifference that was unusual for the popular recording star.

Lee slipped by in silence, but behind her, the man who had arrived on the same plane unwittingly created a commotion as he sauntered past the departure gates. Passengers with cameras loaded with film for their vacations hurriedly snapped away, the click of the shutter and the pop of the flash adding to a hubbub that had sprung to life in an instant. "Who is this bearded man?" people asked even as they took his picture. With shoulder-length hair, scruffy beard, leather boots, and tattered jacket—purple knapsack slung over one shoulder and oversized tape recorder draped over the other—Allen Ginsberg appeared to have arrived at Berry Field from another planet.

Ginsberg was oblivious to the gawkers, but eventually he stopped to talk to the reporters who had camped out to meet the eccentric "Beat poet" and the latest guest to arrive in Nashville to speak at Vanderbilt University's highly regarded, student-run "Impact" speakers' symposium. The bohemian lifestyle was taking root in San Francisco's Haight-Ashbury district that spring, but in Nashville, everything about Ginsberg was so conspicuously different that even his facial hair made headlines ("Bearded Ginsberg in Spotlight," the *Tennessean* proclaimed). A tape recorder? What's it for? reporters asked. "So I can record poetry anytime I feel like writing something, and just in case I run into the police," he answered. The purple knapsack, what's in it? "A notebook, address book, and parka, just in case I decide to go mountain climbing," he replied.

Hippie appearance aside, that Ginsberg's presence attracted attention was quite an accomplishment, considering the eclectic roster of notables who had also arrived in Nashville for the two-day affair. There was Hedley Donovan, editor-in-chief of *Time* magazine, Indian ambassador P. K. Banerjee, syndicated columnist and author Rowland Evans, and the headliner of that evening's opening session, the thirty-eight-year-old Nobel Peace Prize–winning minister from Atlanta, Martin Luther King Jr. Almost exactly one year later, King would be assassinated on another visit to Tennessee, and on this visit to Nashville, he was in the midst of one of the most contentious periods of his career, drawing criticism from the left and the right, from blacks and whites. Already losing favor among younger, more radical blacks, King created a rift within traditional civil rights circles in the days leading up to his Vanderbilt appearance by becoming increasingly outspoken in his opposition to the war in Vietnam. He claimed that the cost of the war was diverting resources from the poor in America and that the United States, as the "world's leading exporter of violence," was losing its moral compass. Some black critics feared that adding a strong antiwar message to the civil rights agenda could endanger tenuous political alliances, undermine white support for the movement, and lend ammunition to opponents on the right who portrayed King and other civil rights advocates as un-American. Strom Thurmond, the states-rights, anti–"big government" senator from South Carolina who was also scheduled to speak at Impact the following day, took the bait. "King is openly espousing Communist aims and goals for the world revolution," the segregationist and former presidential candidate claimed. "He has dropped the pretense that he is fighting for human rights."

But whatever commotion Ginsberg stirred, whatever interest there was in the charismatic and controversial King, nothing compared to the howls of outrage swirling around an Impact speaker who had arrived in Nashville several days early, twenty-five-year-old Stokely Carmichael, the country's most outspoken and polarizing advocate for "Black Power."

Born in Trinidad, Carmichael moved to New York as an eleven-year-old (becoming a US citizen in the process) and later attended the prestigious Bronx High School of Science before enrolling at Howard University. After graduating from Howard, Carmichael joined the Student Non-Violent Coordinating Committee (SNCC), an organization founded in North Carolina in 1960. SNCC originally was committed to nonviolence and desegregation, counting among its early leaders Nashville civil rights icons such as James Lawson, Marion Barry, John Lewis, and Diane Nash. By the mid-1960s, the influence of this core group had waned; and, disillusioned by what they saw as the ambivalence or ineffectiveness of Democratic Party allies, mainstream civil rights organizations, and white SNCC volunteers, Carmichael and other young black SNCC members began leading the organization in a more militant direction. In May 1966 Carmichael was elected SNCC chairman at an organizational meeting in Kingston Springs, Tennessee, outside Nashville, representing what historian Clayborne Carson described as "a group of

SNCC activists [who] began to see racial separatism as an ideal that would awaken the consciousness of black people and begin a new phase of the black struggle."

Though he didn't coin the phrase, Carmichael discovered the electricity generated by the term "Black Power" when he shouted it repeatedly at a rally in Greenwood, Mississippi, in June 1966—and six hundred people shouted it right back at him. While a case reasonably can be made that Carmichael intended "Black Power" to stand for principles such as self-determination, the amassing of political clout, and the building of strong black institutions more than the violent connotations of the phrase, he was purposely ambiguous in its use. "SNCC workers' satisfaction with the black power slogan," Carson wrote, "was based largely on the extent to which it aroused blacks and disturbed whites." Carmichael's historical role, Carson wrote, was to "arouse large segments of the black populace by reflecting their repressed anger and candidly describing previously obscured aspects of their racial oppression." When established civil rights leaders and their white supporters denounced the Black Power message, Carmichael became more provocative, furthering his reputation as a highly quotable demagogue. Speaking in Cleveland in August 1966, Carmichael was in rare form: "When you talk about black power, you talk about bringing this country to its knees," he proclaimed. "When you talk of black power, you talk of building a movement that will smash everything Western civilization has created."

At a time when Perry Wallace, Godfrey Dillard, and the other black students at Vanderbilt were dealing with injustices big and small, discovering that promises of equal treatment were often hollow, searching for opportunities to express themselves on a southern, white campus, and taking the first steps to organize themselves in a meaningful way, they looked outward for cues on how to proceed. King and Carmichael embodied the two most likely paths. The fact that those two men were about to set foot on the Vanderbilt campus, about the last place in the world anyone would expect to find them, was as mind-boggling as it was welcome. "It was really daring and innovative and radical," Eileen Carpenter recalled, "and that was amazing for Vanderbilt at that time." Though King's appeal was diminishing among many of their generation, some students still were drawn to his belief in nonviolence and the inherent benefits of an integrated society. Others found Carmichael's provocative brand of rhetoric more in tune with the times. Wallace was attracted to certain elements of each approach but understood how his role as a pioneer constrained his options. "Stokely Carmichael represented the kind of romantic, overtly courageous presence that attracts people in a group who feel unfairly treated. Old and young alike may fall under the spell of an outrageously unapologetic champion of justice for black people," Wallace said. "For me, however, there was the effect of the past—and my clear, albeit modestly expressed, focus on the harsh realities of the present. I couldn't act out those romantic dramas because of what I knew would be the consequences."

While Wallace, Carpenter, and their classmates eagerly anticipated hearing from Carmichael and King, the white organizers of Impact were equally enthused to have landed such compelling speakers. The attendance record of thirty-five hundred set when Barry Goldwater spoke at the 1966 symposium was sure to fall; Impact '67 was certain to be a rousing success. Beyond the campus borders, however, reaction to the Carmichael invitation was ferociously negative. At the *Nashville Banner*, publisher Jimmy Stahlman was apoplectic over the thought of a "hate-spieling interloper" like Carmichael taking the podium at Memorial Gym of all places, a building (vacant now that basketball season had ended) dedicated to Vanderbilt's greatest heroes, the students and alumni who had given their lives in World War II. That Vanderbilt would extend an invitation to "subversion's circuit-rider" so he could "spew his venom and huckster his inflammatory wares" was to invite "the anarchy of mob rule." Chancellor Heard could say all he wanted about academic freedom and claim that it was the students who ran Impact who had extended the invitation to "the Jamaica-born [sic] firebrand," but Stahlman placed the blame squarely on the shoulders of the chancellor.

The newspaperman wasn't alone in his deliciously colorful brand of hyperbolic outrage. WLAC radio managing editor F. C. Sowell mailed listeners a postcard protesting Carmichael's appearance, claiming that Carmichael's aim was to "take over this country by force." Rather than sit idly by like the Germans who "laughed at Adolph Hitler when he was screaming his way to the top," Sowell encouraged his followers to sign and return the postcard to the chancellor. From Vanderbilt alumni and supporters came more mail: Marvin Wright, Class of '26, sent Heard a ten-dollar check along with a note claiming that "rabble rousers" like Carmichael and Reverend Asbury had tarnished the university's reputation, while Eula Donnell sent a postcard from Nashville's Sylvan Park neighborhood with a simple, if slightly inaccurate, plea: "Please!! Don't let that scum Carmichael Stokely contaminate your campus!" Nashville Chamber of Commerce executive vice president Edward Shea said that Carmichael was no more welcome in town than "the head of the Ku Klux Klan, or the head of the Nazi party, or a head Communist." At American Legion Post 5, members adopted a resolution scolding Vanderbilt for dignifying through its invitation "an individual . . . that reeks of scum, a veritable cesspool of treasonous un-Americanism." Not to be outdone, the Tennessee state senate passed a resolution disapproving of Vanderbilt's invitation to a demagogue who "spread[s] his racist poison and his anti-American doctrine throughout the length and breadth of the United States."

From the left came calls for tolerance. Nashville rabbi Randall Falk dismissed Carmichael as "an immature youngster" who thrived on publicity. "We shouldn't play into his hands," Falk warned. "The less notice he receives, the sooner he will depart." John Seigenthaler's *Tennessean* editorial page took a swipe at the *Banner* and the legislature, claiming that "those who would ban Mr. Carmichael fail to understand the significance of the phenomena that give him standing. . . . The problem is not Stokely Carmichael—he is just the voice. The problem is that more than a few people listen to him. Society needs to find out why." Vanderbilt Board of Trust member Mary Jane Werthan wrote Impact chairman Robert Eager to praise him for assembling such a rousing group of speakers. "I am so happy when I see evidence of 'stirrings' among the students; I am convinced that opportunities must be increasingly found for the airing of controversial as well as purely academic topics." For Eager, a senior from Valdosta, Georgia, who among other responsibilities was charged with selling enough tickets to fill Memorial Gym and cover the event's expenses, the more controversial the speakers, the better. Eager, a friend would say years later, was no radical 1960s hippie bent on re-creating Cal-Berkeley in Nashville. Rather, he was a "stereotypical Deep South college student, except that he ran this wild speakers program," said former *Hustler* editor Chuck Offenburger. "He had enough showman in him to recognize that it was A-OK if someone was absolutely outrageous in what they were saying, because he knew that meant it would be a great program."

The 1967 Impact session was just Vanderbilt's fourth such symposium, but already the event had gained national acclaim. Goldwater was so impressed with the 1966 session that he deemed it the "best college presentation of its kind in the country." Inspired by Heard's credo that "we consider the nation to be our campus and the world to be our proper concern," students had launched Impact in 1964 around the topic of "The South in Transition," featuring speakers Ralph McGill, publisher of the *Atlanta Constitution*, and William Vaughn, president of Eastman Kodak. The ante was raised significantly the following year, when Governor George Wallace of Alabama and NAACP executive secretary Roy Wilkins presented divergent views on race. Gaillard, whose father had served as an Alabama judge with Wallace, had been eager to hear his home-state governor, and had the honor of accompanying Governor Wallace backstage prior to his remarks. Any admiration he felt for the man evaporated once Wallace, just two years removed from his infamous segregationist stand at the University of Alabama, opened his mouth. "My father had told me that it wasn't about race with Wallace, that it was about state's rights, and so that's what I was hoping to find, a man who was much more moderate than you might be led to believe," Gaillard recalled. "But I didn't find that at all. As we were walking out to where he was going to speak, he said to me, 'Do you think there will be any niggers tonight?' There was a young [black] woman from Fisk University who came over to hear him speak, and she got up to ask a question, and [Wallace] was very condescending. Her voice was trembling, and he said, 'What's that honey, you'll have to speak up. I can't hear you.' He leered at her, and said, 'You're mighty pretty, though.' It was just mean, and it was embarrassing to be around this crude little racist. Then at that same Impact, Roy Wilkins spoke and he was just the consummate gentleman. He was intelligent and erudite, and you put these things together, and it was like, 'God this is embarrassing, this guy is governor of Alabama, this is where we're from and this is who we picked to be our leader.'"

Gaillard wasn't alone in being profoundly moved by what he experienced. By 1966 the event had become so popular that the Impact committee's budget more than doubled to eighty-five hundred dollars; more than forty visiting college delegations came to Nashville to hear speakers including Goldwater, former Russian prime minister Alexander Kerensky, and South Vietnamese statesman Tran Van Dinh; the event was covered by the AP and UPI wire services; and seven hundred students turned out for a series of lunches with the speakers.

Led by Eager, preparations for the April 1967 Impact began as soon as the school year started in the fall of 1966, with the first round of invitations mailed on October 5 to potential speakers including Robert F. Kennedy, William F. Buckley, Arthur Schlesinger, and Eugene McCarthy. Carmichael's invitation was sent October 6, King's November 2. A total of eighty-seven speakers were invited over the next five months, including President Lyndon Johnson, John Steinbeck, J. Edgar Hoover, John Updike, Norman Mailer, Edward Albee, U Thant, Henry Ford II, Ayn Rand, Sidney Poitier, and Vladimir Nabokov. In the end eight men accepted the invitation and the two-hundred-dollar honorarium (this at a time when the going rate for comparable speakers ranged from twelve hundred dollars for Senator Jacob Javits to three thousand dollars for radio personality Paul Harvey).

Chairman Eager left nothing to chance, with around two hundred students assigned to committees in charge of everything from publicity, displays, and ticket sales to research, security, and speaker hospitality. Students assigned to welcome each speaker were provided detailed instructions to ensure the guest's comfort: "The host and hostess should go to the Holiday Inn and register for their speaker before they go to meet him at the airport. When they have registered, they should go to the room to (1) set the thermostat at the appropriate temperature setting (2) check the television set to make sure that the sound and picture are good (3) check the bathroom to make sure that soap has been provided (4) check to make sure that there are several clean glasses and (5) request another room if the one which has been assigned is not located in a quiet section of the motel."

Correspondence with confirmed speakers was naïvely earnest; one wonders about the reaction of Martin Luther King Jr. when he received a letter from Eager with a helpful list of possible topics to consider, as if one of the greatest public speakers of the twentieth century may have suddenly been at a loss for words when faced with the prospect of speaking to Vanderbilt students. (Eager's list read: "Suggestions for Speech to Impact Symposium: 1. What do you view as the probable culmination of the civil rights movement? 2. What do you see as the ideal role of the Negro individual in American society? 3. What are the major problems which still face the civil rights movement?") Eager was calculating when it served his purposes, however. On March 13, a few weeks after Carmichael had accepted his invitation but before it was announced publicly, Eager mailed a letter to the parents of Vanderbilt students seeking financial contributions to underwrite the program. "We are most pleased that Senator Strom Thurmond of South Carolina is the fifth speaker to accept our invitation," Eager wrote to this mostly conservative audience, leaving the remaining roster of speakers to the imagination.

By the time Ginsberg, King, and Thurmond arrived in Nashville, the transformation of Memorial Gymnasium was complete. Basketballs were put into storage, practice hoops set aside in the sweltering bowels of the arena. As Perry Wallace, Godfrey Dillard, and thousands of other attendees entered the north lobby of the gym for that night's opening session (featuring remarks by Rowland Evans and King), they were greeted by forty-by-sixty-inch black-and-white photographs depicting various current events. Straight ahead, a statue entitled "Young Man" was flanked by original *Time* magazine cover portraits, and behind that display, the Vanderbilt bookstore had set up shop to sell copies of books written by the Impact speakers. Members of the Metro Police Department's intelligence division had cased the joint on two separate occasions, and eighty-five officers, including forty in plain clothes, were scattered throughout the lobby and the bleachers. Six traffic officers were stationed outside the gym, and patrol cars circled the perimeter, ready for any disturbances.

Passing through the lobby and into the expanse of the gymnasium, visitors were greeted by an awe-inspiring sight: above and behind the wooden stage and the speakers' podium emblazoned with the university seal, stretching the entire width of the basketball court and towering from ceiling to floor, hung what was dubbed the "world's largest" American flag, lending an imposing splash of color and gravitas to the scene.

In the weeks leading up to the symposium, Carmichael and his staffers were highly interested in King's itinerary, phoning Eager to ascertain the preachers' plans. One suspects it was a photo opportunity that Carmichael was after: the rare chance to be seen in the same frame with the esteemed King would cast an air of heightened legitimacy upon the upstart. So it was no surprise that on Impact's opening night, after walking into the gym, Carmichael made a beeline for King. Carmichael talked up King before the program started and sat beside him in the second row of seats as Evans delivered Impact's opening speech, a rundown of the syndicated columnist's opinions on LBJ (Johnson, who had recently visited Nashville in celebration of Andrew Jackson's 200th birthday, "would certainly be a candidate in 1968"), possible Republican challengers (Richard Nixon was too much of a "wheeler-dealer and tricky politician to win"), and the Vietnam War (a "continued stalemate" appeared likely, Evans said, finally getting one right).

Conspicuous in a light summer suit, white shirt, and dark sunglasses, it was Carmichael who was first to leap to his feet to lead a standing ovation when King was introduced following Evans' remarks. Before King could make his way to the podium, Carmichael tugged the Reverend by his arm—and indeed a photo of the forced embrace ran in the next morning's *Tennessean*. King appeared none too pleased with Carmichael's maneuver. "You could tell that he did not want to be seen shaking hands with Stokely Carmichael, but Stokely nailed him anyway. I could read that face," Assistant Dean of Men K. C. Potter recalled. Everyone, it seemed, had an agenda for King's introduction. Reverend Asbury noticed that about half the crowd participated in the standing ovation, a group that included Vice Chancellor Rob Roy Purdy but not Chancellor Heard. "Now, how could you not stand in that situation?" Asbury recalled. "Heard was a diplomat, and that would have been tipping his hand."

Just three days earlier, King had delivered what would become known as one of his most important and controversial speeches, a sermon at the Riverside Church in New York in which he condemned the "madness" of the war in Vietnam and its disproportionate toll on America's poor. Finding it ever harder to convince the "desperate rejected and angry young men" in the northern ghettos that social change could come most meaningfully through nonviolent action, King was struck by the hypocrisy that was so visible to those youth. "They asked if our own nation wasn't using massive doses of violence to solve its problems, to bring about the changes it wanted," King said at Riverside. "Their questions hit home, and I knew that I could never again raise my voice against the violence of the oppressed in the ghettos without having first spoken clearly to the greatest purveyor of violence in the world today—my own government." When asked by reporters in Nashville about having to appear on the same program with Carmichael, King shrugged aside his differences with the militant. "[I would] rather appear with Carmichael than Thurmond," he said.

Dressed in his familiar dark suit and tie, King steered clear of the antiwar message in his remarks at Vanderbilt, though he noted that if the country could spend "$35 billion on an ill-considered war in Vietnam" and "$20 billion to put a man on the moon . . . surely we can spend a few billions of dollars to put God's children on their own two feet right here on earth." He defended his belief in nonviolence ("I abhor violence," he said. "I think God made all of us for something higher and nobler") while acknowledging the forces that led to violent outbursts in urban areas. "I will continue to condemn riots because they cause more social problems than they solve," he said. "But we must condemn the conditions which make people feel compelled to riot. As long as justice for all people is postponed, there will continue to be riots. . . . The summers of riots are caused by the winters of delay." Some observers said they felt King appeared tired on stage, and forty years after the fact, only one passage in his speech stood out: he correctly predicted that in Thurmond's remarks the next day, the senator would quote a passage from the Bible calling on servants to obey their masters. A serviceable speech in King's long anthology, but one that resonated deeply with certain members of the audience.

"You just walked out of there so mesmerized and inspired that there was hope," Bedford Waters recalled. "It was the first time I had seen him, and it was an overwhelming experience."

As King left campus and returned to the airport, the bearded man who had made his triumphant entrance to Nashville that morning capped off the eventful day in signature style. Repeatedly chanting "Allah" and jingling small cymbals, Ginsberg led a group of one hundred students in a three-hour séance in the basement of the Branscomb Quadrangle dormitory in which he "extolled the virtues of LSD, the fantasy of masturbation and the complete awareness achieved during sexual intercourse," according to a *Hustler* account of the bizarre session. Impact '67 was only a few hours old and already it had stirred the campus like never before. As monumental as the day's events had seemed at the time they were occurring, however, nearly everything that happened on this first day of Impact would almost immediately be forgotten, overshadowed by what would take place on Saturday, April 8. As Ginsberg's cymbals rang, King's flight back to Atlanta soared south, and Waters returned to his dormitory energized by King's remarks, a time bomb was already ticking. The worst race riot in Nashville history was about to explode.

For the students who volunteered to help put on the speakers' series, the prospect of arriving early at the Holiday Inn to check the thermostat was a challenge they could handle; fielding bomb threats, not so much. Yet as he stood outside Reverend Asbury's campus office, Frye Gaillard, twenty-year-old history major and descendent of southern aristocracy, found himself trying to convince four young men that they could trust him, that he had everything taken care of.

That those men were George Ware (SNCC's campus coordinator), Willie Ricks (credited with popularizing the "Black Power" slogan), Eldridge Cleaver (Black Panther and author of the soon-to-be-published book of essays *Soul on Ice*), and Stokely Carmichael made the task just a little difficult.

"We have received death threats [against Carmichael], but we've arranged

Carmichael made a beeline for Martin Luther King Jr. as soon as he arrived at Memorial Gym. "You could tell that [King] did not want to be seen shaking hands with Stokely Carmichael," Assistant Dean of Men K. C. Potter recalled. "But Stokely nailed him anyway." Vanderbilt University Special Collections and University Archives.

for police protection, and everything will be fine," Gaillard told the black militants.

"Police protection is a contradiction in terms," Gaillard remembers one of the men replying with obvious irritation. "The police are an occupying army."

"But there's this black officer we've worked with before," Gaillard said, "and he's very good and professional and I know it will be OK."

Gaillard sensed this made no difference. He feared the men might walk out, that Carmichael might give up on Impact.

"Look guys, we've stuck our necks out here, too, and you need to trust us on this," he said. "There's no hidden agenda. We want [Carmichael] to be safe here."

Grudgingly, the entourage consented. Carmichael would stay.

"They must have thought I was the dumbest white kid they had ever en-

Stokely Carmichael and Vanderbilt chaplain Bev Asbury eat lunch with a group of students at a frat house prior to Carmichael's Impact speech on April 8, 1967. "At first [Carmichael and Eldridge Cleaver] wouldn't really talk to me," Asbury recalled, "but I persisted and they relaxed and opened up and talked about Black Power and the weakness of the King movement." Courtesy of Bev Asbury.

countered," Gaillard recalled. "I think I was protected by being so incredibly naïve. They must have thought, 'This guy may be really dumb, but I don't think he's lying.'"

Problem averted, Gaillard and the foursome hung out for a while, touring the campus and eventually making their way inside Memorial Gym.

"That," one of the visitors proclaimed, "is a big fucking flag."

Having arrived in Nashville in late March so that he could spend time on the Tennessee A&I and Fisk campuses recruiting student volunteers for SNCC, and then returning to town two days before his Impact speech, Carmichael had drawn large crowds at both black schools for impromptu rallies: the administrations at each university refused to extend official invitations for him to speak. Carmichael challenged these black students to break out of their comfort zones and become more politically active. "You let your administration run your entire lives," he told students at Tennessee A&I on March 24. "You ought to be ashamed." On April 6, Carmichael needled students at Fisk University: "You don't have the guts to stand up and say we are black, our noses are broad, our lips are thick, our hair is matty and we are

beauuuuuutiful," he said, and this time, the crowd cheered; shouts of "Black
Power" rang out. Tie undone, collar open, yellow shirt clinging to his back
with perspiration, he questioned the relevance of nonviolence. "It's okay to
fight in Vietnam," he told the students, "but don't you touch no honky who
calls you nigger on the streets of Nashville. . . . The *Banner* says we have
come to Nashville to stir up trouble. They lie all the time. But this is the
one time they spoke the truth." The next night, on the eve of his Vanderbilt
speech, he implored twelve hundred TSU students to take over Nashville by
"whatever means necessary. Your duty is to organize these [Negro] people to
take over this city lock, stock and barrel. That's power," he shouted. "That's
black power. . . . Victims of violence should never ever apologize for their use
of violence."

Just a few hours before his speech was set to begin at Memorial Gym,
the man supposedly bent on fomenting revolution found himself in the unlikeliest of environments—sitting down for lunch at Vanderbilt's Kappa Sig
fraternity house with scores of (nearly all white) Vandy students. Reverend
Asbury had met Carmichael and his entourage when they discussed security
concerns with Gaillard, and was invited to tag along for lunch. "I sat at the
table in the frat house between Stokely and Eldridge Cleaver, and at first they
wouldn't really talk to me, but I persisted and they relaxed and opened up
and talked about Black Power and the weaknesses of the King movement,
and some of their analysis was very cogent," Asbury recalled. Wallace attended the lunch as well, and though he believed that his role as a trailblazer
left him in no position to assume a radical stance, he was intrigued by the
forceful tone struck by Carmichael and Cleaver.

"Like a lot of the black radicals, [Cleaver] had a lot of true insights about
race, about the racial experience, and the positive part about what they did
was that they were very emphatic about it and unapologetic," Wallace recalled. "Before then, there was an attitude that you were proper and well
dressed and presented yourself the very best you could. You didn't just step
out and say, 'Damn it, racism is bullshit, it's fucked up and we've just got to
stop this.' With Cleaver and Carmichael, there was a certain catharsis and
release, a certain sense of vindication. That was what those guys brought to
the picture and what was so powerful to many people."

For Wallace, part of the cathartic experience that afternoon was to live
vicariously through the retorts Carmichael issued to his white classmates.
One nattily dressed young man of the South told Carmichael that whites
would be more accepting of reasonable, "articulate" blacks than they would
of Black Power types. "No, you're still not going to let them in," Carmichael
replied. "You're still going to treat them like a bunch of niggers." The student
grew visibly angry. "That's all right, you can get mad and upset," Carmichael
continued, "just don't burn down my churches." Wallace was stunned to

see this exchange taking place on his campus. "It was really striking to have these Vanderbilt students, whom we knew well, have to confront the idea of an outrageous black man who talked about race forcefully and did not back off."

Any time traveler looking for the most condensed snapshot of the divergent and bizarre worldviews shaping American discourse in the 1960s would be hard pressed to pick a better time and place than the hours between 11:00 a.m. and 4:00 p.m. Central Time on Saturday, April 8, 1967, in Nashville, Tennessee. Before the fraternity house luncheons, Senator Thurmond had laid out his conservative case; Ginsberg took the stage at 2:00 p.m. and Carmichael would speak at 3:00.

In an address interrupted alternately by applause and snickering, Thurmond called for law and order, condemned King's tactics of civil disobedience, and drew unintentional laughter when he indeed cited the passage of scripture King had predicted the night before. Arguing that civil rights protestors had no right to break the law, Thurmond (who, unbeknownst to the public at the time, had fathered a child with his family's sixteen-year-old black housekeeper at age twenty-two) quoted St. Paul from Ephesians: "Slaves, obey your earthly masters, with fear and trembling, single-mindedly, as serving Christ." He went on to warn of an international Communist conspiracy and called for an escalation of bombing in Vietnam. With that final pronouncement, Ginsberg, seated in front of Chancellor Heard, directed a flamboyant hand gesture at the senator that he had taught the gyrating students the night before—a hex resembling a bird in flight that he called a "mudrah." And with that, Thurmond was gone less than six hours after he had arrived, telling Vanderbilt students that he refused to share a platform with King or Carmichael.

Ginsberg was up next. "A lot of the language you've heard here has been confused bullshit," he began, before continuing the very theme, rambling on about the size of President Johnson's penis and reading his recently published antiwar poem, "Wichita Vortex Sutra" ("The war is over now / Except for the souls / held prisoner in Niggertown / still pining for love of your tender white bodies O children of Wichita!").

And then, there he was, the man who had inspired death threats and the ire of American Legionnaires and the legislature. There was Stokely Carmichael in the flesh, walking to the podium, cheers bouncing off cinderblocks, his shadow dancing against the red, white, and blue backdrop.

"The honkies of the *Banner* can now leave because you will not even begin to comprehend the lecture I am about to give," he said. "You see, the lecture is on an intellectual level." Someone in the upper balcony unfurled a Confederate flag. Plainclothes police quickly snatched up the Stars and Bars,

Carmichael speaks at Memorial Gym on April 8, 1967. While Carmichael's remarks at Vanderbilt earned rave reviews for their persuasiveness, he was later blamed for riots that night in North Nashville. *Nashville Banner* Archives, Nashville Public Library, Special Collections.

and Carmichael repeated the line he had used at lunch. "That's OK, you can express your views, just don't burn down my churches." Carmichael began reading his prepared remarks, primarily lifted from an article titled "Toward Black Liberation" that he had written for the *Massachusetts Review*. As he was known to do, Carmichael matched his message to his audience, forgoing the more provocative statements he made earlier to black student audiences in favor of a more didactic explanation of the causes and goals of the Black Power movement and a critique of the supposed benefits of integration.

"The program that evolved out of the civil rights coalition was really limited and inadequate in the long run, and one affecting only a small, select portion of the black community," Carmichael said. "Its goal was to make the white community more accessible to qualified black people. And presumably each year a few more blacks, armed with their passports—a couple of university degrees—would escape into white, middle-class America, adopt the attitudes and lifestyle of that group and one day the Harlems and Wattses would stand empty—a monument to the success of integration. This approach is neither realistic nor is it particularly desirable. Even if such a program were possible, the result would be not to develop the black community as a functional and honorable segment of the total society with its own cultural identity and life patterns, but to abolish it. What we need to abolish is not the black community but the dependent and colonial status that has been inflicted upon us. That racial and cultural personality of the black community must be preserved. The community must win its liberation while preserving its cultural identity. This is the essential difference between integration as it is currently practiced and the concept of Black Power."

Carmichael's speech was widely hailed by white observers as unexpectedly persuasive and levelheaded. While only a third of the crowd stood for his introduction, two-thirds rose from their seats and cheered at the conclusion of his remarks. "He makes a compelling case for his 'black power' program," concluded *Hustler* reporter Frank Allen Philpot. "He certainly helped those who attended the symposium better understand the problems

During Carmichael's remarks, a member of the audience unfurled a Confederate flag. "That's OK, you can express your views," Carmichael responded, "just don't burn down my churches." *Nashville Banner* Archives, Nashville Public Library, Special Collections.

and frustrations of the Negro community." Bruce Nichols, a student reporter visiting from Auburn University, heaped praise on Vanderbilt for hosting the controversial speakers, calling Carmichael's address "mild but impressive." Dr. Frank Rose, the president of the University of Alabama who delivered the event's closing address, had submitted his speech to Impact leaders ahead of time, remarks that had included two paragraphs slamming what he *thought* Carmichael would say. Just days earlier, Carmichael had made inflammatory remarks at Birmingham's Miles College ("To hell with the laws of the United States. . . . If a white man tries to walk over you, kill him. One match and you can retaliate. Burn, baby, burn"), and Rose expected more of the same. When he delivered his speech, Rose dropped the references to Carmichael. "Carmichael's speech," Gaillard told colleagues that day, "was not as militant as [Rose] expected that it would be."

Impact '67 was over, a rousing success. Despite concerns over bomb threats, demonstrations, and general unruliness, the most serious offense turned out to be more of a juvenile prank than anything: one of the *Time* magazine portraits had been stolen from the Memorial Gym lobby, but it was soon returned. "Everything went just beautifully," said John Lea, chairman of the Impact student security committee. "The speakers and people who attended were extraordinarily responsible."

Eileen Carpenter drove back home to her parents' house on Whites Creek Boulevard to straighten up the place before her friends—and hopefully Carmichael, whom she had invited earlier in the week—came over to share ideas on how the students could best organize an Afro-American student association. Chancellor Heard drove home to Belle Meade for dinner, where Jean and the kids were prepared to host a meal for Hedley Donovan from *Time*, along with the *Tennessean*'s John Seigenthaler and his wife, Dolores, to celebrate the conclusion of a successful weekend. The group, which included Donovan's daughter, a student at Vanderbilt, enjoyed drinks and conversation about the day, everyone remarking about how civil Carmichael's remarks had been. Then an attendant appeared at the table, telling Seigenthaler he had a phone call. He excused himself and took the call. It was the newsroom, a frantic voice on the other end: "One of our photographers has called in—there's a riot in North Nashville!" Seigenthaler rushed back to the table to say his goodbyes; a story like this demanded his presence at the paper. He made his way around the table, shaking hands with Donovan, hugging his daughter, kissing Dolores. Heard had left the table to take a call of his own, but there was no time to wait for his return, so the editor made his way to the door. On his way, he passed a small alcove, and out stepped the chancellor, "white as a ghost."

"That was Jimmy [Stahlman]," Heard said to Seigenthaler. "He just called me a Goddamn fool."

More than four hundred members of the Nashville police took to Jefferson Street and other parts of North Nashville on the night of Carmichael's Impact speech and the ensuing riots. "The riots were the first major social disorders in the nation in 1967," historian Paul Conkin wrote, "and the worst ever in Nashville." *Nashville Banner* Archives, Nashville Public Library, Special Collections.

The photographer who called the newsroom was Dale Ernsberger, one of the first to arrive at the scene of the riots in North Nashville. No sooner had Ernsberger arrived to meet *Tennessean* reporter Frank Sutherland than the back windshield of his car was smashed to pieces by a rock thrown by rioters. Another rock bounced off the car and hit Sutherland in the head, the first of nine blows the reporter would take from rocks, bottles, and bricks that night. Later, when a cab driver hired to run film back to the paper from the scene was asked to return to the area of violence, his reply was predictable: "You haven't got enough money to pay me to go back there." Problems had started around 8:00 p.m. when the black proprietor of the University Dinner Club near Fisk University called police to remove a disorderly student from the premises. Within minutes, word spread about the incident, and a group of students, perhaps primed for action after Carmichael's poking and prodding all week, began picketing outside the restaurant. Tensions grew more heated when Nashville police arrived on the scene around 9:00 p.m., a force that eventually exceeded four hundred officers, many of whom were itching for a confrontation in this part of town after being repeatedly warned about the potential for Carmichael to cause trouble. Skirmishes between police and roving bands of students lasted well into the early morning (and continued again the following night). The riots were the "first major social disorders in the nation in 1967 and the worst ever in Nashville," historian Paul Conkin later wrote. "Whatever the several necessary conditions for what happened, the city had an easy answer—Stokely Carmichael."

Walter Murray's girlfriend, Donna, was studying in her dorm room at Fisk when some classmates entered to tell her that Carmichael was down at the restaurant and that a big crowd was building outside. She put down her biology book and headed out to see what all the commotion was about. Carmichael was nowhere to be seen ("He was probably long gone if he had ever even been there at all," she recalled), but Donna noticed a man, too old to be a student, walking back and forth through the crowd picking up rocks. Just as she said to herself, "What's he doing?" the guy began throwing the rocks at the police. Donna was stunned, and found herself glued to the spot, trying to figure out what was going on. "Cease and desist!" came the call from the police. But more rocks came flying, the cops started firing their guns into the air, and BAM!, someone threw Donna to the ground to protect her, her glasses tumbling out of sight. "I'm going to be blind in the middle of a riot!" she thought, but then she found her glasses and took off running for the safety of her dorm, passing by a group of students who were pushing a car back and forth in an attempt to flip it over. Back in her dormitory, she saw girls throwing glass bottles out their windows to their boyfriends below, encouraging them to join the fray. "It was one scary night," she recalled. Perry Wallace had been in the area, too, having followed the Carmichael entourage back to Fisk following the Vanderbilt speech when he heard that Stokely would be making one more address to students there. As Carmichael's rhetoric grew more heated, even before the incident at the restaurant, Wallace began to suspect he was in the wrong place at the wrong time and walked back to Vanderbilt.

"Stokely was talking and the students were getting fired up," Wallace recalled. "A lot of times, you can feel the thing brewing, and you can tell something is going to blow. For me there were extra dangers in getting caught up in something like that, so I just took off."

Students—nearly eight hundred strong, according to some estimates—shouted "Black Power," threw rocks and bottles, and fired pellet guns off the metal helmets of police officers, hand-me-down helmets that had been purchased from another state and thus still had "Michigan" printed on them. Police retaliated by firing shots into the air, and in at least one case, aiming a tear gas canister into a dormitory that one large band of rioters had "converted into a bastion against the police," the *Tennessean* reported. FBI agents arrived on the scene and called for reinforcements soon after midnight. Remarkably, there were relatively few injuries or arrests considering the scope of the unrest—around a dozen injuries and forty arrests.

Back at her parents' house, Carpenter had been unaware of what was happening down the street. She had the place to herself; her parents were upset that she had invited Carmichael and found something else to do for the evening. Her father, a professor at Tennessee A&I, was concerned he might lose his job if word got out that Carmichael was at his home. Carpenter considered this more of a working session than a social gathering, so as students arrived, including Godfrey Dillard, she had nothing more to offer than Kool-Aid and potato chips. Mostly she was concerned about the kinds of questions they'd ask Carmichael if he showed up. The students had been making plans to launch an Afro-American association, and Carpenter figured Carmichael would have ideas on how to organize the group. Her guests waited for Carmichael, milling around the kitchen, dining room, and living room of the Carpenters' split-level house, until Eileen's friend Cynthia McClennon came through the door, and by the look on her face, Carpenter knew something was wrong. "They're rioting at Fisk and it's really wild!" McClennon announced to the group. Carpenter turned on the radio and heard reports of the uprising, including rumors that Carmichael had started it all. She turned down the volume. "Well, because of all this," she said dejectedly, "I guess Stokely is not coming." Then, another knock on the door. In walked Allen Ginsberg, Eldridge Cleaver, and Stokely Carmichael. "I will always remember that," Dillard recalled. "We're listening to the radio about how Stokely Carmichael is out leading a riot, and the guy is standing right across from me."

Carmichael arrived at Carpenter's house expecting more action than punch, chips, and a discussion of best practices for campus organizing; he and his buddies mistakenly thought the attractive Vanderbilt student had invited them over for some socializing. Carpenter later recalled hearing some discussion of the fact that with the situation near Fisk disintegrating, Carmichael's entourage figured the Carpenter house might be a good place to lie low for a while. Cleaver seemed especially disappointed that the hostess was serving Kool-Aid rather than liquor, Carpenter recalled. "I think my parents may have had some beer in the fridge so I went looking for some, but he wasn't very gracious about it. It was supposed to be an educational meeting."

Ginsberg was relaxed and just seemed happy to be there, Carpenter recalled, and Carmichael tried to smooth things over. "I thought we were at a party," he said. "Does anybody have Aretha Franklin's new record?"

"We did have the record," recalled one of Carpenter's friends, Bobbie Jean Perdue. "So that's what we did. We didn't ask any questions, we just partied and danced with Stokely Carmichael [during] the riots at Fisk." Finally, Carmichael and crew departed, and the Vanderbilt students drove back across town to their dorms. Even at Vanderbilt, a few miles from the rioting, the situation was tense. K. C. Potter drove around town with campus police until 4:00 a.m., patrolling the area near the riots to see if the violence would spill over toward the Vanderbilt campus, and to gather intelligence in case a march against Vanderbilt was planned. Nothing of the sort ever happened, although Potter returned to campus when several bomb threats against one of the school's dormitories were called in to the campus security desk. The decision was made to evacuate the building, and bleary-eyed students began to congregate in front of the fourteen-story, red-brick dormitory that had opened in March. Its name? Carmichael Towers. Seems that the would-be bombers were unaware that the building was named for former chancellor Oliver Carmichael, believing instead that the school had so quickly fallen head over heels in love with its Impact speaker that it had already named a building for Stokely Carmichael.

"I remember after it was over I went back to my dorm room and I was scared to death," Carpenter recalled. "I thought my father might get fired, and I said, 'Oh my God, what have I done.' My intent was simply to get some information from Stokely Carmichael about what was going on at other colleges with their Afro-American associations, and I can't even remember if we discussed any of that. We had a party."

Years later, the Vanderbilt English professor Vereen Bell ran into Ginsberg at an academic conference. He asked whether the poet might ever make a return appearance to Vanderbilt for another reading.

"He said, yeah, he'd love to come back, for one thing to explain that Stokely Carmichael could not possibly have caused those riots because he and Stokely were driving around stoned," Bell recalled. "He said, 'Is there a place near Nashville called something like Murphy's Town,' and I said, 'Yes, Murfreesboro.' He said, 'We ended up in Murfreesboro and we were too stoned to get out of the car and ask anybody where we were, so we just drove around until we found our way back to Nashville.' It was somewhere the next morning after dawn had broken that they found their way back to Nashville and to all these riots that Stokely had supposedly been the fomenter and leader of."

Whether Ginsberg's tale was apocryphal or not, the historical record seems clear. While Carmichael certainly helped create an atmosphere ripe for a disturbance with his remarks on Nashville's black college campuses dating back to March, he wasn't out leading any riots, and the violence was in no way sparked by his words at Impact. "It is impossible to relate Carmichael's Vanderbilt speech to the riots," Vanderbilt historian Paul Conkin concluded, "except insofar as publicity about him increased racial tensions." Nevertheless, the "I-told-you-so" reaction from Stahlman and others who had been opposed to Carmichael's appearance was relentless.

With his typically colorful brand of outrage, Stahlman scorched Heard and Impact's student organizers in a *Banner* editorial titled "What Price Folly?" The violence, it declared, "occurred precisely as planned, and concerning it the public had been amply warned."

"The stupidity of a campus group's explanation that [Carmichael] was brought here as part of a 'search for truth' was more than matched—it was exceeded—by Vanderbilt administrative officers," read the editorial. "It is colossal stupidity indeed, to suggest that one must lift the lid of a garbage can to discover that there is garbage in it. . . . For boundless arrogance in preachment of hate and anarchy, there is for this free-wheeling, treason-minded alien no parallel in America's history."

Stahlman left no doubt that, in his role as Board of Trust chairman, he would work to ensure that the riots spelled the end of Heard's tenure. "In the final analysis," he wrote, "the ultimate responsibility for what occurred lies at the door of the Chancellor, and fellow-administrative authorities at Vanderbilt University."

15

Trouble in Paradise

Climbing the stairs outside Kirkland Hall, Perry Wallace appeared so calm that the students following him gained strength and confidence with each step. Wallace had performed in front of hostile crowds across the Deep South over the course of the season, had even endured the hell of Starkville, Mississippi. He was six foot five, 220 pounds, and as smart as anyone on campus. This was a man to follow. And yet, here, in his hometown, on his own college campus, flanked by friends who admired him, and headed to a meeting with a man he respected, Perry Wallace felt one overwhelming sensation: he was "scared as hell."

Only eighteen years old and just seven months into the experiment to desegregate the Southeastern Conference, Wallace was afraid because he understood how explosive this meeting could be: a dozen black students, walking into Chancellor Heard's office, sitting down with Heard and a few university administrators—some of them sympathetic to their cause, others likely not—and daring to tell these older white men what was wrong with their university. The North Nashville riot was still fresh in everyone's minds; tensions in the city remained high. These kinds of encounters typically didn't end well, Wallace thought. Still, he knew this meeting was necessary, and more than that, he understood how symbolically important it was that he, the admired and high-profile basketball star, not just be part of the group but lead it into the room.

Carmichael's and King's speeches had a profound impact on Wallace and many of his black classmates. The irony was not lost on them: here were the two most visible black leaders in the country, speaking more freely about race than had ever been done on the Vanderbilt campus, their words earning standing ovations from white crowds; and yet for the black students themselves, nothing about their day-to-day experience changed. In the days that followed Impact, they still felt marginalized, still had a hard time finding receptive audiences for *their* stories. In response, they began to turn to each other more than ever, continuing the steps Eileen Carpenter initiated before the Carmichael visit. Whereas previously many black students were hesitant to talk—even to each other—about the racism they encountered, whether out of denial or as a way to cope and stay strong, in the wake of Impact they began to speak honestly about their common experiences and accelerate their plans to organize themselves more formally.

"We admitted that while many people were the finest of people, the overwhelming number of students and many others either ignored us or were hostile," Wallace said in a speech decades later. "You must know that the impact of this realization on many of us was devastating. What about the promise of equality? Of opportunity? Of justice? Just when we thought America had begun to make good on its grand democratic promises, we were issued, once again, what Dr. King called a 'bad check.'"

It wasn't as if the campus realities came as a complete shock to Wallace. As a high school senior, he gave Vanderbilt "the hardest look" that he could. But that hard look, Wallace began to realize, had been through a lens made narrow by circumstances beyond his control. He had been looking from a distance. From segregation. Through the eyes of a seventeen-year-old. As a boy, Wallace had once lived out a cliché when he climbed out too far on a limb to fetch a pear and had fallen. Now, here was another cliché come to life and met with a jolt: his eyes were opening, his lens widening, but much of what became visible was ugly.

"Even if you grew up in segregation, you would hear the national anthem and hear about the constitution and there was all this talk about equality and fairness and justice," he recalled. "And there were beginning to be overt, explicit kinds of comments and statements that said, 'Come out and live in America and have equal opportunity like everybody else.' But what happened in reality was that sometimes that was true and sometimes it wasn't. You really hoped that America was not just some place that plays a cruel joke on you. We were on campus and had our hopes and dreams like everybody else, and what we were seeing was that in coming into mainstream America, there were some disappointing things, some disappointing realities that were rather harsh. And we discovered that we needed to pull together."

There was an alternative to banding together that also carried appeal, and that was to remove oneself from the situation. It would be a lot easier to leave Vanderbilt than to change it. As the end of the school year approached, Wallace and Dillard broached this subject with *Hustler* columnist Paul Kurtz. In the April 25, 1967, edition of his regular "From the Pressbox" column, headlined "Trouble in Paradise," Kurtz explored the notion that Wallace and Dillard might not be long for Vanderbilt.

"Don't place any money on it yet," the column began, "but there's a good chance that when Perry Wallace and Godfrey Dillard receive their college diplomas, Vanderbilt's name will not appear on them."

Three years later, when Wallace would give a lengthy interview to the *Tennessean* following his final game as a Commodore, his comments about race were met with great hostility, as if he had unfairly dropped a bomb at that late stage after years of silence. Yet, here he was as a freshman, sitting down with a student reporter and airing many of the same grievances, expanding on the themes he had raised in his interview with Billy Reed. In their interview with Kurtz, Wallace and Dillard were unhesitatingly honest about their disillusionment. Kurtz asked simple questions and received direct answers. First, he asked Wallace whether he was happy at Vanderbilt.

"You'll have to categorize that question into three parts," Wallace replied. "You'd have to put it into academic, athletic, and social aspects and I could give you only two thirds of a yes answer to the question." Dillard expanded on Wallace's point: "When you're younger, you look forward to your college days for social contacts which will last you all your life. Instead, we never get a chance to loosen up or relax and it's hard for us to face the new week after being cooped up in our dorm room all weekend. Everybody else gets a chance to let off steam, but we don't. We find it hard to be ourselves. We simply can't get lost in the crowd and become anonymous, like most of the whites on the campus."

In what must have been a startling passage for Coach Skinner and Chancellor Heard to read, Kurtz described the reaction to his follow-up question: Knowing what you know now, would you make the decision to come to Vanderbilt again?

Perry declined to answer, while Dillard would only reply, "I've learned a lot about the South since I've come to Vanderbilt and would think seriously about making the same decision."

Finally, mimicking the language Carmichael had used when describing what he saw as the inadequacies of the civil rights movement, Wallace shared his frustration with the scant attention paid to the process of integration at Vanderbilt and the impact this was having on the black students who were left to fend for themselves.

"This [whole situation] makes us wonder about this thing called integration," he said. "It seems to me that integration is defined by NAACP-oriented status-seeking Negroes and federal fund–seeking whites and is really very little more than selective placement with little regard to one of the basic rules of human health, social well-being."

The article ran on page 8 of the *Hustler*, dwarfed by a three-column story on the intramural softball pennant race. Still, the column was a bombshell, and it caught the attention of Chancellor Heard. Grabbing a small piece of stationery bearing the logo of the Mayflower Hotel in Washington, DC, Heard scribbled off a note to his dean of students, Sid Boutwell.

"Can anything be done to help with this?" he asked.

I n surmising that Wallace or Dillard could leave Vanderbilt, Kurtz had been closer to the truth than he knew. While Dillard would come to this point again in a little more than a year, it was here in the spring of 1967 that Wallace was as close to quitting as he ever would be during his four years on West End. Coming off a freshman season in which he averaged twenty points and seventeen rebounds per game, Wallace appeared destined for stardom the following year when he joined the varsity. But dealing with the isolation on campus and the hostile gyms on the road for another season, and then two more years on top of that, was more than Wallace had bargained for, more painful than he cared to endure.

While Dillard's predicament was largely similar to Wallace's, there was one key difference: he began to sense that while the administration and coaching staff were invested in Wallace's success, he, the *second* black player to sign, the brasher black kid from the North, was becoming expendable. The moment this feeling really hit him, he recalled, came during a scrimmage at Memorial Gym when Dillard was leading the freshman team to a romp over a group of former Commodore players.

As Dillard remembers it, the freshmen were matched up against many of the players who had won the SEC title in 1965 in a scrimmage that preceded a varsity game against Georgia. Dillard was on fire, hitting shot after shot—ten points, twenty points, thirty. "I was killing them. I had thirty points with ten minutes left to go, and there was no question in my mind that I was going to break the forty-point [Memorial Gym] scoring record, and everybody knew it," he recalled. "Now, keep in mind, in the second half the fans are coming in for the varsity game. Everything I threw up was going in. I was out of my mind against these guys who won the SEC." Layups, jumpers, bank shots, they were all going in. "And then about halfway through the second half, as the crowd starts coming in, [Skinner] pulls me. Boom. I sit down on the bench and I think he's just giving me a [rest]. They never put me back in. And that's when I said, you know, these people aren't supportive of me. That's when I came to the conclusion they didn't really want me. I knew they were not interested in me reaching my true potential as a player. I'm playing at a high level; why would you pull me down?"

F or both Wallace and Dillard, their interest in transferring to other colleges was genuine. When Wallace thought about where he might go, the first place that came to mind was Purdue University, the school he had crossed off his list in high school after controversy erupted when he played pickup basketball with Rick Mount. "I felt the Purdue situation had been cleansed enough with one year in between," Wallace recalled. "They had finished the investigation with Rick Mount, and my having gone to Vanderbilt probably had to show that anything anybody may have done to get me to try to go to Purdue didn't work."

Skinner read Kurtz's article and immediately summoned Wallace to his office. He told Wallace he hoped he would stay at Vanderbilt and asked why Perry had not mentioned anything about this before. "I had enough of a sense of dedication and responsibility than to bring up all of these problems in the midst of a season when we're trying to win games," Wallace recalled. "That wasn't responsible or fair to the university or the coaches. But after the season—that's what that period was about."

Following Wallace's meeting with the coach, he and Dillard talked it over, and in addition to a lengthy list of reasons to transfer, they both recognized compelling reasons to stay. "We both knew the symbolic reasons why we were there," Dillard recalled, "and even though we wanted to quit, we wanted to leave, it was just like, 'We can't do that, we just have to tough it out.'"

Before he made a final decision, Wallace also sought advice from his old friend Walter Murray, who had already met with other black students considering transferring that spring. As he would do for years to come with other disillusioned students (first as a student himself and later as a Vanderbilt administrator), Murray encouraged Wallace to stay the course.

"Walter could always see the big picture, and he understood that there were those who had admitted blacks to school thinking it was a grand experiment, and if it didn't work out, then 'Oh, well, too bad,'" said his widow, Donna. "He would always talk to the kids who were thinking about leaving and say, 'You've got to stick it out. We will support you, but it's important that you stay.'"

After speaking with Skinner, Dillard, and Murray, Wallace made up his mind. He would not transfer. "I decided that it was something I started, and I did want to see it through because important things were at stake," he recalled.

At the same time Wallace and others experienced feelings of isolation and disillusionment strong enough to cause them to seriously question their decisions to attend Vanderbilt, there remained pockets of support among certain white professors and administrators. As the black students became more organized in the spring of 1967, this support from sympathetic whites played a direct role in making their Kirkland Hall meeting with the chancellor, the one led by Perry Wallace, possible.

One such ally was English professor Vereen Bell, who would become a friend for life to Wallace. A native of south Georgia, Bell was a rare progressive in the famously conservative Vanderbilt English Department, having come to Nashville in 1961 after teaching for two years at Louisiana State University. At LSU, Bell had become active in civil rights, joining a movement that opposed the state legislature's desire to shut down the entire Louisiana public school system lest it be forced to integrate.

"I was a member of an organization that thought it wasn't a very good idea to close the public school system, and that was about as radical as you were able to be," Bell recalled. "That was still considered insurrection at the time. The only place you could assemble with black people was in a church; otherwise, it was legally forbidden for black people and white people to assemble together. That's clearly a violation of the Constitution, not that they gave a shit about that. So we had to meet at a Quaker church, and my phone was tapped by some American Legion subversive activities board. I knew I had to get out of there, or I was going to get myself, or my family, killed."

Bell found a job at Vanderbilt and arrived on campus soon after James Lawson had been expelled from the university for leading the downtown lunch-counter sit-ins. Despite this recent history and despite witnessing pickets against restaurants that still refused to integrate, including Morrison's Cafeteria and Pancake Pantry, Bell found Nashville to be a welcome relief from the oppressive Baton Rouge. "Even though there was racial disorder, it was a rational disorder in a way that you could get a handle on," he said. "It wasn't like a nightmare. It was a place where intelligent people could have a discourse about things. On the other hand, I was a white person, so I was fully accepted even with my strange views."

Given the harassment he endured in Baton Rouge and the badgering he took from his colleagues in the English Department, Bell was not particularly concerned about any flak he might catch for befriending Vanderbilt's first waves of black students, including Wallace and Dillard. He understood the wide gulf that separated these new students from the majority of professors leading their studies and sought ways to signal that he was different. By the time Wallace entered his senior year, the Bell home on Graybar Lane would become the site of frequent casual dinner parties for black students, a safe haven where Wallace and Murray in particular would relax and laugh for hours on end.

While Bell's role with these students would increase in the years to come, his friend Reverend Beverly Asbury, still in his first semester at Vanderbilt, was already heavily involved with Wallace and his classmates. Introduced to Wallace through a mutual acquaintance at the school's Baptist Student Union, which was next door to the old house where Asbury had set up shop, Asbury invited Wallace and several other black students to his office to talk about their day-to-day experiences at Vanderbilt. The discussion was so chilling that Asbury asked the students whether they'd like to come to his home, six miles west of campus in the suburb of West Meade, to talk further.

A few days later, what Asbury recalled as "an astonishing number" of students, many of whom he was meeting for the first time, arrived at 6852 Pennywell Drive for a Sunday evening dinner with Asbury, his wife, and three young children.

"After we ate, we sat down and I just asked, 'What has your first year at Vanderbilt been like?' and their answers were just stunning," Asbury recalled. He heard stories of signs placed on dormitory doors reading, "Nigger go home." Confederate flags and swastikas, too. Walter Murray told the story of his profane welcome to English class. Bedford Waters told Asbury that black students "were torn because you wanted to be a part of the campus, and you also wanted to bond with the other African American students, and yet there was a perception that if a group of us were together, there was going to be a race riot or something."

As Asbury sat and listened to these stories, he was struck by the courage it took for these "normal kids" simply to exist at Vanderbilt. Helping them was why he had come to the university in the first place, and he knew one man who needed to hear their stories.

"All these reports went on, and I listened and listened," Asbury recalled. "And then I said, 'Would you like the opportunity to tell the chancellor all of this?' And they said, 'Yes, we would; nobody has heard our story.' And so I picked up the phone and called Chancellor Heard that night. He asked me to come by his office the next day and give him a full report, and then for the next Sunday, which was the last Sunday of the school year, he called a meeting for his entire cabinet to meet these students."

With a week to prepare for the meeting, the students thought carefully about what they would say and who should serve as the leader of the delegation. Even most of the upperclassmen among them sensed there was just one option. The question was whether the freshman, Perry Wallace, would accept. Eileen Carpenter, for one, had mixed feelings. She thought Wallace was a little too conservative, too soft-spoken, too diplomatic, and at the time she "wasn't into diplomats." But she also understood that he gave the group legitimacy. "I remember that it was very important that Perry be a part of our group, and I have a lot of respect for Perry because he did not hesitate when we asked," she recalled. "He didn't have to—in fact, it would have been a lot easier on him if he didn't. But even though he wasn't vocal or flamboyant, he stepped right up. I really admired him for that, because he had a lot more to lose than anybody."

Then, as now, it was unusual for any athlete to take a high-profile stand in politics or other controversial issues, let alone a freshman in Wallace's situation. As he looked for role models in the world of sports, Wallace recognized that three prominent African American athletes were taking very different approaches.

First, there was Arthur Ashe, the young tennis star from Richmond, Virginia, who opted to play it safe. Later in his career, Ashe dramatically

Wallace was conscious of how his actions on the court could be perceived by teammates, opponents, and spectators. Early in his career, he limited his aggressiveness to prevent accidental blows that could ignite fights. Photo by Robert Johnson, *The Tennessean*.

changed course, becoming a respected, eloquent, and fearless voice of reason on controversial issues related to race and to AIDS, the disease that would take his life. But as a young athlete trying to make a living in the white, country club sport of tennis, Ashe was hesitant to make waves.

Essayist Damion Thomas later wrote that this early version of Ashe represented the most palatable archetype of a black male for white society, a model with which Wallace was quite familiar. "Because African American males have had to be very conscious about offending white America," Thomas explained, "black men have had to 'play it cool': be passive, nonassertive, and nonaggressive. The politics of 'playing it cool' meant that African American males had to always present a serene exterior in the face of injustice perpetrated by whites, as was required of Ashe. Southern African Americans were painfully aware that aggression against whites could be cause for swift punishment. A central virtue of the 'paradigmatic man' was his ingratiating and compliant manner, thus for many whites this became the standard by which all African Americans are measured. Because of his reputation as 'unflappable' and 'ultra-relaxed,' Ashe became for many whites the embodiment of the perfect integrated black man."

Wallace saw many similarities between his predicament and Ashe's, and grew to appreciate those consistencies over time. They were both, Wallace would say, from the old school, what were colloquially known as "race people," blacks who acted in a way that was intended to "show the world the best side of black people." The older generation of "race people" were the teachers at school or the deacons at church or the grandfather next door who said this is how you act in this environment, this is how you dress in this situation, these are the manners you have, these are the negative things white people think about you that you must disprove when you have the opportunity. "And when you come in as a pioneer, you have to up that game even more, your pioneer game, the you-represent-your-race game," Wallace recalled. "That's how Arthur Ashe started off, and that's what I pretty much did also. He was conscious of his role as a pioneer, and I got that."

In contrast to the approach taken by Ashe, Bill Russell of the Boston Celtics pulled no punches. Black sociologist Harry Edwards credited Russell's 1966 book, *Go Up for Glory*, as one of the "first publicly acknowledged indications that a revolt by black athletes was imminent." Russell, wrote author David Wiggins, was a man of "enormous conviction and intelligence. He inspired younger African American athletes by refusing to acquiesce to the white power structure and speaking out passionately about black pride. Unlike any African American athlete before him and with great effect, Russell articulated the frustrations of many in the African American community and passionately voiced how proud he was to be a black man in American culture and sharing in the problem of those of his race."

Around the same time that Wallace was preparing for the meeting with Chancellor Heard, Russell (then the center and head coach for the Celtics, the NBA having reached this milestone before the SEC fielded its first varsity player) wrote an article for *Sports Illustrated* about a recent encounter with another prominent and outspoken black athlete, Muhammad Ali.

Wallace deeply admired Russell and Ali, both for their athletic prowess and their willingness to speak their minds, even when that meant risking their popularity. "They actually stepped forward," Wallace said. "They used their positions to press more strongly than many athletes or many others did, and they took some risks in doing that. And so I respected them for what they did. I felt it was important." Wallace recognized that there were two sides to Ali, and he was drawn to both of them. There was the boxer, who "brought the spirit and the flash of the black athlete, and he took it to places we had never seen it taken," Wallace recalled. The Pearl Tiger basketball team had exhibited some of that panache, but in his role as a "race person" in the

Southeastern Conference, Wallace felt unable to incorporate much of that style into his game at Vanderbilt. Then there was the political side of Ali, which Wallace said he respected just as much. "Among black folk, including me, he wasn't just some guy who was just performing as an athlete and nothing else," Wallace said. "He had a sense of conscience, and he was willing to give it all up for what he believed in, and he believed in the right thing."

As Wallace ascended the stairs to the chancellor's office, he carried with him a bit of what he had absorbed from Ashe, Russell, and Ali. He was selected by his peers in large part because they recognized that he, like Ashe, was seen by whites as the kind of young black man they could work with. But his classmates also knew that, like Russell, he cared deeply about the plight of others and was willing to speak his mind. And finally, like Ali, there was no doubt that Wallace was a man of principle. "I was scared as hell to lead our group to see the chancellor," Wallace recalled, "but I took the step."

Through the tall wooden doors outside Kirkland Hall and into the chancellor's office came Reverend Asbury, Wallace, and the other students, met on this Sunday evening by Heard and members of his administration, including Senior Vice Chancellor Rob Roy Purdy, the school's treasurer, and the deans of Arts and Science, Law, Divinity, and Medicine.

Heard was more secure in his position than at any point in years, having just won a contentious battle with his antagonistic Board of Trust chairman, Jimmy Stahlman, in the aftermath of the riots. Though Stahlman had argued that Heard's policies spelled doom for the university, the chancellor's position was in fact good for business: the $55 million fundraising campaign sailed along and was successfully completed by 1970. Equally important during a time of campus unrest across the country, Heard's defense of Impact also "cemented a deeper alliance between students and their chancellor," Vanderbilt historian Paul Conkin wrote. "Heard, in seemingly placing his career on the line in support of student interests, became a hero." When the chancellor sent his memo to Dean Boutwell asking whether there was anything that could be done to help the school's black students, and when he agreed with Reverend Asbury's request to meet with the delegation Wallace led into his office, the chancellor once again demonstrated why he was so popular with undergraduates. He wasn't the type of administrator who took high-profile public positions on controversial issues for love of the spotlight, while simultaneously ignoring the university's core constituency, its students. Here he was, willing to speak out on racial issues in a very public way but also willing to sit down for an uncomfortable but important conversation with his black undergraduates.

Wallace spoke first, telling the administrators that the students simply wanted to explain—by relaying incidents and anecdotes—what it was like to be black at Vanderbilt. The esteemed English faculty? Might call you a nigger on your first day of class. The Greek system? Didn't mind hiring black bands on weekends, but wouldn't dare admit a black member. The new dormitories? The kind of place where the father of a white student might protest his daughter's assigned roommate, if the roommate happened to be black. The free thinkers on campus? Often condescending, saying they supported blacks, but doing very little. The stories went on and on, all told in a matter-of-fact style. "The students did a wonderful job," Asbury recalled. "All they had to do was tell what they had gone through. They had a receptive audience. Everybody listened in astonishment and sorrow."

As the session unfolded, the students sensed that their voices finally were being heard. The chancellor asked good questions, allowed the students to speak their minds, listened without judgment. "All the black students had immense respect for Chancellor Heard," Wallace recalled. "He was not only a true intellectual, but he was a statesman. And in that sense, he did listen and he actually understood."

Up to this point, the chancellor's philosophy on integration at Vanderbilt had been based on a simple, seemingly logical precept: the university should treat the black students just like everybody else. That meant no segregated dorms or classes, but also no special orientation sessions, no black fraternities or sororities, no black student association, no black history classes. As the students' stories made clear, this hands-off approach was not only ineffective; it was creating tremendous suffering and disillusionment. Paying no special attention to the school's first waves of black students, but then subjecting them to racist professors, hostile classmates, and a segregated Greek system was, it began to dawn on the chancellor, a form of cruel and unusual punishment. At a gathering of university faculty the following fall, Heard explained the epiphany he experienced while listening to Wallace, Dillard, and their classmates, articulating a line of thinking that informed affirmative action and racial sensitivity efforts on college campuses for decades to come.

"It seems to me that the principle on which we have been operating—that all Vanderbilt students shall be treated alike by Vanderbilt without regard to race or color—may have proved insufficient," he said. "We may be in the ironic position of needing to treat our Negro students differently in order to treat them equally—that is, in order to afford them a reasonable opportunity to gain a personal and educational experience equivalent in its general value to that we believe we afford to most other students. . . . I urge your careful and sympathetic consideration of their sensitivities and of their needs."

For Wallace, the encounter was an empowering experience, a bookend of sorts to his meeting with Coach Skinner in the wake of the Kurtz article. Within the span of weeks, he had spoken frankly with the two most important authority figures in his life at Vanderbilt. More important, he had thought deeply about the totality of his first year at the school, had questioned his decision to attend Vanderbilt, and had given serious consideration to transferring. He had experienced the worst of human nature in the South and knew that this had just been a warm-up act, a freshman season that wouldn't even register in the record books. His first year of varsity ball—and all the torment that would surely come with it—was still six months away. When he made the decision to attend Vanderbilt, it had been a naïve one, but now he knew exactly what he was in for. "I knew what could be bad about it. I knew I didn't like it," Wallace recalled. "I knew that change wasn't going to happen overnight. And I knew that if I stayed, I'd be making a commitment to making some change, and that I'd have to fight the battles to make it happen."

It was a shift in Wallace's mindset that would change his life forever, giving his every action a higher purpose. "I hadn't really embraced the situation I had placed myself in, because I hadn't known what it really meant. I hadn't really said to myself, 'This is what you've agreed to do, to try to help work for change.' But in the spring of 1967, it finally congealed.

"This," Wallace recalled, "is when I finally became a real pioneer."

16

Season of Loss

Morris Morgan and Henry Robinson were hiding in the shadows in the back of the gym when they saw it happen.

Finding himself somewhere he wasn't supposed to be was nothing new for Morgan, the black junior from Cedartown, Georgia. He was just fifteen years old when he entered Vanderbilt, a perpetually curious whiz kid who loved sneaking around campus just to see what was going on. The girls thought he was too young to date but plenty wise enough to ask for help with math or science questions. Thanks to his discovery of "beverages on campus," Morgan gained nearly one hundred pounds over the course of his first two years at Vanderbilt, but on the evening of October 31, 1967, he was still inconspicuous enough to slip into Memorial Gym just before the doors closed for a Commodore basketball practice session.

Morgan and his roommate Robinson wanted to see firsthand whether the news reports were true: the first game of the season was still five weeks away, but prognosticators were saying that Vanderbilt would be a strong contender to win the Southeastern Conference. Only two players were gone from the 1966–67 team that won twenty-one games, and Dillard and Wallace were set to join the varsity. As Morgan could see from his hidden vantage point far above the action, the two heralded sophomores were already making a big impact. Dillard was all over the place on offense and defense, whizzing from one end of the court to the other, pressuring the dribbler one minute and pushing the ball on the break the next, reacting to the defense and either stopping, rising, and popping a jumper or feeding the ball to Wallace on the wing for an easy layup.

Then it happened. Forty years later, Morgan could still picture the scene in his mind's eye: Dillard quickly pushing the ball on the break, flashing down the left side of the court on his way to the hoop. A defender darts across the court to cut him off, so Dillard plants on his left leg, a quick stop to al-

Hal Bartch Bob Bundy Godfrey Dillard Dan Due Tom Hagan

Gene Lockyear Perry Wallace Bob Warren Art Welhoelter Bo Wyenandt

In this publicity slick created before the 1967–68 season, Godfrey Dillard is still depicted as a member of the varsity. He would injure his knee during an October 31 practice and never play a varsity game in a Commodore uniform. Vanderbilt University Athletic Department.

low him to go behind the defender and take the ball to the basket. boooom! Dillard's left knee buckles, and Morgan is stunned as he watches his friend collapse in pain on the hardwood. "My knee, my knee!" Dillard yells. Student manager Paul Wilson is the first to rush to Dillard's aid. "I think I still have his fingerprints in my leg," Wilson recalled decades later. "He was holding on and grimacing in great pain."

Morgan looked on as Wallace rushed over and helped Dillard to his feet, pulled an arm over his shoulder, and walked him back to the locker room. Dillard's knee felt numb, but he was no longer suffering. He showered, put his clothes back on, and walked back to his dorm, unsure about the extent of the injury. While his classmates headed out to parties on this Halloween evening, Dillard tried to get some sleep, but he awakened in the middle of the night to a ghoulish sight: his left leg grotesquely swollen.

The next day, Wallace and his teammates arrived at Memorial Gym and slipped on their white game uniforms, lining up in two neat rows for the team picture. This was the history-making shot, the first time an African American appeared with a varsity SEC basketball team. Warren, Hagan, Easley, Wyenandt, Beavers, and Due knelt in the front row; Bartch, LaFevor,

Bundy, Lockyear and Welhoelter stood in the back. And in the middle of the second row, there was Perry Wallace, the lone black face. Because he was injured, Dillard was not invited to pose for the camera. "Once again, it was fate," Dillard said years later. "The picture; I'm not in it. I was becoming invisible."

Less than twenty-four hours before that photo was taken, Wallace and Dillard had blazed down the court together. But Wallace had walked off it, inching closer to his place in history, while Dillard limped away, speeding toward obscurity. Two steps forward, one step back; as with so many things on the Vanderbilt campus that fall, change was happening, the 1960s were finally arriving, but only in fits and starts.

It was as if the campus were a stage with a major overhaul of the production underway—scenery, props, musical score, and costumes changing. It was in 1967, Vanderbilt biographer Bill Carey noted, that "male students start[ed] to wear blue jeans and T-shirts instead of slacks, pressed shirts and monogrammed sweaters." A letter writer to the *Hustler* noted a sudden paucity of crew cuts. Female students protested the dorm visitation policy and their strict dress code. K. C. Potter recalled this as the year when Vanderbilt students began branching out beyond NoDoz to experiment with marijuana, peyote, and morning glory seeds. Still, this was not a campus suddenly overrun by sky-high hippies. An October *Hustler* editorial complained that there were in fact "no hippies at Vanderbilt. There may be several students with hippie sentiments and sympathies and even a few who try to adopt the outward appearance, but the value-orientation of the status-based, materialistic Vanderbilt community is incapable of sustaining the Love Generation." In some cases, the more traditional students were having a hard time coping even with the music of their generation, let alone the love. One student penned a guest column for the *Hustler* blasting the administration for bringing pop music acts to campus (Otis Redding was among the artists scheduled to appear that semester), arguing that rather than presenting Vanderbilt students with a "demented, cheapened view of our culture," the money would be better spent on classical music performances.

If the scenery was changing at Vanderbilt in 1967, so too was the dialogue. In his sermons and *Hustler* editorials, Reverend Asbury practically begged students to get involved in the social and moral issues of the day and even to protest. Building on the philosophy of the open forum that was the foundation of Chancellor Heard's defense of Impact, Asbury told students that "the function of a university does not lie in suppressing dissent and discouraging involvement in controversial issues but in stimulating both dissent and involvement and responding positively to them." For Asbury in particular, this meant prodding Vanderbilt students to question their views on race ("Am I giving others a chance at life's chances equal to my own?") and the war in Vietnam. Never one to back away from controversy, Asbury chose the occasion of Vanderbilt's 1967 homecoming weekend to deliver, at the Divinity School's Benton Chapel, his first strident antiwar sermon, building on many of the themes King had explored in his sermon at New York's Riverside Church. "As a Christian and a patriot, I want out of the war in Vietnam," he declared before pulling out a Peter, Paul and Mary record and laying the needle down on the song, "Bob Dylan's Dream." "We cannot pretend to be ideal-loving," he said, "while overpowering small nations."

A line of angry parents descended on Asbury after his sermon. One man, Asbury said, was literally "quivering with rage." A mother promised that her daughter would never attend another service at the chapel. Another father said he'd be contacting the chancellor to protest Asbury's remarks. The reaction was predictable, but it wasn't just Vanderbilt parents who held dramatically different beliefs from the university chaplain. A *Hustler* poll released immediately after the sermon revealed that nearly one-third of sorority girls were in favor of using nuclear weapons in Vietnam. While the *Hustler* increasingly took antiwar positions in the months and years to come, its first in-depth reporting on student resistance to the war was decidedly promilitary. *Hustler* reporter Chuck Offenburger traveled to Washington, DC, in October for the National Mobilization Committee to End the War in Vietnam's march on the Pentagon—a protest that attracted an estimated two hundred thousand antiwar demonstrators to the nation's capital, including nine other Vanderbilt students.

"Protestors came face to face with the soldiers," Offenburger wrote in a first-person account for the *Hustler*. "One bearded and flop-headed boy blew smoke in a soldier's face and challenged him with: 'Hey, mercenary, did you rape any Vietnam women? . . . Kill any babies? . . . When nigger officers tell you to do something, do you like doing it? Come on, big man, hit me with your stick.'" Had he been the soldier, Offenburger concluded, he would have done just that. As darkness fell and the capital city's monuments became bathed in light, Offenburger said he had "no qualms" about removing his peace button and armband, disturbed by the destructiveness of the spectacle. Still, despite his disgust with the actions of some of the protestors, he sympathized with the causes of their discontent.

"There will be demonstrations as long as men, women, and children are dying in a war which cannot be won because of policies which our leaders cannot justify," he wrote. "There will be riots as long as the American Dream is unattainable for many Americans; there will be social drop-outs as long as our society is unable to meet the psychological needs of its youth."

Back on campus in the weeks that followed, a small cadre of antiwar students began to gain confidence and make waves, picketing ROTC drills and the appearance of a CIA campus recruiter with a handful of homemade signs. ("We think that the CIA got the message that we don't like their activities," one protest leader said earnestly after a few students held up their small signs in the back of a conference room while a crew-cut CIA recruiter conducted his interviews.) When a representative from Dow Chemical, the maker of napalm, was scheduled to appear on campus to recruit students, an anonymous press release was circulated on campus threatening that if Dow was allowed to come to the university, demonstrators would burn a dog in protest. The stunt never materialized, and while occasional protests were carried out on campus, they were marked by a spirit of polite respect for, and nearly quaint cooperation with, authority. It was a result, Potter concluded, of the administration's tolerance for dissent.

"One of my roles was that I was expected to be at any protest that happened on campus," he recalled. "As long as the protest was peaceful, no matter what positions the people were taking, and as long as they were Vanderbilt people, then my instructions were to let it proceed." At times, Potter even found himself in the unusual position of encouraging even more speech than protest organizers desired. "I don't know the countless times that I stood up when some person who was in charge of a speak-out would say, 'No, we're not going to hear from anybody with that point of view,' and I would walk up to the microphone and say, 'We're going to hear all points of view, no matter what.' And they would generally agree and say, 'Of course, you're right,' and then I would sit back down and let them protest. That was all guidance from Chancellor Heard. Free speech."

As was the case for many students during this period, Perry Wallace's views on Vietnam were evolving. At first the war felt like a faraway thing, not relevant to his life. His views changed, he said, when two things began happening: there were the high school friends who never made it back from the jungles of Southeast Asia, and there were the guys who did make it back but were profoundly troubled by the experience. "That began to open my eyes," Wallace recalled. "Some of the students on campus who were protesting or who had problems with the war were people whom I respected, because those were the same students who were more likely to be friendly with the black students. I just kind of respected that they were bright and committed, and they seemed to be very good people, and if they thought the war was bad, then I thought there were problems with it myself."

Yet, ever mindful of his predicament as a trailblazer, Wallace imposed limits on his involvement with the antiwar set. "I understood that they were seen as communists and hippies, and I had a different position. I had a certain set of responsibilities in regard to the university and the community, and the whole set of stakeholders who were conservative whites who didn't understand about race or the war. They had a certain attitude, and I had to make peace with them. So, there was only so much I could do. I didn't need another battlefield."

As dramatic and exhilarating as the antiwar activity may have been for some Vanderbilt students—threatening to set dogs ablaze, marching in DC, standing up to the CIA—the fact was that racial issues were more top of mind. More than one Vanderbilt student described the campus aura in the fall of 1967 as "an awakening," a time when it was dawning on many white students that black people wished to be treated as equals. The first tentative efforts to do so were often painfully awkward.

The fact that Wallace was so well spoken was seen as something of a novelty even by some of his friends. As if encouraging a baby to crawl for unsuspecting grandparents, one of Wallace's white classmates begged Wallace to talk—just say something, anything!—when the student's parents came to campus for a visit. When a white *Hustler* reporter named Barbara Crosby sat down with a group of black female students to discuss their attitudes about Vanderbilt, she found the encounter excruciatingly uncomfortable. "We've botched," she wrote. "The realization comes to you as you sit with six Negro girls and prepare to ask them the same old inane questions about the life of a Negro at Vanderbilt. It is roughly equivalent to asking a white student you don't know how his sex life has been lately and expecting a serious answer."

While a handful of white students had attended integrated high schools, the vast majority had grown up in environments in which the idea of interacting on equal footing with blacks was a foreign concept. Bob Warren, Wallace's teammate from rural Kentucky, had encountered just two black people in his entire life before enrolling at Vanderbilt and meeting Wallace. "[Perry] was the first African American person that I'd ever done anything with socially," Warren recalled many years later. "I did have an aunt in Tennessee who had a lady who worked for her who was black, and there was a blacksmith in the neighboring county in Kentucky who shoed my horse for me. That was the extent of my exposure."

For every student like Warren who simply had never seen many blacks, there were others like coed Marshall Chapman at the other extreme—constant exposure, but still no equality. The daughter of a South Carolina cotton mill owner, Chapman had literally been raised by black women. "You grew up with blacks in your house, but it was an upstairs, downstairs thing," she recalled. "I grew up with so many blacks in the house, bathing you, dressing you, combing your hair, cooking all the food you ate. There are home movies of us in Florida, and they break your heart in the way my grandfather was only interested in his grandchildren. So there are all these little towheaded blonde white children [holding onto] these black arms, and you never saw their faces. That kind of says it all."

Even the hesitant, largely nonproductive attempts at bridging these cultural gaps were too much for some students and parents to stomach; resistance to integration reflected a broader sentiment in some segments of society that saw blacks "overreaching" in their quest for equality. The white backlash took many forms. A *Nashville Banner* editorial cartoon depicted

Martin Luther King Jr. and Stokely Carmichael angrily shaking their fists and shouting at a beleaguered Uncle Sam; the caption asked readers the question, "How much of this is *too much*?" The father of one Vanderbilt student decided that King and Carmichael's presence on the campus the previous spring was indeed too much; he refused to pay his son's tuition in the fall of 1967 and encouraged his boy to distance himself from a "pinkie" like Heard and transfer to Brigham Young University. Another father, having read about the plight of Vanderbilt's black students in the *Hustler*, was sufficiently enraged to write a letter to the paper. "So far I have received three copies and each one has an article about the poor, mistreated, misunderstood nigger," wrote W. L. Sefton of Jacksonville, Florida. "I happen to be one person who is sick and tired of seeing nothing but nigger trouble on TV and reading same in every paper one picks up. If each issue of your publication is going to have articles defending these people just take my name off your mailing list." Another letter writer ridiculed the *Hustler*'s "deep concern" over the university's black students, reminding "Vandy's Negro community" that if the situation on campus was so tough, no one was forcing them to attend the school. Why not just leave? Among the school's biggest boosters, the backlash took subtler forms. Joel Gordon, a Jewish Nashville businessman who had played under Adolph Rupp at Kentucky and supported the recruitment of Wallace, heard other prominent Nashvillians, including members of Vanderbilt's Board of Trust, say that they would boycott Commodore games to protest Wallace's presence.

While the black students came to expect hostility from some quarters, another source of frustration were the pockets of seemingly sympathetic white students whose actions didn't live up to their words. Dillard found it maddening to be told, "I'll do whatever I can to help," only to be dealt a cold shoulder when he came calling. Robert Moore told a *Hustler* reporter that Vanderbilt's black students "detest and disdain condescending liberals and conservatives" who took it upon themselves to define goals for blacks. "Whites are afraid that if they accept the Negro, they won't be accepted by their white friends," claimed another black student. "In the dorm it is alright to talk to me, but outside when they're with their friends they don't want to be bothered with me. It's taboo to associate with the Negro." Walter Murray and many of his black classmates sensed that administrators and faculty members such as Heard, Asbury, and Bell were committed to improving campus life for black students, but the problem, Murray told a *Hustler* reporter, was that "we don't live with the administration; we live with the student body, and that is where the ultimate change must come. We are not begging for the white student's love or pity. We are just interested in seeing Vanderbilt become a place where any individual will feel free to participate."

Speaking to a *Hustler* reporter, Wallace explained that even with good intentions, the administration's efforts were by their nature long-term approaches—a frustrating reality for students looking for change in their own lives. "We are interested in immediate action that will improve our college life while we are students here," he said. "While Vanderbilt is changing from a University that accommodates only Southern whites to a cosmopolitan institution that brings in many ethnic groups, the social norms are not changing. They still accommodate predominantly the white Southerner. Many of these kids think the Negroes here are just like the ones they have known in their home environments. They may try to adjust and may intend fairness, but the result is usually deception." Then, turning to his own situation, Wallace explained that he continued to have reservations about remaining at Vanderbilt. "It was reported that I was ready to leave Vanderbilt because of the many problems I faced last year," he said. "There were many things that I just didn't see when I visited here in high school. But finally, a [combination] of values convinced me to come back. So I'm back—for this year at least."

The importance of Wallace's presence on campus and the basketball team was not lost on those who recognized that he—the sophomore looking for present-day changes—symbolized the long-term culture shift Heard desired. A graduate student who had spent the previous eight years working on various civil rights projects told the *Hustler* (under conditions of anonymity) that a worst-case scenario for Vanderbilt would not be racial violence—there simply weren't enough blacks on campus to create that kind of stir—but high-profile discontent: "I can see ugly publicity, Perry Wallace leaving, the school never getting another Negro athlete, the school getting a name as a place where Negroes must not go, and I can see the school turning back the clock 50 years if changes aren't made."

Even as they experienced loneliness and "deception" that caused them to consider either scattering—by transferring to other schools—or clinging closer together—by creating a formal black student association—many of Vanderbilt's first black students recognized there were dangers in either scenario that contradicted the very reason they had chosen Vanderbilt in the first place. In reaction to the segregated social system, "the Negro students on campus tend to form a close-knit group," said senior Diann White, who had been one of the first two black female students to live in a campus dormitory. "This robs the student of the experience of meeting and comparing different kinds of people, an experience that should constitute a large part of a college education. I chose an integrated campus because I know my life will be in an integrated society."

Despite some concerns about self-segregating, plans for the Afro-American Student Association, which Eileen Carpenter had intended to discuss with Stokely Carmichael the previous spring, began to crystallize in the fall of 1967. "We are not going to sit back and be stagnant until the white student decides to hand us our freedom," Dillard said. While waiting for the association to gain official university approval, the black students began to organize more formal social gatherings on weekends. The hub of activity was a student lounge on the eleventh floor of one of the Carmichael Towers buildings. Morris Morgan, the underage kid who loved sneaking around campus, turned the study lounge into a party room on Saturday nights. Morgan would carry his Marantz stereo system down the hall; students, including Wallace and Dillard, would bring their records; the lights would be turned down low; and the kids would hang out, drink, and dance. "That lounge on the eleventh floor became our social center on the Vanderbilt campus," Morgan recalled. "We used to have people from Fisk and TSU come over. I tell you, we were all poor, but we had a good time. We'd listen to Aretha, the Four Tops, Temptations, Marvin Gaye." The lounge became so synonymous with black life on campus that when the students launched their own literary magazine, filled with poetry, essays, and other commentary on the black experience, they called it *Rap from the 11th Floor*.

While the black students gained confidence and began to organize, the university administration also took formal steps to address their concerns. In the meeting with the chancellor the previous spring, the idea of forming a permanent race-relations council of students, faculty, and administrators had been discussed. Conversations about such a group became more serious when the students returned to campus in the fall of 1967. Wallace, Dillard, Robert Moore, and Wesley Bradby met with Heard on October 10 to press the issue, carrying to the chancellor's office a list of faculty members and administrators they would like to see on the council, six of whom were ultimately chosen. Not only did Wallace and Murray essentially select the committee members; they were given the power to call the group to order. "It is understood by Wallace and Murray," Purdy concluded in a memo to Heard, "that they would initiate steps for the first meeting of the Council, probably sometime in early December."

Wallace, it turns out, would not get around to scheduling the first gathering of the group until April.

First, he had a basketball league to desegregate.

Sports Illustrated picked the Commodores to win the SEC.
So, too, did the AP and UPI wire services.

If Perry Wallace had any notions of flying under the radar as he toured the South, that wasn't going to be the case. All eyes were on the Commodores.

The team's publicity man, Bill Stewart, tried his hardest to walk the standard tightrope—generating excitement while not raising expectations so high that they would become a burden to Skinner. "Cautious optimism is the watchword for Coach Roy Skinner," Stewart wrote in the introduction to the Commodore media guide. "The team looks good on paper, stronger than last year's 21–5 edition, but paper appearances can be deceiving."

Flip through the press guide, however, and Stewart's mini-biographies of the team's key players belie any caution to his optimism.

Bob Warren, senior, height six five, Hardin, Kentucky: *One of the most underrated players in the game today . . . A coach's dream with the ability to make something happen all the time . . . Has fine speed and almost unbelievable jumping ability . . .*

Bo Wyenandt, senior, height six four, Cincinnati, Ohio: *Has been one of the most talented players ever to wear the Black and Gold . . . A natural player with fine moves and an outstanding shooting eye . . .*

Tom Hagan, junior, height six three, Louisville, Kentucky: *A truly remarkable basketball player . . . A real winner and has the ability to come up with the big basket when the team really needs it . . .*

Perry Wallace, sophomore, height six five, Nashville, Tennessee: *One of the bright new stars to burst on the round ball scene . . . Has the potential to be a great one . . . Amazing jumping ability with outstanding hands for rebounding . . . Started his athletic career in the marching band, but has come a long way since then . . . Has to be one of the finest jumpers in the game today . . .*

Skinner told the *Hustler* that this team was probably the best fast-breaking squad he'd ever coached. He worried about a tough schedule—four of the first five opponents were ranked in the top twenty in the nation—and he knew the team would miss the leadership of Jerry Southwood, the guard who had graduated and was now helping coach the freshman team. But he loved the fact that the top three scorers from the previous year—Warren, Wyenandt, and Hagan—all returned. In the team's earliest preseason scrimmages, he had been impressed with the play of Dillard. The team's fortunes depended on someone stepping up to fill Southwood's shoes; until the last day of October, it appeared that person might be the sophomore from Detroit.

Dillard's injury left an already thin roster even thinner, and when it became obvious that there was no chance he would return to action during the season, it also meant that Wallace would be going it alone in his first varsity season in the SEC. While the Commodores' white players and coaches were largely oblivious to the harassment Wallace and Dillard had received on the road as freshmen, the duo had given each other strength in the most hostile of environments. Where would Wallace now turn for support?

It wasn't the loss of his fellow trailblazer, however, that threatened the greatest disruption to Wallace's season; it was the loss of his favorite shot. Just three days after the UCLA Bruins completed a perfect 30–0 season and won the 1967 national championship, and right around the time Stokely Carmichael was stirring racial tensions with calls of "Black Power" in Nashville, a committee of coaches and administrators met in Louisville and outlawed the slam dunk. "Henceforth," proclaimed Rule 9, Section 11, "the ball cannot be thrown into the basket. It will be a violation for the offense to touch the ball or basket when the ball is in or on the basket and to touch the ball when any part of the ball is in the cylinder above the basket." The "stuff shot" was Wallace's most reliable offensive move, the "freedom song" that had carried him from the playgrounds of North Nashville to the frenzied gym at Pearl High and across town to Vanderbilt. Now, just before he was to play his first varsity game, that song had been silenced.

While the ban wasn't explicitly directed at Wallace, it was more than just a coincidence that the rules of the game changed just as the first black player—a prolific dunker—was about to enter the league that Adolph Rupp had dominated for decades. If the rabid crowd in Starkville had demonstrated a raw, vitriolic reaction to the emergence of blacks in the game, the coaches and administrators who banned the dunk were equally motivated by race—erasing a form of "Black Power" with the stroke of a pen. At the time, it seemed obvious that the rule change was meant to blunt the impact of UCLA's seven-foot center Lew Alcindor. Just a year earlier, UCLA coach John Wooden was still mispronouncing the kid's name, saying AL-sindoor. Now, an All-American sophomore season and national championship later, the intellectually curious, saxophone-playing student of African history and culture was so well known—and dominant—he was getting rules changed. A *Sports Illustrated* article on the subject dismissed the rules committee's three dubious explanations for the ban: (1) there was no defense against it, (2) it was a dangerous maneuver, and (3) it led to broken backboards and rims. "What the committee is upset about," *SI* countered, "is Lew Alcindor." In his 1983 autobiography, Alcindor (by then Kareem Abdul-Jabbar) described his reaction to the ban: "Clearly, they did it to undermine my dominance in the game. Equally clearly, if I'd been white they never would have done it. The dunk is one of basketball's great crowd pleasers, and there was no good reason to give it up except that this and other niggers were running away with the sport."

As William Rhoden wrote in *Forty Million Dollar Slaves*, this wasn't the first time that the "ostensibly level playing field of sport" had been tilted. "Black athletes across the board have been faced with ever-changing rules designed to maintain white dominance," he wrote, "Mostly this has meant using power to change the rules of engagement." In horse racing, black jockeys had systematically been locked out of the sport. In the NFL, after R. C. Owens of the Baltimore Colts blocked a field goal by leaping above the goalpost's cross bar, a rule was changed to prevent such maneuvers. In basketball, the dominant play of big men such as Wilt Chamberlain and Bill Russell led to the widening of the foul lane and the creation of offensive goaltending. While the national media then—and in years since—have attributed the ban solely to the dominance of Alcindor, an entirely plausible theory is that Perry

Wallace had as much to do with the ban as anyone. Abdul-Jabbar himself hinted at the notion: "this and other niggers." While Rupp was no longer on the rules committee when the dunk was banned, he had been the committee's most powerful member for many years prior and still held great sway. David Lattin had embarrassed Rupp's Wildcats with a powerful dunk over Pat Riley, setting the tone in the 1966 NCAA title game. The next season, Lattin's protégé, Wallace, embarrassed Rupp's freshman team with his slam over Dan Issel. Kentucky didn't have UCLA on its schedule, but it did have to play Vanderbilt twice a year.

"Some people have expressed to me that I had something to do with the banning of the dunk, but I would never make that attribution," Wallace said years later. "At the time, I didn't have that level of paranoia or self-importance. I just found out that somebody changed the rules. I'm more comfortable that the major person was Kareem, and in general black players were doing most of the dunking. I was part of that equation, just part of the formula. When you look back, you see it was a silly, suspicious rule, and I think it said a whole lot about the times. I'm like a lot of people; without any evidence, I strongly suspect that it was racially motivated, and like many things that you look back on, it really stands out like your proverbial sore thumb."

Wooden was philosophical about the rule change ("It's bound to affect our play some, but we'll adjust to it," he told Bill Becker of the *New York Times*), but Skinner was less generous. "The NCAA," he said, "crapped on Perry." Looking back on the ban from the distance of decades, Skinner was convinced of two things. First, that his rival at Kentucky had a lot to do with it—and by extension, so did Wallace—and second, that the ban eventually made Wallace a better player. "Oh, my God, it made me just sick for [Perry] when they banned the dunk," Skinner said. "I was for the dunk and was really opposed to the no-dunk rule. Rupp and a few of them scattered around were against it. Rupp was a big part of it because the dunk was hurting him. It took away Perry's game. When he first came [to Vanderbilt], Perry couldn't do anything but dunk and rebound. The ban forced him to become a basketball player."

Wallace agrees with that assessment, saying that the prohibition of the dunk compelled him to work on his skills away from the basket, something he'd need to do anyway if he wanted to play at the next level. There weren't many six-five centers in the NBA.

"Here I am, a player influenced primarily by Wilt Chamberlain and Bill Russell, the big men who could dunk the ball," Wallace recalled. "But I'm six-four, six-five, and I'm playing under the basket because that's what was helpful for my high school and college teams. I wasn't dead-set on making it to the pros; I didn't have that level of self-confidence. But if I wanted to do that, what I needed to do was add in the game of a forward who plays out on the wing. I needed to learn to shoot the ball, handle the ball, dribble, and move. And so in that regard, outlawing the dunk forced me to develop a better all-around game."

Wallace believed there was a second benefit to the ban: a reduced chance of injury. Despite his ability to leap high into the air to throw down rim-rattling dunks, the joy he took in these jams was tempered by fear. In a junior high school game, Wallace had jumped up to block a shot, only to have the shooter "low bridge" him, clipping his legs and causing him to land flat on his back. Though he played through the pain and finished the game, Wallace went to bed that night feeling a strange, painful sensation in his back and legs. When he woke up the next morning, he could not move. His mother asked why he was still in bed, and Wallace pretended he had a cold. Unable to stand, he crawled to the bathroom down the hall when no one was looking.

"I had some paralysis," Wallace recalled. "That period where I could not walk had a huge impact on me. I tried to work my way back by doing exercises and stretching and that sort of stuff, and the feeling gradually came back. But that whole episode taught me about playing defensively; still being a leaper, but playing defensively."

Having played through rough games as a freshman, Wallace knew he'd be even more of a target—especially if he were high in the air about to dunk—during his first year on the varsity. "By having the dunk outlawed, I could leap," he said, "but I didn't have to leap to try to dunk and create a situation where people could physically really do me in."

Wallace was particularly attuned to the possibility of injuring his back because he had taken another hard fall while working a summer construction job at Memorial Gym. Two years earlier, the "balconies Clyde Lee built" had been installed at Memorial Gym, expanding the building's capacity, and though a pocket of alums made noise about staying away from the gym after Skinner recruited Wallace and Dillard, the Commodores' popularity continued to rise after Lee's departure, in part because of the excitement surrounding Wallace's arrival. Some Vanderbilt administrators even expected Nashville's black community to come out in droves to watch Wallace. Whatever the motivation, when the university decided to spend $768,000 to expand the gymnasium's south side by another 1,864 seats prior to the 1967–68 season (all of the new spots immediately sold to eager season-ticket holders), these new bleachers literally became the "balconies Perry Wallace built."

For several weeks Wallace found himself trying to maintain his balance on narrow, greased beams high above the gym floor as the only student-employee of Foster and Creighton contractors, a job he had hoped would be a welcome break from summer school. But between a "redneck" foreman "constantly picking on" him and the precariousness of his assignment, the job turned into a nightmare. The day before his stint was to end, Wallace and another worker stood on a scaffold holding a steel beam when Wallace lost his balance, falling flat on his back onto a concrete and steel surface seven feet below. The beam came crashing down but missed Wallace, and he walked away with only scrapes and bruises.

When practice began in October, the bruises were gone, but something else he picked up on the summer job remained: a somewhat controversial way of thinking about the world that would help carry him through three more tense years at Vanderbilt. As hard as he had tried to please his tall, red-haired foreman, Wallace was constantly on the receiving end of the man's barbs. "He was very tough on me, very, very rough," Wallace recalled. "I seemed not to be able to please him. He said I was lazy, and I was just kind of befuddled. I really tried to step up my game, but he kept picking on me. I tried this and tried that, but it didn't seem to matter."

Finding himself at wit's end, Wallace was approached by an old, black construction worker known simply as Mr. Jake. A deeply religious man with a gentle smile and slow gait, Jake grew vegetables on his farm outside Nashville and struck Wallace as a man who was at peace with the world. Taking a seat next to Wallace during a lunch break, Jake offered helpful advice to the teenager who was struggling so mightily.

"This is what I want you to do," he said. "You have got to figure out how to look like you're working hard, but you have got to stay peaceful and you have got to stay calm. You just keep on working steadily, keep on moving, and don't sit down. When the man asks you to do something, you do what you need to do, but have to be as calm as you can be about this."

For Wallace, Mr. Jake's words reminded him of his mother's approach to survival—an enduring, slow, and steady quiet confidence that carried her through the toughest days. "Mr. Jake helped me with how to appear on the job and what attitude to show," Wallace recalled, "but more than that, deep inside, to not allow this foreman to get the best of me."

The lesson was especially poignant for Wallace, because he recognized something about the elderly gentleman: many in the black community would deride the sage old man—smiling, polite, quiet, head down—as an Uncle Tom.

"The Toms were the ultimate nonthreatening blacks, and the ones most despised by most black folks as being weak and cowardly and too deferential," Wallace said. "But the reality was that not all Toms were alike, and some of them were really strong people who had to make difficult choices. And almost always, they were a lot smarter than a lot of other black folks. All you need to do is to see the very short stories, because they're always very short, about the blacks in that era who stood up and put their fingers in white people's faces. They always tell those stories heroically, but they don't tell *many* of those stories because they're usually tragic. And more often than not, they're just lies. Perhaps cathartic lies, 'freedom' lies, but lies just the same."

In recalling the wise counsel he received from Mr. Jake, Wallace began to develop a philosophy that he'd refer to from time to time for decades to come. He calls it "What the Toms Knew." "Their sense of survival goes much deeper than people understand. They make very hard choices in the world. They're in the South, and they have to figure out some way to make a living, to put food on the table, and get by," Wallace recalled. "A whole lot of their behavior is the maximum amount of assertiveness they can show and still hold on to those jobs. But they found peace, and a sense of fulfillment and a sense of strength, even within that world. Many blacks would call them Toms. But in effect, they were people who were doing their best in a tough situation and had a lot more strength, a lot more substance, a lot more wisdom, than you'd imagine."

As Wallace participated in his first practices as a member of the Vanderbilt varsity, his teammates thought he was unusually quiet. Wallace played hard and was a good kid. There was nothing Skinner could complain about, but the coach wondered why his prized sophomore wasn't more aggressive. The practices wore on, October turning to November, canvas high tops squeaking on the hardwood floor, Wallace keeping his cool, making no waves, pacing himself for a season of the unknown, sneaking a glance at the balconies, and remembering the lesson he learned up there, high above the fray.

Soon the team would fly off to Dallas for the season opener against SMU, and Perry Wallace would make history.

Sort of.

As Wallace set out to blaze a historic trail, faint footprints remained from brief and largely forgotten journeys by his predecessors in New Orleans and Lexington.

17

Ghosts

New Orleans, Louisiana, 1965.

The freshman thought it was funny the way his father and the baseball coach talked about his future, as if he weren't even in the room. The baseball coach, Ben Abadie, had learned that an athletic administrator was lobbying the freshman to join the football team for spring practice. Abadie wanted the kid to commit to baseball instead: he'd played well in "fall ball," and the 1965 regular season was just around the corner. The freshman sat beside his father and listened as Abadie earnestly made his case for baseball, the coach trying to build a personal connection with the student's father, telling stories about the sandlot leagues in tiny West We Go, Louisiana, the town near New Orleans where they both had once lived. He was making his best sales pitch, and that's what made the boy smile. A Latin major and math minor, he was attending college on an academic scholarship, not an athletic one. As much as he loved both baseball and football, he was content to focus on academics and didn't have to listen to what Abadie thought was best for him; his future at the school was secure no matter what decision he made. In his gut he figured he'd stick with baseball, the sport that had been as important a part of his childhood as sermons and school. The Sunday afternoon routine had been the same his whole life: after church, he would head to the ball diamond with his dad and swing for the fences like his hero, Hank Aaron of the Milwaukee Braves.

After several more minutes of lobbying and one final piece of advice from Abadie that he would remember for the rest of his life, the freshman got up from his chair, thanked the coach for his opinion, and announced his decision.

When the Southeastern Conference's color barrier was broken, it didn't require a head coach to make a controversial public decision, and the young trailblazer didn't have the opportunity to ponder the difficulties of pioneering. He wasn't even aware that he'd be the first. History wasn't made in a high-profile sport like football or basketball, and it didn't happen at a powerhouse program like Alabama or Kentucky or LSU. The first African American athlete in the SEC was a speedy walk-on outfielder and Rockefeller Scholar at Tulane University, a school that had already announced it was quitting the league.

It's little wonder so few people remember Steve Martin.

Martin had earned varsity letters in four sports at St. Augustine High School in New Orleans, an all-male, all-black prep school known for its strong academics. Though he was a talented athlete and student, earning the Purple Knight football team's Athlete-Scholar Award as a senior when he averaged more than seven yards per carry as the team's halfback, Martin was unaware that college recruiters had any interest in him. The Catholic school's white principal, Father Robert Grant, held on to the letters that arrived for Martin from coaches around the country, determined that his star pupil would become one of the first black students at Tulane. It wasn't until a friend came running up to Martin with news that an article in the newspaper claimed that Michigan State football coach Duffy Daugherty was "hot after Steve Martin" that he had any idea he was on the radar of the Big Ten school that was gaining a reputation for recruiting black players from the South. And it wasn't until the night of his graduation from St. Augustine that Martin learned from Grant that he had earned a Rockefeller grant to Tulane. "Don't get me wrong, I admired him like he was my father," Martin recalled, "but [Grant] had decided my fate, thinking I was the kind of student who could go to Tulane and play sports and make the grades. I was surprised about the scholarship, and I had no idea what was ahead of me."

Tulane admitted its first black undergraduates just a year before Martin's arrival, and there were only about a dozen black students on campus. Martin felt painfully alone; he didn't even feel he had much in common with the few other black students other than the color of his skin. White classmates walked right by him without saying hello; dormitory hallmates were unwilling to cross the plane of his doorframe, preferring to talk to him from just outside his room. Though there were a few notable exceptions, Martin's teammates weren't especially welcoming, and one or two were outright hostile to his arrival. As a result, Martin felt "robbed of the camaraderie that the other guys on the team had. It was more like a job than going out and having fun and playing with the people that you like and grow with."

After a successful season on the freshman baseball team in 1965 (oblivious to the history he made when he took the field for the first time in a game against a team from the Pensacola air force base), Martin joined the Tulane varsity as a walk-on in the spring of 1966. By this time, university president Dr. Herbert Longenecker had already announced that Tulane, a charter member of the Southeastern Conference, was leaving the league as of June 1. The same concern that had troubled Chancellors Branscomb and Heard at Vanderbilt—that athletics were overshadowing academics in the SEC—had first led then-president Rufus Harris in 1951 to reduce Tulane's football scholarships by a third, cut coaches' salaries, and eliminate a physical education major. Predictably, the Greenies' football fortunes declined as a result, and now Tulane was on its way out, leaving Vanderbilt as the only private school in the conference. The Green Wave football team had closed out its SEC run in the fall semester, an ignominious swan song that concluded with a 62–0 shellacking by LSU. All that remained in the spring of 1966 was for Coach Abadie's team to wrap up its season; then Tulane would be gone for good.

Martin began the season on the bench, occasionally pinch-hitting or entering a game as a defensive replacement in the outfield. Eventually, his speed and what Martin's brother once described as "his gift" earned him a starting job: Martin had an uncanny ability to predict the flight of any ball hit to the outfield. Abadie would hear the crack of the bat, look up, and there was Martin, racing to just the right spot to make the catch. Martin's glove work was such an asset that occasionally Abadie would switch him from left field to right field in the middle of an inning, depending on whether the batter was a lefty or righty.

In this last SEC season for Tulane, Martin vividly remembered the "firsts." His first at-bat against an SEC opponent came against Ole Miss pitcher Scotty Haslet; Martin singled up the middle and then stole second base. Tulane's first road trip to Alabama was canceled after someone called Coach Abadie and said Martin would be killed if the team made the trip.

The first conference road trip, then, was to Mississippi State. Martin had not taken much abuse at road games as a member of the freshman team, but here in Starkville, as would be the case for Wallace and Dillard on the basketball court the following spring, the scene was ugly right from the start. The game hadn't even begun when the racial epithets came raining down from the stands. To Martin the fans seemed incredibly close to the field, as if they were hovering above it. The Tulane players, in their gray road uniforms, were sprawled out on the green grass, running through their pregame stretching exercises. As the insults and threats grew louder and uglier, Martin sensed that his teammates were inching farther and farther away, leaving him exposed in a way he had never felt before. Finally, John Devlin, a teammate from Houston who had befriended Martin, scooted closer and tried to distract him. "Martin," he said. "These people are assholes, but some of what they're saying is pretty funny." The comment "took the edge off," Martin recalled, and he and his teammate busted out laughing. "All throughout the rest of that trip to Starkville, he stuck by me. It's like God had sent him as an angel to make things a little better."

"Then, of course, there was the trip to Ole Miss," Martin recalled. "Oh, Lord, they were waiting for me." Martin sensed something was wrong soon after the team arrived in Oxford: Coach Abadie wouldn't even talk to him. Finally, the coach gathered his team to announce the starting lineup for the first game of the series. "I hear him say, 'I'm not starting Martin, I'm starting such-and-such,'" Martin recalled, "and he did it in such a way that I thought it was just a strategic baseball move that coaches make. We had other good players." But Abadie's demeanor suggested that something else was going on. Martin never got off the bench during the game, not even as a defensive replacement. When the last out was made, Abadie took Martin aside. "I got a phone call," the coach said, "and they told me that if I started you in this game, they would kill me and they would kill you. They didn't say anything about the second game, so I'm going to go ahead and play you tomorrow." Martin agreed to play, and he never forgot his introduction to the fans of the Ole Miss Rebels.

Martin walked up to the plate, stepped into the precisely drawn chalk lines that confined the batter's box. The pitcher stood on the mound, looking in for his sign from the catcher. Suddenly, the pitcher stepped off the rubber, walked to the back of the pitcher's mound, and grabbed the resin bag, flipping it around in his hand. As if on cue (and Martin suspects it was a scripted maneuver), the Rebel crowd began to chant.

N!
I!
G!
G!
E!
R!
What does it spell?! Nigger!!

Martin tried to concentrate on the fact that this was still just a baseball game, like so many he'd played in before. He stepped out of the batter's box and looked down at Abadie in the third base coach's box. The coach was clapping his hands, offering the slightest bit of encouragement in the midst of the chaos. Martin set his gaze on Abadie, but then his eyes were diverted to something just beyond his coach. There in the Ole Miss bleachers was a solitary black man, staring right at Martin. "I looked at him, and he looked back at me, and it was kind of like a feeling of 'Don't worry about it, just play your game,'" Martin recalled.

Martin's concentration narrowed, and he began to feel as if he were in a trance. The pitcher stepped back up on the mound and fired a pitch toward the plate; Martin began to swing, but then abruptly stopped. Still, ball hit bat, caroming safely into the right-field grass. "Run!!!!" Martin was snapped out of his trance by the voice of Bobby Duhon, the Tulane quarterback who was also a member of the baseball team. Bolting away from the plate, Martin was safe at first with a check-swing single. He looked back toward the stands behind third base, hoping to make eye contact again with the man who had silently encouraged him, but he was gone. "I promised myself," Martin recalled, "that I'd find out one day who he was." Nearly a half century later, he still hoped to get that chance.

Twenty-five years after graduating, Martin was invited back to campus to speak about his experience. Martin told students and faculty members that at Tulane he received two educations. On one hand, he had received a degree from a prestigious university, a degree that opened doors and created opportunities for himself and his family that would not have been possible otherwise. He talked about his position with an international corporation that allowed him to move his family to Brussels. His children learned to ski in the Alps, a long, long way from West We Go, Louisiana. He was a hero to his kids, children who had gone on to earn fine educations of their own. His youngest daughter earned a PhD in French, his middle child became an emergency room doctor, and his oldest son earned a PhD and became an epidemiologist. All of this was possible, he believed, because of the first kind of education he had received at Tulane: the purely academic one.

The second kind of education, he told the group, was one he would not wish on anyone. For a teenager entering manhood, his experience at Tulane had been a cruel, psychologically devastating experience, one that continually threatened to sap the joy out of life. If he had to do it all over again, he wouldn't. "The verbal abuse," he recalled, "was something that an eighteen- or nineteen-year-old kid should never have to endure." He discussed his experience as a student on campus, and one scene in particular stood out. He and a friend had arrived in calculus class early, and Martin had grabbed a piece of chalk and was explaining a problem on the board when another white student entered the room. He, too, asked for Martin's help, and Martin gladly explained how to work through the problem. A few days later, Martin was walking across campus when the second student came walking down the sidewalk in the opposite direction. Martin prepared to say hello, but just as they approached each other, the white student turned and looked away.

Decades later, Martin lived outside Dallas in the suburb of Grapevine, Texas. He was proud of his children and also a little envious of the friends they made in college, black and white. Lasting friendships, he said, were something he did not take away from his experience. He coached a Little League baseball team and made it a point to play every kid in every game, regardless of talent. If an adult couldn't develop a kid's skills enough to feel comfortable putting the boy on the field, the grown-up, he believed, had no business coaching. Tulane had left the SEC so long ago that most people Martin met no longer remembered the school was ever in the conference. No one from the SEC came calling to honor the trailblazer. Martin was alone with his experience. In the smallest of ways, he kept his own story alive: the prefix to his email address was "firstbathlete." Every ten years or so, when he was feeling down, he would pull out the old scrapbook that his mother began keeping back in high school, the one with the newspaper clippings about his exploits at St. Augustine, the story about Coach Daugherty wanting him at Michigan State, the articles about him making history at Tulane. He would think back to the sandlot days, to the joy of learning the game from his father. And he would remember that afternoon back in Coach Abadie's office, when the coach convinced him to choose baseball over football.

"Mr. Martin," Abadie told his father, "if he goes out there and plays football, they're not going to block for him. They're going to kill him."

Sports Illustrated
"Scorecard"
September 4, 1967
NO CAUSE FOR ALARM

Kentucky will be the first Southeastern Conference [football] team to have a Negro on its varsity this fall. So promised Wildcat Coach Charlie Bradshaw in listing his tentative lineup for Kentucky's opening game against Indiana Sept. 23.

Nat Northington, a 5′11″ 170-pounder from Louisville, will see action as a defensive halfback and safety for Kentucky, and another Negro player, Greg Page, was down for second-string defensive end duty but got hurt.

When the September 4 *SI* arrived in mailboxes around the country, Greg Page was more than hurt; he was dying, confined to a hospital bed, paralyzed from the nose down. He had undergone a tracheotomy, and was hooked to a respirator. In a matter of weeks he was dead, and a distraught Northington had transferred to Western Kentucky University. If the first black athlete in the SEC had been an unrecruited outfielder on a ghost of a team lost to history, the experience of the first recruited black athletes was even briefer, and more painful. One died before ever playing a game; the other quit after playing briefly in just four.

Friends described Page as a gentle giant. At six foot two, two hundred pounds, his size was intimidating, but his easy smile prevented him from pulling off any kind of tough-guy act. Hailing from the small, eastern Kentucky mining town of Middlesboro, Page was proud to be a trailblazer. As a senior in high school, he answered a question provided by UK's publicity office.

Why did you choose Kentucky?

"I wanted to play football for UK," he said, "and to help open the way for more Negro athletes to play ball here."

Northington was actually the first black player to sign scholarship papers. Kentucky president Oswald, who leaned hard on Rupp to recruit blacks for the basketball team, also encouraged Bradshaw to integrate his team, at one point allegedly reassuring the coach that he'd have a job for life at the university if he successfully landed a black player. Northington, from Louisville, emerged as a logical candidate to break the color line: not only was he a great defensive back, but he was also quiet, thoughtful, polite, and a fantastic student, earning straight A's in high school. Northington and Page became close friends during their freshman year, and as summer camp unfolded prior to the 1967 varsity campaign, they both eagerly anticipated the chance to earn some playing time.

Page's fatal injury occurred during what was considered a routine part of Kentucky's preseason practices, a pursuit drill the defense had run many times—the ball tossed to a running back who would run right or left, the defenders pursuing the ball carrier and giving him a thud. Whether he hit the running back at the wrong angle, whether someone fell on his neck, no one quite knows why Greg Page wasn't able to get up from the pile.

With his friend lying paralyzed in the hospital, Nat Northington was left to become the first black scholarship athlete—and the first black football player—to play for an SEC team when he appeared in Kentucky's 12–10 season-opening loss to Indiana. There was nothing glorious about the historic moment for Northington—a low-scoring loss in a nonconference game while his best friend lay dying. Northington grew increasingly despondent and lonely, spending his nights staring blankly at the brick walls in his room. Page died on a Friday night, thirty-eight days after entering the hospital. Kentucky played its first SEC game against Ole Miss the next day, and Northington appeared in the game, making more league history. Two weeks later, after losses to Auburn and Virginia Tech, he stuffed his clothes into a suitcase and announced he was leaving school. Kentucky's experiment had failed miserably.

By the time Perry Wallace stepped on the court for his first varsity game two months later, the Southeastern Conference was again—except for him—all white.

18

Memorial Magic

First came Samantha, the hobbling basset hound and unofficial team mascot. Then the pep band struck up "Dynamite," the Vandy fight song, and the fans roared. The cheerleaders, hand in hand in a V-formation like a flock of birds, came charging out onto the court, girls in white skirts and gold nautical-style shirts, guys with black sweater vests over white pants, everyone in saddle shoes.

And then came the Commodore players, guards in front, big men in the back, jogging and dribbling, through a small doorway and onto the court, and the crowd grew louder still.

Around the perimeter of the gym, twenty-four doormen welcomed the last-minute arrivals, and forty-four ushers showed the fans to their seats. Lieutenant Charles Kimbrough's squad of Metro policemen kept an eye out for trouble (a "hippie" murder suspect was on the loose, according to the *Banner*), but their most important job was already complete: hours before game time, the cops had scanned the bathrooms and closets for stowaways. Tickets were so tough to get to Vanderbilt games that there were always a few fans who tried to sneak in early without a ticket.

Concessions man J. G. Kyle walked the perimeter of the gym, making sure each stand was fully stocked. At a typical game, 11,094 Vandy fans would eat one thousand hot dogs, munch on eighteen hundred boxes of popcorn, and sip on seven thousand icy cups of Coke and 7-Up. The last thing Kyle wanted was a close game: fans, he had learned from experience, not only didn't want to leave their seats when the outcome was in doubt, they were too nervous to eat anyway. Blowouts were good for business. Gym manager George Baines craned his neck to check the scoreboards—all eight of them—and what he saw was good: all the lightbulbs were burning.

Over on the north side of the gym, Vanderbilt students squeezed into each row of wooden bleachers from courtside all the way to the back of the building—boys in V-neck sweaters or sport coats and slacks, girls in turtle-necks and skirts. Many students had arrived hours early, before the freshman game, even, to get the best seats; now they tucked away the decks of playing cards they brought along to pass the time. Souvenir barkers walked the aisles selling Styrofoam, political convention–style skimmers emblazoned with "Go Vandy" ribbons, and because the temperature had dipped into the low forties, fans with first-row seats hung their winter coats over the balconies.

Public-address announcer Herman Grizzard introduced the visiting Auburn Tigers, and each player was met with a loud round of boos as he ran out to midcourt to grudgingly shake hands with the Commodore mascot. Then it was time to meet the Vanderbilt starters—Bo Wyenandt, Bob Warren, Kenny Campbell, Tom Hagan, and Perry Wallace—and the crowd greeted their boys with pent-up gusto, this being the first home game of the 1967–68 season.

Grizzard then uttered the phrase that always drew more boos: "Hello, referees, how are you?" The men in stripes nodded back at the PA man, knowing that for the next two hours, every move they made would be scrutinized by the Vandy faithful: every single call, it seemed, drew a reaction from the fans in black and gold.

Then the crowd grew quiet, the only sounds the rhythmic stomp of feet and the thud of rifle butts as members of the Vanderbilt ROTC stepped slowly out toward center court, where a small trapeze came fluttering down from the gym's rafters. A student-soldier affixed an American flag to the trapeze, and fans stood for the national anthem.

It was now 7:30 p.m. on Monday, December 4, 1967. Time for tip-off, time for Perry Wallace to play his first game at Memorial Gym as a member of the Commodore varsity and his first varsity game against a Southeastern Conference opponent. For there to be a Shaquille O'Neal at LSU, a Charles Barkley at Auburn, a John Wall at Kentucky, a Dominique Wilkins at Georgia, a Joakim Noah at Florida, a Robert Horry at Alabama, a Bernard King at Tennessee, an Erick Dampier at Mississippi State, or a Gerald Glass at Ole Miss, there had to be this moment in the winter of 1967. Perry Wallace walked to midcourt and leaped high for the jump ball that began the game, soaring into the air right where Martin Luther King and Stokely Carmichael had stood eight months earlier.

The significance of the moment may have been lost on the local media (the *Banner* noted that there would be something different about this game—a 7:30 rather than 8:00 p.m. start time), but Bedford Waters, the black student from Knoxville, looked out at Wallace with great pride, he recalled decades later. Wallace's good friend Walter Murray was so excited he began to lead the student section in a cheer his friends would long remember: "Hey, hey, hey, big V, you sure look good to me!"

Wallace was literally the center of attention, an effect made more pronounced by the unique layout of the fifteen-year-old gymnasium. Whereas at some conference gyms the fans sat so close to the court they could—and often did—reach out and touch (or pinch) the players, at Memorial there was a vast amount of open hardwood separating the out-of-bounds lines from the first row of seats, creating a stage-like effect. This was no accident, and, improbably, it all had to do with the lack of showers in 1920s-era apartment buildings in Paris, France.

Returning from a World War II tour of duty in the navy, Vanderbilt alum and architect Edwin Keeble approached Jimmy Stahlman for advice on how to win a contract to build a new government building in Nashville. Stahlman, who had been lobbying for an on-campus auditorium at Vanderbilt that would host track, theater, opera, and basketball, told Keeble to forget the federal building project and design the gym at Vanderbilt, a building that would serve as a memorial to students and alumni killed in the war. After touring fieldhouses at the University of Michigan and Indiana and traveling to New York to visit Madison Square Garden, Keeble, who later designed Nashville's first skyscraper, the L&C Tower, drew up his plans for the gym. The architect heard news reports out of Lexington, where the University of Kentucky was building a four-million-dollar, 11,500-seat gym that Adolph Rupp was already saying would be too small. Keeble wanted to build something "at least that big," but university administrators kept cutting back his budget. In what would be a gift to Commodore fans for generations to come, Keeble dealt with the budget cuts by creating a building that could easily be expanded. Along each sideline, he added twenty feet of extra height to allow for the eventual construction of two balconies. And along each baseline, he created secret plans to tear out the end walls to allow for the addition of four thousand seats.

Because the building was intended to be used for concerts, plays, and operas in addition to basketball, Keeble built an elevated playing surface, leaving room for orchestra pits along the sides, meaning that for fans in the first few rows along each sideline, eye-level was court-level. While at just about every other basketball arena in the country the teams sat in folding chairs along the sidelines, such an arrangement blocked the view of courtside ticketholders at Memorial Gym, so the team benches were moved to the endlines next to the baskets, creating an unusual vantage point that continues to flummox visiting coaches to this day.

And then there was the ring of open space encircling the court, which traced its roots back to 1920s Paris. It was there that Keeble had moved to study architecture after graduating from Vanderbilt in 1924. "I was playing in a Saturday night basketball league just so I could get a shower once a week—there were no facilities in my apartment," Keeble told Vanderbilt basketball historian Roy Neel. "In this little place we played, the playing floor ran right up to the wall and fellows were always getting hurt as they ran into it. The reason we've got so much space around the floor in the Vanderbilt gym is that I had learned what it was like running into that wall in Paris."

Whether it was the unusual layout of the gym, the vocal crowd support, or the talent of the Commodore players, Vanderbilt was nearly impossible to beat at Memorial ever since the gym opened on December 6, 1952. Heading into the 1967–68 season, the team had won 88 percent of its games there (a 181–25 home record over fifteen seasons). The challenge of topping the Commodores at home was even more daunting for the out-of-conference foes that made infrequent visits to the gym: only five non-SEC schools had ever beaten Vanderbilt at Memorial. The winning created increasingly high expectations. After enduring football season upon football season of disappointment, Commodore fans came to Memorial primed for victory, and any deviations from the script—bad calls by referees, boisterous visiting fans (especially those wearing Tennessee orange)—were dealt with harshly. A student reporter from the University of Tennessee found a visit to Memorial unsettling. "Crowd noise is to be expected at any opposing school's gym," he wrote, "and this is how it should be. However, crowd abuse is another matter. Booing opponents, telling them to go to hell, throwing things on the floor and being rude to visiting spectators is not only grossly unsportsmanlike, but also tends to intimidate the referees, causing them to call an uneven game."

For fans of the home team, the thrill of attending a game at the raucous gym was unlike any other experience in Nashville. "It was like the roof was coming off the place," said Jim Combs, the football player from Detroit. "We wouldn't sit down the entire game, just screaming. You'd walk in there and I'm telling you, from the time the ball was tipped off until the end of the game, people were out of their seats screaming. Then when Tennessee came to town, you'd leave there and your ears would still be ringing."

Chancellor Heard may have been interested in limiting the influence of athletics on his university, but that didn't mean he could temper the enthusiasm of his own daughter. Young Cornelia Heard would dress up in a Vanderbilt sweater ("I was dying for a Vanderbilt cheerleader's outfit, but I never got one," she recalled) and scream her head off. "I remember the other team would be shooting a foul shot," she said, "and in my squeaky little voice, I would yell 'Miss it!' I was probably pretty obnoxious."

These fans expected greatness from their Commodores, and they expected big things from Wallace. While he still had a lot to learn offensively, especially now that the dunk had been taken away, he had dominated games as a defender and rebounder as a freshman, and his early work prior to the home opener was encouraging. In the annual freshman-versus-varsity scrimmage in late November, Wallace was the most productive player on the court, scoring ten points in the first ten minutes of the game and ultimately leading the varsity with eighteen points and twelve rebounds. In the season opener

December 2, a road game at Southern Methodist University in Dallas, Wallace picked up two fouls in the game's first five minutes, and he scored just four points in a cautious first half—his first official basket as a Commodore was a tip-in with 15:35 left in the half, giving VU an 11–9 lead. But after a pep talk from Coach Skinner ("I want to see you rebounding like I'm used to seeing!" the coach told the sophomore before sending him into the game for the final time), Wallace picked up the pace late in the second half, collecting ten rebounds, and Vanderbilt won in overtime, 88–84.

Needing overtime to beat the inferior Mustangs was cause for some concern among the Commodore faithful, and the Auburn game did little to ease their worries. Though Auburn was clearly overmatched, the Tigers forced a sloppy and rough style of play, and Vanderbilt never got its smooth, fast-break style into high gear. Dudley Green of the *Banner* wrote that the "Vanderbilt attack spit and sputtered a goodly portion of the night," and the ragged first half was marred by turnovers and a total of twenty-four fouls, including fifteen by Auburn. In all, referees Ralph Stout and Joe Caldwell whistled a total of forty-four fouls on the night, including a technical against Vanderbilt's Wyenandt and a flagrant foul on Auburn's Ronnie Jackson that led to his ejection from the game. "The boos," Green wrote, "were loud and frequent."

Whistles everywhere, it seemed, except in one of the most obvious cases. Wallace had played tentatively in Dallas, careful not to accidentally throw an elbow or shove a Mustang player and set off a fight. Playing in front of the home crowd, he felt more comfortable against Auburn, gaining confidence with every minute. But then he took a flagrant karate chop to the back, and the crowd howled as Stroud and Caldwell let the game continue with no foul called against Auburn's Wally Tinker. For Wallace, the incident was a shocking introduction to the treatment he would frequently receive from players and referees alike over the course of the season. "After that [blow]," Wallace told a *Hustler* reporter a few months later, "I was always a bit leery." Just one incident in one ballgame, but in its particulars and in its aftermath, a telling glimpse into the realities of pioneering.

Just before Tinker hit him, Wallace had blocked his jump shot, a flat-out playground block at about five feet from the basket that sent the ball flying out to the back court. "No doubt he was embarrassed and angered at this 'black block,'" Wallace recalled. "So, yes, Wally and the boys were pissed—but they were also intimidated, and by a black."

Back in the Vanderbilt huddle immediately after Tinker's hack job, Wallace collected his thoughts, pondering the likely outcomes if he retaliated in kind. How could he "get" Wally Tinker and get away with it? Would Vanderbilt fans support him if he engaged in outright aggression against a white player? How would Tiger fans treat him when Vandy traveled to Auburn?

Wallace's leaping ability and court sense made him one of the greatest rebounders ever to wear a Commodore uniform. He ended his career with 894 boards, ranking second in school history behind only Clyde Lee. Vanderbilt University Athletic Department.

"These three questions were real to me, and I had no choice but to act accordingly," Wallace recalled, ultimately deciding that the best way to get back at Auburn was to play his hardest and win the game. "That may not have been clear to many people," he observed. "Some blacks called my reaction weak and Tomish, and some whites who congratulated me for my 'character' were just phonies who were happy to avoid dealing with race and who really didn't care if a black suffered."

(And a postscript to the Tinker story: About twenty years later, at an SEC event where Wallace was honored, he ran into a gracious Wally Tinker. "After we had talked a few minutes, he did an amazing thing," Wallace recalled. "He related that he had heard about how that famous blow had affected me, and he apologized. I accepted, and we continued to chat like old friends—two men, two southerners, two Americans. He had reflected and America had begun to change. I call that a victory, a much greater and transformative one than 'getting' Wally Tinker.")

Despite Tinker's blow, Wallace's SEC debut was ultimately successful, as Vanderbilt won 78–65 and improved to 2–0, good enough for a Number 8 national ranking in the Associated Press poll. In the moments after the game, however, Skinner was concerned.

By this point, the fans had all gone home, leaving their popcorn boxes and Coke cups scattered throughout the bleachers. Gym manager Baines cut out all the lights except for a few banks toward the back, and the dim, soft-yellow glow of the cavernous building was interrupted only by the exit signs that shone above each doorway. Hagan signed autographs for a few kids who had stuck around to meet their hero, and up in the press box, high above the court (another anomaly for a basketball gymnasium; at most arenas, members of the press sat courtside), the silence of the now-deserted gym was broken by the clickety-clack of typewriters and the voices of sportswriters calling their stories back to their copy desks. In the locker room, Skinner chatted with a lingering writer. His team was 2–0, but if they continued to play this sloppily, he worried, they'd be 2–3 in a matter of days. On their way to Nashville over the course of just eight days were North Carolina, Davidson, and Duke, three powerhouses from one state, all nationally ranked. "I can't remember three tougher games in a row," Skinner said.

For Wallace, the three-game stretch would be especially gratifying. After playing as a freshman in cracker-box gyms at schools that cared a lot more about football than basketball, this, he believed, was big-time basketball. And, more meaningfully, each of the teams coming to Memorial would bring along a pioneer of its own. Charlie Scott at North Carolina, Mike Maloy at Davidson, and C. B. Claiborne at Duke were each the first black players to play for those universities, adding to the list of black luminaries who appeared in Memorial Gymnasium in 1967.

Two days after the Auburn game, Wallace and his classmates received news that the Afro-American Student Association they had petitioned for had been approved unanimously by the student body's Board of Presidents. The group would have thirty-six charter members and would temporarily be chaired by Bob Moore, a senior about to begin his final semester on campus. The *Hustler* reported that the association would plan projects in the "cultural, social, and political spheres," and the group's constitution explained its reason for being: "As it is evident that the Negro will be improved only as much as he improves himself, and as it is evident that the performance and welfare of the Negro becomes stifled in a racially restrictive society, no matter how subtle that racism may be, it becomes necessary for the Negro to adopt a position of self-assertion and determination to maintain himself as a unit of action." Or, as Wes Bradby said at the time, "We prefer segregation as a group to segregation as individuals, if we must have segregation."

In contrast to Bradby, Godfrey Dillard, who had been a popular student at his integrated high school, held out hope that some of Vanderbilt's white students would come to meetings or even join the association. "It is really open," he said, "and will only become a segregated organization if no white students come."

Wallace, more attuned to southern realities, had no such hope. "The AAA will serve a multiplicity of values for the Negroes and perhaps fewer for the white students," he told Brad Edgerton of the *Hustler*. "It could serve an important function as a meaningful dialogue, but I expect to see disapproval among the students. . . . I don't have much faith in the AAA as a vehicle to bring about true interracial understanding. But, meanwhile, it will serve many purposes for us." Among those purposes was to continue to host parties on the eleventh floor of Carmichael Towers West, and among the guests at the association's first official party three days later was Charlie Scott of the North Carolina Tar Heels.

Before that party, however, came another opportunity to celebrate. On the eve of the UNC game, yet another black legend made his way to Memorial Gym. It was Otis Redding, the twenty-six-year-old soul sensation from Macon, Georgia, performing in concert between gigs in Memphis and Cleveland, Ohio. For those who were there, including Wallace, who considered Redding the "embodiment of soul," the performance was unforgettable. "Oh, God, it was a fabulous concert," Bedford Waters recalled. "'Try a Little Tenderness.' It was amazing."

Redding flew away, his stage dismantled, and the following day the three-game gauntlet began. First up were the Tar Heels, ranked fifth in the country and coming off a Final Four appearance in the previous season's NCAA Tournament. UNC was led by thirty-six-year-old Dean Smith, beginning the seventh of thirty-six seasons as the head coach in Chapel Hill. In addition to

Scott, who along with Wallace had been tabbed as one of "eight sophomores to watch" by *Sports Illustrated*, North Carolina's stars included high-scoring All-America candidate Larry Miller and six-foot-ten center Rusty Clark. To *Hustler* columnist Bill Livingston, the game looked like a complete mismatch. "Any team with a 2–0 record and a position on the Top 10 nationally is far from on its deathbed," he wrote of the Commodores. "Yet if the play of the first two games is to be the seasonal trend, Vanderbilt will have no need to ask for whom the bells toll Saturday when UNC comes to town." Skinner was only slightly more positive when he met with the media before the game. "We'll have to play the best game we can play and then play a little better," he said. "North Carolina is one of the top teams in the nation and they have a complete team: speed, size and shooting."

Energized by an uncommonly boisterous crowd, even by Memorial Gym standards, Vanderbilt eliminated the sloppy play that had plagued it against SMU and Auburn, getting its fast-break game into high gear and crashing the boards to collect key rebounds against the bigger, stronger, North Carolina team. Acknowledging the size disadvantage, Skinner chose not to double-team the UNC big men but instead put extra pressure on the Tar Heel guards, making it difficult for them to feed the inside scorers. The strategy worked, as the Commodores forced twenty-two turnovers, including fourteen in a decisive first half. Vanderbilt led by seven points at halftime, the crowd's screams bouncing off the Memorial Gym cinderblocks with such force as the first-half clock expired that Warren and Hagan said their ears were still ringing when they reached the Commodore locker room. In the second half Skinner pulled Wyenandt away from the basket when VU had the ball, drawing his defender, Miller, with him, unclogging the lanes for Warren, who led the way with eighteen points, and Hagan, who scored sixteen of his eighteen points in the final twenty minutes. UNC's full-court press was ineffective, and with Hagan leading the way, the Commodores were nearly unstoppable offensively, hitting on eighteen of twenty-eight field goals and twenty of twenty-two free throws in the second half. Vanderbilt won 89–76.

In the locker room, Warren was jubilant. "This was the biggest win for me since I've been here," the senior said. Wallace, rubbing the bridge of his nose, was perplexed: a distressing trend was emerging. "I believe [my nose] is broken," he said. "Why is it every time one of the big centers turns toward the basket his elbow catches me in the nose?" Not only had Wallace taken a blow to the face, he'd also been targeted by the referees, drawing his fourth foul early in the second half. Still, he altered the game on the defensive end, blocking one UNC shot twenty feet out of bounds and holding the Tar Heels' talented center, Clark, below his scoring average. Skinner heard Wallace's lament but offered little consolation. "You have to learn to duck," he told his undersized center. "If you thought Carolina was tall, wait until Davidson comes in here Tuesday night."

The following evening, as Wallace nursed his aching nose and prepared to battle Davidson's three big men, shocking news spread across the Vanderbilt campus. Marshall Chapman had just returned to her dorm when the phone rang. It was Jim Cunningham, the kicker on the Commodore football team. "He said, 'The Big O has gone down,' and I said, 'What are you talking about?'" Chapman recalled. "He said, 'Otis Redding. The whole band. They crashed going to the University of Wisconsin.'" Redding's concert at Memorial Gym had been the next-to-last appearance of his life: the plane crashed carrying Redding and his band from Cleveland, Ohio, to a show at The Factory in Madison, Wisconsin. While Redding had been in Nashville, a mechanic warned band members that the Beechcraft plane's battery was not producing full power. Now, the plane lay silently on the bottom of Madison's Lake Monona. For many students, returning to Memorial Gym two days later for the Davidson game carried an eerie sensation. Otis had just put on an unforgettable show there. Now he was dead.

Better news arrived on campus in the form of the latest Associated Press poll, which after the Carolina victory listed the Commodores at Number 3 in the country, trailing only top-ranked UCLA, led by Alcindor, and Number 2 Houston, starring Elvin Hayes. With undefeated, Number 8–ranked Davidson on the way to town, anticipation for the game reached a fever pitch. "From the frying pan into the fire" was how Skinner put it, trying his best to convince his players, and Commodore fans, that the upcoming foe from the unheralded Southern Conference would be every bit as tough to beat as the Tar Heels. "Davidson is deeper and has more height than North Carolina. I'm hoping we aren't too tired."

While Skinner engaged in typical coach-speak, downplaying his team's chances, Davidson coach Lefty Driesell, who would go on to fame as the longtime, colorful coach at the University of Maryland, talked up his team's talents without hesitation. "My best ever," he said. "We have excellent depth, good speed, good scoring and strong backboard strength." If anyone could snap Vanderbilt's thirty-two-game, nonconference home winning streak, Driesell believed he had the team to do it.

He also had the good luck charm. As he paced the Davidson bench area, Driesell carried a black, plastic cat in his pants pocket, a talisman named Mojo that had been with him since the late 1950s. Over in the Vanderbilt student section, Godfrey Dillard was without a good luck charm of his own. He was just beginning to rehabilitate from knee surgery, and though he had been able to walk without crutches for a little over a week, Dillard had brought his crutch to the North Carolina game and held it aloft during the game's most exciting moments. Though he wouldn't be able to run for another three or four weeks, he felt confident enough to leave the crutch at home for the Davidson game.

It was a decision that appeared to be a huge mistake. With Wyenandt and Hagan each getting into early foul trouble, Davidson controlled the game offensively, taking a seven-point lead into the halftime break. Unable to contribute to the team in any other way—relegated to the student section, at that—Dillard realized there was one thing he had to do. As his fellow students headed for the concession stands at intermission, Dillard made his way through the bleachers, walked out the door onto 25th Avenue, and hobbled back to his dormitory in search of his lucky crutch. But by the time he returned to the Gym, Davidson had taken a thirteen-point lead.

While Wallace once again racked up double-digit rebounds, it was Warren (seventeen points), Wyenandt (also seventeen), and Hagan (twenty-three) who carried the scoring load. An injection of offense also came from an unexpected source. Back-up center Bob Bundy, whom Skinner had earlier suspended for violating team rules, returned to the lineup for the first time all season and scored seven points off the bench in relief of Wallace. With Dillard waving his crutch, Murray leading the "Hey Hey" cheer, and Commodore PR man Bill Stewart up in the press box twisting, turning, jumping, yelling, and grimacing with every basket or change of possession, Vanderbilt whittled the Wildcat lead down to three points with three minutes to go. It was at that point, Driesell said later, that his players began to force bad shots under pressure. The Commodores tied the score, and Hagan had a chance to win the game in regulation but missed a fifteen-foot jumper as time expired, sending the game into overtime. In the extra session, Wallace controlled a jump ball with ninety seconds remaining and the score tied, and Vanderbilt held the ball for one final shot. Once again, Hagan took the big shot with the game on the line—his one-handed jumper hit nothing but net and sent students flooding onto the court. Skinner, Driesell, and assistant coaches from both teams got caught up in the stampede ("I hate to think what might happen to some of our players in a jam like that," Skinner said later), and rising above all the commotion was a bobbing and weaving crutch—a joyful Godfrey Dillard in the center of it all. "I feel bad that I can't play this year, so I try to do something to help. So far the crutch has done the job," he told a *Hustler* reporter after the game.

As the Commodore players shed their sweat-soaked uniforms in front of their green metal lockers, an unexpected visitor walked into the square-shaped room: Lefty Driesell. "You boys did a great job," he said, scanning the room for Bundy, whom Driesell had unsuccessfully tried to recruit to Davidson. He found him in the shower. "Big Boy," the coach said, "You hurt us. I didn't know you could hit from out there." Driesell's generous praise seemed genuine, but there may have also been some gamesmanship involved. Both Davidson and Vanderbilt were set to participate in the Sugar Bowl Tournament in New Orleans later in the month, and there was a good chance they'd face each other again there. Hours later, well after the players had showered and dressed, after the sportswriters had filed their articles, after the Davidson bus had departed, Vanderbilt student manager Paul Wilson walked into the visitors' locker room to make a final sweep. Scrawled across the chalkboard was one last message from Driesell: "We'll see you in New Orleans."

Two powerhouses defeated, one more—Duke—left to go. While UCLA and Houston had captured most of the national attention to this point in the season and were set to square off in one of the most highly anticipated college basketball games in history on January 20 at the Astrodome, Skinner's club was attracting notice of its own. *Sports Illustrated* sent Curry Kirkpatrick to Nashville for ten days to find out the secret to the Commodores' success, but even the local sportswriters struggled to pinpoint how it was possible for such a mild-mannered coach to have his team playing so well.

"The amazing thing about Roy Skinner . . . is the way he brings out the best in his basketball players," wrote Waxo Green. "He doesn't use mirrors, LSD or strong talk. If you ask any of the present Commodores what Coach Skinner's secret is, they couldn't tell you to save their lives." Skinner's own players may have been at a loss ("I can't put it into words," Warren offered), but there was one group of men on the face of the planet who could very specifically outline Skinner's approach: youth coaches on the island of Taiwan. While on a State Department–sponsored tour there in 1964, Skinner shared his eleven-point coaching philosophy:

1. Be honest to the press
2. Be fair to the players
3. Teach sportsmanship
4. Winning is most important
5. Have confidence
6. Don't be a good loser, just act like one
7. Only dress players who can help
8. Best way to improve your team is to improve yourself
9. End every practice on a happy note
10. New things first in practice
11. Mental and moral condition of vital importance

Skinner's man-of-few-words approach didn't work with all of his players. "He'd give us pearls of wisdom such as, 'To beat these guys, we're going to have to hit our shots and we're going to have to get more rebounds than they do and play good defense,'" said one former player. "Words weren't his strong suit." But one thing Skinner innately understood was how to take pressure off his players. For one thing, he rarely looked like he felt any pressure himself. His cool demeanor likely came at a cost: his jacket pockets were full of cigarette butts, he was known to throw down more than a few beers, and players often spotted the telltale chalky white ring of the antacid Gelusil around his lips. With six kids at home and by all accounts a difficult relationship with his first wife, Skinner no doubt was churning on the inside. But he rarely raised his voice, had few team rules, and let his players stay out late and have fun on road trips. During games, he did little to draw attention to himself. He sat rather than stood, and unlike most coaches who positioned themselves at the far end of the team's bench, Skinner chose instead to sit right in the middle, an equal number of his players on either side. As the action unfolded, Skinner sipped from a cup of ice water; the only betrayal of nerves was the way he shuffled his feet and rubbed his hands together. As Kirkpatrick wrote in his *SI* profile, "Vanderbilt's poise under fire seems a direct reflection of the personality of its leader, but anything more stoic than his present state would make Skinner nearly a dead man." Skinner maintained his low-key style at the expense of a certain amount of popularity. Even though his teams were successful, there was a perception among a segment of Vanderbilt fans that his teams won in spite of their no-frills coach. "What you saw is what you got with Roy," said booster Joel Gordon, a supporter of Skinner's. "Roy was not any back slapper. He was very humble, very laid back. Maybe too much laid back. A lot of people were critical of Roy because they thought he didn't have a very creative offense, wasn't active off the bench, didn't make a lot of tactical decisions. The criticism would be that Roy just rolled the basketball out on the floor and said, 'Go get it.' But he won. He was a hard-working guy." Bottom line, the Skinner style worked. There was something to be said for recruiting well and otherwise keeping things simple.

Heading into the third and final leg of the gauntlet against Duke, one thing out of Skinner's control was the health of his players. Warren had injured a leg against Davidson, but more troubling was a citywide flu epidemic that was threatening to decimate his team. (It was only much later that several players, including Wallace and Bo Wyenandt, discovered that they had actually been struck with mononucleosis, an illness that limited their strength and stamina for much of the season.) First the bug and high fevers hit Warren and Wyenandt; then, on the eve of the Duke game, Kenny Campbell placed a call to team trainer Joe Worden to ask for help. "Even if they get out [of bed] before game time, they'll be rubbery-legged and unable to go full speed for any length of time," Skinner worried. "I'm no doctor, but I'm afraid they'll not be in first-class shape to play against a team as good as Duke."

At 4–0, Vic Bubas' Duke team was led by an imposing front court featuring six-foot-seven Mike Lewis, six-foot-seven Steve Vandenberg, and six-foot-six Joe Kennedy, a trio that promised to give the undersized Wallace problems. Though the Blue Devils were coming off a relatively down year in 1967 (an 18–9 overall record and second-place finish in the ACC), Duke had risen to national prominence under Bubas, reaching NCAA Final Fours in 1963 and 1966 and the national title game in 1964.

By game time, team trainer Worden had given the weary Warren and Wy-enandt the OK to play, but Campbell was a no-go. Skinner opened the game defensively in a passive 2-1-2 zone, hoping to conserve what little energy his depleted team had left, but Duke's Kennedy and Joe Golden took advantage of Vanderbilt's packed-in defense by hitting a series of outside jumpers. Skinner reluctantly switched to a more aggressive man-to-man defense, but the Duke guards capitalized by feeding the ball to the Blue Devils' big men inside. With Hagan picking up four quick fouls, Duke led by as many as eleven points in the first half, took a 44–37 lead into halftime, and extended the lead back to ten points over the first several minutes of the second half. But just as it appeared that the Commodores would succumb to Duke and the flu, a last-gasp burst of energy appeared out of nowhere. Wallace outmuscled Duke's frontline for rebound after rebound, collecting a season-high fifteen by game's end. Hagan shook off his foul trouble to begin pouring in points. Wyenandt forgot about his illness and started draining jumpers. Over an eight-minute stretch midway through the second half, Vanderbilt outscored the Blue Devils 19–7 to take the lead. The crowd was raucous, an improbable victory close at hand, but then a whistle with just over two minutes left. The fifth, disqualifying foul was called on Hagan, who was leading the team with twenty-six points. Boos came cascading down from the balconies, and then students began hurling ice cubes onto the floor in protest. Referee Harold Johnson signaled toward the Vanderbilt bench. Skinner got up from his chair and walked, head down, toward the scorer's table. He grabbed the microphone from Grizzard.

"We've got a chance to win this game," he calmly told the crowd. "If you continue to throw stuff out here you can cost us a technical foul and the game. Please help us." The lead seesawed in the final seconds, Duke recovering from a 74–70 deficit with 1:32 remaining to take a 75–74 lead with seventeen seconds left. One final possession for Vanderbilt. With Hagan on the bench, it would be up to Wyenandt to take the game winner. He dribbled into the corner of the court but was cut off by Duke defenders. A quick pass, then the ball returned to Wyenandt just above the foul circle. A couple of dribbles to collect himself, and he let loose from twenty-five feet. Bucket! Ball game. More pandemonium. ("You hit from that spot, or you aren't too much of a shooter," Wyenandt said afterward.) As Duke players stood with hands on hips or sunk in their seats, Hagan leaped off the Commodore bench to embrace Wyenandt, joined by students and cheerleaders mobbing the game's hero. Vanderbilt players made their way off the court toward the small door that led to their locker room, walking arm in arm beneath the Coca-Cola scoreboard reading Vanderbilt 76, Visitors 75. Policemen ringing the court stood and watched as students continued to streak onto the floor.

One student remained virtually alone. Standing on top of a wooden bleacher in the first row, there was Godfrey Dillard, casting his gaze toward his would-be teammates as they exited the floor, lifting his single crutch high into the air. Wallace sought out Duke's Claiborne, and invited him to come by the eleventh-floor party later that night. At this moment, more than at any other time since he had meditated on that rock at White City Park, Wallace felt at peace with his decision to attend Vanderbilt. From a basketball perspective, things could not be better. In his piece for *Sports Illustrated*, Kirkpatrick gushed that "Vanderbilt . . . plays the game the way it was meant to be played. The Commodores prosper on diligent execution of basic patterns and marvelous insouciance under pressure." Duke assistant Chuck Daly, who would go on to fame as the "Bad Boys"–era coach of the Detroit Pistons, was impressed with Vandy's hard-nosed style. "They shock you with fantastic scrap and hustle," Daly said, "and they get loose balls and come off the floor at you like animals."

The impressed national sportswriters, the admiring opposing coaches, Skinner, Wallace, Hagan, Warren, Wyenandt, the jubilant fans—none of them could have anticipated that Commodore basketball had arrived at a precipice from which it would almost immediately descend. Five games into his varsity career, Wallace had experienced the best it would ever get. It all started with a queasy feeling in his stomach after the Duke game. The bug had caught up with him.

The first signs of the fall were evident in the visitors' locker room at the University of Florida. It was halftime of Vanderbilt's first game since the win over Duke, and although Vanderbilt led the Gators 44–30, the ominous signals were hard to miss. First, the room was emptier than it should have been. Assistant Coach Homer Garr was in bed back in Nashville, too sick with the flu to make the flight south. More important, Bob Warren, who had spent the morning soaking in a whirlpool, had been left behind at the team hotel, hobbling on crutches and nursing injuries to his wrist, shoulder, and leg. Just a few days removed from a 102-degree fever that kept him out of the Duke game, Kenny Campbell slumped in his chair, sick as a dog. How his undermanned bunch would continue to outpace six-foot-ten Gator center Neal Walk, averaging thirty points and leading the nation in rebounding, was hard for Skinner to fathom.

Florida opened the second half with an aggressive pressing defense, wearing Campbell down and forcing a series of Vanderbilt turnovers. Held scoreless in the first half and badly outplayed by Wallace and his backup, Bundy, Walk stayed out of foul trouble in the second half and poured in seventeen points. Little by little, the Commodores' lead drifted away, and when the clock hit :00, the scoreboard read Florida 74, Vanderbilt 72. As team manager Gene Smitherman collected sweaty uniforms in the postgame locker room, he felt that the outcome represented more than just one loss; it punctured the team's self-confidence. "It was a bad letdown," he recalled. "I had been in awe over our wins against Duke, Davidson, and North Carolina, because frankly

I didn't know we were that good. And then here was a sign that we may not have been."

The Commodores bounced back from the loss in Gainesville by winning two holiday tournaments, the hometown Vanderbilt Invitational and the Sugar Bowl Tournament in New Orleans. Other than picking up a second win over Davidson in the Big Easy, the competition in the tournaments hadn't been too challenging. It was two upcoming games—back-to-back matchups against archrivals Kentucky and Tennessee—that would be the true test of the team's mettle.

First up was the January 6 game against the Wildcats in Nashville. With both teams ranked in the Top 5, the game was second in national implications only to the upcoming UCLA-Houston game. In his thirty-eighth season as Kentucky coach, Rupp would be coaching his 939th career game when UK visited Memorial Gym, and with 667 career victories, he trailed all-time leader Phog Allen, his former coach at Kansas, by just five wins. Vanderbilt and Kentucky had engaged in a highly entertaining rivalry in their previous seven matchups: twenty-one years after Rupp had taught Norm Cooper's Vanderbilt team a lesson with the 98–29 rout, the Commodores had emerged as a respected threat to Kentucky's dominance. Over the previous three seasons, the average score of a Vandy-Kentucky game had been a blistering 99–86, including a 120-point effort by the Commodores the previous season that marked the most points an SEC team ever scored against Kentucky. Still, even as Vanderbilt gradually closed the gap on Kentucky's dominant position in the league, there remained among most Commodore fans a feeling of immense admiration, bordering on awe, for Rupp and his program. "I had a lot more respect for Kentucky and a lot more hate for Tennessee," recalled Commodore fan Don Dahlinger. "I'm *proud* of my hatred for Tennessee. But we looked forward to the man in the brown suit [Rupp] coming to town. They were the standard."

In the days leading up to the Vanderbilt game, Rupp informed Nashville reporters that his team would not arrive early to practice at Memorial Gym, as had been standard procedure in previous years. "Too many people around," he said. Finding a way into a Kentucky practice session was a favorite pastime among some of the most die-hard Commodore fans. As leaders of the Vanderbilt booster club, Bob Calton and John Thorpe had organized a speakers' series where opposing coaches were invited to speak to Vanderbilt fans over lunch prior to games. ("It was a lot more fun than football, where our coach would come out every Monday and explain why we lost," Calton deadpanned.) Whenever Kentucky came to town, Calton and Thorpe would drive out to the airport and greet the Wildcats as they got off their plane, and escort the team to Memorial Gym for a practice session. "I remember asking Harry Lancaster if it would be all right if we stayed to watch practice," Calton recalled, "and he said, 'That's fine, there's nothing to this game. All you try to do is get the ball in the hole and keep the other team from scoring.'" With this uncommon level of access, Calton and Thorpe witnessed a scene that provides an interesting glimpse into the way the Baron ran his program.

"We were watching them and they were shooting at two ends of the floor," Calton recalled. "None of the players said anything. They didn't shoot any funny-looking shots; they were shooting serious stuff. There wasn't a coach on the floor; they were all sitting up on the side. And they shot for about fifteen minutes, and then all of a sudden they went to the other end and started shooting. No whistle blew, it was precision. And then one of the managers went to the jump circle at midcourt. And he put down a box of Kleenex, and a wet towel and a dry towel. And one at a time, the players would go over, and wipe their hands with the wet towel, dry their hands with the dry towel, blow their nose or whatever, and then they went down to one end and they had a drill that they ran. My recollection is they had one post player and in each corner where the forwards were, there would be two or three guys, and at the guard position would be two or three more guys. They'd have one guard take the ball, throw it to the other guard. The post man flashed out high, he got it. The two forwards crisscrossed and then he'd toss it to one of them, and they'd jump up and make a fifteen-foot shot. And again, Rupp hadn't said a word, he's just sitting there with us. As soon as one shot went in, the second ball was put in play. Bam, bam, bam, bam, the shot goes in. Bam, bam, bam, bam, the shot goes in. They must have made about eight or nine straight jump shots. And the next shot, the guy shot it, it hits the rim, bounces around, and hits the floor. The first one to miss. Adolph Rupp jumped straight out of his chair, walked out on the floor, and he cussed at them, he yelled at them. 'Goddamn, they're not all going to go in, you've got to follow your shot, I don't want to see that ball hit the floor!' And then when anybody's shot didn't go in, they all went toward the basket to get the rebound. It was fun to see." When the Kentucky practice session wrapped up, Calton and Thorpe, impressed with what they had witnessed, stuck around for Skinner's Vanderbilt walk-through.

"With Kentucky, everything was precision," Thorpe recalled. "Just a well-oiled machine. They go off, we come on, and we're running *backwards*. We have a scrimmage, big men versus short men, and everybody's laughing, goofing around, and hell, we looked not quite like clowns, but not very serious. And [Vanderbilt] beat 'em the next day. Sure did. I said, "Boy, there's just no justice."

In January 1968, there was no practice session, no Calton and Thorpe in the gym, but perhaps, from a Kentucky point of view, there was justice. Bam, bam, bam, bam, the shot goes in. Bam, bam, bam, bam, the shot goes in, only this time the display of precision was in the game itself. Kentucky came out and hit its first seven shots and fifteen of its first eighteen, jumping out to an improbable 51–21 lead with three minutes still remaining in the first half. "I've never had a bunch of boys go up and down the floor like [that]," Rupp beamed after the game, which Kentucky won 94–78. "I've never seen execution any better than they had that first half," said Skinner. The loss dropped Vanderbilt's conference record to 2–2, the winning streak against the trio of North Carolina teams fading into memory, then all but forgotten when the Commodores dropped their next game, a 64–62 loss at archrival Tennessee.

In the wake of the back-to-back defeats, the mood on campus and around Nashville had grown sour, the conventional wisdom holding that the season, with nearly two months still left to go, was effectively over. While some observers, including Henry Hecht of the *Hustler*, attributed the team's slide to the absence of a playmaking guard in the mold of the graduated Jerry Southwood, other fans pinned their frustrations on Wallace, calling for him to be more offensively assertive. Wallace said he heard the complaints from both the black and white communities—two sides of the same coin. From white fans, including some of the diehards sitting in the rows immediately behind the Vanderbilt bench, came jeers urging him to mix it up under the boards. "You're not aggressive enough, Wallace!" "You're lazy!" "Jump, boy, jump!" Some black observers, meanwhile, felt that Wallace was overly deferential in his new surroundings and urged him to let loose and take more shots.

To say that Wallace considered himself in a no-win situation is an understatement of three-ply variety. First, because he was suffering from mono, he simply wasn't able to jump and run as he normally could. Second, there was an extra level of hesitation to his game for two reasons: he imposed some of it on himself in an effort to avoid starting a melee in which he knew he'd be outnumbered; and there was the growing uncertainty he began to feel when officials overlooked the cheap shots thrown his way. Third, Wallace resisted the calls to shoot more often for the most logical of reasons: he knew he simply wasn't very good at it. His best offensive move, the dunk, had been legislated away. To suddenly start launching—and missing—jump shots, Wallace believed, would reinforce stereotypes that blacks played a "wild" brand of basketball. Whatever the reason, the cohesion that had marked the Commodores' fast start to the season was tearing apart as the losses mounted. Wallace felt his portion of the blame came with an extra dose of disdain.

"I'm not saying it was all racial, some of it was just the frustration of the people who were screaming," Wallace recalled. "But I am saying the parts where they're saying, 'Nigger, you better jump!' I guarantee you it's hard to take race out of that. Some of these people were really nasty, and my parents had to hear some of that stuff. There were some games where I didn't play well, there's no question about that, but some of these people weren't able to apply an ordinary level of criticism. They were foaming at the mouth and took it right to the bottom. The words you heard people use were the same ones you heard down in Mississippi or Alabama." Wallace endured the criticism, and in the aftermath he'd hear from old friends and acquaintances from his neighborhood or over at Tennessee State University (as Tennessee A&I was officially renamed that year), not with words of encouragement but with another brand of condemnation, disparaging his decision to attend Vanderbilt. He shouldn't be playing with those white boys, they'd say; he should have gone to TSU or Grambling.

"You'd have black people—sometimes black people with college degrees and sometimes black guys on Jefferson Street who were chemically assisted—saying, 'You ought to get the ball, take more shots, be more confrontational, to hell with them white boys.' Think of what those people didn't understand," Wallace recalled. "All of them, the ones who were doctors or schoolteachers and the ones who were hanging out at 18th and Jefferson, were all safely ensconced in segregation. They didn't know shit from Shinola about what I was doing, but they had a lot of advice. I was smart enough not to take it, but they thought less of me. Those people had no idea what I was doing. Do you know I'm helping to integrate the SEC? The only way I could have done what I did was to have a measure of real restraint—because at the same time I'm really pushing the envelope. I'm doing it in a way that you call nonthreatening, but it creates a real possibility to get it done. I couldn't do it with a clenched fist."

D o you have any idea of the humiliation of a youth subjected to a non-integrated society, reminded on all sides of his inferiority and told to keep his place?"

It was a jarring question for Jean Heard, wife of the chancellor, and not one she had fielded before at a dinner party. Then again, the home on Welbeck Road where she had been invited to dine at 8:00 p.m. on January 11 wasn't in Belle Meade; it was in Nairobi. She and Chancellor Heard were in Africa on a sixteen-day tour of Kenya, Ethiopia, Tanzania, and Uganda sponsored by the Ford Foundation, of which Heard was president.

The questions from Haile Selassie had been a lot easier to answer. Two days earlier, the Heards had been allowed a thirty-minute audience with the seventy-six-year-old Ethiopian leader in Addis Ababa. Not that there weren't awkward moments. Mrs. Heard wasn't sure whether to curtsy or shake hands with Selassie, so she did both. Welcomed into a richly furnished room—oriental rugs, a fireplace, and a tall, brocade armchair with a silver crown on top for the emperor—the Heards were not allowed to sit directly opposite their host. Seated to Selassie's right, the chancellor and his wife listened as the emperor talked of the necessity to harness the energy of youth, to encourage ambition but to direct it in proper channels. How, he wondered, did Heard handle student riots and demonstrations at Vanderbilt? The issue was fresh on Selassie's mind; an appearance in Ethiopia by US vice president Hubert Humphrey had been canceled recently after students picketed with anti-American posters. The question was one Heard had answered many times back on his home turf. "We try to anticipate student grievances and to keep the lines of communication open between students, faculty and the administration," he said. "We protect the rights of students, but on the other hand the abuse of those rights in the name of freedom is not tolerated and even demonstrators must proceed in an orderly fashion." The emperor was impressed, suggesting that Heard return to speak at Haile Selassie University. "You have wisdom that would help our students," he said.

In Nairobi the conversation was more uncomfortable. Phil Ndegwa, a top Kenyan government economist seated beside Mrs. Heard, continued to remind her that minority status was a relative thing. Vanderbilt, he told her, was a fine university, but he would never send a Kenyan there because of the state of race relations in Nashville. Maybe so, but just five years removed from British colonial rule, higher educational opportunities for native Kenyans were so scarce that planeloads were arriving in the United States each year to attend college. It is possible that one such Kenyan, who had briefly attended the University of Hawaii and Harvard and had collaborated with Ndegwa on an influential economic blueprint for the country, was at the party. Mrs. Heard noted in her diary that "several government officials" were there. Could it have been that a colleague of Ndegwa's who had attended college in the United States and whose own son was living in Hawaii would have been invited to dine with the Americans? Impossible to know, but if one of the Kenyans the Heards met that night was Barack Hussein Obama, it surely would have been utterly unimaginable to them that the man's son could grow up to become the president of the United States.

Back in Nashville, Heard's administration was attempting to answer Ndegwa's question in its own way—reporting to university faculty and staff on its progress integrating black students into the campus culture. On January 18 Dean Sidney Boutwell issued a "Report on Negro Students" to the university's Arts and Science faculty members, a nine-page document that was considered timely because members of that spring's graduating Class of '68 included the first black undergraduates to live in university dormitories.

Writing of those first tentative encounters between black students and white administrators, Boutwell erred in concluding that there had been no problematic incidents, but uncannily captured the degree of hesitation involved, as if aliens from two distant planets were meeting for the first time: "Perhaps it was luck, perhaps it was because we prepared as carefully as we could, but, in any event, we avoided any serious problems which might have been caused by well-intentioned persons who had little or no previous associations with Negroes on this level and who might, therefore, have impulsively (they were too nervous) or intuitively done the wrong thing."

Boutwell proudly listed the extracurricular activities of the fourteen most recently admitted black students (one in fencing, two in the Glee Club, three in the band) and informed the faculty that, "off the record and for your private information," Vanderbilt was faring better than Duke, Emory, and Tulane in this regard. Still, Vanderbilt's black students, Boutwell wrote, could not be conveniently considered either all "friendly Negroes" or "militant Negroes."

"I think that most of our Negro students do not want to hide their blackness and wish to develop not only personal pride but to cause their white associates to be appreciative of the distinctive and worthwhile characteristics of Negro or African culture," he continued. "They wish to maintain communication with the white man and to work for an environment in which both white and black can feel comfortable. On the other hand, some of our Negro students are more militant, sometimes hostile, and tend to be separatists."

In making the point that "patience and a sense of humor" had been important ingredients in the integration process, Boutwell related a story about a conversation he had with a black student nearly three years earlier. Over dinner, Boutwell had asked the student "what observations he had made about Vanderbilt now that his freshman year was nearly over. He replied with a twinkle in his eye that 'Vanderbilt has improved a lot since I came.' I am sure he recognized that his statement had more than one possible meaning."

The dean attempted to make an observation about the difficulty some black students faced in their home communities after enrolling at Vanderbilt. Wallace and others indeed took more than a small amount of heat from some blacks for attending a white school at a time when leaders like Carmichael were issuing cries for Black Power, but Boutwell's read on this point progressed in one paragraph from uncommonly insightful (picking up on the emotional "tug of war" many of these students confronted) to paternalistically off-base: "Our Negro students . . . have the unhappy experience of living in two environments—the campus community and the Negro community—and not being really comfortable in either situation. It is understandable that they would not feel completely at home in a predominantly white University, particularly one which has only integrated in recent years. Interestingly enough, many of them feel more comfortable on the campus than they do when they visit friends and parents. Vanderbilt has caused them or at least afforded them the opportunity to add another dimension to their personal experiences so they now find little of common interest to discuss with the folks back home."

Boutwell needed to do no deeper research than to read the local papers to see that on this last point, he was misguided. Rather than becoming estranged from their communities, many black students were becoming more resolute in their commitment to effect change. The university's most prominent black student, Wallace—taking cues from national figures like Russell and Ali—stepped out beyond the boundaries of sport, even as he was acting so carefully within those lines, to speak up on an issue of social justice in black Nashville.

The issue was the imminent construction of a freeway, Interstate 40, the

planned route of which would be most disruptive to the thriving black neighborhoods near Tennessee State and Fisk, including the all-important Jefferson
Street. The problem was three fold: First, during construction, the necessary
road closures would stifle commerce on and around Jefferson Street. Second,
because of the way the completed three-mile stretch of I-40 would wind its
way through North Nashville, the neighborhood would become almost entirely cut off from the rest of the city. And finally, the highway would perma-
nently isolate or destroy huge portions of the neighborhood, decimating the
heart of black Nashville by wiping out dozens of businesses and separating
residents from their jobs, churches, and schools. Similar scenarios had played
out in cities all over the country, with politically marginalized blacks forced
to sacrifice what little they had for the "progress" of the community at large.
In a courageously direct speech before a skeptical breakfast gathering of the
Nashville Area Chamber of Commerce's membership, Dr. Edwin Mitchell, a
black professor at Meharry Medical College, called out the city's white power
structure for ignoring the destructive impact the highway and downtown
urban renewal projects had on black neighborhoods and the economic self-
sufficiency of the people who lived in them. "Superhighways," Mitchell said,
"form concrete moats between Negro and white communities and tear their
way, with no concern for the problems they create, through the heart of the
existing Negro communities, converting the majority of their streets into
blind alleyways and affording almost no access." After confronting his audience with a litany of wrongs committed recently against Nashville's black
residents (discriminatory hiring practices, segregated schools, gentrification,
police brutality), Mitchell warned that after riots in Cairo, Illinois, Milwaukee, and Louisville, "Nashville's time was coming."

"Gentlemen," he said, "Nashville is indeed fashioning a new face. And
it has begun by upgrading the downtown business area. But tall buildings
which allow you to gaze outward upon the green grass of suburbia cannot
long shelter you from the despair, frustration and bitterness that continue to
build around you. In a city that unites its governments but leaves its people
divided, in a city that provides in the midst of want elegant show houses of
luxuries, a cruel mockery is made. But sitting as they are in the midst of all
this poverty, your businesses are just such a mockery to so many. What brave
and unthinking men you are."

The I-40 debate posed a dilemma for Wallace. Here was a sophomore so
conscious of his predicament as a pioneer that he purposely held himself
back in the one venue where he might have felt most at home, the basketball
court. In so doing, he invited taunts from white detractors and black militants. Yet as he played it safe (or smart) on the court, he also demonstrated a
willingness to place himself in the dangerous position of student leader when
it came to confronting Vanderbilt administrators. And he admired athletes
who, rather than remaining silent on social issues, risked their popularity by

speaking up for the powerless. Here he was, thrust into a new world, trying to prove himself in the heart of white Nashville, steering clear of danger, struggling to succeed at the sport he loved, sick with mono, his parents hearing the jeers directed his way. And right at this very moment, the community he grew up in was about to be irrevocably scarred.

If he chose to speak out, Wallace risked alienating the large segment of white Vanderbilt fans who perceived him as the type of "friendly Negro" Boutwell described in his report to faculty. Looking back on this moment forty years later, Wallace saw it as a pivotal time in his intellectual growth. "Believe me, I didn't know anything about politics, economics, international affairs or anything, but I had a real interest in knowing [about those things]," he said. "Part of being at Vanderbilt on the positive side was a growing knowledge of the world, and that included the whole impact of political and social upheaval. There was a lot of learning and thinking. Some of it was just mimicking, but you actually did learn stuff, and there was a sense of urgency to the issues of the day. People were engaged."

On a typical day back in the old neighborhood, Wallace estimated that he would cross Jefferson Street no less than ten times. He believed that if the political, social, and economic center of black Nashville were decimated by the interstate, violence would be inevitable. Few people in Nashville straddled the white and black communities as he did. Now, in February 1968 he feared that those factions were about to go to war. He decided to speak his mind.

"Wherever there are low economic conditions, there is hidden desperation, and all it needs to manifest itself is something like the highway," he told *Hustler* reporter Brad Sabel. "The college kids would be the most violent. . . . There would be some who would want to fight it out to the death. . . . The white community would retaliate with even more violence and power. In the end, it would hurt everyone."

Racial tensions were growing so strong that the *Hustler*'s news editor, Chuck Offenburger, warned that unless the city's power structure changed course quickly, "Nashville is likely to be in a state of racial strife unparalleled in history by this summer." Citing "unconfirmed" rumors that were "scary as hell," Offenburger hinted that black Tennesseans had hidden away some three thousand rifles for "riot purposes."

"If white Nashville—and for that matter white America—wants to avert something near total racial war in the near future," he wrote, "it better sit up and listen."

Deepest Sense of Dread

The Commodores Travel First Class

For over ten years the Vanderbilt team has traveled in style to games throughout the South on Southern Air Lines. This winter will be no exception, as the Commodores will fly on a Martin 404 to nine cities which are connected by the Southern system.

As always the team will stay in some of America's finest hotels and motor inns. Among others, accommodations have been made in Holiday Inns, Ramada Inns, and the Sheraton Inns.

The Commodores leave Nashville in mid-afternoon on the day before the game for their destination, and, after checking into a motel, go through a short workout in the home team's gym. After dinner is eaten as a team, the players then relax at a local theatre.

The day of the game is begun with breakfast, and then another short workout takes place. A team meeting is next, followed by lunch, and the players then go back to their rooms to study or watch television before the game.

A campus magazine's description of life on the road for a Commodore must have sounded positively idyllic to its student readers, what with the chartered planes, fine motels, catered meals, and practically mandatory TV watching. And this was only the G-rated version, no mention of the trysts with stewardesses, late-night poker games, or French Quarter escapades that spiced up many a Vanderbilt road trip. For most players, these trips were highly anticipated departures from the ordinary, an opportunity to pocket some meal money, catch a movie, have a few beers, and impress some coeds, all far from the prying eyes of girlfriends, professors, or potential employers back in Nashville.

But perhaps nothing illustrated the starkly different worlds in which

Perry Wallace and the rest of his teammates existed than the emotions evoked by these swings through the small towns of the SEC. For all but one Commodore, the trips were about trying to win a game and having some fun; for Wallace they were about survival. The very idea of traveling south was a source of enormous stress for the league's only black player, and the trips themselves were variations on the theme that began in Starkville the year before—the stuff of nightmares.

"There were waves of tension that accompanied those road trips," Wallace recalled. "There was a long wave that started back in the summer before the season, and this eerie note or eerie voice that would come in about what I was going to have to deal with down there, and what could happen—what's the worst that can happen. And then the next wave came in the weeks before the games, when I started to think about the specific places that we had to go: Mississippi State, Ole Miss, Auburn, Alabama, Georgia, LSU. I would just try to get ready emotionally."

Wallace's teammates remained oblivious to his plight, caught up in their own mini-vacations, a tone that was set from the top. For years, Skinner had encouraged his players to enjoy themselves on the road. The coach had rules on these trips, but they essentially boiled down to this: don't do anything to embarrass the team, and show up on time for the game. While most of his peers practically locked their players in their hotel rooms, Skinner had two reasons why he wanted his guys to go out and have fun: he believed it was a good stress reliever for players coping with the academic rigors of Vanderbilt, and he believed it was good for recruiting. "These boys had never been anywhere before," he recalled decades later. For a coach who concentrated his scouting efforts mainly on small-town kids from the Midwest, creating the perception that Vanderbilt players saw the world and were allowed to party didn't hurt his cause.

On game-day mornings, Skinner instituted a quirky routine for the team's obligatory "shootaround." Most teams—with the exception of a lock-step Kentucky—would use the practice session to familiarize themselves with a gymnasium by running through a series of plays at three-quarters speed. Skinner, on the other hand, loved to arrange a "Big Man, Little Man" scrimmage, a carefree matchup of the tall guys against the short ones, with Waxo Green from the *Banner* and John Bibb from the *Tennessean* serving as referees. The scrimmages were a fun distraction, temporarily relieving some of the pressure of trying to win a game in a hostile environment, but they were nothing compared to the postgame action Skinner often sanctioned. When Vanderbilt played LSU in Baton Rouge, for example, the coach's motivational speech typically went something like this: "Win this ballgame tonight, and the plane will pick us up in the morning in New Orleans instead." The ploy worked more often than not; after beating the Tigers, changing into street clothes, and making the eighty-mile drive to the French Quarter, Commodore players, not exactly the most inconspicuous bunch, would stay up all night downing Hurricanes at Pat O'Brien's and charging into piano bars, where they'd ask the piano man to play the Vanderbilt fight song, a request usually met with a blank stare. Skinner, meanwhile, would host late-night poker games in his hotel room, joined by team trainer Joe Worden, the team's radio broadcaster, and Green and Bibb, men who traveled on the same flights as the team and were considered part of the family. The student managers, tasked with doling out meal money to each of the players at the start of each trip, also made sure there was a cooler of cold beer in Skinner's room for the card games.

In towns where there wasn't much to do (which at the time would have been the majority of SEC locales), the players' entertainment typically consisted of nothing more than dinner and a movie. In late January 1968, during a three-game road trip to Auburn, Mississippi State, and LSU, it was during these seemingly routine outings that some players began to take notice, for the first time, that Wallace faced an entirely different set of circumstances than they did. In his *Sports Illustrated* article on Vanderbilt's quick start, Curry Kirkpatrick opined that of the four pioneers who would play at Memorial Gym that season (Wallace, Maloy, Claiborne, and Scott), it was Wallace, facing road trips to the "deep, deep South," who would confront the toughest challenge.

Drawing upon his own life experiences, the collective black experience in the South, and what he knew about Emmett Till, James Meredith, the Freedom Riders, and the civil rights workers murdered in Philadelphia, Mississippi, Wallace approached the team's three-game foray into Alabama, Mississippi, and Louisiana with what he later described as "the deepest sense of dread." No one had ever done what he was doing before, and no one in the traveling party could relate to what he was feeling. He dreamed of the worst that could happen and took deliberate steps to avoid such a fate. And in Wallace's mind, the worst that could happen was getting shot and killed, either on the court or around town before the game.

Bill LaFevor remembered a scene at a Mississippi movie theater at a screening of *Cool Hand Luke*. "As I remember it, we were at Mississippi State. We got in and practiced, and then we drove somewhere to the movie," he recalled. "About two or three minutes before the movie was over, somebody behind me mentioned that Perry had gotten up and gone out of the theater. When the movie was over, we all went back to the cars and Perry was there waiting for us. My feeling was that he realized it had gotten dark and that he was in Mississippi. There was a saying: 'Nigger, don't let the sun set on your ass in Mississippi.' We went to the theater when it was light, and while we were watching the movie it got dark. And he was out there trying to get into that car. It was locked and he couldn't get in, and he was concerned about it. And looking back on it now, realistically concerned about it."

Wallace remembers the scene well. "I was concerned about a 'failure to communicate' between me and some Mississippi bigots," he recalled. "What I had thought was a relatively tiny, 'safe' little movie theater was apparently actually a popular Friday night attraction for the community—the white community. I knew my teammates meant well, but I also knew that they hadn't a single clue. I had to provide for my own protection."

Whenever his teammates departed for dinner on this three-game swing, Wallace chose to stay in his room, telling the others that he had a stomach ache or needed to stay in and study. "I remember in Starkville, he would not go out to dinner with us," Wyenandt recalled. "We could not talk him into going. We were like, 'Come on, Perry,' but he was not going to go out of that room. I couldn't imagine it."

On most nights, Wallace remained in his room alone, Coach Skinner and his buddies playing poker down the hall, but occasionally he had company. Bob Warren, the straight arrow from Hardin, Kentucky, whose prior experience with blacks was limited to childhood encounters with a blacksmith and a maid, was assigned to room with Wallace on a number of trips. Feeling challenged academically at Vanderbilt, Warren often used his free time on the road to study. Not one to allow his body to suffer the effects of late nights or hard drinking, Warren had once heard that ketchup had a bad effect on one's "wind," so he went so far as to stay off the red stuff. Warren said he and Wallace spent many nights reading until they turned out the lights.

Alone with his thoughts, Wallace spent long nights (on the eve of games) at the Heart of Auburn Hotel on January 14, the Holiday Inn in Starkville on January 26, and the Capital House in Baton Rouge on January 28. All offered finer accommodations than could be found in the SEC's cracker-box gymnasiums. The gyms were small, and more often than not so were the crowds, but the effect was counterintuitive. For Wallace, especially, but in some cases for all his teammates, these were hostile places to play. Whereas at a large arena with a big crowd, the noise became muffled into one constant, unintelligible din, the atmosphere in the bandboxes of the SEC was unrefined, intimate, and intense. Some players, such as Wyenandt, enjoyed the taunting; the "us against them" mentality made him play harder, he believed.

"They were abusive, but that's what fans do," he said. "I always enjoyed playing in front of a full house or a tough crowd. The noise got you pumped up. The worst thing I can imagine is playing in a gym with no fans, no matter home or away. The fans get you going."

Emotions were especially intense whenever Vanderbilt traveled to Knoxville to take on the rival Vols; the provocateurs weren't always in the stands. "In Knoxville, they hated us," Wilson recalled. "One of my first basketball memories my freshman year was sitting there in Knoxville, and the Tennessee football team was right there behind our bench. The whole place was full

Wallace and teammate Bob Warren listen to Coach Skinner during a game in 1968. Thirty-eight years later, Warren visited Wallace in Washington, DC, seeking forgiveness for not offering more support to Wallace during his first varsity season. Photo by Jimmy Ellis, *The Tennessean.*

of these orange-clad people, and they were foaming at the mouth. [Former Commodore] Snake [Grace] was then our unofficial freshman coach, and I remember him walking back and forth behind our bench, giving them the finger and challenging them to come down to the court and fight."

Irritating the Vols was something Grace enjoyed to no end. During the Tennessee game at Memorial Gym that same season, he set off a melee that sounds like slapstick in retrospect. "It was a very close game, tied near the end, and Tennessee had stolen the ball and their big center was going in for an uncontested layup," Wilson recalled. "Southwood chased him down the floor and screamed at him and scared him, and he missed the layup. We won, and Snake was just agitating him as we walked off the court. As [Tennessee] was trying to get off the court, Snake precipitated the fight and quickly made his exit. Fans were pouring out of the stands, and the Tennessee players started grabbing the folding chairs from our bench and were swinging them at the crowd, fighting off the crowd. I remember this perfect scene of one guy the Vols had gotten ahold of. One player grabbed him and slapped him and passed him on to the next guy."

Context, of course, was everything. For the first three decades of SEC basketball, when all the players and fans were white, the taunts that inspired Wyenandt, the jeers aimed at Snake, and the Keystone Cops–like postgame brawls all took on the air of good old-fashioned college pranks—no harm, no foul. But when Wallace came on the scene, the tone changed considerably. With the country's mounting racial tensions adding fuel to an already combustible environment, the atmosphere turned ugly. From opposing fans and cheerleaders alike came the most vile of epithets, directed at Wallace, from the pregame warm-ups to the final buzzer:

Nigger!
Jigaboo!
Charcoal!
Leroy!
Coon!
We're gonna lynch you, boy!

The words rained down on Wallace, but that wasn't all. He was spit on and pelted with Cokes, ice, and coins. At LSU, some Vanderbilt players claimed, a dagger was thrown on the court in Wallace's direction (an event he cannot recall). In Knoxville, teammates remember, fans dangled a noose near the Vanderbilt bench. Wallace understood that there was a fundamental irony pervading the "hellish dramas" unfolding at these southern gymnasiums. The same values his tormentors claimed to be at their core were the very ones that sustained him, even as the hecklers defaulted on their own claims. "They claimed to be good Americans," Wallace recalled, "yet they were viciously attacking a fellow American's right to 'life, liberty, and the pursuit of happiness.' They also claimed to be good Christians, yet one couldn't call their reactions to me acts of 'Christian love.' Finally, people like these believed they were racially 'superior,' yet their behavior wouldn't have qualified as even minimally 'civilized.' So, they failed at all of their most fundamental claims about themselves, while I embodied quite well the first two—which after all are the only valid ones."

Unlike the incident in the Duke game when Skinner took the microphone to plead with Vanderbilt fans to quit throwing ice on the floor, there were no such calls for respect when Wallace was the target on the road. Most disconcerting to Wallace was the fact that his teammates and coaches proceeded as if nothing was amiss. While Chancellor Heard was coming to the conclusion that in order for blacks to have the same positive experience on campus as white students, they'd have to be treated differently, Skinner had not had the same epiphany. Treating Wallace the same as the rest of his teammates meant no talks with the team about what Wallace was encountering on the road, no pleas for the team to band together in support of one of their own.

One of the enduring images of Jackie Robinson's rookie season is that of Pee Wee Reese theatrically putting his arm around his black teammate's shoulder in defiance of a heckling crowd in Cincinnati. There was no equivalent gesture of support for Wallace. In the decades that have followed Wallace's playing days, he has always gone to great lengths to say that he holds no hard feelings toward his teammates, saying that they were decent kids doing the best they could, having had no more experience with trailblazing than he had. In extreme circumstances, he says, it's not realistic or practical to expect ordinary people to always see injustice, get the point, and then act heroically. Still, Wallace says, "The facts were dramatic, even poignant, and they certainly beg the question: why the hell didn't anyone ever say anything—or do anything—about the nightmarish things goings on?"

The lack of acknowledgment that bizarre things were happening all around him nearly drove Wallace to a breakdown. "It was as if you were walking down the street and you see a purple man coming toward you, and nobody else sees him," Wallace recalled. "You start to think that maybe you're the one who's crazy."

Earlier in the season, when Vanderbilt had beaten North Carolina, Davidson, and Duke, Wallace had been part of the greatest three-game stretch in the history of Vanderbilt basketball. By January 29, when the Commodores had beaten LSU to sweep the three-game Deep South road trip, Wallace had endured arguably the most emotionally taxing three-game stretch of games any African American had ever experienced in American sports.

He'd seen the worst of human nature and felt lucky to be alive.

Again, he asked himself the question that had haunted him for weeks: what's the worst thing that could happen?

The answer was right there on the Vanderbilt schedule. February 9, 1968: at Ole Miss.

20

A Long, Hellish Trauma

The traditional practice in Mississippi has been to eliminate potential troublemakers before they get a chance to cause trouble. Far more Negroes have been lynched for having a bad or wrong attitude (by Mississippi "White Supremacy" standards) than for committing a particular crime. Whenever a Negro questioned the status quo in Mississippi, he just simply disappeared.

James Meredith, *Three Years in Mississippi*

Back in high school, during the period when he was taking the first flights of his life and enjoying the attention lavished upon him by college recruiters, Perry Wallace experienced the unlikeliest of conversations while walking down the aisle of one particular plane.

A middle-aged man recognized him and struck up a conversation. The man, it turned out, was a former high school sports star from Jackson, Tennessee. He had gone on to great success in college, becoming the finest all-around athlete in the history of his school, starring in baseball, basketball, and football (and even running a little track), earning all-conference honors as a centerfielder and leading his football team to two conference titles as a running back and defensive back. In one game, he dazzled the crowd by scoring four touchdowns in just about every way possible—one rushing, two receiving, and one by interception—and not surprisingly, he had been drafted by the NFL's New York Giants. An injury cut short his professional football career, and now he was back at his alma mater, coaching the basketball team. When he spotted Wallace walking down the aisle, he introduced himself and casually asked the Pearl High School star whether he would be interested in coming down to play for him.

The man was Eddie Crawford from Ole Miss.

Two years later, as Wallace boarded Vanderbilt's charter flight to Mississippi, the idea of playing a single game in Oxford, let alone an entire career there, was fraught with a sense of danger unlike anything he had ever experienced. Going back to his childhood days when he walked to the Hadley Park library to read about southern lynchings, Wallace had learned too much about Mississippi—and had experienced some of what the Magnolia State had to offer in Starkville a year earlier—to believe that he was headed south for anything remotely resembling a simple game of basketball. If his worst nightmare was going to come true, this is where it would happen. Oxford, Mississippi, was where he'd be shot.

In the decades that followed this trip, the University of Mississippi attempted to change its image in ways that would have stunned its most ardent supporters in 1968. The school erected a statue of James Meredith, disowned the Confederate flag as a university symbol, hired two African American head basketball coaches, and traded in mascot "Colonel Reb" in favor of a black bear.

But in the winter of 1968, the university, and the state's white citizens, remained engaged in frantic efforts to maintain and celebrate the "Southern Way of Life," a cause that had manifested itself in ways ranging from unashamedly politically incorrect to brutally violent.

Here was a state where 534 recorded lynchings of blacks took place between 1882 and 1952 and where a manual for public-school fourth graders in the 1950s proclaimed: "God wanted the white people to live alone. And He wanted the colored people to live alone. . . . Negroes use their own bathrooms. They do not use the white people's bathroom. The Negro has his own part of town to live in. This is called our Southern Way of Life. Do you know that some people want the Negroes to live with white people? These people want us to be unhappy. . . . God made us different. And God knows best."

Between its Gestapo-like Sovereignty Commission and influential White Citizens' Councils (known as "uptown Klans"), here was a citizenry that looked suspiciously upon not just blacks but other presumed subversives such as the "Air Force, YMCA, FBI and Methodist Church," according to one historian. Another called the Mississippi of the first two-thirds of the twentieth century "as close to being a police state as anything we've ever seen."

In a state with the highest proportion of blacks in the country, sports had played a prominent role in perpetuating the status quo. Six years after the riots that accompanied Meredith's desegregation of the university, the Rebels' athletic teams still remained all white, and Wallace would be the first black opposing player to take the court in front of the school's basketball fans. Perhaps the most emotional and defiant public display of segregationist pride took place at halftime of an Ole Miss football game against Kentucky in late September 1962, a game held off campus in the state capital of Jackson at the height of the Meredith controversy. Just a day before President Kennedy sent in US marshals and the National Guard as riots engulfed the Ole

Miss campus in protest of Meredith's enrollment, Governor Ross Barnett, who had already personally blocked Meredith from enrolling at Ole Miss two times, earned thunderous applause from Rebel fans by uttering just seventeen words. Following a halftime performance that featured the Ole Miss band (dressed in traditional Rebel-grey uniforms) unfurling the "world's largest Confederate flag" while dancing girls waved miniature versions, Barnett stepped forward to a tall microphone near midfield. "I love Mississippi," he said in his slow, Mississippi drawl. "I love her people. Our customs. And I love and I respect our heritage." The next night, violence erupted in the heart of the Ole Miss campus. Four years later, as he attempted to walk the length of the state to draw attention to black voting rights, James Meredith was shot and wounded by a roadside sniper.

Barnett's halftime remarks were all about code. His audience at the football game understood them as a defense of the Southern Way and a rejection of federal authority and all that went along with those concepts. Barnett wasn't always so indirect, and neither were other Mississippi governors. The tenth son of a Confederate Civil War veteran, Barnett had once said he'd "rot in jail" before allowing "one nigra [to] cross the threshold of our sacred white schools," and another governor, James Vardaman, "The Great White Chief," had called blacks "savage, lazy, lying, lustful animal[s]." Theodore Bilbo, a two-time governor (1916–20, 1928–32) from Juniper Grove, Mississippi, who briefly attended Vanderbilt Law School and was a member of the Ku Klux Klan, left no doubt about his racial sensibilities when he authored a book titled *Take Your Choice: Separation or Mongrelization*. Barnett's successor, Paul Johnson Jr., who left office just weeks prior to Vanderbilt's trip to Oxford, found political success with a recurring line in his stump speeches, telling audiences that NAACP stood for "niggers, alligators, apes, coons, and possums."

By the time Wallace and the rest of the Vanderbilt traveling party checked into Oxford's Holiday Inn at 400 North Lamar, bullet holes from the Meredith riot still pocked the campus' iconic Lyceum building, but memories of the event six years prior had given way to the exigencies of the current student body of nearly seven thousand, about 1 percent of whom were now black. Some elements of life on the magnolia- and dogwood-lined campus retained a sense of normalcy. The university's coeds were as beautiful as ever—Ole Miss had produced back-to-back Miss Americas in the late 1950s—and the Oxford Floral Shop next door to the Holiday Inn was busy taking Valentine's Day orders from the beauties' suitors. At nearby Leslie Drugs two-pound boxes of Russell Stover chocolates were selling for $3.50. The campus culture was rife with reminders of the centuries-old social order. Confederate flags, which had gained favor on campus in the late 1940s along with the rise of the segregationist Dixiecrats, were everywhere—adorning dorm room walls, study lounges, and student government campaign posters. Attending costume parties in blackface was such a routine matter that the 1967 and 1968 Ole Miss yearbooks prominently featured photos of coeds dressed as Aunt Jemima and a black railroad worker, onlookers laughing in the margins of the photos. The school's reputation as an intellectually uncurious, football- and Greek-focused country club remained intact. Walter Rugaber, a visiting reporter from the *New York Times*, tried to get a rise out of one classroom of students by telling them that "Mississippi seems little more than a party school attended by the empty-headed offspring of planters and bankers" and received little challenge.

Still, even if Ole Miss students resisted change, it was impossible for them to ignore the changes taking place all around them. A student newspaper editor lamented the fact that outsiders continually attempted to impose their political sensibilities on campus leaders by asking them to endorse antiwar positions, and a yearbook article complained that too many liberal speakers were invited to campus. On the morning of the Vanderbilt game, readers of the *Jackson Clarion-Ledger* were treated to an opinion piece claiming that the United States, "obsessed with the loser," had "reached an age of tolerance that marks the decline of empires," citing hippies, draft dodgers, welfare, Stokely Carmichael, and the Supreme Court as the greatest public enemies. For southerners who agreed that tolerance had run amok, there was hope. Former Alabama governor George Wallace had announced his third-party candidacy for president just two days earlier, vowing to build his campaign around the issues of states' rights, law and order, free enterprise, and hawkish foreign policy. On the day that Governor Wallace made his announcement, the college town of Orangeburg, South Carolina, exploded in violence with three students killed and thirty-seven people injured when blacks and police exchanged gunfire in the wake of a student protest of the whites-only All-Star Bowling Lanes.

As the Commodore players unpacked their bags in the Holiday Inn and prepared for dinner in the hotel's El Centro restaurant, tensions were also rising on the Ole Miss campus. Earlier in the week, five of the eight varsity cheerleaders had resigned, exacerbating the fact that "Ole Miss school spirit has one foot in the grave already," according to one student journalist; as the VU game approached, "anything to put some life and zing in our spirit" was desperately needed. And while the Commodore players dined, the second act of a drug bust was in motion, with seven students arrested for marijuana possession on Friday after three had been busted the night before, culminating a thirty-day investigation. All told, an unusual discontent pervaded the campus in the chill of early February. It was as if the Vanderbilt contingent were the first unwitting guests to arrive at a dinner party where the hosts had stopped arguing just in time to open the door. Whether they were in for any hospitality was another matter.

Commodore student manager Paul Wilson doubted it. Having grown up in Jackson, Mississippi—attending a segregated Murrah High School that sent dozens of students to Ole Miss every year—Wilson was the rare member of the Vanderbilt entourage who seemed to understand what Wallace was about to endure, and unbeknownst to Wallace, he took two steps to try to prevent a Starkville-like nightmare.

First, in creating the travel itinerary for the trip, he assigned himself to be Wallace's roommate at the Holiday Inn. Wilson had been impressed by both Carmichael and King at Impact, and though he had been raised "not to hate," seeing the black speakers state their case for equal rights had further shifted his sensibilities. When Wallace joined the Black and Gold, Wilson said his concern for the plight of blacks evolved from a "struggle *they* were going through, to one *we* were going through. He was our teammate." When the Commodores arrived at the Holiday Inn after driving in from the airport, Wilson was surprised to see a number of police cars parked out front: "I remembered the Meredith riots, so I had a real tense feeling. It had to be one hundred times worse for Perry."

Whatever apprehensions Wilson had about the long night ahead, he was more concerned about the treatment Wallace would receive the following evening from Ole Miss partisans at the Coliseum. He desperately wanted to avoid another Starkville, but he knew from personal experience that such hopes were dubious. Whereas at a basketball school like Kentucky, the fans respected the game and were mainly concerned about the fortunes of their own players, Wilson knew the atmosphere at Ole Miss had traditionally been just the opposite. It had only been in the five years since Crawford's arrival that seemingly any emphasis had been placed on basketball at all. The Rebel basketball team had a reputation as the place where beefy football players banged around all winter to stay in shape for the gridiron. Before the eighty-five-hundred-seat Coliseum opened in 1966, the team played in the tiny Old Gym (capacity twenty-four hundred), where the fans' disinterest in basketball was exceeded only by their willingness to scrap. Clyde Lee recalled a game in 1965 when Vanderbilt's Wayne Taylor caught one of the basketball-playing footballers with an elbow, knocking the Rebel to the ground. Within seconds, a sea of Ole Miss football players, clad in letterman jackets, came pouring out onto the court to take up for their comrade, who had gotten up to retaliate. "Security ran out and circled us in the jump circle at center court until they got everybody settled down," Lee said. "The security guards stayed close to us for the rest of the game. It was intimidating for us; we were a little worried. Put that into context with the animosity toward Perry and his color, and I can't imagine."

Even student managers were not spared the football players' wrath. "That was the most verbally abusive spot that I remember, even for managers," recalled Wilson's cohort Gene Smitherman. "The Ole Miss football players sat right behind our team bench, and they would 'talk' to you the entire game. I was verbally harassed in a way that I have never been harassed before. But for me, as a white manager, I didn't have a reason to feel threatened."

Whether it was his idea or that of Steven Ammann, an elementary and high school pal enrolled as a junior at Ole Miss, has been forgotten over the ensuing decades, but Wilson's next perceptive act was to help create a buffer zone around the Commodore bench. In the days leading up to the game, Wilson got in touch with Ammann, a kid who had moved to Mississippi with his family from the Cincinnati area and who had more open-minded views on race than many of his peers. As a fourth and fifth grader, Ammann had taken grief from his new friends in Jackson over his choice of favorite football player, the outspoken Jim Brown of the Cleveland Browns. The plan hatched by the two old friends called for Ammann to assemble a group of like-minded Ole Miss students and snatch up tickets in the row immediately behind the Vanderbilt bench. "It was one of those little things that one person can do to try to make things better," recalled Wilson. More than forty years later, Ammann recalled that his overriding concern was that Wallace not be harassed by hecklers. He and a group of friends walked over from the Lester dormitory to the Coliseum well before game time and took their positions. "I had a great deal of respect for what Perry Wallace was doing," Ammann said, "so our hope was to create a little distance, to put some people there who would be close to the scene and would not be verbally abusive. There's something inside of you at a moment like that that says, 'This should go right for this person.'"

If we lose to Ole Miss, we are out of it," Skinner told the *Tennessean*'s Bibb before the squad left freezing Nashville for Oxford. "There is no doubt, or at least there shouldn't be, that Ole Miss is a tough basketball team, particularly at home." An unbiased observer, however, would have had a hard time imagining an Ole Miss victory under any circumstances. The Commodores had rebounded from a midseason skid and stood at 15–4 overall, 7–4 in the conference, and remained ranked Number 9 in the country. VU had crushed the Rebels 96–70 in the teams' prior game in Nashville, a January 13 contest that saw the ailing Wallace relegated to the bench. (Bob Bundy took over the starting center position in that game and led the team with twenty-three points, and Wallace had yet to regain the starting job.) Despite the fact that Crawford had injected life into the Ole Miss program when he took over as head coach in 1962–63, filling his roster not with football players but with real basketball recruits from as far away as Illinois and Pennsylvania, the results were much the same as always. The Rebels limped into the Vanderbilt game just days removed from a five-games-in-ten-days stretch that concluded with UM solidly in last place in the SEC, 1–11 in the conference and 4–14 overall. In anticipation of a Vanderbilt victory, and with an awareness that Rebel fans were unlikely to fill their big, new arena to watch a last-place team lose again, a large contingent of Vanderbilt fans made the trip to Oxford for the game, a select few hitching a ride on the Vanderbilt charter flight and the rest making the drive south.

Situated on the southwest side of the Ole Miss campus, the Coliseum presented a stark contrast between old and new. The building itself was on the cutting edge of a style of sports architecture taking hold not just in basketball arenas, but also in multiuse football and baseball stadiums. Out with quirkiness, in with efficiency. Perfectly round ("for easy circulation"), the building featured theater-style seats and air-conditioning. The roof topped out eighty-nine feet above the playing surface, the court sitting twelve feet below ground-level, with eighteen ramps entering the seating area at mid-height, sixteen rows of seats above the entry level, and thirteen below. A mathematical ode to modernity. And yet, immediately adjacent to the space-age gymnasium peacefully sat a haunting reminder of the university's past: a cemetery holding the bodies of seven hundred Union and Confederate soldiers from the bloody 1862 Battle of Shiloh. The school was just thirteen years old when it temporarily shut down from 1861 to 1865 so that virtually the entire student body, all but four men, could go off to war. Several buildings were converted into hospital wards, with the dead buried in the nearby cemetery. Slave labor had been commonplace before the war, with blacks living on campus and serving the white students, staff, and faculty by building fires, cleaning rooms, and maintaining buildings, among other forced duties. The school's very name—then and now, one hears "Ole Miss" far more frequently than "University of Mississippi"—is a perverse but pervasive nod to the days of slavery. In 1897 the school's yearbook was dubbed "the Ole Miss," a term used by slaves to identify the senior mistress of a plantation, and by the turn of the century, students were referring to the university itself by the name. Well into the twentieth century, Ole Miss students participated in Dixie Week, a celebration whose activities included a ceremonial reading of the Orders of Secession and the auctioning off of cheerleaders as slaves. Historians had called the Meredith riots "an echo of the Civil War's last battle." If so, it was an echo that still reverberated as Wallace walked into the Coliseum on the night of February 10, 1968.

Almost to a man, Wallace and his teammates can recall the scene in Oxford when Wallace came running out on the court for the first time, white socks pulled up high, short black shorts and black jersey, VANDERBILT etched out in white and gold letters in a horseshoe shape above his number 25. In Starkville a year earlier, Wallace had clasped hands with Godfrey Dillard to gain strength to face the hostile crowd. In Oxford he was on his own.

The jeers and the cursing started the moment Wallace emerged from the tunnel that connected the locker room area to the playing court, louder, more sustained, and uglier than any of the Commodores had heard since Starkville. But there was something different about the Ole Miss brand of abuse. Steve Martin, the Tulane baseball player, had experienced some of this when he dug into the batter's box for the first time in Oxford, and the crowd spelled out N-I-G-G-E-R in a boisterous, preorchestrated fashion. Here on the basketball court, the effect was similar: the words themselves were ugly, but they were made far uglier by the blithe enthusiasm with which they were delivered. For the next two hours, Wallace would serve as this crowd's entertainment.

As Wallace and his teammates ran through their layup line and shot jumpers while the clock ticked down toward tip-off, Bob Warren noticed something he had never heard before in warm-ups: laughter. Every time Wallace missed a shot, fumbled a rebound, or made even the slightest misstep, the Ole Miss fans near courtside exploded in delight. Every time Wallace made a shot, the crowd booed. And in between, it was, *Go, home, nigger! We're gonna kill you, nigger! We'll lynch you, boy!* Forty years later, Warren was still shaken by the memory. "Those warm-ups," he said, "were really bad." Bundy stopped shooting long enough to look into the crowd to see who was doing the yelling, and by the size and appearance of the hecklers, assumed the ringleaders were Rebel football players, a squad described in the Ole Miss yearbook as a "well-bred" bunch far more refined than the "redneck meats" at other conference schools. Wallace heard the laughter and the threats, "the usual stuff," he recalled, and he heard another taunt that would remain with him for decades. "There was this group of guys harassing me in warm-ups, and one of them made his voice into what he thought was a black woman's voice, and he said: 'I'm from Jackson State. Do you want to come over and [be with] me?' It was just ugly." Even the *Banner* and *Tennessean* reporters, Green and Bibb, who were not particularly sensitive to Wallace's treatment by opposing fans and had not written about it all year, noted the pregame abuse, with Bibb writing in his story the next day that Wallace had endured "occasional catcalls" during warm-ups. The game hadn't even started yet, and already things were out of control. And perhaps worst of all for Wallace, he knew he would begin the game on the bench. He'd just have to sit there and wait for the inevitable: when Skinner turned to him and summoned him into the game, the fans would be ready, and the barrage would begin anew.

Tip-off came as scheduled at 7:30 p.m., temperatures outside the Coliseum dipping to near freezing. Bundy, Warren, Wyenandt, Campbell, and Hagan on the court for the Commodores; Larry Martindale, Eddie Miller, Jerry Brawner, Dale Stevens, and Ken Turner for the Rebels. (With nine Mississippians on the UM roster, of the starters only Brawner hailed from the state.) Ammann and his friends settled into their seats behind the Vanderbilt bench, their plan to protect Wallace from the vilest elements of the crowd already an apparent failure. Commodore fans from Nashville were scattered in pockets around the gym; tickets had been easier to come by than they had even imagined. In all, 3,318 fans showed up to watch, the crowd packed in close to the court, with the yellow-seated upper sections and red middle sections virtually empty. Wallace watched from the bench as the teams traded baskets, the underdog Rebels sticking close to favored Vanderbilt throughout the early going.

Finally, Wallace entered the game for the first time, greeted by the "high-pitched yip, yip, yip of the Rebel yell," according to journalist Scott Stroud. Immediately, the catcalls grew louder. "I checked into the game and they raised holy hell," Wallace recalled. "Every time I made a mistake, everybody clapped, everybody laughed." With just over nine minutes remaining in the first half, Wallace scored his first and only basket of the half, tying the score at 19. On both ends of the court, Wallace and his teammates felt that he was being bumped and bruised more than usual, enduring a physical style of play that referees Ralph Stout and Joe Long overlooked.

Then it happened, a blow that came so fast no one knows who threw the elbow. Fighting for a rebound, Wallace was struck underneath the left eye by an Ole Miss bruiser, knocked so hard in the head that he momentarily lost his vision and staggered to regain his footing. Neither Stout nor Long whistled a foul, nor did they call a halt to the game to allow Wallace to be treated. On the Commodore bench, Bill LaFevor was startled by the Ole Miss cheers, the crowd rising to its feet in delight. Wallace felt "fuzzy," but no matter how bad he was hurt, the one thing he was not going to do was leave the court. But as he regained his sight, he looked down and saw blood. At the next dead ball, trainer Joe Worden came off the bench to check on Wallace and saw his eye swelling shut. He summoned manager Wilson, asking him to help Wallace back to the locker room. As Wilson grabbed Wallace's arm and handed him an ice pack, the Mississippian heard the crowd still cheering, still laughing, still cursing "nigger," a father and son spitting in their direction, one fan yelling, "We're going to kill you," and forty years later Wilson said that at that moment, his body was shaking, he was seething, never so angry and embarrassed in his entire life, then or since. Not quite sure what to say to Wallace as they approached the tunnel to the locker room, he simply said, "I'm sorry, Perry." Wallace, head held high in pride and to stunt the bleeding, kept on walking, looking straight ahead. "It's OK," he said.

The halftime buzzer sounded, Vanderbilt leading 41–35, and soon the rest of the team filed into the locker room. Worden checked on Wallace, but the minutes ran by quickly, and Wallace was left on the training table with a bag of ice as coaches, teammates, and managers returned to the court before the second half began. Eye swollen and hands cold from the ice, Wallace was shaken not just by the physical blow but by the relentless taunting, nineteen years old and black and alone in another Mississippi theater of the absurd. He could hear the Ole Miss crowd react when his teammates returned to the court without him: *Did the nigger go home? Where's the nigger? Did he quit?*

Despite their awareness of the abuse their teammate had endured during warm-ups and the first half of the game, not one member of the Vanderbilt traveling party stayed behind to accompany Wallace back onto the court. As he walked toward the tunnel to return to the bench for the second half, Wallace understood more clearly than ever that his journey as a pioneer was one that he would be making alone. He asked himself, "Who's on *my* side?" and came to the conclusion that the only person he could rely on was himself. Speaking to Chancellor Heard a few months later, he described what came next: "Now, I don't expect you to attach much significance to merely having to run out on a basketball floor, but what I remember most in my life is standing at that huge doorway with that crowd waiting on me with my teammates completely at the opposite end of the floor," he said, according to a transcript of his remarks. "What would have merely been an occurrence of no consequence for a white player was transformed into a nightmare and a long, hellish trauma for me."

This moment in time was as dramatic as any in the story of Perry Wallace. But as with so many other solo acts of courage throughout history, Wallace said it didn't need to happen, shouldn't have happened if those surrounding him had elevated the situation "to the proper level of seriousness." "Somebody should have said, 'This guy is going through some turmoil, and if we want to do anything to help, somebody will stay back with him as he's getting his eye patched up and walk with him back out there to join the rest of the team,'" Wallace recalled. "In other words, if people had been willing to accept this is something very important, that these are outrageous shows of bigotry, then they would have done more."

As Wallace emerged from the tunnel, a group of Vanderbilt fans were the first to see him, and they stood and cheered. Their cheers were soon drowned out by boos.

Steven Ammann said he felt in his heart that a night like this "should go right" for a person in Wallace's situation, and perhaps Coach Skinner felt a similar calling as the second half approached. Though he kept Wallace on the bench to begin the game and though Wallace was now injured, Skinner made the unusual move of putting Wallace in the starting lineup to begin the second half. In the Hollywood rendition of what would happen next, Wallace would rise above the madness of the crowd, not give a damn about whether somebody wanted to shoot him, soar above the floor for every rebound, shake off another hard blow to the head, score one basket after another, and lead Vanderbilt to a convincing victory.

In real life, yes, he did all that, and he also unleashed a perfect, left-handed behind-the-back pass to Warren on a fast-break for an easy layup. The circumstances, Wallace said later, created a stark mandate for him to play well in the second half, and he more than delivered.

Playing his most aggressive and focused ball of the season, Wallace scored Vanderbilt's first two baskets of the second half, an eight-foot jumper at the

19:13 mark and a ten-footer that gave the Commodores a 45–39 lead with 17:55 remaining. In his random encounter with Coach Crawford on an airplane two years earlier, Wallace posed a question to the Ole Miss coach: if I decide to go to Vanderbilt, what is the atmosphere going to be like in your arena? Crawford told him the fans would be hard on him, as they would throughout the South, and Wallace's only remedy would be to tune out the hecklers and let his performance on the court do the talking. "You're a great basketball player," Crawford said, "and if you're as good as I think you are, you're going to shut them all up." Whether or not Crawford remembered giving that advice, Wallace was heeding it, playing with a "steady, calm sense of determination," grabbing rebounds like he was back at Pearl High, and looking for chances to score. With 14:33 remaining, he tipped in his own missed shot, then did exactly the same thing a minute later to ignite a 20–4 Vanderbilt run that put the game away for good. With just over two minutes left in the game, now playing completely without fear, Wallace stormed down court on a fast break and whipped the behind-the-back pass to Warren for an easy layup, a move that was completely out of character. This was all apparently too much to take for the Rebs, and on Vanderbilt's next possession, Wallace was hacked in the back of the head by UM's Martindale, sending Wallace sprawling out of bounds. The foolishness of retaliation, Wallace said later, was "nonnegotiable and obvious." Woozy from the blow, all he could do was stride to the free throw line and sink two shots. Finally, Skinner pulled him from the game, his line score reading six for twelve on field goals, two for two on free throws, three fouls, eleven rebounds, four turnovers, one assist, and fourteen points. Final score, Vanderbilt 90, Ole Miss 72. James Meredith had written that the most remarkable achievement of his time in Oxford was that he had survived. As he took a seat on the bench, Perry Wallace could relate.

Though the Ole Miss student newspaper acknowledged none of what had transpired that night (noting only that the teams had "fought tooth and nail through first-half skirmishes"), both Bibb and Green were impressed by Wallace's gutty performance, even if they didn't grasp the poignancy of it. Over the next two days, readers of both papers saw headlines such as *Commodores Rip Ole Miss: Perry Wallace Leads Second Half Romp*; *Wallace Got the Mouse, And Lion's Share of Praise*; *Vanderbilt's SEC Hopes Rejuvenated By Wallace*; and *Hustle, Wallace, Keep Vandy In*. In the locker room after the game, Skinner was encouraged by his sophomore's performance. "It was one of [Perry's] better efforts," he said. "He got after the ball and never quit hustling. Perry had been down on himself. I never had lost faith in his ability. This should do a lot for his confidence."

Nearly four decades later, the coach remembered the fearlessness with which Wallace played in that second half. "It was just real loud, and anybody could understand the things they were saying to Perry," he said. "You know he got called a lot of ugly things; they just rode him like the black player that he was. And [Ole Miss] had about three players that were giving him a real hard time physically on the rebounds, bumping him around and knocking him around. He knew they were cheating, and the refs weren't calling anything. So he got mad. That's the only time I ever saw him get mad. And he fought the boards with intensity, he was so fired up. He's not that kind of person normally. He cleaned the backboards and we won the game because of it. He was unbelievable. God, he got every shot that went up there, almost."

Reflecting on the game, Wallace agreed with his coach's assessment—to a point. Yes, he had reacted to the abuse with an uncommon brand of basketball vengeance, but he said no teenager should ever have to experience that sort of motivation.

"Things were so bad, it was so oppressive, and so much bad stuff had happened, that sure, it pushed me to another level," Wallace recalled. "But I don't think that's the way you ought to have to play ball, to have that kind of challenge. It did shut a lot of those people up. It was so bad that I just sort of loosened up, so they started seeing me leap and do different things I wouldn't normally do like the behind-the-back pass, floating in high for a layup. It was interesting how that shut them up. They had never seen anybody jump that high. And what they saw is what they had produced. With all those taunts and jeers, this is what they had produced."

In the decades that followed this landmark game, Wallace's teammate Bill LaFevor reflected on the composure Wallace showed in the face of verbal and physical abuse. He said there's no doubt in his mind that the elbows thrown in Wallace's direction were "intentional attempts to injure him." He thought about comparisons to Jackie Robinson, how the baseball trailblazer had been praised for turning the other cheek in similar circumstances. And he concluded that the standard storyline, including the one passed along by generations of Vanderbilt fans when recalling Wallace's career—black pioneer keeps his cool under fire, proves haters wrong—is a bit too neat, lets the antagonists off the hook too easily, to accept at face value.

"It's just another stereotype," LaFevor said. "Think about what Perry did. He was being pushed and shoved and he took an elbow smack in the face, and the crowd stood and cheered as he bled and walked off the floor. He refused to acknowledge the pain. He walked off the court looking straight up. The injury offered him a chance to stay down in the locker room, but he came back and wanted to get in the game. Is it not condescending in a way to refer to the dignity in which he carried himself? It was so much more than that."

21

Destiny of Dissent

Perry Wallace sat in front of his locker in the hot underbelly of Memorial Gym, victorious yet completely depleted, his uniform drenched in sweat.

Nearly a month had passed since the game at Ole Miss, and Vanderbilt had just beaten LSU in the final game of the season, a 116–86 shootout that gave the Commodores their twentieth win of the year, the fourth straight time Skinner had led his team to that plateau. Wallace continued to play his best ball of the season after the emotional performance in Oxford, notching his first twenty-point scoring game in an 84–73 home win over Mississippi State, regaining his starting position, and scoring eighteen points and grabbing twenty rebounds in the LSU victory—a fine performance but one that was overshadowed by a forty-two-point outburst by Tiger sophomore sensation Pete Maravich.

Hustler sportswriter Henry Hecht considered the LSU game as wild an affair as he had ever witnessed, with 201 points scored and fast breaks galore, and the pace of the game accounted for some of Wallace's perspiration. But there was more to it than that. As he sat on the folding chair, surrounded by teammates but all alone, a long, torturous season now over, it was finally time to exhale, to expel the physical, mental, and emotional pain he had endured all winter. The rivers of sweat, he said many years later, might as well have been tears.

Wallace sat alone with his thoughts, paying no mind as a Commodore booster and DuPont executive named Bob Bundy charged into the locker room to greet the Vanderbilt player of the same name, a coincidence that had spawned a friendship. But then another visitor arrived, and Wallace stood to greet a man who rarely entered the locker room.

"Perry," said Alexander Heard in his aristocratic Savannah accent. "I'd like to shake hands with you. Congratulations on the game and congratulations on the year." Wallace remembered the words decades later, but more than anything, he remembered the look in the chancellor's eyes.

"He was standing there in his usual gracious, elegant, patrician way, but there was also a great sense of sincerity," Wallace recalled. "He was quite the gentleman, but he also had these penetrating, knowing eyes. And as he stood there, something in his eyes told me that he really understood. No one else approached me with that kind of serious, sober, and sincere look. Nobody else seemed to understand that this had been a tremendously difficult year, a poignant year, and that I was as drenched with the effects of the whole experience as I was drenched with sweat from playing that game."

One other person who recognized what Wallace had endured was Henry Hecht, the young sportswriter. A few days after the season finale, Hecht sat down with Wallace to discuss—as he headlined his *Sportsbeat* column— "Perry's Long Season." Wallace had invited Hecht to his dorm room for the interview; with some of Wallace's jazz playing on the record player he brought from home, Hecht was "impressed with the maturity and depth of this talented athlete as he gave himself a rigorous self-examination."

Wallace's season, Hecht surmised, could be divided into four parts. The first being the first month of the year, when Wallace played "reasonably well" as the Commodores rose to Number 3 in the national rankings. The second part came when Wallace (suffering from mono) fell into his slump, scoring a total of just two points in losses to Tennessee and Kentucky. The third stage, Wallace told Hecht, was the most important: when he lost his starting job to Bundy and was relegated to the bench.

"The pressure definitely decreased once I didn't start," said Wallace, a statement that was only partly true at best, considering that Wallace hadn't started the game at Ole Miss. "I was getting tired, mentally and physically, and was disappointed in myself. Once I sat down, I could look at myself and ask what was the matter physically and what was the matter mentally. I got more sleep. I started taking vitamins, and also started to mentally prepare myself for each game, but I also tried to make sure I kept my poise. By the end of the season I felt much more comfortable."

Wallace made no specific references to his painful experiences on the road, saying only that it "took me most of the season to get used to [it]." Wallace also minimized his disappointment when discussing his treatment on campus. Though his life was unfolding in a far different way than he had imagined, Wallace downplayed his original high hopes. "I didn't sign [at Vanderbilt] to show or prove anything. It just happened that the school I wanted to go to was in the SEC. But once I got here I knew I couldn't be accepted as Perry Wallace, basketball player, who just happens to be Negro. You just have to deal with practicalities. Socially, I don't depend on campus. I can't. How can you expect people to accept me as Perry Wallace, a person? You can't expect them to, and I don't expect them to."

Wallace told Hecht that his teammates were "really a great bunch of guys" who did accept him as a person, and credited Coach Skinner for never losing confidence in his abilities. In fact, Wallace said, "I wouldn't want to play for anyone else."

That confidence, Hecht wrote, propelled Wallace into the fourth stage of the season, the final seven games, when he regained his form and played more aggressively. "One was almost awed by [Wallace's] tremendous leaping ability, timing and strength," wrote Hecht.

Given the four stages of his season, the young reporter wondered, how would Wallace rate the year as a whole? "I guess I would have to say that it tended toward disappointing," Wallace said. "But I think I have made the adjustment; I had to, and unraveled everything, and placed it in the right perspective."

Hecht posed one final question, one that Wallace would continue to be asked countless times over the ensuing decades: Are you glad you came to Vanderbilt?

Wallace thought of how his life had changed since he had meditated on that rock at White City Park and decided to sign with Coach Skinner and Vanderbilt. And he answered honestly.

"I probably won't know that," he said, "for many, many years."

Hecht's story, perceptive as it was, was buried on page 10 of the March 19 *Hustler*. Dominating the news was word that forty-two-year-old Senator Robert F. Kennedy, who had just a few days earlier announced his candidacy for president, would be speaking at Memorial Gym in two days in a specially arranged advance session of the 1968 Impact symposium, which wasn't formally to begin until April 5. The theme of Impact '68 was "The Destiny of Dissent," and Frye Gaillard, the young Alabamian who had spent so much time with Stokely Carmichael a year earlier and had since risen to the position of Impact chairman, described Kennedy as "the most prominent dissenter in the country at this moment," given the senator's opposition to the Vietnam War.

Landing the New York senator was a major coup for Gaillard and the Impact organizers, and the theme of the symposium left no doubt that Chancellor Heard would not be influenced by those who may have preferred a tamer Impact after the previous year's riots. Once again, Vanderbilt, for many the unlikeliest place to be at the forefront of the zeitgeist, would place itself squarely there. The young Kennedy's opposition to President Johnson and the war made him a favorite on college campuses, though he was still trailing Democratic challenger Eugene McCarthy. In a year in which the number of US troops in Vietnam reached an all-time high, opposition to the war was also escalating. Less than a month before Kennedy's appearance in Nashville, antiwar rhetoric had begun gaining traction at Vanderbilt, where most undergraduates still supported the war. When in late February it was publicly announced that eleven hundred Tennesseans would be drafted into service in April, a small antiwar group on campus passed a resolution supporting draft resistance and circulated an antidraft petition. A *Hustler* column noted the inequities of the selective service system, declaring college deferments "the most flagrant form of economic class discrimination now affecting young adults. Those unable to finance college education are assured of induction." Adjacent to the column ran two opposing letters to the editor. H. G. Bradley, a Nashville doctor who lost his only child in World War II, wrote that "it takes a lot more guts to go to Vietnam and fight than it does to stay home and criticize." Michael Grey, of the Newfoundland Committee to Aid American War Objectors, urged young men to move to Canada rather than submit to the draft.

If the 1960s were arriving at Vanderbilt in the form of these tensions over the war, there were other manifestations of the flash points taking place nationwide. Late February brought Vanderbilt's first-ever marijuana bust, with four students suspended and thirty-eight placed on probation. Racial tensions continued to percolate on campus and around town. Reverend Asbury was embroiled in a running public debate with a local television personality, Jud Collins, who thought Asbury was veering too far to the left in his sermons (including one in which Asbury said that "to say 'nigger' is taking the Lord's name in vain more surely than to say 'God damn it'"). A white Vanderbilt student who entered the Big T Drive-In near Fisk University to order a couple of Pepsis and fried pumpkin pies was verbally harassed by a group of Fisk students until he hurriedly left the restaurant. Still, there were signs of progress. Walter Murray, already known as the ultimate peacemaker, deal broker, and most politically savvy sophomore on campus, had his friends shaking their heads in disbelief and admiration when he convinced Student Government Association presidential candidate Al Hubbard that he, Murray, could help Hubbard win Vanderbilt's "black vote," about as miniscule a bloc as one can imagine. Yet there was Hubbard, future policy advisor in both Bush White Houses, earnestly meeting with the Afro-American Student Association on his way to winning the SGA presidency.

Politics, drugs, race, war, generational conflicts: Vanderbilt was ready for a visit from RFK. One by one, students, including Perry Wallace, filed into Memorial Gym on the evening of March 21, having paid $1.50 for a ticket. By 7:30, the scheduled time of Kennedy's speech, more than twelve thousand people had squeezed into the gymnasium's wooden bleachers, but Kennedy and his traveling party were still hours away. The senator was flying to Nashville from Tuscaloosa, home of the University of Alabama, the campus where Governor George Wallace had confronted Kennedy's Justice Department deputies just five years earlier. But Kennedy found a receptive audience in Alabama, just as he had in Oxford, Mississippi, when he had ventured

In his first speech at Vanderbilt, Chancellor Alexander Heard vowed that the Vanderbilt campus would "be a place of intellectual freedom." Here, he listens to a speaker at the 1968 Impact Symposium, where Robert F. Kennedy, William F. Buckley, and Julian Bond were headliners. Vanderbilt University Special Collections and University Archives.

south for a speech two years prior. With Kennedy's flight to Nashville delayed by storms, country crooner George Hamilton took the stage and occupied the crowd with an impromptu set. Finally, the plane arrived; Gaillard met the entourage amid an admiring mob at the airport, and crammed into the backseat of a waiting car along with Kennedy and astronaut John Glenn for the ride back to campus.

Waiting in the crowd, Wallace was eager to see the younger brother of John F. Kennedy.

"Many of us were really enthusiastic about his coming down to Vanderbilt, and about him running for president," Wallace recalled. "It was just five years before that his brother had gotten assassinated, and during that time, certainly for a lot of blacks and whites who were in favor of change, JFK loomed really large and was very much respected and admired. We had a place in our hearts for him, and so it was almost by extension that we admired Robert Kennedy, too. I wouldn't learn more about him until later on, but the basic point was that he was a Kennedy, JFK's brother, and so I was glad to get a chance to hear him. But I was already 'in the choir' when he gave his speech."

Finally, after 9:00 p.m., as an icy rain fell outside, Kennedy took the stage, accompanied by his sons Michael and David. In one of the first speeches of his campaign, Kennedy eloquently stirred the hopes of young voters who were troubled by the direction of the country. "During a time of war and division, of urban riots and racial injustice . . . he talked about the patriotism of dissent," Gaillard later wrote, "It was, he thought, the duty of the people who loved their country to speak out strongly against its imperfections."

"Today, as the world seems almost to unravel all around us, there is much to dissent from," Kennedy said.

> So when we are told to forego all dissent and division, we must ask: Who is it that is truly dividing this country? I believe it is not those who call for change, but it is those who make present policy, those who bear the responsibility for our present course, who have removed themselves from the American tradition, from the enduring and generous impulses that are the soul of this nation. They are the ones—the President of this nation, President Johnson is the one—they are the ones who make this policy. Those who now call for an end to dissent, moreover, seem not to comprehend what this country is all about. For debate and dissent are the very heart of the American process. . . .
>
> Only broad and fundamental dissent will allow us to confront—not only material poverty—but the poverty of satisfaction, purpose, and dignity that afflicts us all. Too much and for too long, we seem to have surrendered personal excellence and community values in the mere accumulation of material things. For if the Gross National Product now soars above $800 billion a year, still that counts air pollution and cigarette advertising, and ambulances to clear the highways of carnage. It counts special locks for our doors and jails for the people who break them. It counts the destruction of the redwoods and the loss of natural wonder to chaotic sprawl. It counts napalm and nuclear warheads, and armored cars for the police to fight riots in our cities. It counts Whitman's rifle and Speck's knife, and television programs which glorify violence to sell toys to our children. Yet the Gross National Product does not allow for the health of our children, the quality of their education, or the joy of their play. It does not include the beauty of poetry or the strength of our marriages, the intelligence of our public debates, or the integrity of our public officials. It measures neither our will nor our courage, neither our wisdom nor our learning, neither our compassion nor our devotion to country. It measures everything, in short, except that which makes life worthwhile, and it can tell us everything about America except why we are proud to be Americans. . . .
>
> There is a contest on, not for the rule of America, but for the heart of America. . . . I ask your help to give us back our heart, to give us back our spirit, to give us back our soul. I ask your help.

The speech was an exhilarating affirmation for students who desperately wanted political and social change, so much so that those seated closest to the podium nearly pummeled the senator in delight. "I was so close to him, but I made the decision not to shake his hand because he was getting so beat up in the crowd," said Patrick Gilpin, a graduate student seated in the front row. "I felt so sorry for him, so I didn't even try, just out of respect." Kennedy quickly clasped dozens of outstretched hands, but soon, wrote *Hustler* reporter Chuck Offenburger, "escorts had to ward off an intensely admiring crowd . . . to get him out. There were reports that his suit coat was damaged in the crush."

Among the black students in attendance, "there was a huge amount of enthusiasm" for Kennedy's speech, Wallace recalled. (Within a matter of weeks, Eileen Carpenter, Carolyn Bradshaw, and others drove up to Indiana to volunteer for Kennedy's campaign there.) But it wasn't just awestruck Vanderbilt students who created the ruckus. Basketball team manager Gene Smitherman, who later called the night one of the most exciting moments of his life, was amused by the sight of a group of nuns "treating Kennedy like a rock star, complete with screaming and swooning."

What Smitherman didn't know was that Kennedy stopped briefly to speak with one of the nuns; Offenburger overheard the parting words of their conversation.

"Sister," Kennedy said, "put in a word to that One you're close to, please."

Just seventy-seven days later, Kennedy was shot dead in Los Angeles after winning the California primary.

If Kennedy's idealistic speech made it possible for his admirers to imagine themselves living in a new, more progressive America, one of the crucial tests of that new society would come in the arena of race relations. And integration, carried to its logical conclusion, would mean an increasing number of interracial relationships. But for Wallace, who dated a black coed during part of his Vanderbilt years, the idea of an intimate relationship with a white girl at Vanderbilt was fraught with dangers. He believed that as a pioneer under intense scrutiny, creating controversy over anything remotely sexual would mean the end of his Vanderbilt career. All over the country, black athletes on predominantly white campuses were told by their coaches to "stay away from the white women." Wallace did go on a few dates with white girls at Vanderbilt, but "those relationships ended up being fairly limited," he recalled. "Having to always look over your shoulder in a relationship was simply not peaceful."

There was, however, an interracial relationship involving a Vanderbilt athlete that came to light less than two weeks after Kennedy's speech. The scrutiny, public humiliation, and pain inflicted upon Terry Thomas, a white football player from New England's prestigious Phillips Academy, and Evangeline "Gail" Canty, a black military brat from Jacksonville, Florida, demonstrated what a tightrope Wallace had to walk in all aspects of his life just to make it through four years at Vanderbilt. Deviations from the norm, especially in the jock culture, were dealt with quickly and harshly.

Thomas' northern accent and liberal sensibilities caused some of his teammates and assistant coaches to dismiss him as a "Goddamn Communist," a "nigger lover," a "pinko Commie faggot," and a "Yankee troublemaker." These detractors may have been surprised to know more about their teammate's complicated background. His father had used an older brother's birth certificate to join the navy during World War II at age fifteen, and was serving in combat as a gunner's mate on an aircraft carrier in the South Pacific a year later. He saw action at Okinawa and Iwo Jima and lived through a kamikaze attack that sank his ship. Scarred by his experience in the war, he left his wife and children when Terry was just five years old. Two years later, Thomas' mother moved her sons from Long Island to a rented house on a farm in Georgia, where her family tree traced back to colonial days. As a hard-nosed northern kid transplanted to the segregated South, Thomas said he had to "fight the Civil War all over a few times, but when the North kept winning, they finally left me alone." Thomas channeled his energy into constructive pursuits as well, emerging as one of his junior high's top football players and a state champion swimmer in the breaststroke. His athletic prowess caught the eye of a local alumnus of the prestigious Phillips Academy in Andover, Massachusetts, and after scoring well on an entrance exam, Thomas was awarded a full scholarship to the prep school. After being hospitalized for a month with a severe case of mononucleosis, Thomas experienced a tremendous growth spurt—and began lifting weights seriously for the first time—transforming himself from a scrawny 140-pound swimmer into a chiseled 175-pound football player in less than a year. Though Thomas had lived in Georgia for several years by the time he arrived in Andover, his upper-crust classmates considered him a "full-scholarship, working-class kid from Long Island," never really welcoming him into their social circles, but, thanks to his muscular frame, opting not to pick on him too harshly. Thomas long remembered sharing a pep rally podium before a game with rival Exeter with one such classmate, a cheerleader from Texas. "He was very nice to me, and he introduced me as a 'very formidable football player,'" Thomas recalled of his encounter with future president George W. Bush.

With no father around and his mother working as a payroll clerk for an airline, Thomas was flattered but ultimately dismayed to receive only partial scholarship offers from Harvard and Columbia, wanting no part of "Ivy League debt." He was more intrigued by full-scholarship offers from Tulane and Vanderbilt, but as a self-described straight arrow at the time, he was turned off by the "poverty and seediness of New Orleans." So, over the objections of his Andover teachers who considered Vanderbilt a "big-time football factory" (if only they knew), he came to Nashville in the fall of 1965. Shunned as a Yankee in Georgia and a working-class kid in Andover, Thomas once again found himself playing the role of outsider when he arrived on campus. About all he knew about Nashville and Vanderbilt came from a lecture he had attended in Massachusetts by none other than Reverend James Lawson. Lawson told the kids about the civil rights movement in the South and urged them to encourage their parents to support the cause. Enough time had passed since then, Thomas figured, that Nashville would be a changed place; he would "play hard, study hard, and keep [his] damn mouth shut." But, as Thomas wrote decades later, his experience in Nashville turned out to be like nothing he had imagined, "like a fairy tale come true one day where I'm off to college like an All-American hero to play football for a few years, and then suddenly it all turns to shit and I'm lost in a . . . nightmare, where I'm hated and hounded and hunted by a fascist, demon, alien, Southern white race, some who want to kill me just for falling in love . . . and daring to think differently about race and war and politics . . . in America of all places!"

Here's what happened.

During his first two years on campus, Thomas seemed to be doing just fine. He was performing well in school and quite well socially, first dating a cheerleader from Atlanta and then a future homecoming queen from Dallas. He became far less of a straight arrow, developing a counterculture reputation by riding around campus on a motorcycle and posing nude for an art class. Football was tough. First there was the losing—lots of it. Then there was the coaching style—negative and berating—far different from what he had experienced in high school. Though he was strong, fit, and "recklessly aggressive," Thomas wasn't a great football player: he didn't have the best hands and he wasn't all that fast. But on a team that struggled mightily, it wasn't a lack of football skills that set Thomas, a fullback, so far apart from his teammates. It was all cultural. Thomas felt like he didn't fit in with the good ol' boys on the team; the southern kids and coaches made sure he knew they felt the same way. The first clues came during his freshman year on a trip to play Ole Miss, before Thomas had even "done anything to arouse suspicions," when on the bus ride to Oxford a couple of coaches told him not to talk too much lest the Rebels pick up on the fact that Vanderbilt had a Yankee on the team. Thomas had been classmates with African Americans and Africans alike, had played bass guitar in a rock band with a black kid. At Vanderbilt it dawned on him that virtually the only black faces he saw were those cleaning the tables at the dining hall. In his dormitory, surrounded by fellow football players, Thomas said he was considered a representative of "Northern Liberal Yankee Ideology."

"I'd hear this big commotion and I'd open my door, and they'd say, 'Terry Thomas, get your ass down here, we want to talk to you,'" he recalled. His teammates would try to antagonize him by telling racist jokes, or would attempt to lure him into debates about the merits of the most violent aspects of the Southern Way of Life. Thomas was never at a loss for words. "They would shout at me and they'd hear what I had to say, and then I'd say, 'Enough of this ridiculous debate, you guys are lost in the fucking stone age. I'm going back to my room to get some studying done.'" Thomas could stand up for himself, and on at least one occasion he stood up for a less-muscular outsider who wasn't faring so well against the jocks. "There were some attacks on some of the geeky longhaired protestors in the dormitories by one of the largest football players on the team," Thomas recalled. "[The player] found one kid and dragged him into the bathroom and flushed his hair in the urinal and cut off his hair." Thomas entered the bathroom to find the victim crying. Within seconds, Thomas pinned his teammate to the ground and threatened to choke him. Message delivered, Thomas walked back to his room and locked the door. A half-hour later, the bully returned and banged on the door. "If you break into this door," Thomas said, "I will kill you."

Thomas' ability to identify and lend support to the outcast or the ignored took other forms. Carolyn Bradshaw, the black student from Winston-Salem, found herself sitting alone in a physics lab, watching as student after student entered the room and walked past the seat next to hers, seeking out other lab partners. When Thomas walked in the room, Bradshaw was startled by the size of the "big football player" and relieved when he took the seat beside her. "When nobody else wanted to be my partner, he sat next to me," Bradshaw recalled. "I would have preferred to have a stronger partner academically, but he was a nice guy and we did the best we could. Those were the kinds of issues you faced; who's going to be your partner?"

Thomas was both bothered and intrigued when he heard his dorm mates talking crudely about a black female student he had not yet met—Gail Canty. More than four decades later, one thing just about anyone who was on the Vanderbilt campus in 1968 can agree upon is that Gail Canty was a knockout. At the mere mention of Terry Thomas' name, a seventy-something former university official blurted out, "She was the most beautiful woman you ever met in your life. I don't remember her name, but she was gorgeous. Flat-out gorgeous."

Thomas' teammates didn't talk about Canty in such flattering terms. "Even before I met her, some of the good ol' boys on the team kept repeatedly bringing her up in our all-male, jock dorm, bull-session debates," Thomas wrote in an oral history he collaborated on with his daughter decades later. "At first, I had no idea who she was, but they were always talking about how damn sexy she was, and how they thought she had a fabulous ass . . . but how she pissed them off by being such a 'stuck up nigger bitch,' and a 'tease,' strutting her stuff all around campus in such tight jeans and dark sunglasses, never saying hello to anybody, even when they'd say something to her first." When Thomas said he didn't blame the girl for ignoring a bunch of "big hairy white guys coming on to her," his teammates ribbed him for sticking up for Canty, saying what she really needed was some "good old fashioned, animal-style [action] out behind the barn or outhouse somewhere."

It was, Thomas wrote, "against this absurdly obscene backdrop" that he ran into Canty alone on campus between classes. He struck up a conversation with her, "a perfect 10 in ebony," and it turned out Canty had noticed the muscle-bound Thomas on campus before. She had seen his leering teammates, too, and told Thomas that she had purposely ignored them. The chance meeting soon turned into a long conversation, Canty and Thomas exchanging stories about their alienation on campus, and eventually phone numbers. Finally, Thomas asked Canty if she would take off her infamous, large sunglasses; she did, and as Thomas later wrote, he was stunned. "I felt like bolts of lightning flashed between us. As I found out later, so did she.... It was your classic love at first sight, if such a thing exists."

The couple soon found themselves having long conversations on the phone, meeting in hidden corners of the library. On weekends, when most students partied at the frat houses, they'd snuggle in vacant study lounges around campus. Eventually, as their relationship grew intimate, they'd head off campus to an out-of-town friend's apartment. Over time, they became less cautious and more willing to be seen together. Some of Thomas' black male friends let it be known that it was fine with them if Thomas and Canty wanted to join them for parties on the eleventh floor of Carmichael Towers. Perry Wallace and Godfrey Dillard were often in the crowd, and both had an easy relationship with Thomas, who in turn greatly admired both trailblazing athletes. But even with their acceptance, this environment wasn't always hospitable. Canty, Thomas said, felt looked down upon by many of the other black girls on campus, young women who were more conservative by nature, TVC types who resented Canty's more overt sexuality and believed that her miniskirts, tall boots, and flirtatious nature fed into white stereotypes of blacks as overly sexual beings. Thomas would also run into his share of trouble at the parties, most often from Black Power types visiting from other campuses. "They would just come right out and accuse me of playing the role of just another plantation white boy out to take advantage of a gullible young 'sister,' and accuse Gail of wanting to use her spectacular good looks just to 'get out of the field and move to the big house,'" he recalled. Thomas and Canty would argue the point, asking if their love was so "morally doomed, then what future was there for anyone in peace and integration?" The arguments drew the couple closer together, Thomas believed, but also drove home competing realities. "We began to realize that, as a couple, we could upset hate-filled, hate-damaged folks of either color. Anywhere. Anytime. Just by our mere presence," he recalled. "On the other hand, we were a source of inspiration and hope for many less damaged people, black and white, who hoped for eventual understanding and conciliation between our two races. It was a heavy role to play, and we often just wanted to be simply human, you know, ordinary and not so special."

Thomas' football teammates and coaches were aware of his relationship with Canty, and though there was some grumbling from the coaches and ribbing from his dorm antagonists, a kind of don't-ask-don't-tell peace existed as long as Thomas kept the relationship relatively quiet and out of the public eye. In practical terms, that meant no kissing, handholding, or hugging in plain sight, even at the familiar make-out spot outside the women's dorms at curfew. But on a wintry night in February of 1968, Thomas wrote, "it just became just too painfully obvious how utterly dehumanizing and demeaning it was to Gail and to me to continue on in that secretive, hypocritical way."

On this Sunday night, Thomas and Canty noticed that a group of football coaches were paying a surprise bed check on the eve of the start of a winter conditioning program. Wanting to avoid the lobby of his dormitory and the arriving coaches, Thomas escorted Canty to the building's basement, and out a back service door next to a pile of garbage. The reality and the symbolism overwhelmed Canty, and she began to cry. Thomas about-faced, squeezed Canty's hand, and marched her upstairs and through the lobby, smiling and "unashamedly" greeting several of his "wide-eyed coaches." Emboldened by their act of bravado, Canty and Thomas, for the first time, kissed each other good night in front of the Branscomb Quadrangle women's dorm, "just like all the other well-established couples on campus."

A housemother who saw the kiss was enraged, placing Canty on "social probation" and calling an assistant football coach to report on Thomas. The next day at the team's workout, Thomas saw his name moved down the depth chart to fifth string. This was worrisome to Thomas on multiple levels, but most of all because he knew that the easiest way for the coaching staff to solve this problem was to kick him off the team or make life so hellish for him that he'd quit. And without a scholarship, without college, Thomas would lose his student deferment and become eligible for the draft and Vietnam.

And here begins the other side of Terry Thomas' complicated story. Thomas was a student in an introductory philosophy class at the time, a class with a teaching assistant named Paul Menzel. Menzel might have come out of central casting as the "liberal grad student," sporting a beard and longer hair than your typical frat boy. He came from Michigan, had done his undergraduate work at Yale, had worked a summer in Georgia on a voting-rights campaign, had turned against the war in Vietnam, and loved debating the issues of the day with his students outside class. He found the atmosphere at Vanderbilt stimulating; even the students who disagreed with him were willing to talk.

Thomas was conflicted about the war when he first met Menzel. His younger brother was serving in Vietnam, and Thomas himself had been participating in Vanderbilt's Marine Corps Platoon Leader Corps/Aviation program. Most of his teammates, he believed, were extremely hawkish on the war. But Thomas had his doubts, doubts that were cemented when Menzel asked him whether he had ever heard Martin Luther King's position on Vietnam, and shared with him a copy of the speech King had delivered in April 1967, just days before his Vanderbilt Impact appearance, at the Riverside Church in New York. Thomas cried as he read the speech over and over. He thought about his brother risking his life every day, and he contemplated what drove Buddhist monks to set themselves on fire to protest the immorality of war. When Menzel asked Thomas if he'd be willing to sign an antidraft petition, he gave it serious consideration. On one hand, he believed that protesting the war and ending it was the best way to save his brother's life. On the other, he knew that coming out against the war, on top of dating Gail Canty, would further estrange him from his coaches and increase the likelihood that he would be booted from the team, lose his deferment, and get drafted. In the end, he decided to drop out of the Marine program and sign the petition, one of just twenty-three Vanderbilt students (and the only athlete) to do so. Menzel was impressed.

"What social penalty did we [graduate students] pay for signing that petition?" he recalled. "We weren't in frats; we weren't on the football team. For him to sign it was a whole different order, and he had a brother in Vietnam, to boot. Terry's action meant a lot. He was living the talk, walking the walk."

"It was hard for me to decide what to do," Thomas recalled. "I felt my decision was not the same as everybody else's. Either I had to go over there in the Marine Corps, or I had to decide to publicly do whatever I could to end the war because I didn't want my brother to die in Vietnam. But I couldn't do the other thing—which was to do nothing; continue to just quietly avoid the war and party like everybody else."

As had been the case when Thomas kissed Gail Canty in public for the first time, hostile reaction was nearly instantaneous when on March 12 the *Hustler* printed the names of the students who had signed the petition. Assistant Coach Pat Patterson found Thomas and told him his actions reflected badly on the team—players and coaches alike. Thomas argued that he had signed the document as an individual, not as a representative of any group, and that it was debatable in any case whether opposing the war was something that should reflect badly on anyone. In the dining hall that night, Thomas overhead a group of coaches talking about him. One assistant came by and told him to get a haircut or he'd be out running sprints at 5:30 the next morning. "We don't want any hippies on our football team," the coach said. "We want that All-American, clean-cut look." Continuing to eavesdrop on the coaches' conversation, Thomas heard one of them remark that not only had he signed the petition, he was dating a "colored girl."

After an uncomfortable dinner, Thomas returned to his dormitory. Taped to his door was a note: "Coach Pace wants to see you." Thomas peeled the note off the door and settled into his room, exhausted from a draining day, but not more than a few minutes went by before there was a knock at the door. It was another assistant coach, there to warn Thomas that he had stepped outside the football family. Thomas, he said, was going to have to make an important decision: what was more important, his beliefs or football? Anticipating the answer, the coach told Thomas he should expect to be run off the team one way or another.

The next day at practice, Thomas sought out Pace for what he expected to be a confrontational discussion. Instead, the conversation was "pleasant," with Pace telling Thomas that he had a right to his own opinions but suggesting he might be better served expressing his views on the war as a *former* member of the football team. If it was a gentle way of kicking Thomas off the team, it didn't take hold immediately. Thomas continued to practice the rest of the week, and talk of the petition gradually tapered off. By the time workouts were suspended briefly for Spring Break, Thomas was still on the team and fully intended to return for the resumption of drills.

But on the first day back from break, Monday, April 1, Pace called Thomas over for another chat. This time, the subject was Gail Canty. "Are you planning to attend the football and basketball dinner/dance?" Pace asked. Thomas replied that he was indeed planning on going to the April 12 banquet, which was hosted by the Nashville Quarterback Club at the Hillwood Country Club. "Are you planning on bringing a date?" the coach asked. Thomas said that he was. "Are you planning on taking that colored girl as your date?" Pace continued. Thomas said that he was. "You know this time doing that would cause trouble," said Pace. Thomas' beliefs were up to him and he had every right to them, Pace reiterated, but he simply could not take the "colored girl" to the banquet. The alumni wouldn't stand for it. Thomas told Pace that while the coaching staff had a right to their own opinions, "the prospect of spending another year at Vanderbilt under the supervision and control of men who thought so lowly of [him] seemed too dismal and bleak to be worth it." Pace eased the way out. "Your first obligation," he told Thomas, "is to yourself."

Here was the clash of values Kennedy had spoken of, a jumble of disparate views on race, war, speech, tradition, and authority playing itself out on the gridiron. Was it the men in power who were betraying American ideals, or the dissenter? Thomas quit on the spot, walked off the field and met up with Canty to tell her what had happened and to talk about what they might do next. One thing they could do almost immediately, they decided, was to drive over to Memphis and join Martin Luther King's march on behalf of the city's striking sanitation workers. If their opportunities to express themselves on campus were becoming narrower and narrower by the hour, in Memphis, at least, they could join the great civil rights leader and demonstrate publicly on behalf of equality.

K ing was shot around 6:00 p.m. on April 4 as he stood on the balcony outside Room 306 of Memphis' Lorraine Motel, waiting for Ralph Abernathy to finish shaving so they could head out to dinner. Word of his assassination—at the hands of an unknown white suspect—spread quickly. Perry Wallace's sister Jessie, a Memphis schoolteacher, was distraught over the news, but she wasn't surprised. When King had come to Memphis several days earlier to lead the first attempted march, local black toughs marred the event with violence, and Jessie called her mother to say she feared that if King were to come back to town, he'd be killed. With nightfall, tensions rose, young blacks took to the streets, and the National Guard closed in. Jessie felt like it was "the end of the world," a feeling made eerier when the power and telephone lines went out in her neighborhood and other black parts of town.

Wallace had been alone in his dormitory when Walter Murray showed up to break the news. At first, he refused to believe that what his best friend was telling him was true. As he began to process the news, everything seemed to go into slow motion, Murray's words becoming muffled, the room closing in, the *world* closing in. "Things just started to sink," Wallace recalled. "It was obviously just shocking at first, and then it became a feeling of profound sadness. We just sat there and asked each other questions like, 'What are we going to do? What's going to happen now? Is this going to be the end of the civil rights movement?'" Wallace and, to a greater extent, Murray, felt a personal connection to King. They had seen him up close at Vanderbilt almost exactly a year earlier, and while other young blacks had become enamored with more militant figures, Wallace and Murray remained devoted followers, invested in King's dream and his nonviolent approach.

"Walter had a great sense of dedication and commitment to civil rights and to social justice, and King was the prime representative and symbol of that kind of commitment," Wallace recalled. "And then the fact that Walter's [late] father had been a preacher like King, that had made quite a mark on Walter; it was the indelible mark on him. So in those multiple ways, Martin Luther King was a huge figure to him and so he was very, very much hurt. But at the same time, Walter was a leader. He was resilient, and much wiser than the rest of us. He knew that he needed to be strong and be there for us."

As scattered acts of destruction broke out in North Nashville, Murray grabbed his buddy Morris Morgan and took off for the neighborhood in his Ford Fairlane, not to participate in the rioting, or even merely to watch it, but to gather information for the *Vanderbilt Hustler*. Murray wasn't even a writer for the paper, but he overcame his profound sadness over King's death to recognize an opportunity to bring a different perspective to his fellow students by reporting on the reactions of black Nashvillians. "I was walking into the Towers [dormitory] and the person who told me King had been shot was Walter Murray," Morgan recalled. "We went out to interview folks in the community about the assassination, and things were really brewing around town."

For Morgan and Murray, an unspoken motivation for their one-night career in journalism was simply to get off campus and to grieve in the company of other blacks. In that regard, they were exactly where they wanted and needed to be. On another, more practical level, they were completely unprepared for what they were doing—"young and dumb," as Morgan later described it. For one thing, driving with Murray was always an adventure. One of Morris' favorite pastimes was to watch his buddy try to parallel park—back and forth, screech and boom, every time. On this night, however, the bumbling led them into dangerous territory. At one point, the budding reporters were walking around North Nashville—looking for interviews with rocks whizzing by and stores being looted all around them—when they stumbled across an armed guardsman in an army personnel carrier. "He told us to move on," Morgan recalled, "so we did." Later that evening, the scribes were sitting in Murray's car when they were approached by a man waving a gun. "We thought he wanted to shoot us, but it turned out he just wanted a ride down the street," Morgan recalled. "We dropped him off and just looked at each other and said, 'Oh, my goodness.'"

Closer to campus, reaction was far different. At Ireland's restaurant, some patrons cheered when news of the assassination appeared on television. Wallace's teammate Bob Warren was walking back to his dormitory from the library when it occurred to him that the night was much quieter than usual. The only sounds he could hear were trucks moving along West End Avenue, vehicles that turned out to be army tanks. At Carmichael Towers a group of frat boys hauled a keg up to the dormitory's roof so they could enjoy some cold beers while they surveyed the action on West End and strained to see what was happening across the tracks in North Nashville. Sara Hume was so frightened by the presence of tanks, her whole body went numb. Tom Hagan's hair stood on end. Marshall Chapman stood on the roof of the Towers, disgusted by the partiers. She heard what sounded like fireworks coming from North Nashville, and saw the tanks rolling down West End from 21st Avenue. All she could think was, "We're at war, and the world's going to end."

The looting, the rock throwing, the scattered gunfire, the arrival of federal troops—the scenes Murray and Morgan were witnessing in North Nashville and that others were hearing from the dormitory roof were simultaneously taking place in urban areas from coast to coast, continuing for nearly a week after the assassination. Just a year removed from his appearance in Nashville, Stokely Carmichael stoked the fire by calling on blacks to arm themselves and take to the streets. Other voices noted the sad irony that the death of the chief proponent of nonviolence may have brought about the death of nonviolent protest itself. "The philosophy [of reason and nonviolence] that Dr.

National Guardsmen ring the Tennessee State Capitol with fixed bayonets in the wake of the assassination of Martin Luther King. Students on the Vanderbilt campus noted the eerie silence on their side of town, the only sounds the grumbling roll of army tanks barreling down West End. *Nashville Banner* Archives, Nashville Public Library, Special Collections.

Martin Luther King shouted across this land," said Dr. Dorothy Brown of Meharry Medical College, "is so right and so expedient that the very thought of the absence of his voice in our midst is terrifying." Thousands of national guardsmen were called in not just to Memphis and Nashville, but to Detroit, Chicago, Raleigh, Washington, DC, and other cities.

A day after the assassination, Nashville mayor Beverly Briley ordered a citywide curfew, allowing only police, fire, and medical personnel, or citizens traveling to or from work, out on Nashville roads between the hours of 10:00 p.m. and 5:00 a.m. A day later, the curfew was extended to begin at 7:00 p.m. Briley also ordered the temporary closing of all liquor stores and beer taverns, and prohibited the sale of firearms and ammunition. With nobody able to drive downtown to the Ryman Auditorium, Nashville's iconic Grand Ole Opry radio program was canceled for the first time in forty-three years, breaking a string of 2,203 consecutive shows. When Wallace saw photographs and television coverage of the scene in Memphis, he was reminded of an eerie coincidence: when his Pearl Tigers had played a game in Memphis two years earlier, the team had stayed at the Lorraine Motel—on the same floor and on the same side of the building as King. "It might seem silly and I'm not a superstitious person," Wallace recalled, "but that coincidence only multiplied the blinding, stultifying impact of King's assassination."

Memorials to King began to take shape around the country, including in Nashville, where Reverend Asbury worked to organize a service on the Vanderbilt campus, culminating in a march down West End Avenue to the St. Mary's Catholic Church. The plan called for Vanderbilt students and faculty to meet at the church with other Nashville mourners, where they'd then have the option of continuing on to Mayor Briley's office at the Metro Courthouse to protest the presence of the National Guard in black neighborhoods.

When he heard of the memorial service and the march, Wallace knew he wanted to participate, but he was also acutely aware of the escalating racial tensions nationwide and on campus. A story detailing the Terry Thomas saga had broken in the *Hustler* the day after King's assassination, and Wallace feared that his precarious pioneering experiment could be derailed by even the slightest of misunderstandings. If Thomas, a white prep school kid, could be run off the football team, what might happen if the school's lone black varsity athlete was seen participating in a march, a march that could be misconstrued as a protest, a protest taking place in a city under curfew, where tanks rolled down West End and soldiers stood guard around the state capitol with fixed bayonets? So while others around him and peers nationwide acted out of rage or sorrow, fear, or revenge, Wallace chose another course, mindful of what he considered his responsibilities as a trailblazer, fully conscious of what he represented to blacks and whites alike. Some may have called it cautiousness, but to Wallace it was keen insight. By working inside the system, he was able to do what he wanted *and* stay on track to complete the historic journey he had started.

"I actually went down and talked to one of the folks in the Athletic Department, [Sports Information Director] Bill Stewart, and I told him I wanted to participate in the march," Wallace recalled. "I saw Bill as a responsible adult that I could consult, and I told him that this was a peaceful march, expressing our sadness. This was different, not an angry march, not a riot, not violence-related. He said it was OK with him."

Those who were there say they will always remember the tears streaming down Walter Murray's face as Vanderbilt students, black and white, gathered outside Rand Hall for the on-campus memorial. Soon the mourners were on the move, walking down to the edge of campus onto West End Avenue. The group was more than two hundred strong, large enough to occupy the length of two city blocks as they made their way to St. Mary's at the corner of 5th and Church.

Wallace walked along in silence, impressed by the spirit of the group, a collection of young people who he believed had a great sense of responsibility and respect for the moment and for their country. "We wanted to in effect represent what Martin Luther King had represented, which was a calm, thoughtful, committed presence, with America's best interests in mind, and with the notion of human dignity and equality in mind," he recalled. "It was a wonderful coming together that we had, and we had a certain sense of calm as we marched. It was reassuring to us in a way, because we were really sad and distressed, and truly worried about what was going to happen now to our country."

As the procession made its way farther from the Vanderbilt campus and closer to the downtown business district, the reassuring calm of the march was interrupted when a car came screeching by. Wallace turned to see a carload of white teenagers hollering Rebel yells, and then one voice called out from the sedan, "Your king is dead!" Wallace continued walking, reminded of a similar episode that occurred five years earlier, when John F. Kennedy was assassinated. Wallace had been walking home from Pearl High on Jefferson Street near 18th Avenue when another carload of celebrating rednecks zoomed by, one shouting, "Your nigger-loving leader is dead!"

With the city under curfew and two thousand guardsmen blockading North Nashville, the 1968 Impact Symposium went on as scheduled at Memorial Gym, beginning with speeches by black Georgia legislator Julian Bond and conservative *National Review* editor William F. Buckley on the evening of April 5, just a day after the assassination and hours after the march downtown. Bond worried that nonviolent protest died along with King, predicting a "tidal wave of destruction" that would bring on days and nights of fear. Buckley said that it was unfair to blame all of white America for King's murder. It was, he said, a "profanation" for Bond to say that violence was the "official policy" of the United States, a theme King had also advanced in his final months. "The tragedy still is," Buckley said, "that they look upon an America which is so different from the America we know. . . . America is a virtuous country." The next day brought a last-minute addition to the roster of speakers in the form of Tom Hayden, president of the left-wing student group Students for a Democratic Society. Hayden flew to Nashville with less than twenty-four hours' notice and a clean shirt in his hand when both New York mayor John Lindsay and Deputy Secretary of State Nicholas Katzenbach backed out, Lindsay to deal with riots in his city and Katzenbach to engage in peace talks with Hanoi. It was not hard to understand why youth rebellion and violence erupted, Hayden said, when one considered that the country's approach to law and order was directed at one side and one interest. "Our efforts to correct situations are basically directed at keeping peace in America and in our white neighborhoods," he said, "but not directed at justice."

As the Impact panelists came and went, black Nashville continued to burn. At Tennessee State, more than two hundred students stood and watched as the school's ROTC building went up in flames, resulting in one of twenty-five incidents the Metro Fire Department responded to in a span of seven hours. Other than walking downtown for the memorial march, Wallace had not ventured off campus since the assassination when it came time for church on Sunday, April 7. On this day, Wallace carefully made his way to the Schrader Lane Church of Christ, avoiding streets where it looked like there might be trouble. Inside the sanctuary, preacher David Jones, who had for a time picked up Wallace on the Vanderbilt campus and driven him to his small chapel after Wallace was kicked out of the church near Vanderbilt, confirmed the wisdom of Wallace's cautious journey. In these tense days, young black men should be extra careful, Jones warned. The police and National Guard were suspicious of you just for being young, black, and male. They'll snatch you right out of your car, search you indiscriminately, and violate your rights. Wallace appreciated his preacher's warning, and he heeded his advice, avoiding that part of town for a few more days until tensions eased. Godfrey Dillard, meanwhile, took a different approach. The whole reason he had come to Nashville had been to play his part in the civil rights movement. Now, with the leader of that movement dead, Dillard wasn't going to sit around in his dorm on campus; he had to get out and at least see what was happening with his own eyes.

"They basically circled the black community with the National Guard, and over at Vanderbilt, it was just quiet," Dillard recalled. "There were no cars moving or anything; all the activity was about containment of the Afro-American community across the tracks. I went over there and I could see the rioting and I could see a few buildings burning. And I could see the police. And when I crossed the railroad tracks, in the white community everyone was in their house, nobody was in their cars, and the campus was just quiet. It was a voluntary lockdown. But as crazy as it was, I was out there. I was trying to figure out what to do. And I was the only one out there. My fellow black classmates said I was crazy. *What are you doing over there, man?* I said, 'Man, I had to go check it out.'"

During this first week of April 1968, Wallace and Dillard were among the few Nashvillians who had the opportunity to function on both sides of town. Just a day or two after the Sunday sermon, Wallace attended a reception in the wealthy Belle Meade neighborhood, where a number of white adults were consumed by a "hysterical level of worry they did not need to have," he recalled. Their concern was that the blacks looting and rioting in North Nashville would next aim their anger and violence on Belle Meade. The notion, Wallace believed, was so preposterous that he could only reply with a dose of sarcasm. "If you are afraid that those black folks rioting are going to come out this way, think of two things," he told the group that had gathered around him. "One, if you had a mob of angry blacks headed out this way, don't you think they would stand out? Don't you think that somewhere before they got to your house, the police or the National Guard would apprehend them? And the second thing," he continued, "even if these people wanted to come out here and get you, they wouldn't know which Goddamn way to come because they've never been here before. Believe me, the people working out here as servants are not the people who are rioting."

On Tuesday, April 9, in Atlanta, dignitaries by the dozens arrived at Ebenezer Baptist Church for the official memorial service for King. There were Jackie Kennedy, Hubert Humphrey, and Thurgood Marshall. Senator Robert Kennedy, Governor George Romney, and Mayor Henry Maier of Milwaukee. Harry Belafonte, Sammy Davis Jr., and Stevie Wonder. Marlon Brando, Bill Cosby, and Paul Newman. As family, friends, and celebrities mourned one death, another occurred back in Memphis: Loree Bailey, wife of the owner of the Lorraine Motel, died of the stroke she had suffered the night of the killing. Back at Vanderbilt, classes were suspended from 10:00 a.m. to noon, and televisions were temporarily installed in campus lounges so students and faculty could watch the funeral services. Not everyone was happy about this, including a student named Richard Ransom. "If I am paying $4,000 a year for the 'honor' of attending this university, then I'll be damned if I expect Vanderbilt officials to call off classes as a tribute to some damn riot-rouser," he wrote to the *Hustler*. Another student didn't watch on television for entirely different reasons. In addition to the celebrities, politicians, and other dignitaries, more than fifty thousand citizens jammed the streets of Atlanta to be near the memorial service, including one young man who had to be there, as if his own father were lying in that casket, one Walter Murray. Ever curious, Murray somehow worked his way through the throngs of mourners and found himself standing face to face with one of the many politicians who had come to Atlanta to pay respects to King. The next thing Murray knew, he was shaking hands with the man who would be elected president in seven months, Richard Nixon.

22

Revolt

The revolt of the black athlete in America as a phase of the overall black liberation movement is as legitimate as the sit-ins, the freedom rides, or any other manifestation of Afro-American efforts to gain freedom.
—Harry Edwards, *The Revolt of the Black Athlete*

Whether it was out of respect for King or in fear of continued riots, many segments of American life, big and small, shut down in the days before and after his memorial service. In Nashville not only were bars closed and the Grand Ole Opry given a night off, but the Junior League suspended its annual paper sale. Around the country, the sports world came largely to a halt, with NHL and NBA playoff games postponed and Major League Baseball home openers called off in Detroit, New York, Cincinnati, Houston, and Washington, DC.

Though it was highly unusual for so many games to be canceled following the death of a private citizen, the worlds of sports, politics, and civil rights were converging in myriad ways in the spring of 1968, a mix that became increasingly volatile as the months got hotter. Muhammad Ali and Jackie Robinson had attended King's funeral, and when Robert Kennedy was shot fifty-seven days later, two of the men by his side in the kitchen of the Ambassador Hotel were the Olympic gold medalist Rafer Johnson and NFL star Rosey Grier, two of the most prominent blacks in American sports. King himself had expressed support for a political movement gaining momentum among black athletes around the time of his death. And though Wallace continued to operate in near isolation in Dixie, the "plight of the black athlete" became one of the most discussed topics in other parts of the country during a tumultuous and disruptive summer of 1968. At the heart of this discussion, and at the center of the movement in which King had shown an interest, was a twenty-five-year-old sociology professor at San Jose State University named Harry Edwards.

Edwards was Black Power personified. He cut a provocative and imposing figure, standing an athletic six foot eight (he had first come to San Jose to play basketball and compete in track and field) and wearing a black beret and black sunglasses wherever he went. He came with street cred—growing up dirt poor in East St. Louis, Illinois, and spending time in jail, as had his father and brother. His mom disappeared when he was eight years old. Edwards, who told reporters he maintained an arsenal of guns in his apartment, didn't just have the requisite look and background; he talked the talk, too. As national media interest in his activities grew, Edwards never lacked for a provocative quote. He referred to whites not just as "crackers" but as "the blue-eyed devil," made half-serious allusions to "killing honkies," and referred to the president as Lynchin' Baines Johnson. He had no use, either, for prominent blacks he chose to characterize as Uncle Toms, regularly updating a "Traitor (Negro) of the Week" poster on his office wall. Despite the hyperbole and bravado (or perhaps because of it), Edwards, who had earned a master's at Cornell University, was a popular figure among white administrators and students at San Jose State: his classes were jam-packed (eight hundred students in three classes), mostly with white kids, and his department head, Dr. Harold Hodges, confirmed that "even those initially hostile [to Edwards] were won over." However much the people of San Jose State may have been fascinated by him, his primary audience, and his main concern, was the black athlete nationwide.

At times, Edwards simply cited stark statistics to make his point that the sports world was no oasis of racial equality: no black managers in the Major Leagues or head coaches in the NFL; just one black head coach in the NBA; no blacks in the front office of any big league sport. Other times, he'd tell stories about how black stars like Willie Mays and Bob Gibson—highly recognizable professional athletes—were nonetheless denied homes and loans. He'd look at the world of collegiate athletics and point to acts of exploitation, of athletes steered toward Mickey Mouse courses, coaches too quick to demote or run off black players. Edwards made it his mission not just to confront the American public with these stories and statistics, but to encourage black athletes themselves to stand up and demand change, not just in sports but in society. "The revolt of the black athlete arises from his new awareness of his responsibilities in an increasingly more desperate, violent and unstable America," he said. "He is for the first time reacting in human and masculine fashion to the disparities between the heady artificial world of newspaper clippings, photographers, and screaming spectators and the real world of degradation, humiliation, and horror that confronts the overwhelming majority of Afro-Americans."

Edwards first organized a protest by black San Jose State football players in the fall of 1967, then expanded his efforts by creating the Olympic Project for Human Rights with the express purpose of organizing a black boycott of the upcoming Summer Olympics in Mexico City. Why should black athletes compete for the glory of the red, white, and blue on the world stage, Edwards asked, when they weren't treated as equal citizens at home? On Thanksgiving Day 1967, Edwards led a discussion with sixty black athletes in the Sunday School room at Los Angeles' Second Baptist Church, speaking to a group that included basketball phenom Lew Alcindor and track stars Tommie Smith and Lee Evans. Alcindor explained why he would join the boycott, despite his status as the country's best amateur player. "Everybody knows me. I'm the big basketball star, the weekend hero, everybody's All-American," he said. "Well, last summer I was almost killed by a racist cop shooting at a black [man] in Harlem. He was shooting on the street—where masses of black people were standing around or just taking a walk. But he didn't care. After all we were just niggers. I found out last summer that we don't catch hell because we aren't basketball stars or because we don't have money. We catch hell because we are black. Somewhere each of us has got to make a stand against this kind of thing." While others in the group spoke out against the boycott, saying that sports had been good for blacks in America, the majority of the athletes in attendance backed Edwards' plan. "For years we have participated in the Olympic Games, carrying the United States on our backs with our victories, and race relations are now worse than ever," Edwards told members of the media immediately following the meeting. "Now they are even shooting people in the streets. We're not trying to lose the Olympics for the Americans. What happens to them is immaterial. . . . But it's time for the black people to stand up as men and women and refuse to be utilized as performing animals for a little extra dog food." Reaction was predictably polarized: Edwards was called a "black Hitler" by one member of the media, received numerous death threats, and found the letters "KKK" scratched into his car. Martin Luther King, meanwhile, had stated before his death that he supported the concept of the boycott. King's support wasn't a sure thing; other prominent blacks, including gold medalists Rafer Johnson and Jesse Owens, came out against the idea, arguing either that it simply wouldn't work as intended, that athletics were an area for blacks and whites to come together, or that the effort was too political for the sports world. (In the end, the doubts of Johnson and Owens proved true, as the boycott was called off in favor of small acts of protest to be decided upon by participating athletes. Alcindor kept his word and did not play for the US basketball team).

Edwards' influence wasn't just limited to the elite athletes who might have the rare opportunity to compete in Mexico City. He also directly organized or indirectly influenced activity on nearly forty college campuses, mostly in the North and West. When black athletes at Cal-Berkeley threatened to boycott if racial conditions weren't improved, both men's basketball coach Rene

Herrerias and Athletic Director Pete Newell resigned. At Princeton four black football players pledged not to play after alleging that six of the last seven black players to suit up for the Tigers quit before their senior years because of racial discrimination. At Western Michigan, sixteen black athletes called for the dismissal of the basketball coach and the hiring of black assistants in basketball and football. Edwards never approached Perry Wallace, the only black athlete suiting up for a white college in the Deep South, but Wallace was well aware of Edwards' activities elsewhere.

"I never had any personal exposure to him," Wallace recalled, "but as with most blacks, he was kind of a hero because here was a guy standing up, talking straight, and talking pretty tough. Part of it was just black radical chic; for a whole lot of people, that's how superficial their take.was. The idea being that you're supposed to be tough and strong, and he was wreaking havoc on the system and making them have to pay attention to racial issues. He was really quite an orchestrator. But I would have to say that I had a positive view of him, even though he was diametrically the opposite of me in the approach. He was precisely 180 degrees different, and it wouldn't have been politic of me to say things supportive about him and what he was doing at the time."

Though Wallace felt constrained in what he could say publicly, the combination of heightened racial sensitivities in the aftermath of King's assassination and Edwards' work on college campuses was making an impact at Vanderbilt among some whites sympathetic to issues of race. In an April 22 memo to the Arts and Science faculty on the status of integration at Vanderbilt, Professor Cal Izard wrote that racial divisions left the country in its most perilous state since the Civil War and that token steps to integrate the campus were insufficient. "There is a monstrous gulf between the minimal desegregation necessary for a Negro student to exist on campus (sleep, eat, attend classes) and real integration that enables a Negro student to experience the personal and social freedom that is dependent upon his being accepted as fully human," Izard wrote. At the same time, a group of graduate students and professors stood up for Terry Thomas, arguing that he had been run off the football team over matters of free speech related to war and race, a clear violation, as they saw it, of the university's principles. On the second point, the group (led in part by Paul Menzel, the philosophy teaching assistant who had befriended Thomas) picked up on Harry Edwards' rhetoric, calling for Athletic Director Jess Neely not only to clarify the Athletic Department's policy on its athletes' freedom of expression but also to explain its poor record in recruiting black athletes. Menzel and three other graduate students canvassed the campus and collected the signatures of more than five hundred students on a petition headlined, "Let Freedom Ring: Toward Racial and Academic Freedom." It read:

We the undersigned:

1. Question why the Vanderbilt coaching staff has not recruited a significant number of Negro athletes when in a number of professional sports Negro athletes recruited from colleges increasingly play a predominant role.

2. Request a public policy statement from Athletic Director Jess Neely, Coach Bill Pace, and the coaching staff stating their specific policies on civil liberties and the recruitment of black athletes.

Among the students to sign the petition, which was printed as a full-page ad in the April 26 *Hustler*, were many of the school's black students (but not Wallace or Dillard) and SGA president Al Hubbard, perhaps returning a political favor after Walter Murray had delivered Vanderbilt's black vote to him. Hubbard and the newly elected student Board of Presidents soon proposed a "policy statement" for the Athletic Department, at the core of which was language confirming that "all players and coaches have the right to public and private expression of their opinions on social and political issues" and that coaches should not voice disapproval of students' positions. Grad student Pat Gilpin and others pressed the matter further, meeting with Neely to present the petition. Neely was unimpressed with the number of signatures ("People will sign anything," he said. "I could go out tomorrow and get just as many signatures on a statement of the opposite view"), but he took a conciliatory stance on the Thomas matter. "When this thing first came up, I told the coaches that Terry Thomas had signed the statement as an individual, and that wasn't bad," he said. As for the questions on race, Neely was about as unequipped as one could be to lead the Athletic Department through the social changes occurring all around him.

Born in 1898, Neely was one of the all-time greatest football players in Vanderbilt history. He was fondly remembered as a member of the undefeated 1922 team that tied Michigan 0–0 in the first game ever played at Vanderbilt's Dudley Field, a game in which Coach Dan McGugin had inspired Neely and his fellow Commodores by reminding the southerners that the Yankee Wolverines' grandfathers had shot at their ancestors in the Civil War. After a long, successful coaching career at Clemson and Rice (which eventually earned him induction into the College Football Hall of Fame), Neely returned to Nashville in 1967 to wrap up his career as the school's first full-time athletic director. He helped expand and improve Vanderbilt's athletic facilities and boosted performance in a number of "non-revenue sports," but was not inclined to provide leadership in the area of race relations. "Neely was a very old man, and he was from the Old South," Gilpin recalled. "I think he did try to grow, but it was tough for him." Neely told Gilpin and his compatriots that "many Negro prospects are sought every year but that it is a real problem finding those academically qualified for admittance to Vanderbilt." When the group suggested that Vanderbilt hire a black assistant coach, Neely said he didn't believe that doing so would make any difference.

Though the aging athletic director and the grad students clearly did not see eye to eye on a number of issues, the mere fact that Neely took the meeting helped avert further student action; in fact, the matter was resolved so quickly that no wider-spread "revolt" ever took place at Vanderbilt. By April 29 Neely had adopted the Board of Presidents' suggested policy statement as official Athletic Department policy, and by May 3 Heard had dipped into his discretionary funds to award Terry Thomas a scholarship to continue his Vanderbilt studies. Heard had remained out of the public debate in this episode, a classic case of his working behind the scenes to quietly ensure his desired outcome. In the end, he said that he accepted the conclusion of the matter (as if he had no say in it) and issued a statement regarding the adoption of the civil liberties policy that further confirmed—as if with a knowing wink—that he knew where the whole thing had been headed all along: "Mr. Neely and the coaching staff—it should go without saying—are following basic University policy."

Godfrey Dillard maintains that there have always been two sides to his personality. Ever since his mom brought home every conceivable type of sporting equipment when he was a kid, there has been the athletic side. But there has also been a political side, the aspect to his character that made him such a popular student at Visitation High School and that compelled him to travel south to college to play his part in the civil rights movement. When his injured knee rendered his athletic side irrelevant for the winter and spring of 1968, he looked for other opportunities to make his mark. He became more heavily involved in the activities of the Afro-American Student Association, helping launch the organization's arts and commentary newsletter, *Rap from the 11th Floor*. His peers respected his brains and his ambition, electing him president of the association, and it was because he held this title that he was invited to address Vanderbilt's Arts and Science faculty, along with Walter Murray, Robert Moore, and Eileen Carpenter, in a specially called meeting on May 2. Dillard had grown increasingly frustrated with the slow progress of race relations on campus, particularly with what he saw as a lack of urgency to bring blacks and whites together to foster greater understanding. While he found Heard's Human Relations Council meetings a step in the right direction, he was especially energized to have the opportunity to address the entire faculty. This was his opportunity to speak truth to power, and he had no fear.

Standing before the professors in Room 114 of the gray stone Furman Hall, Dillard drew distinctions between King's collaborative approach to racial progress and the confrontational Black Power style. Black students needed to be involved—and feel welcome—in all aspects of campus life, Dillard said. It was the Vanderbilt community's choice at this moment to decide how the necessary changes would come about, how painful the process would be.

In subsequent interviews with the *Hustler*, Dillard expanded on his remarks. He expressed frustration that even though the Afro-American Student Association had opened its meetings to white students, none had attended. "Next year we are going to take the issues to the campus," he said. "Next year our organization will be much more forceful. We know what we've got to do now and we are going to do it." Among his plans were to hold "African culture days"—with black students wearing African clothes, displaying African art, and selling African literature—and to expand the publishing frequency of *Rap from the 11th Floor* after the magazine's inaugural issue sold out all eight hundred copies. He said he wanted to work with the administration to ensure that black contributions to American society were dealt with more fully and honestly in introductory history courses and that more black writers were studied in English classes. Explaining that part of his goal was to help white students understand that they were "part of the racial problem," he gave his thoughts on why the civil rights movement had evolved from nonviolence to Black Power. "Demonstrations have outlived themselves as a force to build good attitudes in whites," he said. "Now, everyone demonstrates and it is no longer radical and shocking. . . . I can't condemn anyone in the Black Power movement because the conditions of white society today made them what they are. If white society had not been the way it is the movement wouldn't have developed. The blame for Black Power falls on the white man, because he has suppressed the black race to the extent that it will resort to violence. . . . If white society makes stable and programmed advances that people can see, then Black Power will die out. . . . It all depends on white society if the movement goes to revolution. Blacks are not content to stand still anymore."

Like Wallace, Dillard was attempting to work within the system to effect change on campus. Matters of style, however, created entirely different perceptions of the two sophomores. Wallace, having grown up in the segregated South, maintained a constant surveillance on his own life, thinking two or three steps ahead about how anything he did or said might be interpreted. Dillard, having lived and studied among successful blacks and whites in Detroit, charged full steam ahead into any situation, emboldened by his unshakeable self-confidence. In this regard, Dillard was the ideal Harry Edwards protégé; the problem was, even Edwards himself hadn't organized any revolts in the Deep South.

Dillard's comments were persuasive enough that the A&S faculty members adopted his resolution to form their own race relations council just minutes after he concluded his remarks. Still, by speaking of "violence" and "revolution," no matter the context, Dillard's comments to the faculty members and to the *Hustler* raised eyebrows. While he merely attempted to relay *warnings* about what might happen if progress weren't made, many at Vanderbilt interpreted his words as threats. A few weeks earlier, football coach Pace had tightened the reins on Terry Thomas when Thomas "stepped outside the family" with his words and deeds. When basketball coach Skinner heard that Dillard was making controversial statements, he called Dillard into his office for a warning of his own.

Skinner told Dillard that he needed to back off his political activities and focus just on basketball. Dillard replied with an obligatory, "OK," but in truth, the coach's words fell on deaf ears. "By that time, in my mind I sensed that they had soured on me," Dillard recalled. "They benched me, and then after I got hurt I didn't feel like he wanted me back on the team, so I didn't feel very good about Skinner. I didn't respect him as a person. So, if you can imagine a young man walking into an office with a white man he doesn't respect, who he probably detests, and then he tells the kid to stop doing something, it was like, *Are you finished? See you later, coach.* I didn't say much to him, because I didn't really have much to say to him at that point, and I didn't care that much about what he was talking about." Within a matter of days, there were whispers on campus that Dillard's days on the Commodore basketball team were numbered.

While Dillard spent some time in the spotlight, even driving around campus in a new red Mustang convertible he had convinced his mother to help him purchase, Wallace took a brief step out of the public eye. The effects of the long and painful season and the assassinations of King and Kennedy (the latter coming two days after Dillard's remarks) left him physically and emotionally spent.

Events surrounding the Ole Miss game, in particular, still weighed heavily on his mind, leading to periods of deep reflection on the course of his life and on broader, complex issues of race. In fact, it wasn't only the game itself that haunted him. He later termed the experience "Four Days in Hell," a series of events so bothersome and potentially misunderstood he didn't speak of them in their totality for more than forty-five years. First, Friday, February 9, 1968. Before the team left for Mississippi, Wallace stopped by Pearl High to see old friends and to gain strength and inspiration for the journey south. Instead, walking down the hallway of his old school, he was met by an older female staff member. "Perry Wallace, you're nothing but a token," she said, startling him. "Those white folks are just using you and you're allowing it to happen." While Wallace eventually discovered that the woman's barbs were born of jealousy (her own son, an athlete, was not being recruited by Vanderbilt), her words—delivered in a building that had previously only brought warmth and comfort—added to his state of anxiety as he prepared for the trip. For

Wallace such encounters with black detractors were surprisingly frequent during his Vanderbilt days. *You're nothing, Perry Wallace. Perry Wallace, you make me sick. Perry Wallace, you're just an Uncle Tom.* He never aired this "dirty laundry" in public, believing many whites in the media and elsewhere would "happily substitute these revelations for any honest consideration of racial problems." Still, he considered the mentality of his black critics a form of "super-slavery," self-destructive behavior where people pulled each other down rather than "work[ing] like hell to heal past wounds and move forward." As he walked out of Pearl High that day, he said he remained determined to continue his journey, even for the benefit of people like that woman, but "at a very long distance from them."

Wallace's second—and most obvious—day in hell came on Saturday, February 10, in Oxford. He looked back on the game and could still feel the heat of a "massive, intense, and unapologetic hatred." The scale was so large and the effect was so glaring and garish, he said, that he was "as dazzled as I was afraid. It struck me to my very core."

Emerging from the inferno that was Mississippi, Wallace's third day in hell came on Sunday, February 11, at his familiar Schrader Lane Church of Christ. Initially, he was comforted by the words of his preacher, the Reverend David Jones, and found it reassuring to spend time back in his old neighborhood. Then, as he stopped to greet Reverend Jones on his way out of the church, someone in the crowd called his name: "Perry! I heard they about lynched you down there in Mississippi!" The parishioners around him exploded in laughter. Wallace was shocked and angered by what he considered the "ignorant" and "outrageous" insensitivity of the moment. Leaving the church grounds, Wallace drove out deep into the country, to get away and think in solitude. "Nature was always healing," he recalled, "and in fact it now seemed to be about the only thing I could count on." As he reflected on the episode at church, Wallace concluded that it highlighted the growing difference between his worldview and that of many of his old neighbors. "These were good, decent, hard-working southern black people. But they were also poor, uneducated, and largely unconscious of their own blackness," Wallace said. "All this made me appreciate more than ever why Reverend Lawson and other civil rights leaders did so much teaching and training. These folks were masters of faith, endurance, and survival, but they were not masters of racial pride and progress. They needed leaders, advocates, and teachers to raise their consciousness and show them the way forward. Otherwise, they would continue on in life, but there would be no improvements for blacks on a large scale." As different as people like Wallace and his family already were from most of his neighbors, Wallace came to believe, his experience at Vanderbilt was making him even more different. "Not only the positive features of a high-quality education, but also the deepening, strengthening effects of my struggles with the university's negative features were producing a more thoughtful, sensitive, and demanding person," he recalled. "And I would have to figure out how to mesh this emerging person with the masses of my people."

The fourth and final day in hell came on Monday, February 12, in the familiar confines of Memorial Gym in the minutes before the Commodores' first practice since the win in Oxford. A voice rang out: "Hey Leroy! Hey Willie! We're going to get you, boy!" A white student, thinking it was funny, began shouting out some of the same threats Wallace had endured at Ole Miss. "It was bizarre and insulting," Wallace recalled. "This guy had actually been at the game and was a supporter down there. How could he have witnessed the horror of that event and still think it was funny to retrieve those moments with his mockery?"

As Wallace reflected on that moment in the weeks that followed, he "placed" the guy in a small category of people he occasionally encountered: the types who, because they had befriended Wallace and were generally inclined to favor equality and racial justice, believed that treating him well was proof positive that they were fully free of prejudice, so that any spontaneous thoughts, words, or acts from them—such as the "joking" taunts at practice—were naturally acceptable. "They seemed to think they owned me. I was their 'pet project,'" Wallace recalled. "Or maybe just their pet. My big problem with them was that, however humble and respectful I was taught to be, the idea of being owned by anyone was deeply repulsive."

Wallace later recalled his "four days in hell" as the most symbolic and impactful ninety-six hours of his Vanderbilt career. "These four days stand out as the most formative ones shaping my views about the entire experience," he later recalled, "including my views, attitudes, and approaches about race. I was forced to be tougher, more protective of myself, and smarter about people. I was changed greatly." Wallace began to watch people more carefully, trying to anticipate any obnoxious, arrogant, or simply innocent hamhanded insults that might be headed his way, either by whites or blacks. His friends and his privacy became more "precious" than ever before. "Emotional recovery," he said, "became an art and a science that I cultivated daily."

When he had spoken with Henry Hecht of the *Hustler*, Wallace had carefully examined each aspect of the basketball season. In the weeks that followed, as he continued to reflect intensely on his overall well-being, his place in society, and the future of the country, he was as disillusioned as he'd ever be in life. There was no easy way out; no matter how bad things got, he would have to find the strength to endure. It was during this time of enlightening but melancholy reflection that two unexpected visitors arrived at his door—one welcome, the other not.

The first visitor was more accurately a group of visitors, white men in dark suits and fedoras who looked like G-men out of an old black-and-white movie. Wallace had been sitting in his room on a Sunday night, talking to a white friend who was smoking a cigar, when he got up to answer a knock at the door. At the sight of the stern and solemn-looking men, Wallace had a brief thought that "this could be the end." Instead, the men told Wallace that they represented the Church of Christ, not the individual church he had been kicked out of, but the church in a broader sense. They told Wallace that they had come in hopes that they could work out some sort of arrangement: "We'd love for you to come to one of our churches, look around, get to know some of the people, see if you're interested, and maybe at this church you'd be able to join." Wallace didn't have to think about the offer for long. His dream of equality in a new America wasn't real, he had concluded, or at the very least it was complicated. He was worn down physically. He was sick of being around people who thought he wasn't good enough. "So I just said, 'Man, I'm just tired of all this and the last thing I want to do is add in any more of this crazy stuff where people say one thing and mean another,'" Wallace recalled. "I appreciate what you all are doing, but I really don't want to do any more experimenting."

The second visitor was more welcome, a black reporter from *Sports Illustrated* who was helping compile research for a series *SI*'s Jack Olsen was writing on the status of black athletes in America, inspired in part by the work of Harry Edwards. The correspondent who came to Nashville was one of many the magazine sent out around the country to speak with athletes, coaches, educators, and prominent blacks over a span of four months, a research project that led to 150,000 words of notes for Olsen to assimilate. Wallace agreed to sit down for an extensive interview, but under the condition he not be quoted in the story. There could be reprisals, he said, mindful of the recent experiences of Thomas and Dillard. "We talked about a number of different things—what it was like, what I was going through, what did I think of it, was I being let down, did I ever feel like leaving, and that kind of thing," Wallace recalled. "I gave him a sense of the difficulties that faced me in even speaking about these subjects, and I told him that what I was experiencing was that either people were pretending that [racism] didn't exist, were denying it, or were getting angry if I said much about it."

When Olsen's series "The Black Athlete: A Shameful Story" ran in five consecutive issues in the month of July 1968, it instantly became the most controversial and talked-about piece in the magazine's fourteen-year history, generating nearly one thousand letters to the editor. In a letter to readers accompanying the first article, *SI* publisher Garry Valk wrote that "the revelations contained in the series will bring the reader a new appreciation of the problems and attitudes of the black athletes whose performances all of us sports fans cheer so enthusiastically but about whom we know so little." Valk's comments were by definition aimed at white readers, but the series had a profound impact on Wallace. He read every word of every article in the series, and though he was never mentioned by name, he recognized himself throughout, both because some of the material he provided was incorporated and because his experiences at Vanderbilt were so similar to the stories of the other black athletes Olsen wrote about. The author came into the project sensitive to issues of race—among the six books he had written was one on Cassius Clay (later to become Muhammad Ali)—and more important, he had covered the 1957 integration of Little Rock's Central High School for *Time* magazine. Olsen wrote of the frustrating social lives of black college athletes, the "vast gulf between black and white sportsmen," the limited job opportunities for former players, and coaches' limited tolerance for mistakes. ("A white kid can make five or six mistakes and stay in," said the future NBA coach Don Chaney, then a basketball player at the University of Houston. "We make one and we're on the bench.") He told stories about black football players at Kansas having to endure a team banquet where the theme was "Dixie," with boosters singing about the "land of cotton" while waving Confederate flags, oblivious to how it made the Jayhawks' twelve black players feel. Five straight weeks of eye-opening details, all intended, *SI* proclaimed, to challenge the widely held assumption that sports was the one part of American society in which blacks had found opportunity and equality.

"Almost to a man, [black athletes] are dissatisfied, disgruntled and disillusioned," Olsen wrote. "Black collegiate athletes say they are dehumanized, exploited and discarded, and some even say they were happier back in the ghetto. Black professional athletes say they are underpaid, shunted into certain stereotyped positions and treated like sub-humans by Paleolithic coaches who regard them as watermelon-eating idiots. . . . Has sport in America deceived itself? Is its liberality a myth, its tolerance a deceit?"

One passage that particularly resonated with Wallace dealt with an athlete forced to play through a serious injury. The account reminded Wallace so much of his own experience, when he had been barked at by Commodore fans as he played through a painful groin injury as a freshman, that he was brought to tears.

In some regards the content of the articles drove Wallace into a deeper funk; on top of all the violence and hate in the world, here were five weeks of evidence that, in purely athletic terms, the situation was as bad or worse for other blacks as it was for him; as Olsen wrote, "There is one thing every last [black athlete] discovers. Life for a Negro athlete on an average American college campus isn't what they thought it was going to be. No, sir." But in another sense, Wallace was energized by Olsen's series, just as he was by the movement organized by Harry Edwards, the words of Senator Kennedy, the mourning for Reverend King. In the midst of the madness that was 1968, at least people were talking about serious problems; at least they were confronting racial division as they never had before.

"There was a huge amount of negative excitement and a sense of turmoil at that time, but it came in the midst of some increased hope in terms of racial conditions," Wallace later recalled. "There was a sense of finally being noticed as opposed to being ignored and invisible. Plus, even with the riots and all the violence and the radical Black Power advocates like Stokely Carmichael and Eldridge Cleaver, there was a certain sense of excitement and adventure. People were paying attention to blacks and issues that affected us. In and around the Vanderbilt campus, there were all these intelligent people and many of them were really being stimulated into exploring these topics. They began to talk to us."

23

The Cruel Deception

Every Negro athlete is a potential messenger from the white world
to the ghetto—a messenger who can help bridge the intolerable
communications gap that exists today. Sport and the universities and
business must all ask: What news do we want these messengers to
deliver? News that in this field, a black man is recognized as a man,
that exploitation has been replaced by human consideration and that
equality is more than just a word? Or do we want the message to be:
burn, baby burn? The choice is ours and—as Prentice Gautt said in the
last article of the Olsen series—"The change should start today. Not
tomorrow. Today."

—*Sports Illustrated* editorial, August 5, 1968

Even before *SI* ran an editorial following the Olsen series in which it described black athletes as important intermediaries between white and
black America, Perry Wallace was on to that notion. Rather than seeing himself as a conduit of news from white America back to the black community,
however, he knew that at this moment in history, the most important thing
he could do was just the opposite: to share black perspectives with white faculty and administrators at Vanderbilt. In early July, Wallace had been asked
to organize a meeting of the university's Human Relations Council for the
morning of July 25. As he read the *Sports Illustrated* articles over the course
of the month, he realized that they could not have appeared at a better time,
that he could use his opportunity to speak at the HRC meeting as a chance
to show that the incidents described in Olsen's stories weren't just easily
dismissed, isolated problems at far-off schools. Wallace worked for days
on his remarks, first writing out notes by hand and eventually typing out
a seven-page script. As prepared as the remarks may have been, they built

to a crescendo of raw emotion, clearly articulating his disillusionment, sadness, anger, and confusion. At the same time, the very fact that he planned to speak these words pointed to two other important realities: first, that despite his disappointment, he cared enough about Vanderbilt to try to improve the situation there; and second, that despite his inherent caution, he was confident enough—buoyed on one side by the words of Edwards and the athletes quoted in the *SI* series and on the other side by a feeling that Chancellor Heard, at least, understood his pain—to speak his mind and bare his soul in the most emotional address of his life. While he had been purposely guarded in his comments to the *Hustler*'s Hecht, he understood that if he held back in this setting, he would only be hurting the chances that things would change for the better, either for him or future black student-athletes at Vanderbilt.

Temperatures were climbing to 90 degrees on a humid Nashville morning when Wallace carried his notes into Chancellor Heard's office at Kirkland Hall. The morning *Tennessean* had run a front-page story saying that in Cleveland, Ohio, black community leaders had begun patrolling the city's East Side in place of National Guardsmen, hoping to bring peace to an area where ten people were killed in racially motivated rioting and gunfire two days earlier. In Washington, DC, the House of Representatives, in response to increased gun involvement in riots nationwide, voted to ban interstate gun sales, and in Cincinnati the nation's governors passed a gun-control resolution. And here, standing before nine white men and women, stood a disillusioned young black man who decided to use words, calmly spoken, to make a case not just for himself but for his classmates and those who would follow. "We didn't riot, we didn't get angry, and I didn't get up and scream," Wallace recalled. "At that moment, I was more passionate and sad than anything else."

Wallace began his remarks with a reference to the graduate students' recent encounter with Jess Neely and the resolution of the Terry Thomas affair, noting that neither the students nor the administrator had bothered to ask his opinion on the recruitment of black athletes to Vanderbilt:

> Last spring, considerable interest was given to issues involving the civil liberties of athletes and the recruitment of black athletes. Certain members of the administration and the head of the athletic department were met with by an interested group from the Vanderbilt community. It has come to my attention that some doubt was expressed as to whether I shared some of the views and attitudes toward the recruitment and probable treatment—considering the composition of racial attitudes within the athletic department—of black athletes that the group of graduate students expressed. Because of this doubt, and because none of these meetings involved or requested the impressions of this school's

only black participant in a varsity sport with regard to recruitment and the capabilities of the athletic department in this area, I feel that this might be an excellent opportunity for you to see a side of the issue that amazingly everyone seemed to overlook. My report deals with Vanderbilt's first recruitment of a black athlete. I plan, briefly, to follow this recruitment from the beginning to the present, highlighting and describing events and situations which are of prime importance to the area to which we address ourselves. Hopefully, this information will be of assistance in future attempts for recruitment of Negroes at Vanderbilt.

Wallace then referred to the *Sports Illustrated* series, a deliberate attempt to give his otherwise emotional comments a foundation in a respected third-party source. Wallace had told Hecht that he had unraveled his painful experiences and placed them in perspective, but here in his remarks to the committee was evidence that the unraveling process had nearly broken him, and in fact would take many years to complete:

I'm sure you are all familiar with the recent series of articles in *Sports Illustrated* on blacks in the field of athletics, so without any summary of this series, I will refer, at times, to it. 'The cruel deception' happens to be the title of the first part. I suppose it would seem difficult for you to perceive of it being a deception to pull a black out of a ghetto and to place him in an academic community where he has a chance to step right into the world of success. But much more is involved and your future efforts at recruitment must carefully address themselves at this important aspect.

The entrance of your first black athlete involved deception. As I was sought after to attend Vanderbilt, many aspects of Vanderbilt life were not mentioned. Social life was one of them. No mention was made of the degree of fraternity participation at the school, my possibilities of joining one, or my alternatives if I chose not to consider them. I was simply brought in and expected to survive in an alien culture with no outlets for the originality of my own culture on campus. One of my other concerns was the degree of racism I would be shown in deep southern states. Certainly, I did not expect to have been given an experienced answer, but there was no need to avoid and cover up the issue by saying that it wasn't any worry at all. I was soon to find that this issue and the previous issue governing the social attitudes were to hamper my career and to affect my life viciously; and to emphasize the effect of the dishonesty, I was stifled most by my disillusionment. For you see, I trusted you and almost destroyed myself trying to prove that you were right.

I read painfully through the series of articles finding it easy in instances to understand the feelings of the blacks speaking and I was amazed at some of our striking similarities. One athlete talked of having to play half a season with a painful groin injury. His pelvic area pained him in practice with each turn and hurt until they gave him a pain depressant for games. I remember the last half of my first season at Vanderbilt with my groin injury which was not shot with Novocain. Like the other athlete in the article, the most painful thing about it was the fact that no one seemed very concerned. I was lucky enough to have a few understanding people around who let me rest as much as possible, but the fact is that I still had to play and not much was said of it. Maybe this doesn't seem to be a valid complaint, but it's a remarkable similarity.

As he progressed deeper into his prepared remarks, Wallace moved into especially nuanced and potentially dangerous territory, telling stories about his own mistreatment on campus, not for sympathy, but to make the brave point that the school's athletic director was wrong: if Vanderbilt was serious about recruiting more black basketball or football players, a black assistant coach would be a great asset.

My first year here involved a battle with my teammates to defeat their knowing and unknowing attempts to categorize me as the "team nigger." The fact that the coaches were not aware that certain things tended to stereotype me made it an even harder battle. I have already related to some of you the story of a teammate telling me of how I would surely have enjoyed the old slave breeding camps and asking me about picking cotton. What I didn't tell you was that a coach was present and they all had a big laugh. Through some informing, and some battling, some of this treatment and some of these attitudes have at least cut themselves out to make the department of basketball a potentially safe area in which a black might be able to work with some people who are slowly becoming aware of the black man's need for understanding and equal treatment.

I have worked in the seeking of athletes for football. And while I am not in full-time association with this department, my judgment of a black athlete's possibility of a smooth relationship with this department is the closest to the real thing that is possible. I am of the opinion that this is the most critical area in your interest for blacks in Vanderbilt athletics. As a matter of fact, to recruit a black football athlete with the present vagueness of policies regarding racial treatment and the present set of attitudes is to recruit that black into certain death.

My association with this department reveals no outrightness on their part, of course, but the set of attitudes is the most viciously dangerous to any black who has to associate with them. My participation in this recruitment so far has been completely a protective measure for the recruits themselves. I have tried to see that they were not deceived and that they knew the issues. This type of attitude extends to many of the athletes of this department, making it doubly difficult on any athlete who is black. The articles made mention about sex myths and white responses. It is from the previously mentioned department that I encountered the most difficulty. It is not uncommon for one of these athletes to ask me about my sex life or to insinuate lewd things about my dates. Once when helping to recruit one of the black football athletes, some mention was made of how I would entertain him. When a house of prostitutes was mentioned, the coach did not laugh as if this were a joke, but gave a grin that gave the impression that he might have believed I might do this.

So, from this incident, we see that not only a strong statement of policy is needed, but other measures must be taken to protect blacks brought in. The question might be asked: How would a black coach be helpful in recruiting? He certainly would have better suggestions about entertainment. It has been stated that a black coach would not help recruiting. In high school, I remember visiting and considering attending two schools simply because they had black football coaching assistants who were there not just to recruit blacks but helped very much. The problems of a black would certainly be better understood by someone who had been through what the younger fellow is going through.

Wallace saved his most profound and emotional words for last. In describing his experience at Ole Miss, he showed that he knew his history was already being written. Here was an opportunity to infuse the feel-good story under development (*Pioneer Overcomes Taunts to Succeed!*) with the truth: He may have overcome adversity, but the "overcoming" was a daily chore, adding up to the unhappiest weeks and months of his life. The sum effect was to cause him to believe that the promise of equality in America was a lie, a lie that stung especially hard because he had so thoroughly bought into the dream. Wallace realized that his challenge at this moment was to not allow himself to be forever damaged by the ordeal, and become, in his words, a "monster."

"The basic point is that if you impose or allow a person to go through so much, it dehumanizes them, and they become more like an animal, the worst type of animal, like a monster," Wallace said years later. "And there are two kinds of monsters, a monster who fails and a monster who succeeds. And that's the news: they're both monsters. You destroy yourself one way or another. When I talk about becoming a monster, I talk about the putrid soul that can get created by an oppressive process, but how if you don't watch out in your resistance to those forces, you can still become a monster. So you've got to watch out twice. If I could have written it better, I would have referred to those two types of monsters, and I was saying I'd rather turn into my own monster than let you turn me into one."

> Let me give you an example of where a black coach might have been helpful to me. My game at the University of Mississippi is often lauded as one in which I bravely fought the racist catcalls and pestering to perform well and be cheered for at the end. But my thoughts of that experience hover around one series of events. I was hit in the eye during the first half (no foul was called and no officials' time out was called when it could be easily seen that I was temporarily blinded in my left eye). In the locker room I got treatment at halftime, but my teammates did not bother to wait and see whether the length of my treatment would allow me to return to the floor with them, and they forgot that I would have to return alone. No trainers or managers returned with me either. Now, I don't expect you to attach much significance to merely having to run out on a basketball floor, but what I remember most in my life is standing at that huge doorway with that crowd waiting on me with my teammates completely at the opposite end of the floor. What would have merely been an occurrence of no consequence for a white player was transformed into a nightmare and a long, hellish trauma for me.
>
> So, I come home to Vanderbilt, with its fraternities and its other attributes which make for a student body unable to imagine my experience or have any understanding. Slowly Vanderbilt became a well-mannered extension of the University of Mississippi and I found no place to really call home. This affected my play at home when I considered that the same people cheered for me who invited me to parties at frats I couldn't join, and these same

people stood up and cheered when the band played "Dixie." (It sounds the same to me in Mississippi as it does at Vanderbilt.) The same man cheered for me who intimidated me after the blacks' first meeting with the administration in the spring of 1967 with subtle things like, "Where are you going, boy?" or "What are you doing?" instead of saying hello, or good morning. I became intimidated by a number of these things but I was expected to perform like a superhuman despite the pressure of a load on my back that belonged to a University who set out on a monumental undertaking (recruitment) and took the road of least resistance (or least assistance).

For the past two years, no athletic department official or athletic committee official has made an effort to formally explore the world of the black Vanderbilt athlete for future usage and improvement. Recruitment this fall involved two black athletes; approximately 30 whites were signed in football. This department brings three to four times the number it plans to sign to the campus. This number figures at 90 to 120 visitations—two of which were black. The black community is aware that at some point there is a prejudicial insertion in recruitment. In black informal language we call it a "nigger-every-four-year-program" while you shuffle and shuck and jive in between.

To sum it up, people, somebody has lied to me, somebody has deceived me and it has resulted in the two unhappiest years of my life. I have felt the strain and even people close to me have felt it. I speak in this case of family, including a mother who has gained a state of bad health in two years and even waited out one of my trips to Mississippi on an operating table in the hospital during a sickness. I don't say any of this to bring your sympathy and granted this has been a lengthy report, but surprisingly you have ignored much and the more blacks you have here, the more people you set up to face destruction.

I wouldn't be surprised if my report is briefly dismissed as my effort to keep in step with current trends among black people. But maybe this is part of my despondency.

I ask, will you continue to try to destroy me and will you try to destroy others? Do you also think I'm going to sit and watch you destroy my black brothers and me? I'd rather turn into the monster you're making me than to go down without making some impact on what you've done.

The articles in the magazine point out the problems and it would be to Vanderbilt's advantage to take heed to them.

With these heartfelt remarks, Wallace at once exposed the shortsightedness of the blacks who considered him an Uncle Tom for even attending Vanderbilt and of prejudiced whites who berated him with the worst of epithets, unable to see past the color of his skin. His words were at once painful, daring, and profound, but as he concluded his speech, his biggest worry was that his advice would go unheeded. Indeed, it soon became clear that some in the room simply did not understand the depth of what he was saying.

In response to Wallace's soliloquy, one Vanderbilt administrator attempted to persuade Wallace that he was overreacting. "You know, Perry," the man said, "in these games, you might have the crowd giving a guy a hard time because he has red hair. They might call out, 'Red!'" Wallace was angered by the comparison, and he shot back at the official in a way that was uncharacteristically direct. "There's a difference between calling a guy Red or whatever and calling me nigger. 'Red' is different than nigger."

The administrator was visibly upset by Wallace's retort, as was a senior Athletic Department official who called Wallace into his office days later. "You've got to admit that what we don't need is protest," the official said. "What we need is law and order." Wallace saw the hypocrisy inherent in the statement, and he came back with a variation of the line Tom Hayden had used during his Impact remarks. "Yes, we do, any society needs law and order, but we also need justice," Wallace replied. "And the problem is that racism doesn't amount to justice. Bigotry doesn't amount to justice."

"If you feel so strongly about that, then why don't you leave?" the official said testily.

This could have been the end, the experiment over, the integration of the SEC instantly rendered unfinished business. But Wallace understood the significance of his journey, even when this Vanderbilt leader did not.

"Sir, it's not my job to leave," Wallace replied. "It's not my job to get up and leave injustice in a country that claims to have justice. I have a right to be here like anybody else, and I'm not going to leave Vanderbilt."

24

Black Fists

A global television audience of 400 million watched as American sprinters Tommie Smith and John Carlos bowed their heads and raised their black-gloved fists into the air, a gesture that turned an ordinary medal ceremony into a provocative statement for racial equality. Smith and Carlos, teammates at San Jose State University and protégés of Harry Edwards, had just earned Olympic gold and bronze medals in the two hundred meters, Smith winning in a world-record time of 19.83 seconds. As their arms remained raised, their heads down, boos cascaded down from the crowd at Mexico City's Estadio Olimpico.

When the national anthem was over, Smith and Carlos stepped down from the medal stand, each wearing long black socks but no shoes, and the boos grew louder. They raised their fists again.

When Edwards' boycott plans faltered, many black American athletes competing in the 1968 Summer Olympics devised their own methods of protest. Smith and Carlos shared a single pair of gloves—Carlos wore one on his left hand, Smith on his right—and their names would be forever linked, even as their friendship frayed in the decades to come. Their silent but defiant act was instantly iconic and polarizing, carrying so much symbolism—in the sports world and beyond—that author Amy Bass concluded that the pose "sealed the metamorphosis from Negro to black." It was not an immediately peaceful transition. Under pressure from International Olympic Committee president Avery Brundage, the US Olympic Committee immediately suspended Smith and Carlos from the American team, ordering them to vacate the Olympic village and to leave Mexico within forty-eight hours.

The date was October 16, the Summer Games taking place in the fall as a concession to the Mexican heat and to American television viewers, ensuring that there would be no conflict with the World Series.

Fourteen hundred miles northeast of the Olympic stadium, at Memorial

Gymnasium in Nashville, October 16, 1968, also happened to be the second day of official preseason basketball practice for Roy Skinner's Commodores. On the same day that Smith and Carlos made an iconic gesture that became seared into the national consciousness, a nearly imperceptible act took place on the wide, hardwood court in Tennessee, just one decision made and a few words spoken, none of it of much consequence to the world outside the brick-walled gymnasium. But on this day, when Coach Skinner told Godfrey Dillard to join the "B-team" for practice, it set in motion a series of events that not only would have a profound and disturbing impact on the lives of two men for decades to come, but also would add another layer of complexity and pain to the pioneering experiment then underway at Vanderbilt and to the telling of that story well into the twenty-first century.

Ever since suffering the injury that sidelined him a year earlier, Dillard had worked hard to rehabilitate his knee, preparing to regain a spot on the varsity team. Given no structured rehab regimen, Dillard devised one himself, spending long, hot days running up and down the steep, cement aisles of the Vanderbilt football stadium. When he wasn't running, he was riding a stationary bike to improve his stamina, or playing in pickup basketball games all over town—at Vanderbilt, TSU, Fisk—wherever and whenever he could find a game. "I was determined to come back," Dillard recalled, and by all accounts, he was succeeding. In those summer games and in unsanctioned scrimmages with his Vanderbilt teammates before the official start of practice, Dillard was playing the same brand of ball as ever before. In a September 29 *Hustler* article on the team's summer workouts and prospects for the season ahead, Henry Hecht declared that "Godfrey Dillard looks to have made a complete recovery."

It could have been a simple storyline: injured player works hard to rehabilitate, earns respect for his determination, and is welcomed back with open arms. In reality, Dillard's reemergence was complicated in nearly every possible way. First, there was the matter of his remarks to the Arts and Science faculty the previous spring, and his follow-up comments to the *Hustler*. As president of the Afro-American Student Association, Dillard had become an outspoken student leader, a role he enjoyed and one that was in keeping with the sensibilities on race, politics, and student involvement that he had developed in Detroit. While Dillard remained in Nashville for most of the summer of 1968 to continue his rehabilitation, his hometown continued to smolder with racial unrest. When school started again in the fall, talk began to swirl among some pockets of alumni: *Did Skinner really need to have this radical black kid from Detroit on the team? What good could come of it?* Somewhat related was the matter of Dillard's style of ball and his demeanor on the court—a flashier, brasher, more individualistic brand of guard play than Skinner was comfortable with. While Wallace could pound away in the paint to collect rebounds, block shots, and occasionally score, he would never be the engine driving the Commodore machine. Dillard, a guard, presented a different prospect altogether. With the ball in his hands on virtually every possession, Dillard would be the face of the squad in many ways, at a time when even integrated professional and northern collegiate teams often restricted the number of blacks on their rosters, especially at the guard position.

There was also the simple matter of numbers: sixteen players in camp competing for no more than eleven or twelve—possibly as few as ten—spots on the varsity roster. In today's game, this scenario no longer exists; teams have thirteen scholarships to use at any one time, and every one of those thirteen players is either an active member of the varsity or sits out the season as a redshirt. There are no leftovers, no need for a B-team. In 1968, however, Skinner had more players than roster spots, a problem compounded by the fact that one player, Rudy Thacker, was returning to the team from academic suspension, and another, Rick Cammarata, had returned after serving two years in the Marine Corps, including a thirteen-month tour in Vietnam. And in Cammarata's story lies the final piece of Skinner's dilemma. When deciding who would make the varsity and who would be relegated to obscurity on the B-team, Skinner would, in some measure, have to weigh Dillard versus Cammarata, the "black radical" versus the war veteran with shrapnel in his leg and two Purple Hearts in his pocket.

Though Cammarata was no basketball star—the only schools that had recruited him besides Vanderbilt had been Dayton and Wisconsin-Stout—he presented an especially sympathetic case to Skinner. He arrived at Vanderbilt as a freshman in the 1965 season, watching with wonder as Clyde Lee and the varsity advanced to the Elite Eight of the NCAA Tournament before dropping the heartbreaker to Michigan. He redshirted the following season—and then his life changed forever. An engineering major, Cammarata made the mistake of allowing a football player to copy from his differential equations exam. Caught, Cammarata was suspended from school by the university's student-run Honor Council, an act that cost him his student deferment from the draft. Rather than submit to that fate, Cammarata enlisted in the Marine Corps, with Skinner reassuring him that he'd probably have the chance to play basketball and stay in shape before returning to Vanderbilt. Instead, Cammarata was sent from basic training to Vietnamese language school, and then on to Vietnam and the war. In one firefight, nearly all the men in his company were killed; the Purple Hearts came from wounds suffered in other battles. All in all, it was a heavy price to pay for allowing a friend to cheat off his exam. When he returned to Vanderbilt in time for the fall semester in 1968, Cammarata sensed that Skinner was giving him every chance to earn a spot on the varsity. During the darkest hours of his tour in Vietnam, Cammarata lifted his spirits by imagining himself back on the hardwood at Memorial Gym. He had survived Vietnam and now he was running free on that court, never happier to be surrounded by a new group of teammates in the safety and comfort of a basketball team. He paid no special attention to Wallace or Dillard; Cammarata had played high school ball on an integrated team in St. Louis and had served with dozens of black soldiers in Vietnam. He had departed for the Marines before either of his future black teammates arrived on campus, and was unaware of the drama surrounding Dillard when camp opened.

In speaking to the press after assigning Dillard and four other teammates (each of whom had previously seen varsity action) to the B-team on the second day of practice, Skinner said that the decision had been agonizing and that the B-teamers would have the opportunity to work their way onto the varsity through stellar practice play; nothing was final. Dillard, however, felt that he hadn't been given a fair chance. The first day of practice, after all, had not even involved a scrimmage. On what basis was Skinner making his judgment? "When they put me on the B-team on the second day of practice, it was obvious they did not want anyone to see me play," he recalled. "They had to shut the door. Because if they had allowed me to be out there on the floor, playing in front of the alumni, practice after practice, showing my talent in the scrimmages, they could not have kept me off the team. So they had to bench me right off the bat. Immediately." Dillard believed that despite the coach's statement that varsity jobs were still up for grabs, there would be little opportunity to force such a decision. B-teamers were forgotten men in the Skinner practice system, watching from the sidelines for nearly the entirety of any practice session before finally getting a chance to play against the subs or the freshman team during the workouts' final minutes. Often, Skinner himself had left the court by this point, leaving his assistants to direct the action. One of those assistants was former Commodore Jerry Southwood, a heady, talented player who had been the prototypical Skinner guard and who believed that Skinner and Dillard were never likely to see eye to eye.

"Godfrey's style didn't lend itself to Skinner," he recalled. "He was a little more flashy than Roy probably was comfortable with. They didn't mesh. You had Perry, where just about everything Roy would want you to do was done by Perry. There was never a cross word or a funny look or anything. Godfrey was a little different. He was a good guy, don't misunderstand me. But you saw Nashville, and you saw Detroit. It was a different upbringing, a different style, and Roy didn't know how to deal with it. It was more than he was ready for."

Dillard believed he was fighting a losing battle, but he decided that all he could do was to accept the demotion, at least until the season started. He would play his hardest and see if he could earn a call-up to the varsity. As the December 2 season opener against SMU approached, it wasn't as if the varsity players were doing anything all that special in practice. Though the team had earned a preseason national ranking of Number 13 by both

Sports Illustrated and the AP, Skinner didn't think his squad deserved the accolades, telling anyone who would listen that with his "youngest team ever," this would be a rebuilding year. As practices continued into November, Wallace was the team's most improved player ("Perry has shown at least a 50 percent improvement over last year," Skinner boasted), and Dillard took advantage of a rare opportunity to attract attention in a scrimmage, leading the B-team back from a twenty-point deficit to beat the varsity substitutes. Assistant Coach Bobby Bland, a popular former Vanderbilt player suffering from kidney problems that kept him shuttling in and out of the hospital, took note of Dillard's exemplary play and offered words of encouragement. "He said, 'Great game, Godfrey, just continue to stay with it. Just hang in there and keep working,'" Dillard recalled. Within a matter of weeks, however, Bland would be forced to take leave from the team because of his kidney ailment, and he'd be dead by spring, leaving three young daughters behind.

On November 24, with Thanksgiving and the early-December season opener approaching, Skinner took stock of his roster, compared the performances of his varsity and B-team players, and announced his final varsity lineup: Perry Wallace, Thorpe Weber, Bob Bundy, Rudy Thacker, and pre-season All-SEC selection Tom Hagan in the starting five, with Van Oliver, Dave Richardson, Les Yates, Ralph Mayes, and Rick Cammarata on the bench. On the B-team: Dan Due, Art Welhoelter, Bill LaFevor, Hal Bartch, Gary Fowler, and Godfrey Dillard. None of the B-teamers were happy about their predicament, but Dillard felt there was more to it than the explanation he was given. Nearly forty years after the fact, Skinner maintained that Dillard simply hadn't recovered fully from his injury, that he lacked the speed that was such a critical part of his game. "He came back but he wasn't good enough," Skinner recalled. "He wouldn't have played any, I don't think. He could have maybe worked his way into a substitute role." Dillard believes there was nothing more he could have done to prove himself. "It had been decided de facto since the second day of practice that no matter what I did, no matter how I played, I was not going to be on the team," he recalled. "I think a lot of people knew ahead of time they weren't going to play me." Southwood believes that the demotion to the B-team was a way of Skinner showing Dillard an early exit from Nashville.

"When Godfrey says he was run out of the program," Southwood said, "he's probably right. It was just a passive-aggressive way to handle it. But that was not unlike Roy. Roy did not like confrontation. It was just his personality, and that's not necessarily always bad or good. So, in effect, a no-decision [placing Dillard on the B-team rather than cutting him] makes a decision for you. You don't have to come out and say, 'We don't like Godfrey's style, so he's out.' You just say, 'He's injured, he's not coming back as well as we'd like, so he's not playing.' And if he's not playing, he's probably going to leave."

And that's just what happened. If he wasn't going to be playing basketball,

Dillard believed there was no reason to stay at Vanderbilt, period. "The whole reason I came to Vanderbilt was to do this, to play basketball and be a pioneer," he recalled. "I didn't care about graduating from Vanderbilt; I wasn't that impressed with it anyway. If I'm not going to be able to play basketball, there was no reason for me to stay in that negative environment, so I decided to withdraw from classes."

First, though, Dillard felt he needed to get Wallace's blessing. Without Dillard around the previous season, Wallace had faced his tormenters around the conference alone. Now, not only would Dillard not be joining him on the team, he wouldn't even be on campus to offer support from a distance. "That, to me, was the worst part of it—leaving Perry," Dillard recalled. "I knew he didn't want me to go, but he also knew what they were doing to me." Dillard sat down with Wallace to talk about the reasons he must leave. Wallace agreed that claims about Dillard's loss of speed were dubious; even if he had lost a step, he was still faster than his teammates. "Perry, you know they're doing me up," Dillard told his friend. "I just can't sit around here and be abused like this. You know they're not going to play me the whole year. If anything, I'll be back up in the stands." Wallace told Dillard that he understood, that he respected him for the decision he was making, that things would only get worse if he stayed. Chaos would be inevitable, he believed; the people angered by his outspokenness would feel "forced to destroy him."

"I didn't see it as abandoning me. He left because he needed to leave," Wallace recalled. "He had a very disappointing thing happen to him, and he couldn't really square it. Quite frankly, even though he had had the knee injury, as he worked his way back from it during the preseason, it came to the point where he was outplaying most of the people on the team. What really shot into my mind was that during one scrimmage, at one point I went up for a rebound and Godfrey went up and snatched it away from me. And that *never* happened. I looked around, and it was Godfrey. So, from everything I saw, he was playing really well. He felt it was irrational, that he had been wronged and mistreated, and that it was all political and racial."

After meeting with Wallace, Dillard called together the members of the Afro-American Student Association—essentially all the other black students on campus—and told them of his plans to leave the school. Finally, Dillard called Detroit, and talked to his mother and older brother, Kenneth, about what had happened. "Godfrey," his mother said, "you need to come on home." Soon, Kenneth arrived in Nashville to pick up his little brother, Wallace noting that "in his very essence, [Ken] reflected that fierce determination of a family that had pledged 'no more' to southern racial abuse." At this point, Skinner didn't know that Dillard planned to quit the team and withdraw from school, so Godfrey and his brother paid a visit to the coach's office to break the news.

"We went down there and I said to Skinner, 'You know you are doing me wrong, and I can't play for you again because you are discriminating against me. I don't know why you dislike me,'" Dillard recalled. "And he didn't say anything. He didn't say, 'Why don't you try to stick it out, maybe you can make it again.' He didn't give me any indication that there was any chance, which confirmed for me that nothing was going to happen. So, I went back and formally withdrew from all my classes and got on a plane and flew back with my brother."

Though he felt he had been unjustly treated, Dillard did not make any public statements. This could have been an opportunity to mount a protest like black athletes on other campuses, but Dillard had his reasons not to speak out: he had already spoken his mind on numerous occasions; since he had already decided to leave, he didn't have much to gain in attempting to force Vanderbilt to make changes; and he didn't want to make the situation worse for his friend, Wallace, who would be left behind. Instead, he quietly left Nashville. With the Thanksgiving and Christmas holidays coming, coupled with the fact that he wasn't going to be on the varsity anyway, hardly anyone around town even noticed he was gone. Wallace felt the loss acutely, however, and it was a two-pronged hurt. He had lost a confidant, once again left to tour the South alone. But more significant, he was left to function within a team structure that he believed had just mistreated his fellow trailblazer. Unlike Dillard, however, Wallace did not hold Skinner, a man he admired until the coach's death in 2010, responsible for the episode, believing instead that Skinner, a largely apolitical man, was boxed into a corner by more fervent alumni. "I never thought it was only Coach Skinner, quite frankly," he recalled. Still, the episode shook him to the core.

"The whole thing with Godfrey was huge for me," Wallace said. "We came in and planned to go through it together. The Mississippi State experience had been a bonding experience, in the face of all that hell. I come back the next year and I was by myself, but then I'm coming into my junior year thinking, 'Well, at least Godfrey and I are going to go through this thing together.' Then, not only is he not going to be on the team, but under these disturbing circumstances. These are the kinds of things that challenge your sense of faith. You don't know what to believe. I'm playing on a team that got Godfrey out because of race and politics? I just felt alone. And it was alone after trouble. I didn't need any more trouble. I had already gone through a trouble-filled year. How do you then put yourself together? It was just the start to another awful year. It was not what I'd imagined as I had dreamt of playing college basketball. And I would say, 'What the hell happened? What the hell happened?' And this is all in America."

Wallace's anguish was compounded by the rapidly deteriorating physical condition of his mother, Hattie, who had undergone surgery a year earlier. The colon problems identified when she gave birth to Perry had lingered ever since, and the cancer was now more rapidly withering her body. When Perry's sisters noticed that their mother was looking uncommonly frail, Perry Sr. sought to reassure his daughters by claiming that all the Haynes women aged that way. Still, the Wallace children knew their mother's health was failing. For Perry, who had always been so close to his mom, her illness added another heavy load to the mental burden he carried as he contemplated another long year of basketball and an unforgiving engineering curriculum. And as Wallace looked out upon the world for signs of normalcy or comfort, there was little to be found. His former freshman hoops teammate Pat Toomay would later describe this period as one of tremendous "vibrations," a time when a seemingly endless barrage of alcohol-fueled violence and vandalism cast a strange aura over the entire Vanderbilt campus. Whether precipitated by anxieties related to race or war, the pressures of school, or the transformation into adulthood, the surreal nature of the times was evident even to those living through it. "Culturally, it was crazy," Toomay recalled. "There was tremendous dissonance. Weird things would happen. People behaved strangely." For Commodore fans, things weren't even going to plan in Memorial Gym. This team rated so highly by national prognosticators began to have the type of uneven season that Skinner had worried about. Seven of the ten varsity players were sophomores, and Wallace continued to labor through the same stresses that had plagued his sophomore season. He even suffered another eye injury, though this time accidentally at the hands of teammate Bob Bundy.

Road trips through the Deep South continued to create angst for Wallace. He long remembered a night at the Heart of Auburn Hotel on February 21, 1969, before a game against the Tigers. As the players left the hotel's dining room after dinner, Wallace noticed a group of long-haired white kids arguing with another group of white men in the hallway outside a crowded meeting room. "I couldn't verify it, but from the arguments it sounded very much like the meeting was a White Citizens' Council gathering and the white kids were protesting it," Wallace recalled. "I obviously didn't investigate." But the point was clear: whether it was leaving a movie early in Starkville or declining dinner invitations to avoid potential run-ins with the more dangerous elements of southern society, Wallace recalled, "it wasn't out of the question that my suspicions were true, and it was prudent for me to act accordingly." Another general point, one he says most people had no sense of, was that Wallace wasn't just relying on common sense or gut instinct; he often had help gathering clues as to the nature of his surroundings. Just as he had been tipped off by black domestic workers when he was being recruited by Vanderbilt, the black workers he encountered on the road often quietly provided him with valuable information. "This didn't happen all the time, as many of them were either scared or not particularly interested," Wallace recalled. "But here and there, some would give me advice—always in that classic black, southern way: heads down, looking away, speaking quietly, often in a near mumble and with a certain cadence and with some words missing and with certain gestures. As was always true historically, it was a way of 'talking without talking.'"

A junior season that looked promising at the start—7–2 in non-conference play and 5–1 in the first six SEC games—entered a tailspin, with a string of six consecutive defeats. Bill Livingston, a *Hustler* writer who would go on to a distinguished career as a sportswriter for the *Cleveland Plain Dealer*, echoed the anti-Skinner sentiment starting to percolate around town: Skinner had lost his touch. "The suspicion lingers that Skinner's coaching abilities are somewhat less than top-drawer," he wrote. "One is at a loss to explain all the adulation and hero worship." While history would show that Skinner had not entirely lost his formula for success—his teams would post back-to-back twenty-win seasons in 1973 and 1974, including an SEC championship in 1974—there was no denying that as a new generation of ballplayers arrived on campus, perhaps a little less square, a little less self-disciplined than the crew-cut types of the early 1960s, Skinner's low-key style became more and more of an anachronism.

In mid-February, Vanderbilt students and administrators scheduled a series of activities for Negro History week, a celebration that met a mostly lukewarm reaction on campus. A group of professors and students were invited from historically black Alabama A&M to lead a series of seminars, but turnout was sparse. Far more successful was an appearance at Reverend Asbury's Benton Chapel by Fannie Lou Hamer, the famed Mississippi political activist who led the state's Freedom Democratic Party to the Democratic Convention in 1964. Plans called for Hamer to talk about her religious and political perspectives; in return, the chapel choir and congregation would join in singing "Amazing Grace." Asbury later recalled that some black students were not thrilled when they first learned that he had invited Hamer to campus; in their minds, the "uneducated field hand" was already a relic from a day gone by. Others, however, including Perry Wallace and Bobbie Jean Perdue, who served as an usher in the church that day, were enthralled. Hamer brought a touch of soul to the service, unlike anything Perdue had experienced.

"I will never forget Reverend Asbury, because he introduced us to Fannie Lou Hamer, and I was very moved by her testimony," Perdue recalled. "My mother died when I was a junior in high school, and here I was at Vanderbilt for the first time learning that I was poor, being told that my culture was poor. I lost a lot of confidence in what my parents had taught me. And here this woman comes. And one of the things that happened in that church service was that we sang "Amazing Grace." And we sang in a typical white style. And then Fannie Lou Hamer shared her experience with us, and it was a struggle that I could feel." Hamer spoke of church burnings and bombings in her state, of the time highway patrolmen ordered two black prisoners to beat her senseless, of being fired from her job after helping blacks register to vote. Her remarks finished, she told the congregation that she'd like to sing the song again. Perdue recalled the deep, soulful exclamation that came next. "She reaches down with this southern black voice and said, 'Amaaaazing Graaace,' and for the first time, I understood why our cultures were different, and I was not ashamed to be a part of that difference. That was a pivotal moment in my life. I always credited [Asbury] with providing the context for me to understand my life in a different way."

As the service ended and people milled around or made their way to the exits, Wallace found himself standing alone for several minutes with Hamer, a figure who in her demeanor and appearance reminded Wallace of women he had grown up around. In what he later called "one of the transformative moments in my life," Wallace and Hamer talked to each other about their struggles. "I had the good sense," Wallace recalled, "to listen carefully. I knew the story, and about her, but to hear and see her in person was both mesmerizing and chilling. I found myself saying, 'This woman is not afraid of anything—anything.' Now, I had seen strong people, and others who claimed to be strong. But this little woman—once you paid attention—was such a powerful persona that I actually found myself standing an extra step away out of awe."

Wallace and Perdue found their encounters with Hamer life changing, and with her newfound strength, Perdue also began questioning the fate of her former classmate Godfrey Dillard. She talked to Eileen Carpenter about the fact that the story circulating around campus simply wasn't true: the rumor was that Godfrey had been cut because he was not skilled enough to play at Vanderbilt, but the students who had heard Dillard's side of the story believed a different truth. She asked Carpenter if they should write a letter to the *Hustler* presenting a counterargument. Carpenter wasn't as keen on the idea, believing it was a no-win proposition, but another close friend agreed to do it. It was Patrick Gilpin, the graduate student who had presented the petition to Athletic Director Jess Neely. In a letter to the editor the *Hustler* headlined "The Great White Father," Gilpin wrote that "it seems that Dillard . . . 'didn't fit into the plans' for this year's GREAT SKINNER TEAM—at least not after he stood up like a man . . . me thinks Skinner, Pace, and Neely speak with forked tongues when they talk of their serious concern to recruit black athletes." Decades later, Gilpin said that he didn't think Skinner was a racist, but he felt a point needed to be made.

The letter was purposely provocative, full of equal parts truth, sarcasm, and hyperbole, and in its criticism of Coach Skinner it offended the sensibilities of *Hustler* sportswriter Henry Hecht, the senior from New Haven, Connecticut, who had covered Skinner and the Vanderbilt basketball team seemingly since the day he arrived on campus in the fall of 1965. Hecht loved sportswriting, loved Vanderbilt, and loved being around Commodore basketball—points not all that notable except for the fact that, as one buddy later declared, "I say this with love, but Henry Hecht did not belong at Vanderbilt."

Hecht's background was far different from those of most of his classmates. His mother died just before his twelfth birthday, and he was raised by his father, Izzy, with help from his older sister, Lois. Izzy worked two jobs to support his kids, running a struggling liquor store in a decaying neighborhood during the day and cleaning out railroad cars at night. Young Henry devoured the *New York Post* sports pages, dreaming of growing up to be like Mickey Mantle or Whitey Ford, his Yankee heroes, but by the age of fourteen he realized he had a lot better chance of growing up to be like one of the guys writing the articles. He became the assistant sports editor of his high school paper, and when a guidance counselor suggested he apply to Vanderbilt, he decided that if the school had been good enough for Chicago Bears quarterback Bill Wade, it was worth looking into. Combining student loans, savings scraped together by his father, and the Social Security check that had come each month since his mother died, Hecht was not the typical wealthy Vanderbilt student, and the fact that he was Jewish further separated him from most of his classmates. Still, he was smitten by Vanderbilt, joining the AEPi fraternity and throwing himself into his work for the *Hustler*. Hecht brought a bit of New York flair to his columns, making casual references to Casey Stengel and Yogi Berra as if all his Vandy classmates cared as deeply as he did about the New York baseball scene. He enjoyed hanging around Commodore basketball practices with the *Banner* and *Tennessean* scribes Waxo Green and John Bibb, men who treated him as kindly as they did Skinner and his players. Whereas Green and Bibb rarely wrote a negative word about the teams they covered, Hecht was less protective of his subjects, a fact that didn't necessarily endear him to the Vanderbilt players (who on at least one occasion in Starkville threw Hecht into their motel's swimming pool). Standing about five foot four and weighing 150 pounds, Hecht compensated for his small stature with an occasionally wicked tongue. "He could be a contentious little bastard," lovingly recalled *Hustler* colleague Chuck Offenburger. Fellow *Hustler* writer Kathleen Gallagher recalled that "Henry could dish it out as well as he could take it," often punctuating his pontifications with four-letter expletives.

Henry became friends with many of the black students on campus, including Perry Wallace and Walter Murray. One of his favorite excursions was to hop in the car with them and head out to a local drive-in on the black side of town, where they'd enjoy cheap but delicious fast food. But there was nothing Hecht liked better than Vanderbilt basketball. He was a fixture at practices and games, and accompanied the team on many a road trip. Once he tagged along on a trip to Lexington for a game against Kentucky without a press pass. Coach Skinner admired his pluck ("He liked me right off the bat,"

Hecht recalled), telling Henry that if he showed up at a certain entrance at a certain time, he'd allow him to carry a bag into UK's gymnasium as if he were a member of the Vanderbilt traveling party.

All of this played into his response to Gilpin's letter: his affection for Skinner, his familiarity with Commodore basketball, his willingness to call it as he saw it. A year and a half earlier, he had joined in the criticism of the football staff and the Athletic Department in the wake of the Terry Thomas episode. In a scathing column, Hecht wrote that "some of the people in the athletic department are bigoted in their racial views," fingering a segment of intolerant coaches and administrators who "[do] not belong at Vanderbilt." But in this case, he expressed little sympathy for Dillard, forcefully defending Skinner's decision:

> First and foremost about Skinner is that he's about as color blind a person as you're going to find. He has one object—win basketball games—and he does not consider race, color, nose shape or any such other criteria to decide who plays for him. If you can put the ball in the hole and play the game you get a uniform. . . .
>
> I've been around the Vanderbilt athletic department for four years now, and especially this past year, I've about camped out in Skinner's office covering the basketball team. The more I've gotten to know the man, the more I've realized that he is a fair, generous, friendly person, free of malicious motives of any type. He has class. He may be from Kentucky and belongs more at the Grand Ole Opry than the Met, but he has class.
>
> Now last year Godfrey Dillard was the third guard on the squad in the early part of the pre-season drills. He hurt his knee midway in the drills and needed an operation. . . .
>
> Maybe Mr. Gilpin doesn't realize it, but after a knee operation, the chances of coming back 100% are two—slim and none. A player in any sport will lose some mobility and speed after such an operation.
>
> This was Godfrey's big problem, as he relied on his speed to be effective. He had to, for he was a poor defensive player and a weak outside shot. When he lost that little bit from the operation he was in trouble.
>
> So he came back this year and in pre-season practice did not decide to go all out until he realized that he was in danger of not making the varsity. So the last week and a half of practice he played as hard as he could. But it wasn't enough and he was put on the B-team—not dropped from the team. He just didn't hustle all the time.
>
> Instead of trying harder to get elevated—like Dan Due and Hal Bartch were—Godfrey quit. He quit because he could not face the fact that he had not shown enough, and he was enough of a spoiled kid to react by running away. Godfrey was a friend of mine, but as I think back on the whole situation I realize that he did have an attitude problem besides the fact that

what he showed wasn't good enough. I saw more than three fourths of the pre-season practice sessions and I knew Godfrey was on the borderline, and I knew Skinner, being the man he is, would decide on talent.

No sooner had Hecht's article appeared in the paper than Dillard's phone began to ring off the hook in Detroit, his old buddies at Vanderbilt calling to tell him what Hecht had written. Dillard was both incensed and embarrassed.

"They said, 'Godfrey you won't believe this article he wrote on you. It's a pack of lies,'" Dillard recalled. "Coming from Henry Hecht, it was the worst. This nothing is going to write this after I leave, when I'm not even there to defend myself, and make it the centerpiece of an article? My feeling was that he did it to confirm the Athletic Department's version of my departure. He was a mouthpiece for them. Because everybody was asking, 'Where's Godfrey? Where is he?' Most kids didn't even realize I had left school. The local community didn't know I had left school. All of a sudden, I'm nowhere to be found, and they had to come up with an explanation."

Hecht's points about Dillard's basketball skills, or lack thereof, were the most upsetting to Dillard, who felt he was one of the most talented players on the team.

"I fundamentally saw myself as an athlete at that time, so it was that embarrassment, the total defeat as an athlete, that bothered me more than anything," he recalled. "You're telling me I'm not good enough for this team? Come on. These guys? Give me a break. I know what my talent is. I know what talent looks like. I'm not going to say Maravich or Charlie Scott were bad players—I know what talent is. But you're telling me I can't make this team here? And the record proved out that it was not a great team. There weren't any outstanding players on that team. So in my mind, it was insulting to the lowest level."

Dillard saw only one way to deal with the situation: to confront Hecht directly. Consumed with frustration and anger, he drove all the way from Detroit to Nashville, a trip of more than five hundred miles. Arriving on campus, friends showed him the article. When he held the paper in his hands and read words he felt were untrue, Dillard "blew [his] top. I was determined to slap him around to make him understand that I'm a human being and you just can't write lies and not have any consequences for it."

Dillard called over to the AEPi house and announced that he was in town, telling whoever answered the phone that he was coming over to pay Hecht a visit. It was early on a Sunday morning, around 9:00 a.m., when one of Hecht's fraternity brothers stirred him awake and said that Dillard was at the door. While the rest of his buddies slept, Hecht took Dillard up a short flight of stairs to the frat's TV room. Hecht recalled Dillard making a threatening gesture and telling Hecht not to leave. "You're a journalist, and every journalist has to experience something like this," Dillard recalled saying. "You're never going to be an experienced journalist until one of the athletes that you write an article about kicks your ass. You're never going to be a good journalist until this happens, because then you'll be able to respect and understand athletes, and you'll be more conscious about what you're doing."

The next thing Hecht knew, Dillard was punching him in the face, five or six times, and eventually blood began to run out of the corners of his mouth. In Hecht, Dillard had found a punching bag to absorb the blows he couldn't deliver to the fans who abused him in Starkville, the students who ignored him on campus, the coach who wouldn't allow him to play after he had worked so hard to get back in shape. He had come to Nashville thinking the sky was the limit; when he left he had been branded a quitter. His pride would not allow that to be the end of his story. After dispatching with Hecht, he climbed in his car and drove back to Detroit. A departure set in motion on the same day a statement was made with black fists in Mexico City concluded with a flurry of them in Nashville. The emotions from that ugly encounter still run deep.

"There's no question that I took my frustrations out on Henry, that he bore the brunt of it," Dillard recalled. "It was the fact that he wrote the article after I left the school. I didn't dog the school when I left. I didn't give an interview when I left. I voluntarily withdrew. I had relinquished my scholarship. I said, 'You don't have to pay for my education no more. You don't owe nothing to me. I'm out of here.' So now, after I'm gone, you're going to write negative about me when you've written articles before that don't give any suggestion of that? For me, it was like, 'That's it, somebody's going to have to pay,' and it turned out to be Henry."

Hecht maintains that he simply wrote what he believed to be true: that Dillard was not as good a player as he made himself out to be before the injury, and was even less of a player after it. Though friends noticed his bruised face in the days after the incident, he never wrote about the assault in the *Hustler*, never pressed charges against Dillard. "I did not write anything about it, because that would have meant getting him arrested," Hecht says. "I just thought that would be horrible for the whole state of the university, the black athlete, and the black student. Which Godfrey Dillard probably doesn't understand to this day. He owes me an apology on so many different levels." While Dillard maintains that when word spread among the basketball team that he had "beaten Henry's ass," the players and coaches laughed, Hecht says that the opposite is true. "They were appalled," he says. In retrospect, it's entirely possible that both men are correct in their recollections: people told them what they wanted to hear.

For Wallace, who considers both Dillard and Hecht friends (and who believed that "Henry and Godfrey were close friends" before the incident, though neither characterizes their previous relationship that way today), the episode was the latest nightmare stacked upon nightmare. Though Wallace could not condone Dillard's act of violence and told Hecht he was troubled by what Dillard had done, he disagreed with Hecht's opinion of Dillard's talent and mindset, and understood the frustration and rage behind Dillard's reaction. He believes that both Dillard and Hecht, one from Michigan, the other from Connecticut, fell victim to a certain naïveté, a lack of awareness about how things operated in the South. Dillard, Wallace believes, never fully appreciated how his persona would be perceived by southern whites, how words and actions not carefully chosen could derail his mission as a pioneer. Hecht, he believes, was blind to some of the racial biases that turned popular opinion—especially the perceptions of the professional sportswriters—against Dillard.

Within a matter of weeks, Hecht would play a role in another event that turned horribly wrong, this time with Wallace as the target.

Nevermore

RAVEN! The air is clear of doubts.
Regroup and prepare for the long flight.

—Gustav

Tucked away on the bottom of page 2 of the February 18, 1969, *Hustler*, just above another small advertisment encouraging Vanderbilt coeds to apply to become stewardesses for Pan American World Airways, the nonsensical, fifteen-word Raven ad, quoting some unknown "Gustav," was mysterious. Then again, for the uninitiated, everything about Raven was shrouded in secrecy.

Despite the occasional perplexing advertisement in the *Hustler*, very few people on campus, just a handful of students, faculty, administrators, and alums, even knew that Raven existed. Moreover, the lucky few who were aware of Raven knew that in fact there *was no* Raven. It was a secret society—a fictitious one at that, Vanderbilt's farcical answer to the infamous Ivy League clubs. Created during the mid-1950s as a way to poke fun at and deflate the oversized egos of the school's biggest overachievers, Raven had evolved into an elaborate annual prank, complete with its own set of rituals, lore, and vows of secrecy. In the spring of 1969, however, it turned into a disaster of epic proportions, a classic case of arguably good—but unthinkingly naïve— intentions gone terribly wrong, a wincingly embarrassing and painful illustration of the awkward scenes that played out all too often in the first days of integration on the Vanderbilt campus. And for Perry Wallace, it was the last straw that drove him off the campus for his final months as a Commodore.

Here's how Raven worked.

Each year, the existing members of Raven identified thirteen unsuspecting upperclassmen to invite—or more accurately, lure—into their fictitious club. The group was open to males only, and just a certain type of Vanderbilt man at that: the fraternity presidents, *Hustler* editors, student government leaders, Honor Council representatives, and top athletes who acted as if they owned the place and whose oversized self-worth made them most likely to fall for a prank that would look ridiculous to them in retrospect.

Once identified, these big men on campus were approached by a current member of the group, a process known as "fishing." Hecht recalled being grabbed by a group of seniors as he approached the end of his junior year. "They said, 'Come with us, this is about Raven.' They lead you to believe this is basically a parallel administration of the university." Offenburger remembered a similar introduction to the group: "They would explain to you that administrators and coaches and leading students were members of Raven, and that Raven was responsible for every big thing that had ever happened at Vanderbilt. And we were swallowing every bit of this." To prove that they could be trusted to follow directions, on the Thursday of the week that they had first been contacted, the initiates were ordered to wear a white short-sleeve shirt with a black ball point pen tucked into their left breast pocket. A handful of the new recruits were sent on what were called "business trips," off-campus expeditions where they were given a research assignment and asked to prepare a report to deliver at the upcoming Raven initiation banquet. Offenburger was given an assignment that he concluded was shaded with a "tinge of racism," but one that he embraced. He was asked to travel by bus down to Alabama A&M University in Huntsville and talk to school officials about setting up an exchange program between the historically black college and Vanderbilt, one where students and professors from both schools would transfer to the other college to foster better understanding between the races. "I went down there and spent a day and a half and talked to everybody who was anybody, except for the president of the university," Offenburger recalled. "So I came back and rattled off my Raven report at the induction ceremony." Another time, an inductee was told to bus down to Huntsville and talk his way into NASA's Marshall Space Flight Center under the guise that Vanderbilt's engineering school was going to launch its own rocket technology laboratory at a time when NASA was planning its moon expedition.

In the spring of 1969, near the end of Wallace's junior year, talk began to circulate among Raven members about which students should be "fished." One name that came up repeatedly, Raven leader Kevin Grady recalled, was Walter Murray's. Though the organization had never inducted a black member before, there was little doubt that Murray was the ideal recruit, with his many extracurricular activities and gregarious ways. "We were sitting around saying, 'Who is the next crop of suckers to bring in,' and Walter was an obvious choice," said Grady, a high-achieving student from Atlanta who served as president of the Honor Council and later attended Harvard Law School. "He was very involved in student government, very confident—everybody liked Walter. He used to wear a suit and tie everywhere and was so officious.

Walter was clearly within the zone to be fished. So we're sitting around and dadgum if Henry Hecht says, 'I think we ought to go for Perry Wallace, too.' And we said, 'We don't know him that well,' and Henry said, 'I know Perry, he'd be great. This would be wonderful for Perry.' So we said, 'OK, Henry, it's up to you, you're in charge of fishing him and getting him in.'"

And, with that, the process of recruiting Wallace and Murray began. On Murray's first day of class nearly three years earlier, he had been greeted as a "nigger." Wallace had endured taunts in one gymnasium after another throughout the South. Both had spent countless hours with members of the Vanderbilt administration pleading for better treatment of black students. Now, they were told that they were being invited to join an elite organization that had the power to make bold changes on the Vanderbilt campus, led to believe that they could accomplish things through Raven that had been impossible to achieve before. And, as with all the other fresh Raven recruits, they were invited to attend the group's upcoming Sunday evening initiation ceremony at the Holiday Inn on Murfreesboro Road, ordered to wear white tuxedos for the occasion and to arrive with a fifth of scotch or bourbon and a stack of thirteen fresh $1 bills to pay for the evening's dinner.

As they entered the hotel's dining room, Wallace and Murray were greeted by an assortment of familiar faces, including Hecht, Offenburger, and other student notables, as well as alums including the sports editor Fred Russell and administrators Purdy and Boutwell. As the Honorable Raven, Grady called the group to order. "And the whole thing was routinized," Grady recalled. "We would be eating dinner, and someone would say, 'I guess we ought to go ahead and induct the new members of Raven.' And then another member would say, 'Let's give them an idea of what we're doing,' so we'd have bogus reports being made."

Grady told the attendees that he had received some letters from philosophy professor Charles Scott, who had taken a semester's absence to work in Athens, Greece. Scott was in on the joke. "He sent letters reporting on his Raven project, which was the possibility of contacting Aristotle Onassis and having him invest in Vanderbilt to buy [Nashville's] Parthenon [a full-scale replica of the building sits in Centennial Park across the street from the Vanderbilt campus] and convert it into a Hellenic cultural center," Grady recalled. "And Scott is sending these letters, and I have to read them to the members, and it turns out he is concerned that Jackie Kennedy Onassis has become smitten with him, and this is causing some problems in his relationship with Aristotle Onassis. He's asking for instructions from me on how to extricate himself from Mrs. Kennedy's desire to go to bed with him. And I had to read that with a straight face." Next, a member reported that "the NBC project had come to fruition," and that later in the month, Chancellor Heard would be a guest on *The Tonight Show* with Johnny Carson, and everyone stood and applauded. Next, the still-unsuspecting students who had been sent on 'business trips' were asked to give their reports. As Wallace and Murray watched, John Seward reported on his expedition to Lexington, Kentucky. Grady and his Raven compatriots had convinced Seward that Raven was considering tearing down a Catholic girls' school and constructing a horseracing track on the grounds, complete with pari-mutuel betting. Seward's job had been to travel to the Keeneland thoroughbred track in Lexington, Kentucky, to learn the business and then meet with members of the Tennessee General Assembly to explore the prospects of getting a bill passed to allow betting in Tennessee. "And he did it," Grady recalled with amazement. "He went up to Keeneland, talked to members of the legislature, he had zoning plans that he'd gotten, and he gave a report about how this would cost $10 to $12 million bucks, but money was no object to Raven."

Following the business trip recaps, the other recruits were asked to stand and speak about what they hoped to accomplish through their participation with Raven. "We go around the room," Grady recalled, "and when it comes to Walter Murray, he talks about his involvement at Vanderbilt and that he wants the university to become much more active in recruiting African-American students. And then Perry stands up and says he'd never really felt comfortable at Vanderbilt, but that now he understood there was a lot he could do that he couldn't do before. He said it was very important to him to increase the number of African American students at Vanderbilt, that he was now at the center of power at Vanderbilt, and that we needed to do more to cooperate with Fisk. He opened his heart and it quickly became clear that Perry was really serious about all this."

After all the students had spoken, it was time for the official acts of induction, carried out in an over-the-top fashion fitting for the occasion. "They would lead you out of the room and put a bandana over your eyes, and have you carry a little candle, and then they'd lead you back into the room," Offenburger recalled. "And then they'd swear you into Raven. Rob Roy Purdy would lead the vows, saying something about upholding Vanderbilt's honor at all costs, and a bunch of crap like that, and all the while somebody is drawing something on your forehead. Meanwhile, the candles are burning down and they start to burn your fingers, and what starts happening is that people drop their candles. And then they quickly finish reading the vows and remove the bandanas, and you can see that we all have fish drawn on our foreheads. Purdy would say, 'Gentlemen, you can see that you all have a fish on your forehead, and the reason is that you have all been hooked.' And then they tell you that Raven is all mumbo-jumbo bullshit, and that you're sworn to eternal secrecy." There was no Raven organization; it was just a drinking party.

And this is when Raven's spring of 1969 initiation ceremony veered off script. This was typically the point when the gullible young men who had been fooled into believing that they were about to join a powerful secret society realized that they had been duped and began to smile at the preposterousness of it all. Maybe a few of the guys would be embarrassed or angry for just a few minutes, but with the punch line delivered and the tension let out of the room, the affair would quickly turn into a night of drinking and laughing and storytelling, everyone now in on the joke, bonding over their common experience, beginning to plot over whom to fish next.

Perry Wallace and Walter Murray reacted differently. They got up and left.

Chancellor Heard had reached the conclusion that in order for Vanderbilt's black students to have the same positive experience on campus as their white counterparts, special efforts would need to be taken to ensure their safe passage. It simply wasn't good enough to drop a handful of black kids into a white, southern environment and hope for the best. And here at the Holiday Inn, a variation on that theme was playing out in dramatic fashion, proving the wisdom of Heard's philosophy. Hecht, Grady, Offenburger, and others had assumed that by treating Wallace and Murray just the same as the other classmates they were fishing, they were doing a good thing—fully oblivious to the circumstances that called for a different approach. It was one thing to mislead a big man on campus who was part of the in-crowd, a white kid who felt comfortable at the university, was fully accepted by his peers and the administration, had a wide variety of social outlets, whose largest obstacle was his own ego. It was quite another to lead on a pair of students who were denied entry into the fraternities, who were greeted by slammed doors in their dormitories, who had experienced uncomfortable moments with the same administrators who now mocked them.

"We did not have the privilege, the security, the protection in America to tolerate such playing around with our dignity," Wallace recalled. Where others could laugh at the fact that their "business trips" had just been elaborate hoaxes, Wallace and Murray were terribly disappointed to realize that they had poured their hearts out merely for the entertainment of the white men surrounding them: Raven offered no promise of making life better for Vanderbilt's black students. They were angry and embarrassed, and they quickly made their way to the exit.

"It was very clear that Perry didn't like it at all," Grady recalled. "In retrospect, we had naïvely misunderstood the incredible pain that he had gone through, and how hard it was to be a black student and athlete at Vanderbilt. At the time, I really had no idea of the incredible degradation that blacks went through in the Deep South. And then to stand up and unburden your soul, only to realize it's all a joke and to be laughed at—he didn't appreciate that one bit. So Perry and Walter didn't hang around and have a good time like the rest of us."

In the days after the ceremony, Wallace said the question he kept asking himself was, "What on earth should I do now?" These "talented and well-educated white guys were going to be powerful, influential white men in just a few years," he recalled. "They would be my colleagues—and my bosses. What made me tremble—literally—was the thought that this was the world I was working so hard to get into." While Wallace dealt with those anxieties, Hecht and a few other Raven compatriots approached Grady and said that they would talk to Wallace and Murray and encourage them to discuss the incident. The decision was made to invite them to Grady's dorm room.

"Perry sits down," Grady recalled, "and I tried to explain that the whole purpose was not to embarrass any one person, and this was all an exercise in teaching people humility. I said we had tried to honor them by bringing them in. Perry said that he didn't appreciate what we had done, that he had been made a fool of, and that he didn't consider it an honor and that we had played a joke on him that wasn't funny."

And before he got up and left, Wallace said one last thing to Grady: "Give me my motherfucking thirteen dollars back."

Looking back on the incident from a distance of more than forty years, the men involved each took away slightly different memories. Hecht is saddened by the role he played in setting up his friend for such a disappointment. "In our naïveté and immaturity, we didn't realize that it was a terrible thing to get his hopes up about changes at Vanderbilt. He thought it was something where he'd be able to help black kids at Vanderbilt," Hecht recalled. "It wasn't a joke to him. It was too important, especially to someone as thoughtful and mature as Perry."

Offenburger feels much the same way: "We intended nothing but admiration for Perry and Walter. We looked on it as a neat deal and a good deal that they were becoming Raven members. In my case, I was so puffed up and all that crap that it was good for me to be [hazed] like that. In Perry Wallace's case, he didn't need anyone to make fun of him. We look back and say, 'Jesus, what were we thinking?' I feel sick about it."

Grady, while acknowledging that he grossly underestimated the pain Vanderbilt's black students had gone through and the impact the ruse would have on Wallace, nevertheless recalls his own Raven experience as one of the most joyful and special memories of his days at Vanderbilt, and regrets that Wallace missed out on new friendships by leaving the party. Decades later, he remains conflicted over the episode.

"Because Perry reacted the way he did, it was a missed opportunity to get more involved in the leadership outside the athletic arena," he said. "Whether he would look at it as a missed opportunity, I don't know. Maybe he doesn't regret it; maybe he's still pissed off. It was well intentioned. Here we were trying to integrate the organization, and we just have a cream pie thrown back in our faces. He said, 'This wasn't funny, we shouldn't be kidding about this'—even though everybody else for the last twenty years had gone through the same thing. But unfortunately for Perry and Walter, it was too sensitive. Other than cheering [Perry] on the court, I didn't know him, and I think that was the problem. We didn't fully appreciate all that he had gone through. If we had limited it to Walter, and then had Walter make a decision the following semester whether to fish Perry or not, that would have been more appropriate. We tried to do too much too quickly. We were trying to say this is the most we can do for you at Vanderbilt, this is the ultimate from one student to another, but it fell on deaf ears."

Wallace looks at the incident as a painful but instructive illustration of the problems of race at that time in history, in both symbol and substance.

Hecht and Offenburger, he believed, could be given the benefit of the doubt. Not only had they apologized, but they also had a consistent record of awareness, sensitivity, and openness on issues of race. Others, he believed, presented a more complicated case. "In their view," he recalled, "it was I who created, or at least worsened, the problem by having gotten upset and left. They noted that they were trying to integrate and yet the blacks remained disgruntled. This all made for a classic conflict between the races in their impressions about the same event: what Walter and I viewed as a grossly humiliating act they viewed as a well-intentioned one that just backfired."

The "Raven incident" occurred in the final days of Wallace's junior year, meaning that he was nearly three-fourths of the way through his pioneering experiment at Vanderbilt. By this point, he had been stunned by the racism in Starkville, bloodied in Oxford. He had been booted from a church, asked to leave campus by a senior athletic official. Men he admired like King and Kennedy had been shot. His best friend had been run off the team, and his mother was dying. Ever since kindergarten, when he sat quietly in his chair at Jewel's Academy while his classmates went berserk all around him, Perry Wallace had tried to do the right thing. He had listened to those foreign language records, walked to the library, practiced his trumpet four hours a day. He had strengthened his legs, overcome his asthma, outrun bullies. He had listened to his teachers, obeyed his coaches, respected his parents, carefully measured his every word and action. And where had it gotten him? Rock bottom. It was at this point, when the burdens of his responsibilities as a pioneer and the weight of the world threatened to overwhelm him, that Perry Wallace once again did just the right thing at just the right time. He began to free himself from the shackles that constrained him, to do what was necessary for himself, to worry less about the expectations and judgment of others. Two years earlier, when he and Dillard decided not to transfer after their freshman season, had been the time, Wallace later recalled, when he became a pioneer. And now, as he hit bottom and began a slow and steady rise back up, he became a man.

26

Bachelor of Ugliness

Six months after Godfrey Dillard walked into Roy Skinner's office and announced his decision to leave Vanderbilt, Perry Wallace approached the coach to say that he, too, wanted to leave the campus.

But there was a twist. In the first days of the summer of 1969, Wallace sat down with Skinner and posed a question: if he focused only on basketball, didn't get involved in extracurricular activities, bring up any racial issues, or complain about anything during the season, would Skinner allow him to move into an off-campus apartment, to remove himself from the daily disappointments that had eroded his happiness? Wallace knew that Skinner rarely granted such requests—protocol called for athletes to live in campus dormitories—but he promised he'd play the best basketball of his career if the coach agreed to his plan.

Skinner believed that Wallace was "mature enough" to thrive outside the structure the campus dorms ostensibly provided and told Wallace that he had his blessing to find a new place to live. But he didn't stop there. He asked Wallace to stay in his office for a while, and together they devised a practice regimen for the summer. During a period when coaches were prohibited from working directly with their players, Wallace would have a roadmap to improvement, a series of solitary drills, mostly ball-handling and repetitive shooting exercises from various spots on the court, dozens and then hundreds and then thousands of shots, three hours every day in a steaming-hot gym with no air conditioning, all while Wallace's mother lay sick in bed. Skinner often took heat from critics for not being particularly innovative, but in developing this meat-and-potatoes program, he provided exactly what his best player needed.

"He had me at five, seven, ten feet out, at the free throw line, so many hundreds of free throws every day, by myself in the gym, just for hours," Wallace recalled. "And that repetition was important. I say good things about

Coach Skinner, and I mean all of it, but if I were to give an example of a real important contribution he made in my life, it would be the 'Roy Skinner ten-thousand-times rule,' and ten thousand times was how many times it seems that I shot that basketball every day." Wallace believed that these solitary workouts benefited him in more than just a basketball sense. They also offered a therapeutic way to deal with the impending loss of his mother, a way of fighting back against whatever forces were taking her away. Working out by himself in the hot gym, Wallace found himself recapturing some of the "sweet peace" of the little boy who learned the game on the North High playground. "It sounds strange, but I obviously was feeling disappointed, let down, betrayed, or something like that by a lot of different sources," he recalled. "And I guess I was asking, 'America, Vanderbilt, you represent that big world and what's the deal here? I come here and see my mother end up like this, how do you explain that?' You tend to approach it like somebody is taking something from you. And so in a sense one of my ways of fighting it was to get my act together and to perform in a way that would do honor to the things that she gave me."

Surrounded by family members rotating in shifts, Hattie lay dying at Vanderbilt Hospital in the early days of August, almost entirely motionless. Jessie forever remembered standing with her young son Chuck beside her mother's bed and watching in disbelief as Chuck reached out his tiny hand toward his grandmother. Out from underneath the sheets came Hattie's own frail hand, young and old touching fingers ever so briefly. Within hours, Hattie was dead. Her funeral was held at her beloved Schrader Lane Church of Christ, with Coach Skinner and team trainer Joe Worden there among the mourners.

Wallace said that while his mother's death was a huge event in his life, it was accompanied by a certain loss of innocence that had the ironic effect of freeing him up. "It was a kind of liberation for me to go for broke for certain things," he recalled. "I wanted to get off campus and stop even playing around with integration. I didn't condemn integration, but basically I had to take myself out of that game on campus to push for change that either wasn't going to occur or was going to occur so slowly that I couldn't put maximum effort behind it. There wasn't the bang for the buck."

One surprising motivation for Wallace's newfound strength was the way some of his old friends and neighbors reacted to his mother's death: they laughed, taunting the "mama's boy" with statements like, "This ought to bring you down," or "Can't go on now, can you?" "This was one of the lowest expressions of human behavior that I had ever experienced," Wallace recalled. "It was about as ugly as could be, and the only possible laudatory aspect of it was that it showed that low human behavior knows no race, gender, age, or social status. I remember well the way they searched my face as they talked to me, hoping to detect any signs of defeat, pain, or suffering." The final blow, he said, came when he heard there was a rumor that he had suffered a nervous breakdown, dropped out of Vanderbilt, and given up on life. Already emotional, Wallace said he became "angry as hell" about the rumors. "But, ironically, it was just what I needed, in that I sort of exploded inside—and then calmed down, as happens after an explosion. What remained was a steely determination, one that, as was usual with me, I never really showed externally, and one that I did not share with a single soul."

Wallace sensed that as his senior year began, he had become a different person, more focused and released from certain burdens, but entering a potentially dangerous period, unsure of all that he had been released *from*. Coming to embrace his role as a pioneer had given him a certain abiding energy, discipline, and purpose. Now he felt less compelled to behave in any prescribed manner, to be the Super Negro skeptical whites couldn't help but accept. Nevertheless, he was aware that he had just one last chance to accomplish many things: to prove himself as a basketball player, to graduate with his engineering degree, to maintain his sanity. As someone with a keen awareness that his history was already being written, the subject of media scrutiny dating back to his days at Pearl, Wallace knew that the conclusion to the "college days" portion of his story was yet to be determined. He had become more cynical about his ability to effect change, but he still felt an obligation to close out this chapter with pride, to pave the way for others to follow, to ensure that his experience amounted to something positive. And though he often felt enveloped by bitter disappointment, there were glimmers of hope that buoyed him.

For one thing, he found happiness working with children. Joel Gordon, the former Kentucky player who had built a career in Nashville and was a fervent supporter of the Commodore basketball program, had taken a liking to Wallace and made a conscious effort to introduce him to supportive alumni and other members of Nashville's Jewish community. Gordon and Wallace first met at Roy Skinner's summer basketball camp after Wallace's sophomore year. Gordon's sons had participated in the camp and so enjoyed interacting with Wallace, who served as a camp counselor along with other players, that they asked their dad whether they could have him over for dinner. Gordon gladly obliged, and it became an annual tradition for Wallace to join the Gordon family for two or three summer cookouts, a relaxing time with stories and jokes, hamburgers and steaks. Later in Wallace's career, he occasionally was joined by Commodore guard Tom Arnholt, an artist at heart, who would wow the Gordon children with lifelike sketches. Gordon helped Wallace land a summer job as a day camp counselor at Nashville's Jewish Community Center, introducing him to other prominent members of the Jewish community such as the doctor Stanley Bernard and the dentist Don Goodman and his wife, Adrienne. "I was trying to do my small part to

Wallace said his interaction with kids—unburdened by racial prejudices—buoyed him during his darkest days at Vanderbilt. "Here's reassurance about humanity," he said. Vanderbilt University Athletic Department.

get him involved," Gordon recalled. "I thought it was very important that he get involved with people who would support him. And the kids all loved him." In the summer before his senior year, in between his long workouts and as he recovered from his mother's death, Wallace also found time to work with special-needs children in the Nashville public schools. The unconditional acceptance of those children, and the kids at the Jewish Community Center, had a profound impact on his outlook on life, mitigating some of the disillusionment he felt toward his fellow man. "It was a wonderful experience," Wallace recalled. "The people [at the JCC] were really friendly and they received me well. They saw how well I got along with the kids, and that we just had this symbiotic relationship. The kids were very important. Here's reassurance about humanity. About human beings. We grown-ups sometimes can let humanity down, but these kids were just fresh and wonderful, so it was just great. I discovered a real affinity for being with and working with young people, so it was just a win-win-win-win-win."

Even as he increasingly looked off campus for support, Wallace found peace in the presence of two campus figures, the English professor Vereen Bell and the chaplain Bev Asbury. Asbury, who had attended Mrs. Wallace's funeral, had been a particularly important source of strength as Wallace dealt with the loss of his mother. Bell also offered words of solace, but perhaps more important, he opened up his home to Wallace and other students, black and white. Bell was well known to Vanderbilt's black students as a supportive voice among the university faculty, and he was also known to throw a helluva party. Students would arrive at his house on Graybar Lane in Green Hills and drink beer, maybe smoke a little dope (though Wallace did neither), and tell stories late into the night, stopping only occasionally when one of Bell's five children would climb out of bed and down the stairs to check out all the commotion. "I could not believe how close these students—white and black—were to their professor," recalled Donna Murray, who attended one of Bell's parties while a student at Fisk University. "I didn't have that at my school, even though it was a black school. It was very interesting, and to me I thought it was pretty wonderful to have that kind of relationship with a professor." Bell knew the loneliness that Wallace was experiencing in the aftermath of his mother's death—"His mom was the only person who really knew what he was going through," Bell recalled—and he took special delight in watching Wallace lose himself among his friends, casting his worries aside in the presence of compatriots such as his longtime pal Walter Murray, the one person, it seemed, who could make Wallace laugh as if he had no cares in the world.

"Perry and Walter were just wonderful the way they would tell stories and just feed off each other like a comedy team," Bell recalled. "And then they would start getting tickled with each other, and each other's stories, and neither of them could talk. It was just wonderful."

Bell long remembered one particular story that Wallace and Murray loved to tell, a sprawling, improvised fable to which they would add new twists and turns and exaggerations with every telling, eventually reaching a payoff that in its gallows humor at once poked fun at their own often fruitless efforts to combat the forces that conspired against them and the hollow boasting of their more militant peers. "There was a story they liked to tell about 'The Man in Black,'" Bell recalled. "It was a long, long-winded story. It used to take what seemed like an hour to get this story told because they would be rolling around on the floor laughing and everybody else would, too. It's about a guy who comes home, he's a rancher and he comes home and his house has been burned down and all of his livestock have been slaughtered and his children have been murdered and his wife has been crucified against the barn wall. And he rides out to her and he takes her down in his arms, and she says with her dying breath, 'It was a man in black.' So he loads up his supplies and gets on his horse and rides off in search of the man in black. And he rides to one town after another, rides through snow and many seasons pass and he becomes gaunt and his horse has died and he gets a new horse, and the story keeps getting embellished. And one day he rides into town and he sees this black horse reined outside a saloon with a black saddle, and he goes inside and at the bar is a man dressed in all black. So he goes up to him and he says,

'Are you the man in black?' And the man turns to him and sneers and says, 'Yes.' And the guy says, 'You better cut that shit out.' And that was the whole story. And they would just think it was hilarious. They would interrupt each other and add other parts and make this story more complicated every time. It was almost sort of a musical thing or a jazz thing that was going on."

As Wallace was in many ways removing himself from the day-to-day Vanderbilt experience even with an academic year and a basketball season left to complete, there was an increasing anxiety among some Vanderbilt administrators, staff, and students over the slow pace of racial progress within the university as a whole, and the Athletic Department in particular. It was as if it was suddenly dawning on people that in a matter of months, Wallace would graduate and there might not be another black athlete in line to join the basketball or football teams. The school's grand experiment—and the pain and progress that had come with it—would not have led to any visible, substantial, longer-term gains.

Pat Gilpin, the graduate student who set the Dillard-Hecht feud in motion with his letter to the *Hustler*, continued to beat the drum for a more purposeful approach to recruiting black athletes and hiring black coaches. In a letter to Chancellor Heard, Gilpin asked the chancellor to follow through on his pledge to "work in good faith behind the scenes in order to bring about more meaningful changes." Claiming that the Athletic Department was more segregated now than it had been a year earlier (because of Dillard's departure), Gilpin called on Heard to take immediate action. "For with the graduation of Mr. Wallace . . . Vanderbilt's athletic program could conceivably be 'lily white' again. If this were the case, Vandy's Athletic Department could not even defend itself with its current tokenism." Striking a balance between truth, polite condescension, and veiled threat, Gilpin concluded his letter by reminding Heard that the hiring of a black coach would be a "splendid opportunity for you to further demonstrate your continuing interest in tackling the problems we discussed with you last year."

Heard had monitored the continuing protests by black athletes and their supporters on other college campuses. Most prominently, in the summer of 1969 black students at the University of Alabama filed a lawsuit against the university, claiming, their attorney said, that the university, "a state school, has not pursued black athletes with the same determination that it has pursued white athletes, and thereby has denied the black equal protection under the law." Coupling news of this sort with his own frustration over the apathy of Vanderbilt Athletic Department officials in recruiting black athletes, coaches, and staff, Heard drafted a confidential, three-page memo to Vice Chancellor Purdy on August 8, 1969, in which he left no room for doubt that the matter of "blacks and the athletic department" was of utmost importance to him. "Of the numerous subjects that I have sought to identify as possible points of friction during the coming year (the list was 29 when I last went over it), I think the whole question of athletics and blacks shows the least promise of amelioration or solution," he wrote to Purdy. "I am thinking here both of substance and of the way the situation may be perceived by sympathetic and unsympathetic observers. I therefore want to give very heavy emphasis to this question in hopes that we can do what we want to do and also in hopes that it will not unnecessarily get out of hand."

Heard went on to tell Purdy that the fact Gilpin was unaware that a black football player recently had been signed to a scholarship meant two things: first, that the graduate student was not well informed about a matter that meant a great deal to him, but second, that "we—Heard, or the Athletic Department, or the Council on Human Relations, or whatever—have not succeeded in making [him] better informed. You and I cannot do everything and I think that a decisive part of this difficulty may lie, quite understandably, but nevertheless clearly, with Jess Neely. Jess does not understand the kind of motivation and interest taken by someone like Pat Gilpin in a matter of this sort. His efforts to communicate with Pat do not seem to be productive. So here is one problem: we need to find a better way of informing interested persons about the Athletic Department's efforts toward black recruitment, etc."

The chancellor then proposed a solution that was classic Heard, a way to achieve his goals—altruistic as they may have been—while simultaneously diverting student energy away from more inflammatory alternatives. He proposed a committee. "Do you think we should, or usefully could, assemble various persons concerned with the athletic program and concerned with blacks in an effort to better inform and educate all sides?" he wrote. "I want to do something affirmative that tackles this problem and that makes people know we are tackling it."

Heard further expressed his exasperation over Neely's reluctance to actively pursue even a single black person for a position within the Athletic Department, relaying some of the details of a phone conversation with Neely in which the athletic director told the chancellor he didn't think a black assistant coach was necessary because, he believed, so few black athletes were academically qualified to attend Vanderbilt, and that a black ticket office or other 'front office' employee would undermine the department's public relations efforts. "I believe his judgment is incorrect on this subject," Heard wrote, "although I understand why he holds it. I did not take issue with him in my all-too-brief telephone conversation although I have no reluctance to go into the whole thing fully with him at such time as you feel would be desirable."

Heard then posed a simple question to Purdy, one that got to the heart of his anxiety—the university needed to make visible public progress, even in a token sense, and quick—but also one that in retrospect comes across as sadly comical, betraying the apparent helplessness of a powerful and educated man, and a racially sensitive one at that.

"Where," he beseeched Purdy, "can we find a qualified and appropriate black person, and soon?"

The irony of Perry Wallace's quest to move off campus to remove himself from the daily pressures and disappointments of integration was the fact that two of his three roommates in his new off-campus apartment, Paul Watermulder and Hal McClain, were white. And the other occupant of the small space, a black student from New Orleans named David Lombard, had been a running buddy of Godfrey Dillard's and was more interested in partying than studying. As Wallace sought to distance himself from the constant frustrations of integrating a campus and an athletic conference, his happiness at the most basic level now depended on the irregular daily rhythms of an integrated, two-bedroom apartment.

There wasn't anything special about the place itself, a two-story brick apartment house near the corner of 17th and Edgehill, not far from the hub of Nashville's recording industry activity, known as Music Row. The apartment these four roommates shared was in the back of the building, on the second floor, and everyone entered from the back staircase, never using the front door. There was a small kitchen by the door with a small table and a couple of chairs, then a living room with a sofa, one bathroom, and two bedrooms, one shared by Watermulder and McClain and the other belonging to Wallace and Lombard, though more often than not Lombard would just fall asleep on the living room couch. The apartment was, as Watermulder later recalled it, "a student dive." And that meant all the accoutrements of such a joint—a fridge stocked with beer and iced tea, a stove used for nothing fancier than hamburgers and hot dogs, a girl often on the couch with Lombard. Watermulder and McClain had lived in the apartment for a year by the time Wallace and Lombard arrived, and one of their previous roommates had been the black student Wes Bradby, an active member of the Afro-American Student Association. Lombard had visited the apartment many times to hang out with Bradby and listen to his voluminous reel-to-reel music collection—recordings he had made from other friends' albums.

In Watermulder and McClain, Lombard and Wallace could not have found two more welcoming white roommates. Watermulder, whom Lombard considered a "hippie," was a Presbyterian minister's son from the North, having grown up in New York, Illinois, and Pennsylvania, going to high school in the same Pennsylvania town, Bryn Mawr, where Wallace's high school girlfriend, Jackie Akins, had gone to college. Watermulder had long hair and a beard and immersed himself in the black community, serving as a teaching assistant at Tennessee State, attending Vanderbilt's Afro-

American Student Association meetings, even dating black coed Brenda Perry for two years. He would long remember driving in a car with her one day and nearly being run off the road by a truck full of "rednecks with rifles in the back window." On another occasion, he stopped at a restaurant one Sunday afternoon with Bradby and waited for what seemed like an eternity to be offered a menu before the friends were finally told that they would not be served. As a freshman, Watermulder had pledged the Sigma Nu fraternity. A week before initiation, he talked to Bradby about his experience with the frat. Bradby told Watermulder that the fraternity would never allow a black student to join; Watermulder argued the point. "So I ended up challenging Sigma Nu and they said, 'Of course we would, if the right person came along," Watermulder recalled. "So I said, 'I'll nominate someone.' And they wouldn't do it. I wrote a long letter of protest and resignation to the local chapter and the national chapter. They call themselves the 'Legion of Honor,' so I made a bit of a grandstand and said nobody of honor would ever join an organization that excludes people just because they're of a different race, and until you change your policies I won't be a part of this. I took the injustice of racism to heart very deeply." Watermulder's appetite for racial reconciliation was matched only by his appetite for dinner. Lombard had a job at a nearby Friday's restaurant, and often brought home food when he returned from work. Whether it was Friday's leftovers or something simple he had made in the kitchen, Lombard was constantly on guard to protect his meals from Watermulder. "I was always fascinated that Paul would eat anything off anybody's plate," Lombard recalled. "And you knew the question was coming. No matter how thoroughly you were killing it, he would say, 'Are you going to eat all that?'" Lombard considered McClain more of a straight arrow than Watermulder, but one with a surprising sense of humor. "At first you thought he was all serious, but then it was joke after joke after joke," he recalled. "They expanded my vision of what the world was all about. The world was full of characters of all types, and you can't judge a book by its cover. I really enjoyed the atmosphere."

Lombard came to Nashville from St. Augustine High School in New Orleans, the same school that had graduated Steve Martin, the Tulane baseball player who broke the SEC's color barrier. While Lombard was there, St. Augustine had played a "secret" basketball game against New Orleans' top white team, Jesuit, in front of no spectators, to determine which team really was the Crescent City's best, and St. Augustine came out on top. Lombard recalled St. Augustine as a "super college-prep type of place," where the white Josephite priests "were on a mission to show the world that black students and black student-athletes could compete on every level." Students prepared for college entrance exams as early as eighth grade, "and the whole thing was, 'We don't want you going to LSU or Texas, we want you going to Harvard, Yale, Princeton, Duke, Tulane, Vanderbilt.' They were forcing the issue." When Vanderbilt offered Lombard the largest scholarship, he chose to head up to Nashville in the fall of 1968, putting him two classes behind Wallace and Dillard. Though that fall semester was Dillard's last on the Vanderbilt campus, Lombard and Dillard became fast friends. "Godfrey was a party guy, he was a guy having a good time, the guy with all the girls, he was driving a Shelby GT Mustang, which was scarce anywhere, but extremely scarce in Nashville, so he was that guy who was attracting everybody's attention," Lombard recalled. "He was like, 'What are you up to? Why don't we go to Fisk and TSU and hang out? Let's go meet some girls.' I loved the vibe hanging out with Godfrey, and I got to see the other campuses and go over there in style, and you know how much that means to a young kid trying to meet the girls and all that stuff."

It was by watching his friend Dillard become marginalized by the basketball team and then eventually quit the team and drop out of school that Lombard came to develop a greater appreciation for what Wallace faced as a pioneer. "There was a lot of conversation going on among the black students that Godfrey had been the victim of a conspiracy," Lombard recalled. "And at that point, being caught up in what was happening to Godfrey, it kind of made me focus more on what was happening for black folks in general, and in particular what Perry was going through. It's difficult to understand at first because so few people have been in that position. Originally, I'm thinking more about the injustice to Godfrey, but then it was like, 'Damn, Perry has to really be going through it.' He's on the front line, and he's on the front line alone. He has his teammates, but ultimately when things get really bad, they're white and he's black. They can opt out of being a supporter if it gets too hot in the kitchen. And the other part is that they might not truly understand. It's easy to say let things roll off your back if it's not you."

As much as Lombard understood the nuances of Wallace's predicament and offered some measure of support, he also created his share of headaches for his roommate. Released from the strict oversight that had funneled his energies into academics in high school, Lombard luxuriated in the freedom he enjoyed away from home and began to suffer terribly with his grades. "My focus was, 'Where is the party?' I probably set some kind of record for absences," he recalled. By the time he moved in with Wallace, Lombard had in fact flunked out of school. He was working his way back to Vanderbilt by taking classes at Peabody College across the street; because he was no longer a Vandy student, he needed a place to live and found refuge with his friends in the second-story apartment. Wallace became something between a wise older brother and a father figure to Lombard, which, as Lombard recalls it, was just what he needed at that moment. If Wallace was worried that, by loosening himself from the straitjacket that was his "pioneer suit" he had entered a danger zone with no focus, Lombard offered him a new purpose—helping to straighten out the life of a talented but confused young man.

"David was a good kid," Wallace recalled. "He was kind of like a little brother in that you just love him no matter what he does. He had trouble getting his act together, and the racial climate didn't help, but he didn't have good habits. He would oversleep. He had a bunch of alarm clocks, but none of them would work. They'd all be going off and he'd still be sleeping."

Without much money himself, Wallace was continually dismayed that Lombard wasn't contributing his fair share to the rent payments. The deal was that Watermulder and McClain paid half the rent and Wallace and Lombard paid the other half, but more often than not Wallace ended up covering for Lombard. To make matters worse, while he wasn't kicking in on the rent, Lombard came home one day with a new stereo. "That became a point of contention," Lombard recalled. "Perry was like, 'You ain't got no money but you've got new stereo equipment?' He was always diplomatic when he spoke about things that were an issue. I thought he was a really nice guy who let me get away with murder. Looking back, I would have whooped my ass."

Gradually, Wallace began to have a tremendous impact on Lombard, both in the way he handled Lombard's indiscretions and the way he conducted his own life. Just as on the basketball court, Wallace was a leader by example.

"What I really appreciate about Perry is that he had my back when he really didn't need to, when other people would have said, 'No man, I ain't doing that,'" Lombard recalled. "And this was all while he was dealing with all the other stuff he was dealing with. It was no walk in the park doing his homework and playing basketball when so much was expected of him. Just by being the person he was, it gave me a better vision about what it takes to make it. I really didn't understand work ethic at that age. I had enough going intellectually to get by halfway by bullshitting my way through everything. But Perry was one of those people that I saw actually studying. He was doing the work, and you'd say, 'As smart as he is, he shouldn't work that hard. And he's a star basketball player, why is he working so hard?' Just having that presence around you, almost through osmosis, through guilt or whatever, it rubs off on you. You're trying to figure out which party to go to and Perry is sitting there studying."

Thanks in large part to the lessons he learned from Wallace, Lombard made the most of this second opportunity. He studied harder, earning grades good enough to reenroll at Vanderbilt for the second semester. He dated (and then later married) Vanderbilt's first black homecoming queen and immersed himself in the music scene on campus, helping bring Bob Marley to Vanderbilt to perform. Later he developed a sterling reputation in Nashville as both a disc jockey (at WVOL, the station that launched Oprah Winfrey's career) and concert promoter. His success promoting shows in Nashville led to an introduction to legendary producer and promoter Dick Griffey and then to bigger and bigger assignments—the Jacksons, Stevie Wonder—and soon Lombard was off to Hollywood to join Griffey, a Nashvillian who had found success in Los Angeles. Out west, he moved in the same circles as Marvin Gaye and Michael Jackson and went on to work with Tony Toni Toné and Johnny Gill, helped create En Vogue, eventually comanaged Britney Spears, produced movies, and created a poetry show for BET. Bringing that stereo equipment back to the apartment at 17th and Edgehill, losing himself in music while the world spun around him, may not have been such a bad idea, after all.

As colleges across the country opened their preseason basketball practices in October 1969, sportswriters identified the nation's top players. Despite the hours of work he had put in over the summer improving his game, Wallace, who had been one of the most highly touted sophomores in the country when he joined the Vanderbilt varsity, was no longer on the watch lists. He did have connections to most of the top players in the game. There was Rick Mount, the Purdue star he had scrimmaged against as a Pearl High senior; fellow pioneers Charlie Scott of North Carolina and Mike Maloy at Davidson; and Dan Issel of Kentucky, the player he had dunked on as a freshman. Bob Lanier at St. Bonaventure and Calvin Murphy at Niagara also drew praise, but there was one player who stood out from the crowd, one player who the scribes said was revolutionizing the sport. In many ways, it was Pete Maravich, the white star at LSU, and not the league's first black player, who ushered in a new brand of basketball in the Southeastern Conference, a frenetic style of play that was in a galaxy of its own and yet most resembled the future of the game, a future dominated by black players.

Whereas Wallace had imposed a significant amount of self-restraint on his game and had been banned from employing his most potent move, the slam dunk, Maravich was the polar opposite of restraint. As the son of the Tigers' coach, Press Maravich, one could imagine a situation where the son would play a strictly-by-the-book style of basketball, but the young Maravich discarded the book entirely. With his trademark floppy socks and mop of hair, Maravich was the center of attention wherever he went. When the Tigers came to Nashville later in the year, no fewer than six *Hustler* reporters attempted to corner him for an interview and a hundred kids swarmed around him seeking autographs. Jess Neely presented him with a trophy honoring his exploits, a rare gesture of appreciation for an opposing player. Maravich said his favorite part of the game was passing, and he drew more than a few oohs and aahs for his no-look, behind-the-back assists, but it was his prolific shooting—in terms of the quantity of shots taken, the varying degrees of difficulty of those shots, and the ridiculous number of points he scored—that made him such a sensation. That the Tigers weren't all that good—Maravich never played in the NCAA Tournament—hardly seemed to matter. As the 1969–70 season unfolded, it wasn't Wallace, the pioneer taking his last lap around the league, who drew the most attention. It was Maravich, and by a long shot. "He really was a great player, and he brought a lot to the

SEC, I think, because he helped to make it a more lively, more exciting game that the crowds could get excited about," Wallace recalled. "In some respects he may have had a style that's more associated with the black style, and that was a good thing for the conference, because you had styles of play that were very old fashioned, and this was the 1960s and things were changing. I think Maravich helped [white people] get used to the idea of a more lively game."

While Maravich occupied the spotlight from a league perspective, attracting some of the harsh glare away from Wallace, it was also true that Wallace was no longer even the most conspicuous member of his own team. That distinction now belonged to a sophomore from Memphis named Steve Turner, a highly recruited player who had chosen Vanderbilt over more than one hundred other suitors. When the *New York Times* decided to run a feature on a Commodore player that season, a rare enough occurrence, the paper didn't choose to chronicle the history Wallace had made but instead focused on Turner. Why? Standing seven feet four inches tall, Turner was the tallest player in the history of the SEC and one of the tallest ever to play the college game. Ever sensitive to the experiences of those around him, Wallace felt a certain kinship with both Maravich and Turner, basketball brothers whom he could sense were dealing with their own doubts and demons.

"With Pete, his father pushed him and pushed him and pushed him," Wallace recalled. "We never had any extended talks, but I think that one thing we had in common is that we both knew what it was like to be under pressure and to feel really alone, in the spotlight, under fire. He was alone because he was this star with all this pressure to be a superstar, to score all these points, pressured by his father to be good, and then the whole notion of it being very lonely at the top. It's not like his teammates were going to give him a hug, because they're really just the cast, the supporting cast."

"It was very similar with Steve," said Wallace, who switched to the power forward position upon Turner's arrival. "I had worked in recruiting him, and I had played center before he did, so in many respects I sort of felt like a little big brother to him. He was under the gun with a huge amount of pressure and expectations. We had a certain affinity because we understood what it was like to be in that situation. I did my best to encourage him and try to help where I could."

As the season opened, Wallace was no longer the only black player in the league—Henry Harris had joined the varsity at Auburn—and he wasn't the only African American associated with the Commodore basketball team. Finally, after much prodding from Chancellor Heard, the Athletic Department hired a black staffer. Headlines welcomed former Tennessee State coach Harold Hunter aboard Skinner's staff, not as an assistant coach, but as a part-time recruiter. "Roy told me, 'I want a recruiter for athletes—I don't care if they're black, white, or polka dot,'" Hunter said at the time of his hire, "and he said he wanted another [assistant coach]. But I haven't agreed

Wallace blocks the shot of "Pistol" Pete Maravich, the high-scoring LSU sensation. Wallace said he and Maravich shared the common bond of dealing with the pressures of isolation and high expectations. Photo by Frank Empson, *The Tennessean*.

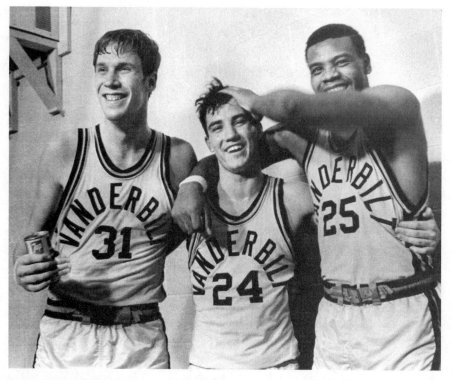

Perry Wallace, Rudy Thacker, and Thorpe Weber celebrate after Vanderbilt's victory over Kentucky during Wallace's senior season of 1970. Wallace was voted team captain and said he got along better with his senior-year teammates than any other group. Vanderbilt University Athletic Department.

to accept anything except to go look at any ballplayers anywhere, especially during the peak season, and to see and talk with as many athletes who meet the entrance requirements as I can." Curiously, Vanderbilt downplayed the significance and potential of Hunter's hiring. He was no ordinary part-time recruiter. A pioneer of note himself, Hunter was the first African American to sign a contract with an NBA team (in 1950 with the Washington Capitols, though he was cut before the season began), and he went on to a successful nine-year run as head coach at TSU, winning 172 games and losing just 67. And while he had a relationship with Perry Wallace dating back to the days when an adolescent Wallace played pickup games at the TSU gym with the likes of Big Daddy Lattin, Hunter's role with Vanderbilt was apparently so small that forty years later, Wallace had no memory of it. Vanderbilt officials failed to capitalize on the buzz Hunter could have given the school in African American communities, content to allow him to devote much of his energy to his business interests, which included ownership of a cosmetics company.

The atmosphere surrounding Vanderbilt's program was changing in other ways as well. Skinner brought on an entirely new set of assistant coaches,

Perry Wallace remains the lone black player in this senior-year team photo. Across the entire SEC, Auburn's Henry Harris was the only other black varsity basketball player. "It almost makes me wonder about the so-called gains of my having been here," Wallace said. Vanderbilt University Special Collections and University Archives.

including former Indiana high school coach Ray Estes, who was known as a "holler guy," and instituted a new level of discipline for the players, including such basics as more frequent bed checks. Sophomore guard Tom Arnholt told a *Hustler* reporter that "it might not seem like as much fun as last year, but it'll be a lot more fun if we win." Despite a mediocre finish (15–11) in 1969, fans and prognosticators were optimistic that the team would rebound; *Southern Basketball* magazine picked the Commodores to win the SEC, citing the home-court advantage at Memorial Gym as a significant factor, an edge that promised to grow more pronounced thanks to the addition of forty-four hundred new seats, bringing capacity up to more than fifteen thousand, making Memorial the biggest building in the SEC and one of the largest on-campus arenas in the country.

While Wallace stuck by his pledge to Skinner and remained quiet, black athletes around the country continued to make waves. In an article he collaborated on with Jack Olsen for *Sports Illustrated*, Lew Alcindor, by then a rookie with the Milwaukee Bucks, talked openly about his decision to boycott the Olympic Games and the reaction to his protest. "For a while I was deluged with hate mail," Alcindor said. "People said I was an uppity nigger.

They said I was a traitor . . . when the sport had done so much for me. They said I should be thrown out of UCLA and barred from professional basketball." In Nashville, Wallace noted Alcindor's comments but maintained his focus on playing the best basketball of his career. He had put on fifteen pounds of muscle over the off-season and it was impossible not to notice that he had markedly improved his shooting ability. "Wallace, famed for his leaping abilities, is virtually unstoppable once he gets the ball inside and his shot from 10–15 feet out is vastly improved since last year," noted *Hustler* scribe David Turner. "Wallace has worked hard on his shot this fall and may see himself rise to new scoring heights." Wallace's extra weight had not diminished his legendary leaping ability; he was still able to reach eleven feet, two inches on the rebounding machine (more than a foot above rim-level). His teammates respected him deeply—and as the team's only senior, they should have—and when they elected him team captain (another bit of history), Skinner assembled his squad and declared his satisfaction with the vote by saying that Wallace "possesses all the qualities of leadership required of being a captain of a Southeastern Conference basketball team." As his teammates cheered, Wallace told a visitor that he was "quite pleased" with the honor. "It is particularly rewarding to have been elected by this group, many of whom I helped recruit when they came to visit the Vanderbilt campus," he said. "I believe we have the experience, depth, and potential on this team to give us a fine season."

Wallace continued to take an active role in recruiting throughout his senior season, particularly in the case of the few black basketball and football players who visited the Vanderbilt campus. It would be a false assumption to believe that Wallace, with all his frustrations, did his best to steer these black high schoolers away from Vanderbilt.

"The notion that there were better places they could go—that is an overrated notion," Wallace recalled. First, he said, black colleges were becoming less competitive athletically due to the "brawn drain," with top players opting to attend the historically white schools—which boasted bigger budgets and more dazzling facilities—that had previously excluded them. But despite the advantages the white schools offered, they also posed problems, the same ones Wallace had witnessed on his recruiting trips. "I saw those black guys there, and they were just walking around and they weren't taking classes that were worth much," Wallace recalled. "When you put that all together, these were the reasons why it wasn't the wrong thing to do to help these guys think positively about the possibility of going to Vanderbilt."

Which isn't to say that Wallace covered up the truth of his Vanderbilt experience. When a black basketball recruit named Tony Jenkins came down from Detroit to pay a visit to Vanderbilt, Wallace explained what had happened with Dillard. "I talked a lot about the northern-southern thing," Wallace recalled, "and how a lot of times the culture was still tied enough to the old southern world that if you didn't understand what I call 'The Song of the South,' then you could be in some danger. Tony was someone who was bright and talented and spectacular, but he had some real reservations about coming down to a southern school. I told him that you've got some challenges on campus, you've got some difficulties here, but it's workable." In the end, Jenkins chose to enroll at Harvard.

Wallace was more successful in recruiting Walter Overton, Doug Nettles, and Taylor Stokes, who would become Vanderbilt's first black football players, and the next black basketball player to follow him, Bill Ligon of nearby Gallatin, Tennessee. And just as he felt a certain responsibility to keep an eye out for people like David Lombard and Steve Turner, Wallace went out of his way to make other vulnerable figures comfortable. Rod Freeman, a white high school star from Indiana who came to Vanderbilt during Wallace's senior year, long remembered the initiative Wallace took to help him enroll in his first-semester engineering classes. Walking into a third-floor classroom in Buttrick Hall, Freeman had no idea how to sign up for his course schedule. Standing across the room registering for his own course load, Wallace picked up on the freshman's confusion. Though the two had never met, Wallace walked across the room, introduced himself to Freeman, and asked if he could help him out. "I said, 'Yes, sir, you sure can,'" Freeman recalled. "He knew all the ins and outs because he was a senior. He said, 'Take this class here, don't take this class.' It was a matter of scheduling and professors, and it was valuable insight. That was my first exposure to Perry Wallace. From a freshman's perspective, he was the epitome of a gentleman. He couldn't have been nicer to me, more friendly to me, more helpful and encouraging."

Wallace, too, remembered the encounter decades later, and he said that this scene, and others like it that played out over the course of his life, carried a more profound meaning than might be expected. "I remember when Rod came into that room, and helping him out, that was the idea, you know?" he recalled. "There was what I had learned from old people and from the 'Toms' and others who didn't have a lot of education, but who were so much wiser than a whole lot of people. The idea that people don't understand is that you're reaffirming your humanity in the midst of situations that would take it away. By extending the humanity, you reaffirm your own. You might just call it decency, but there's sometimes more to it than some might imagine."

As the season rolled along—a loss to Dartmouth one week, a fifty-one-point margin of victory over Portland the next—three trends began to take shape. First, it was apparent that Wallace had broken out of his shell as a player. Most noticeably, he played with far less trepidation away from Memorial Gym: a handful of SEC schools had blacks on their freshman squads, and the crowds became less rabid in their taunting. Memories of harsher experiences the previous three years served as motivation. Wallace would fondly remember walking off the court after playing in his final game in the state of Mississippi, looking up into the crowd, smiling, and thinking, "You didn't get me. And now I'm gone." Home or away, he was blocking shots and rebounding as well as ever, but now his shooting had improved so much that he had become the team's most consistent scorer, showing so much offensive prowess that Skinner often called on him to shoot technical foul shots, the last thing the coach would have done the previous two seasons.

Wallace took special delight in demonstrating that he was more than just a one-dimensional basketball player, later saying that most observers failed to understand the nuances that shaped his playing style. Given the pressure he was under, he said that he initially limited his game to what he knew were his strengths—defense, rebounding, passing, setting screens, tipping in missed shots. Meanwhile, he patiently expanded his offensive skills, gradually improving his game through an emphasis on mastering the fundamentals. As he became a more well-rounded player, Wallace relished silencing black and white critics alike (even Godfrey Dillard had been critical of his game when they played together as freshmen), a phenomenon taking place off the court as well. By that point, he recalled, all doubts about whether he could successfully negotiate the complex courses in math, physics, and chemistry necessary to complete a double major in electrical engineering and engineering mathematics had long subsided.

But even as Wallace excelled on the court, the second trend to emerge was that the team—despite widespread belief that it would reverse the slide of the 1969 squad—wasn't very good. Nobody seemed to be able to put their finger on the cause, but something just wasn't right: despite outscoring and outrebounding their opponents for the entire season, despite totaling more assists and shooting higher field goal and free throw percentages than their foes, despite all those positive numbers, the team would win just twelve games and lose fourteen, the first losing season for Vanderbilt since 1948. "They never could get any chemistry, and I don't know why that was," Southwood recalled. "I could see it happening. For some reason, people couldn't adjust to their roles. They were great kids and they could play great one night, but they never could put it together consistently."

The third and final theme of the year for Wallace, one that became more pronounced as the season went along, was that he began to think more seriously about his legacy, a task that became more difficult, not easier, as a slew of honors began coming his way. Not surprisingly, given his productivity on the court, Wallace would be named to the All-SEC second team upon the completion of the season. He would also receive the league's Sportsmanship Award and would be presented with Vanderbilt's Jim Robins Award, given annually to the senior athlete "in whose life is evident devotion to learning, to honor, to participation in the manly sports and to service to youth and alma mater." The university's faculty would present Wallace with an award of appreciation, recognizing his achievements in the classroom. But it was another award, this one voted on by Vanderbilt's students, the award with the funny name, that created the greatest amount of angst for Wallace. When he edged out his good friend Walter Murray to earn the Bachelor of Ugliness Award on February 25, Wallace understood more clearly than ever that the final chapter of his Vanderbilt story—as written by others—might be whitewashed with a happy ending that would forever hide the true nature of his experience. Though the name of the award seemingly carries a negative connotation, the honor was actually considered the highest attainable to a male Vanderbilt student, bestowed since 1892 to the student who had "made the most significant contributions to the university." A similar award, Lady of the Bracelet, was presented to the leading female student.

At a time when students were questioning many of the university's traditions, the purpose of both of these honors came under fire even as students were voting on them. One *Hustler* columnist derided the process as a "superficial popularity contest," arguing that both awards should be abolished. Other students argued that the school should even do away with its ODK honors society, arguing that in its elitism it divided, rather than brought together, the student body. Still, when the *Hustler* commissioned a survey to gauge opinion on whether to continue with the Bachelor of Ugliness and Lady of the Bracelet awards, 75 percent of students voted in favor of continuing the traditions. But in winning the award, becoming the fourth basketball player in the last six years to earn the title, Wallace had multiple reasons to feel some ambivalence. While there was no doubt that many students voted for Wallace with the best of intentions, in true admiration of all that he had accomplished and endured, he couldn't help but believe that in some respects, given the controversy over the very existence of the award, that he had been the beneficiary of a half-serious protest vote. More important, he saw the sad irony in being declared the winner of a popularity contest when so few people on campus had taken the initiative to get to know him. "I remember when Perry started getting a lot of campus-wide honors, he felt it was a kind of tokenism," his teammate Bill LaFevor recalled. "It was a nice gesture, but there was a feeling that it was to make him feel better than he really needed to feel." The greatest danger of all, Wallace believed, was that so few people recognized all of this. Rather, the narrative taking shape was that the Bachelor of Ugliness recognition represented the final triumphant act of Wallace's career, the ultimate nod of respect from his admiring peers, something for everyone to feel good about as Wallace departed. In a March 4 column in the *Tennessean*, John Bibb wrote glowingly about the selection, linking Wallace to a Vanderbilt lineage of exemplary sportsmen dating back to Grantland Rice, the sportswriting legend who declared that it wasn't winning or losing that ultimately mattered, but how one played the game. While Wallace was flattered by the "sense of fair play" and "sincerity" of some of those who had voted for him, he understood that "on one level, people can vote for you for an honor but never have any deeper relationship." The literal and figurative backslapping that accompanied the award left Wallace feeling uneasy. "I began to feel that I needed to give people, give the world or whatever, some idea about how things really had been because there was so much that people didn't know. People were about to wrap this thing up, this whole experience, into a nice, neat little package, just a quick civil rights success, like a pretty picture, and then put it away so they can forget about it and let it be like a trophy, as opposed to a work in progress where there is a tremendous amount of work that still remains."

On March 7, 1970, the day of Perry Wallace's final game as a Commodore, even the sun paid its respects, hiding behind the moon so that Wallace alone could shine. The last solar eclipse of the twentieth century visible in the southeastern United States dimmed all of Nashville from 11:35 a.m. until 2:35 p.m.; residents were warned not to look directly at the shrouded sun, lest they be blinded for life. Jimmy Davy, the young reporter who had once counseled Wallace when the Pearl High senior first began considering Vanderbilt, quoted Skinner calling on Commodore fans to gaze admiringly upon a different star. At game time, the coach said, fans should look at Wallace and appreciate what they were witnessing for the final time. "It has been a most frustrating season," Skinner said. "I can't say I'm sorry to see the season end, but I'm certainly not happy that this is the last game we'll have Perry with us. He's been an outstanding young man both on and off the floor for four years." In the afternoon *Banner*, Skinner picked up on the same theme. "We would like to leave the fans with a sweet taste, but most of all we would like to win this one for Perry Wallace," he said. "Perry has been a fine one for us. He has made great improvement every year. This year he reached his peak. He has worked hard. His improved scoring this year is a perfect example of what one can gain by hard work."

As Harold Huggins settled into his seat just before the 8:00 p.m. tip-off, he wondered whether Wallace had read the letter he had mailed to him. The son of former Commodore player Harold "Skinny" Huggins (who had captained the 1934 Commodores), the younger Huggins covered high school sports for the *Banner*, but when it came to Vanderbilt basketball, his "Vanderbilt colors outweighed his journalist colors." And as a hard-core fan of the Black and Gold, what Huggins wanted to see more than anything in Wallace's final game was a flash of the brilliance that Wallace, and Commodore fans, had been denied the last three years. "Dear Perry," his letter began, "I've enjoyed your three years of varsity play at Vanderbilt, and I wish the best for you. What I would like for you to do in this last home game, and I know the rules say you can't dunk the ball, but I wish in the second half if Vanderbilt is ahead that you'd slam one in, and if the refs turn blue in the face calling technical fouls, then so be it."

The opponent for the finale was Mississippi State, an appropriate enough foe. Here was the team that had spoiled Clyde Lee Day in 1966, a Maroon victory that remained MSU's only win in Nashville since the founding of the SEC. (Making an uncommon editorial statement in an otherwise objective game-preview story, Davy wished Wallace a more fitting farewell: "Clyde deserved a better ending to his career," he wrote, "and so does Perry!") Here, too, was the team that Tom Hagan had torn to shreds in his final game a year earlier, scoring a school-record forty-four points as his teammates took every opportunity to feed him the ball. And here, too, was the team from Starkville that would forever occupy a haunted and poignant place in the minds of both Wallace and Godfrey Dillard, memories indelibly etched of clutching each other's hands in a cramped, dirty locker room as courtside hecklers howled. As he prepared himself for this final game, Wallace thought back to that first game in Starkville and how his mother had heard the jeers on the radio as she lay sick in the hospital. He thought about all the other scars he had accumulated over the last four years, the opportunities he had been denied; and most of all he felt the pain of his mother's death. He decided that there was just one thing he could do to honor Hattie Wallace's memory, and that was to dedicate this game to her, to play with extraordinary purpose and focus, to show the fans, and himself, what might have been possible had he been able to play free and easy all along. For one game, at least, it would be as if Perry Wallace were back on the court with the Pearl High Tigers, bringing a bit of the old woomp show to Memorial Gymnasium.

The ball was tipped and at first it seemed that Wallace's dream of a dazzling performance in honor of his mother had been transformed into a nightmare of epic proportions. Everything was out of sorts—he was taking quick shots (and missing them), making mistakes that were completely out of character. Skinner recognized that Wallace was trying too hard, and he removed him from the game to regain his composure. "And then," Wallace recalled, "I went to work." Playing like a man possessed, he scooped up every missed shot. By game's end he had collected twenty-seven rebounds, just one short of Clyde Lee's school record. But Wallace didn't just rebound; his twenty-nine points were the most he had ever scored in a varsity game. Watching the game from the sidelines, freshman Rod Freeman noticed that "the whole undertone in that game was to get Perry the ball." John Bibb couldn't find enough adjectives to describe Wallace's stellar play. "The long arms, strong legs and big heart of Vanderbilt Capt. Perry Wallace led the Commodores," he wrote. "Without Wallace . . . there can be little doubt in the minds of the 13,855 in attendance that Vandy's disappointing campaign was destined to finish in a dismally inept defeat. But, the Vanderbilt senior captain who swept in the highest honor on campus recently by being selected as Bachelor of Ugliness, picked up the ragged effort through brilliant individual dedication. . . . It was Wallace's obvious determination to go out a winner that triggered the victory." When the game was over, a 78–72 Commodore squeaker, the crowd serenaded Wallace with a rousing standing ovation, the third such ovation he earned from the Vanderbilt faithful on this night. Joel Gordon recalled the prevailing mood among the team's most well-heeled fans. "People were saying that *in spite* of him being black, he's a good guy," Gordon recalled. "He's smart, he handles himself well, he has not reacted to terrible things that have been done to him. He had the ability to maintain his composure under some trying circumstances, which got him into good graces with a lot of people."

As he stood and cheered while Wallace acknowledged the ovation, Harold Huggins had just one thing on his mind: had Perry actually read his letter? It sure seemed like it. With Vanderbilt leading 74–70 with twenty-one seconds left in the game, Wallace found his opportunity to dunk when a Ralph Mayes jumper skipped off to the left side of the rim. Wallace leaped high for the rebound, caught the ball with one hand, and stuffed it in the basket. "He did it because of me!" Huggins screamed to anyone who would listen. In the postgame locker room, Wallace's teammate Tom Arnholt called the dunk "about as legal as marijuana," but referees Reggie Copeland and Julius Sneed swallowed their whistles as the crowd roared with delight, allowing the bucket to stand. "I had planned to dunk, but I couldn't find the right moment. I took the first one that showed up, but I was really surprised they didn't call it," Wallace recalled. "But one part of me said I think the referees understand enough about this journey that they had decided to let that one pass. They all knew me and what I had done by that point." The dunk was a crowd pleaser, bringing thousands to their feet in a moment of collective surprise and joy, but it carried a far deeper meaning to Wallace. Learning to play ball on the streets of North Nashville, leading an entire team of showstoppers at Pearl, the dunk had been Wallace's "freedom song," a provocative, forceful, and in its own way *violent* statement against the forces that threatened to tether him to a lifetime of emasculated anonymity. Godfrey Dillard had exited Vanderbilt with a show of misguided violence, asserting his will with his fists. Here was Wallace's own departing exclamation point, taunting authority with the final points of his collegiate career, a crowning spike delivered with cathartic power.

As the crowd continued to bathe Wallace and his teammates in postgame cheers, Steve Turner draped an arm over Wallace's shoulder, as if to protect his mentor. Wallace maneuvered his way through a crush of children and fans who had stormed the court, stopping to sign autographs along the way, including one for Huggins, the letter writer. In the minds of those who watched him escape the court and duck through a doorway that led to a hallway and the Commodore locker room, Wallace had completed his final act in grand style. But Wallace had an uneasy feeling in the pit of his stomach. "It was a sense of relief, but it was not an overwhelming joy," Wallace recalled. "It was more somber, because too much had gone on. It had been too involved, too difficult, and too unresolved. I knew too much and it weighed heavily on me." While Wallace understood that it would be a long-term challenge to unearth the feelings he had kept bottled inside for so long, he also recognized that in the short term he had some unfinished business to take care of, the substance of which, he knew, would dramatically alter the perception of those cheering for him.

That business, however, could wait a day. For now, Wallace retreated to the embrace of family and friends in the locker room. His young nephew, Willie Sweet, romped in with a camera: "Big Junior! Keep your uniform on! I want to take a picture!" Exhausted, Wallace took a seat on the floor in front of his locker, signing more autographs for kids who had flooded into the locker room and answering questions from reporters. "I dedicated this game to my mother," he told Davy. "I thought all day about her and how proud she would be if I could play well in my last game. My mom was a great influence on my decision to come to Vanderbilt. She wanted me to stay at home. Her whole life was one of sacrifice for me and the other children." Davy asked Wallace what the high and low points had been in his career. He recounted the ordeal at Ole Miss as the most painful experience but recalled a recent encounter with a young black boy on the Vanderbilt campus as his most pleasant memory. Walking across campus to class, Wallace had been approached by the boy, who told him he was from Mississippi and had seen Wallace play basketball on television. Ever since then, the boy told him, he had dreamed of going to college and playing basketball on TV just like Wallace. "That youngster and his determination to go to college is something that time will never erase from my memories of the last four years," he said. "It means something to inspire someone to climb up and do better things. Suddenly, all the hardships of being the first black athlete in the SEC [are] worthwhile."

Finally, after the kids had collected their autographs and the reporters had gotten their quotes, Wallace showered and dressed. As he walked out the back door of Memorial Gym and into a chilly Nashville night, his Vanderbilt basketball career now over, he had never been more popular in this city. The irony, he knew, was that in less than twenty-four hours, he would sit down for an interview with a young *Tennessean* reporter and would, in effect, "write his ticket out of town." His most important contribution to Vanderbilt would come a day after he'd played his final game, and it would make him persona non grata for decades to come.

27

Ticket Out of Town

Frank Sutherland was prepared to cook dinner if necessary. However long Perry Wallace wanted to talk, he'd listen, even if it meant taking a quick break to whip something up in his kitchen. Sutherland, who lived on the second floor of a house at 3436 Love Circle, just west of the Vanderbilt campus, had invited Wallace to his apartment for their afternoon talk, figuring an off-campus locale was best for this kind of interview. Sutherland knew all about Perry Wallace but not because he covered sports. He wrote about education matters for the *Tennessean* and had been the paper's Vanderbilt correspondent, covering campus issues, not athletics. He knew all about Perry Wallace because he was a big Commodore fan and a regular at Memorial Gym, which made sense when one considered that Sutherland was completing his eighth and final year as a Vanderbilt undergraduate. But he was no slacker; just the opposite. His lengthy path to a degree was because of the fact that he was paying for his education by working full-time at the *Tennessean* at the same time he was taking classes, from two to five courses per semester.

Though Sutherland would go on to a long and successful career at the newspaper, eventually becoming its editor, at this point he was not yet considered a rising superstar. He had, however, impressed John Seigenthaler with his work ethic and initiative, first catching the editor's eye with a story he had written for the *Hustler* on a 1962 Vanderbilt appearance by Martin Luther King. A freshman at the time, he pestered *Hustler* editor Roy Blount Jr. for an opportunity to write for the paper, a rarity then for newcomers. Blount, who went on to fame as an author and humorist, repeatedly rebuffed Sutherland's requests, until finally he relented and let the Nashville-area native cover the King speech because all the other *Hustler* writers would be out of town, gone home for Christmas break.

When, during the final weeks of the basketball season, Wallace decided that he wanted to publicly discuss the true nature of his pioneering experience, it only made sense that he would look to tell his story to the *Tennessean*. While Jimmy Stahlman's afternoon *Banner* had taken reactionary editorial positions on the civil rights movement and other social issues, the morning *Tennessean* had a long progressive tradition, a reputation that was strengthened under the watch of Seigenthaler, who had worked for a time in Robert F. Kennedy's Justice Department. Though no one quite remembers the exact chronology of events, the recollections of the people involved suggest that Wallace first approached Jimmy Davy with the idea that he had some important things to say about his experience once the season was over. Davy felt the story would be better suited to a news reporter who wasn't writing about Vanderbilt sports on a regular basis; penning a controversial story about Wallace could make ongoing coverage of Commodore athletics a dicey proposition for a beat writer like Davy. Though he had never met Wallace, Sutherland emerged as a logical alternative because of his familiarity with the university and with issues of race. When Davy walked into the Vanderbilt locker room after the season finale against Mississippi State, he brought Sutherland with him and introduced him to Wallace. They made arrangements to talk the next afternoon.

Wallace arrived at Sutherland's apartment just after lunch, dressed in a Vandy basketball T-shirt and a light jacket. Wallace had a keen understanding of the power of the media to influence public opinion, which in this case, he knew, was a double-edged sword. He had been the subject of newspaper and magazine coverage since his high school days, and he understood that the narrative of his life didn't just belong to himself anymore but had become a part of the public domain. He felt that for the most part reporters had treated him fairly, and he understood that if he wanted the everlasting record to reflect his feelings at this moment in history, the best way to accomplish that was not by having long talks with administrators, coaches, and recruits but by speaking to a sympathetic member of the press. He also understood, however, that what he planned to talk about would anger a lot of people—so much so, he believed, that he would almost certainly not have the option of living and working in Nashville after graduation. As he walked through Sutherland's door and took a seat on the couch, he was fully in control of what he wanted to say and how he wanted to say it. This was not a case of a reporter steering a naïve subject in a controversial direction to sell papers, of an athlete veering off into subject matter he knew little about, or of being quoted out of context. Wallace began to talk, and Sutherland scribbled in his notebook—no prepared questions, just a conversation. Wallace was as thoughtful and determined as he'd ever been on the basketball court, and as focused as ever, paying no mind to *Tennessean* photographer Robert Johnson, who snapped pictures during the first ten minutes of the interview, nor to Pyewacket, Sutherland's small black kitten, which took a special liking to Wallace, climbing all over his arms, chest, and legs for the duration of the talk.

"My thinking was that I wanted to tell enough of the truth for people to get some sense of what had happened," Wallace recalled four decades after the interview, meaning not that some of what he said was false but that he didn't tell Sutherland about *everything* he had been through. "I didn't want to attack or indict people and I didn't want to bash the university, but I did want to speak in a way that objective people would see that this guy tried to tell the truth because it needed to be told, and he did it for the right reasons. Somewhat more perceptive people would say that this guy obviously took a lot for four years without speaking out or lashing out or caving in. People who understand catharsis, who understand the aftermath of traumatic events— they would understand the need for some expression. I also felt I had enough of a sense of history as I could at that time, and how things change, to know that for some people at that time, but for a lot more people as things moved forward, that they would have an appreciation for what I did and what I was willing to sacrifice and risk doing so."

Stroking Pyewacket's soft black fur, Wallace began to speak.

"It is ironic to be elected Bachelor of Ugliness," he told Sutherland, "because I have been a very lonely person at Vanderbilt. I can't say it any other way. I have been there by myself. Of course, the fact that I, as a black man, was elected Bachelor of Ugliness shows something good about how the school has progressed. Things have gotten a lot better over the years, but it has been a lonesome thing."

Wallace expanded on this counterintuitive notion of isolation in the midst of fame, telling Sutherland that the pattern started during his very first days on campus. "Most people introduced themselves and talked to me when I first came," he said. "My welcome was like that for some messiah. Many of them thought they were sincere. Over the years many people knew my name but they were not interested in knowing me."

Sutherland was taken aback by much of what Wallace said. "To be honest, I was really surprised about all of this at first, because I had just assumed, as had many other folks, that everything was all right," he recalled. "He was popular on campus, he won the election, and so when I heard this, I said, 'Oh, really?' Once I thought about it, I could understand it, but I had not thought about it [before], like a lot of other people."

Wallace picked up on the themes he had focused on in his emotional address to Chancellor Heard and the Human Relations Council two years earlier, telling Sutherland that his recruiters had "tricked" him into believing that the racial situation at Vanderbilt would present no problems. He talked of dormitory hall mates who were incapable of treating him as an equal: "It was depressing to have people like this around me. . . . They respected my basketball ability but they still considered me a person who sweeps floors.

They meant well but they didn't come off too well." Wallace talked about the toll the departure of Dillard took on his psyche—"He was one of the people I could look to for some understanding and friendship"—and of the difficulties of dealing with "racist" teachers. For the first time, he publicly shared the story of his banishment from the University Church of Christ and of the church's later attempt to woo him back.

Wallace told Sutherland that his experience had not been all bad, claiming that "the fans have really been great" and that he had become closer to his senior-year teammates than he had with any other group. "I have gotten along better with the guys on the team this year," he said. "I regret this didn't help our team play better." Not once did he name names, nor did he mention the Raven experience, nor the athletic administrator's suggestion that he quit Vanderbilt if he was so unhappy. He could have said so much more, yet he anticipated the backlash that was sure to come. "I know some people will say I am ungrateful," he told Sutherland, "but that's the way it has been. If I don't say this at some time in my life, it would be too much unbearable pressure."

And in his most poignant and telling remarks, he attempted to convey to Sutherland and those who would read his article that the very fact that he was sitting there, holding the kitten, speaking his mind, preparing to graduate, still functioning, not diminished by bitterness, having completed a four-year tour of duty through a hostile South, all during a time of riots, war, and assassinations, had been no foregone conclusion. "I have to say there were a lot of times in the four years I was trying hard when I got some bad breaks and a lot of disappointments—things went the wrong way," he said. "There is even now a thin line between success and failure. I would hate to have to do it again depending on just luck."

The interview went on for a couple of hours, Sutherland gaining confidence by the minute that he was on to something big. The young reporter was struck by Wallace's composure throughout the interview, feeling that the man he was talking to was "articulate, sensitive, aware, and hurt," more disappointed than angry. "He opened up immediately, and he was candid and direct the entire interview," Sutherland recalled. "It was not a difficult interview in that regard. I had no list of questions. I just started talking to him and he didn't hold anything back."

As long as the interview was, it did end before dinnertime; Sutherland wouldn't have to cook anything for his guest. Closing his notepad, he thanked Wallace for his time and sped down to the *Tennessean*'s office at 1100 Broadway to begin writing his story, believing it was imperative that the article appear the next morning to guarantee that he could not get scooped by the afternoon *Banner*. He sat down at a small desk in the back of the newsroom and banged away at a Royal typewriter in his hunt-and-peck style, no thumbs, eventually handing his copy over to the weekend city editor. While Sutherland typed, Wallace returned to his apartment satisfied that he had accomplished his goals on two fronts. One, he had brought the university's racial difficulties out into the open, beyond in-house venues such as the Human Relations Council that had proven limited, he believed, in their effectiveness. Lifting the lid, exposing the school's challenges to daylight, could only help improve things in the long run, he thought. Two, he had experienced a bit of the catharsis he had hoped for, with "bit" being the operative word, considering all he had not said. "It was amazingly contained as I look back at it," he recalled decades later. "But it was still bringing the message out and being less of the good, quiet, obedient Negro."

The front page of the *Tennessean* on Monday, March 9, 1970, carried news of tragedy the world over: an American soldier killed in Laos, three Vietnamese civilians killed by an "accidental" barrage of fourteen rockets fired from an American helicopter, four Nashvillians killed in weekend traffic accidents, the president of Cyprus barely eluding an assassination attempt. And tucked in the lower left-hand corner, a photo of Perry Wallace with a kitten on his shoulder. One can imagine the progression of thought for the unsuspecting reader:

Why is there a picture of Perry Wallace on the front page?

Then again, that Mississippi State game was amazing, with all those standing ovations.

But what's with this headline? "Lonely 4 Years for VU Star: 'They Meant Well.'"

And what about the continuation of the story on Page 12? "Perry Wallace Spent 4 Lonely Years at Vanderbilt."

And the photo captions: "No place to go. Been there by myself. A few subtle surprises. The school has progressed."

Wait a minute, what is this all about? Why is he saying these things?

Wallace had woken up early to go buy a copy of the paper, and soon Walter Murray showed up at his door with a copy of his own. Murray joked that all around town, people were probably picking up their morning *Tennessean* and running away in shock over what Wallace had said. He was just about right. Down at the newspaper office, the phones began to ring as soon as the papers hit the street, and they rang all day. Sutherland took a call from a woman who fumed that Wallace was an "ungrateful son of a bitch." Seigenthaler fielded more than a few calls from irate Vanderbilt fans phoning in to cancel their subscriptions. As editor, he hated to lose readers, but he couldn't help but take some pride. Pride in what Wallace had said, and in the fact that his paper had this story, relishing the fact that his rivals at the *Banner* never would have touched it. Jimmy Stahlman had attached a moniker to his columns, "From The Shoulder," as if his opinions were rifle shots; in this case, Seigenthaler believed, Wallace had returned fire.

Walking around campus, moving around town, answering more phone calls, Sutherland heard mixed reactions to what he knew was a bombshell of a story. There were those who were angry at what they considered Wallace's lack of appreciation for the opportunities Vanderbilt had afforded him. Given his background covering civil rights, Sutherland was accused by some of manipulating Wallace's words, or goading him into making controversial statements. One disgruntled reader called Sutherland a "troublemaker," another wished Wallace "good riddance." Many of Sutherland's black friends called with words of support, telling him that nobody in their right mind should be surprised by anything Wallace had said. Others were more curious than upset, surprised that Wallace had experienced such loneliness on campus: every time they had seen him, after all, he'd been surrounded by thousands of people in Memorial Gym. More than anything, Sutherland began to realize, reader reaction was some combination of disappointment, sadness, anger, and exasperation. Just two days earlier, these people had felt a measure of pride and satisfaction in their own tangential roles in Wallace's story. They were Vanderbilt fans, Vanderbilt had done a good thing in recruiting Wallace, Wallace had overcome adversity, and his final act as a player had gone perfectly—the slam dunk, the victory, the ovations. But now, with his words, it seemed to these people that Wallace was nullifying the feel-good story. "I had been proud of Vanderbilt for being the first to bring in a black athlete, as had a lot of other people, but what this did in a lot of people's minds was negate some of the pride in that step because he wasn't happy," Sutherland recalled. "If this had been a male version of the Cinderella story, where he went off and was happy the rest of his life, they'd be able to say, 'Look what we did,' but the truth was that he had endured a lot more than people ever knew, so they couldn't be as proud of it, and that's what hurt a lot of the people who called me. They thought, as many folks did in the sixties and seventies, that once you've integrated with one person you've done your job. There were a lot of 'firsts'—the first black man to do this, the first black woman to do this. The paper was full of that. But that didn't mean the problems were solved, though. That's the point, and that was the perceptual problem that people had."

Wallace's friends, teammates, and acquaintances each viewed the article and the fallout from slightly different vantage points. Vereen Bell, the English professor, was surprised by the reaction; to him what Wallace had endured "was so obvious." Rod Freeman, the freshman who felt such a debt of gratitude for Wallace's academic assistance, was perplexed. "I was like, 'Where did this come from?' I never knew that, never saw that, but by the time I got there (in 1969–70), it was probably much easier for Perry," he recalled. David Lombard felt that if anything, Wallace had offered a "watered down" version of the truth. Joel Gordon listened to alums say things like "Vanderbilt gave him an education; why is he so derogatory toward them?" Chancellor Heard was crestfallen (surprising given his ongoing dialogue with Wallace and other black students), initially doubting the credibility of the article and later asking Seigenthaler, "How did I miss this? How could this have happened and I didn't have a sense of it?" Frye Gaillard, the Impact organizer, was disappointed in himself when he read Wallace's quotes. "I didn't know about all the stuff he was saying, but I felt like I should have." Vice Chancellor Purdy was "surprisingly angry" at Wallace, Gaillard recalled, telling Gaillard in an interview that "Perry has become quite bitter. . . . He seems to remember the trauma and not the good side of it. He has made a lot of people unhappy."

And then there was the reaction of Roy Skinner, the country boy from Paducah, the plain-talking, salt-of-the-earth, nonconfrontational coach who couldn't quite deal with Godfrey Dillard. It was this man who read the story and came away with an opinion that was not all that popular on campus or in most corners of the white community at the time, an opinion that wouldn't take hold as the lasting lesson from the whole episode for years to come. It was Roy Skinner who believed that with his words, Perry Wallace had been trying to help Vanderbilt, that he had done the school a favor, that the basketball program and the university would be better for it in the long run. "At first, I thought, 'How can he say all this stuff when they just voted you the most popular student?'" he recalled. "But then the more I thought about it, I got real mad over how he talked about how he had been treated on campus. God, I don't know how he took it for four years. It was a lot worse than I thought it was. I felt for him, and I really admired him for doing it. He was trying to help us understand."

For Chancellor Heard, worried since the previous summer that a controversy related to blacks and athletics was nearly certain to break out at Vanderbilt during the 1969–70 school year, here, as a Nashville spring blossomed, his fear was coming true. Heard's reputation as the rare administrator who maintained a peaceful campus while universities from Manhattan to Madison to Berkeley boiled with unrest was well known—even Haile Selassie was impressed by it—and while that reputation continued to grow, it came with an increasing burden of responsibility. Heard was highly regarded both locally and nationally as an expert on the roots—and future— of student expression and protest, an area of expertise that surely would lose some of its luster if Wallace's statements ignited a high-profile controversy at Vanderbilt. When Columbia University of the Ivy League launched a nationwide search for a new president in the wake of student disruptions that had forced the temporary closing of the university, Heard interviewed for the position, and by the summer of 1969 he was widely considered to be the school's top choice. Decades later, his daughter Cornelia said that he came so close to accepting the offer that they had even discussed where she would take violin lessons in New York. But Heard, who had earned his PhD at Columbia, chose to remain at Vanderbilt, saying later that one of the chief reasons he stayed in Nashville was to continue to work on the racial issues that he believed were so important to the university's—and the nation's—progress.

On the very day that Sutherland's front-page article ran in the *Tennessean*, Heard delivered a speech at the Vanderbilt University Club addressing the question, "Why do the young behave the way they do?" In classic Heard style, he cleverly cautioned the group of alumni not to overreact. "'What is happening to our young people? They disrespect their elders, they disobey their parents. They ignore laws. They riot in the streets inflamed with wild notions. Their morals are decaying. What is to become of them?' Thus," he said, revealing a twist to his audience, "wrote Plato twenty-three hundred years ago." Heard said he saw students taking two divergent paths. There were those who fled society and its problems, taking refuge in "the caves of drugs, the caves of anger," and others who made "strident demands for solution," asserting themselves in ways that were "unfamiliarly vigorous." This assertion of "individual personality against organized institutions," he said, was "often iconoclastic, sometimes courageous, often egocentric, sometimes generous, often puritanical and moralistic. It may be constructive or destructive and it is frequently maddening, but it is there."

In his remarks, scripted before he had any idea of what Wallace would say in that morning's paper, one can see how, on one level, Heard would have understood Wallace's words to be part of a generational, even millennial, tradition. And yet, on another level, one can also see why he might deem them unnecessarily divisive, or "maddening." A passage from a column Heard wrote for the Vanderbilt alumni magazine four years later offers another clue to why he—and perhaps other university administrators such as Purdy—may have been frustrated by Wallace's public comments. A student's perspective, Heard wrote, is narrow by definition, while his perspective as chancellor was far broader. And in that context, he believed, a tipping point leading to continued progress over the long haul had been reached, even if the gains were slowly felt, and even if student demands continually escalated. "Sometimes," he wrote, "persons with a long view become impatient with others, sometimes students, whose span is two or four or six years. A Chancellor soon learns that every step up the ladder simply raises the ground level, and the more rapid the steps the faster the ladder extends into the sky."

In choosing what messages to convey to Sutherland, Wallace had consciously taken the most universal path possible. By focusing on his loneliness and the lack of social opportunities on campus—rather than his treatment around the SEC or other aspects of his basketball career—he called attention to the kinds of problems that, if solved, would improve the lives not just of Vanderbilt's future black athletes, but of black students as a whole. Since his earliest days at Vanderbilt, Wallace understood that while legislation, broad social changes, and administrative initiatives had their place, it was improvements in the day-to-day campus experience, the routine interactions with individuals, and the attitudes of fellow students that would have the most direct and profound impact on him and other black classmates. To that end, he felt it was important that he not just share his feelings with the *Tennessean*, in hopes that a broad, community-wide understanding of his ordeal might lead to changes at Vanderbilt, but also that he speak directly to his fellow students via the *Vanderbilt Hustler*. Nine days after Sutherland's front-page article in the *Tennessean*, the *Hustler* devoted three pages to a feature on Wallace written by Steve Kendall, a sophomore from Massachusetts with long sideburns and longer hair, perpetually dressed in bell bottoms and T-shirt, who "wanted to change the world."

While Sutherland felt that Wallace opened up immediately, Kendall, somewhat awed by Wallace's mature and "distinguished" demeanor in what was their first-ever meeting, later recalled that Wallace spent a good bit of time "feeling him out," choosing his words carefully. In this interview, Wallace hit on many of the same themes he had covered with Sutherland, but he also expanded on his rationale for speaking out at all. Though Sutherland's piece was read by far more people and would be well remembered for decades by Vanderbilt alums and other Nashvillians, in some ways Kendall's story provides an even deeper view into Wallace's emotions. Whether because he was more relaxed speaking to the student paper or because he benefited from the experience of speaking first to Sutherland, Wallace was more direct in his criticisms and spoke in greater detail about his experiences on the basketball court. Once again, the interview took place in the home of the reporter, this time a small, narrow dorm room with a single bed, a dresser, mirror, desk, and chair. Kendall sat on the edge of his bed and Wallace on the wooden chair, striking such a mature pose that Kendall found himself awestruck by the "larger than life" figure before him. Wallace began to speak.

"I've thought pretty carefully about how I was going to present my feelings, not only because I know that there are a lot of people who will say, 'There goes an ungrateful nigger' and because I will face some unjust vindictiveness because of it, but also because I [am] concerned about black athletes in the future. I think it's important that a kid know what the deal is before he comes," Wallace told Kendall. "I don't think it's moral for me to have gone through this, for me to have seen the things I've seen, and for me to know the things I know about the people I've worked with and around at Vanderbilt, and to never say anything about it."

He went on to take one of the only shots at the media of his entire life, lamenting the fact that none of the professional sportswriters covering the team ever made an effort to accurately portray the abuse he received on the road until his final days as a Commodore. He later called the lack of acknowledgment of even the obscene catcalls at Mississippi "timid and weak to the point of grossly mischaracterizing the horror of the actual event. They made the 'mouse' [as his eye injury was described in print] barely more than a bee sting at a barbecue."

"I don't know whether a lot of publicity in a few weeks can make up for no publicity for three and a half years," he told Kendall. "I don't think people would believe the way they were the first few times I went down to the Deep South. The whole time I was on a trip—not just during the games—I was very uncomfortable. There were the trips where I just wanted to get back, to get the game over with. How can you play good basketball when you're trying to look past the game? I just lost hope in people. And even when I had good games I didn't feel good a lot of the time after it was over. I am very disappointed that no one has been willing to mention until now the problems I've had at other schools in the South. Nobody, the newspapers or any other media, has openly attacked these people and places for allowing overt prejudice to be demonstrated. Everybody has kept quiet about it and mentioned it only when they had to and only really very quietly. I think that that should say something for how much confidence I might have felt in the people who supposedly were on my side."

He spoke of the deep disappointments he had endured, the sad realization that he had overcome so many obstacles only to arrive at an empty place.

"I sacrificed a lot of myself that I'll never really be able to regain," he said. "You risk being destroyed. Godfrey Dillard got destroyed. He wasn't able to accept some of the sacrifices a pioneer has to make. But it's very human for a person to feel that he doesn't have to accept certain injustices.

"When I think that there is only one other black basketball player in the conference, I tend to think that the gains have been small. To think that there has not been another black player at Vanderbilt almost makes me wonder about the so-called gains of my having been here."

And finally, much to the disappointment of Kendall, who had hoped for a happier ending to the story, Wallace offered another answer to the same question Henry Hecht posed at the end of Wallace's sophomore season. If he had to do it all over again, would he? When Hecht asked the question, Wallace demurred, saying he wouldn't know the answer for a long, long time. This time, there was no hesitation. The answer was "no." "If I had to do it over again," he told Kendall, "I would go to school somewhere in the East or the West."

While Wallace's interviews with Sutherland and Kendall were his parting shots from a media perspective, he still had two months of school before Vanderbilt's commencement ceremonies on May 31. With his views on Vanderbilt's racial progress and problems firmly on the record, he turned his sights to equally important matters that would have a profound impact on the course of his life. He made sure he properly closed out his coursework, ensuring that he would receive his engineering degree. He also wanted to give professional basketball a shot, should he get the opportunity. Though he understood the limitations to his game, with dunking allowed and black players commonplace, pro ball would be a completely different ballgame.

With a potential basketball future on his mind, Wallace participated in a college All-Star game in Kentucky, where his coach for the exhibition was none other than Adolph Rupp. It was the first time Wallace spent any time around the man who had been—always from a distance—a significant actor in his life, given Rupp's role in the banning of the dunk and his halfhearted efforts to recruit Wallace to Lexington. Wallace would take away only pleasant memories of his encounter with the legendary coach. "It was a very special meeting, out on the floor at the first practice. He was extremely welcoming and gracious. If you think about it, by that point it was clear that Texas Western, my efforts, all were part of a great flood of progress. And in our talks, I discovered something compelling that I knew many people would not understand," Wallace recalled. "For all of his reputation as a classic racist power figure, I hadn't the facts to decide whether or not that was true. What I could see in those short talks and moments was an American man—yes, white, but more important, a product of all of America's good, bad, and ugly. And more curiously, I found myself comparing him with older patriarchal men, both black and white. My father, my high school coach, and many others all seemed eerily similar in certain basic ways. Tough, not hugely emotional. The good ones pushed you, goaded you, but toward honorable goals and good conduct. Tough love personified."

In late March, Wallace was selected in professional drafts by both the Philadelphia 76ers of the NBA and the Kentucky Colonels of the upstart ABA. Four years earlier, he'd agonized over whether to remain in the South for college or whether to fulfill his dreams of finding opportunity in an integrated, northern setting, and he had decided to stay home. This time, he didn't have to think twice: he'd join Dr. Jack Ramsay's 76ers right after graduation.

Wallace also had concerns, however, about another kind of draft—the one that could send him straight from Vanderbilt to Vietnam. With a draft number that matched his uniform number, 25, Wallace decided he would enlist in the National Guard, a commitment that would begin the following winter and might very well derail his shot at a professional basketball career.

Even as he prepared to leave the campus for good, Wallace continued to assist Vanderbilt's athletic recruiting efforts. That real progress came in this area was immensely important to his psyche. "To a large degree a part of my life still hinges on the success of integration at Vanderbilt and elsewhere in the South," he'd later tell journalist Bill Hiles, "because if the program of integrating athletics is not successful, much of what I did will have been for nothing." Skinner began to pursue an increasing number of black high schoolers, though the visible results were paltry. Frye Gaillard broke down Vanderbilt's basketball recruiting efforts in a special report titled *The Black Athlete—1970*, which he coauthored in August of that year on behalf of Nashville's Race Relations Information Center: forty-four black recruits contacted, thirty-seven not interested in Vanderbilt, four not academically qualified for admittance, three offered scholarships, and one accepted. The one commitment was from Bill Ligon, the local star from Gallatin Union High School who had grown up traveling to Detroit each summer, becoming a fan of none other than Godfrey Dillard when Dillard was starring at Visitation High School. After committing to Vanderbilt, Ligon made one last visit to the campus before Vanderbilt's graduation day. Just weeks after Wallace had taken a great risk to help ease the way for future black athletes at Vanderbilt by speaking to Sutherland, Ligon preferred not to engage in any deep discussions with Wallace about his experiences. "I already knew based on the articles what Perry's attitude was all about," Ligon recalled. "I was thinking, 'I've got to do four years here. I don't want to hear that!'"

Ligon may not have wanted to rehash Wallace's examination of the state of race relations on campus, but he did embrace the opportunity to pick up where Wallace had left off. "I committed to Vanderbilt to be a pioneer," he recalled. "If I wanted to go somewhere where there were a bunch of black guys on the team, I could have gone to the University of Kansas or somewhere like that, or Tennessee State. I was [at Vanderbilt] for the education and for that experience. That experience is the American experience for any upwardly mobile African American man. You're not going to see many people who look like you, talk like you, or sympathize with what you're going through as you're going along doing it." During his Vanderbilt visit, however, Ligon didn't even see much of the one guy on campus who did share a few similar characteristics. Wallace was assigned to host Ligon, though to hear Ligon tell it, the senior didn't take a very hands-on approach as a chaperone, which suited Ligon just fine.

"Perry met me, we went over to the Holiday Inn, I checked in, got me a shrimp cocktail, and then Perry disappeared," Ligon recalled. "I stayed from Friday evening until Wednesday all by myself. We went to the Temptations show downtown, I'll never forget it, and then I never could find him again. It didn't bother me. I knew every beer joint in town. My uncle was a bootlegger in Gallatin, so I knew all the crazy spots."

Wallace does not dispute Ligon's recollection, saying he was suffering from a case of "senioritis." "I didn't mean any offense," Wallace recalled. "I'm a senior figuring out what I'm going to do, and I have this whole mix of feelings and all these dynamics to my situation, and so I had my own version of the senior's dilemma. I didn't mean any harm. I certainly wanted to spend good time with Bill. Mainly, what I tried to do with Bill and the others was to tell them about the good things and the possibilities, and also to try to prepare them, to give them a sense that the world is not perfect here, you have got challenges. They do have a ways to go."

The skies were heavy with thunder on May 31, 1970, Vanderbilt's graduation day, forcing the commencement ceremonies inside. While Wallace wasn't enthused about making the walk across stage to receive his diploma, he knew how much this moment meant to his father, how much it would have meant to his mother. He put on his cap and gown and, along with 1,412 fellow graduates, made one final appearance in Memorial Gym. As was Vanderbilt tradition, Chancellor Heard delivered the commencement speech, making the case once again for the value of intellectual freedom on campus, claiming that it was under fire from those opposed to "diversity and discussion."

Wallace had been ambivalent about the graduation ceremony, understanding that a few burdens were lifted the very second he accepted his diploma but knowing, too, that the heaviest of them would require far more time to process and might in fact never disappear. He could, however, begin to look ahead to what he hoped would be a happier existence, a process that had begun twenty-four hours earlier with an event that would carry a sweet glow for decades to come: the marriage of his best friend Walter Murray to his high school sweetheart, Donna. Coming just a day before graduation, at the church where Walter's father had been preacher, the wedding was a "joyous" occasion for Wallace, a chance to be surrounded by the warmth of close friends. A year earlier, Wallace had created a stir—just for being black—by showing up as a guest at a teammate's Nashville wedding ceremony. His presence at the Murray wedding also generated some buzz, but this time it was good natured: at six foot five, Wallace, the best man, towered over the rest of the wedding party, presenting a challenge for the photographer.

Wallace could not have been happier for his good friend, the "cheerful little clarinet player" he first met back in the All-City Band in elementary school, the unsung hero who selflessly supported Wallace's high-profile existence while at the same time speaking up for the students with no profile at all. Murray had married the love of his life, had earned a job in the Vanderbilt admissions department to help recruit black students, and had accepted a "young alumni" post on the school's Board of Trust, the first African American ever to serve on the panel. Wallace had survived an experiment that might have ended tragically if not for his uncommon self-awareness, intelligence, sensitivity, strength, and grace. They both had graduated from an esteemed university. There was much to celebrate. But as Wallace and Murray hurriedly left the gym and changed out of their caps and gowns, Murray taking the wheel of his green Dodge, Wallace riding shotgun for a trip to the airport and a flight to Philadelphia and rookie camp with the 76ers, any joy he felt was bittersweet, tempered by the death of his mother, the experiences of the last four years, and the knowledge that once his plane lifted off, time and distance would forever change the nature of his relationship with his best friend, no matter how much they swore it wouldn't.

As they drove on toward the airport, Murray leaned over and turned on the car radio. On came a song by Peter, Paul and Mary. The two old friends turned toward each other, smiled, and shared one last laugh as they listened to the chorus.

I'm leaving on a jet plane, I don't know when I'll be back again.

28

Time and Space

The danger of being a pioneer is not in the immediate experience,
but reconciling the experience for the rest of your life—
hoping it does some good.

—Perry Wallace, *The Tennessean*, July 31, 1973

As Perry Wallace flew north to Philadelphia, he knew he was leaving more than friends and family behind. The fallout from the Sutherland article, he believed, would make it impossible for him to remain in Nashville and build a life there, or even look forward to returning to visit. He had the resume of a hometown hero—Bachelor of Ugliness, team captain, NBA draft pick, engineering scholar, valedictorian, state champion—but even before his flight landed, before he had set foot on Pennsylvania soil, he felt ostracized from Nashville and separated from his experience at Vanderbilt, for better and worse. He was enormously excited about resuming his childhood dream of escaping to a more enlightened and cosmopolitan world, but he also understood that he had not achieved any closure. The Vanderbilt chapter was over, but the lifelong reconciliation had not even begun. He'd live his life in the unknown chapters to come, a prospect that was at once both scary and exhilarating.

Wallace yearned to prove his basketball doubters wrong, to see if he could thrive in a league where dunking was allowed and he could play without apprehension, where the color of his uniform would be a bigger issue than the color of his skin. He would indeed play well at rookie camp but remained levelheaded enough to listen when 76ers coach Jack Ramsay, a true intellectual who had earned a doctorate at Penn, told him that while he would invite him back for fall camp with the veteran players, his chances of making the team were slim. Wallace's shooting ability and ball handling weren't up to NBA standards for a man his size (six foot five was considered small for a "big man" in the pro ranks), and besides, Ramsay said, his 76ers roster was loaded with too many veterans—including Hal Greer of Marshall, Billy Cunningham of North Carolina, and Bailey Howell of, of all places, Mississippi State—for Wallace to break into the lineup. Still, Ramsay admired Wallace's intellect and appreciated his rebounding and shot-blocking skills, and in conversations that were longer and more frequent than one might have expected between a future Hall of Fame coach and a fifth-round draft pick, he told Wallace that after training camp was over in the fall, if he didn't make the 76er roster he'd line him up with a spot on a minor league team in nearby Wilmington, Delaware.

Wallace returned to Philadelphia for preseason camp in the fall, and the flowering of his game continued as he had hoped. Rather than feeling overwhelmed when scrimmaging, he grew comfortable in his surroundings, at one point making a dramatic statement by swatting away veteran Billy Cunningham's shot. "Obviously, I still had my shortcomings," he recalled, "but they were getting less short by the day. In a way, it was a great pleasure to see the maturity, but it was also a bit frustrating." As expected, despite his progress, Wallace was dismissed from the team before the regular season started.

As he made the transition from 76er to Delaware Bluebomber, Wallace simultaneously took his first steps toward a professional career not just outside basketball but outside the world of engineering, his major at Vanderbilt. He had always found satisfaction working with young people, and now he added a dose of social justice to the equation. At night he played pro ball in Delaware, and during the day he taught math in Philadelphia as a semipermanent substitute teacher at John Bartram High School, a position Ramsay helped him land. "It was quite a baptism into an inner-city, northern school with a lot of tough characters and gangs," Wallace recalled, "but I developed a rapport with the kids, and I probably learned more than they did." Inevitably, the one math teacher who also played minor-league basketball and could throw down a ferocious slam dunk found himself working briefly with Bartram High's basketball team. This was a school with a rich basketball tradition, most notably claiming legendary NBA star Earl "The Pearl" Monroe among its alumni. Brief as his experience with the 76ers had been, Wallace knew NBA talent when he saw it, and he found himself transfixed by the smooth playing style and deft ball-handling skills of a slim, polite tenth grader named Joe Bryant. In the years that followed, Joe would become better known by his nickname, Jellybean, and he would prove Wallace correct by playing seventeen years of professional basketball, including eight in the NBA and nine in Italy. Future generations of basketball fans would come to know him as the father of a son who speaks fluent Italian, a kid who would grow up to become one of the greatest players in the history of the game, a kid named Kobe.

Wallace enjoyed his fleeting interactions with Bryant and the other Bartram basketball players, but he felt a greater sense of purpose working with the kids in the classroom, helping them see beyond their circumstances, a feeling that took on a more profound meaning in comparison to what he witnessed night after night in half-full gymnasiums in the working-class towns of the Eastern League. As a high school recruit, Wallace had been turned off by the lives he saw so many athletes leading at many colleges in the North. In the minor leagues, the reality was different in its particulars but the same in its fatalism. Here Wallace saw players hanging on well into their thirties, playing ball because it was all they knew how to do, masking their pain with drugs and alcohol. "Their paths were frightening," Wallace recalled. "Years of trying to make it, hanging out, a job here and there, some women here and there, some drugs and parties more than here and there, and then bad backs and knees and broken dreams foisted them into retirement." Wallace talked to Ramsay about what he was seeing and feeling, and the coach told Wallace that he knew he had a brighter future ahead of him outside basketball. If he ever wanted to apply to law school, Ramsay said he'd be happy to write a letter of recommendation.

While Wallace could see the dangers in the excessive partying of some of his teammates, he also took advantage of his newfound freedoms in Philadelphia. "Jazz at last, jazz at last, thank God Almighty, I could listen to jazz at last," he later recalled. During his off-campus year at Vanderbilt, he had begun to break free from the social constraints of his upbringing, and that process accelerated now that he was on his own in what was then the nation's fourth-largest city. Wallace discovered that his intellect, his sense of humor, and his diverse interests allowed him to fit in better with his new neighbors than he originally anticipated. One night, in a bar on the west side of Philadelphia, he experienced a moment that he would never forget, the first meaningful bit of closure to the Nashville chapters of his life. Ironically, this episode did not involve race in the sense of any comeuppance for whites—just the opposite. As a kid, and even through his high school and college years, Wallace endured everything from playful mocking to outright hostility from some black classmates and neighbors for his studious, straitlaced nature. His dad wouldn't let him have a "cool walk," his mom made him dress up and carry his Bible to Sunday School, his sisters shared their foreign language records, his teachers encouraged his trumpeting and his schoolwork. For years, an earnest young Perry took his lumps from the "in" crowd as he pursued a different path, clinging to a faith that there would come a day when this disciplined, patient approach paid off. He was determined to live his life in a way that would prepare him—years down the road—to succeed outside the constraints of North Nashville. Little did he know that his delayed gratification would arrive in dramatic style in an East Coast nightclub, when a group of young black men from Nashville, some of the ones who had often made fun of the way he talked and dressed, came up north for a football game. Wallace ran into the guys at a West Philly nightclub known as the Coupe de Ville, a popular establishment on a part of West 52nd Street known as The Strip, an active commercial corridor that attracted a large black middle-class clientele. Standing beside some of his new black Philadelphia friends, Wallace enjoyed more than a little bit of schadenfreude as he listened to how the visiting Nashvillians were perceived by their northern peers.

"These guys come up to Philly with their southern, Nashville ghetto clothes that they thought were cool clothes, and with their speech that they thought was cool down in Nashville, and they were viewed as a bunch of country bumpkins," Wallace recalled. "[The Philadelphia crowd] called them 'Bamas,' for Alabama. And in those days, 'Bama' had an even more pejorative connotation than it does today, where it might be said more jokingly. And the idea was that you were a backward, stupid, southern black. Here were blacks, some educated and some not, at a West Philadelphia nightclub, and they didn't want to be associated with these other guys from Nashville. And it made me feel so good: bad for them, but good for me. It was really a dramatic pronouncement, like I could hear an orchestra playing. It was that revealing. It showed that I had not only grown more sophisticated and smoother, but also that the tools I had acquired put me in position to be 'cool' in much higher-quality places than most of the people who used to laugh at me. That whole pattern was going to continue in more places during my career. I have looked back on that night in West Philly at the Coupe de Ville as really kind of a celebration party of the path I had chosen."

As a senior at Vanderbilt, Wallace had grown uneasy with the accolades that started to come his way, aware that painful, necessary truths needed to be told before he graduated. Now, just a few months later, at the very moment when he was beginning to loosen up and enjoy life in Philadelphia (even thinking about growing a goatee like Bill Russell), he knew once again that a dramatic turn of events was on the horizon. Virtually all his independence was about to vanish, as was his professional basketball career. He had a military obligation to fulfill.

In those final days in Nashville, Wallace had enlisted in the National Guard as an honorable way to serve the country while hoping to avoid service in Vietnam, and now, on a frigid January night, he reported to Fort Leonard Wood, Missouri, for four months of basic training. Wallace would long remember arriving at the camp on that bitterly cold winter night, and he recalled the weeks of drills and training exercises as exhausting, dirty work. "All of a sudden you lose your freedom," Wallace recalled. "It was not what

I would have preferred." By this point, Wallace had begun to think seriously about attending law school, and as he marched through the cold, muddy fields of south central Missouri, he thought about how different his daily routines must be from those of the upscale, East Coast kids also preparing to apply to elite universities. Still, training in Missouri was a far cry from service in Vietnam, a sobering realization that buffeted Wallace from too many feelings of self-pity. At Vanderbilt he had spent lonely nights in his dormitory, but solitude wasn't an option in the military barracks. In another sign that he was becoming increasingly self-confident, shedding the insecurities that were part and parcel of his pioneering stint, he became known as one of the funniest guys in the camp. Even more than his basketball background, it was Wallace's sense of humor, he said, that ingratiated him with his comrades. "I could make people howl," Wallace recalled, "and this made me feel good."

As the first signs of spring signaled the end of basic training, Wallace decided not to return to Philadelphia to take another shot at making the 76ers' roster in the fall or to make another run with the Bluebombers. Though he would play semiserious recreational ball for another fifteen years, his days of competitive basketball were over. For many athletes, the end of their playing days marks the end of their living, the rest of their existence either a long postgame show, old glories retold until their dying day, or a sad slide into obscurity, their one and only true talent rendered worthless by age. For Wallace, however, the game he once loved carried mostly painful connotations, and he also suspected that his biggest contributions to society would come off the basketball court. "My body could probably allow me to run up and down the floor for maybe five years," he told his young nephew Willie Sweet, "but my brain will carry me for a lifetime." Though he had sacrificed and suffered just to play the game, he felt no great emptiness in leaving it. Bill Russell had written that playing basketball was a shallow endeavor in a society with so many problems, and Wallace concurred. He also believed that the best way he could bring about the changes he wanted to see in the world was to work within the system on behalf of the less powerful, and like many others of his generation, he concluded that a law degree was a prerequisite for the kinds of social change he wanted to influence. He knew he'd be a stronger candidate for an elite law school if he had more real-world experience on his résumé than a stint of minor league basketball and a few months of hiking around in the mud, but before starting a serious job search, he briefly returned home to Nashville to visit his family and collect his thoughts. It was on this trip back south, and in reconnecting with his hometown, that he began to realize, he later recalled, that he "really was becoming a citizen of somewhere else." After seeing the potential for a happier life on the East Coast, the fear that he'd alienated himself from potential Nashville employers was largely irrelevant; he didn't want to stay, anyway. Eventually he landed an interview with the National Urban League for a job that would involve traveling the country and working as a liaison between inner-city nonprofits, government agencies, and corporate sponsors to promote community development programs. The interview would take place in Washington, DC, where his job would nominally be based. Because it entailed equal parts exposure to law, government, politics, and business, Wallace thought the position was ideal preparation for law school, and though he had little work experience, he believed he was qualified for this sort of liaison position, given his recent history trying to bring together disparate communities in Nashville.

Everything lined up nicely.

And yet, after driving to DC to make his best case for the job, Wallace walked out of his interview with the Urban League's Ron Brown depressed, convinced he had squandered the opportunity. For years, Wallace had painstakingly planned his every move, thought carefully about his choice of words, rarely let his emotions overwhelm his intellect. But sitting in Brown's office, Wallace sensed that he was speaking to a man who understood exactly what he had been through to arrive at this moment in time, and he let loose with what he later described as a "torrent of emotions." Brown, who would go on to a respected, high-profile career in politics and government (serving as chair of the Democratic National Committee before becoming the country's first African American commerce secretary under President Clinton), had at this point just graduated from St. John's law school and was serving as the Urban League's director of youth and student affairs. Like Wallace, he had been a pioneering athlete (at Middlebury College) and had recent military experience, serving a five-year stint in the army. He and Wallace had much in common, and on one point, Wallace's instinct about the kindred spirit sitting across from him was correct: Brown did understand Wallace's pain and confusion at a deep, unspoken level. But on the matter of whether Wallace had torpedoed his job prospects by becoming too introspective and emotional during the interview, Wallace's intuition was off-base. If there was one job screener in the nation's capital who would be impressed, and not unnerved, by Wallace's soul baring, it was Brown. Though Wallace left the interview convinced he had blown it, Brown knew he had found just the right guy for the job, and he hired him.

Under the guidance of Brown, Wallace traveled to some of the toughest parts of the country, working with Urban League–funded organizations that dealt with gangs and teens in trouble with the law, with neighborhoods looking to better themselves economically. "It was just one year," Wallace recalled, "but it was a very important year." In Philadelphia, Wallace had recognized that working with the students at Bartram High School had been as much a learning experience for him as it had been for the students, and here, too, with the Urban League, the benefits flowed both ways. At a time when Wallace still battled demons from his past, this would have been the period in his life—young, unattached, on his own, living out of hotels, surrounded by trouble—that he could have lost his way, sliding into the bad habits he had warded off for a lifetime. Ever conscious of this possibility, he avoided wallowing in depression or acting out in dangerous ways by losing himself in his work, helping solve the problems of other people even as he struggled to come to terms with his own. On the streets of Watts, Trenton, Chicago, and Boston, Wallace once again reaffirmed his own humanity by extending it to others. "At this time, I was just beginning to recognize some of the different feelings that I had kept inside, and was doing some searching and some working and scrambling and struggling," Wallace recalled. "I had these feelings of hurt and shame and sometimes anger. I needed time and space to move beyond it, so this was a critical period for me."

Wallace found the work fulfilling, but all along he knew it was a short-term gig, so even as he traveled for his assignments, he prepared law school applications to five schools in New York and Washington, DC: George Washington, Georgetown, Catholic, Columbia, and NYU. In the end, he was accepted at all but GW, and he ultimately decided to enroll at the school where two prominent figures in his life—Alexander Heard and Paul Robeson, the pioneer his father admired—had studied. In some ways, Columbia University, on the Upper West Side of Manhattan, was everything that Vanderbilt was not. While Heard maintained campus peace so successfully that at times he was disappointed in Vanderbilt students' apathy, Columbia had been a bubbling stew of activism in the late 1960s, a major reason Heard had been such an intriguing candidate when the school went looking for a new president. For Wallace, who enjoyed the exposure to big city life in DC, Philadelphia, and the cities he visited with the Urban League, the opportunity to live and study in New York City was a huge draw. If he was intimidated by the prospects of enrolling in one of the country's most prestigious law schools, he balanced that fear with the knowledge that he had succeeded academically at every stage of his schooling, and with the hope that here in New York, in the North, at a progressive Ivy League university, he would be free from the constant racial frustrations that had filled his Vanderbilt days with such anguish. But if Vanderbilt and Columbia had their differences, Wallace was soon to discover that not only were there more similarities than he imagined, but also that not all the differences were for the better. Whereas at Vanderbilt he had found pockets of comfort in allies such as Vereen Bell and Reverend Asbury, had experienced a special camaraderie with his fellow black students, and had believed that there was a genuine—if uneven and often unsuccessful—interest from Heard and other administrators in listening to the concerns of black students, at Columbia he initially found the atmosphere surprisingly cold, competitive, and distrusting. It was so unlike what Wallace had expected to find—a thoughtful, collegial, collaborative intellectual environment bent on social change—that as the naïveté of his expectations became more apparent, he was reminded of a childhood encounter with an aggressive raccoon, a real-life varmint who wasn't nearly as fun and cuddly as the Rocky Raccoon cartoon version he enjoyed watching on television.

"I come into this hard-core, single-minded environment that is very cold, very aloof, very serious, very intimidating," Wallace recalled. "It's really a huge amount of work, the people are very smart and intimidating, everybody is kind of Ivy League elite, and they're so focused and bright. Sure, at Vanderbilt you had people who ignored you and didn't have anything to do with you, but you also had people who were warmer. But with so many of these people [at Columbia], the white ones and even the black ones, the whole idea of ascension to the highest professional positions, wealth, social class, and status were so much more important. And the racial element, prejudice, was surprisingly there."

Even his trip up to New York City from Washington, DC, had involved the issue of race. Wallace had rented a U-Haul van to move his belongings, and the truck broke down on the New Jersey Turnpike outside the city. After pulling over to the side of the road, Wallace was relieved when he saw a New Jersey state trooper park behind him: help had arrived. But when the two cops approached Wallace's vehicle and took a look at him, one of them blurted out, "What's in the van? Drugs? Stereos?" Wallace realized what was happening and moved, he said, into what was his standard strategy to avoid trouble. "No," he said, inviting the troopers to look through the van all they wanted. "Why don't you check it out?" As the cops took him up on his offer, Wallace chatted amiably about his background and where he was headed. "Before it was over," Wallace recalled, "they became friendly, calling a tow-truck for me and giving me a ride to a motel in the nearest town so I could spend the night. I think I surprised the hell out of them by almost demanding they search the van. At that point, I was just trying to get to New York City and didn't have time to carry on a civil rights movement. It worked out."

Once he settled in on campus, Wallace discovered an added dimension to the "racial element" at Columbia, one that had never been a part of his experience in Nashville: even some of the most prominent professors at the law school would take one look at their first-year student, a black man standing six foot five, and fear for their own physical safety. In the years that have followed his studies at Columbia, Wallace says he has "worked really hard to be fair to some of these people," to try to understand why they would have felt such irrational fear toward one of their students. New York City was rife with crime in the early 1970s, he said, a fact that wasn't just some abstract statistical truth but was part of one's daily considerations on the Morningside Heights campus. Just a week into his first semester at Columbia, one of the school's most renowned law professors, Wolfgang Friedmann, had been robbed, stabbed, and killed by a group of black Puerto Rican kids in broad daylight, a violent act that accentuated the climate of unrest on an already unpredictable campus. "Only a park separated us from Harlem," Wallace recalled. "Black students who looked more like me—that is, black men who had more of a 'physical' presence—noticed the tension especially. It would show in how some people looked at and reacted to us, and this even included some of the professors."

One professor, Wallace recalled, was so nervous around him that he visibly shook when Wallace visited during office hours. "At first I was offended," Wallace recalled, "but it occurred to me after some thought that fear, as opposed to racism, may have been the main problem." The professor, Wallace knew, had long been a strong advocate of equality and social justice. "This was a short, small guy. He's in New York City, one of his colleagues has been stabbed viciously to death just down the street from the law school. So, I could understand," Wallace said. "I'm not making excuses for the guy, but what I am saying is that there is a lot of power—the power of wisdom, the power of insight, and the power of peace—in understanding how people find their way to some limitations, even outrageous limitations. And, going further, I knew that this guy actually stood for the right kind of things. He had a very practical concern, and a type of fear that had overtaken him because once outside the law school, on Amsterdam or Broadway, if somebody wanted to take him out, they could do it. For all his status and stature, he had to be concerned about that."

This professor wasn't alone in his fears. On one occasion, Wallace walked toward a bank of elevators after an afternoon of studying at the library. As he waited in the lobby, Wallace was met by an eminent scholar whom Wallace considered "a brilliant guy." "God, you're big," the professor said to him, nervously. "I'd hate to be caught in a dark alley one night with you." Wallace corrected the esteemed lecturer. "Professor," he said, "I'm just the one you would want to be with you in that alley, because I'd protect you." If there was one thing these accomplished men did not understand, Wallace concluded, it was race. Still, Wallace believed, it was vital to his success at Columbia that he try to understand the people and the environment in which he was now operating. In Nashville, Wallace had recognized that as a pioneer, he simply couldn't quit. Now, he came to the conclusion that if he truly wanted to realize his full potential in life, he would have to dispassionately assess the benefits of remaining at Columbia and look for silver linings wherever he could find them. Columbia offered a powerful, transcendent opportunity, even if the challenges were equally large. Not only would he not quit, he'd rise above the negative people and circumstances.

"I went ahead and adjusted, because I knew this was a profession worth pursuing, and these were the kinds of people who come with the profession, especially at this level," Wallace recalled. He turned his skeptical eyes inward, asking himself if he was giving the place and the people a fair chance: *Are*

*all of these people cold and aloof? Have you tried enough, or are you just hid-
ing out in your own insecurities? What lesson did you learn from Vanderbilt?*
Answering his own questions, Wallace set out to find people who were approachable, and began to cultivate new relationships, ultimately discovering
students and faculty outside the mold in terms of their civility, people who
went out of their way to help him adjust to his surroundings. As a recipient
of the Charles Evans Hughes Fellowship (awarded annually to a handful of
law students showing promise in the area of social justice and human rights),
Wallace had the opportunity to study under and work with Jack Greenberg
of the NAACP Legal Defense and Education Fund, a legendary attorney who
had argued as co-counsel with Thurgood Marshall in the *Brown v. Board
of Education* case. "This obviously was one of the high points in my life,"
Wallace recalled. "And as a bonus, Professor Greenberg was not the least bit
afraid of me; on the contrary, he worked with me very well and encouraged
me."

Thanks to the influence of Greenberg and other supportive professors
and students at Columbia, Wallace said he was able to face up to an important truth: rigorous intellectual inquiry not only does not promise always to
be warm and fuzzy, it may often not be so. Ditto for the people who practice
those high arts—whether they are for, against, or neutral to social justice.
"Not that I hadn't always had intellectual abilities and inclinations. But this
was the real deal, the real world of thinkers and doers," Wallace recalled. "I
embraced the lesson, even while reaffirming my own original values of respect and humanity toward people." Wallace believed it was imperative that
he demonstrate he could succeed in such a challenging environment, both
to himself and to others who may have had doubts. "From Nashville to New
York, many thought I wouldn't—couldn't—make it," he recalled. "Including
the benign observers, the 'pretty-good-for-a-colored-guy' crowd." And, as he
had done in Nashville, Wallace chose to deal with the frustrations of campus
life not only by finding islands of support and channeling his energy into his
work but by physically removing himself from the sources of discomfort.

Which in this case meant moving to the Bronx.

During his year with the Urban League, Wallace befriended a coworker
named Leonard "Lenny" Burg, "an African-American with a Jewish
name," as Wallace puts it. Though Burg had been with the organization
longer and was Wallace's superior, they hit it off as friends, sharing an interest
in social justice and an appreciation for freewheeling conversations and just
plain laughter. In the summer before his third and final year of law school,
Wallace reconnected with Burg, who by this point had left the Urban League
and was living in Apartment 7A of the red-brick Mitchell-Lama co-op
at 665 East 181st Street in the Bronx, a stone's throw from the Bronx Zoo.
The apartment was sparsely furnished with pillows, blankets, milk crates,

and a four-speaker stereo system, and it actually belonged to Burg's cousin, who was off living in Westchester, so Burg had extra space and he invited Wallace to move in. Wallace accepted the offer, and he took a keen interest in Burg's way of living, which while outside the mainstream, was rooted in the fundamental concepts of physical, mental, and spiritual health.

At this point in his life, Burg was on a mission of healing and self-awareness, recovering from the loss of a serious girlfriend and quitting what had been a fairly heavy marijuana habit. Like many of his contemporaries, Burg had been shaken by the assassinations of Malcolm X, Martin Luther King, and the Kennedys, was troubled by the Vietnam War, and had lost confidence in both the leaders and transformative possibilities of religion and politics. He discovered a community of like-minded people in and around the Tree of Life bookstore in Harlem, gaining exposure to yoga, meditation, fasting, vegetarianism, and other forms of spiritualism. Searching for peace in his life, but also to restore feelings of confidence and identity, he found it in this new milieu, coming to understand that he was more than black, more than just a member of a particular religion or political party, more than mortal: he and all humans, he believed, possessed immortal spirits. Burg retained a natural skepticism even as he began to put these discoveries into practice, and when Wallace moved into his apartment, he never attempted to proselytize. "Lenny was a super-intelligent guy and he had developed his own study of philosophy and meditation and that sort of thing," Wallace recalled. "I was giving him a sense of what was going on in my life, and that I had decided to stick it out at Columbia. I told him how I found the people to be aloof, tight-ass lawyers, but that still I was making my peace with it and adjusting to it." Burg, who was cobbling together various jobs (massage therapist, taxi driver, grant writer) to support his new passions, understood Wallace's determination to avoid sacrificing his own values as he pursued his degree. "He was preparing for a career in law, but he didn't want to get corrupted," Burg recalled. "He wanted to stay true to himself. He was trying to see a way of being a part of the system, but he's trying to figure out a way to be a lawyer and really serve people and not be tainted by the negative aspects of the process. To be *in* that world but not *of* it."

Wallace could see how Burg's pursuits—particularly meditation—were helping him deal with his demons, and he began to join Burg for half-hour meditation sessions in the apartment. (He even became a vegetarian for a time, losing more than sixty pounds in what he deemed "worry weight.") "It almost seemed like this was a balm for Perry," Burg recalled. "The kinds of things I was involved in were a healing balm, and he soaked up things like a sponge. He wasn't expressing frustrations or whining about his life and what he had been through. It was more like he was absorbing; this is Perry's strength. People don't realize he's always seeing and picking up on things, because he may not talk about it much, but he's incorporating it into his toolbox and retaining enough to use to his advantage." Though Burg was occasionally perplexed by what seemed to be his roommate's one annoying habit—using too much of Burg's Dr. Bronner's liquid peppermint soap in the shower—he found that in exchange for whatever therapeutic effect he was having on Wallace, the Columbia law student more than returned the favor. "Perry just totally accepted you for who you are, without judgment, and he had a beautiful sense of humor. At that time in my life, that's what I needed," Burg recalled. Wallace felt much the same way about Burg, appreciating that Burg was a good listener, asked good questions. "Lenny was a person with uncommon wisdom and maturity, tremendous integrity and compassion and goodness," Wallace recalled. "He was a New York version of Walter Murray, and through his intellectual inquiry and friendship, he helped me deconstruct a lot of my experiences going back to Vanderbilt, the insecurities I still struggled with." Burg's spiritual, peaceful nature was just the right tonic for Wallace, who on top of the stresses of law school and the lingering shadows of Vanderbilt was dealing with the impending death of his father, Perry Sr., back in Nashville.

Wallace visited his dad briefly that summer, but it was his sisters who spent the most time with their father. Though he kept driving his 1964 Impala to job sites around the city, by this time the elder Wallace had been diagnosed with cancer by the same doctor, Anderson Spickard, who had treated his wife. In fact, the sisters later learned that their dad had known about his prostate cancer for years, but had kept quiet about it so the family could focus on Hattie's health. As it became clear that his days were numbered, the patriarch summoned Jessie home to help him organize his paperwork. She searched through a desk drawer for some insurance documents, freezing in place when she discovered several letters addressed to her brother Perry. She didn't recognize any of the return addresses on the envelopes, but had suspicions about what they might be. "I said, 'Daddy, what are these?'" Jessie recalled. "And he said, 'Oh, I didn't intend for you to see those.' I looked at the postmark dates and I said, 'Oh, no, no, no, these do not belong in this house; it's a bad spirit in this house and I do not want them in here with you." Jessie's mind raced back to Perry's high school days, when letters from hateful strangers arrived all too frequently. Daddy would say that Perry didn't need to know the letters had ever arrived, and she had assumed he'd thrown them out. But now here they were, in her hands, letters that threatened to kill her baby brother. "I don't know why he kept them," Jessie recalled. "Maybe he had been hiding them from Mama." Whatever the reason her father had kept those letters, Jessie "didn't want anybody's evil in that house while Daddy was laying there dying." She scooped up the letters, walked to the alley behind the house, and as her father watched through a window, set them ablaze. Within weeks Perry Wallace Sr. passed away.

Just as he had found an unexpected release of pressure after the death of his mother, Wallace discovered that the passing of his father presented an opportunity and incentive for renewal. Through periods of meditation with Burg and old-fashioned prayer, through the daily real-life rhythms of the eclectic Bronx, riding crowded buses and subways and walking through vibrant neighborhoods bustling with bodegas and pizza joints, Wallace gradually felt himself not so much in conflict with the world and his immediate environment, more at peace, more determined to finish his final year of law school on a strong note. And with the passing of one role model, the father who had started his business in a bucket, came the appearance of two more: one in flesh and blood, the other as inspiration from the past. While his classmates found summer internships at law firms and corporations, Wallace took a job at the Recruitment and Training Program, an organization founded by Bayard Rustin to increase minority participation in the building and construction trades. While Wallace enjoyed a few conversations with Rustin, a civil rights legend who had been one of the architects of the 1963 March on Washington, it was Rustin's deputy, Ernest Green, who made the biggest impact. If Wallace's pioneering at Vanderbilt represented an overlooked, relatively late episode in the civil rights pantheon, Green had been a key figure in one of the movement's earliest, most enduring dramas. When President Eisenhower sent in troops of the 101st Airborne Division into Little Rock, Arkansas, to enforce the integration of Central High School in 1957, Green was one of the young black students, known as the Little Rock Nine, who made history. In Green, Wallace could learn from a man who represented what he hoped to accomplish in his own life. Here was a pioneer who had seen hate up close, had survived it, had achieved a level of peace, and had built a successful career that allowed him to lift up other people.

As summer ended and Wallace's final year of law school began, he held on to the hope that Green embodied and the peace of mind that Burg helped him achieve, and he also picked up another inspiration as classes commenced, this one bringing a message from the past, delivered at just the right moment, as if from his departed father. All through Wallace's days at Vanderbilt, his dad had made references that Perry was "just like Paul Robeson." A student of music and of history, Wallace knew a bit of Robeson's story as a trailblazing athlete, actor, and outspoken political activist and a 1923 graduate of the Columbia Law School. What he hadn't fully understood was the pain Robeson's words caused him, how he was ostracized from a society that had once flocked to see his shows and listen to his music. Wallace could now see parallels that even his father hadn't anticipated. During Wallace's third year at Columbia, Robeson's son came to campus to host the Paul Robeson Film Festival, speaking to students about his father's life before the screening of each film. The son spoke of Robeson's resistance to the House Un-American Activities Committee and his regret over some of the demeaning roles he had accepted.

"It was a real eye-opener for me, just so inspiring, and at a time when I really needed it after my father died," Wallace recalled. "It just so happened that [Robeson] and I were physically the same size, and we had some similar elements to our lives. I said to one of my friends as we watched the movies, 'If somebody like Robeson can pass through this place, then I guess there is enough that is good about it to stick it through.' He made a huge sacrifice and paid quite a price. He was smeared and America has never given him his due. And I understood the notion of ostracism, and exile, in a certain way. It was just very helpful, and it allowed me to move along and shape my life."

He had always thought it would be some redneck in Mississippi. But now, as he quickly but calmly walked away from the men with the guns, Perry Wallace faced the very real prospect that he wouldn't be shot and killed by a white Christian on a basketball court in Starkville or Oxford, but by a black Muslim in a government building in Washington, DC. After graduating from Columbia in the spring of 1975, Wallace returned to the nation's capital to begin his career. He believed that in Washington, a city with a large black middle class and its first-ever black mayor, he had situated himself in a spot where he could thrive. He'd accepted a job as a legislative aide to Mayor Walter E. Washington with the same understanding that had led him to apply for the Urban League position three years earlier: the lessons he'd learned as a pioneer, he believed, would serve him well in a job that required him to communicate messages from one constituency to another and, perhaps more important, to bridge the gap between black and white.

One of Wallace's responsibilities was to attend meetings of the DC City Council on the top floor of the District Building. On the afternoon of March 9, 1977, Wallace stepped out of the council meeting to use the restroom and was stunned by what he saw as he walked back out of the bathroom into the hallway. Down at the far end of the floor, a group of men were climbing up the stairs with "big ass rifles, and they were not smiling." Calling on both common sense and a knack for spotting trouble and taking steps to avoid it, developed as a defense mechanism as a youngster in the Jim Crow South, Wallace stepped to the side, kept his head down, walked calmly down the stairwell (*Don't get caught in the elevator*, he said to himself), rushed out of the building, and continued all the way home, right past the White House to his apartment at 21st and F streets in Foggy Bottom. "I turned on the television to see what had happened," he recalled, "and by that point, all hell had broken loose." The men Wallace had seen were part of a group of twelve Hanafi Muslims who raided the City Council hall, the B'nai B'rith International Center, and DC's Islamic Center, taking 149 hostages, killing two people, and injuring dozens more. The wounded included another DC figure who had once studied in Nashville, Marion Barry, shot in the chest, a city councilman who would be elected the mayor of Washington the next year. A twenty-four-year-old radio reporter, Maurice Williams, was shot and killed stepping off the elevator that Wallace had decided to avoid. The thirty-nine-hour siege would later be looked upon as one of the first high-profile cases of Islamic terrorism in the United States; hostages at the B'nai B'rith building were told they'd be beheaded if they made any wrong moves. Wallace's bladder, and his commonsense approach to danger, may have saved his life. "My reaction was very simple—get the hell out as fast as possible," Wallace recalled. "Marion Barry got shot [in the hallway], and that could have been me."

Wallace left the mayor's office just before the election of Barry in 1978 (a campaign that gained momentum in no small part because of Barry's wounds in the shooting), taking a position at the one school that had rejected his law school application, George Washington University. It was here that Wallace first became a university administrator and began to teach law courses to undergraduates and law students. But it was his encounters with two figures, one a coach and the other a student, that had the most meaningful impact on the next phase of his life.

The coach was Bob Tallent, in his fourth year at the helm of the Colonials basketball team. Tallent had begun his collegiate playing career at the University of Kentucky in 1965, but after a run-in with Adolph Rupp, he transferred to GW, becoming the nation's fifth-leading scorer in 1969. Wallace and Tallent had crossed paths a few times over the years, and when the coach learned that Wallace had taken a position at the university, he invited him to speak to his players about his experiences at Vanderbilt and to serve as a mentor to some of them. "It was very gratifying to have someone appreciate me and what I could contribute," Wallace recalled. "And it was great to get together with Bob, someone from 'down home.'" Nearly a decade removed from Nashville, this was the first time Wallace had ever been asked by a coach—anywhere—to share the lessons he learned about pioneering, a void that Wallace had long found curious. Back in his Vanderbilt days, he was dismayed that more white students didn't take the opportunity to initiate discussions with the handful of black students on campus, believing they missed out on a relatively easy chance to learn "the other half of the story about race," and during the decade of the 1970s, as collegiate basketball became an increasingly African American game, he believed that coaches struggling to mentor black players would have been well served to call on him to share what had worked—and what hadn't—during his time at Vanderbilt. "I marveled at the failure of so many leaders in sports to draw upon obviously rich sources of help," Wallace recalled. "The adjustment problems and other challenges for black athletes could have been helped measurably by people like me who could talk to the young people, who understood them, who came from their same neighborhoods. In effect, those leaders should have scoured the country for people like me, brought us in, and asked us to speak to the central question: 'How'd you do that?'"

The other figure Wallace encountered at George Washington, the student, was none other than Godfrey Dillard, who after earning his undergraduate degree at Eastern Michigan, had received a law degree from the University of Michigan. He then spent time as a criminal defense attorney in Detroit but, yearning to accomplish something bigger and better, had come to DC to earn a master's degree from George Washington's International Affairs program. Dillard and Wallace, who was auditing classes while working at the university, sat next to each other in an evening class dealing with strategic planning for international business, the first time they had seen each other, or even spoken, since Dillard had left Vanderbilt. After class, the old friends would head out to dinner at a popular bar on M Street called Rumors, where they'd catch up on what they'd each been doing over the previous decade and talk about their hopes for the future.

The two pioneers had frequently arrived at the same locales and stations in life by different paths, and that pattern continued as Dillard caught Wallace up on his life since Vanderbilt—similar themes, approached from slightly different angles. Immediately after withdrawing from Vanderbilt, Dillard was shocked to be drafted into military service, having never thought about the fact that he'd lose his student deferment. He remedied that situation quickly by appealing to the head coach at Eastern Michigan, who had known Dillard since his high school days and immediately offered him a scholarship. Dillard never did return to his former self on the court, not because he hadn't recovered from his knee injury, he says, but because he had been so psychologically damaged by the Vanderbilt experience. "My heart was out of it in terms of sports in a lot of ways," he recalled. "I lost the passion for the game and I could never get it back like I had before. I started to look to do other things, and that's when the idea of law school took hold."

Dillard was determined to graduate on schedule, in four years, despite the disruption of his transfer. He took eighteen hours of classes each semester and attended summer school, ultimately achieving his goal, earning a degree in philosophy and collecting his diploma on time in the spring of 1970. When it came time to apply for law school, Dillard had no desire to leave home again. "I was so devastated by the Vanderbilt experience, I needed to ground myself," he recalled. "The University of Michigan was close to home and to my mother. I could rebuild myself there. It's interesting, Perry grew up [in the South], so he needed to get away. I had been there and needed to go back [to the North]."

Dillard excelled in his studies, just as he always had, but he could feel that he was a changed man in other respects. The kid who had grown up playing backyard sports with white neighbors, attended an integrated Catholic school, and hoped white students would join Vandy's Afro-American Association, found himself filled with rage. "I hated white folks," he said. "I had been discriminated against, and it was white folks who discriminated against me. I had never felt that way about white people before. For a long time [after Nashville], I was wary of white folks. I was not going to be taken in like I had been taken in before. Just because you had a smile on your face did not necessarily mean you had my best interests in mind. So, in a lot of ways I was very cautious in my dealings with people. That doesn't mean I didn't have white friends, but I knew someone could claim to be your friend—and not be your friend. It was depression, bitterness, hate, and it took me years to get over it."

Wallace found his conversations with Dillard cathartic, and he took delight in discovering how their experiences had propelled their journeys along similar trajectories—an interest in the law, in civil rights work, and in international affairs. He took the opportunity to impress upon Dillard that their distinctly different approaches to the racial climate in Nashville had led to the same painful conclusion. "We got a chance to deconstruct the Vanderbilt experience, and it was helpful to put our notes together," Wallace said. "I think if I could say so, it was important for Godfrey to see that however much he was the more threatening one and I was the less threatening type, one of the things he got to see was that it only took another year [after he left] for people to start hating me, too. Then *I* was the 'nigger non grata.'"

Dillard still retained resentment toward Vanderbilt, but there was also a bit of confusion mixed in. He'd ask himself over and over again, "Was it me, or was it them?" If there was one thing he believed about himself, it was that he was not a quitter, and he agonized over the chain of events that had led to his departure. "For a long time, it was a sense of failure, that I wasn't able to close the deal, that I wasn't able to complete my career there. I didn't think the injury should have stopped me. I always questioned that as a young person, that maybe I was misreading the situation. But I was coming to the point where I could see that I was like a virus. They really looked at me like a virus. It wasn't just me; it was them."

Just as Wallace found it easier to come to terms with racial injustices, past and present, by taking a detached look at a situation and trying to understand the motivations of others, Dillard also took a philosophical stance—in his case, literally, recalling from his philosophy training that change often comes from the interaction of opposites. "Change needs a dialectical interchange—a pro and a con," he said. "A choice between the two is necessary for a decision to be made, and thus cause change to take place." Thinking back to their Vanderbilt days, Dillard surmised, he and Wallace represented different sides of the same coin. "We were both the first black basketball players at Vanderbilt and in the SEC," he said, "yet we were two very different personalities. Heads and tails." In the racially charged atmosphere of the late 1960s, Dillard believed, he and Wallace provided Vanderbilt's white power structure a choice as to what kind of black player and student they wanted on campus. "They wanted to be viewed as progressive and nonracist," he said. "They wanted change, but they wanted to personally determine what kind of change would occur. Their history and culture of racial bigotry would not let them go too far or too fast in reaching a point of accommodation or equilibrium. In this framework, the contradictions that Perry and I presented allowed Vanderbilt to fundamentally change for the better. They remained integrationists while still making a choice—a black, Nashville, favorite son who respected them or a black, northern, outsider who disrespected them. In this paradigm, they could not lose and had no problem kicking me to the curb. In making that choice, however, they could not ignore my impact on them. I was real and a vision of what the immediate future looked like."

What was it Godfrey Dillard said about providing a vision of the immediate future at Vanderbilt? Bill Ligon hadn't been on campus more than a few days in the fall of 1970 when some of the black upperclassmen started telling him that he reminded them of their old friend Godfrey. Their backgrounds were different—Dillard from the Motor City, Ligon from the small town of Gallatin, north of Nashville—but in their approach to life, the next black player to wear a Commodore uniform was a lot more like Godfrey Dillard than Perry Wallace. Ligon's attitude when he arrived on campus was that he was not going to take abuse from anybody—not students, not coaches, not opponents, not hecklers. "My background was you whup everybody," Ligon later recalled. "Take no stuff, don't back up. You get your lick in before they get theirs." Whereas Wallace had arrived on campus with his record player and his jazz albums, Ligon brought two gifts from his uncle: a pistol and a bottle of whiskey. "You take these and I'm going to get out of here," the uncle said as he dropped Ligon off at his freshman dormitory. "You're going to need both of these down here."

Ligon had followed Wallace's career for years, had been impressed with Pearl High's undefeated teams and Wallace's comments in interviews, but it was Dillard who wowed him most with his flashy guard play. Given his similarities to Dillard, it was no shocker that Ligon and Skinner never got along, their relationship deteriorating into an almost comical game of cat and mouse. Ligon felt Skinner didn't appreciate his skills, would only play him on the road away from the home fans, when the game was out of reach, or when he desperately needed Ligon's scoring. In response, Ligon tuned Skinner out in practices and games, and when he did see playing time, he'd take as many shots as possible. "I'd come off the bench and start shooting," Ligon recalled. "The name of the game was how many can I shoot. It was kind of like psychological warfare." Skinner would then use Ligon's questionable shot selection as a reason to bench him, and the cycle would continue.

"I had my mind made up early on not to listen to the coaches," Ligon recalled. "I got my scholarship because I brought certain skills to the table, and I used those skills. Memorial Gym, the way it's laid out, you never could hear the coaches anyway. So therefore I never had to listen to them. It was great. I never listened. [Skinner] would start yelling, and I'd move down to the other end of the floor, wave at the crowd, whatever I wanted to do."

Ligon's sense of humor obscures the complexity of the situation. He was a supremely talented player, drafted by the NBA's Detroit Pistons despite the fact that Skinner kept him out of the starting lineup. He never had a black teammate his entire career at Vandy, and he felt his teammates were just as oblivious to his plight on Deep South road trips as Wallace's had been years earlier. "We'd be in Oxford and my teammates would say, 'We're going to get a few beers, do you want to go?' And I'd say, 'Are you trying to get me killed?' They just didn't know. So I told them, 'I don't need to go anywhere with you guys because you literally do not have a clue as to what danger I may be in. You're going to get drunk, start talking to the girls, and as you move away from me, the good ol' boys will move toward me and I will have to do something real crazy to get out of there, and later you're going to ask me what is the problem. If you don't know what the problem is, I can't go nowhere with you.'"

Beneath his salty exterior, Ligon had a nuanced view of American race relations quite similar to Wallace's, developed at an early age. As a kid he had taken the bus up to Detroit to spend the summer with relatives, and he'd long remember the freedoms that accumulated as the odometer rolled. "You'd sit in the back of the bus until you got to Louisville," he recalled. "When you got to Louisville and everybody got off the bus, you could use the bathroom. When you got to Cincinnati, you could move up to the front of the bus. When you got to Dayton or Toledo, you could actually go into the place to buy yourself a cheeseburger. When you got to Detroit, you could catch a cab. I'd take a cab to the house. But when I got back to [Tennessee], you'd ride in the back of the bus again, and you'd have to be very cautious."

He understood the losing battle he was facing with Skinner, coming to peace with the situation by accepting his frequent benching as long as the Commodores were playing well. "I have no problems sitting as long as we win," he'd tell Skinner. "But let's not lose ballgames for bullshit like this." He also understood how his antagonists in the bleachers across the SEC perceived him, and rather than try to disabuse a redneck of prejudiced notions by assuming the role of the Super Negro, he'd throw their stereotypes back in their face by creating an oversized caricature of their worst nightmare. "A couple of good ol' boys sitting in the stands at Georgia started yelling and calling me monkey and all kinds of stuff," Ligon recalled. "I'm on the bench, these guys are screaming, and they had these big wooden crates with our water cups in them. I go over and take the water out, one at a time. And I looked up in the stands and said, "I want you guys to take a vote. When I get all of this water out of here, I'm going to take this wooden crate, and jump this Goddamn rail, and I'm going to get one of you. Y'all vote. Vote for the one to get got.' Word went straight up to the top of the stadium, and the word was that from then on, 'Don't bother the nigger. He's crazy.' But that's the kind of person I was."

If Skinner had a difficult time relating to Ligon, he did display some flashes of understanding. When Vanderbilt played at Auburn during Ligon's sophomore year, Henry Harris, the first black player at Auburn and the only black SEC opponent Wallace ever played against, was rounding out his senior year. Understanding the symbolism of the moment, Skinner tabbed Ligon as the "game captain" for the Commodores, and the two pioneers met at center court for a pregame handshake. Ligon never developed a passionate dislike for Skinner as Dillard had; instead, he looked at the coach with a mixture of sympathy and amusement, got along with him well enough to join the Commodore coaching staff as a graduate assistant while attending Vanderbilt Law School when his NBA career was over. He could only imagine what was going through the coach's mind when two black freshmen Skinner had recruited played in their very first freshman game in the late fall of 1971. Billy "World" Smith and Ben Skipper, both from New York City, had decided to make a splash in their first ballgame. Before the game, Smith stopped by a Nashville drugstore and bought some Christmas bells, and as the newcomers laced up their sneakers before tip-off, they tied the bells to their shoes. And then proceeded to jingle all the way to sixty shot attempts. "World took thirty-nine and Skip took twenty-one," Ligon recalled in disbelief. "Sixty shots between them. In their very first game. Even I thought that was a lot." Skinner could only shake his head. Five years later, at the age of forty-five, he'd retire from coaching.

While the pace of change remained slow at Vanderbilt, the league's other nine schools began walking through the door Wallace had opened. Harris played his first varsity game at Auburn in the 1969–70 season, and the other SEC universities fell in line: Alabama, Florida, Georgia, and Kentucky integrating in 1970–71, LSU, Ole Miss, and Tennessee following in 1971–72, and Mississippi State holding out the longest, with Larry Fry and Jerry Jenkins joining the Bulldog varsity in 1972–73, a full half decade after Wallace had broken the color line. Ten years after Alabama governor George Wallace's stand in the schoolhouse door, it was the Alabama basketball program, under Coach C. M. Newton, a former player under Rupp at Kentucky, that truly integrated the league in a big way, becoming the first SEC squad to start an all-black lineup in the 1973–74 season. Even Ligon could sense the changes that were underway in Alabama during a Commodore road trip to Tuscaloosa his sophomore year. The night before the game, Ligon took Smith and Skipper to a black beer joint down the street from the team hotel to play some pool. "This is when I knew things were changing," Ligon recalled. "Skip and I were standing there drinking beer and chain-smoking our cigarettes, and World's shooting pool and he's killing these guys. And this one guy pulls out a Street & Smith's [basketball magazine]. And he says, 'All you all in here, Alabama's going to tear you up.' And Alabama had four or five black guys by that point. C. M. Newton had gotten everybody in there. So these are black guys at a black pool hall rooting for the University of Alabama, and I'm sitting there going, 'Whoa, times have really changed around here.'"

As William Reed (the same Billy Reed who had interviewed Wallace during a freshman trip to Lexington) later noted in *Sports Illustrated*, "no league benefited as much from integration as the SEC, the league that had resisted it the hardest." No longer content to watch southern black athletes migrate to northern schools, SEC coaches in both basketball and football began to load up their rosters with black players, and the results were undeniable: most notably, C. M. Newton's Alabama teams racked up three consecutive SEC basketball titles between 1974 and 1976, the school's first basketball championships since 1956. Whatever advantage Vanderbilt might have enjoyed as the first school to successfully integrate one of its major programs was squandered as the university made no attempts to capitalize on its place in history, ceding the recruitment of black athletes to the same universities that had been most hostile to Wallace. Some coaches, especially Newton, were conscious of the difficulties these first waves of black athletes were forced to overcome. When he recruited Alabama's first black player, Wendell Hudson, Newton gave Hudson a copy of Frank Sutherland's *Tennessean* article, telling Hudson he wanted to keep lines of communication open in hopes of avoiding some of the problems of isolation and discrimination that Wallace had encountered. Other coaches simply wanted to win games, and if black players could help them do it, they were instant integrationists. The same fans who had heaped abuse on Wallace were curiously and suddenly ardent supporters of "their" black stars, at least for a few hours on Saturdays. White institutions, wrote William Rhoden in *Forty Million Dollar Slaves*, began to understand that they could exploit black muscle and talent while at the same time giving themselves credit as humanitarians. "The key to the ultimate appeal of integration for white coaches," Rhoden said, "was that it would not mean a corresponding loss of power; in essence, whites could have their cake and eat it, too. Integration on the sports field would not mean the transfer of power from whites to blacks any more than the black workforce in the cotton fields threatened white control of antebellum plantations." No matter to what degree one buys into the notion of exploitation, the onslaught of black talent into the SEC between the mid-seventies and mid-eighties, made possible by Wallace's pioneering, was monumental, with basketball and football stars such as Bernard King, Charles Barkley, Herschel Walker, and Bo Jackson becoming household names around the South and across the country.

Karen Smyley was skeptical. Her childhood friend Muriel and Muriel's husband, Jerry, a former basketball player at Tennessee State University, kept telling her how nice Jerry's friend was: *He's a really nice guy. You've got to meet him.* A nice guy. That was usually a red flag. What was wrong with this guy from Nashville, really?

But then she thought back to Senegal, and she began to warm up to the idea. It was while doing research on, and in, West Africa that she first contemplated the notion of dating a man from Tennessee. She was there doing translation (from French to English) for an author from Henning, Tennessee, Alex Haley, who had gained acclaim for his collaboration with Malcolm X and had traveled to Africa to do genealogical research for a book he planned to write on his own family's experience. Though she saw him only infrequently, Smyley enjoyed Haley's company, appreciated his manners, his humor, and his laid-back way. The future author of the landmark book (and TV miniseries) *Roots* would often joke that what Karen really needed was a nice southern man of her own. Years later, she remembered those conversations with Haley, and finally accepted an invitation to meet Perry Wallace at a 1981 gathering of TSU alums and others from Nashville at Howard University in Washington, DC.

Smyley had been born in New Orleans, where her parents met as students at Xavier University. Returning from World War II service overseas, her father recognized the limitations of raising a black family in the South, and he moved his wife and young daughter up to New York City, where they moved into a brand-new public housing project on the Lower East Side, near Delancey Street. Her father, Newton Smyley, earned a master's in electrical engineering at Brooklyn Polytechnic, and young Karen soaked up the sights and sounds of her new home. As she grew older, she became friends with the other black kids in the neighborhood, but also with the Italians and the Puerto Ricans, and with the Eastern European Jews, forever remembering the telltale markings on the arms of the Jewish kids' parents and grandparents. His eyes firmly set on the American Dream, Smyley's father patiently saved his money until he could move the family to the suburbs, and as she entered sixth grade Karen settled into a new life in Hempstead on Long Island. Here she noticed more friction between blacks and whites than back in the old neighborhood, where everybody commiserated in their struggles. Still, this was the "suburban dream," her days filled with music and dance lessons, her brother often off at some Boy Scout, sports, or music function. Newton Smyley was a Renaissance Man, complementing his aptitude in math and science with a deep love for the arts. He could play the violin and the bass and was fluent in French. As long as Karen could remember, her father had read her bedtime stories in French, had asked her to say her bedtime prayers *en français*, planting the seeds that would last a lifetime. When it came time for college, Karen accepted an invitation to an affordable all-girls school close to home, Hunter College in New York, where she paid one hundred dollars a semester to major in French and minor in Spanish. She performed so well in her studies that she earned a Fulbright scholarship that allowed her to earn her French master's at the elite Sorbonne in Paris, a city she came to love. She returned to the United States in 1967, just as the country seemed to be breaking apart. Teaching French on Long Island, she experienced a "reawakening" as she watched coverage of riots and protests. On the way to earning her PhD in French from City University of New York, she decided she wanted to live in a smaller, more accessible urban environment, and she moved to Washington, DC, to conduct research at the Library of Congress (where she met one of Haley's assistants), then took a job in the Black Studies Department at the University of Maryland, and finally landed a professorship at Howard.

Single, living in DC, and vaguely wanting to meet a man from the South, Smyley made her way to the TSU alumni event, and almost immediately, she was smitten by her blind date. Things clicked with Perry from the very beginning. "He was a southern gentleman, very smart, funny, and kind, and just with so much perspective," Smyley recalled. "We talked about everything from jazz to our love of New York City." In Smyley, Wallace had found the kind of woman he had been looking for ever since college. During parts of his Vanderbilt days, he had dated a preacher's daughter from South Carolina, a devout and "very fine young woman" attending Nashville's David Lipscomb College. "Everything seemed just perfect," Wallace said years later, "nice southern colored boy and girl, both members of the same church denomination, both college students. I'm sure everyone just assumed things would quite naturally lead to marriage, family, and settling down in Nashville." The problem, Wallace realized, was himself. The benefits and burdens of his college experience and his "need for a more profound philosophy of life and religion" were stretching him to the point that "this safe little world didn't cut it anymore." When he met Karen Smyley years later, he realized she was exactly the kind of sophisticated woman he desired. They went on dates to restaurants and art galleries and took drives in the country, and more often than not, their conversations turned to their shared interests in language and music. "Perhaps most important, we both believed in treating people nicely and giving others plenty of room and respect," Wallace recalled. "Her humanity impressed me. We both had a true and abiding interest in civil rights and the betterment of the black community. This was key. Our families both were solid black families with traditional values but with a strong interest in advancement in a modern world."

As the couple grew closer, Wallace shared stories about his experiences as a child in segregated Nashville, at Vanderbilt, and at Columbia. For Wallace, Karen's "humanity, intelligence, and patience were valuable" attributes in understanding his journey; from her perspective, "Perry's a good teller and I'm a good listener." Wallace began to share more about his experiences, adding new, deeper detail each time he told the same anecdote. "I had the sense that maybe he had opened up to other people before and maybe others had made harsh comments," she recalled, "or would try to wrap things up quickly and say, 'Well, that's over. Why do you still think about that? How bad was it?' I would just listen and he opened up more and more, and he began to feel that he could open up and not feel thwarted."

Wallace and Smyley were kindred spirits, and as Wallace fell deeper and deeper in love, his thoughts turned to marriage. In deciding to propose to his soul mate after two years of dating, he shed yet another insecurity. Smyley, it so happened, was a light-skinned black woman. Meeting her for the first time, some people assumed she was white. "There were two reasons why this created problems," Wallace later wrote. "First, during those days, some people would stare at (even only *apparently*) interracial couples and some people exhibited intense feelings. Second, coming up in the South during the time of Emmett Till, and having had the special scrutiny of a racial pioneer, I was almost seized with fear about the life prospects of what would look like an interracial marriage in that type of America. The problem was mostly with whites who had problems with us (and they were not only rednecks but also some highly educated, well-placed whites), but some blacks were hostile to a black man marrying either a white woman or a light-skinned black woman.

"This was a serious matter for me, and it posed a fundamental challenge for me about who I was and how I was going to function in America. As I struggled with it personally, one question—combined with one realization—occurred to me: How far should I go in shaping my life—whom I should love and marry, etc.—to satisfy people who, after all, obviously didn't think much of me as a human being? It occurred to me how much and how long in my life I had tried to please and pacify other people—especially in the context of race.

"So, I decided they could (1) back up about 20 feet, (2) get a running start, and (3) go straight to hell. I wasn't going to proceed in fear and self-denial about my most important decision in life, just to satisfy myriad and sundry idiots who insisted essentially on being spontaneously unfair and unjust."

Having achieved this life-defining epiphany, Perry asked Karen to marry him—a happy enough occasion but for the fact that in the giddiness of the moment Karen forgot she had some peas on the stove and burned them to a crisp. Wallace had come to Karen's tiny apartment off Dupont Circle for their usual Sunday night dinner date, popping the question in the kitchen as she cooked. "It was such a magic moment," Karen recalled. "I had to sit down and think, 'What would it all mean? Where would we go?' But the answers didn't really matter to me. Perry had a red Ford [Mustang] at the time, and I had no car. We used to get in that car and just drive and talk and enjoy each other's company, and I said to myself that marrying Perry would be just like getting inside that red Ford and going off we don't know where. We had both met people in our lives who were critical, who might be in that car saying, 'Turn left,' or 'Why didn't you bring the map?' I didn't do any of that, and Perry liked that. It was easy. We just enjoyed each other's company. We'd talk and listen and maybe turn around. It was no big deal. It mattered not to me where we were going; as long as we were hanging out, that was great."

The wedding took place at Howard's historic Rankin Memorial Chapel in June 1983, a relatively low-key affair spiced up by the company that was present, most notably Perry's best friends from Vanderbilt, including Godfrey Dillard, Walter Murray, who was the best man, and a younger former classmate named Larry Wallace, who had been elected Vanderbilt's first black Student Government president. For Karen, who had commuted to college in New York, it was a treat to meet this group of friends who had forged such strong bonds in a traditional—as if anything about their collegiate experience had been traditional—college setting. She was especially gratified to meet and gain the approval of Murray, her new husband's close friend, whom she had heard so much about.

At the time of the wedding, Wallace had recently taken a new job as a senior trial attorney at the US Department of Justice, and he had to appear in court for oral arguments in a high-profile environmental case two days after the ceremony. He was worried that his new bride would be upset, but in typical style Karen was gracious about it. A delayed honeymoon would be for the best, she said, because she was busy with a writing assignment in her pursuit of tenure at Howard, anyway. During the first week of marriage, with unpacked boxes piled up in their small apartment, Perry prepared for his case and Karen set her typewriter atop a crate and finished her paper. The following weekend, they rented a car and drove up to New York, where they stayed for several days in her brother's temporarily vacant apartment on Central Park West, enjoying an eclectic experience in the Big Apple. "It was a great New York City moment," Karen recalled. "We went everywhere, saw every movie, saw basketball games, listened to jazz, browsed in bookstores, ate in restaurants. In other words, it was a wonderful time."

Finally, Wallace could exhale. The kid from Short 26th had come a long way. Once on the receiving end of government-sanctioned segregation, he now represented the federal government in courtrooms across America. As a trial attorney in the Justice Department's Division of Lands and Natural Resources, it gave him profound pleasure to open a session with these words: "May it please the Court. My name is Perry Wallace, and I represent the United States in this matter." The shy, asthmatic kid had blossomed socially, found the woman of his dreams, and situated his new family in a part of the country and among a circle of friends and coworkers where issues of race would not be a daily battle. It was, however, still a factor, even within the halls of justice. In one Montana courtroom, was it a mere coincidence that Wallace was the only attorney or witness to be searched by security guards? And why was it that one federal judge in the nation's capital refused to believe that Wallace was who he said he was even after Wallace showed him his Justice Department ID tag, his bar card, his social security card, and his driver's license?

Still, these types of episodes were becoming less frequent. He felt that he and Karen were the subject of less staring, that society was progressing. He was still essentially a forgotten man at Vanderbilt—no one from the university had contacted him in more than ten years—but he had prepared himself for this possibility before granting the interview to Frank Sutherland. If the situation in Nashville ever thawed, that would be great. After years of deconstruction and healing, he was ready to begin a new relationship with the school, but he was now more focused on the next steps in his career than on the traumatic events of his past.

And then a middle-aged, southern newspaperman called, out of the blue, and asked him what he'd been up to all these years.

29

Embrace

Perry Wallace was twenty-two years old when Vanderbilt fans showered him with a rousing ovation following his final game as a Commodore.

It wasn't until the day before his forty-first birthday that he was invited back to campus.

And even this low-key appearance—a 10:00 a.m. speech to Athletic Department boosters on the day of a basketball game against LSU—likely would never have happened if not for the nostalgic initiative of a Sunday features writer in Atlanta who was itching to write about sports. When Perry Wallace decided to speak to Frank Sutherland on March 8, 1970, he knew he was writing his ticket out of town. Nearly two decades later, on February 18, 1989, his return ticket was finally stamped. Wallace's speech to the Commodore Club marked the culmination of a series of events that can be traced back to a call he had received a year earlier from a journalist named Sam Heys.

Heys had grown up in Chattanooga, and though he was two years younger than Wallace, he had closely followed the Mid-State star's high school career, watching with curiosity as Pearl High won the first integrated TSSAA tournament and recognizing the historical significance when Wallace signed with Vanderbilt. As an undergraduate at the University of Georgia, Heys made a point of witnessing Wallace's games in Athens, and when he became a professional journalist for the *Atlanta Constitution*, he included Wallace in a 1980 Sunday magazine story on the SEC's black pioneers.

Eight years later, it was Heys who called attention to the significance of the year 1988, the twentieth anniversary of Wallace's 1967–68 varsity debut. In their interviews for the 1980 story, Heys was struck by Wallace's eloquence, believing that among all the pioneers with whom he spoke, it was Wallace who described his experiences in the most insightful, transcendent ways. Now, as he called Wallace to commemorate a historic accomplishment nobody else chose to acknowledge, Heys was again impressed by Wallace's perspective but bewildered that the significance of his pioneering experience had been so overlooked.

Wallace shared a few of the anecdotes he had relayed to Sutherland and the *Hustler*'s Kendall eighteen years earlier, but he also plunged deeper into his past, speaking of the flood of hatred in Starkville, the enthusiastic bigotry in Oxford, memories of Vanderbilt boosters yelling "jump, boy, jump," awkward encounters with fellow students—their silence and avoidance in many instances, their condescension or insults in others. The passage of time had given Wallace a more nuanced perspective on his own experience, his extensive work with national civil rights organizations and the exercises in "deconstruction" with friends like Burg in New York and Dillard at George Washington yielding fresh insights.

Heys was the first journalist to explicitly frame Wallace's basketball pioneering as a significant, even monumental storyline in the larger civil rights struggle in the South. "Sport," he wrote, "a cherished ground of honor on which only white males could tread, was the region's final citadel of segregation. Buses, theaters, restaurants, swimming pools and, in some places, even schools were integrated before college athletics." Wallace, Heys wrote, had "entered the Southern sanctuary of sport" at age eighteen and left that subculture forever changed. As his article went to press on January 12, 1988, 83 of the league's 134 basketball players were black. Which made it all the sadder, Heys posited, that probably no player in the league could correctly answer the question "Who was Perry Wallace?" and all the more disappointing that no one from Vanderbilt, over the entire span of the 1970s and now nearing the end of the 1980s, had ever called Wallace to say, "Come on down. Tell us of your time. What was it really like? Perhaps there is a message to be heard?"

Heys' article ran on the front page of the *Atlanta Constitution*'s Lifestyle section, and within two weeks, the longtime pastor at one of Nashville's historic black churches, the Reverend William Alexander of St. Andrew's Presbyterian, had written a letter to the editor of the *Nashville Banner*, bringing Wallace's name back to life in his hometown. Alexander's son, living in Atlanta, had sent him a copy of the Heys story. What a shame it was, the clergyman wrote, that Vanderbilt had never invited Perry Wallace back to campus. "I hope that Vanderbilt will," Alexander concluded. "He is 39 years old and a very successful young man. Wallace is quiet but fiercely proud of what he did."

If Heys' article and Alexander's reference to it in Nashville were the shouts that finally woke up the echoes, they found a receptive ear in Vanderbilt's basketball coach, C. M. Newton, the same man who had accelerated the pace of change in the SEC during his twelve-year tenure at Alabama. Following Skinner's retirement in 1976, Vanderbilt struggled under coaches Wayne Dobbs and Richard Schmidt, famously hiring Schmidt, an assistant at Virginia, rather than Mike Krzyzewski, then coach at West Point. Newton came to Nashville in 1981, slowly returning the program to respectability and leading the Commodores to a Sweet 16 appearance in 1988. The star of that team was a seven-foot center named Will Perdue, who entered Vanderbilt as a gangly project but blossomed under the tutelage of Commodore assistant coach Ed Martin. Though his protégé, Perdue, was white, the fact that Martin was at Vanderbilt was further evidence of Newton's sensitivity to race. The African American Martin had served as head coach at Tennessee State University for seventeen years (succeeding Harold Hunter) before winding down his career on Newton's staff. At Vanderbilt, Martin was encouraged by Newton to serve as a mentor and confidant to the team's black players, many of whom struggled with variations of the social problems Wallace had endured decades earlier.

Despite the school's place in history and Newton's racial awareness, Vanderbilt continually fielded the whitest team in the league, a fact that sportswriters (and opposing recruiters) highlighted throughout the 1980s and even into the early 1990s. By the second half of the 1989 season, Newton had announced that he'd be stepping down as Vanderbilt coach after the season to return to the University of Kentucky, where he had played for Adolph Rupp and where he would become athletic director. Before he left Nashville, he acted on Vanderbilt's behalf with a gesture that was long overdue, writing to Wallace and inviting him back to campus to speak. Wallace, who by then had left the Justice Department to teach law at the University of Baltimore (where he was the Law School's first tenured black faculty member), accepted without hesitation.

When he returned to Nashville in February 1989, Wallace checked into a hotel directly across the street from the dormitory in which he had lived as a freshman, just a few blocks north of the former site of the University Church of Christ. Before heading over to a campus banquet room for his speech, Wallace came across members of the LSU basketball team in the lobby of the Vanderbilt Plaza hotel, where the visiting Tigers had also spent the night. Someone introduced Wallace to Tiger freshman Chris Jackson, the phenom who was pictured on the cover of that week's *Sports Illustrated* and was on his way to setting an NCAA single-season scoring record for freshmen. Jimmy Davy, the *Tennessean* reporter who had known Wallace since high school, observed the encounter, noting that it was clear that Jackson, an African American from Gulfport, Mississippi, had never heard of Wallace. It was also obvious, Davy sensed, that he appreciated the history lesson.

The first time Wallace ever stood before a roomful of Commodore boosters was in 1966, when as a high school senior he had been invited by Skinner to attend the Commodores' postseason banquet. Vanderbilt supporter Richard Philpot would long remember an uncomfortable stir, like the air had been taken out of the room, when Skinner introduced Wallace to the crowd. Everyone knew the kid from Pearl was a good player, but in the hubbub around the tables, people wondered aloud what their friends would say about Vanderbilt recruiting a Negro. What will the alumni think? Was this the end of Commodore basketball?

Twenty-three years later, Wallace was unsure of how he would be greeted upon his return. He had been cheered in his last public appearance in Nashville, but that was before the Sutherland article. During his Columbia Law years, Wallace once attended a Vanderbilt alumni reception in New York City. Everyone was cordial—except for one alumnus. "He was a prototype of the usual confronter: white male, successful, confident (arrogant) enough to be confrontational and loud, and obviously very angry," Wallace recalled. "Also, there were other traits that I had meticulously observed over the years, quietly, as these types of people ranted on: they didn't know Jack about race, about me, about what a specific day was like for me at Vanderbilt, or anything else relevant to what they were talking about. Obviously, they never let me talk and had no interest in listening—or learning anything." After a certain amount of experience with these figures, Wallace said he came to three powerful conclusions that brought him a certain satisfaction: First, these people couldn't harm him. Second, these people—fueled by arrogance and with limited to no experience with race—were on their way to being "outrageously unprepared for the new America that was emerging." Third, his remedy for this lingering type of hostile expression was simple: stop going to Vanderbilt alumni events. "And," he said, "but for a few precious exceptions years later, I did."

But Wallace accepted Newton's invitation, and the coach, already a highly respected figure who had become even more beloved by Vanderbilt fans since announcing his plans to leave, set a tone in his introductory remarks that assured nothing but a warm embrace for his guest. Newton told the boosters that even watching from a distance, he had admired Wallace's "willingness to blaze a trail. I marveled at the time at his willingness to take a risk." More impressive than Wallace's courage on the court, Newton continued, were his achievements as a scholar, attorney, and teacher. "What he has done with his life since [Vanderbilt] is an even more impressive statement." As Newton concluded his remarks and welcomed Wallace to the podium, the crowd rose in unison and cheered.

Acknowledging the well-wishers, Wallace took the high road, speaking in broad strokes about the lessons he learned at Vanderbilt, drawing his listeners in close with a comforting tone that allowed him to be heard, not tuned out, when he did speak of the hardships he overcame. "Because of athletics I can now deal with people on all levels and dictate the quality of my life," he said. "Clay Street in North Nashville was my home and it was good. But it's a broader world." Looking back on his college experience, he told the fans that "the high points were the times I was able to relate best to people who were so different from me. These times came on the basketball practice floor, the dorm room, or just on campus. The low points were the times when this clearly wasn't happening." He paused to let that point linger and concluded with a crowd-pleaser: "And apart from all that, beating Kentucky was a high point. I still remember hugging my teammate, Rudy Thacker." The boosters stood and cheered again as Wallace concluded his remarks, and the applause seemed to linger all day, the underdog Commodores handing nationally ranked LSU its biggest loss of the season, 108–74, before a raucous crowd at Memorial Gym. "The fans are amazing," Wallace told Davy after the game. "They always have been."

Wallace's appearance was a revelation to a new generation of Vanderbilt students, most of whom had never heard of this black man who had made history at their school. Where administrators had failed for years to honor the significance of Wallace's and Vanderbilt's place in history, clinging to a belief that Wallace was "angry," this new wave of students, raised in the years since Wallace left Nashville—and in a culture that had grown comfortable celebrating civil rights icons—wasted no time in retelling his story once they had heard it. A feature on Wallace and Dillard soon appeared in the campus literary magazine, *Versus,* and in the weeks that followed, the editorial staff of the *Vanderbilt Hustler* and leaders of the Student Government Association pushed for the school's new student recreation center to be named in Wallace's honor. University administrators (under the leadership of Chancellor Joe B. Wyatt, a Texan who succeeded Heard in 1982) declined to entertain the idea, explaining that naming rights to campus buildings were given to those who contributed a significant sum of money to the school, a claim *Hustler* editors branded hypocritical and not entirely accurate. "By holding out for a donor, University officials are promoting the idea that Vanderbilt values people more for the money they contribute than what they have accomplished for the school," read an April 19, 1991, editorial that anchored a two-page spread on Wallace and the rec center. "Past VU chancellors have been honored for their actions, not donations, and this pattern should be followed with Wallace. Vanderbilt has placed more value on diversity of late, and now would seem an opportune time to honor a man who just twenty years ago helped integrate the SEC and Vanderbilt itself. Who knows, maybe by honoring Wallace now, the University will attract new donors impressed by the commitment to diversity." Wallace told the young journalists he was flattered by the suggestion, but less idealistic in his hopes. "I'm a lawyer," he said. "I know about these cost benefit analyses of naming buildings."

Still, Wallace's name had been reinserted into the conversation in Nashville and around the South. While Vanderbilt administrators continued to keep their distance (Roy Kramer, athletic director from 1978-90, could only offer that he didn't know why Wallace had not been invited back to campus more often, while Wallace's friend and former teammate Thorpe Weber said there remained "a lot of hard feelings" toward Wallace among school officials and many alumni), that stance became increasingly uncomfortable. In June 1991, a short-lived publication known as *Nashville Business & Lifestyles* ran a cover story on Wallace, noting that he'd only been invited back to speak on campus one time, for the private Commodore Club event. "I've remained available, but how much can I initiate?" Wallace asked journalist Shelley Liles. "That's the university's job. It could be some people might have figured, 'Hey, having this guy come in and speak wouldn't be a pleasant occasion. So let's leave him alone.' What many people down there do not know is that for the last 10 years things have been all right. I've said the right things. I've moved along in my life and I have been a perfect candidate for someone to be asked to come back to participate in one sense or another." (It wasn't just Wallace who felt marginalized by his alma mater. Around the same time Wallace spoke to Liles, a group of former black Vanderbilt players attempted to create their own letterman's club, saying they didn't feel welcome at the official Vanderbilt football reunion events.) That Vanderbilt, a university with Ivy League–style aspirations, chose not to proactively claim Wallace as one of its own appeared especially baffling given the article's portrayal of him as a true Renaissance Man. "I try consciously not to be the old jock type—not to have to lean on it for fulfillment," he told Liles, and that was evident in a story that informed readers that Wallace held a brown belt in karate and sang opera in Italian, German, and French. He quoted from Shakespeare in describing the deceptions inherent in a culture that professed to reward people who worked hard and played by the rules—and yet spurned Wallace when he spent a lifetime doing just that. Wallace explained that growing up black in the South meant existing in a "reverse America," coming to understand "how insane and inane the world can be, in that a lot of the rules are not what they're said to be. Shakespeare's Iago says something that at first glance doesn't seem to make sense. At one point in *Othello* he says, 'I am not what I am.' And in some ways the rules of the game have said that to me. I am not what I am."

A few months after the Nashville magazine story, Wallace left his position at the University of Baltimore to join the faculty at American University's Washington College of Law, a highly respected law school in the northwest quadrant of DC. Wallace's life was coming together in all the ways he had envisioned as a child reading the magazines his mother brought home from work: a brilliant and loving wife, a rewarding profession, a comfortable home in a cosmopolitan city. He and Karen took the next logical step by starting a family, choosing to adopt a daughter in early 1992. The African American baby had been born to a single teen mother in the District on December 30, 1991; her new parents named her Gabrielle Eugenie Wallace, a tribute to Karen's mother's maiden name, Gabriel, and a French spin on the middle name Perry had inherited from his father: Eugene.

Like most first-time parents, Perry and Karen did the best they could with their infant daughter, learning by trial and error, experiencing together the joys and frustrations brought on by the new addition to their family. Perry considered fatherhood the "best version of this crazy life" that one could have. As Gabrielle reached toddler stage, however, it became obvious that she was lagging well behind the milestones spelled out in the parenting guidebooks. She wasn't talking, wouldn't answer when her parents called her name. After a series of appointments and tests came the diagnosis: Gabby had Asperger's Syndrome, a high-functioning form of autism marked by extreme social challenges and an all-absorbing focus on certain tasks or topics to the exclusion of others. In the years following Gabby's diagnosis, far more became known about Asperger's, but at the time the condition was much more mysterious, a discovery made worse by the fact that the doctor who initially met with Perry and Karen seemed to have difficulty dealing with a black family, frowning as she spoke in simplistic terms as if the Wallaces couldn't possibly comprehend what she had to say.

For Perry and Karen, the news was shocking. Their minds raced with contradictions: questions, fears, love, unknowns, anxieties, hope, determination, pain, curiosity, exasperation. And here, at this low point, is where the trajectory of Perry Wallace's life turned back upon itself. All that he had experienced as a child growing up in a segregated society, all the suffering as a pioneer, all the healing in the years since—he now saw all of this in a new context. His experiences made him the ideal adoptive father for this little girl. Wallace's own parents had lived with a determination that their children would not be confined by the circumstances of their birth, and now it was his turn to take the same approach to fatherhood. Along with Karen, he would draw upon lessons learned from the most painful of his own experiences to create the best possible world for his daughter.

Gabby would not make eye contact. It reminded Wallace of his childhood in Nashville, where looking a white man in the eye was inviting trouble and where, even aside from this, people often looked down or away either out of ignorance or shame. Gabby was taunted by some of her schoolmates for being different, reminding Wallace of the threats he had received his whole life, from the black kids who thought he was a Goody Two-shoes, to the white kids who didn't like him walking past their school, to the crowds in places like Athens and Knoxville and Baton Rouge. Gabby had the hardest time learning to tie her shoes. Patiently working with his daughter reminded Wallace of the remedial work that was so common in the schools of North Nashville, where teachers were determined to help their students overcome generations of slavery and discrimination, and of his own embrace of Coach

Skinner's ten-thousand-times rule, understanding the importance of focus and repetition.

As there had been at Vanderbilt, there were good days and bad days, fits and starts, moments of joy and crushing disappointment, lots of hard work with no guarantees that it would pay off in any larger sense. One step forward and three steps back, frustration heaped upon tears. At their lowest points, Perry and Karen held hands, like Wallace and Dillard in Starkville, and vowed that together they'd find the strength to make it through. This would either make them or break them. "Once again in life," Wallace recalled, "we learned more about faith—the substance of things hoped for, the evidence of things not seen."

Gabby was so easily distracted, getting her from the car to her classroom was a torturous journey. Wallace improvised, hauling a little red wagon in the back of his car on the drive to her school each morning, pulling his daughter down the hall straight to her desk. One day even this strategy backfired. A struggle just to make it inside the school, Gabby still crying. Wallace turned to a teacher, sweating as if he'd just played a full basketball game, and looked down at Gabby. "She wants her mama," he sighed, "and I want mine, too." And then he had to clear his mind and drive off to teach his law students. Perry and Karen both made sacrifices in their careers; the unrelenting focus on academic publishing that many of their peers maintained was not possible. Every step of his career, Wallace had worked extra hard to disprove stereotypes; now he had to accept the fact that he would do what he could professionally but that his family came first. Even then, there was no sanctuary in the magnanimity of his choices; acting out of nothing but love for his daughter, he dealt with indignities of prejudice. There were the doctors who didn't look past the color of his skin to see a Vanderbilt- and Columbia-educated man. Teachers who would turn their backs on him in parent-teacher meetings to speak only to Karen, who they assumed was white. "I had to dance the kind of dance that a lot of black men have understood, and that I understood, the same dance I had been dancing all the while as a black professional," Wallace recalled. "I was dealing with these people who were not willing to work with me as a human being, but in order to find help for my daughter, I chose to put up with it."

Wallace settled into the prime years of his professional career, taking the greatest satisfaction in mentoring his law students. Karen would find him in his home office late at night, on the telephone helping a student with a paper, or scouring a thesaurus to find just the right word for a passage in a student's thesis. He sought opportunities to upend preconceived notions of what black attorneys and professors should specialize in, focusing on environmental law, corporate governance, and international arbitration.

He patiently answered questions from Vanderbilt students calling as they prepared oral histories or wrote term papers for history classes. Occasionally, out-of-town reporters phoned to ask his opinion on the latest issue relating to race and basketball, or about his pioneering days at Vanderbilt. Wallace never grew tired of the calls from strangers. After two decades of silence, suddenly the media would not let his story die, and for that he was thankful. "All you have to do to understand that is to see how little people will listen to you in life in general," he recalled. "And just think, you might actually have something to say. And so to have these openings, where people are actually listening to you, and giving you credit for having accomplished things and having an interest in how you actually did it? That really is golden. I've had a story to tell since before Vanderbilt. I started having more of a story at Vanderbilt. And I tried to tell it. So obviously, personally it was very satisfying, but it was an opportunity to make sure that points were made, that knowledge and inspiration were conveyed and shared to as many people as possible."

Along with the media coverage, recognition arrived in official ways: in 1995 Wallace was named to the National Association of Basketball Coaches' Silver Anniversary team (along with contemporaries such as Calvin Murphy, Charlie Scott, and the late Pete Maravich), and in 1996 he was presented a "sports pioneer" award by Reebok and the National Association of Black Journalists (along with legendary TSU coach John McClendon and, posthumously, Wilma Rudolph, among others). Still, there was no comparable embrace by Vanderbilt, a fact that became increasingly irrelevant to him as he dealt with the responsibilities of marriage, fatherhood, and work. Most of all, Wallace believed that life was too short to sit around waiting for something that might never come. That point was driven home in 1998, when his best friend, Walter Murray, succumbed to cancer in Boston, where he was working after studying at the Harvard Divinity School. Wallace traveled to Boston to be by Murray's side during his final days. "Perry came to see him at a point when Walter needed twenty-four-hour care, and we had called hospice," Donna Murray recalled. "My brother and his family came, and Perry came around the same time. We decided to take shifts and Perry and my brother took a shift together. He and my brother, two tall grown men, taking care of my husband. Walter wasn't eating, and we had all these lollypop sticks to moisten his lips. It was very touching, after all these years, the love Perry still had for his friend."

As he grew increasingly comfortable with his teaching responsibilities at American, Wallace took on a series of significant side projects, organizing annual study-abroad programs in Europe and South America, traveling to Africa as part of an international group of attorneys and mediators assembled to negotiate a sensitive Sharia law case with the government of Nigeria and returning to the continent to represent the Federated States of Micronesia

Wallace is now a professor of law at American University in Washington, DC. Visitors to his office would see no signs of his pioneering past. Photo by Lisa Nipp, *The Tennessean.*

at a United Nations global warming hearing in Kenya. Dating back to his childhood days on Short 26th, Wallace had found fulfillment and satisfaction in the study of foreign languages, his sessions of deep concentration and repetition first providing an exotic escape from the streets of North Nashville and later from the pressures of academia. He drew upon lessons from his father (who *studied* the newspaper every evening) and from Coach Skinner (recalling the summer of the ten-thousand-times rule) in teaching himself French, eventually reaching such a level of fluency that he delivered three lectures at France's Université d'Aix-Marseille III—in French—on topics as intricate as climate change and corporate governance. Karen, the French professor, was duly impressed by her husband's persistence and his knack for the language, developed independently of hers. In the Micronesia case, Wallace was appointed as the formal negotiator to represent the low-lying island nation's concerns over ozone depletion and climate change. His greatest professional satisfaction, however, came on the Nigeria project, where he contributed to one of several advocacy campaigns seeking to spare the life of a young woman sentenced to death by stoning for the crime of sex out of wedlock in the Muslim, northern part of the country. When he was first asked by the dean of American University's law school to join a delegation of international attorneys lobbying to overturn the conviction of the woman, Amina Lawal, Wallace was inclined to say no. He had enough on his plate. Then he went online and searched for more information on Lawal. First married at fourteen, twice divorced, and with three children, she was illiterate and impoverished. The man who impregnated her (and went free without prosecution) had lured her in with promises of marriage and stability. Wallace was intrigued by the particulars of the case and startled by a photo of Lawal, an image that took him back to a summer day near Grandfather Wallace's farm in Murfreesboro, Tennessee.

"In the photo [Lawal] was in her gown, a little small woman. I thought about her case and it was concerning, but very distant. I looked at more photographs of her, and another image came into my mind from maybe fifty years earlier," Wallace recalled. "I was a little boy at one of those old-fashioned baptisms in the country, down by the riverside. They would baptize people down in the river, drape them in sheets, walk them out into a river. When they would lift them out, some people would get happy and shout and sing. This happened in the late afternoon one summer. I was a very little boy, maybe five or six years old. And I remembered the scene because it was so striking, these dark black bodies in white sheets covered in Tennessee red clay, and the sun was glistening off the bodies and the river. I remember one little woman who was so happy when she was baptized. She felt she had been saved. And if you know what you know about America, a young African American woman from the country in the 1950s wasn't going to be saved in this life, and was going to go out into a brutal world and probably have a brutal life. And in my memory, that woman looked so much like Amina Lawal. It appeared that the two women might have faced similar worlds and fates. I couldn't go back to the 1950s in Tennessee and help one woman, but I could go to Nigeria and help the other one. That was striking. So I called my dean and said, 'OK, I'm going to go.'" Like many black civil rights leaders, Wallace saw the connections between oppressed people in the United States and those in other parts of the world, embracing the opportunity to work for justice on an international level. Ultimately, on her second appeal in September 2003, Lawal's conviction was overturned.

David Williams knew so little about Vanderbilt University that when Gordon Gee called to ask him to help run the school, he figured it must be located in some small town called Vanderbilt, Tennessee. Williams, then an administrator and professor of law at Ohio State University, had grown up in Detroit, and though he had a cousin who attended TSU, he hadn't spent much time in the South since he was a kid in the 1950s and 1960s, when he'd visit relatives in Jackson, Mississippi. Those trips had been his first exposure to overt racism and in some respects, to white people, period. In Detroit the black neighborhood he grew up in had every kind of store and amenity his family ever needed, so there weren't many reasons to venture out. In Jackson he knew he couldn't try on clothes at the department stores downtown, but as a kid who hated going on those shopping trips in the first place, he really didn't mind not trying on clothes. One day he and his cousin ventured out alone and raised the ire of a white storekeeper over something insignificant to them, and Williams couldn't quite understand why his grandmother had made such a big deal out of it, hurriedly marching the two boys back down to the store where she told the white store owner that her grandsons "weren't from down here, and didn't understand."

Accepting the offer to serve as Gee's right-hand man when Gee was named Vanderbilt's chancellor in 2000, Williams set out to learn more about his new environs. He asked colleagues what book he should read to get to know Nashville and its history, and someone recommended David Halberstam's chronicle of the 1960 sit-ins, *The Children*. Williams was shocked to read about James Lawson and Vanderbilt's reaction to his role in the protests. He called on other friends to learn more, including an old friend from Detroit named Tony Jenkins, the same Tony Jenkins whom Roy Skinner had unsuccessfully tried to recruit during Wallace's senior year. Jenkins told Williams about his recruiting visit to Nashville, reminded Williams that their fellow Detroiter Godfrey Dillard had played briefly at Vanderbilt, and recommended that Williams learn more about one of Dillard's teammates, the man who integrated the Southeastern Conference and hosted him on his Vanderbilt visit, Perry Wallace. It was the first time Williams had ever heard Wallace's name. He began reading everything he could find about Wallace and that era in Vanderbilt's history, learning about Wallace's career at Pearl, the historic game against Father Ryan, and the Impact Symposium appearances of King and Carmichael. He also picked up on the cold feelings the old Vanderbilt guard still maintained toward Wallace. He was intrigued, but as a newcomer with one of the fullest plates in all of academia (Williams served as vice chancellor, university general counsel, university secretary, and tenured law professor in addition to his duties overseeing athletics), he moved on to other, more pressing tasks and did not pursue any sort of outreach to Wallace until a group of political science students visited him a few years later.

The students (Zach Thomas, Justin Wood, and Sara Ruby), like others before them, had discovered Wallace on their own and were determined to do something to honor him. Along with *Hustler* sportswriter Brad Golder, they brought up the rec center naming idea once again (more than a decade had passed since the idea was first raised, and still the building remained nameless). Williams looked into it and came back with the same answer that had been given for years: university policy on these sorts of things was complex, and it simply wasn't going to happen. Then the students presented Williams with a documentary they had produced on Wallace, and the vice chancellor, he later recalled, was mesmerized. The students talked to Williams about other ways to honor Wallace, and a plausible idea was proposed. What about retiring his jersey? This was a relatively common practice at other universities, but only two jerseys hung from the rafters at Memorial Gym, the number 43 of Clyde Lee and the number 40 of Wendy Scholtens, the first star player on the Commodore women's basketball team. Williams recognized the opportunity to do something powerful, to officially welcome Wallace back into the fold and to take another symbolic step beyond the events of more than four decades earlier, when the university had expelled Lawson. *You get a chance to make a difference so few times in your life*, Williams told himself. *When you get that chance, you seize it.* He picked up the phone, called Wallace, and told him of the students' idea and the university's plans. "This was our way of Vanderbilt saying, 'We got it. We recognize it. We appreciate it. You're one of us.' This was just one of the pieces in reestablishing the relationship with Perry."

There had been times in the late 1960s when Wallace would look into Chancellor Heard's eyes in their Kirkland Hall meetings and feel that Heard truly understood where he was coming from. Now, in his conversations with Williams in the first years of the twenty-first century, that dynamic reappeared in even more powerful ways. Calling from his office in that very same building, Williams drew upon his own life experiences, bringing a nuanced understanding to his conversations with Wallace and coming to deeply respect a man he had never met.

"You listen to Perry and he's talking about playing at Mississippi State in Starkville, Ole Miss cancels its game, that has an impact on you," Williams recalled. "And I think that if you've experienced some of that, you understand it. People don't understand just how much that hurts. To be able to keep going through that is phenomenal. Perry Wallace is a hero. There's no other way to say it. He's a hero. You talk about the [*Tennessean*] story that came out after his last game, and what he endured after that. The ungrateful people were the ones who criticized him. He didn't have to stay here and go to school. Perry did more for Vanderbilt than Vanderbilt ever could have done for him."

Heard had maintained that for integration to work at Vanderbilt, it had to be more than a case of whites accommodating blacks. The effort had to be deeper than that; black culture and consciousness had to become engrained in the Vanderbilt culture itself. In his candid remarks about Vanderbilt's indebtedness to Wallace and in taking the symbolic step to retire his number, Vice Chancellor Williams was carrying out, nearly a half century later, the vision Heard identified. Williams believed that it was only by acknowledging its history, a flawed past in some cases, that Vanderbilt could live up to its full potential as the national university Heard had first imagined it to be.

Wallace was inducted into the Vanderbilt Athletic Hall of Fame as part of the Hall's inaugural class on September 12, 2008, by Commodore athletic director David Williams. "Perry did more for Vanderbilt than Vanderbilt ever could have done for him," Williams said. Vanderbilt University Athletic Department.

"I just think you have to own up to who you were before you can change who you are," Williams said. "When I came in 2000, sitting around the management table, we'd talk about what was the future goal for Vanderbilt. You'd hear that we want to be like the Ivy League, or Stanford, and they were all much more diverse than Vanderbilt. I'm not sure the people here had been told or listened or cared about what was standing in their way, and there were a number of things. If you want to be diverse, and one population is African American, there's some things you have to do as a university. My first year, I went out and talked to a number of black graduates, and I got almost the exact same thing: 'I got a great education, but I hated it there.' Our plan was, how do you change that? I always thought first you have to address the past. You can't redo the past, but you can try to correct some things. My advice was you need to remedy that; it's not too late. And you need to own up to what you were. It was a different time. People can understand that. They're not going to judge you for what you were, they're judging you for what you are. And what you are ain't that good. So change things. And as you do, you'll see people migrate to you."

Part of Williams' strategy was to transform the university's historical low points into pivot points for change. In addition to retiring Wallace's number, Vanderbilt would in future years name a new university dormitory after Walter Murray, welcome Reverend Lawson back to campus as a professor at the Divinity School, and induct Wallace into the inaugural class of the Vanderbilt Athletic Hall of Fame. An especially poignant scene played out quietly at a corner table as guests mingled in the minutes before the Hall of Fame ceremony, when Wallace and Lawson came face to face for the first time ever. Lawson, whom Martin Luther King had once called "the leading theorist and strategist of nonviolence in the world," reached out his hand to an "amazed" Wallace. "You're a real pioneer," Lawson said. "I'm a real pioneer because you were a real pioneer first," Wallace replied.

In Williams' estimation the university's steps to mend relationships with Reverend Lawson and Wallace had a significant impact on African Americans' opinions of the school. "It took a courageous university to stand up and say, 'We did stuff that wasn't cool, but we want to reach out and do what we can now,'" he said. "To me, the whole concept of Perry Wallace and Reverend Lawson, I found that to be absolutely intriguing. You mean the first African American to play basketball in this league was from this city and went to this school and you all aren't waving banners about it? You're not telling stories about it? You're one of the homes of the civil rights movement and you're not proud of that? I remember some older people telling me, 'We don't know if we should retire Perry's number because he was a troublemaker. He said bad things about us.' And my response was, '*You* did bad things to *him*.' It's kind of like truth is always the best defense."

Wallace was more than flattered by the call from Williams; in the days leading up to his return to Nashville, he told one reporter that he was looking forward to the jersey retirement ceremony so much that "it's almost scary." He was proud of the fact that he would return to Nashville in "good shape," not only in a physical sense (which he was), but in every possible way. This was not a case of the old alma mater trotting out a relic with hat in hand, conjuring sympathy for a broken soul. Nor did Wallace return as a bitter man, only grudgingly accepting a welcome that was long overdue. Instead, Wallace returned to town at peace with himself and with his past, not only forgiving of Vanderbilt but proud of the institution for taking a stand in the midst of a reactionary South during a volatile period in American history. He also found forgiveness for the people who had tormented him in gymnasiums around the SEC, characterizing himself as a "staunch defender of their humanity and many fundamental aspects of their culture." In seeking to preserve his own peace of mind in the aftermath of his Vanderbilt experience, to avoid becoming the "monster" he had described in his address to Chancellor

Heard, it was necessary, Wallace believed, that he respect the humanity of his most hurtful adversaries. Learning to be fair and objective in his view of other people, he said, was an exceedingly powerful tool in that it allowed him to "see straight." It was an educational process he started way back on those road trips to the deepest reaches of Dixie. "I tried to observe these people when they weren't trying to destroy me," Wallace recalled. "It helped me demystify the fearful, intimidating image of whites and the resulting sense of inferiority that Jim Crow segregation tended to instill in many of us blacks. I could see whites as people, with both good and bad characteristics. It was very important for me to see these people going about their ordinary lives, to see that in those moments they didn't seem to be devils with horns and tails." And in that respect, Wallace said, he was not only the most ironic defender of southern whites "but also one of the most credible ones."

In his return to Nashville, Wallace recognized the transformational opportunity that came with the spotlight, a chance to use the moral authority the occasion brought with it to make thoughtful statements on race and his personal experience that would continue to foster progress. "So even though [the jersey retirement] was about me, I didn't make it about me," Wallace recalled. "I took it and said, 'OK, this is a glorious thing, this is a wonderful thing, and there is a lot of power. Too much that is too powerful for me to just take it and bask in it and not take it and use it as a moment to inspire, to inform.' My question was, 'What could I do with it that was productive for Vanderbilt and for people in general?'"

In addition to the healing and the sharing and educating, Wallace had other important objectives in returning to Nashville. One goal was to support what Williams and others were accomplishing at Vanderbilt. From a distance he could see that while the university had continued its path toward greater prestige and presence in the world, now there was also progress in terms of diversity and other social justice goals. Wallace believed that his reconnection with Vanderbilt would boost those efforts.

And perhaps most important, there was the impact his return might have on Godfrey Dillard's relationship and legacy with Vanderbilt. Wallace recognized that in the telling of his story, Dillard provided a compelling counterpoint—but unfairly so. The problem was never Godfrey Dillard, he believed. It was the time and place in which Dillard operated. "It still amazes me that Godfrey was so often characterized—actually demonized—as being excessive, or arrogant, or threatening, or something extreme," Wallace said. "The problem was the environment. It was ignorant and unexposed to a personality like his and it was instinctively intolerant of him because he was black." It was during this same time, Wallace said, that many white Americans were similarly outraged at the behavior of Muhammad Ali. Ali's presence, along with the 1968 Olympics protestors, against the backdrop of Black Power and civil rights activities, all generated what Wallace believed to be a particularly paranoid and hysterical reaction to Dillard. "I had never really been able to do something that might really help create some justice for him. Then it occurred to me that if people can be made comfortable with me, maybe that will provide an opportunity for some acknowledgment, some acceptance—some justice—for Godfrey."

In interviews he gave to the Nashville media before he returned for the ceremony, Wallace made it clear that he would strike a conciliatory tone upon his return. Though some friends encouraged Wallace to be outspoken about the injustices he had endured, he resisted the temptation. "I knew what I was doing," he recalled. "It was about principles and practicalities, roots and wings. In both the most practical and the most principled ways, my decision about how to approach this situation was to promote the so many good things." Vanderbilt was to be admired, he said, "for being very good about seeing the future and being willing to take some risks in that direction. I think you have to measure them as much about what they have done and what they're willing to risk doing as you do on what they might not have done. All you need to do is think about all the institutions and people, then and now, who are not willing to take a chance on investing positively in the future. I think it's a very special institution."

Wallace had returned to Nashville alone for the 1989 speech to the Commodore Club, but when it came time for his jersey retirement ceremony, he brought Karen and Gabby along with him. The ceremony was set to take place just before tip-off of the February 21, 2004, game against LSU, "Perry Wallace Day" in Nashville as proclaimed by Mayor Bill Purcell. Wallace made the rounds on campus before the game, joining his old friend Vereen Bell for a panel discussion and a viewing of the students' documentary about him, and then, at the invitation of Commodore basketball coach Kevin Stallings, speaking to the Vanderbilt team for nearly an hour. "[Stallings] wanted me to talk about race as well as basketball," Wallace recalled. "He wanted it to be a learning experience for his team." It was an emotional moment for many of the Commodores, who, unlike previous generations of players, knew Wallace's story. Senior Russell Lakey, an African American point guard from California, said that all he wanted to do was shake Wallace's hand and say thank you. "I told them that I was older than they were, and I have gray hair, but we are part of a family with a magnificent heritage," Wallace recalled. "You've got to understand that there is a line that connects us, that connects us back through time, and it's a line that contains the same kind of ingredients: a certain excellence in education, and an education that has to be used to be productive in society, to help society and others." Stallings, who would go on to break Skinner's record for most victories by a Vanderbilt coach, said the "inspirational" session he and his players spent with Wallace was one of the finest moments he'd ever experienced in basketball.

Waiting courtside for the ceremony to begin before tip-off, Wallace caught up with the friends and family members he had invited to share the moment with him, including a contingent of old friends from Pearl High School, for whom the 1966 title game against Memphis Treadwell remained their strongest memory of Memorial Gym. There, too, were Bill Ligon, by then a successful Nashville attorney, and Godfrey Dillard, an attorney and judge splitting time between Detroit and Atlanta, back on campus for the first time since he had confronted Henry Hecht. Dillard was still bruised by his Vanderbilt experience, but it was now a distant part of an otherwise content and successful life. He had last spent significant time with Wallace back at George Washington University, when he was preparing for a career in international diplomacy, and that dream of serving the country and helping people overseas had come true. Dillard, who, like Wallace, had learned to speak French, joined the State Department and spent two years in the Democratic Republic of the Congo (Zaire) as deputy consul general. He returned to Michigan and resumed a prominent legal career there, reaching the pinnacle of his profession when he argued before the US Supreme Court on the winning side of an Affirmative Action case involving the University of Michigan. By the time he returned to Nashville for Wallace's ceremony, his stint at Vanderbilt seemed remote, like a bad dream. He had overcome the feelings of hatred for whites that threatened to eat him up inside, coming to the conclusion that there was too much to enjoy in life to be consumed by negativity. Still, he credited much of his career success to the motivation his Vanderbilt experience provided him. "They're going to regret it," was his mantra. "Godfrey Dillard will not disappear. I will not be a failure. And when I succeed, they won't be able to claim me."

While the ceremony brought Perry Wallace's Vanderbilt experience full circle, it would only just begin that process for Dillard; but begin it did. Earlier in the day of the jersey retirement, Dillard attended a campus luncheon with Wallace. After the emcee introduced Dillard to the crowd ("I was kind of surprised they did that," he recalled), an aging professor Dillard did not recognize approached him. "Godfrey, I want to apologize for what happened to you," the mystery man said. "Not everybody agrees with what happened to you at that time." Unbeknownst to Dillard, a similar conversation had taken place five years earlier, on the deathbed of John Bibb, the former *Tennessean* sports editor who had covered the Commodores throughout Skinner's tenure. John Seigenthaler, the longtime editor of the paper, recalled sitting beside Bibb and Skinner on what turned out to be Bibb's last living day: "I said, 'Bibb, what mistakes did Skinner make? What were his biggest mistakes?' He said, 'Well, he didn't make many, but he retired too soon' and a couple of

Perry Wallace is flanked by Godfrey Dillard and Bill Ligon at Wallace's jersey retirement ceremony on Feb. 21, 2004. Dillard turned to Wallace and said, "Perry, they've got more black cheerleaders now than there were black students back in our day." Vanderbilt University Athletic Department.

things like that and then he said, 'And then there was Dillard.' And Roy said, 'What do you mean?' And Bibb said, 'I always said you were wrong on that one.' I knew who Dillard was but I didn't even remember how he had left. Bibb knew. He said, 'You were wrong to let him go.' It went over my head. I had thought he had left because of his injury. I woke up at nine o'clock the next morning and Bibb was dead." Slowly, in the years that followed the jersey retirement ceremony, Dillard would be written back into Vanderbilt's history, and he achieved a measure of closure. One year, when Black History Month facts appeared on the Memorial Gym scoreboard, Dillard's name was listed alongside Wallace's. Another year, his photograph appeared on a Vanderbilt game ticket along with other former Commodores, the only instance of a player who never appeared in a varsity game receiving such an honor. And like Wallace, he was occasionally invited back to campus to meet with student groups. Speaking to a black Vanderbilt fraternity several years after the jersey retirement, he told the students that though he believed he had been shortchanged in terms of his athletic career, he did not allow that to stifle his dreams. "I told them failure or setbacks do not have to be the end of the game or a slippery slide down the slope into oblivion," he recalled. "It can be an opportunity, a chance for a fresh start—a new beginning. What is necessary is a realistic assessment of who you are, what you want to be and how to get there. I told them I decided that I was going to make those choices, not somebody else. So, I picked myself up, dusted myself off, and went to work at being happy."

Surrounded by fourteen thousand Vanderbilt fans for the first time since 1970, Wallace stood in the center of the familiar, wide court that Edwin Keeble had dreamed up in Paris. Supporters in the crowd included Kevin Grady, the classmate who had organized the Raven ceremony and had become an attorney in Atlanta, and Rod Freeman, the teammate Wallace had helped register for engineering classes. The year after Wallace graduated, Freeman was given Wallace's number 25 jersey—literally. In those days, uniforms were handed down year after year. Looking out at Wallace, Freeman turned to his wife and joked that it was his jersey, too, that they were retiring that night. A handful of recognizable faces, thousands of people seeing and hearing Wallace for the first time in their lives. The alums in sections A through E, the students in G through K, the hard-core fans up in 3F and 3L—they all stood in respect, most of them wearing round white stickers with the number 25 stamped in black ink. Wallace was handed a microphone.

"Many years ago, Vanderbilt and I set out on a great and ambitious journey," he said. "A journey about progress and about justice. And tonight we celebrate that journey's great success." The crowd erupted in applause, and Wallace turned and waved to each corner of the gymnasium. He can still see the scene in his mind's eye. "At one point, I cheerily point over to one corner of the gym. In that corner, right on the floor, were Godfrey, Bill Ligon, and a host of former Pearl High teammates, coaches, and teachers. It was subtle, but it was a strong expression to them of my special appreciation for them and their support of me over the years. They all smiled joyfully and pointed back."

In a suite reserved for the Wallace family, Karen felt like she couldn't open her eyes wide enough to take in the beautiful sight, thousands of people standing and applauding for her husband. Perry's sisters were smiling, too, Bessie most proud that her brother had "survived the things he encountered," Jessie impressed that he had handled success with modesty and dignity, and Annie hoping that young people could look to Perry's story and realize that if they strived to do things well, developed their capabilities to the fullest extent, that "there shouldn't be anything that could stop you."

Amid the feelings of love that radiated around him, Wallace momentarily felt a combination of sorrow, self-satisfaction, and good fortune. Here he stood, achieving closure in a joyful setting, when in so many cases throughout history, African Americans who had accomplished significant things had ultimately been cut down in tragic ways. He had to look no further than at his fellow SEC pioneers for proof: Greg Page, the Kentucky football player, killed in practice under mysterious circumstances, his friend Nat Northington leaving UK in despair. Godfrey Dillard run out of town. Henry Harris, the first black player at Auburn, dead by suicide. Tom Payne, the first black player recruited by Rupp at Kentucky, serving time in the penitentiary.

Wallace motioned for Ligon and Dillard to join him out on the court; they too, he felt, deserved applause from the crowd. Smiles all around, Dillard clutching a digital camera in one hand (no lucky crutch this time), acknowledging the fans with a wave of the other. He looked over at the pep band and dancers across the court, and turned to Wallace: "Perry, they've got more black cheerleaders now than there were black students back in our day."

Wallace looked up to the southwest corner of the gym, high above section 3K, and soaked in the sight of the black, white, and gold banner, his name printed in black letters above an oversized white jersey—"Vanderbilt 25." He hoped that as people looked upon the jersey that night and in the years to come, they would appreciate the impact of his contribution "as bearing on equality in sports, but, as with Jackie Robinson, extending out to contribute to progress in some larger ways. I would want them to think of a man from humble beginnings, but with a strong family with strong, solid values and a tremendous determination to live a good, productive life. I want them to think of a man who was more ordinary than some would think, in the sense of having had to struggle at times to find strength, unlike the 'hero' types who almost court danger. My hope also is that they will think of a man who possessed more intelligence, wisdom, and integrity than the world generally accords to a black man, and who dedicated himself constantly to fighting against the signals the world often sent—subtly and otherwise—out to people like me to make us believe we weren't worthy. I strongly wish for my family and the broader society to know this."

Up in that corner of the gym now hung one representation of Wallace's legacy, the stitches in the banner telling a tale decades in the making. In the standard American success story, this would be the emotional conclusion: neglected hero finally gets his due and lives happily ever after. But the real story that night went unnoticed. As the crowd cheered, Wallace turned around and looked across to the other side of the gym, up to the suite where Karen and twelve-year-old Gabby waved back. Thirteen thousand

Wallace, his wife, Karen, and their daughter, Gabby, today live in Silver Spring, Maryland. Wallace, Karen said, "has been a spectacular father." Courtesy of Perry Wallace.

eight hundred and ninety-two people cheered for the man standing at center court and for the legacy represented by that banner now hanging above them. The man they cheered for looked up at his wife and daughter, full of pride. At his core, he was more than a pioneer, more than a symbol: he was a husband and father. Though no one in the gym besides Karen and his other family members knew it, it was in his love and devotion to Gabby that Perry Wallace had made his most satisfying—and most difficult—contribution to this world.

At this moment, he realized better than anyone that public recognition wasn't the apex of his story. His happy ending was ultimately not only about public victories but private ones, within his own family. Despite the challenges of Gabby's childhood, the Wallaces continued undaunted, finding extra money each year to pay for special services and tuition at a school that specialized in serving highly intelligent kids with disabilities, and assembling a group of people to help them who had talent, compassion, or both. And gradually, progress. A family vacation to Karen's beloved Paris, nearly ruined by Gabby's frequent behavioral episodes, remembered instead as a watershed breakthrough, Perry and Karen's patience and improvisation rewarded with a child who suddenly began to enjoy the City of Lights. In the years that followed the jersey retirement, understanding of Asperger's began to improve, and along with the scientific milestones came moments of joy at

Wallace and his daughter, Gabby, on one of the family's visits to Paris, a city Karen fell in love with during her college days. Wallace said the family's work to help Gabby overcome Asperger's-related obstacles has been his life's "greatest victory." Courtesy of Perry Wallace.

home, Gabby discovering a love for art and computers. She began to enjoy school and became more comfortable around her teachers and classmates, eventually becoming an honor student, graduating from high school—with her father serving as commencement speaker ("a powerful and satisfying culmination to a long and poignant journey," Wallace recalled)—and enrolling in a nearby community college. For Wallace, Gabby's progress has been his life's most important victory. "It's the closest thing to a miracle we have ever experienced," Wallace said. "We have won, and won big."

Rising

The office where Bob Warren came to ask for Perry Wallace's forgiveness is much like the others on the fourth floor of the law school at American University, filled with books, filing cabinets, an uncluttered desk, and half-filled shelves, with framed family photographs and academic citations on the walls.

As he stood beside his desk and listened to Warren's simple but profound plea, Wallace's mind raced back to the days that nearly destroyed him, that tested his faith in humanity, that drove him thousands of miles from his hometown. But he also thought of the healing and reconciliation that had come later, and he believed that it wasn't the "good, decent, and humble guys like Bob Warren" who needed to go on living with that sort of regret, anyway. It was quite an irony, Wallace believed, that the highest-caliber people were the ones who felt the most pain; the people who really needed to be seeking forgiveness would never even think to ask.

"We are fine," Wallace assured Warren. "Don't think another thing of it. We were all just kids."

In the years that followed Warren's visit, there were other moments when former classmates approached Wallace to express deep feelings of regret—about those times, about some insensitivity or even some attack on him. At one Vanderbilt reunion event, Wallace stood for an hour with a former classmate, a tall, blond Mississippian. "While others listened to music, had cocktails, and reminisced, I listened to this man's tale, recalling the racist environment in which he grew up, the attitudes he had naturally acquired in it, and his sense of horror once he realized what those views had made of him and his culture," Wallace recalled. "As he spoke, at times trembling, it became clear to me that I had the power to give something to this man. As he took this journey into the core of his soul and that of his culture, a journey of remorse and shame about what bigotry had done to them both, it became clear to me that what would help deliver him to the right place was a certain and proper expression of leadership, a property that people often haven't associated with pioneering but that lies, however subtly, at the core of it. To me, the man had been willing to go that rare distance of sincere, deep reflection, admission, and remorse. I could have simply left him hanging, following the advice that some would surely have given to 'let him suffer.' But it, like the moment with Bob [Warren], was an opportunity to affirm the most enduring values and principles that I had learned—in my family, my community, the South, in America. The real victory is in fighting for the proper human values and then bringing them even to those who had been hateful and recalcitrant. So as he finished, I remember looking him in the eye, shaking his hand, and holding it for a few seconds before we parted. He had been unburdened—and he deserved it."

Such has been the arc of life for this pioneer: power attracted and reimagined, transformed from its most grotesque and hurtful applications to its most beautiful and healing. And if the seat of this power is in Professor Wallace's office at the law school at American University, about as far from Short 26th and the basketball courts of the Old South as one can imagine, it's an unassuming place. A visitor sees no evidence of Wallace's past, no signs of the role he played in changing the face of American sports. No trophies, no action photos, no Vanderbilt memorabilia. And yet, in the back of the room, just barely jutting out from behind one of the filing cabinets near the door—a clue. It's the corner of a framed poster, collecting dust. Only Wallace knows it's there. And in this simple poster, the whole story. HIGH ASPIRATIONS, it reads. And above those words, a photograph—a young African American boy holding a basketball, looking up at what appears to be an impossibly tall goal. From time to time, Perry Wallace will get up from his desk and walk over to the filing cabinet, pull out the poster, stare, and reflect. He's that boy again, back on the playground in North Nashville, eyes fixed on the rim, bouncing that ball and running, leaping, rising, rising some more. And as he rises, in pursuit of his "freedom song," the indelible images of a rich and complicated American life flit by, like individual frames in a movie reel gradually picking up steam.

Short 26th, All-City Band,

Big Daddy Lattin,

Pearl High

> Rising

White City Park,

University Church of Christ,

Kirkland Hall

> Rising

Heard, Dillard, Skinner, Murray

> Rising

Starkville, Oxford, Impact, Raven

> Rising

Graduation, Philly, Columbia, DC

> Rising. Rising

And finally, the goal

Karen, Gabby,

Love, Healing

> WOOMP!

> > Slam dunk.

Acknowledgments

The roots of this book trace back to 1989, when I read an article on Perry Wallace and Godfrey Dillard written by my sportswriting mentor at Vanderbilt University, Dave Sheinin (now of the *Washington Post*). Picking up on Dave's work, I called Perry and interviewed him for a term paper for Yollette Jones' black history class. Little did I know that this class existed thanks to the work of Perry, Godfrey, and their classmates, who pushed so hard for such a course in the late 1960s. Professor Jones encouraged me to pursue a topic that brought together three of my greatest interests—sports, history, and writing—and I gained confidence that I could make it as a student at Vanderbilt.

The reason I had come to Vanderbilt was because the university offered one of the most unusual and generous grants anywhere: the full-tuition Fred Russell–Grantland Rice sportswriting scholarship. My father happened to notice a poster on the wall at my high school promoting the scholarship; otherwise, I never would have applied to Vanderbilt or heard the story of Perry Wallace. Thank you to my Austin (Texas) High journalism teacher, Peggy Morton, for preparing me to apply for and win such a life-changing scholarship, and thanks most of all to Fred Russell, as well as Charles Cella and the Thoroughbred Racing Association, for their support of a grant that has made an education at Vanderbilt possible for so many kids over the decades. I had the good fortune to know Mr. Russell for the last fifteen years of his life and was in awe of the man every second I spent around him. The direction of my life has been shaped for the better because of Mr. Russell and his scholarship, and for that I am forever grateful.

I spent most of my time outside class working at the school newspaper, the *Vanderbilt Hustler*. During my term as sports editor, I wrote a few columns on Perry, making the case that the school's recreation center should be named after him. The effort failed, but in spending so much time covering

Vanderbilt sports and hanging around the Athletic Department, I lucked my way into a job in the Sports Information Department. Thanks to Paul Hoolahan, Kevin Kade, Lew Harris, Tony Neely, and Rod Williamson for putting me to work and giving me incredible opportunities as a rookie, and to Jan van Breda Kolff for his kindness and encouragement while I served as the media contact for his Vanderbilt basketball teams.

After five years in the Athletic Department and a year in St. Petersburg, Florida, where I was fortunate to work under Rick Vaughn as the Tampa Bay (Devil) Rays' first media relations manager, I returned to Nashville in late 1998 to join McNeely Pigott & Fox Public Relations, an amazing place that has been my home ever since. Thank you to all my talented colleagues at MP&F over the years, and especially to the other partners—Mark McNeely, Mike Pigott, David Fox, Katy Varney, Keith Miles, and Alice Chapman—for allowing me to pursue my dream of writing this book outside my "day job." Mark, I only printed out the manuscript a few (dozen) times on company copy paper.

While I first talked to Perry as a Vanderbilt student and stayed in intermittent contact with him over the years, the spark that began the book project came in the kitchen at my future in-laws' house, while Alison and I were enjoying some of her mother Cathy Williams' legendary (and bountiful) appetizers. Alison's father, Doug, knew that I was itching to write a book but was having a hard time coming up with a topic. "What about Perry Wallace?" he said. Eureka! The rest, I'm proud to now say, really is history. Thank you for everything, Doug and Cathy; our little family is lucky to have you play such a big role in our lives.

Within days of Doug's prodding, I began placing the first phone calls and sending the first e-mails to begin what became an eight-year process of research and writing. My first interview was with Roy Skinner. Sitting with Coach Skinner and his wife, Tootsie, I was impressed by the same things that those who knew him admired for decades: his kindness, humility, and complete lack of pretense.

One of my greatest regrets in writing this book is that one person profiled in it, the Tulane baseball player Steve Martin, passed away in 2013, before I completed the manuscript. If Perry Wallace's story is too often forgotten, then Martin's is forgotten altogether. He was so surprised when I called him for the first time, and it gives me great pleasure to tell part of his story here.

The book would not have been possible without the help and support of many of Wallace's contemporaries at Vanderbilt, especially Jerry Southwood, a former Commodore player and assistant coach who met with me several times at the outset of the project and gave me an accurate, insiders' view of the program; Paul Wilson and Gene Smitherman, two former student managers, who were constant sources of information and encouragement; and Pat Toomay, one of the smartest and most eclectic men walking the planet, a

Super Bowl champion whose line edits and words of support were golden. Thank you also to all the other former Vanderbilt and Pearl High students, basketball players, coaches, and administrators who shared their memories with me, to the former journalists who gave me the inside stories behind the words I read on microfilm, and to Eddie Crawford, the former Ole Miss basketball coach who was gracious with his time.

I am indebted to the recently retired Vanderbilt historian Lyle Lankford for his tremendous assistance ("Here you go, these are the boxes you need to see") and to Teresa Gray, the university's Special Collections librarian, for her efficient help all these years. Members of the university administration have been eager to see this project succeed from the very beginning, including Vice Chancellor Beth Fortune, Executive Associate Vice Chancellor Robert Early, former Vice Chancellor Michael Schoenfeld, and Vice Chancellor and Athletic Director David Williams, a man who has played as big a role as any in welcoming Perry and Godfrey back into the university community.

Thanks also to the many others who have read the manuscript, assisted with research, or supported the project in other ways, including John Seigenthaler, Bev Asbury, Frye Gaillard, Langston Rogers at Ole Miss, Thomas LeBien, Andrew Blauner, Rafe Sagalyn, Andy Norwood, Geoff Macdonald, Mitch Light, Chad Schmidt, Logan Rogers, Matt Nahay, Willy Daunic, Mike Spayd, Matt Pender, Carl Heinemann, Robert Hicks, John Lombardi, David Stringfellow, Philip Nagy, Meredith Schakel, Maggie Harris, Sandra Adams, Dick Philpot, Andrew Derr, Meg Downey, Maria De Varenne, Scott Stroud, Ricky Rogers, Sam Heys, Demetrius Walker, Linda Wynn, Curtis Wilkie, Matthew Gillespie, Christie Hauck, Rod Freeman, Kevin Grady, Terry Thomas, Richie Weaver at Tulane, Andrea Blackman, Beth Odle, David Ewing, Marcia Masulla, Kendall Hinote, Julie Schoerke, Kevin Kazlauskas, Jim Patterson, James Crumlin, Howard Gentry, Kent Oliver, Beth Gebhard, Niki Coffman, George Largay, Brooks Harper, Jessi Grant, Erin Mercer, Annakate Ross, Megan Robinson, Margaret McCarthy, Nikolett Juhasz, Carrie Morris, Jessica Pawlarczyk, Hayden Williams, and Sarah and Tom Vander Schaaff (and my sweet nieces Heidi and Ava).

I am grateful to my editor at Vanderbilt University Press, Michael Ames, for his deft editing and enthusiastic encouragement. Michael believed in the importance of this book from the very beginning, and it gives me great pride to go to press with Vanderbilt, bringing Perry's story, and in a smaller sense, my own, full circle. Thank you also to Betsy Phillips, Joell Smith-Borne, Dariel Mayer, Gene Adair, Sue Havlish, Grant Maxwell, Jenna Phillips, Mary McClintock, and Bruce Gore for their roles in making this book come to life.

It has given me tremendous pleasure to tell Godfrey Dillard's story in these pages. I spent a memorable day with Godfrey at his Atlanta home and have corresponded with him numerous times over the last eight years. I never fail to be impressed with his graciousness, sense of humor, penetrating insights, and optimism.

There is no finer man than Perry Wallace. He's brilliant, funny, and considerate; compassionate, forgiving, and hopeful. If my two young children grow up with half the character, wisdom, and grace as Perry Wallace, they will succeed beyond measure. Thank you also to Perry's brilliant wife, Karen Smyley, and to three of his equally wonderful sisters—Annie, Bessie, and Jessie—who sat down with me for a memorable group interview.

Thank you to my incredibly supportive (and cool) parents, David and Linda Maraniss. Their encouragement throughout this project is matched only by the lessons they have taught me since birth on the notion of unconditional love. I started tagging along with my mom and dad when they were only twenty years old; how fun it has been to have such a close and easy relationship with them ever since. I am so proud to hand you guys a copy of this book! I regret that my late grandparents, Elliott and Mary Maraniss and Ritchey and Pat Porter, are not around to read this. All four of them loved to read; I suspect heaven has completely gone the e-book route, so maybe they can download a copy.

Finally, where do I begin in thanking my spectacular wife, Alison? I've been working on this book almost as long as we've been together, certainly longer than we've been married. For the last eight years, after dinner or getting the kids to bed, she'd go one way and I'd go another, off to write or conduct an interview. If I had a free moment on the weekend, I'd spend it on the book—all with her encouragement. We got married, bought a house, moved, had two kids; the constants were the book and her love. Not only that, she came through with some crucial edits just as I was completing the manuscript. And to sweet Eliza and Charlie, ages four and one, how lucky Alison and I are to have you in our lives. I hope that one day you will read this book and discover some real heroes. I love you with all my heart.

Notes

CHAPTER 1

1   **Bob Warren sat alone in the back of a taxi.** Interviews with Perry Wallace and Bob Warren.

CHAPTER 2

2   **His parents, Perry Wallace Sr. and Hattie.** Description of Wallace family history and life before Perry was born drawn from a memorable group interview with three of Wallace's sisters, Annie, Bessie, and Jessie.

2   **The South remained overwhelmingly rural.** Nearly thirty thousand people migrated to Nashville's Davidson County in the 1920s, accounting for more than half of the county's population growth in that decade. Doyle, *Nashville since the 1920s* (Knoxville: University of Tennessee Press, 1985), xiii, 35.

3   **As late as 1940.** Ibid., 36.

3   **The city where Perry and Hattie began.** Jesse Burt, *Nashville: Its Life and Times* (Nashville: Tennessee Book Company, 1959), 1, 52, 55, 59, 61, 69.

4   **Rather, there were institutions.** Jefferson Street United Merchants Partnership website, *jumptojefferson.com*.

5   **The Wallaces believed that a strong education.** Hattie enjoyed reading her kids' schoolbooks. "She would often sit by a window, gazing out of it toward the sky and then, with a look of great calm and pleasure, begin to read," Wallace recalled. "I learned from her how to 'steal away' into a place where I could feel secure and good about learning and developing."

6   **the attention of boys at Hadley Park.** Located on the site of a former plantation, the thirty-four-acre Hadley Park was established in 1912 and is considered the first US park built for African-Americans. In 1873 Frederick Douglass addressed former slaves from the front porch of the Hadley house, which stood until 1948. Park history drawn from "Nashville's Civil Rights Movement—A Walking and Driving Tour," published by Historic Nashville, Inc., and available at the Nashville Public Library.

9   **In his voluminous study.** David Halberstam, *The Children* (New York: Random House, 1981), 22, 110. Halberstam covered the sit-ins as a reporter for the *Tennessean*.

9   **True as all this may have been.** Doyle, *Nashville*, 224.

9   "By the 1950s." Ibid., 235.

10   In what became a national model. Halberstam, *The Children*, 53.

10   As gradual and conservative as the plan was. Doyle, *Nashville*, 235.

10   Vanderbilt English professor Donald Davidson. Nashville school integration events, ibid., 237–42.

12   escape to new worlds. Wallace's first music teacher was an accomplished touring musician named J. D. "Chick" Chavis, who at that point, like other fine black musicians in the area, was teaching in the public schools. Chavis invested in his pupil not only his penchant for rigorous, methodical study but also his reflections on music and life.

12   It was a friendship. Interview with Donna Murray.

13   deeper into the heart of black Nashville. "There is a certain metaphoric irony here," Wallace recalled, "in that it was black institutions and communities that would provide me and many others with the protection and nurturing that would empower my journey into the larger American mainstream—which in turn would create a brain drain that would diminish the resources and place of the institutions and communities."

13   James Lawson, a black divinity school student. Doyle, *Nashville*, 245.

15   Perry rode out to the country with his father. "Daddy wanted to toughen me up, fearing that as a mama's boy I would be easy pickings in a tough, cruel world," Wallace recalled. "So in summers during that preteen and teen period, many things got worked in—including stints in the country where I got to work in the fields and spend days outdoors, a cultural aspect of respect for the country that both parents shared strongly and with a certain nostalgic longing."

CHAPTER 3

20   In the days before integration siphoned. David Maraniss, *Rome 1960: The Olympics That Changed the World* (New York: Simon and Schuster, 2008).

20   McClendon would go on. Nelson George, *Elevating the Game: Black Men and Basketball* (Lincoln: University of Nebraska Press, 1992), 86–90.

20   Meanwhile, black high school basketball. Ibid., 83.

21   I was the only white coach in the stands. George, *Elevating the Game*, 134; Gene Pearce, "Tennessee's Glory Road," TSSAA (article PDF e-mailed to author).

22   But for now, Lattin was about to enroll. Frank Fitzpatrick, *And the Walls Came Tumbling Down: Kentucky, Texas Western, and the Game That Changed American Sports* (New York: Simon and Schuster, 1999), 161.

22   his asthma was worsened by fear, nerves, and excitement. "Fear was a primary tool of slavery, and then segregation in the South," Wallace said decades later. "Even when it wasn't spoken about, there was a layer of it in the black community. It played its own hidden role in the way many black people walked, talked, lived. This is a subtle point, but it is true and it is powerful."

25   Pearl traced its roots all the way back to 1883. Pearl High history from Patrick Connolly feature story in the *Tennessean*, July 26, 1996, and interviews with Lee Hayden, Tony Moorman, Donna Murray, Michael Vinsang, and Linda Wynn. Pearl closed in 1983, but the building is now home to the Martin Luther King Magnet High School.

29   Pearl had won its first. Gene Pearce, *Field of Dreamers: Celebrating Tennessee High School Sports* (Hermitage, TN: Tennessee Secondary School Athletic Association, 2005), 178.

30   "Whose cigarettes are those?!" Interview with Tony Moorman.

32   The first stitch had come undone. Writer Andy Telli generously shared a series of articles (in Word document form), the first of which was titled "Ryan-Pearl Game Made History 40 Years Ago," which he wrote on the fortieth anniversary of the Ryan-Pearl game for the *Tennessee Register*, the newspaper of the Diocese of Nashville.

32   In fact, the voluntary merger. Gene Pearce, *Field of Dreamers*, 177.

33   Then, nearly a decade after admitting. Telli, "Ryan-Pearl Game."

33   And then Ryan coach Bill Derrick. Ibid.

34   Interest in the game was so overwhelming. Ibid.

34   On the one hand, he had been invited. *Tennessean*, January 8, 1965.

35   In Washington, DC, President Johnson delivered. The Learning Network, "Lyndon Johnson Outlines 'Great Society' Plans," *New York Times*, learning.blogs.nytimes.com/2012/01/04/jan-4-1965-lyndon-johnson-outlines-great-society-plans.

35   In downtown Nashville, Memphis attorney. *Nashville Banner*, January 5, 1965.

36   I thought if this is the B-team. Telli, "Ryan-Pearl Game."

36   Irish guard Pat Sanders. Ibid.

36   Cue Willie Brown. Brown would become the first African-American basketball player at nearby Middle Tennessee State University. Having preceded Wallace as a pioneer, Brown, Wallace recalled, was "helpful and encouraging about how to operate in integrated settings." Brown died in a motorcycle accident in Stamford, Connecticut, in 1975. Father Ryan High School retired his number, not just in basketball but in all sports, in 2013.

36   One Pearl fan had brought. *Tennessean*, letter to the editor, January 9, 1965.

37   I had a very special place in my heart. Telli, "Ryan-Pearl Game."

37   Ryan's players and fans celebrated. *Banner*, January 5, 1965.

37   fans should have to pay another $1.25. Ibid.

38   "Walt," he said to Fisher. Interview with Walter Fisher.

CHAPTER 4
43   Here's Ted McClain. Interview with Tony Moorman.

46   On his recruiting visit to Iowa. Interview with Perry Wallace.

47   In the story, Russell talked about. *Sports Illustrated*, November 18, 1963.

CHAPTER 5
49   The university had been financed. University history, from Bill Carey, *Commodores, Chancellors and Coeds: A History of Vanderbilt University* (Knoxville, TN: Clearbrook Press Publishing, 2003), 193, 244, 257–72.

56   "For our country," he said. Alexander Heard, *Speaking of the University: Two Decades at Vanderbilt* (Nashville: Vanderbilt University Press, 1995), 35.

56   He was a sports fan. Interview with Connie Heard.

56   On some campuses. Heard, *Speaking of the University*, 32.

56   In a confidential report. Jason Parker, Vanderbilt thesis on Perry Wallace, 1995, Vanderbilt Archives and Special Collections (hereafter referred to as "Archives").

57   When Coach Roy Skinner climbed. Interview with Roy Skinner.

58   That winning basketball games mattered. Story of the Vanderbilt-Kentucky 1947 basketball game and early history of Commodore hoops, from Roy Neel, *Dynamite: 75 Years of Vanderbilt Basketball* (Nashville: Burr-Oak Publishers, 1975), 11–12, 69-76. A onetime basketball team manager and *Nashville Banner*

sportswriter, Neel went on to a career in politics and served as a close advisor to Al Gore. His son, Sam, later became a law student at American University, where Wallace taught.

59   some historians say *the* first. Charles Rosen, in his book *Scandals of '51: How Gamblers Almost Killed College Basketball* (1978; repr., New York: Seven Stories Press, 1999), 10, writes that Vanderbilt fielded the nation's first men's varsity in 1893.

62   Decades later, he attributed his early failures. Interview with Roy Skinner.

63   *This is the dining hall.* Interview with Bill LaFevor.

63   He came into the house. Neel, *Dynamite*, 123.

64   He'd even turned down a scholarship. Interview with Perry Wallace.

64   My parents knew people. Frye Gaillard article on Perry Wallace titled "The Long Road Home," *Vanderbilt Magazine*, Fall 2004, 44–51.

65   Clyde Lee walked him around. Interviews with Clyde Lee and Perry Wallace.

65   Perry Wallace did not want to be. Interview with Perry Wallace.

67   "Listen to what I heard." Interview with Perry Wallace.

CHAPTER 6

69   I think the region will be. *Banner*, March 10, 1966.

69   Beloved *Banner* sports editor. *Banner*, March 11, 1966.

70   The rim itself would be carried back. Interview with Linda Wynn.

70   The rims at Vanderbilt *Banner*, March 11, 1966.

71   They are probably the best. *Banner*, March 12, 1966.

72   In the spring of 1965. Pearce, *Field of Dreamers*, 62.

73   Even football coaches showed up. *Banner*, March 17, 1966.

73   Cub reporter Bob Baldridge. *Tennessean*, March 18, 1966.

73   Roy Skinner from Vanderbilt. *Tennessean*, March 15, 1966.

73   his temperature still read 103 degrees. *Tennessean*, March 19, 1966.

74   "Hampton," he said. *Tennessean*, March 16, 1966.

75   Do you hear them?! *Tennessean*, March 18, 1966.

75   he thought the Pearl coach's grip. Ibid.

76   I think it's the pressure. Ibid.

76   Friday, March 18, 1966. *Banner* and *Tennessean*, March 18, 19, 1966.

77   The locker room scene this time. *Tennessean*, March 19, 1966.

77   Passing by the Pearl team. Ibid.

77   decided to stop taking notes on Treadwell. Ibid.

77   thinking Treadwell had lost. *Banner*, March 19, 1966.

78   I told you we could play. Ibid.

78   five times in the previous seven years. Ibid.

79   You're not only representing. Interview with Walter Fisher.

80   The Tigers wasted no time. Pearl-Treadwell game footage (provided to author in DVD form by TSSAA).

80   He called out. Interview with Walter Fisher.

80   *Did you hear that some of their players.* Interview with Curry Todd.

80   To the modern eye, the black-and-white footage. Game footage.

82   He could read about 1776. Interview with Walter Fisher.

82   *Thank you, Jesus, we pulled this one off.* Ibid.

82   And here comes Richard Baker. Game footage.

83   We weren't leaving without that trophy. *Tennessean*, March 20, 1966.

83   I'm especially happy for the other. *Banner*, March 21, 1966.

86   In the days leading up to the tournament. Interview with Tony Moorman.

86   Perry Wallace drank his chocolate shake. Interview with Perry Wallace.

CHAPTER 7

87   John Oldham, the head coach. *Banner*, March 21, 1966.

88   In El Paso, Lattin was still the intimidator. Don Haskins, *Glory Road: My Story of the 1966 NCAA Basketball Championship and How One Team Triumphed against the Odds and Changed America Forever* (New York: Hyperion, 2006), 130.

88   "Just dunk it like they ain't never seen it dunked." Haskins, *Glory Road*, 183.

88   "Take that, you white honky." Fitzpatrick, *And the Walls*, 210.

89   When a Kentucky baby is born. Michael Bradley, *Big Blue: 100 Years of Kentucky Wildcats Basketball* (Saint Louis: Sporting News, 2002), 12.

89   A point-shaving scheme. Russell Rice, *Adolph Rupp: Kentucky's Basketball Baron* (Champaign, IL: Sagamore Publishing, 1994), 203.

89   We play teams from the Big Ten. Fitzpatrick, *And the Walls*, 46.

89   Rupp was brash, arrogant and antagonistic. Rice, *Adolph Rupp*, 51.

90   In late February 1966, a white Nashville businessman. Interview with Perry Wallace.

90   Both Beard and Unseld had been recruited. Fitzpatrick, *And the Walls*, 144–45.

92   Rather than take the relatively painless step. Rice, *Adolph Rupp*, 152.

92   Put another way, as Lancaster said of Oswald. Fitzpatrick, *And the Walls*, 38.

92   sounded like a bigot. Ibid., 140.

92   "immediate all-out effort." Ibid., 136.

92   Speaking of his contentious conversations. Ibid., 141.

92   If they treat me and my boys like that now. Rice, *Adolph Rupp*, 152.

92   He apparently didn't want to be the first. Ibid., 154.

93   It was quite clear after March 1966. Fitzpatrick, *And the Walls*, 28.

93   Many Kentucky fans wouldn't even point. Rice, *Adolph Rupp*, 172.

94   most of them from the South. Haskins, *Glory Road*, 194.

94   Anybody who tells you that our 1966 team. Ibid., 199.

94   Rupp had assured him. Fitzpatrick, *And the Walls*, 221.

94   Wallace was home in Nashville. Interview with Perry Wallace.

94   There was a visit to the *Tennessean* newsroom. *Tennessean*, March 21, 1966.

95   Frontiers president William Harper lauded. *Tennessean*, March 30, 1966.

95   schools director Dr. John Harris. *Tennessean*, March 23, 1966.

95   I'll be perfectly honest. *Tennessean*, March 21, 1966.

96   It was not too much of a surprise. Interview with Jimmy Davy.

97   Because the school had a history. Interview with Perry Wallace.

97   desegregated way back in 1947–48 by Bill Garrett. Tom Graham and Rachel Graham Cody, *Getting Open: The Unknown Story of Bill Garrett and the Integration of College Basketball* (New York: Atria Books, 2006), 129. Garrett had originally enrolled briefly at Tennessee A&I before transferring to Indiana.

97   During his visit to Purdue. Interview with Perry Wallace.

97   *Sports Illustrated*'s Frank Deford labeled. *Sports Illustrated*, February 14, 1966.

97   One such student was senior Van Magers. Interview with Van Magers.

98   He's probably the best rebounding prospect. *Vanderbilt Hustler*, April 15, 1966.

99   the *Tennessean* devoted a two-page spread. *Tennessean*, May 1, 1966.

101   on a tour of his old neighborhood. Interview with Perry Wallace.

102   Over in the *Nashville Banner* newsroom. Interview with Roy Neel.

104   At 4:00 p.m., Wallace picked up. In his article that appeared in the next morning's paper, Davy couldn't help but throw in a jab at the *Banner*, writing that Wallace

had confirmed that the reports published the day before were unfounded. Until he had called Coach Skinner, Wallace said, no one outside his family knew of his decision.

105   Here, in one frame, the photographers. Photograph, *Tennessean*, May 4, 1966.

CHAPTER 8

106   HISTORIC STAY-AT-HOME. *Sports Illustrated*, May 16, 1966

106   VANDERBILT SIGNS SECOND NEGRO STAR. *Banner*, May 11, 1966

107   Dillard's "reverse migration" from the North. Interview with Godfrey Dillard.

107   the integrated Boston-Edison neighborhood. Neighborhood description, from interview with Dillard and the Historic Boston-Edison Association website, *historicbostonedison.org*. Reflecting on Dillard's upbringing, Wallace noted a striking contrast to his own: "I did not grow up around doctors and lawyers and the like. I can see how this gave Godfrey so much more confidence and exposure—and this quite apart from the typical northern bias that often views the South as less advanced and more backward."

111   On May 10, accompanied by a newspaper photographer. *Banner*, May 11, 1966.

CHAPTER 9

112   *"We're* not prejudiced," the men told him. Interview with Perry Wallace.

114   HE WAS REMINDED OF THE FIRST TIME. Perry Wallace, e-mail to author. "Years later, after the Nashville civil rights movement eliminated formal segregation, one could still see the remaining imprint of the outlines where those 'colored only' signs had been. Impressionistically, this imprint, barely noticeable to many, would effectively be a harbinger of sorts. That is, the formal signs were down, but the essentials had not receded. Also, because of habit and for certain strategic reasons, I always go to the back of any bus that I ride."

114   *July 31* In Chicago,. Litany of events in the late summer of 1966 from *Tennessean*, August 1 through September 15.

116   As dads lug trunks and suitcases. *Tennessean*, September 15, 1966.

116   These Vanderbilt freshmen are smart kids. *Hustler*, September 16, 1966.

117   One freshman tells a *Tennessean* reporter. *Tennessean*, September 15, 1966.

117   How would VUceptors react. Sidney F. Boutwell, "Report on Negro Students Given to Arts & Science Faculty on January 16, 1968," Archives.

117   There were blacks on the Vanderbilt campus. Paul Conkin, *Gone with the Ivy: A Biography of Vanderbilt University* (Knoxville: University of Tennessee Press, 1985), 305. I was fortunate to take at least two classes from Professor Conkin at Vanderbilt; he also served as my freshman advisor. One of my strongest memories is from his class on US geographical history. He asked the class if we knew what tree most baseball bats were made of. My friend Mike Csernovicz and I both yelled out, "Ash!"—quite possibly the only time either of us volunteered an answer all semester.

118   It used to be that to have it made. *New York Times*, January 29, 1967.

118   From the tiny Appalachian town of Red Fox. Interview with Bobbie Jean Perdue.

119   Bedford Waters arrived from Knoxville. Interview with Bedford Waters.

119   Carolyn Bradshaw came to Nashville. Interview with Carolyn Bradshaw Morgan.

119   Morris Morgan, from Cedartown, Georgia. Interview with Morris Morgan.

119   Frye Gaillard was raised. Interview with Frye Gaillard.

120   Not five minutes later. Interviews with Godfrey Dillard and Perry Wallace.

120   Conversation came easily to these two. Article by Scott Stroud in the *Lexington*

Herald-Leader, March 1, 1992. As I was working on the manuscript in 2013, it was a great coincidence and thrill to meet Stroud, by then an editor at the *Tennessean*, and realize that he was the same Scott Stroud who had written the 1992 article on Wallace and Dillard.

121   **our Emmett Till.** From *biography.com*: Fourteen-year-old Emmett Till was visiting [from Chicago] relatives in Money, Mississippi, on August 24, 1955, when he reportedly flirted with a white cashier at a grocery store. Four days later, two white men kidnapped Till, beat him, and shot him in the head. The murder attracted tremendous national attention.

CHAPTER 10

122   **The problem with controversy.** *Hustler*, February 28, 1967.

123   **In the meantime, whether it was cause or effect.** Carey, *Chancellors*, 241.

123   **Pretty much the entire social scene.** Interview with Sara Hume

123   **"Typical Vanderbilt Coed."** *Hustler*, October 31, 1967, referring to the "Princeton publication, 'Where the Girls Are.'"

124   **The 948 TVCs on campus.** "December 1966 Geographical Distribution of Vanderbilt University Women Students, 1966–67," Archives.

124   **a campus so sedate that a girl could cause a stir.** "The implication of this grand reality for blacks was clear," Wallace recalled. "For me, while I was not particularly interested in joining a fraternity, it was the 'what's left' of it all, the void, that was problematic. Many people assumed that I should be happy as a second-class citizen—at least I was allowed to live on campus and function around whites." He was left to deal with a phenomenon he said was well known to blacks who operated in the public eye: "the superhero/nobody nature of one's existence, which can be especially maddening because the hypocrisy is so glaring and pronounced."

125   **The chancellor's own life was quite conventional.** Interview with Connie Heard.

125   **He was a voracious and eclectic reader.** Interview with Heard by Neil Skene, January 5, 1973. Archives.

126   **Heard's workday was as regimented.** *Tennessean*, March 20, 1966. Fantastically detailed feature on Heard headlined, "A Man to Change the Climate," by Larry Daughtrey.

126   **"Each university, on the Charles or on the Cumberland."** Heard, *Speaking*, 36.

127   **A university campus is a lively place.** Heard, *Speaking*, 21. "[It] is our nation's democratic doctrine that if an idea is false it should be exposed, and if an idea is dangerous it should be understood," Heard continued. "Weak ideas that you or I may not agree with will not prosper in the open air nor in free debate. And certainly if we know anything from the history of this century it is that strong ideas cannot be beaten by attempting to deny them circulation."

127   **He brought in Norman Thomas.** *Hustler*, May 6, 1970.

127   **"You can be sure," he told students and faculty.** Heard, *Speaking*, 43.

128   **Over the years, it was Werthan.** Interview with Bedford Waters.

128   **Growing up white in segregated Elberton.** Interview with Bev Asbury.

130   **For all his liberalism.** Connie Heard felt that for many of Belle Meade's elite, the Heards were "their token Democrat friends." An oriental rug dealer in town said as much, she recalled. "Mr. Harb always told my father, 'You're the only Democrat I'll sell any rugs to.'"

130   **Heard once told attendees.** Heard, *Speaking*, 51.

CHAPTER 11

131   "So," the professor smirked. Interviews with Donna Murray, Perry Wallace, Vereen Bell, and K. C. Potter.

131   One Sunday in the summer of 1966. Perry Wallace remarks drawn from interviews with Perry Wallace and transcript provided by Wallace of his speech, "The Promise of the Commons," at the dedication of a Vanderbilt dormitory named after Walter Murray, September 4, 2007.

133   You're the only black in the class. "The academic performance of black students," Wallace recalled, "was a matter of great interest and concern among many whites. I had more than a few instances in which professors scrutinized me personally because they thought I hadn't written a paper or performed the pertinent research myself. The good thing about those inquisitions was that they actually had to sit and listen to me speak and express my thoughts, instead of merely imagining how I sounded. In those moments, as they looked on wide-eyed and amazed at my speech and intelligence, I truly discovered the importance of intelligent thought and expression—at least some whites could see better who you were."

135   As many painful racial slights. "This, to me, was one of the most powerful lessons from that experience," Wallace recalled. "The challenge is to somehow be able to detach from the immediate pain of the discrimination and look around to see who all is around you. When you do this, you see that not all whites are the same, even if a lot of them seem to act the same. It's a lesson I first learned from my father, as he reflected on his harsh journey to success."

136   Given the paucity of black men. Interview with Eileen Carpenter. "I was probably everything the TVC was, except I wasn't white. Most of us were eggheads. I'm sure the guys thought I was a conservative prick."

CHAPTER 12

138   It's always a little humorous. *Tennessean*, November 18, 1966.

138   The previous year, an enormous line. *Banner*, November 17, 1966.

139   A St. Louis Cardinals baseball fan. Interview with Roy Skinner.

140   One of the black players Bundy matched up against. Interview with Bob Bundy.

143   One white teammate who made an effort. Interview with Pat Toomay. Toomay went on to a ten-year NFL career with the Dallas Cowboys (winning Super Bowl VI), Buffalo Bills, Tampa Bay Buccaneers (including the infamous 0–14 team in 1976), and Oakland Raiders. He is the author of two acclaimed books on professional football, *The Crunch* and *On Any Given Sunday*.

145   Down at Printers Alley, Suzette Dupree. *Tennessean*, November 19, 1966.

148   It hadn't always been this way. Description of Vanderbilt football history from Fred Russell, *Fifty Years of Vanderbilt Football* (Nashville: Fred Russell and Maxwell E. Benson Publishers, 1938); and Carey, *Chancellors*, 113–15, 166–67, 221–22.

149   College athletics, he believed. Parker thesis, Archives, quoting Harvie Branscomb, *Purely Academic: An Autobiography* (1978). Branscomb set out to rein in college football's influence, but was rebuffed when he tried to convince fellow conference presidents to de-emphasize the sport by eliminating spring practice and bowl games and reducing scholarships. He later unsuccessfully tried to form a Southern Ivy League with schools such as Georgia Tech, Duke, Rice, and SMU.

149   Even Chancellor Heard wasn't above a joke. Interview with John Seigenthaler.

149   was hit by a delivery truck. *Hustler*, November 4, 1966. While George had not inspired the Commodores to many victories, students would never forget his

moment of glory in 1964, when he chased the University of Tennessee's walking horse all the way out of the stadium, and the Commodores beat the rival Vols 7–0.

149 **Effigy hanging became such.** Football player Christie Hauck recalled arriving at Vanderbilt as a freshman that fall and being startled to see his coach hanging in effigy before the first game had even been played. Also, when the freshmen scrimmaged the varsity in preseason drills, Hauck recalled, the freshman team returned the game's opening kickoff for a touchdown.

150 **With campus-wide malaise reaching a crisis.** *Hustler*, November 11, 1966.

150 **Against this backdrop, Tennessean sportswriter John Bibb.** *Tennessean*, November 21, 1966.

150 **The chartered bus rolled north.** Neel, *Dynamite*, 159.

151 **Wallace played along with the bad joke.** Boutwell, "Report on Negro Students."

151 **The Vanderbilt–Western Kentucky game.** *Tennessean*, December 1, 1966.

151 **the largest gathering of people for any campus event.** *Banner*, December 2, 1966.

151 **Tacked to a bulletin board next to the lockers.** Ibid.

152 **As Wallace passed by Coach Skinner.** Neel, *Dynamite*, 159.

153 **Ole Miss coach Eddie Crawford.** *Hustler*, December 2, 1966; *Sports Illustrated*, December 19, 1966.

157 **It was a dramatic scene in its own right.** Interview with Perry Wallace.

157 **Life isn't one big holiday right now.** *Louisville Courier-Journal*, January 7, 1967.

CHAPTER 13

159 **By 1963 Ben Hilburn had been replaced.** *Sports Illustrated*, March 10, 2003. This scene drawn from a thorough accounting of the episode by Alexander Wolff headlined "Ghosts of Mississippi."

161 **Schoolwork and basketball practice.** *Tennessean*, February 27, 1967.

162 **James Meredith had been shot.** *New York Times*, June 27, 1967.

162 **It is possible that the cramped visitors' locker room.** Description of Mississippi State locker room and fan taunts, from interviews with Perry Wallace and Godfrey Dillard.

162 **And then out of the tunnel and onto the court.** *Lexington Herald-Leader*, March 1, 1992.

163 **Mack Finley, a white graduate student.** *Tennessean*, February 22, 2004.

163 **Dillard's uniform grew cold and wet.** *Lexington Herald-Leader*, March 1, 1992.

163 **Before Jackie Robinson.** Jonathan Eig, *Opening Day: The Story of Jackie Robinson's First Season* (New York: Simon and Schuster, 2007), 23–27.

164 **"We were trying to be in denial."** *Vanderbilt Magazine*, Fall 2004.

164 **Dillard's approach could not have been more different.** *Lexington Herald-Leader*, March 1, 1992.

166 **She could hear the crowd.** Interview with Perry Wallace.

CHAPTER 14

167 **The bearded man attracted so much attention.** Description of airport scene, from *Tennessean*, April 8, 1967.

168 **King is openly espousing Communist aims.** *Banner*, April 7, 1967.

168 **Born in Trinidad, Carmichael moved to New York.** Carmichael and SNCC background. Clayborne Carson, *In Struggle: SNCC and the Black Awakening of the 1960s* (1981; repr., with new introduction and epilogue, Cambridge, MA: Harvard University Press, 1995), 2, 3, 21, 162–63, 203, 215, 221.

170 The attendance record of thirty-five hundred. 1967 Impact program, Archives.

170 At the *Nashville Banner*, publisher Jimmy Stahlman. *Banner*, March 25, 1967.

170 WLAC radio managing editor F. C. Sowell. Postcard, March 31, 1967, Archives.

170 Eula Donnell sent a postcard. Postcard dated April 3, 1967, Archives.

170 Nashville Chamber of Commerce executive vice president. *Banner*, March 29, 1967.

170 At American Legion Post 5. Quoted in the March 31, 1967 *WLAC Comment* newsletter by the station's managing editor F. C. Sowell, Archives.

170 Not to be outdone, the Tennessee state senate. *Banner*, April 6, 1967.

170 Nashville rabbi Randall Falk. *Banner*, March 29, 1967.

171 those who would ban Mr. Carmichael. *Tennessean*, April 8, 1967.

171 Vanderbilt Board of Trust member Mary Jane Werthan. Letter dated April 2, 1967, Archives.

171 best college presentation of its kind in the country. 1967 Impact program, Archives.

172 with the first round of invitations mailed. List of speakers invited to Impact '67, Archives.

172 the going rate for comparable speakers. Letter dated October 10, 1966, from Harry Walker Inc. speakers' bureau, Archives.

172 The host and hostess should go. March 24, 1967, memo from Dean Boutwell to Amanda Griffin, Impact committee, Archives.

172 Correspondence with confirmed speakers. Letter to King dated March 15, 1967, Archives.

173 they were greeted by forty-by-sixty-inch. "Impact '67 Display Committee Report" and Appendix A of same, Archives.

173 eighty-five officers, including forty in plain clothes. April 7, 1967, memo by Robert Eager on security arrangements, Archives.

173 Evans delivered Impact's opening speech. *Hustler*, April 11, 1967.

174 rather appear with Carmichael than Thurmond. *Tennessean*, April 8, 1967.

174 $35 billion on an ill-considered war. *Tennessean*, April 8, 1967.

175 Ginsberg led a group of one hundred students. *Hustler*, April 11, 1967.

175 We have received death threats. Interview with Frye Gaillard.

178 "No, you're still not going to let them in." Interview with Perry Wallace.

179 Slaves, obey your earthly masters. *Hustler*, April 11, 1967.

179 A lot of the language you've heard here. Ibid.

179 Someone in the upper balcony. *Tennessean*, April 9, 1967.

180 an article titled "Toward Black Liberation." *Massachusetts Review*, Autumn 1966, 639–51.

182 Dr. Frank Rose. *Hustler*, April 11, 1967.

182 To hell with the laws of the United States. *Banner*, April 5, 1967.

182 the most serious offense turned out to be. *Hustler*, April 11, 1967.

182 "Everything went just beautifully." Ibid.

182 Jean and the kids were prepared to host a meal. Interview with John Seigenthaler.

183 The photographer who called the newsroom. Description of the riots drawn from contemporaneous coverage by the *Tennessean*, *Banner*, and *New York Times*, as well as Carey, *Chancellors*, and Conkin, *Gone*.

184 first major social disorders in the nation in 1967. Conkin, *Gone*, 621.

185 Back at her parents' house, Carpenter. Interviews with Eileen Carpenter, Godfrey Dillard, Bobbie Jean Perdue, Vereen Bell, and K. C. Potter.

185 Cleaver seemed especially disappointed. Cleaver may not have been impressed with the party, but he did meet his future wife, Kathleen Neal, on this trip to

Nashville. Cleaver was covering the event for *Ramparts* magazine while Neal was accompanying Carmichael as a SNCC worker. *Hustler*, April 15, 1969.

186　**Its name? Carmichael Towers.** Interview with K. C. Potter.

186　**With his typically colorful brand of outrage.** *Banner*, April 10, 1967. Heard and Eager were bombarded with criticism in the form of phone calls, letters, and telegrams; a handwritten note from one mother arrived for Eager blasting him for inviting the "Communists" King and Carmichael to campus and suggested that "he and his nigger buddies" move to Africa. Expressions of support arrived as well. Future Tennessee governor and US senator Lamar Alexander, then an aide to Senator Howard Baker, attended the event and upon his return to Washington wrote Eager a note to thank him and to request a copy of Rowland Evans' speech. "I was extremely impressed with the entire Impact week-end and want to congratulate you for the superb job that you did in handling it," Alexander wrote, with no mention of the riots. "Quite frankly, I don't think that anything like that could have happened four years ago when I was a senior at Vanderbilt." When US Army captain David M. Bullock, Judge Advocate General's Corps, flew back to Savannah, Georgia, after spending the weekend in Nashville, his seatmate spent the flight complaining about Carmichael's appearance and mentioned that he planned to call Heard to make his feelings known. "I do not know whether he ever called, but I decided I should write you, if for no other reason than to counteract his objection," Bullock wrote to Heard from Hunter Army Airfield. "I heartily disagree with Mr. Carmichael's activities and professed beliefs, but I would be disappointed in Vanderbilt if she failed to respect her students' maturity and judgment—and her obligation to provide a forum for diverse points of view, however extreme—by preventing his appearance." These letters found in Vanderbilt Archives.

CHAPTER 15

188　**Climbing the stairs outside Kirkland Hall.** Description of students' meeting with Heard, interviews with Perry Wallace, Bev Asbury, and Eileen Carpenter.

189　**We admitted that while many people.** Perry Wallace remarks at dedication of Walter Murray dormitory.

189　**his eyes were opening, his lens widening.** Wallace described this concept to Vanderbilt student Erin Wolfson in a comprehensive November 16, 2004 oral history, Nashville Public Library.

189　**Even if you grew up in segregation.** Interview with Perry Wallace; Wolfson oral history.

191　**Grabbing a small piece of stationery.** Memo dated April 27, 1967, Archives.

195　**Essayist Damion Thomas later wrote.** Thomas, "'The Quiet Militant': Arthur Ashe and Black Athletic Activism," in *Out of the Shadows: A Biographical History of African American Athletes*, ed. David K. Wiggins (Fayetteville: University of Arkansas Press), 290. Thomas credits the theory of the "paradigmatic black man" to the psychiatrists William Grier and Price Cobbs.

196　**first publicly acknowledged indications.** Maureen Smith, "Bill Russell: Pioneer and Champion of the Sixties," in Wiggins, *Out of the Shadows*, 236.

196　**Russell, wrote author David Wiggins.** Wiggins, *Out of the Shadows*, 184.

196　**Wallace recognized that there were two sides.** Ali had been a larger-than-life figure in Wallace's youth. Wallace had a vivid memory of Cassius Clay's visit to Nashville soon after he had won a gold medal at the 1960 Summer Olympics in Rome.

Clay showed up in North Nashville calling on another gold medalist, the track star Wilma Rudolph, who was a student at Tennessee State. "I was at the barbershop, and some of the older folks said that Cassius Clay had come to town in a big ass pink Cadillac driving down Jefferson Street looking for Wilma Rudolph," Wallace recalled. "And one guy in the barbershop said, 'Shit, I'm looking for Wilma Rudolph, too. I hope if he finds her, he has more luck than me.'"

197   Heard, in seemingly placing his career on the line. Conkin, *Gone*, 623.

197   Wallace spoke first, telling the administrators. Interviews with Perry Wallace and Bev Asbury.

198   It seems to me that the principle. Heard, *Speaking*, 101.

CHAPTER 16

201   While his classmates headed out to parties. Interview with Godfrey Dillard.

202   An October *Hustler* editorial complained. *Hustler*, October 6, 1967.

202   Am I giving others a chance. *Hustler*, September 15, 1967.

203   As a Christian and a patriot. *Hustler*, September 17, 1967.

203   A *Hustler* poll released immediately. *Hustler*, November 17, 1967.

203   *Hustler* reporter Chuck Offenburger traveled. *Hustler*, October 24, 1967.

204   That was all guidance from Chancellor Heard. Free speech. Perhaps the greatest testament to Potter's ability to broker campus peace came during an "only at Vanderbilt" anti-Vietnam protest on May 8, 1969. A group of antiwar students, led in part by Paul Menzel, the philosophy student who had befriended Terry Thomas, had planned to protest the "sins of war" not by burning, but by washing an American flag, during a US Navy ROTC ceremony on Alumni Lawn. The students brought a giant wash tub and oversized box of Tide detergent out to the lawn with them, along with the flag they had purchased at, of all places, a nearby John Birch Society bookstore. As they prepared to wash the flag, a group of counterprotestors, including some football players, encircled them, knocking over the tub and roughing up a few of the antiwar kids. Vanderbilt chief of police Robert Blankenship, a World War II vet, called Potter and asked him to come diffuse the situation. "It was all happening right under the big magnolia trees in front of Rand [Hall]," Potter recalled. "The navy band was pumping along and all the little ladies with their hats on were watching the [ROTC] officers with their crisp uniforms on. And the football players were not going to let them wash the flag. It was very Vanderbilt." Potter was late to speak to a gathering of faculty administrators on a subject he detested, campus parking policy, so he had no problem dragging out the scene on the lawn, believing in any case that the longer the standoff persisted, the more emotions would cool off. Decked out in his trademark suit and bow tie, Potter asked whether he could hold the flag until it was decided how the situation would be resolved, and the protestors, who respected his history of tolerance for dissent, acquiesced. When a recent Law School graduate (and future Vanderbilt administrator) named Jeff Carr appeared on the scene and asked whether he could help, Potter sent him over to the Law School library to "see if washing a flag is a violation of the law." By the time Carr returned, the ROTC review had concluded and all the little old ladies had gone home, leaving only the would-be flag washers and their foes. Carr told the group the lawfulness of flag washing depended on the intent; Potter then told the gathering it would be OK if the protestors' intent was to clean the flag, not deface it. The counterprotestors

argued the point until finally Potter broke the impasse: "What if we just sprinkle the flag? That's the way a lot of people are baptized, you know." Menzel and his friends realized there weren't enough campus police on hand to protect them if things grew violent, so they reluctantly agreed. "It was a pretty faint imitation of washing it, but we wanted to get the loggerhead over with, so we said sure, we'll sprinkle the flag. And someone negotiated with [the football players] that they wouldn't bowl us over. It's laughable in retrospect." The sprinkling complete and the protest over, Potter made his way to the faculty gathering, which had already begun. Chancellor Heard called out to Potter before he could begin his remarks on campus parking. "K.C., nobody's going to listen to a thing you say until you tell us what happened over at the flag pole." "Well," Potter deadpanned, "there was a group of students who wanted to make a Baptist out of the flag, and we decided to make a Methodist out of it instead." Interviews with Paul Menzel and K. C. Potter.

205 As if encouraging a baby to crawl. *Atlanta Constitution*, January 12, 1988.

205 "We've botched," she wrote. *Hustler*, October 13, 1967.

206 The father of one Vanderbilt student. Ibid.

206 wrote W. L. Sefton of Jacksonville. *Hustler*, October 17, 1967.

206 Whites are afraid that if they accept the Negro. Harold Davis, quoted in *Hustler*, October 13, 1967.

206 Murray told a *Hustler* reporter. *Hustler*, October 13, 1967.

207 This robs the student of the experience. Ibid.

208 met with Heard on October 10 to press the issue. Memo from Purdy to Heard dated November 17, 1967, Archives.

209 "Henceforth," proclaimed Rule 9, Section 11. Todd Boyd and Kenneth Shropshire, *Basketball Jones: America above the Rim* (New York: New York University Press, 2000), 152.

210 Just a year earlier, UCLA coach John Wooden. *Sports Illustrated*, December 5, 1966.

210 What the committee is upset about. Kareem Abdul-Jabbar, *Giant Steps: The Autobiography of Kareem Abdul-Jabbar* (New York: Bantam, 1983), 160.

211 Wooden was philosophical. *New York Times*, March 30, 1967.

211 "The NCAA," he said, "crapped on Perry." *Hustler*, February 26, 2002.

211 Oh, my God, it made me just sick. Interview with Roy Skinner.

213 The beam came crashing down. *Hustler*, December 1, 1967.

213 black construction worker known simply as Mr. Jake. "I was delighted to see the film *The Butler* debut in 2013 and be so well received," Wallace said. "Forest Whitaker played a black man from the South who served as a butler in the White House for decades. The movie did a wonderful job of bringing to life the complete character of people like Mr. Jake, and it portrayed especially well the intelligence, dignity, and strength that they discreetly retained at their core. As much as I had learned from Mr. Jake and others like him, the one thing that was different about me was that I didn't plan to endure forever. Some way, somehow, I planned to find an end to a life where all you could do was endure some of this treatment. It needed to stop or I needed to leave."

CHAPTER 17

215 The freshman thought it was funny. Interview with Steve Martin.

216 Tulane, a charter member of the Southeastern Conference. *Tennessean*, January 1, 1965.

220 He had undergone a tracheotomy. David Wharton, "The Great Barrier," *Los Angeles Times*, September 3, 2004.

221   **With his friend lying paralyzed.** Nathaniel Northington, with La Monte McNeese, *Still Running: The Autobiography of Kentucky's Nate Northington, the First African American Football Player in the Southeastern Conference* (Bloomington, IN: iUniverse, 2013). By this time, Northington went by "Nate" rather than "Nat."

CHAPTER 18

222   **First came Samantha, the hobbling basset hound.** Detailed description of the atmosphere at a Vanderbilt basketball game in Jim Andrews, "The Spoilers and the Spoiled," *Tennessean*, February 11, 1968.

224   **This was no accident, and, improbably.** Story of Edwin Keeble and Memorial Gym from Neel, *Dynamite*.

225   **Vanderbilt was nearly impossible to beat.** 2009 Vanderbilt men's basketball media guide, VU Sports Information Department.

225   **A student reporter from the University of Tennessee.** *Hustler*, February 16, 1968.

226   **But after a pep talk from Coach Skinner.** *Banner*, December 5, 1967.

226   **"After that [blow]," Wallace told a *Hustler* reporter.** *Hustler*, March 19, 1968.

228   **"I can't remember three tougher games in a row."** *Banner*, December 7, 1967.

229   **Two days after the Auburn game.** *Hustler*, December 8, 1967.

229   **Charlie Scott of the North Carolina Tar Heels.** "We were honored to have Charlie spend time with us, and we were proud of what we had built," Wallace recalled. "Moreover, Charlie and I could compare notes and boost each other as pioneers. Charlie and I had met as high school seniors. Before deciding to go to UNC, he had committed to play at Davidson for Lefty Driesell. So, it was Charlie who met me and showed me around."

229   **It was Otis Redding.** "Otis was the embodiment of 'soul,' and we had begun to truly love and celebrate our black culture," Wallace recalled in an e-mail to me. "A nice extra was that Otis was a basketball fan. It was also interesting, at the concert, to see that many whites were watching us blacks, and the looks on their faces were intriguing. They seemed to be watching another show, examining us carefully as we moved to the music. Essentially, you could see the stereotypes in their minds, but there was something else going on. Perhaps it was the fact that in all the other settings in their lives where black music was being played, all nearby blacks were either servants or musicians (servants). We were black, so watching us for entertainment (and pointers) was natural to them, but the strange addition was that here we were 'equals.' As always, it made me a bit uncomfortable, because the looks often amounted to leering—especially with one particular category of them where one could see both the disdain directed at us daily and the curiosity at our 'natural rhythm.' Above it all, however, Otis and the boys helped us put such madness aside and enjoy the music. It was great fun, and (despite some of the looks) it was healing."

230   **To *Hustler* columnist Bill Livingston.** *Hustler*, December 8, 1967.

230   **In the locker room, Warren was jubilant.** *Banner*, December 11, 1967.

231   **While Redding had been in Nashville.** *Hustler*, December 12, 1967; *Banner*, December 11, 1967. My parents were standing in line outside The Factory waiting for Redding's concert when word arrived the plane had crashed.

231   **As he paced the Davidson bench area.** *Banner*, December 11, 1967.

232   **"You boys did a great job."** *Banner*, December 13, 1967.

233   **Scrawled across the chalkboard.** Interview with Paul Wilson.

233   **The amazing thing about Roy Skinner.** *Banner*, December 11, 1967.

233   While on a State Department–sponsored tour. *Banner*, December 27, 1967.

234   As Kirkpatrick wrote in his *SI* profile. "Getting the Vandy Treatment," *Sports Illustrated*, December 25, 1967.

234   First the bug and high fevers. *Banner*, December 16, 1967.

235   "We've got a chance to win this game." *Banner*, December 18, 1967.

235   You hit from that spot. Ibid.

236   Assistant Coach Homer Garr was in bed. Ibid.

237   "Too many people around." *Banner*, January 5, 1968. Another story from Calton: "One time we watched practice was when they had Cotton Nash. We were sitting two or three rows behind Adolph, and Kentucky's out there shooting, and they've got six or seven guys firing away and firing away, but no Cotton Nash. Ten minutes went by and no Cotton Nash. We heard Rupp turn to Harry and say 'Coach, where's my star?' And Lancaster said, 'He's coming, Coach.' Well sure enough, here he came. And everybody on Kentucky's team had a basketball, one for each player, but they were old, dirty basketballs. Cotton came out, and his came out of a box. It was a brand new basketball. And he comes out and he starts shooting and if anybody else's ball would get mixed up, they'd get whichever ball bounced to them. But if anybody else got Cotton's ball, they'd throw it right back to him. He was the star."

239   "Jump, boy, jump!" *Atlanta Constitution*, January 12, 1988.

239   To say that Wallace considered himself. Interview with Perry Wallace.

240   Do you have any idea of the humiliation. Memories of Kenya from a scrapbook titled, "The Alex Heards Visit East Africa, January 5–20 1968, With a Narrative by Jean Heard." Heard's daughter Connie gave me access to the scrapbook and also brought me to her father's home during his final months.

241   Perhaps it was luck, perhaps it was because. Boutwell memo, January 16, 1967. Archives.

243   In a courageously direct speech. Transcript of Mitchell's remarks included in report of Metro Human Relations Commission, 1967.

244   Wherever there are low economic conditions. *Hustler*, February 13, 1968. The construction of I-40 mostly cut the old black neighborhoods off from the rest of the city. A major connector road was not built to remedy the situation until 2013.

244   Racial tensions were growing so strong. *Hustler*, February 23, 1968.

CHAPTER 19

245   *The Commodores Travel First Class*. "Vanderbilt Basketball 1969–70: Searching for a Championship," *Versus*, n.d. This preseason publication was way ahead of its time; in its layout, writing and subject matter, it is much more akin to the media guides of the 1980s and 1990s than to the guides of the 1960s.

246   There were waves of tension. Interview with Perry Wallace, November 16, 1989. I first interviewed and wrote about Perry Wallace for a black history class taught by Dr. Yollette Jones when I was a nineteen-year-old sophomore at Vanderbilt. The paper was titled, "When You See a Purple Man: Perry Wallace at Vanderbilt." I later expanded on the paper as a senior in Dr. Jimmie Franklin's black history class my senior year ("The Deepest Sense of Dread," December 3, 1991).

250   From opposing fans and cheerleaders. Interview with Perry Wallace; *Sports Illustrated*, August 5, 1991; *Nashville Business & Lifestyles*, June 1991.

251   The lack of acknowledgment. "In these moments leaders are the ones who should enter the picture," Wallace said. "And I say this even as I have been somewhat

protective of leaders like Coach Skinner and Chancellor Heard. Frankly, they did much more than a world of other so-called leaders (SEC officials, coaches, government and community leaders) who bore responsibility for, to take the most prominent example, outrageous fan behavior in the stands at games."

CHAPTER 20

252   Back in high school. Interviews with Perry Wallace and Eddie Crawford.

252   In one game, he dazzled the crowd. Eddie Crawford biographical fact sheet dated October 7, 1998. Thanks to legendary Ole Miss sports information director Langston Rogers for access to the Rebels' athletics archives.

253   In the decades that followed this trip. "Ole Miss is not the national repository of racial guilt," former university chancellor Dr. Robert Khayat said in the late 1990s, "and we are not the last bastion of the Confederacy." *New York Times*, November 1, 1998.

253   Here was a state where 534 recorded lynchings. William Doyle, *An American Insurrection: The Battle of Oxford, Mississippi, 1962* (New York: Doubleday, 2001), 3.

253   God wanted the white people to live alone. Ibid., 60.

253   Between its Gestapo-like Sovereignty Commission. Ibid., 55, 59.

253   Just a day before President Kennedy. David Sansing, *The University of Mississippi: A Sesquicentennial History* (Jackson: University Press of Mississippi, 1999), 299.

254   Barnett stepped forward to a tall microphone. Videos of scene found on YouTube.

254   Barnett wasn't always so indirect. Doyle, *Insurrection*, 53.

254   James Vardaman, "The Great White Chief." Ibid.

254   Theodore Bilbo, a two-time governor. Internet Archive, *archive.org/details/ TakeYourChoice*. Bilbo's book was published in 1947 by the Dream House Publishing Co. of Poplarville, Mississippi.

254   Barnett's successor, Paul Johnson Jr. *Time*, January 31, 1964.

254   about 1 percent of whom were now black. *New York Times*, October 8, 1967.

254   two-pound boxes of Russell Stover chocolates. *Daily Mississippian*, February 12, 1968.

255   Walter Rugaber, a visiting reporter. *New York Times*, October 8, 1967.

255   A student newspaper editor lamented. *Daily Mississippian*, February 6, 1968.

255   Former Alabama governor George Wallace. *Tennessean*, February 9, 1968.

255   Earlier in the week, five of the eight. *Daily Mississippian*, February 9, 1968.

255   the second act of a drug bust. *Jackson Clarion-Ledger*. February 11, 1968.

257   "If we lose to Ole Miss, we are out of it." *Tennessean*, February 9, 1968.

258   the Coliseum presented a stark contrast. 1968 Ole Miss basketball media guide, Ole Miss athletics archives.

258   a haunting reminder of the university's past. Visit Oxford, MS, website, *visitoxfordms. com*.

258   Slave labor had been commonplace. Sansing, *University of Mississippi*, 54.

258   The school's very name. Ibid., 168–69.

258   an echo of the Civil War's last battle. Ibid., 303, quoting Willie Morris.

259   Tip-off came as scheduled. Description of the game from coverage in the *Tennessean, Banner*, and *Daily Mississippian*, as well as game footage.

260   "high-pitched yip, yip, yip of the Rebel yell." *Lexington Herald-Leader*, March 1, 1992.

260   Then it happened, a blow that came so fast. Interviews with Perry Wallace, Paul Wilson, Bill LaFevor, and Roy Skinner.

261   Speaking to Chancellor Heard. Wallace remarks to Human Relations Council, July 25, 1968, Archives.

261 Playing his most aggressive and focused ball. Play-by-play account of game, Ole Miss athletics archives.

262 Wallace was hacked in the back of the head. Video footage of the game, Archives. Mysteriously, several minutes of the first half have been removed from the video, including the play where Wallace was struck in the eye.

CHAPTER 21

264 Perry Wallace sat in front of his locker. Interview with Perry Wallace.

264 Bob Bundy charged into the locker room. *Banner*, March 5, 1968.

264 I'd like to shake hands with you. Interview with Perry Wallace.

265 One other person who recognized. *Hustler*, March 19, 1968.

267 A *Hustler* column noted the inequities. *Hustler*, February 23, 1968.

267 Late February brought Vanderbilt's first-ever. Interview with K. C. Potter; *Hustler*, March 15, 1968.

267 Walter Murray, already known as the ultimate peacemaker. Interview with Morris Morgan; *Hustler*, March 19, 1968.

267 By 7:30, the scheduled time of Kennedy's speech. *Hustler*, March 22, 1968.

268 During a time of war and division. Frye Gaillard, *With Music and Justice for All: Some Southerners and Their Passions* (Nashville: Vanderbilt University Press, 2008), 57.

269 Today, as the world seems almost to unravel. Transcript of Kennedy's speech, *Hustler*, March 22, 1968; Edwin O. Guthman and C. Richard Allen, eds., *RFK: Collected Speeches* (New York: Viking, 1993), 330–35.

270 The scrutiny, public humiliation, and pain. Background on Terry Thomas and description of his relationship with Gail Canty, from interview with Terry Thomas, as well as oral histories and essays written and e-mailed to me by Thomas.

277 But on the first day back from break. Coverage of the Thomas dismissal, from *Hustler*, April 5, 1968.

278 King was shot around 6:00 p.m. *Summer of '68: The Season That Changed Baseball— and America—Forever* (Cambridge, MA: Da Capo Press), 33. In his famous "Mountaintop" speech delivered the night before his assassination in Memphis, King mentioned Reverend Lawson and Vanderbilt. "And I want to commend the preachers . . . James Lawson, one who has been in this struggle for many years; he's been to jail for struggling; he's been kicked out of Vanderbilt University for this struggle, but he's still going on, fighting for the rights of his people." American Rhetoric website, *www.americanrhetoric.com/speeches/ mlkivebeentothemountaintop.htm*.

279 At Ireland's restaurant, some patrons cheered. *Hustler*, April 12, 1968.

279 Other voices noted the sad irony. *Banner*, April 5, 1968.

280 A day after the assassination. Ibid.

281 The group was more than two hundred strong. Ibid.

282 With the city under curfew. *Banner* and *Tennessean*, April 6, 1968. Whether the National Guard presence helped restore order or merely exacerbated tensions was subject to debate. The *Banner* and *Tennessean* had predictably divergent takes on the root causes of the violence. "It all is the outgrowth of a dangerous appeasing spirit of permissiveness, propagated by mealy-mouthed segments of the press, the pulpit, the campus, and the courts—topped by an ever-growing body of saccharine-lipped demagogues, concerned mainly with the preservation of their own callous political hides," a furious Stahlman wrote in the *Banner*.

"Its climax now is the threat of total destruction. . . . To the ultimatum of surrender to mobocracy, the nation's answer must be NO. . . . If there is surrender to planned insurrection today, there may be no tomorrow." The *Tennessean*, meanwhile, soberly cast its glance at business, labor, and government, saying they all played a role in finding solutions to the problems that plagued the black community and the country as a whole.

282   Our efforts to correct situations. *Tennessean*, April 7, 1968.

282   one of twenty-five incidents. *Tennessean*, April 8, 1968.

284   On Tuesday, April 9, in Atlanta. Coverage of King memorial, *Banner* and *Tennessean*, April 8–9, 1968.

284   Loree Bailey, wife of the owner of the Lorraine Motel. *Banner*, April 9, 1968.

284   If I am paying $4,000 a year. *Hustler*, April 12, 1968.

284   The next thing Murray knew. Interview with Donna Murray.

CHAPTER 22

285   Around the country, the sports world. *Tennessean*, April 7, 1968.

285   King himself had expressed support. *New York Times*, May 12, 1968.

286   Edwards was Black Power personified. Edwards' background drawn from richly detailed *New York Times* feature on May 12, 1968, by Arnold Hano headlined, "The Black Rebel Who 'Whitelists' the Olympics." In her book on the 1968 Olympics, Amy Bass quotes Edwards as saying that he consciously created an oversized persona: "At times it was as much as I could do to keep a straight face, standing before crowded auditoriums, under blazing television lights, delivering a lecture developed for my race relations class from a rostrum festooned with reporters' microphones, or bombarding white America with rhetoric calculated to outrage. When I couldn't bedazzle them with brilliance, I bamboozled them with bull. But the black cap, the beard, the work boots and jeans, the beads, the 'shades' (dark glasses, and the black jacket with the occasional book of matches pinned to the front attracted more attention from more varied sources than I would have ever felt desirable. The mystique just may have worked too well." See Bass, *Not the Triumph, but the Struggle: The 1968 Olympics and the Making of the Black Athlete* (Minneapolis: University of Minnesota Press), 2002, 144.

287   On Thanksgiving Day 1967. *New York Times*, May 12, 1968.

287   Alcindor explained why he would join. Harry Edwards, *Revolt of the Black Athlete* (New York: Free Press, 1969), 53.

288   In an April 22 memo to the Arts and Science faculty. Izard memo to A&S faculty titled, "Some thoughts on rights and responsibilities of the faculty in integrating the university," Archives.

290   By April 29 Neely had adopted. *Hustler*, April 30, 1968.

290   Standing before the professors. Interview with Dillard, Parker thesis, and minutes of faculty meeting, Archives.

291   In subsequent interviews with the *Hustler*. *Hustler*, May 7, 17, 1968.

292   Within a matter of days, there were whispers. Parker thesis, Archives.

294   The first visitor was more accurately a group. Interview with Perry Wallace.

295   The correspondent who came to Nashville. *Sports Illustrated*, July 1, 1968.

295   generating nearly one thousand letters. *Sports Illustrated*, August 5, 1968. SI's editors knew the series would generate so much controversy that just as the first issue hit the stands, according to author Amy Bass, "all those connected with the series left for their summer vacations, rightly assuming that all hell would break loose at Time, Incorporated." Bass, *Not the Triumph*, 233.

295 In a letter to readers accompanying the first article. First installment of the series ran July 1, 1968.

CHAPTER 23

299 Temperatures were climbing. *Tennessean*, July 26, 1968.

299 Last spring, considerable interest was given. "Statement by Perry Wallace to the Council on Human Relations, July 25, 1968," Archives. Discovering these previously unreported remarks was one of the great joys of the research phase of this project.

305 In response to Wallace's soliloquy. Interview with Perry Wallace.

CHAPTER 24

306 A global television audience of 400 million. Bass, *Not the Triumph*, 239.

306 When the national anthem was over. Ibid., 240.

306 Their silent but defiant act. Ibid., 25.

306 ordering them to vacate the Olympic village. Ibid., 260.

307 But on this day, when Coach Skinner. Interview with Godfrey Dillard.

307 *Did Skinner really need to have this radical black kid.* Interviews with Bill LaFevor, Godfrey Dillard, Jerry Southwood, and Perry Wallace.

308 Though Cammarata was no basketball star. Interview with Rick Cammarata.

310 On November 24, with Thanksgiving. *Banner*, November 25, 1968.

310 And that's just what happened. *Banner*, November 27, 1968.

314 Bill Livingston, a *Hustler* writer. *Hustler*, undated clipping, January or February 1969, Archives.

314 Fannie Lou Hamer, the famed Mississippi political activist. Account of Hamer visit, from interviews with Perry Wallace, Bobbie Jean Perdue, and Bev Asbury, and from *Hustler*, February 11, 1969. In a January 28, 1969, memo directed to members of the Human Relations Council shortly after he issued his invitation to Hamer, Asbury explained that he intended for the service to address the question of "why white, affluent Christians seem to be impoverished in 'soul' while less affluent black Christians have 'soul' in worship and elsewhere." Archives.

315 it seems that Dillard . . . 'didn't fit into the plans.' *Hustler*, February 18, 1969. "Pat was a great spirit, a very kind man, and a wonderful advocate," Wallace later recalled. "His presence was substantive and positive, and I always felt reassured by him."

316 Hecht's background was far different. Interview with Henry Hecht. Hecht went on to a distinguished career in sportswriting with the *New York Post* and *Sports Illustrated*, among others. For the *Post*, he covered the New York Yankees during the height of the George Steinbrenner–Reggie Jackson–Billy Martin era, once famously quoting Martin as saying of Jackson and Steinbrenner that "one's a born liar, the other's convicted." Martin was fired the next day but was soon rehired. In the interim, three fans at Yankee Stadium held up a sign that read, "Henry Hecht Sucks. Reggie too."

317 In a scathing column, Hecht wrote. *Hustler*, April 9, 1968.

317 But in this case, he expressed little sympathy. *Hustler*, April 21, 1969.

318 Dillard saw only one way. Account of Dillard-Hecht encounter, from interviews with Godfrey Dillard and Henry Hecht; both remained extremely emotional about the incident. This episode has not been written about previously, and I am thankful to both men for sharing their memories of it.

319 Though Wallace could not condone. "Godfrey decided wisely to do what his parents

did decades earlier—leave an untenable, irreparable situation in the South to seek a better life up North," Wallace said. "At the same time, I respected Henry's right to express his view and our relationship didn't change one bit."

CHAPTER 25

321   **Here's how Raven worked.** Description of Raven lore and rituals, from interviews with Kevin Grady, Kassian Kovalcheck, K. C. Potter, Chuck Offenburger, Henry Hecht, and Perry Wallace. It was Kovalcheck, my former communications professor, who first mentioned Raven to me. I am especially thankful for Grady's detailed and honest recounting of the episode.

325   **In the days after the ceremony, Wallace said.** Wallace said that as he and Murray reflected on the Raven episode, they laughed at what they assumed would have been Godfrey Dillard's reaction to the incident: "He would have kicked [the white students'] asses for doing what they did, and kicked our asses for putting up with it."

326   **"Give me my motherfucking thirteen dollars back."** "My uncharacteristically open display of anger simply reflected the cumulative effect of so many similarly disappointing events and moments over the previous three years," Wallace recalled. "So much laughing. So much ridicule. And from so many white faces."

CHAPTER 26

328   **Six months after Godfrey Dillard walked.** Interview with Perry Wallace.

329   **Surrounded by family members.** Interview with Jessie (Wallace) Jackson.

329   **One surprising motivation.** E-mail, Perry Wallace.

330   **Now he felt less compelled.** In his fascinating book on five 1967 films nominated for Academy Awards, Mark Harris described the formation of the character played by Sidney Poitier in *Guess Who's Coming to Dinner*, perhaps the ultimate portrayal of the Super Negro. "I wanted the prospective black bridegroom to be a person so suitable that if anyone objected to them, it could only be due to racial prejudice," Harris quoted director Stanley Kramer as once writing. "Kramer," Harris wrote, "was sure that if [Poitier's character] had any flaws at all, bigots in the audience would seize on them as a reason to disapprove of the marriage, but in seeking to avoid that trap, he fell right into another one: the return of the exceptional Negro, a character type that had by then become so familiar that even white critics were beginning to react against its persistence. In [William] Rose's script, [Poitier's character] became not just a doctor, but an Ivy League–educated potential Nobel laureate who worked for the United Nations on worldwide health missions." See Harris, *Pictures at a Revolution: Five Movies and the Birth of the New Hollywood* (New York: Penguin, 2008), 188.

330   **Later in Wallace's career.** Interviews with Perry Wallace, Joel Gordon, and Tom Arnholt.

333   **In a letter to Chancellor Heard, Gilpin asked.** Gilpin letter dated March 21, 1969, Archives.

333   **Most prominently, in the summer of 1969.** Bernard E. Garnett and Frye Gaillard, *The Black Athlete—1970*, Special Report (Nashville: Race Relations Information Center, 1970), 22.

333   **Heard drafted a confidential, three-page memo.** Memo dated August 8, 1969, Archives.

335   **The irony of Perry Wallace's quest to move.** Interviews with Perry Wallace, David Lombard, and Paul Watermulder. "The problem wasn't white people. The

problem was white prejudice, personal and institutional," Wallace recalled. "So, it didn't matter who I lived with, as long as they were good and fair. And these guys were great."

339 **it was Pete Maravich, the white star at LSU.** "It was interesting playing in those games against LSU and running down the floor and hearing his own teammates cussing him that 'they could play, too,'" Wallace recalled. "I remember one guy saying, 'This asshole thinks I can't shoot. Let him shoot the whole damn time. I can shoot; why don't I get a chance to score?'"

340 **When the *New York Times* decided to run a feature.** *New York Times*, January 4, 1970.

340 **Henry Harris had joined the varsity at Auburn.** "I obviously was happy to see another black face in the conference," Wallace recalled. "But I was very, very afraid for him. As bad as Auburn had been for me, I frankly was puzzled that they would be the next school to bring a black on board."

340 **former Tennessee State coach Harold Hunter.** *Hustler*, January 9, 1970. "Coach Hunter was one of the important people in my life, one who contributed immensely to my development," Wallace recalled. "I regret that we didn't reconnect."

343 **In an article he collaborated on with Jack Olsen.** *Sports Illustrated*, November 10, 1969.

344 **As his teammates cheered, Wallace told a visitor.** *Vanderbilt Alumnus*, No. 2, 1969.

344 **When a black basketball recruit named Tony Jenkins.** "Tony was just such a fine young man," Wallace recalled. "He needed to know the whole truth and I gave it to him. He made a wise choice, his life went beautifully, and it has made me happy to have spelled things out for him."

345 **Wallace was more successful in recruiting.** "These guys brought the talent, intelligence, and toughness necessary to make it at Vanderbilt," Wallace recalled. "And, topping it all off, they knew the South. Even though I knew they would have challenges, and they would wonder at times what the hell I got them into, I knew Vanderbilt was a good choice for them. They would ultimately have the benefit of a great education, an opportunity to play major college ball, and, equally important, they would be part of a struggle that would take the character that I already saw in them and raise it to an even higher level. They never knew it, but I thought long and hard about each one of them before urging them to come."

346 **"You didn't get me. And now I'm gone."** *Sports Illustrated*, August 5, 1991.

347 **While Wallace was flattered.** *Vanderbilt Alumnus*, March–April 1970.

348 **On March 7, 1970, the day of Perry.** *Tennessean*, March 7, 8, 1970.

348 **As Harold Huggins settled into his seat.** Interviews with Harold Huggins and Don Dahlinger. Wallace later said that he had in fact read Huggins' letter and that it strengthened his resolve to dunk during the game.

350 **Wallace found his opportunity to dunk.** *Tennessean*, March 8, 1970. Wallace ended his Vanderbilt career with 1,010 points, becoming just the sixth Vanderbilt player to eclipse the 1,000-point mark.

351 **"I dedicated this game to my mother."** *Tennessean*, March 8, 1970.

CHAPTER 27

352 **Frank Sutherland was prepared to cook dinner.** Account of Sutherland-Wallace interview, article, and aftermath drawn from interviews with Sutherland, Wallace, John Seigenthaler, and Jimmy Davy.

353 **strengthened under the watch of Seigenthaler.** As special assistant to Robert Kennedy, Seigenthaler acted as an intermediary between the Justice Department, the 1961

civil rights activists known as the "Freedom Riders," and segregationist state officials. He was struck in the head and knocked unconscious by white protestors in Montgomery, Alabama, while traveling with a group of Freedom Riders.

357   **that was the perceptual problem that people had.** The more vitriolic reactions were in keeping with the blowback other black pioneers had experienced. "Jackie Robinson was a national hero when he kept his eyes and mouth shut to injustices," wrote William Rhoden in *Forty Million Dollar Slaves* (p. 216), "but when he began to speak his mind, he was met with a backlash of negativity by whites. When Robinson criticized the baseball establishment for its persistent racism, his popularity plunged. 'You owe a great deal to the game,' The Sporting News instructed him in a 1955 editorial. 'Put down your hammer, Jackie, and pick up a horn.'"

358   **Vice Chancellor Purdy was "surprisingly angry."** Garnett and Gaillard, *The Black Athlete*, 23.

358   **"At first, I thought, 'How can he say all this stuff.'"** Interview with Roy Skinner.

359   **On the very day that Sutherland's front-page article.** Heard, *Speaking*, 135, 143.

359   **A passage from a column Heard wrote.** *Vanderbilt Alumnus*, Spring 1974.

360   **Nine days after Sutherland's front-page article.** *Hustler*, "Wednesday" supplement, March 18, 1970.

360   **Steve Kendall, a sophomore from Massachusetts.** Interview with Steve Kendall.

362   **the Kentucky Colonels of the upstart ABA.** "I went to rookie camp at the Colonels, a couple of weeks after the 76ers camp in June," Wallace recalled. "Dan Issel and Mike Casey were there, along with others whom I remember. I was glad to be included. I understand that they may have been interested in using me to attract some Tennessee people. Remember that the ABA was a fledgling league and they were into big business development. For example, the 76ers held two-a-day sessions in private. The second workout at Kentucky was often an exhibition game at Freedom Hall, with a band, concessions, etc. We were encouraged to be fancy, dunk a lot with the red, white, and blue ball, etc. I found it interesting, and frankly kind of cool. It obviously wasn't as sophisticated as the NBA, but since I knew I wouldn't be going there, it was all right."

364   **His presence at the Murray wedding.** Interview with Donna Murray.

365   **As they drove on toward the airport.** Interview with Perry Wallace.

CHAPTER 28

367   **his 76ers roster was loaded.** One day in training camp in the fall of 1970, Wallace overhead one of the team's trainers describe Wallace to someone else as "the friendly colored guy from down South." The term became Wallace's "rhetorical shorthand" for the simplistic view that some people have had of him over the years, a "potent mixture of their own prejudices and my manner and strategies," Wallace said. "Although it is quite a well-known 'type,' in the black community, my persona has eluded even most blacks—and obviously most others. Only in recent years have some people begun to perceive the nuances."

371   **"torrent of emotions."** *Vanderbilt Magazine*, Fall 2004. Brown's boss at the Urban League was Vernon Jordan. "Vernon knew Alexander Heard," Wallace recalled. "He recounted this to me at a dinner a few years ago as we sat together. Vernon came to NYC from Atlanta, and so was a southern boy who knew the South. Heard probably met Vernon through his work with the Ford Foundation in NYC. Apparently, according to Vernon, Heard invited him to take a position at VU, but nothing ever worked out."

372   **he prepared law school applications.** Wallace's listed references on his law school applications were Ron Brown, Chancellor Heard, and Dr. Jack Ramsay.

372   **at the school where two prominent figures in his life.** Adolph Rupp also earned a master's degree at Columbia.

373   **fear for their own physical safety.** "In the South, as a black I had never encountered a white who appeared to be afraid of me—or any other black," Wallace recalled. "This gives a sense of what kind of culture that had been created down there."

375   **Wallace set out to find people.** For example, one classmate (one year behind) was Eric Holder, the US Attorney General under President Obama.

375   **In the summer before his third and final year.** Interviews with Perry Wallace and Leonard Burg.

377   **Wallace visited his dad briefly that summer.** Interviews with Perry Wallace and Jessie (Wallace) Jackson.

379   **One of Wallace's responsibilities.** *Tennessean*, March 10, 1977; *Washington Post*, January 28, 2006.

380   **The coach was Bob Tallent.** *Washington Post*, January 28, 2006.

383   **They remained integrationists.** "A more profound and similar framework unfolded with Dr. Martin Luther King Jr. and Malcolm X," Dillard said. "The change and progress that has come to America could not have occurred without both of their contributions. America needed more time and a choice in order to fundamentally change for the better."

385   **Skinner tabbed Ligon as the "game captain."** Interview with Bill Ligon.

385   **Billy "World" Smith and Ben Skipper.** Ibid.

385   **While the pace of change remained slow.** Barry Jacobs, *Across the Line: Profiles in Basketball Courage; Tales of the First Black Players in the ACC and SEC* (Guilford, CT: Lyons Press, 2008), 333.

385   **Ten years after Alabama governor.** The "schoolhouse" was the building where Alabama students registered for classes, Foster Auditorium, then the home of the Crimson Tide basketball team.

386   **As William Reed.** *Sports Illustrated*, August 5, 1991.

386   **Alabama teams racked up three consecutive.** In 1974 Alabama and Vanderbilt tied for the SEC title.

386   **When he recruited Alabama's first black player.** *Tennessean*, July 31, 1973.

387   **Karen Smyley was skeptical.** Interview with Karen Smyley.

390   **And why was it that one federal judge.** Interview with Perry Wallace; *Vanderbilt Register*, February 17, 1997.

CHAPTER 29

392   **Heys had grown up in Chattanooga.** Interview with Heys. During his junior year at the prestigious McCallie School on Chattanooga's Missionary Hill, Heys' teacher Spence McCallie III (grandson of one of the school's founders and a 1959 Vanderbilt graduate), began to expose his students to what Heys termed "the bigger world," and through this introduction to a different way of thinking, he became comfortable with more progressive views on race. McCallie tapped Heys to participate in a program called "Project Straight Talk," which paired white high schoolers and college students with their counterparts at Chattanooga's black schools, and Heys further explored this new territory through the prism of sports, buying a ticket to a basketball game between Chattanooga's two powerhouse black high schools, Riverside and Howard, an eye-opening experience he later termed a "revolution on a personal level." At the time this

book went to press, Heys was completing a biography of Henry Harris, the Auburn pioneer who committed suicide.

393   **Reverend William Alexander of St. Andrew's Presbyterian.** *Banner*, January 26, 1988.

394   **The African American Martin had served.** After retiring from coaching, Martin was a frequent visitor to the Vanderbilt Sports Information Department while I worked there. He was full of corny one-liners—"He raced a pregnant lady and came in third"—and also shared his own stories of pioneering as a basketball player and as a pitcher in the Negro Leagues.

394   **Vanderbilt continually fielded the whitest team.** *Tennessean*, June 23, 1991. "I remember being told about this irony by sportswriters and others, with their often joking that I needed to go back and reintegrate the SEC—or at least reintegrate Vanderbilt," Wallace recalled. "I also remember being told by Bill Ligon and others that many VU officials blamed their failures to recruit black athletes on me—that my statements had run them away."

394   **writing to Wallace and inviting him back.** *Banner*, February 18, 1989.

394   **Before heading over to a campus banquet room.** *Tennessean*, February 19, 1989.

394   **The first time Wallace ever stood.** Interview with Richard Philpot.

395   **Newton told the boosters.** *Tennessean*, February 19, 1989. Newton, who did as much to bring about change in the SEC as anyone, later hired the African American Tubby Smith as basketball coach at Kentucky; Smith led the Wildcats to a national championship in his first season, 1998. All three of Smith's sons played basketball in the SEC (at Georgia, Kentucky, and Ole Miss).

396   **clinging to a belief that Wallace was "angry."** "The label 'angry' was a fabrication of certain administrators and alumni," Wallace recalled. "And it was a masterful strategy. The idea was to get people to dismiss me as being angry so they wouldn't listen to what I had to say. The great irony is that they were the ones who were angry as hell."

396   **A feature on Wallace and Dillard.** The February 1989 *Versus* article by Dave Sheinin was the first I heard of Wallace.

396   **I know about these cost benefit analyses.** "Frankly, I gave the most diplomatic answer I could," Wallace recalled. "In reality, I knew what was going on at the top levels but knew it would be impolitic and unstrategic to speak on the matter."

397   **sang opera in Italian, German, and French.** He could also sing opera in Spanish.

398   **Gabby would not make eye contact.** "Early intervention is the fundamental advice with disabilities like this, and then ongoing vigilance and care are a basic part of the formula that may, *may*, lead to some success," Wallace recalled. "I often sum up the basic requirements as 'love, science, and money'—this is what we and other parents have discovered."

399   **there were good days and bad days.** One episode during that sweep of years was especially challenging—the bigot being a "so-called man of God." By the time Gabby reached middle school, the Wallaces had enrolled her in a Catholic school affiliated with what Perry considered a "nice church where many of the people were very good." Gabby thrived on the quality of education and the positive values she was taught, Wallace said, and was surrounded by "many stellar people." The problem was one of the priests. At mass, he would ignore Perry but say hello to Gabby and Karen, whom, with her reddish hair, he, Wallace believes, assumed was white. The priest's affection for Karen, in fact, often crossed a line with her—his hugs too close, lasting too long. On the occasion of Gabby's baptism, Perry, Karen, and Karen's mother stepped forward along with the family members of the other parishioners receiving the holy water. The priest

motioned for Karen and her mother to remain with Gabby, and then pointed
to Perry and the seats and ordered Perry, the proud father, to take a seat in the
pews. "I put up with being shunned, as that happened all the time in many,
many situations," Wallace recalled. "What I didn't know about until after Gabby
graduated and left was the physical touching with Karen. There's no way I would
have put up with that. In fact, even afterwards, I had to struggle a lot within
myself not to lash out at this guy. But as we removed ourselves from all contact,
I had a realization that brought me all the justice I needed: Bigotry and lust are
sins, a basic failure of [the priest's] fundamental vows to God."

400   **recognition arrived in official ways.** *Vanderbilt Register*, February 17, 1997.

402   **David Williams knew so little about Vanderbilt.** Interview with David Williams.

406   **An especially poignant scene played out.** Interview with Perry Wallace. I attended
this event and witnessed the encounter between Lawson and Wallace from afar.
When Vanderbilt administrators first met to discuss possible candidates for the
inaugural class of the Hall of Fame, Associate Athletic Director Rod Williamson
opened the conversation by saying, "Well, let's start with the no-brainer." "Who's
that?" someone asked. "Perry Wallace," Williamson replied, and the discussion
moved on without debate.

408   **Vanderbilt was to be admired.** *Nashville Scene*, February 19, 2004.

408   **I think it's a very special institution.** The Vanderbilt he spoke of had evolved, he
believed, into the place he had hoped it would be when he chose to attend the
school. Under Williams' leadership, the school's athletic fortunes entered a
golden age, achieving the success Vanderbilt administrators dating back to
Chancellors Branscomb and Heard had doubted was possible, with the men's
basketball team winning its first SEC Tournament championship since 1951,
the baseball team winning the 2014 College World Series, and most improbably,
the football team winning nine games in a season for the first time since 1915
and advancing to back-to-back bowl games for the first time in school history.
The head coach of that paradigm-shifting football program—a program that
had once run off a player in part for dating a black girl and that doubted a
black assistant coach would do it much good—was James Franklin, and James
Franklin was black. Most important to Wallace, the university had apparently
achieved all of this success without compromising its commitment to these
students in the classroom. His gut feeling on that point was borne out in a
2012 study of the country's seventy-six major-conference athletic programs
by the University of Pennsylvania's Center for the Study of Race and Equity
in Education, which revealed that 74 percent of black athletes in "revenue
producing sports" (football and men's basketball) graduated within six years at
Vanderbilt, a rate that was fifth-highest in the nation, well ahead of the national
average of 50.2 percent and far ahead of any other school in the SEC. Newton's
old school, Alabama, was the next highest, at 56 percent, and three league
schools (Arkansas, Mississippi State, and Florida) ranked in the bottom ten of
the national rankings, with percentages in the 30s. On a national scale, it was
easy to make the argument that athletic powerhouse universities were merely
exploiting black athletic talent. Between 2007 and 2010, the study revealed, black
men represented just 2.8 percent of full-time, degree-seeking undergraduate
students on these campuses, but 57.1 percent of football players and 64.3 percent
of basketball players.

408   **Senior Russell Lakey, an African American point guard.** *Tennessean*, August 4, 2006.

408   **to help society and others.** *Vanderbilt Magazine*, Fall 2004.

409   finest moments he'd ever experienced in basketball. *Tennessean*, February 22, 2004.

409   John Seigenthaler, the longtime editor. Interview with John Seigenthaler. I was surprised by this story and asked Seigenthaler to clarify whether Bibb meant it was a mistake for Skinner to sign Dillard or to let him go. It was a tremendous honor to interview Mr. Seigenthaler, a Nashville treasure and a tireless advocate for social justice.

411   Many years ago, Vanderbilt and I set out. Perry Wallace e-mail.

412   Amid the feelings of love that radiated. "I had the kind of experience that could have been tragic, because it was for some people who came even after I did," Wallace recalled. "But I figured out how to not let this experience turn into tragedy. Ordinary black people meet tragedy all the time, but there is a special challenge and a special tragedy that may attend black people who are talented and may have achieved above the rest. Robeson was a great example. His story after all was a tragedy. Because he confronted America on race and he wouldn't back down, America punished him in a lot of ways and eventually it drove him down. Many others had the same thing happen. And so for neither the general tragedy, or the special tragedy that can await someone by confronting and dealing with America, I found a way of not succumbing to either one. In that sense it took some effort, it took some living, it took some working, but I rounded my own circle, and [returning to] Vanderbilt was another type of rounding of the circle."

412   the sight of the black, white, and gold banner. *Urban Journal*, February 25, 2004. Vanderbilt fans familiar with Memorial Gym will note the original banner has since been replaced by a higher-quality, black and gold banner.

413   Despite the challenges of Gabby's childhood. "It is quite telling who ended up on the team," Wallace recalled. "They might be as educated and erudite as the psychologists and psychiatrists who made assessments, or as humble as Sara Rojas, a wonderful Nicaraguan woman who, with her husband Fabio, so lovingly cared for Gabby as a little one. Tight, harsh, cynical people were out—and no amount of education, social status, or wealth could counterbalance their 'jerk factor.' They got put on our 'no-fly' list."

CHAPTER 30

415   "We are fine," Wallace assured Warren. Interviews with Perry Wallace and Bob Warren.

416   A visitor sees no evidence of Wallace's past. Author visit to Perry Wallace's office.

Bibliography

NTERVIEWS

Jacqueline Akins, Steven Ammann, Tom Arnholt, Bev Asbury, Bob Baldridge, Hal Bartch, Vereen Bell, Bob Bundy, Leonard Burg, Bob Calton, Rick Cammarata, Eileen Carpenter, Marshall Chapman, Jim Combs, Eddie Crawford, Don Dahlinger, Jimmy Davy, Godfrey Dillard, Dan Due, Walter Fisher, Rod Freeman, Frye Gaillard, Bessie (Wallace) Garrett, Patrick Gilpin, Joel Gordon, Kevin Grady, Tom Hagan, Christie Hauck, Lee Hayden, Cornelia Heard, Henry Hecht, Sam Heys, Harold Huggins, Sara Hume, Jessie (Wallace) Jackson, Kathleen (Gallagher) Kemper, Steven Kendall, Don Knodel, Kassian Kovalcheck, Paul Kurtz, Bill LaFevor, Clyde Lee, Bill Ligon, David Lombard, Van Magers, Steve Martin, Paul Menzel, Tony Moorman, Carolyn (Bradshaw) Morgan, Morris Morgan, Donna Murray, Roy Neel, Chuck Offenburger, Bobbie Jean Perdue, Dick Philpot, K. C. Potter, John Seigenthaler, Roy Skinner, Billy Smith, Gene Smitherman, Karen Smyley, Jerry Southwood, Frank Sutherland, Annie (Wallace) Sweet, Willie Sweet, Keith Thomas, Terry Thomas, John Thorpe, Curry Todd, Pat Toomay, Bill Traughber, Michael Vinsang, Perry Wallace, Bob Warren, Paul Watermulder, Bedford Waters, David Williams, Rod Williamson, Paul Wilson, Bo Wyenandt, Linda Wynn.

BOOKS

Abdul-Jabbar, Kareem, and Peter Knobler. *Giant Steps: The Autobiography of Kareem Abdul-Jabbar*. New York: Bantam Books, 1983.

Bass, Amy. *Not the Triumph, but the Struggle: The 1968 Olympics and the Making of the Black Athlete*. Minneapolis: University of Minnesota Press, 2002.

Boyd, Todd, and Kenneth Shropshire, eds. *Basketball Jones: America above the Rim*. New York: New York University Press, 2000.

Bradley, Michael. *Big Blue: 100 Years of Kentucky Wildcats Basketball*. Saint Louis: Sporting News, 2002.

Burt, Jesse C. *Nashville: Its Life and Times*. Nashville: Tennessee Book Company, 1959.

Carey, Bill. *Chancellors, Commodores, and Coeds: A History of Vanderbilt University*. Knoxville, TN: Clearbrook Press Publishing, 2003.

Carson, Clayborne. *In Struggle: SNCC and the Black Awakening of the 1960s*. 1981. Reprint, with new introduction and epilogue. Cambridge, MA: Harvard University Press, 1995.

Conkin, Paul. *Gone with the Ivy: A Biography of Vanderbilt University*. Knoxville: University of Tennessee Press, 1985.

Doyle, Don H. *Nashville since the 1920s*. Knoxville: University of Tennessee Press, 1985.

Doyle, William. *An American Insurrection: The Battle of Oxford, Mississippi, 1962*. New York: Doubleday, 2001.

Edwards, Harry. *The Revolt of the Black Athlete*. New York: Free Press, 1969.

Eig, Jonathan. *Opening Day: The Story of Jackie Robinson's First Season*. New York: Simon and Schuster, 2007.

Fitzpatrick, Frank. *And the Walls Came Tumbling Down: Kentucky, Texas Western, and the Game That Changed American Sports*. New York: Simon and Schuster, 1999.

Gaillard, Frye. *With Music and Justice for All: Some Southerners and Their Passions*. Nashville: Vanderbilt University Press, 2008.

George, Nelson. *Elevating the Game: Black Men and Basketball*. Lincoln: University of Nebraska Press, 1992.

Graham, Tom, and Rachel Graham Cody. *Getting Open: The Unknown Story of Bill Garrett and the Integration of College Basketball*. New York: Atria Books, 2006.

Guthman, Edwin, O., and C. Richard Allen, eds. *RFK: Collected Speeches*. New York: Viking, 1993.

Halberstam, David. *The Breaks of the Game*. New York: Knopf, 1981.

———. *The Children*. New York: Random House, 1998.

Harris, Mark. *Pictures at a Revolution: Five Movies and the Birth of the New Hollywood*. New York: Penguin, 2008.

Haskins, Clem, with Marc Ryan. *Clem Haskins: Breaking Barriers*. Champaign, IL: Sports Publishing, 1997.

Haskins, Don, with Dan Wetzel. *Glory Road: My Story of the 1966 NCAA Basketball Championship and How One Team Triumphed against the Odds and Changed America Forever*. New York: Hyperion, 2006.

Heard, Alexander. *Speaking of the University: Two Decades at Vanderbilt*. Nashville: Vanderbilt University Press, 1995.

Jacobs, Barry. *Across the Line: Profiles in Basketball Courage; Tales of the First Black Players in the ACC and SEC*. Guilford, CT: Lyons Press, 2008.

Katz, Milton S. *Breaking Through: John B. McClendon, Basketball Legend and Civil Rights Pioneer*. Fayetteville: University of Arkansas Press, 2007.

Maraniss, David. *Rome 1960: The Olympics That Changed the World*. New York: Simon and Schuster, 2008.

Meredith, James. *Three Years in Mississippi*. Bloomington: Indiana University Press, 1966.

Neel, Roy M. *Dynamite: 75 Years of Vanderbilt Basketball*. Nashville: Burr-Oak Publishers, 1975.

Northington, Nathaniel, with La Monte McNeese. *Still Running: The Autobiography of Kentucky's Nate Northington, the First African American Football Player in the Southeastern Conference*. Bloomington, IN: iUniverse, 2013.

Olsen, Jack. *The Black Athlete: A Shameful Story*. New York: Time-Life Books, 1968.

Pearce, Gene. *Field of Dreamers: Celebrating Tennessee High School Sports*. Hermitage, TN: Tennessee Secondary School Athletic Association, 2005.

Ramsay, Dr. Jack. *Dr. Jack's Leadership Lessons Learned from a Lifetime in Basketball*. Hoboken, NJ: John Wiley and Sons, 2004.

Rhoden, William C. *Forty Million Dollar Slaves: The Rise, Fall, and Redemption of the Black Athlete*. New York: Three Rivers Press, 2006.

Rice, Russell. *Adolph Rupp: Kentucky's Basketball Baron*. Champaign, IL: Sagamore Publishing, 1994.

Rosen, Charley. *Scandals of '51: How Gamblers Almost Killed College Basketball*. 1978. Reprint, New York: Seven Stories Press, 1999.

Russell, Fred. *Fifty Years of Vanderbilt Football*. Nashville: Fred Russell and Maxwell E. Benson Publishers, 1938.

Sansing, David G. *The University of Mississippi: A Sesquicentennial History*. Jackson: University Press of Mississippi, 1999.

Traughber, Bill. *Vanderbilt Basketball: Tales of Commodore Hardwood History*. Charleston, SC: History Press, 2012.

Ward, Geoffrey C. *Unforgivable Blackness: The Rise and Fall of Jack Johnson*. New York: Knopf, 2004.

Wendel, Tim. *Summer of '68: The Season That Changed Baseball—and America—Forever*. Cambridge, MA: Da Capo Press, 2012.

Wiggins, David K., ed. *Out of the Shadows: A Biographical History of African American Athletes*. Fayetteville: University of Arkansas Press, 2006.

Index

Page numbers in **bold** refer to illustrations

Meridian Star, 159–60
Merritt, John, 20
Merry High School, 43, 72
Metro Police Department, 173
Middlebury College, 371
Middle Tennessee State University, 155, 425n36
Miles College, 182
military, 262, 267, 276, 362, 369, 381
Miller, Eddie, 259
Miller, Larry, 230
Mississippi State University, 159–60, 161–65, 246, 346, 349, 385
 and black players, 89
 and Martin, 217
 and NCAA Tournament, 154
 and player safety, 92
 and Wallace, 247
Mitchell, Edwin, 243
Mitts, Billy, 160
Mobile, Alabama, 119
mononucleosis, 234
Monroe, Earl "The Pearl," 367
Moore, Robert, 206, 208, 229, 290
Moorman, Tony, 26, 33, 44, 71, 86
 and college recruitment, 45
 and Kingston, 76
 and Pearl-Ryan game, 35
 and practices, 30
Morgan, Morris, 119, 200, 208, 278–79
Morton, Peggy, 419
Moss, Dyer, 118
Mount, Rick, 97, 192, 339
MSU. *See* Mississippi State University
Municipal Auditorium, 34
Munson, Larry, 61
Murfreesboro, Tennessee, 2–3, 186
Murphy, Calvin, 339, 400
Murrah High School, 256
Murray, Donna, 28, 184, 332, 400
Murray, Walter, 101, 223
 and Asbury, 194
 and band, 12
 and church, 131
 and civil rights, 278
 and Donna Murray, 41, 184, 430n131
 and dormitory naming, 406
 and faculty meeting, 290
 after graduation, 364
 and Hecht, 316
 and Hubbard, 267, 289
 humor of, 332
 and King, 278–84
 and racist professor, 131
 and Raven, 322–24
 and riot, 184
 and Smyley, 390
 and Wallace, 41, 192, 356, 400

 and white students, 206
music
 black, 436n229
 jazz, 144, 265, 368, 390
 and Lombard, 338–39
 and Wallace childhood, 12, 14

NAACP Legal Defense and Education Fund, 375
Nabokov, Vladimir, 172
NAIA (National Association of Intercollegiate Athletics), 20
Naismith, James, 20, 59
Nash, Cotton, 437n237
Nash, Diane, 13, 53, 168
Nashville, Tennessee
 and black basketball, 20
 black middle class of, 27
 campaign, 53
 Chamber of Commerce, 170, 243
 and civil rights movement, 13–14, 51, 428n114
 history of, 3–4, 7
 and media, 408
 North, 4, **183,** 184, 188, 243, 279
 and old money, 49
 public schools, 331
 race relations in, 241
 riots in, 175, 180, 182–86, **183,** 188, 197
 segregation in, 9–10
 Wallace return to, 407
 See also *Nashville Banner*; *Tennessean*
Nashville Banner, 71, 170, 171, 393, 428n104
 and Carmichael, 179
 cartoon, 68, 205–6
 and integration, 51
 as reactionary, 353
 and Wallace, 102, 103, 106
Nashville Business & Lifestyles, 397
Nashville Interscholastic League, 33
"Nashville Plan, The," 10
Nashville Quarterback Club, 277
National Association of Basketball Coaches, 400
National Association of Black Journalists, 400
National Association of Intercollegiate Athletics (NAIA), 20
National Collegiate Athletic Association (NCAA), 20, 86, 93, 154, 159–61
National Guard, 279, **280,** 283, 362, 439n282
National High School Athletic Association, 20–21
National Life Insurance, 55
National Urban League, 370–71
NCAA (National Collegiate Athletic Association), 20, 86, 93, 154, 159–61
Ndegwa, Phil, 241
Neal, Kathleen, 432n185

Author Biography

Strong Inside is the first book by Andrew Maraniss. A partner at McNeely Pigott & Fox Public Relations in Nashville, Andrew studied history at Vanderbilt University as a recipient of the Fred Russell–Grantland Rice sportswriting scholarship, earning the school's Alexander Award for excellence in journalism and graduating in 1992. He then worked for five years in Vanderbilt's Athletic Department as the associate director of media relations, dealing primarily with the men's basketball team. In 1998 he served as the media relations manager for the Tampa Bay (Devil) Rays during the team's inaugural season and then returned to Nashville to join MP&F. The son of Pulitzer Prize–winning journalist and best-selling author David Maraniss and trailblazing environmentalist Linda Maraniss, Andrew was born in Madison, Wisconsin, grew up in Washington, DC, and Austin, Texas, and now lives in Brentwood, Tennessee, with his wife, Alison, and their two young children. Follow Andrew on Twitter *@trublu24* and visit his website at *www.andrewmaraniss.com.*